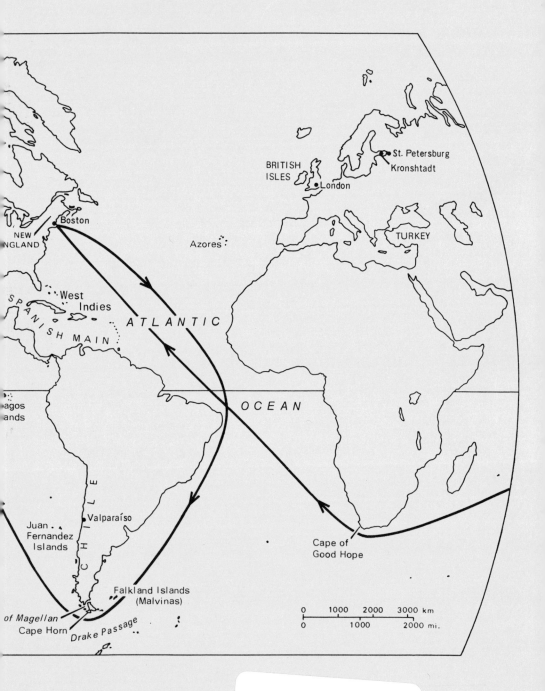

BRITISH
ISLES

• London

St. Petersburg
Kronshtadt

TURKEY

Azores

Boston

NEW
NGLAND

West
Indies

S P A N I S H   M A I N

A T L A N T I C

O C E A N

agos
ands

C H I L E

Valparaíso

Juan
Fernandez
Islands

Cape of
Good Hope

Falkland Islands
(Malvinas)

of Magellan
Cape Horn   Drake Passage

0	1000	2000	3000 km
0	1000		2000 mi.

Otter Skins, Boston Ships, and China Goods

A young male sea otter, 1778, drawn by John Webber.
From Captain James Cook (and Captain James King),
A Voyage to the Pacific Ocean (London: G. Nicol
and T. Cadell 1784), atlas, plate 43.

Otter Skins, Boston Ships, and China Goods

The Maritime Fur Trade of the Northwest Coast, 1785–1841

JAMES R. GIBSON

University of Washington Press
Seattle

Legal deposit first quarter 1992
Bibliothèque nationale du Québec

Printed in Canada on acid-free paper

This book has been published with the help of a
grant from the Social Science Federation of Canada,
using funds provided by the Social Sciences and
Humanities Research Council of Canada.
In recognition of the importance of this work, its
publication has been made possible by a special grant
from the Faculty of Arts and the office of the
Associate Vice-President (Research) at York University.

Library of Congress Cataloging-in-Publication Data

Gibson, James R.
    Otter skins, Boston ships, and China goods: the
    maritime fur trade of the Northwest Coast, 1785–
    1841 / James R. Gibson.

       p.   cm.
    Includes bibliographical references and index.
    ISBN 0-295-97169-x (alk. paper)

    1. Sea otter skin industry – Northwest Coast of North
    America – History. 2. Sea otter skin industry – China
    – History. 3. Pacific Area – Commerce – History.
    4. Voyages to the Pacific Coast. I. Title.

HD9778.5.S4153N74 1992
382'.4397447–dc20   91-34597

Published simultaneously in Canada by
McGill-Queen's University Press,
3430 McTavish Street, Montreal, Quebec H3A 1X9.

Typeset in Baskerville 10/12 by Caractéra inc.,
Quebec City.

For
William Sturgis (1782–1863)
and Frederic Howay (1867–1943)

and all other Nor'westmen

Contents

Tables

Preface

From Mount St. Elias to Monterey, the coast of America presents
nothing to the speculations of our merchants but skins of different kinds, and particularly those of the sea otter, for which
there is in China a certain and ready sale. This fur, so highly
valued in Asia, is more common in America, along an extent of
twelve hundred leagues of coast, and more widely spread, than
even seals are along the coasts of Labrador.

J.F.G. De La Pérouse, 1786

From the middle 1780s, when Russian galiots penetrated the Gulf
of Alaska and British snows (brigs) reached Nootka Sound, the fur
trade was the dominant economic activity on the Northwest Coast, a
well-known but loosely defined stretch of the damp, rugged Pacific
shore of North America between, say, glacier-ringed Icy Bay and red-
wood-studded Cape Mendocino. For more than half a century the
Tlingit, Haida, Tsimshian, Nootka (or West Coast, or Nuu-chah-
nulth), Salish, and Chinook Indians in particular spent much of their
time hunting fur bearers and trading their pelts, especially the "black
skins" of sea otters, to Russian, British, and – above all – American
shipmasters for metals, firearms, textiles, and foodstuffs. The Yankee
Nor'westmen dealt the skins at Canton for teas, silks, and porcelains,
which they then took for sale to European and American customers.
More and more land furs were traded on the Northwest Coast from
the mid-1810s until the early 1840s, by which time the depletion of
all of the fur bearers by over-hunting, the depression of the fur
markets by civil strife or changing fashion, and the depopulation of
the Indians themselves by disease and warfare had reduced the
Northwest trade to insignificance. The history of this far-flung and
many-sided enterprise deserves to be told, not only because of its
inherent interest but also because of its wide-ranging and far-reach-
ing impact; the Northwest Coast itself and the Hawaiian Islands were
particularly affected, both physically and culturally.

The coast trade has been studied before, of course, most prolifi-
cally by Frederic Howay, a county judge and amateur historian who
identified the principal features and changing aspects of the business
and in particular uncovered the bulk of the primary English-language sources.[1] Yet no comprehensive monographic treatment of the
trade has ever been published. And previous studies have suffered
from two shortcomings. First, probably because of their authors' ethnocentric preoccupation with American and British involvement and
their inability to read the Cyrillic sources, they have either neglected
or ignored Russian participation, which lasted longer than that of
any other nationality. Second, they have tended to concentrate on the
early or boom period of the trade before the War of 1812, partly
because it was more salient then and partly because most of the published sources predate that conflict. In fact, however, the Nor'west
trade persisted as late as the 1860s on the northern coast, although
by the end of the 1820s land furs outnumbered sea furs and by the
early 1840s American coasters had withdrawn, leaving the overworked field to the British and the Russians. During the late period
the trade changed considerably, and these changes can be traced in
a number of unpublished American ships' logs and journals from
the first three decades of the 1800s (they have survived partly
because they were used by other skippers as navigational guides), the
records of the Russian-American Company (RAC) and the Hudson's
Bay Company (HBC) for the 1820s and 1830s, and the business correspondence of several Boston shipowners. Howay made considerable
use of these logs and journals and business letters; otherwise they
and the companies' records have been underexploited by investigators
of the coast trade. Most notable in this regard is the recent work of
Robin Fisher, who on the basis of a minority of the extant primary
sources, particularly for the later period, reaches several revisionist
conclusions – for example, that the level of violence in the trade was
low, that the military role of firearms was negligible, and that the
Indians controlled the traffic.[2] Such neglect of the evidence is perhaps understandable in a study of the coast trade which forms but
one chapter of an award-winning dissertation on a broader theme
over a longer period – Indian-European relations in British Columbia
from 1774 until 1890. Nevertheless, that the primary sources are not
quite as "scattered and fragmentary" as Professor Fisher would have
us believe[3] is attested by my own bibliography.

For enabling me to consult the array of sources and allowing me
to quote them, I am grateful to the following repositories and individuals: Baker Library of Harvard University, Boston; Bancroft
Library of the University of California, Berkeley; Beinecke Rare

Book and Manuscript Library of Yale University, New Haven, especially Stephen Jones; British Columbia Provincial Archives, Victoria; California Historical Society, San Francisco; Essex Institute, Salem, MA; Hamilton Library of the University of Hawaii at Manoa, Honolulu, especially Patricia Polansky; Houghton Library of Harvard University, Cambridge, MA; Hudson's Bay Company Archives in the Manitoba Provincial Archives, Winnipeg, especially Shirlee Anne Smith; Kendall Whaling Museum, Sharon, MA; Library Company of Philadelphia, Philadelphia, PA; Massachusetts Historical Society, Boston; Mystic Seaport Museum, Mystic, CT; New York Public Library, Rare Books and Manuscripts Division, New York City; Old Dartmouth Historical Society, New Bedford, MA; Oregon Historical Society, Portland, OR, especially Sherry Crownhart-Vaughan; Pacific Manuscripts Bureau, Research School of Pacific Studies, Australian National University, Canberra, ACT; Peabody Museum, Salem, MA; Public Record Office, Kew, England; Scott Library of York University, Toronto, especially the interlibrary loan service under Mary Hudecki; Sag Harbor Whaling and Historical Museum, Sag Harbor, NY; United States Department of State Library, Washington, DC; United States National Archives and Records Service, Washington, DC; University of British Columbia Library, Special Collections Division, Vancouver; and University of Canterbury Library, Christchurch, NZ, especially the interloans and photographic services.

This monograph is an outgrowth of a study that was commissioned by the Smithsonian Institution for volume four of the revised edition of the *Handbook of North American Indians*, where a much shorter and rather different version appears.[4] It now remains for someone else to tap Indian oral histories and Chinese written records for additional perspectives on the maritime fur trade of the Northwest Coast.

1. Norfolk (Sitka) Sound with Mount Edgecumbe, 1787, by an unknown artist. From Captain George Dixon (William Beresford), *A Voyage Round the World* (London: Geo. Goulding 1789), facing 192.

2. A young Hawaiian woman, 1779, drawn by John Webber. From Captain James Cook (and Captain James King), *A Voyage to the Pacific Ocean* (London: G. Nicol and T. Cadell 1784), atlas, plate 63.

3. Two Hawaiian attractions: girls and hogs, 1792–93, drawn by Sigismund Bacstrom. Courtesy of the Oregon Historical Society, from a private collection.

4. The Canton factories, *circa* 1820, painted by an unknown Chinese artist. From Hosea Ballou Morse, *The Chronicles of the East India Company trading to China 1635–1834* (Oxford: Clarendon Press, 1926–29), 3: facing 368.

5. A labreted Haida woman, 1787, redrawn by an unknown artist from a
sketch by George Dixon. From Captain George Dixon (William Beresford), *A Voyage Round the World* (London: Geo. Goulding 1789),
facing 226.

6. Captain George Vancouver's ship *Discovery* on the rocks in Queen Char-
lotte Sound, 1792, drawn by Zachary Mudge. From Captain George
Vancouver, *A Voyage of Discovery* (London: G.G. and J. Robinson and
J. Edwards 1798), 2: facing 300.

7. A battle between Captain Robert Gray's *Columbia* and some Kwakiutls in Queen Charlotte Sound, 1792, drawn by George Davidson. From Frederic W. Howay, *Voyages of the "Columbia" to the Northwest Coast 1787–1790 and 1790–1793* (Boston: Massachusetts Historical Society 1941), facing 404.

8. New Archangel, or Sitka, in the middle 1820s, drawn by an unknown artist. From K. T. Khlebnikov, "Zapiski o Koloniyakh Rossiisko-Amerikanskoy Kompanii" ("Notes on the Colonies of the Russian-American Company"), Archive of the Russian Geographical Society, raz. 99, op. 1, no. 112, p. 3.

Tammeamea
King of the Sandwich Islands.

9. King Kamehameha I, 1816, drawn by Louis Choris. From Otto Von Kotzebue, *Voyage of Discovery in the South Sea ... in the Years 1815, 16, 17, and 18, in the Ship Rurick* (London: Sir Richard Phillips and Co. 1821], facing 84.

10. Honolulu, 1816–17, drawn by Louis Choris. From M. Louis Choris, *Voyage pittoresque autour du monde* (Paris: Firmin Didot 1822), plate 9.

11. Friendly Cove in Nootka Sound, 1792, drawn by Henry Humphrys. From Captain George Vancouver, *A Voyage of Discovery* (London: G.G. and J. Robinson and J. Edwards 1798), 2: facing 336.

Otter Skins, Boston Ships, and China Goods

Come all you Bold N West men
  thats Doubled round the Cape
O Come & Set down By me and a
  Story i will relate

Ebenezer Clinton, "The Bold N West Man"

Introduction
The Northwest Coast

This numerous [Northwest Coast Indian] population is not to be
wondered at when we consider the abundant means of support
the country affords. The sea yields abundant supply of excellent
fishes of the most agreable kind, every rivulet teeming with myr-
iads of salmon; & the land affords an endless variety of berries
& esculent roots.

Dr John Scouler, 1825

The various Tribes who inhabit the large Extent of Coast from
[Juan] De Fucas Streights to the [Queen] Charlottes Islands
appear to have some Commercial Intercourse with each other.

Lieutenant Peter Puget, 1793

The Northwest Coast is more definable in cultural than physical
terms. Admittedly, the entire coast is damp and mild, but the high
mountains, deep fiords, thick rain forest, and numerous islands of
the northern half are much more muted in the south, which also has
somewhat warmer winters. Culturally, too, the coast displayed not a
little variation; for example, women played a more influential role
among the northern Indians, who, moreover, were usually considered
by Euroamerican visitors to be less swarthy and more handsome,
intelligent, and industrious than their southern brethern.[1] On the
whole, however, the Northwest Coast was one of the most distinctive
aboriginal areas of the continent. The primacy of the autonomous
local kin group, the derivation of social status from heredity and
wealth, the practice of slavery, elaborate ceremonialism, a highly formalized heraldic art form, an emphasis on woodworking, the use of
rectangular plank houses and dugout canoes, the wearing of untai-
lored (slipover or wraparound) garments, barefootedness, the importance of weaving and the unimportance of stone and ceramic
artisanry, the dominance of fishing, the paucity of vegetable foods,
an emphasis on water transportation – these and other traits were

common to the score of Native peoples of the coast and sharply distinguished them from the rest of North American Indian society.[2]

The Northwest Coast was peculiar in that it was able to support a large Indian population with a high level of cultural development without the benefit of farming – "complex" hunters-fishers in the taxonomy of anthropologists. The pre-contact population likely approached 200,000, making the coast one of the most densely peopled non-agricultural parts of the world. The sole domesticated animal was a basenji-like dog, which was kept in large numbers for deer running (especially on the northern coast in winter) and sometimes eating; about 1800 each Haida family owned nearly a dozen, and in 1791 an American sailor noted "the multiplicity of dogs" among the Nootkas.[3] On its way down the Columbia River between the Snake and Willamette Rivers in 1805 the Lewis and Clark expedition bought up to one hundred dogs for food from the Indians, who were unwilling to sell their fish; most of the party became very fond of dog meat, and Meriwether Lewis himself "vastly" preferred dog to deer and elk, which, with fowl, fish, and roots, were available below the Willamette.[4] The Chinook dogs were small and parti-coloured (black, white, brown, and brindle) with a long head, pointed nose, small eyes, erect and pointed ears, and short, smooth hair (except on the tail) and were used for hunting elk.[5] The Coast Salishes bred and clipped a woolly strain for hair for weaving blankets. It resembled a sheep dog, having long, soft, white hair, a bushy tail, a long, pointed muzzle, erect ears, sharp eyes, very large feet, and a thick body, and it stood one and one-half feet high; like all coastal dogs, it tended to howl and yelp rather than bark.[6] (Salish weaving, using sheep wool rather than dog hair, has recently been revived in the Lower Fraser Valley.[7])

The only cultivators on the Northwest Coast were the Yuroks, Haidas, and Tlingits, who grew tobacco.[8] "Haida tobacco," now extinct, was probably a variety of *Nicotiana quadrivalvis*; it was grown and chewed green (with lime from burned clam shells or sometimes with pine cambium and pine resin) as a narcotic stimulant by the Haidas and Tlingits.[9] (By contrast, the Yuroks, as an American seaman noted in 1788, "smoak tobacco out of a small wooden tube about the size of [a] Childs wistle."[10]) Members of Captain Vancouver's expedition (1791–95) observed it growing in "little gardens" among the Tlingits along Kootznahoo Inlet in the Alexander Archipelago; they learned that it was "by no means uncommon amongst the inhabitants of Queen Charlotte's islands, who cultivate much of this plant."[11] These sightings were corroborated by the American trading vessel *Atahualpa* in 1801–02; on Clarence Strait the supercargo, Ralph Haskins (the uncle, incidentally, of Ralph Waldo Emerson), found that the Tlingits had "some small patches of land planted with the weed that serves them for tobacco," and at Massett on the Queen Charlottes the homesick crew was cheered by "the beautiful verdure that covers the little plantations of Y^e tobacco weed about this [Haida] village."[12] American traders were not above buying coarse Haida tobacco. The log of the *Otter* for 4 November 1810 noted: "To day the [Haida] Indians [at Skidegate] sold us a few Skins & a large quaintity of their Tobacco, the other tribes are very fond of it altho it is miserable stuff, but it is only at a few places on this Coast that they can raise any, for it is a rare thing to see a clear spot of Land to contain only a few rods and, that nature must clear for them they being too lazy to doo it themselves, they cultivate no sort of vegetables."[13]

But Chinook and Salish dogs and Tlingit and Haida tobacco were exceptional. The Northwest Coast's rugged terrain and thin soil (save the sedimentated Puget Sound shore and Fraser River delta in particular), and the dearth of sunshine towards the north, did not favour agriculture; indeed this fact was to prove advantageous to the Indians with the coming of white settlers, for their largely unarable ancestral lands were generally shunned by agrarian intruders, although their fishing grounds and timber stands were often usurped. Fortunately, nature was otherwise generous, as well as majestic. The rushing rivers and long "canals" (inlets) teemed with edible fish, including five species of salmon as well as herring, halibut, cod, and "small fish" (oolachen). (Salmon was the most prized food of the Nootkas, and it was one of the few articles that they usually refused to trade, and only very dearly when they consented.[14]) Shellfish (clams, mussels, crabs) and various sea animals (hair seals, sea lions, sea otters, fur seals, porpoises, whales) likewise abounded, and the Pacific flyway afforded numerous waterfowl. Not to be outdone, the abutting mountains, higher and more angular to the north and lower and more rounded to the south but everywhere seldom breached by transverse rivers, offered magnificent forests of workable timber, red and yellow cedar above all, as well as various berries and other food plants.[15] The ubiquitous conifers outcompeted grasses, so big game in the form of ungulates was not plentiful on the coast, except at the southern end (elk and deer in the Willamette valley) and in the northern part (Sitka blacktailed deer in the Alaskan panhandle and Alexander Archipelago). As an early British fur trader remarked, "It is the peculiar happiness of this country, that the sea which washes its coasts, shares with the land the plenty of commercial produce."[16] A later British visitor, Dr John Scouler, ship's surgeon (and botantist) on the HBC's *William and Ann*, concurred: "Certainly few savage tribes have equal

facility in procuring their favourite luxuries as the Indians of the
N. W. Coast," he declared.[17] Fishing and canoeing were emblematic
of the Indian economy. A number of fishing and hunting techniques
and preserving methods were mastered by the Natives,[18] and the food
surpluses enabled them to settle in sizeable villages, to prosper mate-
rially, and to evolve complex social, religious, and artistic values, particularly during the rainy but mild winters.

Not all Northwest Coast Indians, however, had access to sea otters,
which were the mainstay of the maritime fur trade. *Enhydra lutris* is
the largest member of the weasel family but the smallest marine
mammal (Frontispiece). Lacking an insulating layer of body fat, its
fur coat is exceptionally dense (60,000 hairs per square inch) in order
to lend both warmth and bouyancy. The thick, dark, lustrous pelt
became by far the most valuable fur on the world market. "Other
furs bear no proportion, in value, to those of the sea otter," asserted
the owners of one of the earliest British trading voyages.[19] In 1829
it took more than ten beaver pelts, the pillar of the continental fur
trade of North America, to equal the value of a single sea-otter skin.[20]
(Similarly, in 1841 the HBC exchanged sea-otter skins with the RAC
for beaver skins at the rate of one for nine and one-half; and in 1822–
23 at Canton even a sea-otter tail [$5.00] was worth more than a
beaver pelt [$4.50], which in turn was worth only one-ninth as much
as a sea-otter skin [$40.00].[21])

An American trader judged that "the fur of this creature is certainly much finer and more delicate than any heretofore known."[22]
A British competitor agreed: "Their fur is the finest in the world; it
possesses a jetty blackness, and is of exceeding beauty. The peculiar
warmth it affords, renders it a most valuable clothing in the colder
climates; but considered in an ornamental view, it has a rich and
magnificent appearance, and, under a certain arrangement, may vie
even with the royal ermine."[23] Lewis and Clark saw sea-otter skins for
the first time at the mouth of the Columbia in the winter of 1805–
06 at Fort Clatsop. "The fur of them were more butiful than any fur
I had ever Seen," William Clark wrote; "it is the richest and I think
the most delightfull fur in the world at least I cannot form an idea
of any more so. it is deep thick silky in the extream and strong."[24]
William Sturgis, a veteran American Nor'westman, derived more
pleasure from viewing a sea-otter skin than "half the pictures that
are stuck up for exhibition, and puffed up by pretended connois-
seurs." To him only "a beautiful woman and a lovely infant" were
more attractive natural objects.[25]

A prime (adult) pelt of "this beautiful and elegant Fur" was as large
as 5½ feet by 3 feet and glossy black.[26] Cub (juvenile) pelts and tails

were also taken but especially the latter were less valuable; at Canton prime skins brought ten times as much as tails. In addition, adult were thicker and darker than juvenile pelts, male were larger than female skins, and winter were darker than summer coats.[27] The Chinese classified sea-otter fur under eight to ten grades.[28] The Russians divided sea-otter skins into four categories in terms of quality (size of pelt and length and softness of fur) in the following descending order: Kurilian-Kamchatkan, Aleutian, Northwest Coast, and Californian.[29] The last, which came from a distinct subspecies of the animal, generally brought only two-thirds as much as Northwest Coast skins at Canton, being smaller and browner.[30]

Hundreds of thousands of these playful creatures frequented the protective kelp beds of the North Pacific littoral from the Sea of Japan to the Sea of Cortez, feeding on sea urchins, mollusks, and starfish. But there were gaps in this range, especially between Cape Flattery and Trinidad Bay and even in Puget Sound and the Strait of Georgia. Around the mouth of the Columbia River, too, sea otters were not plentiful, although they were large in size and high in quality, so that the Natives set a "great value" on them.[31] Consequently, the maritime fur trade was less marked on the southern half of the Northwest Coast; besides, that stretch was not well sheltered for vessels and its Natives were neither very numerous nor very friendly. This study, then, focuses on the "classic" Northwest Coast of Franz Boas rather than the more extensive North Pacific Coast of more recent specialists like Philip Drucker. The Northern (Tlingit, Haida, Tsimshian), Wakashan (Bella Coola, Kwakiutl [or Kwagulth], Nootka), and Coast Salish–Chinook cultural subdivisions of Drucker, numbering probably up to 100,000 Indians in 1834 – that is, after the malaria epidemic of 1830–33 on the lower Columbia and before the smallpox outbreak of 1835–38 on the northern coast – receive almost all of the attention and the Northwest California subdivision almost none. In fact, after about 1800 the maritime fur trade was largely confined to the Northern subgroup alone.

PRE-CONTACT INDIAN TRADE

Although not all of the coastal Natives had an opportunity to hunt the sea otter, all of them did prize its resplendent coat. Robes of sea-otter fur, like those of mountain-goat "wool" (hair) and whistling-marmot fur, were esteemed as objects of beauty, wealth, and prestige, as well as comfort. Among the Nootkas, only chiefs and nobles hunted sea otters and wore their pelts, which were considered their finest clothing.[32] The animal's flesh was eaten, too. According to Captain John Meares, one of the earliest British traders, sea-otter hunting was even more troublesome and more hazardous for the Nootkas than whaling, for the otter was wary and cunning, an excellent swimmer, and ferocious in defence of its young. Yet "scarce a day passes," he noted, "but numbers are eagerly employed in the pursuit of it."[33] Thus, with the advent of Euroamerican traders the Indians did not have to initiate an untried activity in order to meet white demands; rather, they had simply to intensify a traditional occupation. Hunting singly with harpoon and bow and arrow was replaced by hunting severally via the sweep-and-surround method. And the gun was adopted as a hunting weapon, although as late as 1801 the Haidas, who had been introduced to firearms a decade earlier, were still killing sea otters with "a long dart, barbed like an arrow."[34]

Furthermore, the first Euroamerican coasters certainly did not have to introduce the Indians to commerce, for they already had a strong tradition of barter among themselves and with interior groups. Trade was well suited to Northwest Coast Indian society, for one of its main values and goals was the accumulation, display, and redistribution of material goods. So in Puget Sound in 1792 Captain Vancouver met Natives who most likely had not had any previous contact with whites "but they had a very good idea of bartering and woud not part with anything without the value of it."[35] Vancouver's second lieutenant, Peter Puget, remarked that "the various Tribes who inhabit the large Extent of Coast from De Fucas Streights to the Charlottes Islands appear to have some Commercial Intercourse with each other."[36] In fact, this intracoastal trade was more voluminous and extensive than Puget realized, thanks to the fact that, as one anthropological specialist has noted, "the environment of the Northwest Coast cultures is neither uniformly rich and dependable within any tribal area nor precisely the same from area to area"[37] (like, for that matter, the Indian culture itself). "Southern" were exchanged for "northern" articles and coastal for inland products. If the British shipmaster John Meares had realized the extent of this Native trade he would not have wondered why Nootka Sound in 1788 "appeared ... totally destitute of European articles" despite visits by a number of trading vessels since 1785.[38] The local Indians traded with nine villages to the north of the sound and nine villages to the south (including one on Tatoosh Island across the Strait of Juan de Fuca), according to a 1789 report by a second mate on an American vessel.[39] Captain George Vancouver's expedition noted in 1792 that there was "considerable commercial intercourse" between the Kwakiutls and the Nootkas, whose Chief Maquinna was the "grand agent" of this trans-island traffic; indeed the Kwakiutls had received "almost every article of Traffic in their possession" from Maquinna.[40] And this traffic was to be increased by Euroamerican traders, who were not slow to see the profit in buying items from one tribe and selling them to another for skins.

Both scarce and specialized commodities were traded up and down the coast for decorative and practical purposes alike: mountain-goat hair "blankets" (ceremonial robes), ermine skins, copper plates, and spruceroot baskets from the Tlingits; dugout cedar canoes from the Haidas; mountain-goat horn spoons, raven rattles, dance head-dresses, and oolachen (candlefish or fathomfish because they were oily enough to be burned as candles and because they were dried and smoked on strings and sold by the fathom) and their oil (*ssak*, or shrowton) from the Tsimshians; mountain-goat hair and horn from the Bella Coolas, the best hunters on the coast of that animal; yellow cedarbark robes and wooden utensils from the Kwakiutls; dugout cedar canoes, shark's teeth, and dentalia shells (*Dentalium Indianorum*, or *pretiosum*) from the Nootkas; dog-hair blankets and slaves from the Coast Salishes; elk hides and slaves from the Chinooks; and tobacco, woodpecker scalps, and Monterey (abalone) "ear shells" (*Haliotis cracherodii*) from the Yuroks.[41] Dentalia shells – haiqua – were one of the most popular and widespread articles. They were round and hollow, from one to four inches long and half an inch thick, slightly curved and tapered, milk white, very hard, light, and fragile. They were graded into long, medium, and short sizes (the longest were the most valuable) and traded in cedarbark packets or fathom-long strings (the fixed standard was forty to a strung fathom). Most came from the rich beds off the western coast of Vancouver Island. Haiqua were especially prized by the Yuroks, who used them as money. Among the Chinooks they were also a standard of value.[42] (Monterey shells were as highly prized as haiqua, if not more so. A longtime American trader recalled: "Their [Indian women's] most valuable Ear pendants, their real diamonds & pearls, are made from the central part of a shell, the haliotis, which is found upon the coast of California. They are very particular in selecting these shells; and I have occasionally seen a prime Sea Otter skin given for one in which I could scarcely discover a shade of difference from others, of which 100 would not command a skin."[43]) Equally precious were elk ("moose deer") hides, which probably came mostly from the Willamette valley. These "clamons" or "clemmels" were "always in great demand on the Northern Coast"[44] as "leather war dresses" for use in the frequent intertribal clashes. The hides were dressed and folded double or triple; they could stop arrows and lances and even musket and pistol balls at a distance.

Although the Northwest Coast was rather isolated from the rest of aboriginal North America by mountain ranges and knots (what Captain Vancouver perceived to be "one barrier along the coast"[45]), there was not a little intercourse through the mountain wall, at least wherever arterial rivers afforded routeways (indeed Vancouver carelessly overlooked the two main breakthroughs, the Columbia and the Fraser). There was no transoceanic contact, for the Northwest Coast Indians, unlike the Polynesians, were strictly coastal in their navigation; besides, there were no oceanic islands within striking distance, and the North Pacific belied its name. Transmountain contact was exemplified by the Chinooks, who may have numbered up to 17,000 around the mouth of the Columbia in 1805–06.[46] (When Captain Gray entered the Columbia in the spring of 1792 he was told by the local Chinooks that there were fifty Indian villages on the banks of the river[47] – meaning, perhaps, fifty Chinook villages on the lowermost Columbia.) Their canoeing skill – "Those Indians are certainly the best Canoe navigaters I ever Saw," declared William Clark[48] – enabled them to cope with the high surf, strong tides, swift current, shoals, rapids, whirlpools, and large drift trees of the river's notorious mouth and estuary. The Chinooks had access to more beaver and elk than sea otters; thus in August 1804 the *Caroline* bought 450 beaver, 145 elk hides, and only 31 sea otters in the Columbia.[49] The Chinooks traded Euroamerican goods and coastal products (sea-otter skins, whale blubber and oil, haiqua) to upriver Indians for wappatoos (arrowhead roots) and oolachen.

They also ventured as far up the Columbia as The Dalles, where the Columbia was narrowed to a torrent by the Cascade Mountains. This busy marketplace and prolific fishery was the fulcrum of a native commercial network that reached as far as the Rocky Mountains. "This is the great mart of all this country," observed Captain Clark in 1805; "maney nations visit this place for trade."[50] Alexander Ross; one of the Astorians (employees of John Jacob Astor's Pacific Fur Company (PFC), based at Astoria at the mouth of the Columbia), dubbed The Dalles the "great emporium or mart of the Columbia."[51] Here dried salmon and haiqua and eventually Euroamerican wares (copper tea kettles, brass arm bands, red and blue blankets, and old clothes in 1805[52]) were swapped for land furs, buffalo robes, rabbit-skin robes, mountain-sheep horn, jade celts, obsidian blades, native tobacco, bear grass, camas roots, shappalell (a whitish bread made from sun-baked roots), baskets, horses, and slaves from the Nez Percés and Cayuses (the Sahaptin Indians were called Nez Percés because of their custom of piercing the nose and inserting an ornament of dentalium). Lewis and Clark estimated that between Celilo

Falls and The Dalles 30,000 pounds of salmon were dried for market by the Indians annually.[53] The commercial traffic of the Columbia impressed the two explorers: "In this manner there is a trade continually carried on by the natives of the river each trading some article or other with their neighbours above and below them; and thus articles which are vended by the whites at the entrance of this river, find their way to the most distant nations enhabiting it's waters."[54] Indeed Clark found Indians in the Rockies who had haiqua, cloth, and brass that had come from the mouth of the Columbia.[55] So successful was Chinook commerce that the Chinook jargon became the *lingua franca* of the coast, spoken even by white traders, although Haida also became a "ship dialect."[56] Chinook was a pidgin of typically simple grammar and limited vocabulary, a mixture of Chinook, Salish, Nootka, English, and French which survived into the twentieth century.

Other Northwest Coast Indians were also active intertribal traders. The Coast Salishes trafficked with the Chilcotins and Lower Carriers, the Tsimshians with the Upper Carriers and Sekanis, and the Tlingits with the Tahltans and other Athapaskans; for example, well-worn "grease trails" led from Tsimshian oolachen beaches through river canyons and mountain passes to interior rendezvous.[57] Land furs, moose and caribou hides, ermine skins, jade celts, and porcupine-quill embroidery went from the interior Indians to the coast via the Fraser, Nass, Stikine, and Chilkat river valleys. Control of two of these routeways, the Stikine and the Chilkat, helped to make the Tlingits the strongest and the richest of the coastal groups. And their interior clients were among the last to be tapped by HBC posts; indeed in 1852 a Chilkat Tlingit war party trekked nearly 300 miles inland and captured and destroyed one of these posts, Fort Selkirk at the junction of the Pelly and Lewes rivers, in order to preserve their own intermediary role.[58] Also, the Tlingits virtually monopolized several of the most valuable indigenous trade goods: placer copper, ermine skins, and superior baskets and robes. In addition, they were the closest middlemen to precious Asiatic iron. And, finally, their principal villages, which were situated towards the heads of the long inlets, were less accessible to attack by other Natives or Euroamericans. Unluckily for the latter – specifically, the Russians – the formidable Tlingits were the first Northwest Coast Indians to be encountered.

1 The Russian Headstart and the Spanish Sideline

The constant decrease in the number of sea-otters taken for some years upon the coast of Kamschatka, and the great advantages derived from the trade in these valuable skins, induced the Russians to extend their possessions eastward from the continent of Asia; first, to the [Aleutian] islands between that coast and America; and finally, to the north-west coast of America itself.

Georg H. Von Langsdorff, 1805

In the year 1769, the court of Spain, alarmed at the progress the Russians were making on the north-west coast of America, determined to occupy Upper California, and to establish missions there for the conversion and civilization of its inhabitants.

Captain William Shaler, 1804

THE RUSSIAN ENTRY

The Russians were the first Euroamericans to make contact with the Northwest Coast Indians, although technically speaking they were not the first to enter the coast *trade*, owing in part to their preference for hunting to trading. In 1741, after eight years of arduous and costly preparation, the Vitus Bering–Aleksey Chirikov expedition finally left Kamchatka in two small ships to probe the "big land" across the Bering Sea. Chirikov's party made two landfalls on the Alexander Archipelago, where fifteen well-armed crewmen disappeared; they were likely seized by wary Tlingits – an omen of the future uneasy state of Russian-Tlingit relations. The expedition returned to Petropavlovsk in 1742 without its Danish-born commander, who was fatally shipwrecked, but with hundreds of sea-otter skins instead. They were found to bring handsome prices in north China, whose large and affluent Manchu upper class valued sea-otter fur as both fancy trim and snug garb in winter. "The skin of a sea-otter is preferred in China to every other, but is used only by the opulent," noted a Russian observer.[1] Russian promyshlenniks (freelance entrepreneurs in general and fur traders in particular) launched a fur rush down the Kurile Islands to Yezo (Hokkaido) and across the Aleutian Islands to the Gulf of Alaska in search of what they called "sea beavers." From 1743 to 1800 one hundred ventures obtained more than 8,000,000 silver rubles worth of "soft gold."[2] In 1799, alarmed by the violent competition among the several Russian companies and by the prospect of international entanglement on the Northwest Coast, the tsarist government chartered a joint-stock monopoly, the RAC (modelled upon the British East India Company [EIC] and the HBC), to administer and develop Russian America.

Thus the Muscovites enjoyed a lead in the maritime fur trade of nearly half a century, rival Euroamericans not entering the contest until the middle 1780s. This advantage was compounded by Russian control of the habitats of the most valuable grades of sea otters: Kurilian-Kamchatkan and Aleutian; their fur was blacker, thicker, and glossier than that of the Northwest Coast and Californian otters. The British Captain George Dixon, for example, asserted that the sea otters to the south of the Alexander Archipelago were of a "very inferior quality."[3] It was not until the superior varieties were exhausted that the Russians advanced to the Northwest Coast in 1788, whereupon they engaged other Euroamerican traders in a competition that was eventually to exterminate the local strain (it has only recently been reintroduced from the Aleutians). Until 1795, however, few Russian ships made the coast because of a shortage of both vessels and sailors. In 1794–95 three new ships were built in the Gulf of Alaska and two more arrived from Okhotsk, then Russia's chief Pacific port, and the number of tsar's men more than doubled.[4] In 1794 the reinforced Russians reached Yakutat Bay (Captain Cook's Bering Bay), getting 2,000 sea otters in the process and founding the settlement of Slavorossiya there the following year.[5]

Meanwhile, an expedition under the command of James Shields, a British employee of the Golikov-Shelikhov Company, reconnoitered the coast as far south as the Queen Charlotte Islands and sighted numerous sea otters. In January 1795 Alexander Baranov, the company's colonial manager, sailed in the *Olga* to Sitka Sound, raised a cross on shore, and named the waters Cross Bay. In July of the following year Shields and a party of Aleuts from Kodiak arrived on the *Oryol* and bagged 1,847 sea otters; two years later another party of Kodiak Aleuts killed up to 1,000 otters.[6] Finally, in June 1799 Baranov returned on the *Oryol* with 550 kayaks of Aleuts to hunt, and in late July he established the settlement of Arkhangelsk.[7] (It was destroyed by the Tlingits in July 1802 but re-established on a

nearby *kekur* [rocky promontory] in September 1804 as Novoarkhangelsk [New Archangel], whose population as the colonial capital at
the beginning of 1810 numbered 621, including 199 Russians, 411
Konyagas [Kodiak Eskimos], and 11 Tlingit hostages.[8])

By 1800 three-quarters of the RAC's sea-otter skins were coming
from the vicinity of Sitka Sound;[9] here Aleut hunting parties killed
more than 2,000 otter in July 1800 and up to 4,000 in June 1801.[10]
Here, too, the Russians finally encountered their American rivals,
who were likewise seeking fresh sources of sea otters (this imperialist
overlap was reflected in the area's dual toponomy: the Alexander
Archipelago and Sitka Sound to the Russians but the King George
Archipelago and Norfolk Sound to the Americans and British)
(Fig. 1). In late April 1799 the American ship *Hancock* met "Canoes
coming from all parts of the Sound appearing to have many Skins,"
and in two weeks of trading some 250 pelts were taken from the
Tlingits; at the end of spring the *Hancock* was joined by the *Caroline*
and the *Despatch*, and they hailed a Russian brig, the *Oryol*, whose
commander said that its owners had 1,300 Aleut and Kodiak hunters
"out after Otters."[11] At the end of 1805 the Russian navy's *Neva*, which
was accompanying the *Nadezhda* on the first Russian voyage around
the world and which had helped the Russians recapture New Archangel, or Sitka, left the port for Canton with 442,819 rubles worth
of furs, including 151,000 fur seals, 9,288 foxes, and 4,220 sea
otters.[12]

The Russians enjoyed additional advantages, such as the financial
and political backing of the tsarist government. Some of its highest
officials, including the emperor himself, owned shares in the concern.
Another advantage was the existence of permanent bases on the
coast: Slavorossiya (1796–1805) on Yakutat Bay, the colonial capital
of New Archangel, or Sitka (1799–1802, 1804–   ) on Sitka Sound,
and St Dionysius Redoubt (1834–40) at the mouth of the Stikine
River. They were not matched by American or Spanish settlements;
Fort Clatsop (1805–06) and Astoria (1811–12), both at the mouth of
the Columbia, were shortlived and insubstantial, as were Santa Cruz
de Nutka (1789–95) on Vancouver Island and Nuñez Gaona (1792)
on the Olympic Peninsula. The British did not have a coastal post
until 1812 – Fort George, formerly Astoria; the larger establishments
of Forts Vancouver and Langley were not founded until the middle
1820s, and neither was located right on the coast.

Moreover, the RAC benefitted from the use or, more correctly,
enserfment of the Aleuts and Kodiaks, the world's best hunters of
sea otters. In fact, Russian participation in the Northwest Coast trade
amounted more to hunting than trading, with their ships serving to
transport and protect hunting parties of kayakers. As the British

trader Captain Nathaniel Portlock found at Cook Inlet in 1786, "I could perceive that they procured no furs by bartering with the [native] Americans, and that they got no sea otter skins, nor indeed furs of any kind, but what the Kodiac Indians [Eskimos] caught in hunting."[13] Before the creation of the RAC the natives paid *yasak* (fur tribute, usually so many pelts per man per year); after the company's establishment one-half of all adult males (those eighteen years of age and over) had instead to hunt for the firm, which gave them materials for repairing their kayaks, guns, ammunition, dried fish, and tobacco. The company told the Aleuts and Kodiaks beforehand how many kayaks would be needed, and in December the Native elders made duty rosters, choosing the hunters mainly from villages with more than one man. The kayaks set out in March or April – usually up to 150 from Kodiak, up to 100 from Unalaska, and about 50 from Atka, and even some from Kenai (Cook) Inlet and Chugach (Prince William) Sound, each party under a Russian or Aleut foreman. They proceeded to assigned stations along the mainland and island coasts and stayed until August or September. Upon their return they submitted their catch, receiving 30 rubles per first-grade sea-otter skin, 15 per second-grade skin, and 3 per third-grade skin, minus any expenses for outfitting.[14]

Consequently, the low quantity and quality and the high price of Russian trade goods (stemming from the backwardness of Russian manufacturing) were not crucial, the RAC being able to get skins in return for paltry Aleut and Kodiak wages in kind. Consequently, too, the Russians incurred lower costs than British or American traders in the procurement of skins. The former likewise benefitted from access to more than one market on the Chinese frontier (Kyakhta and Tsurukhaitui), where, moreover, they had no competitors (Captain Vancouver also believed that the Russians had the advantage of being more used to the northern cold and the frontier hardships).[15] So dependent were the Russians upon Native hunters that in 1861 two official inspectors reported that "in chatting with the Aleuts, and in fact with all the natives, we have come to the conclusion that they are not in slavery to the Company at all, but that in fact the Company itself has become a slave to them."[16]

Russian trading voyages *per se* remained infrequent also because of the company's shortage of sound vessels and adept sailors and the difficulty of navigation of the "straits," the maze of often narrow and shallow channels dividing the islands of the Alexander Archipelago, in the face of Tlingit hostility. Another deterrent was corporate inflexibility. Russian prices for Indian furs were set by the RCA's head office in St Petersburg, halfway around the globe, and hence could not be quickly changed to meet competition, whereas American and

British "tariffs" could be adjusted on the spot.[17] It was not until the acquisition of a "sizeable" amount of trade goods in the autumn of 1832 that the Russians were able to break the American and British stranglehold on the coast trade in the following year, when Captain Adolph Etholen, a future colonial governor, took the *Chichagov* on a purely trading voyage in the "straits."[18] This initiative was solidified in 1834 by the founding of St Dionysius Redoubt at the mouth of the Stikine as a commercial base. At the same time, the HBC was pressing the Americans from the south with both ships and posts. The RAC was unable to match the quality or the price of the trade goods of the more efficient British firm. In 1839 Governor Ivan Kupreyanov lamented that "year by year I see the Tlingits drawn more and more from our territory to the English frontier."[19]

Yet another obstacle was the long haul for Russian furs from the Northwest Coast across the North Pacific and through Eastern Siberia to the Mongolian frontier at Kyakhta, the pre-eminent of the two border crossings where Russia was permitted by treaty to traffic with China. As an anonymous merchant stated, because of "the difficulty and heavy expence attending the Transport" from either Sitka or St Petersburg to the Chinese market, "the price requisite to remunerate the Russians must be very great."[20] (For example, around 1800 shipping tea from Canton to England by sea was from two to three times faster and up to eighteen times cheaper [30–40 kopeks per pud] than from Kyakhta to Moscow by land [600 kopeks per pud].[21]) Moreover, competition resulted in lower prices for sea-otter skins at Canton. The influx of British, American, and even Spanish skins there prompted north China's merchants to travel nearly 1,000 miles to reach the city, where they found the skins for sale at prices "much below" those of Kyakhta (they also found that Canton's British woollen imports were superior to those of the Russians at Kyakhta).[22] The Chinese refused to allow the tsar's subjects to ship more quickly and more cheaply to Canton, perhaps because they felt that two points of contact with the expansionist Russian "barbarians" were sufficient (Russia did, after all, border on China) and perhaps because the proud Russian emissaries refused to kowtow. One of the main goals of the abortive mission of Count Yury Golovkin to Peking in 1805–06 was to secure commercial access to Chinese ports, including Canton. At the very same time, two Russian ships tried to break the Cantonese barrier and narrowly avoided seizure; their commander, Captain Adam Von Krusenstern, had sailed in a British vessel to Canton and lived there in 1798–99 and had become acutely aware that Russian access to Canton would obviate the protracted (one-year) and hazardous shipment of pelts from Sitka to Kyakhta. Yet the suspicious Chinese did not relent. They feared that, as one high official stated after the rejection of Captain Von Krusenstern's overture, "now that they had come by sea to Kwangtung [Canton], they might possibly become well acquainted with the sea route to China, and gain information about the Interior."[23]

Equally disadvantageous was the inability of the usually undermanned and often undersupplied RAC to subdue the stalwart Tlingits, who numbered about 10,000 at the beginning of the 1800s.[24] Their strong clan system provided solidarity against a common enemy. As the naturalist Georg Von Langsdorff noted in 1805, "single families, as well as single tribes, have contentions sometimes with each other … but if attacked by a common enemy, suppose the Russians, they unite for their common defence."[25] Moreover, the Russians' Aleut and Kodiak hunters took what the Tlingits regarded as their potential trade goods in the form of sea-otter skins and gave nothing in return.[26] Additionally, unlike American and British traders, the Russians actually infringed Tlingit territory with settlements. As Von Langsdorff again noted: "That they should entertain an unalterable enmity against the Russians is the more natural, since they have not only been driven from their hereditary possessions by them, but they have also been deprived of their great means of wealth, nay, even of subsistence derived from the sea-otters, the fish, and other marine productions, with which the coast they inhabit so richly abound[s]."[27] This enmity was such that Von Langsdorff found that "the Russians cannot properly be said to carry on any trade with the Kaluschians [Tlingits]."[28] As late as 1821 Russian-Tlingit trade was "very insignificant."[29] This situation did not change until the middle 1820s, by which time American trading vessels – the Tlingits' traditional customers – were quitting the Nor'west trade. Even then, however, the HBC outcompeted the RAC for Tlingit furs.

Furthermore, the Tlingits were militarily formidable, employing orderly battle formations, wearing hide and slat cuirasses (which could stop musket shot), gorgets, and bone helmets, and eventually wielding firearms, including cannons. They destroyed Sitka itself in 1802 and threatened it as late as 1855, and periodically they killed unwary Aleut and Kodiak hunters; in the spring of 1818, for example, twenty-three Aleuts were killed and twelve wounded by Tlingit gunfire on Prince of Wales Island.[30] The American trader William Sturgis described the Tlingits in 1799 as the most "daring and insolent" Indians on the Northwest Coast, while the Tongass Tlingits were rated "the bravest people, as well as the best hunters, on the coast" in the middle 1820s by Dr John Scouler, a British surgeon-botanist.[31] The Koloshes, as the Russians called the Tlingits (from the Russian word for "labret"), were never completely pacified by the Muscovites, whose warships could seldom reach the main Indian villages far up the narrow, tortuous inlets.[32]

Thus Russian participation in the maritime fur trade of the Northwest Coast did not extend south of the "straits," and it remained marginal figuratively as well as literally. That marginality was deepened in 1839, when the HBC leased the *lisiére*, or mainland panhandle of Alaska, from the RAC, whose Nor'west activity thereafter was further restricted to the Alexander Archipelago.

THE SPANISH ENTRY

Spain's involvement in the coast trade was even more peripheral than Russia's, although it began auspiciously. In fact, Spain beat both Great Britain and the United States to the coast and, excepting the voyage of Bering and Chirikov, Russia as well. Indeed, before the Russians repeated Chirikov's visit in 1788, the Spanish had sent three expeditions there, beginning in 1774, when Captain Juan Pérez in the *Santiago* reconnoitered as far north as the Alexander Archipelago and obtained some sea-otter skins from the Haidas (in the same year the first permanent Russian settlement in the New World was founded on Unalaska Island in the eastern Aleutians). Alarmed by the relentless Russian advance, as well as by the prospect of Great Britain's discovery of the fancied northwest passages of Juan de Fuca (1592) and Bartholomew de Fonte (1640), His Catholic Majesty outfitted a series of expeditions from the shallow, pestilential port of San Blas on the Mexican isthmus to the Northwest Coast in the last quarter of the eighteenth century to evaluate and forestall Russian and British encroachment. Naval outposts were established to protect New Spain's northwestern frontier: Santa Cruz de Nutka on Nootka Sound and Nuñez Gaona (Neah Bay) on the Strait of Juan de Fuca.

Spanish interest in the Northwest Coast, however, remained strategic. They wanted simply to keep the coast unexplored and undeveloped as a wilderness buffer against foreign penetration of the Californias and México, where their primary concerns lay. They also seem to have been repelled by the coast's wildness, ruggedness, coldness, and raininess; for example, during an excursion with Captain Vancouver in Nootka Sound in 1794 the Spanish commissioner, José Manuel de Álava, frequently expressed his "astonishment" that "a region so wild and inhospitable ... could ever have been an object of contention [the Nootka Sound dispute] between our respective sovereigns."[33] So the pagan Indians were not missionized and the natural resources were not exploited; only one of the Spanish voyages was a trading venture. New Spain, however, had neither the capital nor the labour to sustain such far-flung bastions. Alta California's missions and ranchos produced abundant wheat and beef but foreign trade was prohibited by the Laws of the Indies. Also, the *frontera del norte* was chronically undermanned, an American trader opining in 1804 that "the conquest of this country would be absolutely nothing; it would fall without an effort to the most inconsiderable force."[34] In addition, the Spanish voyages, like their Russian counterparts, remained, in the words of Captain Vancouver's surgeon-botanist, Dr Archibald Menzies, cloaked in an "odium of indolence & secrecy"[35] and hence unappreciated by other imperial powers. Madrid's claims to the coast were further weakened by official caution and eventually retrenchment in the wake of Bourbon dethronement by Napoleon.[36]

Otherwise Spain was in a favourable position to prosecute the Nor'west trade. In 1786 Captain De La Pérouse found it "perfectly unaccountable that the Spaniards, having so near and so frequent intercourse with China from Manilla, should have been hitherto ignorant of the value of this precious trade of furs."[37] In fact, they were well aware of its value, and theoretically, at least, they were well placed to act. Their supply bases (San Blas, Monterey, San Francisco) were found closer to the coast than those of Great Britain or the United States, and for a while, of course, Spain even had two posts on the coast itself; it had ready access to suitable trade goods, particularly abalone shells (*guindas*, or *conchas*), whose pearl was much in demand by the Indians for adornment, as well as Mexican cloth and Chilean copper, besides plenty of provisions from Alta California; it had charted a well-defined trans-Pacific sea lane to the Chinese market from New Spain – the annual "China ship," or Manila galleon; and it would have conserved precious silver by substituting peltry for specie in exchange for Chinese commodities, especially quicksilver (mercury), which was essential in New Spain for refining silver and gold ores.[38] As a Spanish observer noted: "We have, in our possessions, all the items that circulate in this trade: abundant copper in Michoacán; many textiles in Querétaro, Cholula, and other places; crude hats throughout the kingdom [of New Spain]; abalone shells in Monterey; and so forth. Navigation ought to be less costly for us and closer to the port of departure and points of arrival. We have an abundance of foodstuffs which can be obtained from the Californias and the facility to purchase these easily. We can therefore pay more to the Indians for the furs and sell them to the Chinese more cheaply."[39]

But the Spanish source of sea-otter skins remained the Californian coast.[40] Although southern sea otters were lighter in colour and smaller in size than their northern brethern, the difference in the prices of their pelts on the Chinese market – $40 versus $45 each in 1785–86[41] – was not great, at least at first. From 1783 sea-otter skins were shipped to China on the Manila galleon from Acapulco, and between the middle 1780s and the middle 1790s several schemes were advanced for trading Californian sea-otter fur for Chinese quicksilver. One such scheme was proposed in 1784 by the *colonial* Vicente Vasadre y Vega, who argued that such traffic would checkmate Russian and British entrepreneurs in the North Pacific and procure more quicksilver for New Spain's tin miners. The skins were to be shipped from the Californias to San Blas on the returning (and empty) supply vessels and from Acapulco to Canton on the China ship. His plan was approved in early 1786, and at the end of that year he returned to San Blas from San Diego with 1,060 skins, mostly from mission Indians. In 1787 the missions gained exclusive control of Vasadre y Vega's venture, and at the end of that year 1,750 more skins (including 1,133 from Baja California) were delivered to San Blas. This scheme ended in 1789; in four years it had sent 9,729 skins of *nutria de mar* to Manila and made $3,120,000 ($321 each) for the king's treasury.[42] During the late 1780s the Spanish took "several thousand" skins annually along the Californian coast, and in 1791 they had 3,000 awaiting buyers at Macao.[43]

Yet this southern traffic did not flourish. The Californian Indians were neither willing nor skilled hunters of sea otters, the balmy climate obviating the need for fur garments. Besides, they were given low prices for their skins, and trade goods were scarce in the Californias. The Franciscan missionaries, who did not control hunting and did not want their Indian charges distracted, were indisposed. And their eventual monopoly was infringed by illicit private trading on the part of soldiers. Another monopoly, the powerful Royal Philippine Company (established 1785), which had exclusive rights to the importation of Chinese goods into the Americas, was opposed to the trade. Its sole venture involved the *Princesa Real* (the former *Princess Royal*, seized by the Spaniards at Nootka Sound in 1789), which carried 3,333 sea otter skins in 54 boxes in 1791 from San Blas to Manila via Hawaii. The skins were eventually sold in Macao; the ship was wrecked in a typhoon in the autumn of 1791 and sold for scrap.[44]

The inferiority of southern to northern sea-otter skins, the imposition of state duties on the exportation of furs from New Spain, and the glutting of the Canton market by British and American fur traders in the last half of the 1780s and the first half of the 1790s were additional disincentives. After 1800 most of the traffic in Californian sea-otter pelts was conducted partly by American and Russian poachers and partly by licensed Russian hunters (on halves).[45] By then not only Spain but also Great Britain, the initiator of the Nor'west trade, had virtually abandoned the business.

2 The British Disclosure

To Captain Cook ... we are indebted for the commerce of the
North West Coast of America, and its profitable application to
the China market ...

Captain John Meares, 1790

Spain's retreat from the Northwest Coast was signalled by the Nootka
Sound controversy (1789–94), an international territorial dispute
which arose from the Spanish seizure of four British trading vessels
in what Captain James Cook had named King George's Sound. It
was Cook's third (and fatal) voyage that brought his country into the
Nor'west trade before all others.[1] In 1778 his two ships, *Resolution*
and *Discovery*, were refitted for a month in Nootka Sound, where his
crewmen bought sea-otter skins – literally off the Indians's backs –
for scraps of iron; more were purchased later in Cook Inlet for glass
beads. They were used mainly for warm clothing (greatcoats, jacket
linings, caps, gloves) during the expedition's two subsequent probes
of far northern waters in its vain search for an Arctic seaway between
the Pacific and the Atlantic.[2] Upon leaving the Northwest Coast Cook
reflected that "there is no doubt but a very benificial fur trade might
be carried on with the Inhabitants of this vast coast," although he
cautioned that unless a northwest passage were found it would be
"rather too remote for Great Britain to receive any emolument from
it," and that the only available pelt of any value was that of the sea
otter (and most of the skins acquired by his expedition were full of
lice and in the form of clothing). Nevertheless, Cook asserted that,
although the Indians seemed to be quite self-sufficient, "a trade with
Foreigners would increase their wants by introducing new luxuries
amongst them, in order to purchas which they would be the more
assiduous in procuring skins, for I think it is pretty evident they are
not a scarce article in the Country."[3] At the end of 1779 the expedition's prime skins brought $120 apiece in Canton for a return of
£90 on an investment of 1 shilling (or "an astonishing profit" of 1,800

per cent!).[4] Little wonder that the crew's eagerness to return to the Northwest Coast "to make their fortunes" bordered on mutiny; in fact, two men deserted with the *Resolution's* cutter and headed for the coast (but disappeared).

Others, better prepared, followed, alerted by the publication in the first half of the 1780s of both the official and unofficial accounts of Cook's last voyage. In the official version Captain James King, who succeeded to the command after the slaying of Cook in Hawaii and the death of the consumptive Captain Charles Clerke in Kamchatka, noted the "advantages that might be derived from a voyage to that part of the American Coast, undertaken with commercial views." He recommended that the East India Company (EIC) dispatch two ships from Canton with iron, woollen cloth, glass and copper trinkets, and knives to the Northwest Coast in the early spring to trade until the autumn, which would allow it to obtain at least 250 sea-otter skins and realize a profit of more than 400 per cent.[5] King's advice was quickly heeded, but not only by the British. "It was as if a new gold coast had been discovered," wrote Washington Irving. "Individuals from various countries dashed into this lucrative traffic ..."[6] Thus, although it failed to find a northwest passage, Cook's last voyage did reveal the colchian bounty of the Northwest Coast. In addition, incidentally, it demonstrated that scurvy, the longtime bane of seafaring, could be controlled, so that distant voyages like his to the coast need no longer be "objects of terror"; before Cook, one-half and sometimes two-thirds of ships' crews died of scurvy and other ailments.[7]

The first argonauts to exploit the master mariner's findings were his countryman Captain James Hanna with 30 crewmen in 1785 in the 60-ton brig *Harmon*, fittingly renamed the *Sea Otter*. (Captain William Bolts, a Dutch adventurer and a former employee of the EIC in Bengal, had planned commercial-scientific ventures to the coast under the Austrian flag in 1781 in the 700–ton *Cobenzell* and a 45–ton tender and again in 1784 in the *Imperial Eagle*, but both had been aborted, the first by an "intrigue."[8]) Hanna anchored in Nootka Sound for five weeks and procured a "valuable cargo of Furs," 560 skins, which fetched from $20,600 to $24,000 at Canton in 1786 to defray an outlay of $17,000 and launch a "New Fur Trade."[9] By that year there were seven British trading vessels on the coast, including the *Sea Otter* again, Captain Hanna receiving $240 per month plus 6 per cent of the returns and his crew their wages and 6 per cent as well.[10] Only Hanna's death prevented him from undertaking a third voyage to the coast.[11]

In accordance with Captain King's suggestion, half of the ships were outfitted in China or India rather than more distant England,

and they were large vessels of 200 to 300 tons that sailed in pairs for security. They included two ships, the *King George* and the *Queen Charlotte*, skippered by members of Cook's own expeditions: Nathaniel Portlock and George Dixon, whose published accounts further extolled the prospects of the coast trade. Captain Dixon asserted that "the fur trade is inexhaustible wherever there are inhabitants, and they ... are not confined to any particular situation, but are scattered in tribes all along the coast."[12] Captain Portlock declared that "the inestimable value of their [Indians'] furs will ever make it a desirable trade, and ... will become a very valuable and lucrative branch of commerce," and he concluded that "the public may at once perceive that this branch of commerce ... is perhaps the most profitable and lucrative employ that the enterprising merchant can possibly engage in."[13] The two ships' furry cargo brought nearly $55,000 at Canton for their owners, the King George's Sound Company of Richard Etches and partners.[14]

Nevertheless, by the end of the 1780s, as Captain Meares noted, "a very false idea has arisen, that the trade of the North West Coast of America is an unproductive business,"[15] thanks to setbacks to several early ventures from shipwreck, mutiny, and – despite Cook – scurvy.[16] In 1786, for example, the *Sea Otter* and the British snows *Captain Cook* and *Experiment* obtained few skins, while the *Lark* was wrecked on the Commander Islands with the loss of thirty-eight of forty hands and another *Sea Otter* (Captain William Tipping) vanished.[17] Even Portlock and Dixon did not fare as well as they had anticipated, spending too much time in Cook Inlet and Prince William Sound (both of which had already been tapped by Russian promyshlenniks) and reaching the Canton market when it was glutted. Meares still believed, however, that the prospects of the Nor'west trade were bright. He assured his readers that at Nootka Sound he had found the Indians "cloathed in dresses of the most beautiful skins of the sea otter, which covered them from their necks to their ancles," and they were "totally destitute of European articles." He felt certain that, if a "commercial communication," perhaps via the imagined "Great River of the West," were opened between the coast and the continental interior, then a "great and very valuable source of commerce will be unfolded ... forming a chain of trade between the Hudson's Bay, Canada, and the North West Coast of America," with Canadian beaver pelts being exported directly to China instead of through Russian middlemen.[18]

The same idea was to be expressed by Alexander Mackenzie, who in 1793 became the first Euroamerican to cross the continent and reach the Pacific (where he just missed Captain Vancouver); and similar thinking on the part of Thomas Jefferson led to the Lewis and Clark venture of 1803–06. The 1791–95 voyage of Vancouver, who had also accompanied Cook to the north Pacific, demonstrated the absence of any transcontinental waterway, however, although his detailed charting of the coast was to assist trading vessels as late as the 1820s. British traders seemingly ignored the prospect anyway. By the end of the century they had virtually disappeared from the coast trade (Table 1). American dominance was such that when *Le Bordelais* dropped anchor on the coast in 1818, its French master "hoisted American colors, these being the best known to the savages of the coast."[19]

Yet the withdrawal of British Nor'westers was not prompted by the lack of a convenient channel across North America. From the beginning they had been obliged to hurdle the monopolistic privileges of the EIC and the South Sea Company (SSC), which, as Captain Portlock complained, "without carrying on any traffic themselves, stand in the mercantile way of more adventurous merchants."[20] The SSC, although moribund, had been granted the exclusive right to British trade in the Pacific Ocean, and the EIC to British trade in China, so sea-otter skins were procurable only in the preserve of one monopoly and disposable only in that of another. Some British "coasters" obtained licences from both companies, some from either, and some from neither – the last risked becoming "fair and lawful prizes" of licensed vessels; still other ships masqueraded under foreign flags (Austrian, Portuguese, Swedish) to circumvent the restrictions. For example, in 1785 the SSC granted without charge to Richard Etches' King George's Sound Company a five-year licence for the *Prince of Wales* and *Princess Royal* to traffic on the Northwest Coast, and in the same year the EIC licensed the same owner's *King George* and *Queen Charlotte* to traffic at Canton at the cost of a commission on the sale of furs by the company's supercargoes and a freight rate of £11–13 per ton on China goods to England; in 1788 the *Felice Adventurer* and *Iphigenia Nubiana* did not obtain licences from either company and instead sailed under Portuguese colours, just as the *Imperial Eagle* had flown the Austrian flag in 1787.[21]

The "John Company" usually permitted British trading vessels to import furs into Canton, where company supercargoes sold the skins for a percentage. As a result, asserted Portlock, he obtained less than one-quarter of the open-market value of his at least 2,000 skins on the *King George* and *Queen Charlotte* – that is, less than $20 instead of $80–90 each.[22] Moreover, the EIC would normally not issue export licences to other British merchantmen to enable them to import Chinese goods into Great Britain; instead, they were given specie for their furs in the form of bills payable on London. Thus the last and most profitable leg of the England–Northwest Coast–China circuit – the sale of Chinese teas, silks, porcelains, and curios in Western Europe – was denied British Nor'westers, who consequently received 20 per cent less for their skins than their American counterparts.[23] No wonder that after 1793 British shipmasters came to the coast from China, not England, and the sea-otter trade became for them an end in itself, not a furry means to a chinoiserie end, as in the case of American coasters.[24]

The proficient North West Company (NWC), which vied with the HBC for control of the beaver trade of Rupert's Land until their merger in 1821, was faced with similar obstacles in its plan for trans-Pacific commerce. Nevertheless, the Nor'Westers persisted in their "adventure to China," perhaps because of the enduring allure of their old dream of Pacific enterprise as envisioned by Alexander Macken-zie. From 1792 through 1823 the NWC sent furs to China through American firms every year except, apparently, 1802–03 and 1810–12. These shipments annually averaged, for example, 36,822 pelts in 1792–96, 20,000–25,000 in 1804–08, and 15,000 in 1813–23. Despite the "heavy Charges & large Commissions" exacted by the American middlemen, their channel was "more profitable" than that afforded by the EIC because of "the restrictions imposed on the pri-vate Trade by the EICO and the disadvantageous manner of remit-tance," resulting in "expences which the trade could not bear."[25] The NWC saved 50 per cent (in other words, halved its expenses) by ship-ping its trade goods to an American Atlantic port for transshipment in an American vessel to the Columbia and shipping its Cordilleran furs to Canton in the same vessel, rather than sending its goods directly to the Columbia via the Horn in a British ship and its furs to Canton in the same ship for sale to the EIC for bills on London and returning empty to England. The latter course was necessary during the War of 1812–14, when American ships were not obtain-able (the last licensed ship reached Canton in 1815).[26] From 1815 the Boston firm of J. and T.H. Perkins shipped NWC furs from the coast to Canton, exchanging the furs for China goods and conveying the goods to Boston for sale – all in return for 25 per cent of the pro-ceeds. This arrangement ended in 1822, when United States customs officials imposed an *ad valorem* duty of 50 per cent on three-quarters of the proceeds.[27]

Another problem facing the Canadian concern was the fact that its furs were not sea otter but less valuable beaver. Moreover, the NWC sent not fine beaver but felting beaver to China, its Oregon Country beaver being of low quality (the Russians, by contrast, sent only top-grade beaver to China).[28] The distinction among beaver grades should not have been crucial, however, for China was a large market for both luxury and common furs. Also, as the Canton agents of the Perkinses reported in 1822, "from the experience we have had in furs calculated for this market we are decidedly of opinion that with the exception of sea otter skins the ordinary description will generally answer best, as the Chinese do not make those nice distinctions in furs which is done in Europe for instance they will give no more for the fine Northern Beaver of which we have had samples from the U States (& which cost more than double) than for the southern Beaver of the same size."[29] In any case, in the early 1820s the Chinese market for beaver was overdone. The Perkinses were informed by their Canton agents in early 1820 that "the price of Land furrs of all descriptions is represented [in Canton] to be exceedingly depressed in the interior & but little demand either for Land furr or seal skins in the northern provinces; the only article of the furr kind which is demanded is sea otters." In a subsequent letter the agents repeated that "furrs of all descriptions with the exception of sea otters were exceedingly dull this season," adding that "we were fortunate in having effected the sale of most of the NW Company's altho' at a very low price ... & had they been kept till another years collection arrived they would have declined still more."[30] The annual demand for beaver pelts at Canton in the early 1820s was from 12,000 to 15,000, and they usually brought $3.50 each.[31] From 1815 through 1822 beaver fetched only 50–60 per cent as much in Canton as in London.[32]

The HBC, which absorbed the NWC in 1821, faced the same barrier to the China market. In November 1822 the American agent of the "new concern" in Canton sold 16,000 of its beaver skins in one sale, but the company paid "heavy Freight & Commission to the Americans." An anonymous commentator explained the problem and suggested a solution:

From the Restrictions, under which the Trade labors [the EIC's monopoly on British trade with China and Russia's ban on fur imports from Britain], the HBCO have been obliged to employ a House in Boston to ship from thence in an American Vessell the trading Goods, provisions etc necessary for the trade to the Columbia River in the Pacific, where the Vessell receives a cargo of Furs for Canton to be then bartered for a Return Cargo to Boston to be there sold, subjecting the Company to a heavy charge & giving employment to American Shipping, and large profit to the American Merchant, all which by the intervention of the E.I.CO. might be secured to Gt Britain, as in this case the HBCO would send a British Vessell to the Columbia … would bring the Furs to England, which might afterwards be transported to China in the E.I.C.o's Ships.

So in 1824 and 1825 the HBC marketed 20,000 beaver and 7,000 land-otter skins in China through a contract with the EIC, but the arrangement did not prove "advantageous" to either firm, the John Company being "not conversant with the article [beaver]" and deeming such small consignments "unworthy of particular attention."[33] Most important, as long as the NWC or the HBC marketed through the EIC, American shipowners, or even the Russians, it had to pay a middleman. In 1834 the EIC's monopoly was finally abolished but by then there were few sea otter or beaver left to buy or sell, and fur was rapidly losing its lustre on the fashion front.

In addition, Canton's mandarins seemed to prefer the upstart Yankees to the arrogant Limeys.[34] Captain Portlock admitted that his compatriots were "opposed by prejudice and restrained by monopoly."[35] British sailors gained an unenviable reputation at Canton for hooliganism. Granted shore leave after a long voyage, they became inflamed by *samshoo*, a cheap rice liquor, at Whampoa, Canton's outport. Worse, emboldened by their own numbers (as many as 2,000), they not infrequently assaulted other foreigners, particularly the French, Dutch, and Spanish enemies of their country, as well as the local Chinese. American sailors were fewer in number and had enjoyed more cathartic recreation en route, especially on the Hawaiian Islands.

Added to these handicaps were the seizure of British vessels during the Nootka Sound dispute and the disruption of British commerce by the almost constant state of war between Britain and France from 1793 to 1815, as well as by the War of 1812 with the United States.[36] During the 1790s, for instance, French frigates stalked British merchantmen around the Straits of Sunda and Malacca leading from the South China Sea to the Indian Ocean.

British traders, too, may well have been less ruthless, less resourceful, and less efficient than their free-wheeling Yankee rivals, although the vaunted shrewdness of the latter may have been simply the result of their freedom from the former's commercial constraints. This is not to deny the astuteness of the American shipmasters and their supercargoes. A Spanish *commandante* noted early that "the English, and more especially the Americans, give anything they have, or for which the natives may beg, in exchange for the skins of the sea otter."[37] And a Russian commander declared that "the spirit of commerce is, perhaps, no where greater than in America." "The Americans," he continued, "avail themselves quickly of every advantage that is offered to them in trade."[38] In the summer of 1791, for example, when Captain Joseph Ingraham of the Boston brig *Hope* ran short of trade goods, instead of leaving the coast he had his armourer forge twisted iron collars after the fashion of copper ones worn by Haida women, and these newfangled necklaces (and iron bracelets and rings, too) became all the rage; eventually, in order to save time, labour, and sea coal (it took the armourer a day to make five collars), unwrought lengths of iron were traded for skins at one-half the value of the collars.[39]

Similarly, after spending the winter of 1793–94 in Port Cox (Clayoquot Sound), Captain Josiah Roberts of the *Jefferson* dispatched his tender *Resolution* to the Columbia River with 400 iron swords fashioned by his armourer and 160 fathoms of haiqua traded from the Nootkas, as well as 60 sheets of copper, 11 muskets, 8 cutlasses, and 7 pistols – all of which were expected to bring 400 or more sea-otter skins (the *Resolution* bought all available clamons at the Columbia and then sailed to the Queen Charlottes, where it was seized by the Haidas and all hands but one killed); Roberts himself then sailed northwards in the *Jefferson* with 252 clamons that had been traded from the Chinooks and Nootkas since the previous summer. Having exhausted these and other trade goods at the Queen Charlotte Islands by late spring of 1794, with up to 800 skins still available, Captain Roberts resorted desperately but inventively to swapping swivel guns, table-cloths, bed sheets, cabin curtains, deep-sea lines, a longboat, seines, a boat anchor, a powder-horn, ship's crockery, light sails, a cabin looking-glass, officers' trunks, seamen's clothing, rockets, seal oil, women's garments made from old sails, wooden chests and iron bangles wrought by the carpenter, and even a Japanese flag for skins, as well as tin pots, gunpowder, iron collars, chisels, and daggers for fish and eggs – "in short every thing that could be spaired on board were purchass'd up by the natives with the greatest Evidity – seemed in want of Every thing they got thire Eye on." And to curry the favour of the Haidas the ship's doctor made daily visits to patients in Chief Cunneah's village (Cunneah's Harbour [Kuista]), and the carpenter with several hands "went to the village at the request of Cumeah to plane & smooth a monumental pillar of wood," which they also painted and erected. The "pillar" was a mortuary pole, "which they [the Indians] Cut & Carved with a great deal of art." At the chief's invitation the captain and his officers even participated in a potlach celebrating the dedication of the mortuary pole.[40] (Captain Snow of the *La Grange* demonstrated another example of purposeful ingratiation in the fall of 1836 when he corralled all the trade of one

Tsimshian group by saluting with five guns the body of its chief who had died of smallpox – "a contemptible Yankee trick" to the British at Fort Simpson.[41])

At the same place late in the trading season of 1799 the *Hancock*, having run short of muskets and cloth, "sold our Three Royals [the sails above the topgallant] for a Skin apeece and Half of an Old Lower Studingsail for 1 Skin the Cap[t] [Crocker] Sold his Jacket Waistcoat & Trowsers for a Skin"; and on August 18 the ship's longboat was traded for ten skins.[42] (Earlier in Sitka Sound the *Hancock* had to pay a considerable array of goods for a sea-otter skin: on April 27 one greatcoat, one hat, one cartridge of powder, one small looking-glass, and six strings of beads, and on April 28 four yards of cloth or one greatcoat, four yards of ticking, one tin kettle, one knife, two iron combs, six strings of beads, one small cartridge of powder, two pieces of wire, and one key.[43]) Further, in the same year William Sturgis discovered at Kaigani (or Kigarnie, or Kygarny, or Cassarn [or Kasaan, meaning "pretty village" in Tlingit]) that white ermine skins "were really considered here in the same light that we do Silver and Gold, except that they never part with them but hoard them up with great care," so in 1804 as captain of the *Caroline* he took coals to Newcastle by trading European ermine skins for sea-otter pelts at the rate of five for one or $1.50 for $50, thereby procuring 560 prime pelts in one forenoon.[44] About this time, Captain Sturgis recollected many years later, "keys made of brass, copper, or iron, and of every size & form, from a small trunk key to the largest door key," were "greatly in vogue among them [the Indians], and eagerly sought for, both to hang about their persons & attach to their garments." Their popularity prompted him to buy as many as he could find in Boston and New York, thereby raising the suspicions of the New York police, who nearly arrested him, but the contretemps was worthwhile, for the keys were sold to the Natives at twenty times their cost. And on a subsequent voyage Sturgis took some 10,000 brass and copper keys, made to order in Holland and imported specially for the coast trade.[45] The *Lydia's* Captain James Bennett was so diligent that a crewman complained in 1812 that "he often tells us [the crew] he never will go to China as long as he has the price of a Skin remaining on board the Lydia."[46]

American commercial acumen – or British misfortune – was such that in 1799 the "King George's men" lamented at Sitka that they would have to forsake the coast trade, for during the past decade competition from the "Boston men" had raised the price of a sea-otter skin from one to five muskets and from one to six yards of woollen cloth.[47] The encumbered British traders could not afford to keep pace. As an admiring Russian naval commander observed, "no people in the world surpass the citizens of the United States in the boldness, activity, and perserverance of their mercantile speculations."[48] This accolade referred particularly to New Englanders, perhaps because, as one Boston merchant contended with obvious prejudice, to survive in trade in New England a man had either to be a Jew "or stoop to such petty artifices & tricks as would *disgrace a* [seal] *Skinner*."[49]

That American bottoms plied the Northwest Coast trade very efficiently (and hence very profitably) was the result of the vested interest of the captains and the economical outfitting of the vessels. The captains had a proprietary interest in the success of their ventures because they shared directly in their proceeds. As a HBC chief factor noted in 1832, "the American Coasters are masters & part owners of their own vessels & cargoes filled out on the most economical & cheapest manner & who moreover enjoys facilities & privileges on her canton Dealings of which British subjects are deprived."[50] The attraction of a Nor'west voyage for officers (those holding commissions or warrants) was not the wages, which were not high, but the "privilege" (the privilege of having some cargo space on the ship for speculation in China goods on their own account), the "primage" (a percentage commission on the voyage's net profit), and the opportunity for career advancement (William Sturgis, for example, became a seaman at age 16, a chief mate at 17, and a master at 20, all on a Nor'westman). Generally captains and mates received wages of $20–25 per month, a privilege of 0.5–5 tons (20–200 cubic feet), and a primage of 1–8 per cent.[51] Captains Benjamin Swift of the *Hazard* (1796–99), William Bowles of the *Alert* (1799–1801), and John Ebbets of the *Alert* (1801–04) each received $20 per month, as did their first (chief) and second mates.[52] Captain John Suter of the *Mentor* (1816–19) was paid wages plus 7½ per cent of the voyage's net proceeds in the United States.[53] Another Bryant and Sturgis skipper, Captain George Clark of the *Borneo* (1817–19), received wages, $500 worth of China goods as a privilege, and 6½ per cent on both the voyage's net proceeds and the sales of all cargo (except clothing) to the crew.[54] The same shipowners paid Captain James Hale of the *Ann* (1818–21) wages (probably $20 per month), a "priviledge home" of 6 tons, and a commission of 6 per cent on both the net sales in the United States and the sales of cargo to his crewmen; his first mate received $15 per month in wages, 1 percent of the net sales in China, and a privilege of 1 ton.[55] Captain John Suter of the *Lascar* (1820–25), whom Bryant and Sturgis considered their most trustworthy shipmaster, was paid wages, 5 tons of "privilege from Canton in the ship free of expense," and 8 per cent of the net profit; his first mate, James Harris, received wages of $20 per month and a commission of 1 per cent.[56] Some skippers, such as Suter, were also part owners. Captain William Martain of the *Louisa* invested $7,000 of his own money in the 1826–29 voyages of the *Louisa* and *Active*.[57]

The officers were in a minority on a coaster, of course. The *Atahualpa*, Captain Suter, cleared Boston on 1 October 1811 for the coast with twenty men, including the commander, three mates, a clerk, a boatswain (the man responsible for maintenance of the hull), a carpenter, an armourer, a sailmaker, a tailor, a cook, a steward (provisioner), five seamen, and four ordinary seamen.[58] The HBC's Lieutenant Simpson was told by American masters in 1828 that their vessels carried a captain, two mates, a clerk, a boatswain, a carpenter, and from twenty to twenty-five hands; the captain was paid $20 per month plus a 5 per cent commission, the first mate $30 and the second $20 per month, and each of the rest of the crew $10–16 per month.[59] From their wages the crewmen bought goods from the ship's stores. For example, each of the twenty-one hands of the Yankee snow *Sea Otter* on its 1795–98 voyage received $600–750 in wages, from which he bought $100–150 worth of clothing, tobacco, soap, and the like. One sailor, Theodore Carlton, was paid $14 per month for a total of $481.14, from which $35.58 were deducted for purchases of supplies (clothing, footwear, soap, tobacco, knives, and scissors) and $64 for cash advances.[60] The value of these purchases eventually increased substantially and became a source of not a little profit to the shipowners, as Lieutenant Simpson learned in 1828: "As they are in the habit of supplying their people with goods, upon which they charge a large p[r] Centage, they hire them at a cheap rate, their demand for goods being generally equal to their pay, and what tends very much to increase this demand is the connexion they form with the Indian women of the Kygarnie and Tumgasse Tribes who freely grant favours, for which they are liberally rewarded generally."[61]

So the American crewmen did not fare well financially. Fifty-four seamen served on the *Sultan* during its coast venture of September 1821 to August 1824; their monthly wages ranged from $5 to $20, with the average being $10, and at the end of the voyage most of them were owed less than one-half of their wages, and many next to nothing, because of cash advances and shipboard purchases.[62] Bryant and Sturgis told Captain John Suter of the *Mentor* to sell clothing to his men at double the cost price and trade goods at the same prices that he charged the Indians.[63] Similarly, the same owners instructed Captain James Harris of the *Lascar*: "Charge them [crewmen] one hundred per cent on the Invoice price of clothes Boots Shoes and all articles [such as tobacco] necessary for their comfort, and for any thing else that they take up charge the same price as you are selling it for to the natives." Captain Harris was also ordered to "put the Crew on regular allowance and take care that they have full weight and measure."[64] Each crewman was given daily rations of one and one-half pounds of buscuit, one pound of meat, a glass of rum, morning coffee, and evening tea.[65] The hands were expressly prohibited from trading for furs on their own behalf, and periodic searches were made to enforce this band. Thus, when the *Hope* reached China in 1791, "at this time [6:00 PM on 27 November in the Typa] the seamens chest & bedding were strickly searched no furs or any articles were found on them."[66] A search of the *Hamilton* on the coast on 23 November 1820 was more successful: "At 2 pm overholed the peopels chests and bays & births for Furs found in —— Hartshorn 20 cub sea oter tails which was Delivered up to Capt Martain."[67]

Skilful, obedient, and honest crewmen were essential to the success of a voyage, and Yankee sailors seem to have met these requirements. At first, at least, the crewmen of the Boston ships were "Down-Easters" from ports along the New England coast. The Canton commercial agent Sullivan Dorr emphasized to Yankee shipowners the importance of hiring only "Northermen" (New Englanders) as hands, even at the extra cost of $2–3 per month each in wages, for "it will be made up by peace and order on board Ship, without which your vessells will not suceed on the Northwest Coast."[68] Captain Adam Von Krusenstern, the commander of the first Russian circumnavigation in 1803–06, admired the Yankee sailors: "Being skilfull seamen," he said, "they man their ships with a smaller crew, in which respect it appears altogether impossible to excel them," adding, incidentally, that "their vessels are, besides, so admirably constructed, that they sail better than many ships of war."[69] The seamanship of the Bostonians was valued by the RAC, which occasionally hired American sailors and bought American ships. When a Yankee brig avoided shipwreck during a stopover at Sitka in 1825 in spite of the insobriety of the entire crew, including the skipper, Captain Otto Von Kotzebue was not surprised because, in his words, "the North Americans are such clever sailors, that even when drunk they are capable of managing a ship."[70] Canton was to be avoided as a source of seamen, for its recruits were usually deserters from British Indiamen and were "generally the worst of a bad crew," in the opinion of Captain Richard Cleveland.[71] At the beginning of 1799 he hired twenty-one men there for the *Caroline*, mostly British runaways from men of war, Indiamen, and Botany Bay (convict) ships – "as accomplish'd villains as ever disgraced any Country." Indeed, some of them mutinied at Quemoy Island in Formosa Strait en route to the coast.[72] The city was likewise to be avoided as a source of supplies. "It is very expensive in fitting out a Vessel from this place," reported Captain John Kendrick in 1792 to one of his owners.[73]

And the Boston men were particularly adept at keeping expenses to a minimum. A HBC trader asserted that American vessels were "fitted out in the most economical & cheapest manner."[74] A Yankee Nor'west coaster was synonymous with economy; no more cargo was used than was absolutely necessary for the voyage. Bryant and Sturgis reminded Captain Suter in 1816 "how essential is the strictest economy in the expenditure of your Stores & provisions."[75] The same owners issued similar reminders to Captain George Clark of the *Borneo* in 1817 and Captain James Hale of the *Ann* in 1818, adding to the latter: "Let nothing be wasted or squandered and take care there is no pilfering or embezzlement on board."[76] And to Captain Harris of the *Lascar* they wrote in 1820: "You will employ the crew on the passage in getting her [the ship] ready for the coast, always remembering that we want every thing done to keep her tight staunch and in good order, but would not waste a Dollar for show. Be very careful of your stores and provisions put the Crew on regular allowance and take care that they have full weight and measure."[77] Captain Von Kotzebue of the Russian navy toured an American brig (probably the *Lapwing*) at Sitka in 1825 and was impressed by its frugality. He wrote: "On my visit to the ship, I could not help remarking the great economy of all its arrangements: no such thing, for instance, as a looking-glass was to be seen, except the one kept for measuring the angle of the sextant, and that, small as it was, assisted the whole crew in the operation of shaving."[78] The "strictest economy" was also observed in stowage. Captain Robert Forbes described the packing of the homeward cargo of the *Canton Packet* from Canton in 1818 (the ship was not a Nor'west coaster):

A ship of the usual model was floored off with shingle [gravel] ballast, carefully graded; the tea boxes were stripped of the rattan bindings and stowed so closely by Chinese stevedores that a mouse could scarcely find lodging between them, and all spaces between beams and carlines [fore-and-aft timbers supporting the deck] were filled with small mats containing cassia. The silks and crapes were generally stowed under the main hatch in what was called the "silk room," a space between the tea-chests left vacant for the purpose. The cases of camphor and oils were stowed on deck, sometimes in or under the long boat, but more generally around the after hatch, covered by a well-secured mat-house, under which, as I can vouch from an experience of two passages, lived the carpenter, the cook, and sometimes two boys.[79]

So proficient were Yankee Nor'westmen that they dominated the coast trade within a decade of its opening by the British (Table 1). Had it not been for the monopolistic hurdles of the EIC and the SSC, British traders, who were first on the coast, could have continued to dominate the sea-otter trade (and perhaps eventually have provided a stronger British claim to the entire Northwest Coast). They did manage to bring the trade to its first peak in the early 1790s, so that the first American ventures (such as both of the *Columbia Rediviva*'s) were losing ones; however, the market depression of the first peak spelled the end for British participation, and this demise in turn opened the field more and more to American traders.

3 The American Takeover

Mr. Grey [Robert Gray], the master [of the sloop *Washington*], informed us, that he had sailed in company with his consort, the Columbia [*Rediviva*], a ship of three hundred tons, in the month of August, 1787, being equipped, under the patronage of Congress, to examine the Coast of America, and to open a fur-trade between New England and this [northwestern] part of the American Continent, in order to provide funds for their China ships, to enable them to return home teas and China goods.

Captain John Meares, 1788

The Americans of the United States, whose navigation and commerce are daily acquiring fresh extension, have seized with ardour, and without being discouraged by the distance, the new support which the peltry of the north-west coast of America offers to their speculations, to their industry, and to their want of enriching themselves in order to pay the public debt: to the nations of Europe, they are becoming formidable competitors; and their activity is by no means inferior to that of the English.

C.P. Claret Fleurieu, 1791

The Northwest Coast trade was opened at a highly opportune time for New England's merchants, for it enabled them to escape the depression that followed the Revolutionary War, when their main markets for the cod and whale fisheries – the British Isles and the West Indies – were lost. Also, before the American Revolution the Thirteen Colonies had received Oriental goods in amounts and at prices beyond their control, and during the War of Independence very few such goods were available on the Atlantic Seaboard. As soon as the Peace of Verseilles ended the conflict between Britain and her breakway American colonies, as well as France and Spain, in early 1783, Yankee merchants began to test the Asiatic-Pacific trade on their own account. Independence brought new problems for American commerce (the loss of Imperial preference and Royal Navy protection in addition to the closure of British home and colonial ports to most US imports) but also new opportunities, especially in the Far East and the East Indies, where the superiority of American sailing ships and the entrepreneurial daring of American shippers were quickly to make the Yankees the self-styled "Lords of the Pacific."[1] The United States was now freed from the EIC's monopoly on British trade between the Cape of Good Hope and the Straits of Magellan (the penalty had been forefeiture of vessel and cargo). "Since a part of North America had shaken off the yoke of England, and had formed a federative Republic," remarked an anonymous French observer, "her commerce disengaged from the bonds that fettered its operations, had acquired an extension to which she was not allowed to aspire as long as she was in the dependency of an European mother-country, whose privileged countries [colonies] impeded, in both hemispheres, every circulation contrary to the concentered interests of monopoly."[2]

Not only was there still a market in the United States for Asian products that had formerly come in British ships, but there was likewise a market in China for at least one American product – ginseng. Moreover, the new republic, not yet either a manufacturing or a transcontinental nation, was far from self-sufficient and needed a variety of goods, while the country's coffers, which had been drained by a victorious but expensive revolutionary struggle, needed the wealth that commerce could generate.[3] And ships and sailors were available, for peace had idled those engaged in privateering. As Phineas Bond, the British consul in Philadelphia, observed, "in the restricted state of American trade it is natural for men of enterprise to engage in such speculations as are open to them, and which afford a prospect of profit."[4] American shipping was further stimulated by a series of navigation and tariff acts, beginning in 1789, which discriminated against foreign bottoms. The navigation act of 1789 imposed a charge of forty-six cents per ton on foreign vessels, and the tariff act of the same year made tea imports in any but American bottoms prohibitive and levied duties of 12½ per cent on imports of other "East Indian" (Asiatic) goods by foreign ships; in addition, the warehousing system permitted drawbacks (refunds of duties on imports that were subsequently exported or were used to make products for export), and the payment of tea duties was deferable for two years).[4] Yet another impetus was afforded by the uninterrupted (barring one year) European wars of 1792–1815, which enabled the United States to become the world's foremost neutral carrier.[6]

The China trade loomed exotic, if not large, in this mercantile outreach, Yankee merchants finding that they could buy Chinese goods directly themselves rather than more dearly through British and Dutch middlemen. The Canton market, however, preferred precious metals and Oriental products in return. The British possessed both – silver and opium – but the Americans' supply of specie had been depleted by the War of Independence, and only a limited amount of North American ginseng could be acquired and marketed. The search for a saleable substitute was ended by Captain King's disclosure that Canton's hong (security) merchants readily accepted sea-otter skins from the opposite side of the continent to New England. As the anonymous French observer, an obvious admirer of the new republic, rightly noted, "neither the productions of her soil, nor the produce of her industry, afforded her an aliment for a traffic with the Chinese; and silver and gold, which makes up for the deficiency of every sort of commodity and merchandise in trade with that people, were yet too scarce in a rising Republic, for her to be able, without prejudicing her other operations and her engagements with her creditors of EUROPE, to divert from the insufficient mass of her currency the capitals necessary for maintaining an active trade with CHINA: furs might serve in lieu: and the attention of the American congress was ready in aiming at a resource which was to supply the want or the insufficiency of other means."[7] A Connecticut Yankee, John Ledyard, had, like King, become aware of the "astonishing profit" to be made on sea-otter skins while serving on Cook's *Resolution* in 1778–79, and from 1783 until 1785 he had tried unsuccessfully, first in the United States and then in Europe, to organize a trading voyage to the Northwest Coast.[8] It was not until his account was corroborated by others and the British had entered the lists that his countrymen followed suit.

Probably the first shipmaster to ply the New England–Northwest Coast–South China circuit was Captain Robert Gray, who cleared for the coast on the *Columbia Rediviva* in 1788. He returned two years later to become the first American to circumnavigate the globe. On his second voyage in the same 212–ton vessel in 1792 he became the first Euroamerican to enter the "Chinook River" (first sighted by Captain Bruno de Hezeta in 1775[9] and missed by both Cook and Vancouver), which he named after his ship.[10] Gray set the pattern for successive American trading voyages, most of which originated in Boston. Just as Salem dominated American trade in the Indian Ocean, so Boston commanded the nation's traffic in the North Pacific. Nearly all of the owners, captains, and crews of American coasters were from Boston, and all American argonauts were known as "Boston men" or "Bostonians" in the Chinook argot. Their argosies were small (usually less than 300 tons) for navigating the winding, often narrow, and sometimes shallow channels, inlets, and bays of the island-studded and deeply indented coast, well manned and heavily armed (up to thirty hands and as many guns) for repelling Indian attacks, and copper-bottomed for discouraging seaweed, barnacles, and worms. Of the 38 American ships – albeit not all coasters – that put in to Canton between 6 June 1816 and 26 February 1817, the average size was 339 tons and the average complement was 20 hands. Most Nor'westmen were quite small, like the brig *Hope*, which measured 72 tons, mounted 18 guns, and carried 16 men. One of Captain Vancouver's officers, upon seeing the 26-ton, 33-feet-long, and 8-feet-wide schooner *Fair American*, was "Struck with Surprize, at so small a Vessel having been employ'd on such a Commercial pursuit as she had been, and to have travers'd Such an immense tract of Boisterous Ocean as she had done."[11]

The ships stood down Boston harbour in the late summer or early fall, or, as the log of the *Hancock* put it, "weigh'd and Sail'd from Boston bound towards the NW Coast of America."[12] Another ship's log was more detailed: "Sunday Oct. 24 [1824] ... 7 am. got under way, and made sail down the harbour. At 9 am. abreast of Boston light, having discharged the pilot. Set all sail steering S.E. by E. for Cape Cod."[13] Some captains, such as William Martain of the *Louisa*, invoked divine protection: "At 7 am the Pilot Came onbord and got the Ship under Way and Sttod down the harbour with all hands onbord in good health and good spiritts And at ½ Past 8 am discharged the pilot off ... Boston light ... from which we take Ower departure bound Round Cape horn and to the N W Coast of America and I hope that god with his infynat goodness & Kindness will Protect us in ower intended voige and Send us in Safety home to ower friends in his due time."[14] Skippers who were not accustomed to the route from the Atlantic Seaboard around Cape Horn to the Northwest Coast received explicit sailing orders from their owners in order to take full advantage of the prevailing winds and to maximize the safety of the ship and crew. Captain James Harris of the *Lascar* was instructed as follows by Bryant and Sturgis in 1820:

You will shape your course so as to bring you to about the Longitude of 32° or 34° when in Latitude of 30°. Here you may expect to take the N.E. trades. Then steer so as to pass about 2 or 3 degrees to the Westward of the Cape or Verd Islands and endeavor to cross the Line [Equator] any where between Longitude of 23° & 29° You will lose the N.E. trade in Latitude 8° or 10° north and have light Southerly winds, calms and Squalls till you get to about 2° north, where you will probably find the wind incline to SSE and round to SE. You need not be afraid of falling to leeward on the Brazil coast if you cross the line any where to the Eastward of Longitude 30° – but if you get to the Eastward of 23° you will be in danger of long calms. After crossing the line, keep a good fall and run along about 3° or 4° from Cape Rio - *by all means* go to *westward* of the Falkland Islands, pass in sight of the east end of Staten Land (called Cape St. John) and dont be afraid of the land off Cape Horn. It is best not to go much if any to Southward of the little Island of Diego Ramirez as the passage is very good and clear between that and Cape Horn. You will find a Constant current off the Cape, setting to the North East, and the only difficulty is after passing Cape Horn to get a wind that will enable you to make a slant along the shore to the Northward. You had better be on the safe side when approaching the Sandwich Islands and take care to get in their Latitude 3° or 4° to windward as 'tis much easier to run to leeward than to beat up.[15]

Despite the vaunted dangers of doubling the Horn, even in the Antarctic summer, the trickiest navigation occurred immediately afterwards. The *Rob Roy*'s Captain Daniel Cross, who was likewise not used to this route, was warned by Bryant and Sturgis in 1821: "The greatest difficulty will be when standing to the northward, on the western side of the Cape. The wind generally blows fresh from the westward, & one feels apprehensive of a lee shore, but the best way is to push on to the northward as fast as possible, for the further you progress in that direction, the better you will find the climate. After taking the trade winds steer nearly direct for the Sandwich Islands, which will carry you across the equator in about Long. 125°. Make the Island of Owhyee [Hawaii] in Lat. 20° & go round the *North* point."[16] Besides trade goods, ordnance, and ballast, the coasters carried water, bread, and salted meat for the crew, and it was not uncommon to keep a nanny goat aboard or even a cow to provide fresh milk. For example, before leaving Boston at the end of August 1798 the *Hancock* took on 49 tons of ballast; the ration per man on the *Mentor* from Boston to the Northwest Coast in 1816 was 6 pounds of bread per week and 3 quarts of water per day; the *Convoy* left Boston in late October 1824 with 1,940 gallons of water; and in June 1792 the *Jefferson* with 29 hands took on its stock of 6,000 gallons of water at Valparaíso, its first anchorage since leaving Boston six and one-half months earlier.[17]

Stopovers were made en route for fresh food, water, and wood – for spars, "sea coal" (charcoal), and turpentine – at Portugal's Azores (where "St. Jago" [São Jorge] afforded "Sundry supplies ... in plenty good and very cheap"[18]), the British-Spanish contested Falklands/Malvinas (feral cattle, goats, and pigs [weighing up to 140 pounds each], ducks, geese, eggs, wild celery, sea-lion oil, fur-seal skins, driftwood, ballast stones), Robinson Crusoe's Juan Fernández Islands, and

Charles Darwin's Galápagos (Tortoise) Islands (giant tortoises). The passage to the coast was long (half a year) and the shipboard routine was monotonous, as the logkeeper of the sealer *Amethyst* attested in 1806: "One continual sameness awaits our lying down and rising up except a gale of wind to Enrage the ocean and set us tossing on its surface of [or] Gustice calls on the Commander to inflict punishment on some of the offending Crew."[19] Witness, too, the log of the *Paragon* in the middle of February 1819 in the South Atlantic: "All hands employ'd at Ship duty ... Armourer at his forge. Tailor at his needle. Cooper at his adze. Carpente[r] at his Saw."[20] When not working the ship, the crewmen were bending and unbending cables (thick ropes), and blackening their ends, making sennit (braided cord or fabric of plaited rope yarns), knotting yarns (rope strands of twisted fibres), fashioning boarding nets from rope, mending sails, paying the deck with ochre and turpentine, running (melting and molding) bullets, making gun wads, collecting rain water, catching sea turtles, or even salvaging a wreck; in one day the crew of the *Hamilton* made 756 feet of rope.[21] Occasionally the ennui was relieved by an unusual occurrence, such as hailing another ship,[22] seeing an eclipse of the sun, glimpsing a spouting whale, watching a waterspout, having flying fish land on deck to afford a meal, spotting masses of drifting rockweed or balls of entwined sea snakes, throwing a mad dog or dead livestock overboard,[23] being dunked when crossing the Equator for the first time (although on the *Amethyst* the "green hands" "were shav'd in the usual beastly manner ... with an iron hoop for a raizor and ... a lather of human excrement, wine, tar, &c &c" – *Amethyst*, 1806, in the middle Atlantic[24]), watching the sea sparkle at night, or welcoming a sow's farrowing. One morning the crew of the *Paragon* enjoyed the following caper: "At 11. am overhaul'd the Tailor & found him to be full of Lice all over and his cloth[e]s likewise which we hove overboard afterwards we shaerd the hair from his head & all other parts of his Body. gave him cloth to make cloth[e]s."[25] It was more common to disinfect the hold, as occurred on the *Mentor* on 6 May 1823: "At 5 oo this morning commenced smoaking of the Ship with 4 potts of charcoal at 9 oo took off the Hatches as this I hope has effecttually destroyed them [vermin]."[26] Not infrequently the sailors chafed under the boredom and the sometimes arduous and dangerous labour, and in order to maintain harmony on board the captains were cautioned to treat their men firmly but fairly.

Once in the Pacific and nearing the Hawaiian Islands and the Northwest Coast, the crewmen began to mount boarding nets on the sides and guns on the deck while the armourer started to clean and repair muskets. The trading vessels first sighted driftwood, kelp, and gulls and then the snowcapped peaks of the "iron-bound" (rock-girded) Northwest Coast in the spring, just as the Indians were returning to the outer coast from their inland winter villages. The shipmasters spent spring and summer "beating about the coast" between "Sheetka" (Sitka) and "Gray's River," or simply "the River," as the Columbia was known, in search of *quan nuckees* ("plenty of sea otter skins"), eager to "make hay while the sun shone" in "the competition for Nuckies," to use their own words.[27] The shipboard routine on the coast was more variable and more hazardous than during the passage from Boston. The most important new chore was bartering, of course, but much of the time, as the *Hamilton*'s log repeatedly phrases it, the "People [were] variously Employed on Ships duty."[28] The journal of the brig *Otter* illustrates some of the duties during one summer week:

Sunday July 15th 1810 We Anchored here [Skidegate, Queen Charlotte Islands] last thursday and ever since have been busy making alterations in the stowage between decks and shifting the Steerage bulkhead farther forward to make more room & to accomodate the knyackies [Hawaiian hands] with births to sleep in at present likewise to stow our water & provision on the homeward bound passage, which however wont commence in less than twelve or fourteen months from this time unless we [have] better luck than we have had this some time back. Yesterday went on shore once cut a small spar to secure and tighten the lower part of the bulkhead, Opened the Main hold and took up 3 hogsheads [sixty-three-gallon barrels] of Molasses for trade, caulked the hatches down and hoisted in the boats. Indians on board from morning to night but very little trafic going on, to day we fired a Gun for another tribe that are up the inlet a fishing to come and trade with us the weather dry & pleasant, Therm. from 55 to 70° [Fahrenheit].

Monday 16th Finished the births for the Kynackies, the people employed repairing the Sails and other necessary jobs got a boat load of water. The weather remarkably fine.

Tuesday & Wedensday 17th & 18th Very little trade & but a few Indians about us, the people employed in necessary jobs about the sails & rigging, the Armourer cleaning Muskets, & myself preparing stuff to make a wheel. To day we run all the Guns over on cove side and careened the Vessel for scraping her bottom above the copper, at noon finished one side & shifted the Guns & careen'd her the other way. Ends cloudy weather.

Thursday & Friday 19th & 20th Finished the Vessels bottom, run the Guns out in their places cleared the decks and sent the TG [top gallant] Yards aloft and got all ready to go out with the first fair wind, weather thick & rainy, latter part fair, At work on the wheel. To day the weather dark and gloomy with a strong breeze from the Eastd. which blows right into the harbours and prevents our getting out this day, the Indians still sells us two or three skins a day and a few tails. the people necessarily employed about the Vessel. Thermo. at 50°.

Saturday July 21st 1810 Calm & pleasant weather throughout. The Indians informed us that there was to ships off the mouths of the harbour and that one of them was a new comer, Capt. Hill had the cutter man'd & arm'd and went out to meet them. Thermometer at 65°.[29]

Besides the supercargo, who oversaw bartering, the carpenter was kept particularly busy on shore felling spars, making charcoal, sawing boards for "skin boxes" (chests for storing pelts), and cutting firewood. In one month in the summer of 1793 the *Jefferson* loaded up to 300 bushels of charcoal at Bucareli Bay "for working our iron into Collars" as well as for "makeing [four-foot] iron swords for the trade to the south [Columbia River]" (where they brought one clamon or two sea-otter skins each); in October another 500 bushels of charcoal were embarked at Clayoquot Sound.[30] Again, in one November week of 1810 at Kaigani the *Hamilton*'s crew dug a "Coal pitt" and made 18 barrels of wood charcoal.[31] A carpenter was also essential for ship repairs on this hazardous coast. As an American captain asserted in 1825: "I think there is no place in the world w[h]ere one is wanted, more than on this Coast. For Instance; – if a vessel runs ashore and gets injured badly, which is very often the case here, you could not repair the damage immediately, but for want of a Carpenter would have to lay by a month, or more; besides their work adds to the appearance of the vessel, for the expense that is incurred for Stock is no more than the labour to go on shore to obtain it."[32]

By late summer the Indians were shifting inland for the winter for forest hunting, the fall salmon run, and "a more comfortable retreat" (wooded shelter) during the coming inclement weather, and trade was ending.[33] Before quitting the coast the American captains made sure that their golden fleece had been cleaned and packed in chests or casks (100 per container) to prevent contamination by vermin; "in taking a cargo of furs, a vessel takes a cargo of lice," lamented a French trader, although filthy Nootka skins had at least been very well dressed by the Indians.[34] (At Nootka Sound in 1786 James Strange, co-owner and skipper of the *Captain Cook*, was constantly busy cleaning sea-otter skins of vermin and other filth.[35]) In addition, water, wood, and food (fish, venison, wildfowl, berries) were replenished; in the autumn of 1792 the *Columbia Rediviva* with a crew of 30 took on 5,545 gallons of water for its run to Canton; and the *Jefferson* loaded 8 cords of firewood and 300 bushels of charcoal before leaving the Marquesas for the Northwest Coast in the late southern summer of 1792–93, and 4,000 gallons of water before leaving its winter haven of Clayoquot Sound for the northern coast and China at the beginning of the spring of 1794.[36] Also, grass was cut for the ship's nanny goat, sow, or even cow, ballast (sand, stones, boulders) was loaded, and holds were smoked (to kill rats and mice), rigging repaired, decks, spars, and sides blackened (tarred), leaks plugged, seams pitched, bottoms scraped, and bends (the thickest and strongest planks in the sides) coppered for the long voyage to South China. En route crewmen were kept busy "overhauling" (opening and airing) skin casks and powder kegs (and beating and brushing the furs), picking oakum (old rope fibres used for caulking), chinking decks and water barrels, setting and mending sails, taking leads, keeping watch, and varnishing and painting. It was particularly important, of course, that the furs be kept dry, as Captain Lisiansky of the *Neva* ruefully discovered in November 1805 en route to Canton following a typhoon, which helped to wet and rot his cargo, so that "we were obliged to throw overboard thirty thousand sea-bear [furseal] skins [out of 151,000], besides a great quantity of other valuable furs; a loss which I estimated altogether at forty thousand Spanish dollars."[37]

After three weeks "under all sail" the voyage was interrupted and the routine relieved by "the genial climate, the luxurious abundance, and the gratifying pleasures" of the "Western Isles" (Hawaiian Islands), which, Captain Meares added, "offer a station for intermediate repose, where health animates the gales, and every species of refreshment is to be found on the shores."[38] Captain Auguste Duhaut-Cilly of the *Héros* observed in 1828: "These islands seem to have been designed by Providence to become a general entrepôt between Asia and America; a place for the rest and recreation of sailors, after their long, perilous navigations; and, lastly, a haven of refuge and safety for vessels requiring repairs and refurbishing before continuing on their voyages."[39] Here water, wood, salt, and provisions (pigs, yams, sweet potatoes, plantains, breadfruits, taro, coconuts, sugar cane) as well as "island rum" (ti plant liquor) and fibre (for line) could be had plentifully and – at first, at least – inexpensively. An American teenaged sailor lauded the archipelago's attractions during a stopover at Hawaii Island in 1792: "Many Canoes along side containing beautiful *Women* Plenty of Hogs and fowls, together with most of the Tropical fruits in abundance, great quantities of Water and Musk *Mellons*, Sugar Cane, Bread fruit, and salt was brought for sale."[40]

The French naval scholar, Count C. P. Claret de Fleurieu, aptly termed the islands the "great *caravanserai*" on the transoceanic route between North America and Asia.[41] From 1827 through 1829 an average of 125 American ships totalling 40,000 tons and worth $5,275,000 (vessels plus cargoes), including 100 whalers, arrived at, or departed from, the Hawaiian Islands annually.[42] Many ships, such as Captain Dixon's *Queen Charlotte*, enjoyed "a delicious regale among the hogs, yams, and other good chear."[43] The first to do so was Captain Cook, who in return for iron was offered hogs and yams by the inhabitants of what he named the Sandwich Islands (after John Montague [1718–92], the fourth Earl of Sandwich and from 1771 the First Lord of the Admiralty, as well as – perhaps fittingly – a notorious rake).[44] And the first British Nor'westman, Captain Hanna, touched at the islands in the fall of 1785 on his return to China from the coast to initiate a long succession of traders who took advantage of the archipelago's convenient location, balmy climate, abundant output, and proficient people. Indeed the main reason why Captain Vancouver tried so hard in the first half of the 1790s to mediate among the warring chiefs was to ensure the safety and supply of British coasters.[45]

When the British vessels were supplanted by their American competitors, the role of the islands remained the same, as the log of an unidentified Yankee coaster noted during an 1801 stopover: "Bot. hogs, Fowls, [sweet] Potatoes Benannus, Plantin, Sugar Cane Cabages, Water Mellons, Bread fruit and allmost all kinds of Vegetables."[46] An American shipmaster even found "excellent white cordage, of all sizes"; "for running rigging, there is no better rope," he asserted.[47] But especially pork was taken by visiting vessels. Pigs were so numerous on the islands that they were commonly called the "Hog Islands."[48] The animals were large and tasty; one large hog fed the thirty-three crewmen of the Russian ship *Rurik* for more than two days in 1816, and their captain found the pork more flavourful than European pork (perhaps because the pigs were fattened on sugar cane).[49] Large numbers of live hogs were bought and salted. Captain Cook in the *Discovery* set the precedent by buying more than 250 hogs in January 1778, their price ranging from a nail to a spike each.[50] In 1788 en route to China from the Northwest Coast Captain Gray of the *Columbia Rediviva* loaded 150 hogs and 5 puncheons (large casks of up to 1,200 pounds each) of salted pork, and Captain Meares of the *Felice Adventurer* took on more than 400 hogs in the same year.[51] In 1793 the *Jefferson*'s Captain Roberts purchased "about

180 fine hogs, a great quantity of sweet potatoes, some yams, sugar cane, & fowlls" on Hawaii Island; 90 large hogs salted down into 20 barrels.[52] The *Hancock* bought "as Many Hogs & Vegetables as we wanted ... 50 Hogs in all" on Hawaii Island in 1799 (27 of them were subsequently butchered and salted aboard ship en route to Canton), and the *Vancouver* bought 100 on Maui Island in 1805.[53] In 1791 these porkers cost an American ship only 2 iron spikes each; in the same year another American vessel paid 10 inches of old hoop iron for a 100–pound hog.[54]

Other provisions were obtained, too, and just as liberally and cheaply, as in the case of the *King George*, Captain Portlock, in 1786:

we stood off and on under easy sail, which gave the natives an opportunity of bringing us the different produce of their island [Maui], which they presently did in great abundance; such as hogs, plantains, bread-fruit, taro, cocoa nuts, fowls, geese of a wild species, and great quantities of excellent salt: for these articles we bartered with nails, towes [spikes], and trinkets of different kinds; and so brisk a trade went forward, that in the course of four hours we purchased large hogs sufficient, when salted, to fill seven tierces [1 tierce = 1 cask of 35 imperial gallons, or ⅓ of a pipe], besides vast numbers of a smaller sort for daily consumption. Near two tons of vegetables, such as taro and bread-fruit, were also procured; and so amply did the natives supply us with those very useful articles, that we were obliged to turn vast quantities away for want of room to put them in. Indeed, it would not have been proper to purchase more of those kinds of vegetables than what would be sufficient for six or seven days consumption; for after that time they begin to decay very fast. We also got about one ton and a half of fine salt, and I immediately set twenty hands to kill and salt pork.[55]

The tendency of coasters to gorge at the islands was explained by Captain James Colnett, who as master of the *Prince of Wales* sojourned there in early 1788 while sailing for the same owners as Dixon: "great Quantity of Vegetables was bought & the Quantity eat[en] of Greens & Hogs is scarce creditable but great allowances can be given when informed we had scarce tasted fresh flesh for fifteen months." At Kauai every morning 400 coconuts were bought for the crew of 35 to drink, and usually 200 or 300 more were received daily as gifts.[56]

In 1786–87 Captain Dixon found Hawaii the best island for swine and fowl, Kauai for taro, coconuts, and salt, Oahu for wood and water, and Niihau for yams (at, appropriately, Yam Bay).[57] Thirty years later, according to the Russian Captain Vasily Golovnin, Hawaii was the most populous island, Kauai had the most accessible sandalwood, Oahu was the most beautiful and productive island, and Maui afforded the best fresh water with the greatest ease.[58] Usually the favourite of visitors was Oahu; an anonymous sealer called it an "Arcadia" – "a place which I shall ever remember, for the fondness of the Women, the generosity and urbanity of the Men and the delicacy and variety of its refreshments" (its sole drawback, he added, was the "Weeping [rainy] Climate").[59] Yams, incidentally, were an "excellent" substitute for bread and "the best Roots that can be carried to Sea, as they keep superior to any other," according to Captain Clerke, Cook's second-in-command; in 1778 at Niihau Cook bought mostly yams (as a replacement for bread, his "scarcest article of provision") because they could be preserved for two or three months at sea; plantains and bananas were an "indifferent" substitute, with green ones keeping only two or three weeks, sweet potatoes no more than ten days, and breadfruit only two or three days.[60] In the middle of March 1792 Captain Vancouver procured eight tons of yams for the *Chatham* and "a good deal more" for the *Discovery* at Niihau.[61] With the permission of the chiefs, the islanders canoed and swam to the visiting vessels to sell these victuals. When the *Discovery* and *Chatham* put in to Kealakekua Bay on Hawaii Island in early 1793 they were surrounded by 3,000–5,000 Natives in or on the water (although not all of them were provisioners).[62] At Maui's future whaling port of Lahaina on 23 and 24 February 1805 110 canoes hawked foodstuffs to the coaster *Vancouver*.[63]

The Hawaiians also offered themselves. The Elysian archipelago provided a salubrious climate for ailing seamen, competent sailors for shorthanded vessels, and, more famously (or, to the missionaries, more infamously), winsome *wahines* for lustful crewmen – what one British skipper called a "Lap of Pleasures."[64] "Fresh provisions and kind females are the sailors sole delight; and when in possession of these, past hardships are instantly forgotten," declared one of Captain Cook's officers.[65] And lest this view be taken lightly, it is well to remember that the delights of Polynesian shore leave were considered the main cause of the *Bounty* mutiny, not Captain Bligh's brutality. Although the commanders of official expeditions tried to restrict or prevent sexual contact between their men and the Hawaiian Islanders (and without much success, since even their officers, such as David Samwell, surgeon on Cook's *Discovery*, and Thomas Manby, midshipman on Vancouver's *Discovery*, managed to indulge themselves freely), it was common for a visiting trading vessel to have, in the words of the log of the *Hamilton*, "a Number of the Natives on board," particularly women, who, as one coaster's surgeon delicately phrased it, "were in expectation of getting husbands for the night."[66] And they were not disappointed, for the same coaster's steward wrote that "almost every man on board took a native woman for a wife while the vessel remained, the men [the women's husbands] thinking it an honour, or for their gain, as they got many presents of iron, beads, or buttons."[67] Few sailors were able to resist the comely, bare-breasted, and licentious females (Figs. 2–3). As John Boit, fifth mate on the *Columbia Rediviva*, noted in 1792, they were "quite handsome" and "all in a state of Nature"; "not many of the Columbia's Crew prov'd to be *Josepths* [celibates]," he added sardonically.[68] The Astorian Alexander Ross summarized the appeal of the *wahines*: "The women are handsome in person, engaging in their manners, well featured, and have countenances full of joy and tranquillity; but chastity is not their virtue."[69] The coaster *Hope* found the young women of the Marquesas just as attractive, if not more so: "They were in genral small and young quite naked and without excepton the most beutifull people I ever saw ... their beutie and gen[t]leness with the rest of their charms where such that but few could but admire them and none resist the impulce of the moment. They do not appear to have any idea of shame or criminalety in their intercors with any and in that respect it seems to be nothing more thought of then mear cavilety."[70])

The *wahines* were definitely "amorous," as more than one observer expressed it.[71] Samwell found (more to his delight than his dismay) that the Hawaiian women were aggressively sexual: "Indeed we found all the Women of these Islands but little influenced by interested motives in their intercourse with us, as they would almost use violence to force you into their Embrace regardless whether we gave them any thing or not, and in general they were as fine Girls as any we had seen in the south Sea Islands." At Waimea Bay on Kauai "the Young Women, who were in general exceeding beautiful, used all their arts to entice our people into their Houses, and finding they were not to be allured by their blandishments they endeavoured to force them & were so importunate that they absolutely would take no denial." "There came likewise," Samwell added, "many young women alongside who used lascivious Gestures and wanted to come into the Ship [*Resolution*] and seemed much chagrined on being refused; they seem to have no more Sense of Modesty than the Otaheite [Tahiti] women, who cannot be said to have any."[72] The prudish Captain Vancouver was disgusted by the "excessive wantonness" and "licentiousness" of the Kauaian women. He criticized "the readiness of the whole sex, without any exception, to surrender their persons without the least importunity," as well as "the eagerness, nay even avidity, with which the men here assisted in the prostitution of the women."[73] On a single March night in 1792 there were more than 100 women aboard the 100-man *Discovery*.[74]

An officer of the coaster *Atahualpa* declared in 1805 that he had never seen women who were "so obliging."[75] Two years later the log-keeper of the *Amethyst* recorded: "They are very fond of the Whites, for in a little time after our arrival, more than four hundred, come off in Canoes, with every kind of fruit in abundance, and so eager were they to come on board, that numbers jumpt'd overboard and climb'd up the Ships side and without any prelude overwhelm'd us with caresses the men repaid the girls, by returning their embraces with greatest ardour, and being fresh and strong, were capable of doing justice to this heavenly Sex, who in this part of the world, were not averse of bestowing their caresses with redoubled transport."[76] Louis Choris, the French artist on Von Kotzebue's first expedition (1815–18) to the Pacific, reported that the women of the island of Hawaii were reputedly the archipelago's prettiest, and "modesty is not a quality in fashion among many of them, for they make advances to us." He added: "Women can be considered one of the commodities that these islands abundantly furnish to visiting ships; every evening until sunset they are surrounded by hundreds of boats laden with girls belonging to the lower classes ... sometimes as young as ten years, [who] traffic with the men."[77] Adelbert von Chamisso, the naturalist on the same expedition, was equally appalled. "I cannot pass over in silence," he wrote, "the first thing that we, like all other strangers, encountered in these islands: the general, importunate, greedy complaisance of the other sex; the propositions shouted at us by all the women round about and by all the men in the name of all the women." He added more vehemently: "One big brothel of the natives! Every woman, even every matron, is well versed in all the vilest artifices of whores, all the filthiest, dirty tricks of prostitutes. They all lack shame; openly and avidly sex is offered for a fixed price. Openly every husband offers his wife, presses her upon one for a price."[78]

The females often swam several miles to reach moored vessels, even during taboos (temporary bans on specific activities, violated on pain of death),[79] although at first at least they were likely moved as much by curiosity as by cupidity. In Kealakekua Bay on Hawaii Island, where Captain Cook had been killed, the *Gustavus III* (the British snow *Mercury* masquerading under Swedish colours) had in August 1791 "upwards of one hundord Girls unbord at a Time," according to John Bartlett, one of the common sailors. "At Night," he added, "Every man tuck his Girl the Remainer jumpt over Bord to Swim upwards of three mile for the shore."[80] As soon as the Russian sloop *Neva* dropped anchor in the same bay in 1804 it was surrounded by about forty women wanting to spend the night on board.[81] When the *Lydia* reached Kauai on 21 September 1806 the crew were sorely disappointed, "it being Tarboo we Cant get no girls off it makes it dull times." On the 25th the taboo ended, and "at 8 am the Lasses Came off to us & we had fine fun."[82] And the log of the *New Hazard* for 29 September 1811 records: "Towards Woahoo [Oahu]. Not much work done this afternoon, being girls on board: going from ship to ship."[83] Shipmasters invariably remarked the stark (and welcome) contrast between the forbidding Northwest Coast – rainy and chilly and peopled by what they considered dirty, sullen, and hostile Indians – and the inviting Sandwich Islands, which were sunny and warm and inhabited by seemingly clean, cheerful, and friendly Polynesians.[84] No wonder the log of the *Lydia* recorded that in 1805 "the Atahualpa was so long at Woahoo, that not only the Natives were sorry to have us leave them but our own Crew appeared to be unwilling to leave the place."[85] Not a few hands from coasters asked to be discharged at "the Islands" or simply deserted there.

From the Hawaiian Islands the American trading vessels took the NE Trades across the midwestern Pacific, skirted the northernmost of the Ladrone Islands (the Marianas), threaded the Bashi Channel between Formosa (Taiwan) and the outermost Philippines, and in late autumn off the southern coast of China sighted the prominent coastal rock of Pedro Blanco and raised the Asses' Ears, two mainland peaks that guided them to the estuary of the Pearl, or Canton, River. They entered the passage between the Asses' Ears and the Lema Islands, the Grand Lema serving as a landmark, passed little Lintin Island, and anchored in Macao Roads, or the Typa, the outer harbour of the Portuguese island leasehold of Macao, which served as a trading and smuggling base and a resort for Canton's foreign residents in summer, when the latter city's trade was dull and its climate sultry. The trading season did not begin until the middle of November, the earliest date for obtaining a cargo of teas. Besides, during early autumn the squalls and typhoons near the South China coast were "so frequent & So severe that Ships are extremely liable to be blown off the Coast & from their Anchors in Maccao Roads."[86]

At Macao a licensed pilot was hired; in the first half of the 1820s the twin brothers Assee and Attii were "two of the best Pilots of Macao."[87] At Macao, too, an official "chop" (permit) was secured which allowed the trading ships to beat upriver through The Bogue, or Boca Tigris ("Tiger's Mouth" or "Tiger's Gullet" ["Lion's Gate" in Chinese]), the debouchment of the Pearl River, and past the first and second bars to moor off French Island or Dane's Island in Whampoa Roads, or Reach, the "inner anchorage" for all foreign merchantmen (Map 1). Whampoa stood at the head of the river's estuary on Bankshall Island, which was named after the bankshalls, or warehouses,

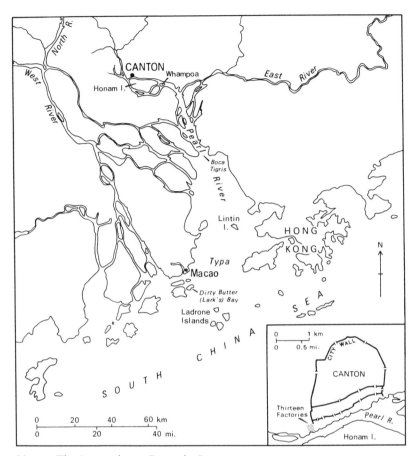

Map 1   The Approaches to Canton by Sea

that were used by visiting vessels for storage and reparation. It was the head of navigation for large ships, which were not permitted to proceed any farther upstream and which were not allowed to depart until they had been issued the "grand chop" (port clearance), which signified that all of the requirements of the Chinese authorities had been met.

As Canton's outport, Whampoa was the bustling gateway to the China trade. Up to 80 foreign ships, including 15 American vessels, were riding anchor here in mid-November of 1789.[88] While they were repaired and refitted, their hands – probably up to 6,000 in 1805–06, for example, when there were 49 British, 37 American, and 4 Continental clearances[89] – could go ashore on Dane's Island at certain times to sightsee and debauch (at Loblob Creek), usually with the aid of *samshoo*, the local rice grog, cheap but usually doctored. At Whampoa the shipmaster submitted a manifest of his cargo to the *fiadors*, or hong merchants, one of whom became security for the proper conduct of his crew and the full payment of all of his charges; the hong also fixed the price of the shipmaster's furs, his ruling being final because nobody else was allowed to bid. In addition, the security merchant appointed a *comprador*, or chandler, to each ship, which bought its "chow-chow" (provisions) from him alone. "Boston Jack" was the favourite comprador of American vessels, being "ever civil and obliging." He once took passage to Boston as a steward and returned in 1817 via the Northwest Coast on the brig *Cossack*. He was regarded as a "great gun" by his countrymen, whom he liked to tell of his passage round the Horn: "Too muchee strong gale; sea all same high masthead – no can see sky, no can see water."[90] The comprador was licensed by the Hoppo, or customs chief, who came aboard at Whampoa to measure the ship for tonnage and to receive "sing-songs" (clockwork presents). Here, too, a "linguist" (interpreter) was hired. An 1807 advisory stated that none of the linguists was "so capable of rendering you real service as Gouqua."[91]

At Whampoa the furry cargoes were unloaded into Hoppo (customs) boats for weighing and then transferred into covered and locked "chop" boats, sampans that lightered trade goods the dozen miles between Whampoa and Canton. Called "watermelons" by the Chinese, they had rounded decks and sides; each could carry 500 piculs (33 ⅓ tons) – 500 chests of tea, for example.[92] (The lightering of inbound cargo cost a ship $15.22 per chop boat at the beginning of the 1800s; outbound cargo was lightered at the seller's expense.[93]) At Canton the furs were unloaded at small docks on Jackass Point and carried across an esplanade – the Respondentia Walk, crowded with beggars, hucksters, and loungers – and deposited in the hongs, or "go-downs" (warehouses), of the "thirteen factories" (so called because they were the headquarters of factors) (Fig. 4). These were long, narrow buildings occupying a dozen acres and extending from the riverfront to the suburbs outside the southwestern corner of the stone and brick wall of Canton, which by 1820 contained 800,000–900,000 Chinese,[94] many of whom were engaged in the city's extensive domestic and foreign trade. Each factory's two or three whitewashed stories were divided vertically into sections, with business facilities (offices, storerooms, scales, vaults) on the first floor, sitting- and dining-rooms on the second, and bedrooms on the third for supercargoes, commission agents, and guests. Space was rented from the hong merchants, who owned the factories. The largest – called simply "The Factory" – was occupied by the EIC; the American factory was the smallest. Along the lanes in the rear and on either side of the factories were the houses and shops of Chinese traders and artisans; Hog Lane, for example, so named because of its dirtiness, offered samshoo and other low wares. In 1833–34 the foreign population of the factories totalled some 250.[95] Their practice of removing to Macao during the warm, or off, season had largely ceased by 1800 because of the "coming and going all the year round" on the part of American vessels.[96]

The furs were sold or, more commonly, bartered for a return cargo, the hong merchant paying all inward and outward duties. So the foreign shipmaster was relieved of all responsibilities except the care of his ship and the control of his crew, and the supercargo had only to follow the cargo to Canton, choose the goods for the return voyage, and avoid being cheated. The language of commerce at Canton was "Pidgin" (broken) English, or business English, a baffling amalgam of English, Portuguese, and Chinese. This trade jargon was devised by the Chinese, who imitated the sounds of English, Portuguese, and even Indian words, used simple Chinese words to convey their meaning, and expressed them monosyllabically with Chinese syntax and duplicatives, for example, "comprador," from Portuguese *compra*, "purchase," go-down, from Chinese *ka-dang*, "warehouse," and chop, from Chinese *cho*, "document." Being spoken but not written, Pidgin English changed rapidly. It arose because the Chinese authorities obstructed the learning of Chinese by foreigners, even once beheading a Chinese teacher for giving lessons.[97] From the turn of the century, however, this discouragement waned, and after 1810 Cantonese was also used to conduct business. "Canton English" nevertheless remained pre-eminent because, as one observer put it, learning Chinese required "a head of oak, lungs of brass, a constitution of iron, the patience of Job, and the lifetime of Methuselah."[98] Or, as the missionaries were wont to say, "the devil invented the Chinese language to keep the Gospel out of China." Each ship paid $250 to hire a "lingoo" (linguist), who in fact spoke only Chinese and Pidgin English. "Old Tom" was perhaps the best known of the interpreters. (Similarly, *moya-tvoya* [literally, "mine-thine"], a Russian-Chinese pidgin derived from eighteenth-century Chinese peddlers in Siberia, came into commercial use on China's northern frontier; later it was much in use in Harbin, where there was a sizeable expatriate Russian community.)

Americans virtually monopolized the sea-otter traffic at Canton, for the "city of rams" was closed to Russian merchants and only open to British coasters at the chary and costly discretion of the EIC. Buyers came from as far as North China to Canton, arriving with teas, silks, and ivory and leaving with peltry and broadcloth. The furs were sold in January, when the buyers arrived from Peking and Nanking.[99] At Canton they could buy the same sea-otter skins from the Americans as at Kyakhta from the Russians but at much lower prices; the "great superiority" of British over Russian broadcloth likewise attracted them.[100] *Hai lung pi* were used mostly in the northern provinces, where they formed the "principal and favourite dress of the inhabitants ... and those of the rarest kind and the highest prices are eagerly purchased by them," a sea-otter fur suit often fetching from $500 to $1,000 and even more.[101]

Fuel was scarce and costly in China, and in North China winters were long and cold. Even at Canton "all the Chinese that can afford it" wore woollens or fur-lined camlets during the cool season of March-April, when frost could occur at night.[102] And South China's houses were unheated.[103] An early British Nor'westman, Captain John Meares, noted that "even there [Canton Province], the cold will often render a fur dress necessary; more particularly as the Chinese are minutely attentive in proportioning their cloathing to the temperature of the moment, whatever it may be; and frequently in the course of the same day, add to or diminish the number or warmth of their garment, as from the varying circumstances of the atmosphere, etc. the air may demand a cooler or a warmer covering."[104] The anonymous editor of a Cantonese English-language annual stated that the consumption of furs was "very great" because "the necessity of restricting the use of fuel to culinary operations and the arts, compels the Chinese to load themselves with garments in the winter." So their winter clothing was lined with fur or stuffed with cotton in order to limit the number of outer garments; fur-lined clothes were carefully preserved and often passed from father to son, usually lasting about twelve years.[105]

Sea-otter was preferred in North China and beaver in South China. Captain Meares explained: "The skin of the sea-otter, from the thickness of its pile and the length of its fur, forms too cumbersome an habiliment for the people of the Southern provinces; they prefer, in general, the Canadian and Hudson's Bay [beaver] furs; but still, such as can afford it, seldom fail of having a cape of the sea-otter's skin to their coats, though perhaps at the extravagant price of six dollars."[106] In general, declared a British commercial agent in Canton, sea-otter skins were "esteemed above all others by the Chinese."[107] The fine, dense pelage of fur seal skins was valued for making caps.[108] And the demand for furs at Canton was "steady & constant."[109] Captain Meares believed that all of Canton's intake of sea-otter skins before 1790 had not even satisfied the demand of Canton Province alone.[110]

The transaction of foreign trade in the Celestial Empire was frequently lengthy and trying, especially for the hustling Yankees, and it was commonly late winter before they had sold their furs and bought a load of China goods for the bourgeoning United States market, as well as Europe: teas, mostly Congo and Bohea blacks with some Young Hyson green; textiles, mostly silk, nankeen (a durable cotton fabric, considered in New England to be the best cotton cloth), and crape (a lightweight, crinkled fabric); porcelains, especially willowware (blue-and-white dinnerware), which served additionally as ballast; sugar, which also made good ballast; cassia in the form of bark or buds, either of which was an inferior and cheaper substitute for true Ceylonese cinnamon; teak; and sundry bric-a-brac. (Chinese dominance of Oriental porcelain was such that all of it became known as chinaware or simply china. The ancient potteries were located 400 miles north of Canton at Ching-te-chen, or Fowliang. Mostly Canton, Fitzhugh, and Nankeen ware [terms describing their decorative patterns] were taken to the United States.) In the words of an anonymous French commentator, "depots of peltry, formed in their [Americans'] ports, and afterwards distributed among their ships which are employed in the expeditions to Asia, give them in return, both teas of which habit has made a want to which perhaps they owe their liberty, and those rich India [Asiatic] goods which republican simplicity scarcely allows of, but which, being necessary to the luxury of Europe and of her western colonies, become, in the trade of the Americans, articles of barter against commodities of real necessity which Nature has refused to their climate."[111] The *Sea Otter* returned to Boston in 1798 with 700 chests (47,558 pounds) of teas, 814 bags (1,087 pounds) of sugar, 70 bales (7,000 pieces) of nankeens, 400 sets (tea and dining) of chinaware, 8 pieces (144 yards) of silk fabrics, and 2 boxes (109 ½ pounds) of sewing silk.[112] In December 1806 and January 1807 the *Pearl* received at Whampoa from 7 chop boats 1,628 chests of teas, 1,246 bales and 2 boxes of nankeens, 343 bundles of cassia, 156 boxes of chinaware, and 62 cases of silks.[113] And in December 1822 at Whampoa the *Hamilton* discharged 135 bags of ginseng, 39 casks of furs, 11 bundles and 2 boxes of fur seal skins, 3 boat loads of rattan, and some sandalwood and ballast, and embarked 2,575 mats of cassia, 1,200 bags of sugar, and 587 chests of tea.[114]

Particularly tea was taken, for the Chinese merchants were usually so overstocked that they would not only sell it at a reasonable price but also accept goods in return at a high rate, as well as do so with dispatch; in 1799 a sea-otter skin brought $23 in cash but $26 in goods.[115] They would even advance a cargo of tea on credit in order to rid themselves of it. Moreover, the American public savoured tea as much as the British.[116] A Russian observer concluded that "this induces the Americans to give the preference to this article, since it affords them the advantage of making a better bargain with the goods they import, and of being the sooner despatched; an object of considerable importance at Canton, the stay there being attended with much expence, while the health of the crew is a good deal at stake."[117]

The trading season ended about the beginning of February, which coincided with the commencement of the Chinese new year. By then the Chinese merchants wanted their accounts settled, for goods which were kept until the next season would lose half of their value, as well as incur interest on capital (normally a rapacious 18–20 per cent per annum, although legally only 12 per cent).[118] So exports usually cost less then – for example, teas were discounted 30–40 per cent[119] – but by the same token imports likewise brought less because the Chinese market had by now been sated. After receiving the "chow-chow chop" (the last chop-load of goods embarked before sailing) and replenishing their water supply and "sea stock" of provisions, the American merchantmen dropped down the Pearl River and out to sea. (In 1792 Captain Charles Barkley's crewmen on the *Halcyon* on its homeward leg each received 1 pound of meat, 1 pound of bread, ½ gallon of water, and 2 drams of liquor per day and 6 pounds of sugar and 1 pound of tea per month.[120]) Few ships dared to sail against the monsoons, which ruled navigation in the China Seas even more than in the Indian Ocean (typhoons were particularly fearsome at the autumnal equinox).[121] The American vessels kept the northeast monsoon down the South China Sea and through Sunda Strait and caught the southeasterlies across the Indian Ocean to the Cape of Good Hope, which was rounded in early spring. Then they followed the SE Trades between Africa and South America and squared away for Cape Cod, taking on a pilot off Boston Light and – some four months after leaving China – coming to at India Wharf to complete the "golden round." As was the custom of the trade, the China goods were sold at auction immediately upon arrival.[122]

Altogether, American ships made at least 127 voyages between the United States and China via the Northwest Coast from 1788 through 1826 – more than three every year.[123] Many a Yankee sailor learned his craft on the decks of a Nor'westman, prompting the American naval historian Samuel Morison to dub the Nor'west trade "Boston's high-school of commerce for forty years."[124] Its high regard is illustrated by an incident recorded by Richard Dana, Jr, in his *Two Years*

Before the Mast, a classic account of the California hide-and-tallow trade in the middle 1830s. Homeward bound with 40,000 hides, 30,000 horns, and several barrels of sea-otter and beaver skins, Dana's ship hailed an American schooner in mid-Atlantic in an effort to procure fresh provisions for the scorbutic crew. He wrote:

The style and gentility of a ship and her crew depend upon the length and character of the voyage. An India or China voyage always is *the thing*, and a voyage to the Northwest coast (the Columbia River or Russian America) for furs is romantic and mysterious, and if it takes the ship round the world, by way of the [Hawaiian] Islands and China, it out-ranks them all. The grave, slab-sided mate of the schooner leaned over the rail, and spoke to the men in our boat: "Where are you from?" Joe answered up quick, "From the Nor'west coast." "What's your cargo?" This was a poser; but Joe was ready with an equivoke. "Skins," said he. "Here and there a *horn*?" asked the mate, in the dryest manner. The boat's crew laughed out, and Joe's glory faded.[125]

The Boston–Northwest Coast–Canton route enjoyed more popularity and more prestige among New England seamen than any other because of its exotic stopovers and – more important – lucrative returns.[126] The expenses of the *Despatch's* first voyage (1794–96) for cargo, outfit, wages, port charges, and duties came to $25,563 and its proceeds to $51,541 for a net profit of $25,978 and a return of approximately 202 per cent on investment.[127] Around 1800 a 200–ton coaster on a two-year voyage cost £5,500–7,000 (£2,000–3,000 for the vessel, £2,000 for its outfit, and £1,500–2,0000 for its cargo) and returned £25,000–30,000, or 250–450 per cent on investment.[128] Between 1804 and 1814 21 American ventures took cargo worth 507,800 piasters (silver dollars) to the coast, exchanged it for furs worth 491,980 piasters, and sold them in China for 11,123,000 piasters for a return of 2,200 per cent;[129] this calculation, however, excluded vessel and outfit costs, which generally constituted five-sevenths of the total costs, which would therefore total 1,777,3000 piasters and leave a return of 525 per cent. In the late 1810s the return on investment reportedly ranged from 300 to 500 per cent,[130] even though the trade's heyday had passed. And in 1821 an EIC employee testified that the American coast trade was "extremely lucrative."[131] Some individuals and firms did exceedingly well by the trade. John Cushing went to China at age sixteen, became a partner in Perkins and Company at nineteen, and retired in middle age with a fortune of nearly $1,000,000; Perkins and Company, the senior new England firm in the China trade, was worth $3,000,000 in the late 1820s; and William Sturgis valued his share of the Bryant and Sturgis partnership at $171,000 in 1827 and at $500,000 twenty years later.[132]

The reasons for the handsome profits are not hard to find. Investors had the opportunity to gain on not one but three transactions: on the Northwest Coast, at Canton, and in Boston. This is what Frederic Howay, the longtime student of the Nor'west trade, called the "triple golden round of profits." "The Americans had," he wrote, "a perfect golden round of profits: first, the profit on the original cargo of trading goods when exchanged for furs; second, the profit when the furs were transmuted into Chinese goods; and, third, the profit on those goods when they reached America."[133] Moreover, in the first and second exchanges the returns were "exceedingly profitable in proportion to the capital invested"[134] because of the very high value of New England goods on the coast in terms of sea-otter skins and the equally high value of sea-otter skins at Canton in terms of Chinese commodities (the third transaction was, of course, an outright sale at Boston for a cash return). In addition, as an anonymous commentator noted, the ships were small and the hands were few, so that "even those who have no capital, may carry it on upon credit," and "if one will share the profit with the ship owner and the captain, it is not necessary to advance any money."[135] The value of American trade goods that were expended on the coast from 1789 through 1817 is given in Table 2, which reveals the changing value of these goods as the number of trading vessels increased and then decreased (and perhaps, too, as Indian customers demanded more substantial and expensive articles such as textiles and guns and as inflation mounted). During the 1790s an average of $62,673 worth of American trade goods were bartered on the coast for furs annually; during the same period the annual value of American shipments of sea-otter skins to Canton averaged some $350,000.[136] During this decade, then, the sea-otter skins were worth from five to six times as much to the American traders as the trade goods that were bartered for them. For the decade from 1804 through 1813 the differential was even greater – twenty-two to one (but this according to an incomplete French inventory).[137] The ratio of the value of sea-otter skins to that of China goods is unknown.

The boom years of the American coast trade were the last decade of the eighteenth and the first decade of the nineteenth centuries (they correspond, incidentally, to the "A", or growth, phase of the first Kondratieff fifty-year economic cycle [1780/90–1810/17], just as the waning years correspond to the "B," or stagnation, phase of the cycle [1810/17–1844/51]). By the beginning of the 1810s American shipping in general and the Nor'west trade in particular were starting to ebb. The slowdown was wrought by restrictive United States legislation in 1808–10 (which was designed to keep the country neutral by curtailing foreign trade), the War of 1812 with Great Britain, the imposition of trade restrictions by several European countries, the replacement of wood and sail by iron and steam (with the steamship lessening the American advantages in ships and shipmasters), and the attractiveness of manufacturing to American investors in a country with a growing supply of both capital and labour (the population doubled every twenty years between 1780 and 1840).[138] On the coast itself the trade was being overdone, with too many ships chasing too few skins. Already by 1801 Sullivan Dorr was advising his clients from Canton "to omitt the Northwest business entirely." "The Bostonians," he added, "are playing a ludicrous farce indeed."[139] Dorr estimated that up to 22 sail in 1801 would have to share 11,000 skins, which would fetch up to $20 each at Canton, so that each vessel would average 500 skins worth $10,000, minus $5,000 for port charges, leaving only $5,000 for investment in a return cargo of China goods.[140] He was right. In fact, in 1801 24 coasters took some 13,000 sea-otter skins to Canton, where they fetched $20–21 each (Tables 1 and 6).[141] In the fall of 1802 Dorr declared that "the Northwest trade is compleatly overdone," and at the end of the year he asserted flatly that "skins cannot now be had on the coast for anything." "It is a lottery," he concluded.[142]

Actually, the outlook was not quite as bleak as Dorr maintained. Fewer shipmasters with better information could still do fairly well, so shipowners kept close track of coastal shipping. But the lifting of Jefferson's 1807–09 Embargo Act, which had prohibited American vessels from leaving Atlantic Seaboard ports, prompted a spate of Nor'west voyages and a flood of furs at Canton, where the price of a sea-otter skin dropped from $30 in 1808–09 to $21.50 in 1811–12 (Table 9). Thus in the fall of 1811 Bryant and Sturgis informed Captain Bennett of the *Lydia* that "the number of Vessels and amt of Cargoes already gone [to the coast] will be more than we think can be profitably employed."[143] And in 1812 a Nor'westman wrote to a prospective investor: "Dear Sir do not engage in the N.W. Business for times never was so Bad Before."[144] By the spring of that year Bryant and Sturgis were "desirous of closing our North West consern," and William Sturgis wrote that "we do not feel much flattered with the prospects of skinners this year – tis literally a lousy 'business' [worm damage to skins] & not worth pursueing."[145] Nevertheless, the firm remained in the coast trade, outfitting ventures whenever circumstances were favourable and adjusting to changing conditions. In

1824 Bryant and Sturgis merged their coast business with that of Boardman and Pope in order "to prevent competition in the N.W. Trade."[146]

During the 1810s the coast trade continued to diminish (by 1817 to less than one-quarter of its former value, according to the firm of Perkins and Company, whose principal owner even advised another investor that "the Northwest Coast trade ... is nearly extinct"[147]), but towards the end of the decade it was reported that American trade between the Northwest Coast and Canton was still "very profitable."[148] As Captain Grimes told Marshall and Wildes in 1822, "there is money to be made in this trade with a good selected cargo,"[149] the important thing being accurate and speedy intelligence. Grimes's owners concurred, for they instructed him the next year to "stick to the N. w. trade as it is our greatest dependence."[150] The importance of up-to-date information was stressed by Bryant and Sturgis in a directive to Captain Suter:

Never neglect an opportunity of writing us by any rout[e], giving an account of your prospects proceedings etc. also an[y] information about trade both with the Russians & the natives that you think may be usefull ... Give us all the particulars of your trade with the Russians and a list of such articles as will answer best with the quantities that can be sold and the prices they will bring, also state what sells best among the Natives, inform us whenever you can what other vesels are doing and what are the prospects for business there in future.[151]

Prospects were still favourable as late as 1824, for in the autumn of that year Captain Grimes reported that "the rage for the N. West runs high."[152] Yet returns were steadily decreasing. A couple of years later Stephen Reynolds, one of Honolulu's leading foreign merchants, noted tersely: "Skins Scarce on the coast." "Business very Dull there," he added.[153] The Honolulu agent of Marshall and Wildes wrote in the autumn of 1827: "The North West Ships have done miserable enough the last year [1827] – not 150 skins each, and what they have got cost on an average Thirty Dollars. That trade is finished for the present, no object for more than two vessels in one season."[154] He added, however, that "amongst the Indians something will be done every year, they are always in want of certain articles for which they will pay a good profit."[155] A French shipmaster reported from Honolulu in 1828 that four American coasters which had arrived there in October had "failed miserably in their northwestern dealings." One, the *Louisa*, had spent two summers and one winter on the coast and had collected only 800 beaver and 100 sea-otter skins, and the latter had cost eight times what they had ten years earlier. The

Frenchman added: "In both 1827 and 1828, trade with ten visiting ships did not furnish half the number of otter skins that a single vessel formerly could purchase in only three months, and those that they were able to obtain cost them five times more than the amount paid before."[156] Bryant, Sturgis, Boardman, and Pope told Captain Pierce in 1828 that "the N. West Trade is in a most miserable state & we see no prospect of its revival," and at the end of the next year their Honolulu agent reported that "the N. w. Coast is nearly abandon'd by Americans."[157] In 1823 the Yankee vessels collected 350 skins each – even then "hardly a saving business," according to Bryant and Sturgis; in 1827 they obtained fewer than 150 each; and in 1829 they procured only 60 skins each.[158] As Captain Dominis informed his owners, Marshall and Wildes, in 1829; "The furs are very scarce every where, and particularly on this Coast. What we do get here is well paid for, and a small prospect of getting much more."[159] Boardman voiced a general sentiment when in 1832 he advised Captain Barker: "I shall not make any outfit this season, the trade apears fairly run out."[160]

Shipowners were already turning their attention to more profitable ventures. At least one-half of the coasters in 1829, for example, went only to Sitka to sell supplies and did not trade elsewhere on the coast at all. John Jacob Astor abandoned the China trade in 1828 and the fur trade in 1834 (he made most of his fortune from Manhattan real estate); Marshall and Wildes had withdrawn from the coast trade by 1831; and the firm of Bryant, Sturgis, Boardman, and Pope was dissolved in 1841.[161] This pullback is reflected in the decline of American fur sales at Canton (Table 3). The author of an 1834 guide to the China trade wrote: "Twenty years ago, the fur trade with China amounted to upwards of a million of dollars annually; but during the last two or three years no skins or furs whatever have been brought to Canton ..."[162]

The turning point in the American coast trade, therefore, seems to have occurred in the late 1820s, even though the depletion of sea otters had begun much earlier. But American shipmasters had been able to compensate to a considerable extent by accepting more and more beaver pelts. In doing so, however, they came up against a new (and formidable) obstacle in the late 1820s in the form of the HBC, which re-entered the coast trade in force in order to protect its monopoly. The capital and expertise of the Honourable Company were to prove too much for the remaining American coasters. In Howay's words, "the triumph of the Boston vessels was, however, merely temporary; in the end the trade fell into the hands of the Hudson's Bay Company."[163]

4 The British Comeback

To secure our Inland trade we must endeavor to destroy com-
petition on the Coast, as these [American] Coasters trade with
Indians who in their turn trade with the Natives of the Interior.
John McLoughlin to George Simpson, 20 March 1827

The Hudsons Bay Co have not interfered as yet but they are
expected next season.
Captain Cotting to James Hunnewell, 7 August 1827

After the War of 1812, in the wake of the over-hunting of sea otters,
American maritime fur traders took more and more beaver skins,
which came via intertribal trade from New Caledonia, the northern
interior of the HBC's Columbia Department (the company's adminis-
trative name for the Oregon Country). By the early 1820s American
Nor'westmen were taking from 3,000 to 5,000 beaver pelts to Canton
from the Northwest Coast annually.[1] This particular traffic did not
trouble the rival British continental fur traders until the middle
1820s, when the HBC, enlarged by the 1821 merger with the NWC
and rejuvenated by George Simpson's reorganization of operations
in the Columbia Department, began to expand westwards and northwards from New Caledonia. Then the coastward diversion of beaver
immediately became apparent. Moreover, by now American fur-trading vessels were returning to the coast in force after a temporary lull
resulting from the tsar's 1821 decree that attempted to ban foreign
ships from Russian America's coast north of 51° N. In 1824 Russia
and the United States signed a convention that readmitted American
vessels to the Alaskan panhandle for a period of ten years. By now,
too, sea otters were even scarcer, and even more beaver pelts were
being taken instead. In 1827 the *Louisa*'s Captain William Martain,
who was considered the best of the "Boston pedlars" on the coast,
spent nearly the entire year trading and managed to obtain only 160
sea-otter but 1,000 beaver skins.[2] By the early 1830s American coast-

ers were getting up to 10,000 beaver pelts annually (as many as the HBC was getting from New Caledonia and half as many as it was getting from the entire Columbia Department!).[3]

Not only were the American vessels siphoning furs that ought, in the HBC's view, to have been going to their inland posts. They were also inflating Indian demands and lowering company profits by giving higher prices for skins and forcing the company to follow suit. Chief Factor John McLoughlin reported from Fort Vancouver in 1827 that the American brig *Owhyhee* had entered the Columbia that summer and offered the Indians double the company price. "She traded at half our Tariff and as you may suppose this had a powerfull effect on the Chinooks," he wrote.[4] The *Owhyhee*, Captain Dominis, returned to the river in the late winter of 1828–29 in company with the *Convoy*, Captain Thompson, and they raised the price that the HBC paid for beaver (1 blanket for 6 beaver or 1 musket for 20 beaver) by 400 per cent to 4 muskets or 4 blankets.[5] A veteran Bay man complained that the price of beaver had risen fivefold on the coast during the 1820s because of increased competition.[6] The *Owhyhee* and *Convoy* returned to the Columbia in 1830, and again, in McLoughlin's words, they "completely spoiled the trade of this place [Fort Vancouver] as we now are obliged to give a Blanket for One [instead of two] Beaver Skin & a Gun for 4 Beaver." "Still," he added, "at this place it would pay but the news spread up into the Interior & will affect the Trade of that quarter."[7] The company had to pay so much for skins that not enough trade goods remained for entering the coast trade.[8] When the company finally did enter the contest it found that the Indians expected high prices because they had been shown "a great deal of indulgence" by American traders, who gave a blanket, a gallon of rum, and two ounces of tobacco for a beaver skin in 1831.[9] That year, after a decade on the coast, the *Owhyhee* under Captain Dominis returned to Boston with from 8,000 to 9,000 beaver skins and a "large number of lesser furs."[10] However, "from the acct. he gives of the Columbia the prospect is unfavourable for getting many Beavers there as the agent of the Compy told him they would rather sacrifice £50,000 than allow the same collection again to be taken out of their hands."[11] The British were determined to undercut the "American opposition."

That determination materialized in the middle of the 1820s. Hitherto the British may have been deterred by the tsarist edict of 1821. And the NWC, which was on the coast (Fort George) as early as 1812, may have deliberately shunned the sea-otter trade by agreement with its Boston agents as part of the price for delivery to the Chinese market. Such collusion was implied in an 1822 report from one of

George Simpson's lieutenants: "This quarter [Fort George] abounds in Beaver, a few land Otters are also procured, but both these and the former mentioned fur, are far inferior to those procured on the east side of the [Rocky] Mountain; the only fine and rich fur I have seen, are the Sea Otter, these surpass anything of the Kind I have hitherto seen, but very few of these are procured, as it has been the policy of the former [North West] Company discouraging the Natives bringing them to Fort George, which if I may be allowed to give my opinion, was rather against the trade."[12]

Initially the HBC, moreover, simply did not want to participate in the coast trade. As late as the summer of 1824 Simpson informed the Governor and Committee in London that the Council of Rupert's Land at York Factory, the company's Canadian headquarters, believed that it would be unprofitable and dangerous to enter the coast trade "on account of the hostile character of the natives."[13] Within a year, however, Simpson himself, during an inspection tour of the Columbia Department, became convinced that the company should unite its "inland business" with the "coasting trade" "with spirit and without delay."[14] He asserted that the coast traffic, which had been "shamefully neglected," was "unquestionably worth contending for" and "if properly cultivated would become an object of the first importance" to the company, and he predicted that the combined coastal and interior trade, "if sufficiently extended and properly managed," would be twice as profitable as that of any of the firm's other North American departments.[15] Simpson told McLoughlin in 1826 that "the first principal objects of attention are the Coasting Trade and the establishing of Frazers River [Fort Langley]."[16] Earlier Simpson had recommended that the "principal Depot" of the Columbia Department be shifted from Fort Vancouver on the lowermost Columbia to the mouth of the Fraser – the future Fort Langley – because the latter would be more central to both the coast and inland trade, so that the company's coastal venture could be extended and its inland posts supplied more easily and cheaply.[17] Fort Langley was established in 1827 but it did not become the headquarters of the Columbia Department because Simpson's journey down the Fraser in 1828 demonstrated that the Fraser Canyon was an even greater obstacle to transport than the Columbia Bar and Columbia Gorge together; in addition, farming proved more productive at Fort Vancouver.

Simpson's opinion of the coast trade was also altered by the fact that in 1825 Russia signed a convention with Great Britain that gave British trading vessels the same access to the Alaskan panhandle that American vessels had won in 1824. The governor was confident that the company could eliminate both Russian and American competition on the coast. The Russians, he believed, did not really matter because their furs were mostly fur seal and sea otter, not beaver, and were not competitive because of the "prodigious" expense of transport to the North China market via Siberia. He forecast that the Columbia Department's returns would double or even treble with the addition of the coast and inland trade of New Caledonia.[18]

The HBC had sufficient capital and resolve for prosecuting the coast trade but it still needed reliable intelligence, suitable ships, skilled seamen, and saleable goods. And these essentials were not gained quickly or easily. The first attempt at intelligence-gathering was a failure. In the winter of 1825–26 the *William and Ann* reconnoitered the coast trade but to little avail because its master, Captain Henry Hanwell, Jr, wasted so much time; he spent one month leaving the Columbia, one month in the Strait of Juan de Fuca (which was already well known to the company and whose furs would mostly go to Fort Langley anyway), and one month trying in vain to find the entrance to Portland Canal. Also, at Skidegate Hanwell met the *Owhyhee*, Captain Kelly, who had spent five years on the coast. He was "very communicative" and told the British that "their vessel was not well arranged for the purpose of trade and defence, invited them on board his Vessel, and offered to shew them how she was arranged, and to shew them his Furs [1,600 sea-otter and 1,000 beaver and land-otter skins], but they did not avail themselves of his invitation." "This loss of time," concluded McLoughlin at Fort Vancouver, "is more to be regretted as he passed going and coming within sight of most of the places I suggested, at which had he stopped we would have known the Articles requisite for the Trade and the Price paid for the Furs – both of which would be important."[19] Simpson agreed, reporting that Captain Hanwell had not obtained "any information of importance" on the coast trade because he had "had little or no communication with the natives and rarely ventured within a sufficient distance of the land to run any risks." His "extraordinary" and "unnecessary" caution, charged the governor, amounted to "pusillanimity."[20]

The company then placed Lieutenant Aemelius Simpson, RN, at McLoughlin's disposal "with a view to establishing a permanent Trade on that Coast." From his services the company expected "to derive much useful information and advantages."[21] It was not disappointed. In 1827 during a visit to California Lieutenant Simpson interviewed a veteran American Nor'westman:

I met here [Monterey] a Mr. [William] Smith who has been engaged in the North West Coast trade for upwards of thirty years, who informed me that the Coasting trade now carried on by the Americans is daily becoming less valuable owing to the number of Vessels they have upon the Coast; last year [1827 season] they had Six who did little or nothing, the competition having completely drained the market of Skins ... and that all made a loosing business of it, thus in fact the Indians are now so abundantly stocked with Goods, that they do not engage in hunting and this too great a use of fire arms has tended very much to frighten away the Sea Otter from the Coast, that the Indians last year more particularly were engaged in wars and consequently furnished no Skins, and that to make that Coast again valuable, Vessels should not visit it for some years.[22]

The lieutenant recommended that the company not enter the coast trade "in its present state."[23] But Beaver House, the HBC's London headquarters, was not deterred. In 1828 Lieutenant Simpson sailed northwards to reconnoiter the coast personally. There he met the *Volunteer*'s Captain Barker, who told him that the coast trade "now proves a losing Trade to all engaged in it." "The Trade upon the Coast," the American shipmaster added, "has been so much overdone by competition that it has now lost its value and importance and would not pay more than two vessels, if they collected all the Skins (which are annually dwindling away in number) even at a moderate tariff."[24] In 1828 no more than 600 sea-otter and 7,000 beaver and land-otter skins were taken on the coast by five American ships; each sea-otter skin cost them $15 in goods but brought them $30 in China (and each beaver and land-otter skin cost one gallon of gunpowder and fetched $3).[25] Simpson reported that the Americans had for "several years back" found the coast trade to be a "losing one," and "it was only their wish to dispose of the goods on hand" – and the Hawaiian market for timber ($200 per 100–foot plank) and cured salmon ($10 per barrel) from the coast – which "induced them to persevere in it."[26] Simpson also verified the diversion of beaver pelts from New Caledonia to American coasters: "The Indians say they Trade a number of them [land furs] from other Indians higher up the [Nass] River, who again say they procure them from others further in the interior, whom they say have intercourse with Whites [Bay men] who come to them upon Horses; in speaking on this subject to the Americans they say the interior Indians are fools, as they dispose of their Furs to those Whites for little or nothing. The Americans know by the Mode of stretching the Skins, those from the interior from those of the Coast – the first are stretched round the latter longways."[27]

The Honourable Company was determined to plug this drain and thereby eliminate American competition on the coast at almost any cost, and Lieutenant Simpson's detailed report on the trade provided the necessary information. At the end of the winter of 1828–29 Captain John Dominis of the *Owhyhee* reported from the Columbia that the American mountain man Jedediah Smith had told him that the company's Fort Vancouver "expect two ships from England daily with North West Cargo, then to establish themselves ... on the North West Coast, on purpose to take all the trade from the Americans."[28]

Meanwhile, however, the requisite vessels, sailors, and goods had still to be acquired. In 1826 the Council of Rupert's Land resolved that a "small vessel" be "outfitted for the Coasting Trade" and assist in the founding of Fort Langley.[29] Accordingly, the thirty-ton sloop *Broughton* was constructed and launched at Fort Vancouver in the summer of the same year, but it proved too small; so did the sixty-ton schooner *Vancouver*, which, moreover, was built of unseasoned timber and was not serviceable until 1828.[30] This disappointment prompted Governor Simpson to recommend that in the future, should the "London ships" (which brought goods to Fort Vancouver and returned to England with furs) be owned by the company and reach the Columbia early enough to make a coasting voyage – that is, any time before 10 May, after which they had three spare months before the proper season for departure – "it may be advisable to instruct the Captains to follow the directions of the Chief Factor [John McLoughlin] superintending the Columbia affairs from the time of arrival until departure."[31] The first London ship to do so was the schooner *Cadboro*. It reached Fort Vancouver in the spring of 1827 and, under the command of Lieutenant Simpson, sailed from there "with the Outfit for [founding] Frasers River [Fort Langley] and from thence to proceed on the coasting trade."[32] The *Cadboro* proved to be a "dull" sailer, however, its captain declaring that "such a vessel must prove the Means of defeating any advantage from the Coasting Trade."[33] Indeed the ship did not get beyond the Strait of Georgia, "saw few furs with the natives and for which they asked a very high price," got only two sea-otter and twenty-eight land-otter and beaver skins, and had one man killed and another wounded by the Indians.[34] "I am sorry," wrote one Bay man to another, 'that the coasting business from which so much was expected has had such an unfavourable beginning.'[35]

Shipping improved after Beaver House in 1828 decided to deploy three vessels for the coast trade, two to make the annual voyages from London to the Columbia and back and the third to stay on the coast, with the ships being interchanged when refits were needed.[36] However, the loss of the brigs *William and Ann* in 1829 and *Isabella* in 1830 on the treacherous bar at the mouth of the Columbia "deranged our plans very much," in Governor Simpson's words.[37] As late as the summer of 1832 he admitted that the company's shipping was still "inadequate" for the coast trade.[38] McLoughlin himself was partly to blame, for he firmly believed that the coast trade should be prosecuted with fewer ships and more posts.[39] Simpson and the Governor and Committee favoured more shipping, however, and by 1836 the company was using seven vessels on the coast and between London and Fort Vancouver.[40] In 1835 alone two new vessels were commissioned (Table 4). One was a steamer, the *Beaver*, which proved to be particularly advantageous in the variable winds and strong currents of the coast. Lieutenant Simpson had stressed the superiority of a steam vessel in 1831: "How valuable a Steam Boat would prove in these inlets – with one of these you might go along the whole coast in a few days."[41] Governor Simpson was persuaded of the advantages of a steamer in the coast trade, and in 1832 he asked Beaver House to provide one:

We are aware that the first cost would be heavy, but we feel assured that she would, in a very short time, become the cheapest craft that could be used, and perform more effective service than any two Sailing Vessels which might be provided. The saving of time in ascending and descending the Columbia and Fraser's Rivers of itself would be a very important object, as it rarely happens that any of the craft we now have perform the trip between Cape Disappointment and [Fort] Vancouver in less than three weeks while the river is high, which, with the detention at Bakers Bay and off the mouth of the river from calms and head winds, occasion a prodigious loss of time; indeed a Vessel entering the Columbia, and having occasion to go up to [Fort] Vancouver, cannot be expected to get to sea again in less than a couple of months, and craft have been known to be windbound in Bakers Bay for six weeks at a time, being unable to work over the bar. Much valuable time is also lost in ascending Fraser's river to Fort Langley owing to the strength of the current when the water is high and calms; and at Nass there will likewise be a considerable loss of time in working out and in to the Establishment; indeed it is ascertained that a Vessel can perform the voyage from the Port of Nass to the Sandwich Islands and back again in less time than from Nass to Vancouver and back. A steam Vessel would afford us incalculable advantages over the Americans, as we could look into every Creek and cove while they were confined to a harbour by head winds and calms, we could ascend every stream of any consequence upon the coast, we could visit our establishments at stated periods, in short a Steam Vessel would, in our opinion, bring the contest to a close very soon, by making us masters of the trade.[42]

Simpson suggested a steamer of no more than 180 tons and of small draft, with the very best machinery and a double set of parts, the whole costing about £6,000.[43] Chief Factor McLoughlin, incidentally, did not agree. Not only did he favour fewer vessels and more posts on the coast, but he especially opposed the use of the *Beaver* because it was costlier and riskier than a sailing vessel.[44] Simpson, however, had his way.

The want of sailors was mainly a want of officers, crewmen being obliged by the terms of their contracts to transfer from the annual supply ship to the coasting vessels whenever necessary.[45] At first the masters were intemperate, incompetent, and insubordinate; they were unwilling to take orders from Fort Vancouver's commandant, a civilian merchant, and they knew too little and drank too much. Captains William Darby (*Eagle*, 1833–34 and *Columbia*, 1836–37), James Davidson (*Vigilant*, 1823–24 and *Dryad*, 1825–26), William Eales (*Ganymede*, 1834–35, 1836–37), Henry Hanwell, Jr (*William and Ann*, 1824–25, 1826–27), Leonard Hayne (*Ganymede*, 1828–29), Charles Kipling (*Vancouver*, 1832), Joseph Langtry (*Nereide*, 1833–34), John Minors (*Dryad*, 1829–30), William Ryan (*Isabella*, 1829–30), and John Swan (*Cadboro*, 1826–27 and *William and Ann*, 1828–29) were of this ilk.[46] Lieutenant Aemelius Simpson was a noteworthy exception, but he served less than five years; on 2 September 1831 he died aboard the *Dryad* at Fort Simpson "after a fortnight's severe illness."[47] Governor Simpson declared that his death was a "very serious loss" because of his "great zeal and ability" in conducting the naval department.[48] At the same time, the governor reported that "the coasting service is miserably lame in effective officers ... in regard to ability & character," and he asked the Governor and Committee to send an officer to supervise the marine department and two lesser officers, warning that the former should be "above all things a man of strict veracity sober habits and good private character" and be engaged for five years.[49] In the same year the company replaced the late Lieutenant Simpson by hiring a fifteen-year veteran of the coast trade, the American captain William McNeill (plus three other experienced American officers), and buying his ship, the *Lama*, as well. The vessel was "a fine new copper brig of 150 tons," bought at the Hawaiian Islands from the proceeds of company sales of salmon and timber there.[50] In 1833 Captain McNeill and the *Lama* collected one-third of all skins traded on the coast.[51] The Bay man John Work, who served in the coast trade with McNeill, told a friend in early 1838 that he was "the most active serviceable captain we ever had on the Coast notwithstanding he is a Yankee"[52] (indeed, McNeill's retention of American citizenship once prompted a mutiny by the British hands on his vessel).

The shortage of trade goods arose from damage to cargo aboard the London ships, the late arrival of the London ships at Fort Vancouver, and shipwreck. The *William and Ann* and its cargo and crew were lost in 1829; in 1830 the *Isabella* and part of its cargo were lost, and the *Eagle* reached Fort Vancouver "with a considerable proportion of her Cargo damaged";[53] and in 1834 the schooner *Vancouver* was lost with its cargo. The company's coast returns were £8,000 lower in 1834 than in 1833 because of the "scarcity of goods" stemming from the wreck of the *Vancouver* and the late arrival of the London ship *Nereide*.[54] Governor Simpson stressed that it was "very desirable" that outfits from London "be dispatched early in September, so as to reach the Columbia early in February, as it is of the utmost importance to be prepared with goods for the business of the coast in March, when the Americans arrive from the Sandwich Islands, where they usually winter." After unloading at Fort Vancouver the London ship could then supply the coastal posts and spend the rest of the summer trading on the coast or making a voyage to the Hawaiian Islands, returning to Fort Vancouver in time to load the returns and leave for England in October.[55] McLoughlin complained to Simpson in 1830 that "the Ganymede arrived so late that by the time our Vessel could get on the Coast the trade would be over."[56] On its next voyage in 1832 the *Ganymede* not only arrived late (July) again but also brought damaged goods. Simpson reported that "many articles were damaged, owing to the leaky state of the decks, and improper stowage"; a "considerable quantity" of woollens in particular suffered "much injury" from rust.[57]

The shortage of tradeable goods lowered fur returns, of course. In 1833 the company collected £13,000 worth of skins on the coast but "certainly left furs in the hands of the natives to the amount of £2000 from the want of goods to trade them."[58] The governor lamented in 1835 that "much loss has arisen of late years from damage arising from bad stowage in the vessels from England"; for example, he added, 1,000 blankets were rendered unsaleable in 1831, several casks of hardware were "much injured" by rust in 1832, several hundred pounds sterling worth of goods were lost in 1833, and £300 worth in 1834.[59] McLoughlin asserted that he had been short of trade goods every year except two (1830 and 1831) from 1825 through 1834, and at the end of the latter he complained that "the only thing we want to carry on the coast trade with energy is goods."[60] As early as 1828 he had suggested that the problem be solved by the simple expedient of London sending the annual outfit one year in advance so as to provide an ample reserve of goods.[61] By the last half of the 1830s the company seems to have been doing just that, and the dearth of goods, like that of vessels and officers, had been largely overcome.

By now, too, the company had buttressed its coast trade with two posts north of Fort Langley. The first (and foremost) was Fort Simpson, founded at the mouth of the Nass River in May 1831 with the assistance of the *Dryad* and *Vancouver*. The site augured well. Every summer an Indian fair, attended by the Tsimshians and Haidas, was held at the mouth of the river.[62] McLoughlin had reported in 1826 that "more land Furs are traded at Nass [the northern side of the entrance to Observatory Inlet] than at any other place along the Coast," and Aemelius Simpson, the post's namesake, had found in 1828 that Nass was the main mart for land furs on the coast.[63] (In 1834 Fort Simpson was moved several miles southwards to the site of the present Port Simpson, which was more convenient for shipping.) Fort McLoughlin was established in May 1833 on an island in Milbanke Sound with the assistance of the *Ganymede*, the company hoping to intercept the 3,000–4,000 beaver pelts that American vessels reportedly collected there annually.[64] In the same year Fort Nisqually was built at the southern end of Puget Sound and linked with Fort Vancouver by a trail over the Cowlitz Portage; company coasters could now unload skins and embark goods at Nisqually and avoid the longer and riskier passage around Cape Flattery, over the Columbia bar, and up the river.

Yet the company still did not enjoy clear sailing on the coast. As John Work wrote in a letter to a friend, "the natives are very numerous, treacherous, daring, savage and ferocious in the extreme; besides the climate is shockingly bad, almost continually raining, and in many other particulars equally unpleasant."[65] The Americans laboured under these conditions, too, of course, but they had dealt with the Indians longer and consequently were more familiar with their seasonal movements, favourite goods, and commercial habits. As Lieutenant Simpson had reported in 1828, "the Americans were well acquainted with these Indians" whereas the Bay men were "perfect strangers."[66] For the same reason the Yankees also knew the coast itself better – its channels, harbours, winds, currents, shallows. Furthermore, not having permanent bases on the coast, they were not exposed to its inclemency year-round, and they did not have to contend with the temperate rain forest. James McMillan, the founder of Fort Langley, found it a formidable barrier in 1827: "The great size of the Timber and the thick growth of underwood have been sadly against us in clearing the ground, the jungle on the banks of the [Fraser] River is almost impenetrable and the trees within are many of them three fathoms [eighteen feet] in circumference, and upwards of two hundred feet high."[67]

The American traders were likewise spared "intermittent fever" (most likely malaria), which erupted at Fort Vancouver for the first time in the late summer of 1830, killing three-quarters of the local Indians and delaying the founding of Fort Simpson.[68] It struck again in 1831 and 1832.[69] In 1831 Fort Vancouver was in a "very unhealthy state ... nearly all the people belonging to the establishment and shipping being more or less affected" by the disease; no whites died but there was a "prodigious mortality" among the Natives as far upriver as The Chutes.[70] Governor Simpson believed that "intermittent fever" was caused by the "putrid exhalations and penetrating damps which issue from the stagnant water left in the neighbouring swamps" by the annual summer overflow of the Columbia, whose crest was unusually high in these years (he was right in the sense that the stagnant flood water bred anopheline mosquitoes). He went so far as to recommend that, if the fever raged again in 1832, the fort should be abandoned and replaced by a new "Grand depôt" on Puget Sound.[71] The disease did return unabated but the post was not moved. Its "sickly state" that year made it "quite impossible" to build a coasting vessel there; indeed the ship carpenter, a Mr Anderson, who was to manage construction, was the first man to succumb to this outbreak.[72] And the stricken condition of the crew of the *Ganymede* prevented it from leaving the Columbia before 8 November, about two months later than usual.[73] In the fall of 1834 McLoughlin acknowledged that "the fever has not been so prevalent this summer as it used to be, but it is a fact that since it first began in 1830 it so much weakened our people that it was with the greatest difficulty we got through our work."[74]

When Lieutenant Simpson had reconnoitered the coast trade in 1828, he had reported as follows on the American traders: "They had the advantage over me in every respect – Ships well arranged for the Trade with an abundant supply of goods suited for the Market – a knowledge of the Indians and their language, and a perfect acquaintance with the several Ports where skins were to be had – besides being in concert, Indians would not attempt any hostility towards them."[75] By the middle 1830s, however, the British, too, knew the coast and the Indians; they had sufficient and suitable vessels, sailors, and goods as well as posts; and "intermittent fever" had abated. Nevertheless, the Yankee coasters still enjoyed two advantages: the skippers had a proprietary interest in the outcome of their voyages, and they offered the Indians more goods for their furs. The British captains were salaried employees with no vested interest in their ventures and therefore no incentive to excel (unless, like Captain McNeill, they became a shareholding chief trader). That their American counterparts were able to continue in the face of the vigour of British opposition and the depletion of fur bearers is a testament to their experience of the trade, their efficiency of operation, and their freedom of action. Certainly nobody knew the coast trade better or dealt more sharply (with the possible exception of the Haidas). And their economy resulted from the keen competition among themselves, for they "were not so much rivals of the [Hudson's Bay] company as they were of one another," noted a company servant.[76] They were able to pay more for skins partly because they outfitted their ships so economically and partly because it was better to dump their remaining cargo on the coast even below cost than, as Chief Factor Duncan Finlayson noted, "be at the trouble and expence of carrying it to China where stowage is an object to them, having to take return cargoes from thence to the States."[77] Or as John Work explained in 1835: "The Americans never calculate on making more than a part of their voyage on the coast. They dispose of part of their cargo at the [Hawaiian] islands, and make further sales to the Russians [at Sitka], and then come on here with the residue here, which is disposed of at almost any price rather than take it home. Their Captains act in the double capacity of Master and supercargo for which they are allowed a very moderate monthly wages, and a percentage upon their sales, so that it is [in] their interest (as they express themselves) to 'get rid of it' even should the owners be no gainers by the bargain."[78]

"This is the way with the Americans," repeated Work, "when they come to a winding up they part with every thing they have, and often at such low prices, as they say to, '*get rid of it*,'" and the situation was unlikely to change, he concluded, "so long as our opponents get worth their whiles for coming on the coast to wind up a voyage, which is all they calculate upon, as they chiefly reckon upon the profit of their sales at the Islands, Sitka, and California."[79] The problem for the HBC, as both Finalyson and Work stressed, was not only the large number of skins that the American coasters took but, more important, the high prices that they paid for them. If the company did not match these "extravagant" prices, the Indians kept their furs until the American traders reappeared. In any case, the British were willing to match and even exceed the American prices in order to deter the Yankees completely and then, having gained a monopoly of the trade, drastically lower prices and quickly recoup the initial heavy outlays.

The company was able to absorb these outlays because of its large capital fund, especially after its merger with the NWC in 1821. And even before the middle 1830s the British enjoyed a couple of other advantages. As George Simpson told the Governor and Committee in 1832, "the facilities we possess for conducting the business, having permanent establishments to co-operate with our Shipping, which are chiefly provisioned from the produce of our farm, give us a decided advantage."[80] In the same report he asserted that New Caledonia was "still well stocked" in fur bearers, particularly beaver, and that "many" of them were still being routed to the coast for "American Adventurers"; "we are now, however," he added, "beginning to divide this trade with our opponents, and I trust will ere long become Masters of it."[81] The company's farms at Forts Vancouver and Langley were especially helpful, yielding surpluses of grain and meat for the Bay men.[82] As early as the summer of 1826, only two years after the post's founding, Simpson declared that the progress of farming at Fort Vancouver was so auspicious that he felt "perfectly easy as to the means of provisioning our Establishments and coasting vessels without the assistance of importation [via the London ship]."[83] The 1830 crop (2,043 bushels of grain, 583 bushels of peas, and 9,000 bushels of potatoes), although damaged by the Columbia's summer crest, was, according to McLoughlin, "sufficient to supply all our wants and enable us to give the new Establishment [Fort Simpson] a full stock of provisions for one year." He added: "We must take into consideration the freight it saves us, and it has been raised at no expence ... as, if the people [servants below the rank of clerk] had not been doing that [farming], they would have been unemployed."[84] In 1833 Fort Vancouver's farm produced more than 10,000 bushels of grain, which left enough for export to the Hawaiian Islands.[85] The next year Simpson rated the farm "an object of vital importance ... as it has enabled us to dispense with imported provisions, for the maintenance of our shipping and establishments, whereas, without this farm, it would have been necessary to import such provisions, at an expense that the trade could not afford."[86] And in 1835 the governor reported that the cattle were so numerous that it was no longer necessary for the London ship to bring provisions for both its outbound and inbound voyages, the farm being able to supply its homeward leg.[87] Fort Langley also produced agricultural surpluses as well as much salmon. "There is no place on the Coast," declared McLoughlin, "where Salmon is so abundant and got so cheap as at Fort Langley."[88]

The company also enjoyed an advantage in trade blankets, its being superior to – albeit slightly dearer than – those of the American coasters. Boardman and Pope advised one of their shipmasters in 1831 that HBC blankets were "*thicker & larger &* of somewhat higher cost than those usually carried to the N West" by American vessels.[89] The Indians, however, may well have preferred the Yankee blankets because they could be had for somewhat fewer skins.

The HBC's strategy for defeating the American coasters was, in the words of Duncan Finlayson, who took charge of the coast trade in 1836 from Peter Skene Ogden, "to oppose them with a well regulated steady opposition,"[90] that is, to offer unbending competition. At first McLoughlin, at least, was content simply to match American prices. "We must expect to sell at a low price," he wrote to Simpson, "and to gain more from the quantity we sell than from the price we sell at."[91] However, by now there were not very many skins left to share, and they were decreasing steadily. Moreover, as long as the company only met rather than beat American prices, it was still profitable for the Bostonians to return to the coast year after year. The British vessels shadowed the American coasters, offering the same prices. In 1836, for example, the *Lama* dogged the *Joseph Peabody* on the northern coast from 9 May until 2 June, when the two ships became separated in foggy weather.[92] The American coasters anchored off the British posts and forced the company to raise its prices to their levels. Thus the *La Grange*, Captain Snow, dropped anchor at Fort Simpson on 17 October 1836 and stayed until 15 November. Relations were nevertheless polite, even friendly: "5 of the la Granges Crew picked up some of our pickets [posts] and brought them on shore for us, much indebted to Capt Snow for his kindness though we wished [him] any where but at Fort Simpson," records the post's journal. And as soon as the *La Grange* left, the Bay men "raised our Tariff to our old standard viz 1 Blkt, 1 Gall. Mixed Rum & 2 Hds [hands (1 hand = several leaves of tobacco tied together)] Tobacco for a Large Beaver and other things in proportion at first the Indians grumbled but as they had no other resource they were obliged to come to our terms."[93]

Sometimes the two sides tried to outbid each other, much to the joy (and profit) of the Indians, who, as John Work put it, "glory in having in having [sic] opposition and know well how to take advantage of it."[94] He described one bidding battle at Fort Simpson in 1835:

Sunday, May 17. Still fine weather. The Indians assembled again in the morning as usual, and kept going between us and our opponents [the American coaster *Europa*] as usual. During the day we traded 94 Beaver, 5 Otters, 28 Bears, 21 Martens. We had more customers than our opponents owing to the superior quality of our Rum and Tobacco. Capt. Allen [of the *Europa*] who must have been perfectly aware of our scale of trade, came aboard [the British vessel *Lama*, Captain McNeill] and enquired what we were giving, and on being told, got in a violent passion and declared that he would do his utmost to rise the price and make us pay as high as possible for all the furs we would trade on the coast this season, that he had plenty of goods to do so (& as our deck was full of Natives busy trading) without waiting to be spoke to went over the side and proclaimed to the Indians that he would give 4 gall. Rum & 8 heads of tobacco with one of his large blankets for a beaver. The Indians received this intimation with several loud hurrahs, and immediately ceased trading, and began to clear off to his vessel. It remained with us now either to lose the beaver or rise our price, the latter was preferred and we accordingly offered 5 gal. Mixed [diluted] rum & 10 heads tobacco with a blanket per beaver, the result of which was that we secured, as we think, the best share of the day's trade. At this rate the furs cost high, but as our expenses are going on the same, let us get beaver or not, and as we have a good stock of goods, it is deemed best rather than let the furs fall into the hands of our Opponents, to secure them even at a light profit. The Indians seem perfectly aware that this is not to last, for they are enquiring how long these prices are likely to continue and were promptly told by us only so long as our Opponents remained.[95]

The only way for the company to maintain the "old standard" was to eliminate its American competitors entirely by outpricing them. So it decided, in Work's words, "to get the furs at any price or at least raise them so high that any which may fall into the hands of our Opponents will yield a loss or at least no profit." "This," he added, "is considered the only means by which the Coast can be kept clear of Opponents."[96] Accordingly, on a trading cruise to the south of Fort Simpson on the *Beaver* in the spring of 1837 Captain McNeill was instructed "should he fall in with Opponents ... to be guided by circumstances as his own judgment may direct taking every means in his power to annoy them and prevent them from getting furs and to raise the price so high that what they do get will yield no profit."[97]

This strategy was only partly successful. Simpson had said in 1832 that "our immediate object is to obtain possession of the [coast] trade," whereupon the company would be able to lower the "exceedingly high" tariff.[98] The next year it was reported that "there were no Americans on the Coast this season [1833]," and in 1838 John Work told a friend that "we had no Yankee opponent last season [1837]," adding that "I have made such arrangements that should they come again they would get so little that they would not be induced to come again and that we would get rid of them altogether."[99] In fact, American traders did ply the coast in 1833 and 1837, but increasingly, as British competition intensified and fur bearers diminished, they were freighters of supplies to the Russians at Sitka rather than traders of goods to the Indians. The Russians were sorely in need of provisions and manufactures, and American coasters had been supplying them since the beginning of the century.[100] Now these supplies were more profitable than skins. Having made Sitka, however, the American skippers were still wont to seek some furs in the "straits," and the company had to be watchful. In 1834, for instance, Fort McLoughlin expected to increase its fur returns by one-third over those of 1833; instead, its returns decreased by two-thirds because bourgeois (commandant) Peter Skene Ogden, thinking mistakenly that the *La Grange*, Captain Snow, had disposed of all of its goods at Sitka, halved the price of beaver pelts from one to two beaver for a blanket, whereupon the *La Grange* appeared and collected all of the skins (at least 2,000).[101] The company had to be watchful of the Indians as well. They resented the weakening of American-British competition, since that meant lower prices for their furs. John Work reported from Fort McLoughlin in the late summer of 1835 that "the disturbed state of the Indians and their discontent, arises from their being under the impression that our being here is the cause of their not getting such high prices for their furs as formerly, in consequence of the Americans not visiting them so frequently." But he also blamed the lower prices on the simplification of the inland trade, for the interior Indians now brought their own furs directly to the fort, thereby eliminating the coastal Native middlemen.[102]

In the middle 1830s even the Sitka market, long a mainstay of American Nor'west traffic, became more precarious. The American traders had been bringing supplies to Sitka since its very establishment in 1799 but they had also been poaching skins and smuggling firearms and spirits in what the Russians considered their territorial waters. St Petersburg's protests had been rejected by Washington, so in 1821 the Russian government unilaterally banned all foreign vessels from the coast of Russian America north of 51° N. The American government objected but, more important, the RAC discovered that its alternative supply line by sea from Kronshtadt was more expensive and less reliable. So in 1824 and 1825 Russia signed conventions with the United States and Great Britain, respectively, that readmitted American and British ships to the coast between 54° 40' N and Lynn Canal (and British vessels to the rivers flowing through the *lisière*, or mainland Alaskan panhandle) and prohibited the sale of ordnance and liquor to the Indians. But these terms were valid for ten years only. On the very day that the American-Russian convention expired two Yankee captains, Snow of the *La Grange* and Allen of the *Europa*, were warned to leave the coast north of 54° 40' N (they ignored the warning).[103] The post journal of Fort Simpson recorded another expulsion: "Saty. 26th [July, 1834] ... Vessel anchored in the bay about 6 p.m. – proved to be the 'Bolivar Liberator' Capt. Dominis, last from Sitcha, where she had disposed of greater part of her cargo ... They recd. orders at Sitcha prohibiting them from entering any of the harbours on Russian territory, and having applied for permission to enter Tomgass, for the purpose of cutting Spars only, they were

refused it."[104] In 1836 the Russians drove the *Loriot* from the coast
and the United States presented a claim for damages but Russia
refused to pay or to renew the 1824 convention.[105]

If the Russians had renewed the two conventions, they would have
been outcompeted by both the Americans and the British. From 1826
to 1829 the RAC collected an annual average of 400 beaver, 300 fox,
80 sea-otter, and 60 black-bear skins in the straits from the Tlingits.[106]
But many others were taken by American traders, who paid more.
The Russians gave the Indians seven medium-size blankets for one
sea-otter skin (which was one-half or two-thirds as much as they paid
their own hunters) but the Americans paid eight large-size blankets
(or six plus presents worth two blankets).[107] The RAC's prices were set
by the head office in St Petersburg, and colonial officials were not
supposed to change them without its consent.[108]

The British also outbid the Russians. In 1832 the RAC admitted
that its British rival had a competitive edge partly because, contrary
to the 1825 convention, it traded firearms and spirits to the Indians
and partly because its trade goods were cheaper on account of lower
transport costs. Indian trade goods sent to Sitka around the world
from Kronshtadt or across Siberia via Okhotsk cost the RAC twice as
much as the same goods sent to Fort Vancouver from London cost
the HBC. Consequently, the British were able to pay the Tlingits from
two to three times as much for skins as the Russians were.[109] The Fort
Simpson post journal acknowledged this advantage: "The Governor
[of Russian America at Sitka] also told them [some Kaigani Haidas]
that whatever we [the British at Fort Simpson] gave them [for furs]
he would give as much. We on our part tell them that whatever the
Russians give we will give a little more. It will be our interest to do
so so long as the skins can be got at a price that will pay, in order to
secure the furs. These furs we may say have been bought from the
Russians' door."[110]

Nevertheless, the Russians were still able to get some furs in the
"straits" from the Tlingits, who in turn were getting them from interior
Indians. The Tlingits at the mouth of the Stikine River travelled 150
miles inland to traffic with the Nahanis.[111] The latter would otherwise
have been trading these skins to the inland posts of the HBC, which
was determined to stop this diversion. In order to do so it decided
(in accordance with the terms of the 1825 British-Russian convention)
to ascend one of the Alaskan panhandle's rivers and erect a post at
least ten marine leagues (thirty miles) upstream and thereby intercept
the flow of peltry. As early as 1832 Simpson had planned to open a
water route from the coast to New Caledonia and capture the 3,000–
4,000 beaver pelts that American ships were collecting annually at

the mouth of the Stikine River.[112] By 1834 the company was ready to act, as the Americans were retreating, leaving only the Russians to challenge the British. Simpson told Beaver House: "We have no apprehension of annoyance on the coast from the Americans, as they now admit that we are masters of the trade, but from the Russians, who it appears look upon our exertions and encroachments with much jealousy and dissatisfaction, it is thought we are likely to meet with opposition, as we are now striking at the very root of their trade."[113] In the spring the company's brig *Dryad* arrived at the mouth of the Stikine to found the new upriver post, which was to be called Fort Drew and which was intended "to cut off from the Russians the invaluable trade they have hitherto enjoyed without interruption, drawn from the British Territory in the interior."[114] But the expedition was blocked by the Russians, who had recently established St Dionysius Redoubt at the river's outlet and stationed the fourteen-gun *Chichagov* there (two local Tlingit chiefs also objected to the British plan, incidentally, because it "would injure their trade with the interior," but they were not averse to the British building a post beside the Russian redoubt, knowing full well that the resultant competition would raise fur prices).[115] The British contended that this action was in breach of the 1825 convention, filing a claim for £22,150 in damages, and appealed to the Foreign Office for assistance. While the Stikine, or *Dryad*, affair simmered, Simpson decided that it would be safer (less resistance from the Russians as well as the Tlingit middlemen) and cheaper (fewer men and less equipment) to approach from the interior via Pelly's (Stikine)River.[116] In 1838 the company established a post on Dease Lake, and in the summer of that year a party of five men from this post met a band of Tlingits under Chief Shakes ten days up the Stikine at the "splendid rendez-vous" where the coastal Indians annually traded with the interior natives.[117]

Meanwhile, American coasters continued to abandon the trade. The HBC's coast returns of outfit 1838–39 were the largest yet, thanks to a two-year absence of American competition.[118] In the summer of 1839 Simpson reported to the Governor and Committee that the company's coast trade was still "undisturbed by opposition" because it had succeeded in mounting a "strict Coast Guard."[119] The Russians were still on the coast, however, and the Russian tariff at St Dionysius Redoubt still set the standard for the company's fur prices.[120] Until both the Americans and the Russians were completely removed from the coast trade, fur prices would remain high. And American trading vessels would continue to come as long as the Russians needed supplies, so the British (Aemelius Simpson in 1828, Peter Skene Ogden in 1832, and Duncan Finalyson in 1836) offered to supply Sitka with provisions and manufactures in place of the troublesome Bostonians. The company's Oregon Country farms, especially Forts Vancouver and Langley, were producing surpluses of grain and meat, and more could be obtained cheaply for goods from the Willamette Valley settlers, while high-quality wares were brought by the London ship to the Columbia. At first the RAC showed little interest in this offer, since it was obtaining sufficient and economical supplies from both the American coasters and Alta California's bountiful missions. By the last half of the 1830s, however, both of these sources had become unreliable. Fewer and fewer American vessels were making the coast in the face of the depletion of fur bearers and the resurgence of British competition; and the Californian missions were secularized, with the *peninsular* padres being removed, the property plundered, and the fields abandoned. So in 1839 the two companies signed an agreement (to take effect in 1840 for a period of ten years) whereby the British undertook to supply Sitka annually with provisions and manufactures, to rent the *lisière* for an annual payment in land otters, and to drop its claim in the *Dryad* incident. The RAC's supply line was again secure, and it could dispense with American suppliers/poachers (the last such order was negotiated in 1839 and delivered in 1841); it could also liquidate its enclave of Russian California around Fort Ross, which had failed to fulfil its agricultural promise. The HBC, for its part, had the coast trade to itself at last as well as a market for its Columbian agricultural surpluses. Simpson noted the significance of the "Russian contract": "And the recent arrangement with the Russian American Company, putting an end to all competition from the northward, we shall forthwith be enabled to reduce the price of Furs, to their fair value, and to discontinue the sale of Arms, Ammunition and spiritous liquors, which will be productive of a great savings in wages, as when deprived of warlike stores, they will no longer be the formidable people, they have been accustomed to be, but be manageable with less force, than it has heretofore been prudent to remain among them; so that our coast trade promises to become more valuable and extensive every succeeding year."[121]

Thus the Indians became more docile and their furs less costly. The coast trade was now, as Simpson put it, "tranquil."[122] It had been a long and dear struggle. At the beginning of 1832 Chief Trader Angus McDonald had written from Fort Langley that "there is Beaver in this quarter [northern coast] but the price is enormous, still the Yankees stick to it and what is more strange they say they make something by their labour."[123] By now, however, the HBC had entered the coast trade in force. At Fort Nisqually, for example, the company raised the price of a two-and-one-half-point blanket from one beaver in the spring to two in the summer after no American coasters appeared. This measure prompted "constant jarrings" from the Natives, the Clallam Salishes of the northern Olympic Peninsula denouncing the increase as "robbing the Indians of one beaver." By late February of 1834, after the worst of the winter was over, trade became "very dull" at the post, the Indians keeping their furs "in hopes of an opposition casting up." But none did and the tariff remained at two beaver for one blanket.[124] Similarly, in the late spring of 1837 on the northern coast "it is arranged that in a short time hence should no Opposition cast up the price paid for furs at Fort McLoughlin and to the South will be reduced to a blanket per large Beaver or lower if it can be done without injury to the trade," although at Fort Simpson "it is doubtful if we can make much reduction on account of the vicinity of the Russians."[125] By the middle of 1840 both the Americans and the Russians had withdrawn. The British replaced St Dionysius Redoubt with Fort Stikine (or Highfield) and added Fort Taku (or Durham) farther north (when twenty Bay men opened the former in mid-June 1840, some 1,000 Tlingits had assembled there to trade).[126] In 1843 the bourgeois of Fort Stikine reported that nine-tenths of the post's fur returns came from the interior.[127]

The British monopoly enabled McLoughlin to make "important changes in the trade on the Coast, an entire suppression of the sale of spirits and raising the price of the [trade] goods to the same scale at which they are sold at Fort Vancouver."[128] The drop in fur prices meant a slowdown in the flow of furs from the interior to the coast and hence a stabilization of the inland trade. It also meant that the Indians on the coast "held back" their skins for a time in the hope that American vessels would return and raise fur prices.[129] But they waited in vain and eventually had no choice but to sell to the company at half the former prices. According to McLoughlin, before the withdrawal of the American coasters the company had to pay ten times as much for Northwest Coast as for New Caledonia furs;[130] afterwards the company presumably paid a common price.

At first the HBC lost money on the coast trade, owing to the necessity of buying vessels, hiring sailors, and matching high American prices. In 1831 the company collected about 3,000 beaver skins on the coast but still lost £1,600.[131] Then its coast trade cleared £1,613 in 1832, the first year to show a profit.[132] The coast traffic compensated for the decline in the early 1830s of the fur trade of the lower Columbia, where the business was "far inferior to what it was some years ago." This "defalcation" in returns resulted from the "great mortality" among the Indians wrought by intermittent fever, "whole villages having ... been swept away."[133] In 1833 the company collected £13,000 worth of furs on the coast, whereas John Work's Snake Country trapping expedition garnered only £1,375 worth – the result of "the exhausted state of the Country and the severe sickness [intermittent fever] with which he and his party were afflicted".[134] The coast trade accounted for 37 per cent of the Columbia Department's gross returns in 1833 (twelve months) and 25 per cent in 1834 (eleven months).[135] The 1834 coast returns were lower because of a "scarcity of goods and opposition."[136] McLoughlin asserted in 1843 that from 1831 through 1834 the company collected £22,348 worth of skins on the coast (with opposition) but still lost £8,436; "in 1835 we began to clear money and have done so ever since ... because we had no opposition." He added that the American traders "went away and never returned for this simple reason[:] as they were mere Adventurers without capital, they could not afford to carry on a losing trade, as we undersold them."[137] The HBC's dominance of the coast trade from 1835 is shown in Table 5. In the early 1840s the company's coast trade amounted annually to up to 10,000 beaver and land-otter pelts, plus small furs.[138] That take may have represented as much as one-half of the Columbia Department's total returns of those skins.[139]

Yet the HBC's capture of the coast trade from the Americans and Russians was rather a hollow victory for Simpson. By the time the company managed to enter the trade, it was already being abandoned anyway by American shipowners in favour of more lucrative ventures, such as whaling in the North Pacific and hiding and tallowing in California. Moreover, the fur trade in general – both maritime and continental – was declining in the face of the depletion of fur bearers and the alienation of fur buyers. "I regret much," reported Work to McLoughlin in 1841, "that ... there is a great falling off in our returns. We have this season received few or no furs from the Northward. Furs appear to be becoming scarce every where."[140] Three years later Work wrote to a friend: "Furs have been selling badly and what is worse greatly decreased in numbers." "Dividends are fallen off greatly," he added.[141] As early as 1841 Simpson recommended that Forts McLoughlin, Stikine, and Taku be abandoned, leaving the coast trade to Fort Simpson and the *Beaver* at an annual saving of £4,000.[142] Stikine was spared (until 1849) but McLoughlin and Taku were vacated in 1843 and their servants transferred to the new post of Fort Victoria on the southern tip of Vancouver Island. (Fort Victoria was intended to replace the district headquarters of Fort Vancouver once the international boundary was settled, Simpson believing that it would follow the Columbia–Snake–Clearwater rivers to the Great Divide.[143]) And then American competitors returned in the form of whalers. In 1843 and 1844 Yankee whaling vessels bought venison and potatoes from the Indians of the northern coast and traded a "large amt" of furs and haiqua on Vancouver Island and the Queen Charlottes.[144] Work lamented in 1844 that "the Yankees are annoying us again, a number of their whalers were on the coast here last summer and two of them winter in Queen Charlotte Island, and have been picking up a good many furs from us."[145]

Fur sales fell partly because of changing fashion. In Europe and North America the eight styles of beaver hat were yielding to the new silk hat. In 1830–31 beaver skins brought $4.00–4.50 each at Canton but $6–8 in the United States; a year later, however, they fetched $6 at Canton and $4 or less in the United States because of the advent of an "immense number" of silk hats.[146] And business was struck by a financial panic in 1837. Early that year the three London banks that handled most American-Chinese trade failed, and the prices of China goods slumped.[147] But for half a century "China fever" had kept these prices high and had drawn traders to Canton, the entrepôt of the China market. That market was not only ancient and exotic but also complex and dynamic, demanding patience, flexibility, and diligence on the part of shipmasters and supercargoes.

5 The China Market

The productions of our Empire are manifold, and in great Abundance; nor do we stand in the least Need of the Produce of other Countries.

      Emperor Chien-lung to King George III, 1793

Speculation at a proper time is my grand motive.

      American commercial agent Sullivan Dorr, Canton, 1799

China presents the most extensive consumption for Skins of any Kingdom in the World.

      Canton commercial agent James Goddard, 1823

THE CHINA TRADE

When the first British coasters made Whampoa with sea-otter skins in the middle of the 1780s, they added another link to a long chain of trade that had tenuously connected China with the barbarian world for at least two millenia. Cathay's foreign trade had flowed via caravans on the Silk Road through Central Asia to the Roman Empire, via Arab dhows on the sea lanes of the Indian Ocean to the Near East, and via Chinese junks to the Spice Islands of the Southern Sea. After the European discovery of the sea route to India by the Portuguese in the fifteenth century, trade between China and the West went by sea, with the exception of the Russian caravan traffic through Mongolia and Siberia. By the late eighteenth century the Celestial Empire's foreign commerce had expanded to include Japan (via Portuguese Macao for bullion), Korea and southern Manchuria, southeastern Asia (via Amoy for spices, rice, and woods), and even New Spain (via Manila and Acapulco for bullion).

Domestically, China was racked by three profound changes in the eighteenth century: the doubling of its territory through the annexation of Mongolia, Sinkiang, and Tibet; the doubling of its population from some 150 million to as many as 340 million through a prolonged period of peace and order and an expansion of agriculture (marked by the double-cropping of rice and the introduction of dryland crops such as corn, potatoes, sorghum, sweet potatoes, and peanuts); and the establishment of a European presence.[1] The advent of Europeans was triggered by the prospect of mercantile profit, for foreign merchants saw the "Central Flowery Land" as a populous and wealthy market. Populous it unquestionably was, the total number of consumers continuing to spiral from 230 million in 1760 to 430 million in 1842.[2] Wealthy, however, it generally was not. Most Chinese had to make do with "weak tea and insipid rice," to use their own expression for poverty.[3] Furthermore, China was nearly self-sufficient, with little need for foreign goods. As Sir Robert Hart, a British customs official, noted:

The Chinese ... lives in its own ring-fence, and covers a country made up of fertile land and teeming waters, with infinite variety of mountain and plain, hill and dale, and every kind of climate and condition, producing on its surface all that a people requires ... Chinese have the best food in the world, rice; the best drink, tea; and the best clothing, cotton, silk, and fur. Possessing these staples, and their innumerable native adjuncts, they do not need to buy a penny's worth elsewhere; while their Empire is in itself so great, and they themselves so numerous, that sales to each other make up an enormous and sufficient trade, and export to foreign countries is unnecessary.[4]

Hart added that "many regard China as a far-distant land, with an immense population, but so wanting in all that others possess as to be ready to purchase, in unlimited quantities, whatever is offered for sale; whereas, what is true is this: China needs neither import nor export, and can do without foreign intercourse."[5] He warned that "foreign traders can only hope to dispose of their merchandise there in proportion to the new tastes they introduce, the new wants they create, and the care they take to supply what the demand really means."[6]

Trade with China was additionally discouraged by slow transportation (coolies, sampans) and transit taxes as well as, perhaps, the anti-commercial bias of Confucian doctrine, which placed the merchant below the farmer and the bureaucrat on the social scale.[7] A mercantilist outlook was wanting in China, whose rulers stressed stability rather than growth, maintenance – of national security, law and order, public works, peasant subsistence, and gentry comfort – rather than development.[8] Moreover, the Son of Heaven's Middle Kingdom was very ethnocentric. "They consider China the centre of civiliza-tion, and their Emperor the sovereign of the universe," testified one British merchant to a parliamentary committee.[9] China's firm belief in the superiority of its civilization rendered foreign trade unimpor-tant, and – to some – even undesirable, since contact with "foreign devils" would sully Chinese culture. The reaction of Western traders, themselves not lacking in ethnocentricity, was predictable; they char-acterized the Chinese as arrogant, supercilious, and anti-commercial. But the Chinese experience with outsiders, especially those from the north, had been far from happy, and a new Great Wall had to be erected at Canton against the "sea barbarians," whose imperialist inroads on the southern periphery of Asia were well known to the Manchus (1644–1912); the latter, in addition, were equally well aware of their own naval weakness.[10]

Notwithstanding all of these impediments, there was still a basis for some foreign trade. China itself did not produce enough silver, furs, or opium. The system of waterways was extensive, if slow, and not all transit taxes were prohibitive. There was, too, a sizeable body of affluent customers – officials, merchants, warlords, scholars, land-owners. And the barbarian entrepreneurs were persistent. So the Chi-nese authorities grudingly allowed foreign trade but, in keeping with their view that foreigners were uncivilized and troublesome inferiors, the mandarins confined them strictly to Canton, Macao, and Kyakhta (Maimachin) and closely regulated their activities, dealing with them at arm's length through a commercial monopoly, just as the equally sensitive Japanese restricted Dutch trade to Deshima Island in Naga-saki Bay, and for the same reasons, namely, to facilitate control, min-imize contact, and maximize profit. In addition, since the Chinese myth of superiority over non-Han cultures presupposed a lord-vassal relationship, foreign traders were required to give gifts – the equiv-alent of the kowtowing demanded of foreign diplomatic emissaries.

THE CANTON SYSTEM

Thus was created the "Canton system" to regulate foreign trade. Its essence was hierarchical subordination. At the bottom stood the Cohong, a monopolistic commercial guild of thirteen members known as hong merchants, or hongists. It was founded in 1720 to supervise the trade of the Southern Sea, and the activities of its mem-bers became concentrated in the suburb outside the southwestern wall of Canton, where a "foreign quarter" had existed since the Sung period (960–1280 AD). In 1745 the hong merchants became security merchants, each hongist having to assume responsibility for the payment of import and export duties by a foreign ship as well as the "obedience" (proper conduct) of its crew. They leased factories, provided interpreters, settled prices, guaranteed duties, arranged loans, restrained foreigners, controlled smuggling, supported charities, and gave presents. The hongists colluded in enforcing control but not in conducting trade, each of them trading on his own capital for his own profit.[11] An American merchant explained their advantages: "They have the exclusive privilege of exporting certain Articles & the Duties are lower to them."[12] At first, the Chinese termed an appointment to the Cohong a "promotion" because it provided the opportunity of realizing a fortune from the Canton trade.[13] And, despite the legendary corruption of China's mandarins, the hong merchants enjoyed a reputation for honesty among their foreign clients. One of the latter asserted that "as a body of merchants, we found them honourable and reliable in all their dealings, faithful to their contracts, and large-minded." He added that "as regards quantity and quality, the Hong merchants fulfilled their part with scrupulous honesty and care."[14]

The wealthiest and hence most famous of them was the "great, good, and rich" Howqua (Houqua), or Wu Tunyuen (1769–1843). He joined the Cohong in 1792 and by 1822 was the senior member.[15] Frail in body and frugal in living, Howqua was extremely generous to his friends and singularly methodical and precise in his accounts.[16] He charged higher prices than other hongists but was very dependable in terms of both punctuality and quality, and in the United States and Great Britain teas bearing his chop (stamp) sold for premium prices. Howqua preferred to deal with the Americans in the first quarter of the nineteenth century[17] but broke completely with them in the last half of the 1820s, when American overinvestment in teas and tighter credit rendered China-US trade unprofitable (the number of American ships at Canton fell from forty-two in 1825–26 to twenty in 1827–28, and in 1830 interest rates in the United States on money borrowed for mercantile ventures were double those in Great Britain[18]). In 1834 Howqua estimated that his assets were worth $26,000,000.[19] He was rich enough to command the market (even shipping his own goods to Europe on chartered vessels), so much so that less astute hongists suffered financial "embarrassments."

Weaker hong merchants had to offer higher prices in order to gain business and therefore ran greater risks.[20] (In 1813–14 the Chinese authorities tried to reduce the size of the Cohong by removing the junior [weaker] members but the EIC, fearful of fewer hongists and higher prices, successfully resisted by suspending trade for two months.[21]) Moreover, all hongists were subjected to frequent and heavy "squeezes" – "voluntary" contributions to finance public works, relieve famines and floods, suppress bandits and rebels, and enrich higher officials. It was reported in 1806 that they had to pay their superiors $3–4 million annually in gratuities.[22] The hongists met these exactions by imposing a surcharge, or tax, on all imports and exports.[23] Nevertheless, bankruptcies became so frequent that Cohong membership, which was bought in Peking for 200,000 taels, or £55,000, came to be regarded as a burden, not a privilege, and the full complement of thirteen members was seldom reached.[24] Even Howqua failed in 1798, although two years earlier he was "supposed to be rich ... in excellent credit ... & very cautious & circumspect in his Actions."[25] In 1828 Manhop went broke owing $1,500,000; only seven hong merchants were then left.[26] For bankruptcy or lawbreaking hong merchants could be "unbuttoned" (deprived of their badge of office, a button atop their cap) and jailed or exiled to Sinkiang, China's Siberia. Corruption among Chinese officials at Canton increased so much in the late eighteenth century that the hongists felt obliged to establish the secret Consoo Fund, which was financed partly by a contribution from each hongist of 10 per cent of his trade profits and, from 1780, partly by a levy of 3 per cent on foreign imports; it was designed originally to meet the increasing exactions of greedy officials but eventually to repay the foreign creditors of "bankrupts" – insolvent hongists.[27] This growing corruption was symptomatic of Manchu, or Ching, dynastic decline, with high offices being sold, local taxes embezzled, and army rolls padded.[28]

The Cohong's monopoly was limited to staples. The other needs of the foreigners were met by the "outside merchants," also known as "shopmen," "China Street men," or "Chinchew men," who operated out of the two-storey shops that flanked the foreign factories, there being no houses in the suburb. Each narrow, paved street was associated with a particular trade, and China Street was the busiest.[29] The shopmen were supposed to restrict themselves to the sale of petty articles for the personal use of foreigners, such as clothes, hats, shoes, and handicrafts. But they came to sell (through the hongists in return for a commission) staples as well, including teas, silks, nankeens, crapes, mats, and drugs (rhubarb, camphor, cassia).[30] Their position was explained by an American merchant: "Altho the Outside Merchants (so called from not being in the Co-hong) are numerous and many of them large & respectable dealers, willing to contract with you to any extent and for any Articles (Bohea Tea excepted) yet are they obliged to connect themselves with a Hong Merchant to land, or Ship the Goods under his Chop; this they easily do by granting part of their profits, Paying certain sums of Money, or by even advancing the duty to a Hong Merchant who has not funds."[31] Especially the Americans preferred to deal with the cheaper "outside men," who had no Consoo Fund to finance and fewer and lighter "squeezes" to remit.[32] As an early American commercial agent, Sullivan Dorr, noted, the hong merchants charged higher prices because they had greater expenses – "such expense that he must have a greater price or not be half juicy enough for the mandarin to squeese."[33]

At the same time, however, the shopmen were less trustworthy and more unscrupulous and therefore riskier than the hongist, although some of them, at least, such as the well-known Yowqua, were "of an integrity and intelligence in business unsurpassed."[34] One American merchant even advised flatly that these "Sharpers" be avoided altogether: "They will offer a much higher price perhaps 50 pct. & more flattering Terms in all respects but will cheat you in the price or Qualities of the Goods you take in return or will get the advantage of you in some part or other of the operation, for at this game this Class of Chinamen, are a match for the Devil."[35] The Americans, then, ran more risk but, if they were careful, could make more money than the less daring British by dealing with the outside merchants. Two of the latter, Ponqua and Gnewqua, were the "only real skin [fur] dealers" at the turn of the century.[36] In 1800–02, of the five hong and shop merchants who dealt with American vessels, Ponqua served more Boston vessels and handled more fur cargoes than any other; and of the sixteen cargoes handled by him in the two trading seasons, twelve comprised furs only, three specie only, and one both furs and specie.[37] Thus the monopoly of the Cohong was broken by the shopmen, just as Canton's was infringed by the "outer anchorages" of the Canton River estuary from 1821, and the EIC's was violated by the Indian "country traders" from 1813. In 1828 the British tried to limit the business of the outside merchants, and thereby undermine their American rivals, but in vain.[38]

Above the Cohong stood the Hoppo, or superintendent of maritime customs at Canton, and above him the viceroy or governor-general of Kwangtung (Canton) and Kwangsi Provinces. The Hoppo was always a Manchu and was appointed by the emperor himself, usually for three years. During his term "it took the net profit of the first year of his tenure to obtain his office, of the second year to keep it, and of the third year to drop it and provide for himself."[39] The Hoppo's job was to collect the duties on Canton's foreign trade and remit them to the Board of Revenue at Peking. The capital expected a fixed sum, so he was free to line his pockets at his own discretion. The exactions of the 1800–01 and 1813–14 autumn-winter trading seasons were particularly overbearing and rapacious.[40] A British trader contended that the Hoppo kept one-half of the port revenue for himself and sent the other half to the emperor.[41] Charged with maintaining this cash flow to Peking, the Hoppo was anxious to prevent disruptions of the Canton trade and bankruptcies among the hong merchants.[42] Such exigencies also depleted his own purse, of course.

The viceroy, or 'John Tuck' to the Euroamerican traders, was the emperor's representative. He could make or break the hong merchants, fining, firing, or even exiling them. The imperial government, for its part, was concerned only that as much trade revenue as possible be forwarded to Peking and that the foreign traders be contained. As early as 1789 the viceroy began to conceal from the emperor the actual number of foreign ships at Canton in order not to alarm the Son of Heaven with the large extent of foreign commercial contact, as well as, of course, to enable himself to retain more of the duties.[43] The emperor nevertheless received from $500,000 to $1,000,000 per year from Canton's foreign commerce at the beginning of the nineteenth century.[44]

At the very bottom of this pecking order chafed the foreign traders. As befit their status as *Untermenschen*, they were isolated, segregated, and surveilled. Their presence was governed by the "Eight Regulations." Foreigners were forbidden, for example, to import opium and saltpetre (except that intended for the imperial government) and to export *sycee* ("fine silk": silver bullion), metal goods, and rice in bulk.[45] They were not allowed inside the wall of Canton and were required to leave the city's factories during the off or dull season (April-October); their females and weapons were not permitted in the factories; the number of their servants was limited; pleasure boating on the Canton River by them was prohibited; the teaching of Chinese to them was forbidden; and all their communication with Chinese officials had to be made indirectly through the hongists in the form of "respectful petitions." Because of the officials' corruption, and perhaps civility, too, some of these restrictions were not enforced and were allowed to lapse. Still, anti-foreign feeling persisted, as indicated by the fact that the offspring of Euroamerican crewmen and Chinese consorts at Canton were sometimes killed by drowning.[46]

These features of China's foreign trade – the supervision and taxation (usually less than 30 per cent *ad valorem*) of trade by officials who were responsible directly to the capital, the restriction of trade to border emporia, and the confinement of foreign traders at these emporia to their own quarter – were manifestations of the tribute system, whereby barbarian nomads (astride horses or aboard ships) acknowledged the material and cultural superiority of the Celestial Empire, mainly but not solely in order to facilitate trade. To ethnocentric Peking, foreign trade was at best a favour granted to barbarians and at worst an opportunity used by them for spying – hence the prohibitions on the export of saltpetre, gunpowder, and ironware and on the bearing of arms by foreigners on Chinese soil, and the restrictions on the study of Chinese life by foreigners (such as the bans on summering at Canton and learning Chinese).[47]

THE BRITISH TRADERS

Several foreign trading nations were kept at bay, but by the late eighteenth and early nineteenth centuries Great Britain and the United States loomed the largest. British commerce was handled by the EIC.[48] It had been chartered by parliament in 1600 to monopolize British trade in the Eastern Hemisphere. After losing the contest for the trade of the East Indies and Pacific islands to the Dutch East India Company (1602–1798), it limited itself to the India and China traffic, concentrating on the export of textiles from the former and teas from the latter. By the late eighteenth century the "John Company" had become primarily a governing body and tax collecting agency in the Indian Presidencies, principally through Calcutta, rather than a trading concern, staffed mostly by overpaid soldiers and bureaucrats instead of cost-conscious merchants and profiting chiefly from its monopoly on tea imports from China.[49] In India the company governed and taxed; in China it traded. The East India Fleet numbered up to 100 sail.[50] Most Indiamen, some as large as 1,500 tons, were constructed, repaired, and refitted by a dozen shipyards on the Thames.[51] They were convoyed and escorted to India and China. From Great Britain the company exported men (cadets and clerks for its own operations and soldiers for the king's regiments in India), military and naval stores, woollens and cottons, metals, and silver bullion.[52] Its income was derived from its monopolies in India on cotton cloth, saltpetre (for gunpowder), raw silk, indigo, rice, and sugar, which were exported to Britain, and opium, which was sold at public auction to private merchants and shipped from the Hooghly to China together with woollens, raw cotton and cotton cloth, and tin.[53] The company bought Chinese teas mainly from bullion revenue on illicit opium sales; its sale of British woollens and cottons at Canton was unprofitable because Chinese cottons were more economical, until the 1820s, at least, and more durable. Long ells of cotton cloth were used in China for clothing by shopkeepers and labourers and for furniture coverings and curtains.[54]

The company's exports to China were converted at Canton into tea imports, mostly chests of black tea from Fukien Province. It has been said that the EIC suckled on spices and matured on teas.[55] "Tea is the grand material of their trade from China," asserted the firm's director in 1820.[56] The importation of tea into Great Britain was stimulated by the Commutation Act of 1784, which sharply reduced the amount of duty, although tea still furnished one-tenth of the country's revenue and all of the company's profit.[57] With this commutation of tea duty, and the advent of American exporters, the demand for tea increased at Canton, where tea prices accordingly rose from 25 to 40 per cent between 1784 and 1787.[58] From 1784 to 1796 Canton annually exported 25–28 million pounds, of which 18–20 million pounds were consumed in Great Britain and its dependencies.[59] Between the middle 1780s and the late 1790s tea became the common beverage of all classes in Britain; the poorer classes afforded tea by adulterating it.[60] By 1819, noted an anonymous observer, its use "has become so habitual to all ranks of society, that it has long ceased to be a luxury, and may be now fairly classed among the chief necessaries of life,"[61] even though in the same year British duty on tea imports had risen to 100 per cent.[62] Britons were so fond of tea that the John Company was required by law to keep one year's supply in stock.[63] At least one-half of the sugar imported into Britain was consumed in tea alone.[64] The Chinese themselves drank mostly black tea; well-to-do Chinese usually drank old tea, which was less pungent and milder than new tea.[65] On the Canton market black were more common and much cheaper than green teas. Most of the black tea was grown in Fukien Province and some in Kwangtung Province, and most of the green tea in Kiangnan (above all) and Kiangsi Provinces and some in Chekiang Province.[66] There were three pickings of tea: early spring, late spring, and late summer, the last yielding an inferior grade.[67] The teas reached Britain a year later and remained another year in storage in order to meet the legal requirement of one year's supply in reserve. Fortunately for British consumers, black tea retained its flavour longer than green tea, keeping two or three years without injury.[68]

The hong merchants bought the teas from "country dealers," or "teamen" (tea merchants), advancing them one-third of the price, and sold them to the EIC at a profit of 25 per cent.[69] The tea merchants were men of "very small capital"; there were up to 400 supplying green tea and a smaller number supplying black tea to Canton.[70] Every February-March the company contracted with the hong merchants for three-fifths of the following winter's tea supply, and the firm advanced money (at interest) to the hongists, who in turn advanced it to the teamen; after the middle 1810s, however, the company desisted, partly because the practice more or less compelled it to accept the forthcoming teas and partly because India House, its London headquarters, wanted to lessen the risk to its capital in China.[71] The hongists preferred dealing in teas because they could get them on credit from the tea merchants for one or two years, whereas few silks and nankeens and little porcelain and sugar was obtainable on credit.[72] The tea merchants also sold teas to the outside merchants.

The teas reached Canton in small, single-masted boats, each carrying up to 150 chests (1 chest = 1 picul, or 133 ⅓ pounds); they suffered a "great deal" of injury in transit from the tea districts to the company's factory.[73] (A "chop" of tea was the amount grown on one plot by one man, usually 600 chests of black and 400 of green tea.[74]) "The Factory" was manned by about twenty well paid supercargoes and clerks, who were employed on commission (2 per cent of the sale of imports and exports) but who had little or nothing to do much of the year.[75] They inspected the teas in the Tea Hall of the factory to determine quality and detect adulteration, such as the admixture of stale tea or chopped willow or elm leaves to increase the bulk, Prussian blue or Chinese yellow to enhance the brilliancy, or iron filings to augment the weight.[76] Because the company carried considerable prestige and weight at Canton, owing to the volume of its trade, it had the first choice of black teas. The main black teas were Pekoe (the best and the dearest), Souchong, Congo, and Bohea (the worst and the cheapest).[77] Because the Russians bought primarily Pekoe tea and freighted it by land rather than by sea, where it was more exposed to moisture, it was superior to that in use in Western Europe and North America.[78] The EIC shipped mostly Bohea and Congo teas.[79] Canton's merchants obtained the easiest credit and realized the most profit on Bohea tea and were therefore more inclined to handle it than any other article.[80] Bohea was the only tea which was not brought to Canton already packed in chests ready for shipping. It was conveyed in baskets because before it could be packed it had to be "fired," that is, baked or fried in large houses in the vicinity of Canton and then spread to cool; cooling required clear, cold, dry weather, which did not occur until the onset of the northeasterly winds in the middle of November (another reason why the trading season did not begin until then). Afterwards it was taken to the hongs and put in chests, whereupon it was trampled by naked coolies in order to pulverize the leaves and pack the maximum amount.[81] Bohea was the everyday tea of Britain's lower classes, who extended it with dry sloe and ash leaves.[82] Chests of inferior Bohea were used as flooring in the company's ships; it was common, too, to take chinaware "for flooring Ships & also in single Tea Setts for stowing under the beams."[83] Tea chests were stowed much more rapidly, and were less liable to breakage, in the large Indiamen than in the smaller American vessels.[84]

Parliament revoked the EIC's monopoly on the India trade in 1813 and allowed it to keep its China trade monopoly for two more decades. A boom ensued in the "country trade" – the private commerce between India and the Orient.[85] By the late 1820s about seventy country trade ships, manned mostly by Lascars, were visiting Canton every year, and they were capable of making two trips each year between India and China.[86] The country traders introduced more and more capital (and contraband opium) into Canton, so that interest rates there fell from 20 to 12 per cent per annum.[87]

THE AMERICAN TRADERS

The chief competitors of the "red-haired devils," whether of the company or country variety, at Canton were the "second-chop Englishmen" from the "flowery flag republic." The United States, by remaining neutral during the protracted Napoleonic Wars, profited from the carrying trade to the belligerents, Britain and France, although occasionally British and French privateers seized and condemned American vessels. The "circuitous voyage," an indirect sailing between Britain or France and their overseas possessions, was devised to avoid capture. An Indiaman skipper remarked that American traders were "in the habit of making the most circuitous voyages of any traders in the world."[88] The boom in American shipping sparked a demand for more seamen, and many British tars deserted their own vessels for the higher wages and better working conditions on American ships. Britain, anxious to maintain naval manpower, responded with impressment.[89]

The circuitous voyage inevitably took American shipmasters to Canton. The first was Captain John Green of the *Empress of China*, whose trial voyage of 1784–85 returned a modest profit of $30,727 or nearly 26 per cent on an investment of $120,000, principally in ginseng.[90] The "new people," as the Chinese called them initially, also gained information and encouragement. As Philadelphia's British consul, Phineas Bond, told Lord Carmarthen, Secretary of State for the Foreign Department, in 1787, "The encouragement the Americans have met with in their trade to China has induced them to enter largely into this speculation."[91] From that year more and more American ships put in to Canton (Table 6). The overwhelming majority of these vessels were out of New England ports, particularly Boston. In 1800–01 and in 1801–02 Boston was the leading home port of American vessels at Canton: eight of twenty-five arrivals in the former season and thirteen of thirty-three arrivals in the latter.[92] Again, of the forty-three ships of United States registry that made Canton between 6 June 1816 and 25 May 1817, eleven cleared from Boston, nine from Philadelphia, seven from New York, six from Salem, four from Baltimore, three from Providence, two from Amsterdam, and one from Newburyport.[93] Bond explained the Yankee dominance: "The people of New England are an enterprizing people, the number of their ports and the locality of their situation, favor the increase of seamen. They navigate their vessels frugally and their outfits are infinitely less expensive than the outfits of Brit. vessels."[94] He added that New Englanders "have more public spirit more enterprize energy and activity of mind and body than their neighbors."[95] The only obstacle, he continued, was "the difficulty of making suitable remittances to obtain the proper investments."[96] That difficulty was overcome with the discovery of the Northwest Coast's sea-otter skins. Boston's shipowners were short of capital, especially specie, unlike, say, Philadelphia's merchants, who used more specie and larger craft in the China trade;[97] hence the coast trade became a Boston trade. And the China trade required a lot of capital because it was tied up for a long time (at least a year and usually two or even three years), and double capital was necessary, since investors could not rely on the sale of the goods – particularly non-furs – for the purchase of the return cargo.[98] So only half a dozen Boston merchants predominated. Indeed the city's wealthiest merchants were those trading to Canton.[99] The foremost house of business was Thomas H. Perkins and Company until it was liquidated in 1830.[100] In that year there were from seven to eight American firms at Canton, some with three or four partners and others with one.[101]

At first all American shippers relied upon supercargoes to handle their transactions at Canton, but soon Boston's shipowners turned to resident commission agents, or *taipans*, instead, while the shipowners of New York, Philadelphia, and Baltimore continued to use supercargoes. The latter were at a disadvantage because they had less experience in, and time for, dealing.[102] (No doubt Boston ships, with more non-specie to trade, had more need of resident agents.) The Yankee merchant Sullivan Dorr, son of a Northwest Coast trader, pleaded some of the advantages of an agent in 1802:

It would have been exceedingly advantageous to our Northwest [Coast] Ships and sealing Ship owners to have had an Agency house establish'd here through whom all Sales of skins should have been made thereby rendering this market less fluctuating by making annual contracts with one or two respecting [*sic*] Merchants who would have been able to manage so large a concern and prevent the bad consequences resulting from skins getting into necessitous mens hands who are not able to hold them, being under the necessity of making sacrifices to face or meet their obligations, causeing a market price for those who would willingly keep theirs. and many respectable characters are prevented from purchaseing for the above reasons when if they could monopolize skins the prices would be fix'd, always knowing themselves to be certain of all that might be brought. the business would become regular and I think vastly more productive; for when three or four Vessels come in at once it often happens that a secrecy and jealousy is observed towards each other of the sellers and in fact often a competition is raised among some Merchants who are glad to grasp at anything so that a few may be benefitted to the prejudice of the many. but such is the disposition of our Merchants who adventure here that the necessity or utility of employing residents is not or cannot be seen.[103]

Most important, agents were cheaper than supercargoes, even though both received a commission of 3 per cent on the Canton purchases.[104] As Dorr advised his shipowning brothers: "I would recommend that you encourage one two or more young men of ability to come here and remain for the purpose of gaining intelligence by which means you will be better served, and the expense of their residence here amply paid by your getting better goods and cheaper than under the conduct of Captains, the Young men at the same time benefitting themselves."[105] Dorr's expenses at Canton for ten months of 1800 were five-eighths those of a supercargo of a Philadelphia ship, enabling him to buy teas for one-eighth to one-half as much the latter.[106] (Dorr stated that annually it would cost $10,000 for an agent plus $800 for a factory; his own business and personal expenses at Canton amounted to $3,900 in 1800 and $3,500 in 1801.[107]) He added, incidentally, that Canton was economical, too, inasmuch as it offered few opportunities for dissipation. "This is a fine place to cure wild young men they have no other incitement here than to be steady," he wrote.[108]

Subsequent agents confirmed the inferiority of supercargoes, even though it took an agent several years to become proficient in trade at Canton.[109] In 1821 the American agent William French, who subsequently prospered in business at Honolulu, counselled a leading Boston merchant, Josiah Marshall, to hire a commission agent at Canton in place of supercargoes because "if you have an agent here to pay proper attention to the business and take advantage of the market ... silk [will] cost him from 10 to 15 pr. ct. less, than those purchased by regular supercargoes who remain here on two & three months."[110] In the same year a Canton dealer paid from 10 to 15 per cent less for silks from a resident agent than from a seasonal super-cargo.[111] In 1827 there were from ten to twelve American and from eight to ten British agents at the city.[112] Probably the most successful of the American agents was John P. Cushing. He arrived at Canton in 1803 at the age of sixteen as an agent for Thomas H. Perkins and Company and remained until 1828, making a fortune of perhaps £500,000.[113] He became a close friend of Howqua, with whom he had more influence than anyone else, including the powerful Select Committee, the EIC's governing body at Canton.[114] American ship-masters also received some assistance from the US consul at Canton. The first was Major Samuel Shaw, who arrived in 1784 as supercargo on the first American ship. The post offered neither salary nor per-quisites, however, the only compensation being the fees and the pres-tige of the office. Until 1854 the holder was merely a merchant[115] and a "complete cypher," carrying no official weight.[116] A ship's papers were deposited with the consul, who also signed any deben-ture and duty certificates, but he had no control over the crew.[117]

The American traders bought a wider array of goods than the British at Canton. Either American consumers liked *chinoiserie* more and tea less than their British counterparts or the East India Com-pany, much more a captive of habit, was unwilling or unable to alter its preoccupation with tea. Whatever the reasons, the difference meant that American shipowners lessened their risk. Their Canton agents generally procured most of their teas from the hong mer-chants and most of their silks and nankeens from the outside or shop merchants; the Americans were the main buyers of nankeens, which fluctuated in price more than any other article at Canton.[118] Whereas the company's Select Committee had its ships secured and tea orders filled by the hongists in order of their rank – the seniors securing more ships and filling more orders than the intermediates, and the intermediates more than the juniors – the American and country traders did not.[119] Rather, they dealt with those hongists who were the most economical and reliable. As Sullivan Dorr noted in 1802, "There is a wide difference in the characters of the merchants now composing the Hong,"[120] despite their official stature. The Yankees often did business with the poorer (junior) hongists because they were keener to trade and offered higher prices than the senior ones.[121] The Americans were also willing to lend money to the poorer hong merchants at the interest rate of 1 per cent per month.[122] But they preferred to truck with the shopmen, who would give the capital-short Yankees credit – as much as $40,000 Spanish at 8 per cent per annum.[123] The shopmen were prohibited by law from trading staples to foreigners, being allowed to sell only ten petty articles like "sing-songs" (clockwork, or automata), footwear, and chinaware; in 1828, however, they were permitted to handle wrought silks, while still being banned from exporting twenty-four items (including raw silks, teas, cassia, and sugar) and from importing fifty-three items (including furs, woollens, cottons, metals, ginseng, and sandalwood).[124] But these restrictions were overcome with bribes. It was rumoured that the outside merchants bribed the hong merchants with payments of $5,000 or $10,000 "for their pass to cover certain [staple] exports."[125] Every two or three years the shopmen were arrested and fined but they soon reappeared in operation.[126] The Americans' preference for the shopmen induced the hongists to let the Yankees share the first choice of teas with the EIC, which then threatened to curtail its voluminous trade unless the hong merchants desisted; consequently, in 1817 the Chinese authorities closed some 200 outside shops.[127]

By dealing with the outside merchants the American traders deprived the hong merchants of business and contributed to the insolvency of some of them, especially the more vulnerable junior hongists, more and more of whom went broke in the 1820s through excessive improvidence and speculation.[128] At the end of 1827, following the successive bankruptcy of three hong merchants, the Hoppo strictly forbade the outside merchants from dealing with foreigners.[129] But this ban, too, was undoubtedly circumvented. The shopmen were also preferred by the Americans because much of their trade involved goods that were more suited to the shop dealers, such as curios and silk piece goods, which were very much a "trade of detail," that is, in design and pattern.[130] Yet it was riskier dealing with the outside merchants and the junior hong merchants. They were more apt to try to cheat, as well as go bankrupt, and the hongists were security for only the duties, not the debts, of the shopmen, who, moreover, had no Consoo Fund.[131] The shopmen were accountable for their goods until they were alongside the trading vessels,[132] so the shipmasters had to check the goods carefully for fraud before they were loaded.

Although American vessels took on a wider array of Chinese goods at Canton than Indiamen, their cargoes were still dominated by teas. A ship could carry ten chests of tea (700–800 pounds) for every ton (forty cubic feet) of capacity; one tea chest weighed from seventy-two to seventy-six pounds.[133] In the early 1820s three-quarters of the value and nine-tenths of the bulk of an American ship's outbound cargo consisted of teas;[134] by then, however, the Americans were taking fewer textiles because Chinese silks were being supplanted by British silk manufactures and French were proving superior to Chinese nankeens.[135] Mostly green teas (Imperial, Gunpowder, Hyson, Hyson Skin, Young Hyson) were embarked, partly because green teas yielded more profit than black teas and partly because American consumers preferred green tea.[136] The EIC was unable to ship much green tea because it was required by law to keep one year's supply in stock (and the tea was already a year old by the time it reached Britain), and green tea lost its flavour faster than black tea, which could be kept for two or three years without deterioration. These circumstances meant that American merchants could outsell the company in Britain with fresher, and therefore stronger, teas, which were preferred by customers.[137]

In the 1828–29 season 80,498 chests of tea were exported from China to the United States, including 52,459 chests (65 per cent) of green tea, all Hysons, that is, intermediate grades.[138] In fact, the American traders embarked generally poorer teas than the British because they found them more marketable and more remunerative,[139] being within reach of the lower classes of both North America and Western Europe, who constituted a very large market. Partly because they bought inferior teas and partly because they bought mostly "in the market" rather than on contract, American traders paid only 50 to 90 per cent as much as the East India Company for teas at Canton.[140]

Americans drank mostly Young Hyson tea, the buds of the first picking of Hyson; moderately priced, it was "in great demand in America."[141] As an American broker noted, however, his countrymen "are not great tea drinkers; they are more generally consumers of coffee."[142] American consumption of coffee increased rapidly during the 1820s because of its falling price (by nearly one-half) and its source, the West Indies, which was not only closer than China but also more willing to accept American products (instead of specie) in exchange.[143] Coffee consumption in both the United States and Great Britain almost doubled between the first and last halves of the 1820s.[144] The contrast remained, however; in the middle 1820s, on an average annual per-capita basis, Britons drank two and one-half times as much tea as Americans, and Americans drank three and one-third times as much coffee as Britons.[145] At the end of the decade Americans were commonly drinking coffee at breakfast and tea in the afternoon.[146] For this reason not a little tea was re-exported from the United States, mainly to Rotterdam, Hamburg, Paris, and Gibraltar, the large British and Russian tea markets being closed to American merchants by high tariffs. As early as 1800 Sullivan Dorr realized that the US tea market was being overdone. "I think so much teas have gone to America a vent must be found elsewhere and Shipments made to Europe," he declared.[147] Already by 1803 more than one-half of all tea that was exported to the United States was re-exported to Europe.[148] By contrast, in the last half of the 1820s Great Britain re-exported only one percent of its tea imports.[149]

Re-exportation was facilitated by the drawback system, whereby from 1791 to 1832 the payment of duties on teas that were re-exported within two years could be deferred by bonding. (American tea duties varied from 20 per cent before 1816 to 40 per cent until 1830 to nil between 1832 and 1842, the rate discriminating in favour of American carriers.[150]) Nevertheless, the profitability of the American tea trade declined from the late 1810s.[151] As the supply of Young Hyson tea, the favourite of American consumers, was increased by the Chinese from 1810, its quality deteriorated, particularly in the last half of the 1820s.[152] More and more American tea drinkers switched to cheaper coffee at breakfast. And in the last half of the 1820s the American market became overstocked, the Canadian market was lost to direct EIC shipments, and the European market was dulled by prohibitive duties.[153] American importers lost from 25 to 30 per cent on teas, and several investors, such as the Philadelphia house of Edward Thompson, the largest American shipowner in the China trade with five or six vessels at Canton, went broke, having overextended themselves by engaging "without sufficient means."[154]

Being poorer than Great Britain, and lacking colonial products, the United States had more difficulty providing the few trade goods that China would accept, especially specie. Initially it was hoped that ginseng would fill the bill. In the Orient, where this medicinal root was prized as a panacea, it was the most valuable drug in the Chinese pharmocopeia.[155] Dorr described its properties: "It promotes digestions, procures appetite, calms the mind thereby the patient obtains sleep; a good diurectic and sudorific; it gives strength to a patient enablling him to conquer any debility, procures easy births, gives vigour to old and young, exciteing them to Coition when nature would not."[156] Ginseng was native to both Asia and North America, so American shipowners had ready access to their own supply. Even the Chinese market was limited, however, the "essence of man" being an expensive luxury. At the turn of the century Canton could absorb from 500 to 600 piculs annually.[157] This demand was soon overmet and the price fell accordingly. Imports and prices at Canton amounted to 800 piculs @ $190–400 in 1799–1800, 1,600 piculs @ $120–200 in 1800–01, and 1,700 piculs @ $50–80 in 1801–02.[158] By the summer of 1801 a picul was bringing only $80, which was at least 10 per cent below cost; by the autumn ginseng was "now a drug" on the market and worth but $60 a picul.[159] (Between 1804–05 and 1832–33 American vessels took an average of 1,850 piculs of ginseng to Canton annually.[160]) Moreover, Tartarian ginseng was "infinitely better" than the North American variety.[161] At Canton the former fetched $3,000 per picul in 1783 but the American ginseng brought by the *Empress of China* in 1784 fetched only $150–350 per picul (whereas the Asiatic variety still sold "for nearly its weight in gold").[162] The Chinese themselves asserted that one root of their own ginseng had "more virtue" than thirteen pounds of the North American plant.[163] This difference stemmed wholly or partly from the fact that North American ginseng was not always gathered or prepared properly.[164] Also, being a prohibited import, like opium, ginseng had to be smuggled into Canton, although this restriction did not absolutely prevent importation.[165]

Long before the Canton ginseng market was saturated, however, Boston's merchants, at least, had found a more acceptable and more lucrative alternative in the form of sea-otter (and fur-seal) skins from the Northwest Coast (Table 7).[166] Yet there was a noticeable, if irregular, decline in fur imports almost from the beginning and especially after 1825. Between the start and the end of the first quarter of the 1800s the value of American fur imports at Canton fell from $1,000,000 to $500,000 annually.[167] By 1830, because of the rising price of furs and the growing importation of woollens at Canton, the us fur trade to China had, in the words of Joshua Bates, an American broker, "dwindled to a very trifling amount; there are very few persons engaged in it; and it does not yield much profit."[168] Also noticeable was the decreasing proportion of sea furs (sea otters and fur seals) and the increasing proportion of land furs after the War of 1812, as the Northwest Coast Indians turned more and more to river otters, foxes, and other land fur bearers to offset depleted sea otters in particular. The declining importation of sea-otter skins was especially significant because of their unmatched value. From 1804–05 through 1817–18 sea otters constituted only one-fifteenth of the number but more than one-half of the value of all furs that were brought to Canton by American ships.[169] Hence an anonymous French observer's exclamation: "A passage of a year [for Gray's first voyage from Boston to Nootka Sound]! This is going very far for skins of animals, for an inhabitant of NORTH AMERICA where they abound! The Americans no doubt have experienced that the furs of the part which they occupy on the continent, and of the parts bordering on it [that is, land furs], are not in much estimation at CHINA, and do not procure a profit so considerable as that which may be expected from the peltry of the NORTHWEST coast."[170]

Their exceptionally high value enabled furs as a whole to form up to one-sixth of the value of all American exports to China.[171] From 1804–05 through 1809–10 furs accounted for 13 per cent (and sea-otter skins 7 per cent) of the value of American imports at Canton, and they were second in rank to silver dollars only (which represented 75 per cent).[172] And furs probably loomed even larger earlier, when less ginseng, sandalwood, and opium were imported (in terms of the trade of *all* nationals at Canton furs were insignificant, however, con-stituting, for example, only $200,000, or less than 2 per cent, of the total of $11,500,000 worth of imports in 1796[173]). After the middle 1810s, of course, the share of furs was appreciably lower, fluctuating between 2 and 8 per cent (Table 8).

What is noticeable from Table 8 is not so much the relative decrease of furs or even the relative increase of opium as, from the middle 1820s, the equally steep fall of silver and the rise of manufactures. Earlier, however, such was not the case. At the turn of the century at Canton Sullivan Dorr had noted "the vast influx of specie here from various quarters."[174] It was primarily silver, and much of it came from New Spain as "Old Heads" (Carlos IV silver dollars). (American were less valuable than Spanish silver dollars at Canton, being discounted by 10 per cent in 1801.[175]) The Manila galleons, or "China ships," annually brought Mexican and Peruvian silver pesos from Acapulco to the Philippines and Macao and returned with Chinese silks and East Indies spices.[176] In a period of 250 years (1571–1821) Manila received some 400 million silver dollars from the Spanish New World, and perhaps one-half of this total reached China.[177] Silver dollars became the circulating medium of coastal South China around Can-ton because silver "shoes" (small oblong ingots) were too heavy and "copper cash" was too low in value.[178] Boston's shipowners successfully substituted furs (and later sandalwood, too) for specie, while those of Philadelphia and New York used the silver dollars that they earned in trade with New Spain (mostly contraband), the West Indies, and the Mediterranean. In 1800–01 two-sixths of the American vessels but only one-sixth of the American tonnage, and in 1801–02 four-tenths of the American vessels but only three-tenths of the American tonnage, at Canton were from Boston; in the former trading season six of the eight, and in the latter ten of the thirteen, Boston vessels brought furs only, while mostly specie was brought by the larger Philadelphia and New York vessels (larger because they carried bulkier cargoes and did not have to manoeuvre the Inside Passage of the Northwest Coast).[179]

From 1805 through 1812 the United States exported $22,000,000 worth of specie and $8,952,000 worth of goods (mostly furs) to China;[180] the latter represents nearly one-third of the total. With the depletion of precious sea otters, however, American merchants shipped more specie. Especially after the War of 1812 the China trade drained the United States of specie.[181] Whereas US vessels took 5,400,000 silver dollars to Canton in 1806–08, they brought 9,872,000 – nearly twice as many – in 1816–18.[182] But Boston's traders continued to avoid specie, as one of their number, perhaps Thomas H. Perkins himself, explained in the middle 1820s:

There has been a strong prejudice existing against the China trade in this country, under the idea that specie was necessarily exported to procure cargoes from China. So far is this from the fact, *in our case*, that, although our importations have averaged more than a million dollars annually for several years, in the products of China, of which silks and nankeens form a considerable portion, that we have not shipped a Spanish dollar for the past *three years* to China. Our funds arise from the export of opium from Turkey, British goods from Great Britain, lead and quick-silver from Gibraltar, and the same articles on a large scale from Trieste.[183]

Even Boston shipmasters, however, were not above using silver dollars, and before sea otters were depleted. The *Eliza*, Captain Rowan, made Canton at the end of October 1799 with 3,000 furs and 23,000 Spanish dollars, the latter derived from the sale of goods on the Spanish Main; Rowan's return cargo consisted of 115,064 pounds of teas, 1,333 pounds of silks, 667 pounds of sugar, and 40,000 pieces of nankeens.[184] And in 1801 the *Diana* and the *Washington* made sales of $40,000 and up to $100,000, respectively, on the Spanish Main.[185]

The British goods were mostly woollens, cottons, and metals. Opium was an illicit import, since, as the Chinese themselves said, "foreign mud" or "vile dirt," as it was called, "poisoned" their country.[186] The Manchu government forbade opium smoking and importing in 1729, and the EIC itself banned the shipping of opium to China on its vessels in 1733.[187] But cladestine trafficking ensued with "ease and regularity" because "so perfect a system of bribery existed."[188] It was bought by the very mandarins who were supposed to combat smuggling. Not a few Chinese were addicted to the narcotic, and it was an extremely profitable commodity, although prices did fluctuate, and the substance was perishable in heat or damp. Opium was invariably sold for cash,[189] so its sale furnished American traders with specie for purchases at Canton.

The opium trade boomed after 1819 in response to keener competition between growers in eastern (Patna) and western (Malawa) India and the resultant falling prices.[190] Imports rose from 3,000 to 12,000–14,000 chests per year between 1810 and 1830; between the early and middle 1820s imports of Indian opium doubled.[191] In 1820 opium was retailing for $1,150–1,200 per picul at Canton, more than double its "old price" of $450–500.[192] During the 1820s opium's price fell by 40 per cent as supply rose,[193] but the decline was temporary. By the middle 1830s the trade in opium was more valuable than that in any other single commodity in the entire world.[194] The Chinese government persisted in trying to suppress this pernicious traffic (its persistence was to lead to the infamous Opium War at the end of the 1830s, with Great Britain compelling the Chinese "paper tiger" to admit opium, open more ports, agree to extraterritoriality, and even cede territory; the opium trade was finally legalized by the terms of the Treaty of Tienstin of 1858). By 1821 the Chinese authorities had succeeded in stopping the opium trade at Whampoa, but it then simply shifted to the "outer anchorages" – the islands in the Canton River estuary (and eventually Hong Kong in particular), especially Lintin, which had a "good anchorage ... without the Chinese limits."[195] Here the so-called depôt, or receiving, ships, up to twenty at a time, anchored to sell contraband goods.[196] With the connivance of the junior customs officials, smuggling thrived, so much so that by 1830 up to one-half of the value of the Canton trade was contraband.[197] The American smugglers brought Turkish opium. It was inferior to, and cheaper than, the Indian product, and the two were blended by Chinese customers.[198] To pay for this expensive drug the Chinese had to use specie, whose exportation was just as illegal as opium's importation. In 1828–29 Canton imported 14,732 chests of opium at a cost of $13,573,115.[199] The drain on China's reserves of specie was such that around 1826 the traditional inflow of specie reversed to an outflow, just as the traditional outflow of textiles reversed to an inflow. The old commercial conundrum of China needing little but offering much had been reversed.

AMERICAN-BRITISH COMPETITION

This transformation was wrought primarily by British (especially country) and American traders. In doing so they vied with each other – just as they did on the Northwest Coast – for the same goods and, to some extent, the same markets, and once again the Americans outdid their competitors. In some respects the Americans were at a disadvantage. Between the Atlantic Seaboard and South China there was hardly a port where they could seek refuge or refreshment without the indulgence of another power, and at Canton they were up to a six-month voyage from their supply base, whereas India, Batavia, Manila, and Macao were much closer for the British, Dutch, Spanish, and Portuguese, respectively.[200] And at first the Americans suffered from inexperience and undercapitalization. Mercantile capital was more plentiful in Britain,[201] and the financial resources of the EIC were enormous. American China merchants did not have much capital.[202] They raised money "on respondentia," a loan made by a financial house at 11 or 12 per cent of the voyage, regardless of length, the house paying the insurance and hypothecating the goods.[203] Because of their smaller reserves, the Americans became heavily involved in credit dealings with the hong merchants, despite a Chinese ban on such transactions.[204] Moreover, with less capital the Americans were in greater need of harmonious relations at Canton, since they faced relatively larger losses in the event of temporary disruptions of trade and even ruin in the case of prolonged disruptions.[205]

The Americans had advantages, too. A director of the EIC testified to a parliamentary committee in 1820 that it was generally known that at Canton American sailors were "far more orderly and better conducted" than British salts.[206] Their good behaviour was partly a reflection of their dependence upon Chinese good will. It also derived from a variety of other factors: American seamen came from higher classes than British seamen; they were usually known personally to the shipowners and shipmasters; most of them had families to support; they were paid from 50 to 100 per cent more than their British brethren; they enjoyed the privilege of being allowed to buy some Chinese goods "on their own account"; and they strove for promotion.[207] Consequently, American crewmen were less disorderly, less drunken, and less quarrelsome than their British counterparts and American trade at Canton was attended with "less inconvenience" than that of the British, being freer of disputes between ships' crews and Chinese authorities.[208]

The contrast was not lost on the Chinese. East Indiamen were "very unpopular" with British sailors because of the low wages and the long voyages, so that the company got the "refuse" of Jack Tars.[209] Company crewmen were inclined to get drunk and start fights with the Chinese; certainly they clashed more with the Chinese than did American sailors, who were more "prudent and wary."[210] On several occasions, as in 1792, 1804, 1807, and 1810, such rowdiness led to

melées and disruptions of trade.[211] As John Shillaber, US consul at
Batavia, reported in 1834: "There will be at Whampoa between September and March, annually, from 2000 to 2200 British sailors, and
I may almost say 'let loose' often under the mad influence of arack
[a rum-like liqour of high alcoholic content widely distilled in the Far
East from the fermented juice of the coconut palm or from a fermented mash of rice and molasses], which may be had for a trifling
cost, or in exchange for any implements etc. stolen from the Ships."[212]
The problem lay not so much with the EIC's ships as with those of
the country traders, "in which class of vessels, there is generally but
too little discipline or command; certainly far less than in American
merchant vessels, or in [the] Company's Ships, where Naval marshal
law was in force."[213]

Not surprisingly, relations between American and British sailors
were not amicable, particularly in the wake of the War of Independence. An American supercargo found in 1799 at Canton that "there
is a jealousy always between the English and Yankees here; there is
much *hauteur* with the English and enough independence in the Yankee to despise it." "The Americans and English are never on good
terms," he repeated, "there is a jealousy between them; the *hauteur*
of the Englishman does not please the Yankees; there is scarcely any
intercourse between them." He cited an example of the mutual sentiment: "As one of our ships was dropping down past an Englishman
he hails in a Yankeefied manner, 'Where are you bound?' and was
answered also Yankeefiedly, 'To Boston with a load of tea; don't you
want to go and see Bunker Hill?'"[214]

The Chinese were more partial to the Americans for other reasons
as well. For one thing, they remained politically neutral during the
protracted European wars of the late eighteenth and early nineteenth
centuries, and for another they were not suspected of imperialistic
designs on the Chinese Empire.[215] The Yankees may also have been
less racist than the colonialistic British and consequently have treated
the Chinese with less disdain and more respect.[216] Certainly the Chinese gave a warmer welcome to the Americans insofar as they were
more willing to submit to Chinese port regulations and protection,
whereas the British sometimes resisted with gunboat diplomacy, as in
1808, when trade was interrupted for six months after Admiral
Drury tried unsuccessfully to force his ship upriver.[217] It should be
remembered, however, that the Chinese preferred to trade with
American vessels primarily because, with the exception of those from
Boston via the Northwest Coast, they were "rich" ships, that is, they
were loaded with specie (silver dollars) rather than manufactures,
which were less welcome.[218] "The Chinese like dollars better than they

do almost anything else," noted one Yankee skipper.[219] And by offering more dollars (or even furs, which were more acceptable than goods) and fewer wares than the British the Americans obtained teas more cheaply.[220] Similarly, in the summer of 1801 American traders paid $55–59 and the EIC Company $96 per hundred for nankeens,[221] although the latter's may have been higher in quality.

But the American traders enjoyed even more important advantages over their British rivals, namely, better ships and lower costs. The most economical vessel for the China trade was one of 450 tons with a crew of 18 to 19 hands.[222] American China ships were much closer to this standard than British Indiamen were; their owners, having less capital, could not afford larger ships or larger cargoes. They were "very handy vessels, from 400 to 500 tons" – about one-half the size of Indiamen.[223] (Each 100 tons required about six men.[224]) The larger British ships – up to 1,300 tons and occasionally even larger – were more comfortable, more healthful, more secure, and more durable, but the smaller American craft were easier to manage in the shallow waters along the coasts of the Americas, around the South Sea islands, and through the Eastern Straits, and they sailed better in light winds; in other words, they were "handier."[225] They were also cheaper to construct, outfit, and operate.

It cost less to build ships in the United States because shipbuilding materials were dearer in Great Britain.[226] In the middle 1780s a ship could be built in New England and sold in the Old Country for one-third less than British-built ships.[227] It was asserted in 1830 that on account of the greater expense of shipbuilding and provisionment in Great Britain it cost £25 per ton (of fifty cubic feet) to have a first-rate ship ready for sea there and £15 per ton in the United States.[228] And in the same year an American broker boasted that "ships cannot be built stronger or better" than American vessels.[229] British ships were not well constructed in that they "cannot carry bulk in proportion to their tonnage"; for example, an American vessel of 450 tons actually carried 750 tons of cargo because in the 1810s they were improved by being built longer, deeper, and narrower.[230] An American bottom of 450 tons of this new type carried 7,500 chests of tea and 18 to 19 hands, while an Indiaman of 1,200 tons carried 15,000–16,000 chests and 120–130 crewmen.[231] American ships cost up to 25 per cent less to operate, since they enjoyed cheaper provisions, carried fewer hands, and exhibited "less parade" or less "style"; for example, they did not need apprentice boys, and their captains had no servants.[232] The EIC employed 10 men on its ships for every 100 tons and American shipowners only 4 men.[233] Thus in the 1820s an American vessel of 400 tons would have a crew of 18 and British and

Dutch ships of the same size up to 25 men.[234] So the American ships had more room for cargo, and their crews had less space but better food.[235] In addition, American merchantmen were generally better sailers.[236] Their captains, too, were "actually sailing masters, and always on the alert, and urging dispatch."[237]

In the 1820s an American ship could sail from Boston to Canton to Boston to Europe to Boston in less than a year, and it took only two-thirds as long as a British ship to make a Britain-China round trip.[238] An American vessel, therefore, could make three voyages to China for every two made by a British vessel.[239] The average turnaround (unloading plus embarking) time for a Boston ship at Canton around 1830 was from five to six weeks.[240] Being more efficient, American vessels were less subject to demurrage (overstaying) charges at their ports of call. And because their home ports were leeward of the trade winds, they took virtually as long to sail directly to China (via the Cape) as through Liverpool to get woollens, and they could also take profitable cargoes of tobacco, cotton, and flour to Britain from the United States.[241] They did so, moreover, with lower insurance and freight charges. Around 1800 insurance from South China to New England cost an American ship up to $6,600.[242] In the 1820s insurance rates ranged between 4 and 6 per cent (of the value of ship and cargo), as much as one-third less than what British ships were charged.[243] (A Russian source for the same period, however, states that American Nor'westers paid from 10 to 30 per cent of the value of their ship and cargo for insurance.[244]) British vessels also paid higher freight charges. The "shipping interest," which owned and operated the EIC's fleet, exacted exorbitant freight rates – from two to three times as much as American ships paid in the 1820s.[245] American shipping charges were so economical that Yankee traders could pay Great Britain's tea tariff and still undersell the company there.[246] And, finally, at Canton American commercial agents charged less than their British counterparts – from 2 to 2½ per cent versus 5 per cent.[247] Little wonder that American traders could "frequently" outbid the mighty EIC's Committee of Supercargoes for green teas.[248]

By 1830, according to the Yankee merchant Charles Everett, American traders even knew the China trade better than British traders.[249] The EIC on the eve of the loss of its China monopoly in 1834 was too large, too rigid, too cautious. By contrast, declared the Liverpool broker William Brown, "There is a very great spirit of enterprise in the United States," adding that "it is pushed frequently too far," as evidenced by the overdoing of the tea trade by some American merchants in 1825 and 1826.[250] But while the sun shone the American trader, being "more a general speculator" than his British rival,[251] was able to make more hay, whether on the South China Coast or on the Northwest Coast, where he faced a very different set of demands. On either coast, however, the Bostonians had all that was necessary to succeed in foreign trade: enough capital, reliable information, sound judgment, and bold enterprise. It is ironic that at Canton they took full advantage of these prerequisites to compete vigorously and successfully with the very British company whose grasping measures had ignited one of the sparks of the American Revolution – the "tea party" in their home port.

6 Modes of Trade

> While three vessels were lying together here [Sitka Sound], it was amusing to observe the adroitness and cunning with which the Indians derived all possible advantage from the competition. They had succeeded in raising the price of their skins so high, that there was a necessity, at last, of our entering into an agreement, respecting the price to be given, which ought to have been made at first; as not less requisite to profit, than to despatch.
>
> Captain Richard Cleveland, 1799

Unlike the rulers of Manchu China, the Indians of the Northwest Coast were eager to trade with foreigners, but the Euroamericans had to adjust their operations to the seasonal round of their Native hosts. One observer of the coastal Indians noted that "they have several villages that they shift to at different seasons of the year" – the Nootkas, for example, moved five times during the year to fish "in accordance with the seasons at which they have had experience that the fish make similar changes,"[1] and they remained inland from the beginning of September until the end of February. So it was advantageous for trading vessels to reach the coast no later than the onset of spring, for by then the Indians had congregated on the outer coast for the herring, halibut, and oolachen runs and had brought their winter accumulation of furs for bartering to the first vessels.[2] About the end of February or the beginning of March the Nass Tsimshians left Lanacoon for Observatory Inlet, the Sebastian (or Sebastiers, or Shebashers) Tsimshians of Principe Channel left their winter village for Nass, and the Cocklane (or Cocklain, or Cocka-thane) Tlingits left their winter quarters for Clemencitty.[3] The Tsim-shians gathered at the mouth of the Nass River every March for oily oolachen. The herring run annually brought nearly 500 Indians to Nootka Sound in February in the early 1790s and up to 2,000 Tlin-gits to Sitka Sound in early April, and in the middle of May 1831 the same number of Tlingits assembled to confer.[4] By late summer the Indians were moving inland to the narrows and falls of the inner coastal rivers for the awesome salmon run, leaving few customers for lagging vessels. The temperate rain forest also provided more shelter from the inclement winter weather, as well as more game, than the exposed outer coast. One of the earliest maritime fur traders, Alexander Walker, reported that the Nootkas moved inland in late summer for the fall salmon run and for "a more comfortable retreat in winter."[5] By the end of July, as Aemelius Simpson of the HBC found in 1828, the coast was "nearly swept of Furs."[6] Similarly, at the end of October 1810 the brig *Otter* learned at Lanacoon that "the Nass [Tsimshian] Indians were not come from Sheen [the Skeena River] where they have been these 3 months past catching Salmon for their winter's provision," so that "Skins has got to be a very scarce article."[7]

Those trading vessels that made the coast first had the advantage, since they had first pick of the choicest skins and did not have to pay as much as they would later in the season, when fur prices rose in response to more competition. Furthermore, as the owners of the *Mentor* advised its master in 1816, the Indians were "always desirous of trading with Vessels just arrived in hopes of getting higher prices and better assortments" than those offered by wintering vessels.[8] An American agent at Canton asked the question "how many [vessels] will make money?" and then answered it himself: "Why those 2 or 3 who get on [the coast] first!"[9] Thus the owners of *Cleopatra's Barge* instructed its captain as follows in 1820: "Tis important for you to make the most of your time in the early part of the season. Let nothing escape you that can be bought at a fair price, so that the Coast may be as bare as possible of Furs when other vessels get on. Skins sold in Canton this year higher than last, so that people will be anxious to get all they can, even if they give more for them."[10] To do well a ship generally had to be on the coast by 1 March at the latest. In 1799, during the heyday of the sea-otter trade, the earliest American vessels on the coast were the *Eliza* (mid-February), which collected 2,800 skins, and the *Caroline* (end of March), which procured 2,200 skins; they were followed in mid-April by the *Hancock* (1,700 skins) and the *Despatch* (1,400 skins). The *Ulysses* had arrived in February but garnered only 1,200 skins, its trade being disrupted by a mutiny.[11] The *Caroline's* skipper, Richard Cleveland, cited these disparate catches as "a proof how much the success of a voyage of this kind depends on being the earliest vessel on the Coast."[12] Once on the coast, a shipmaster had to hustle in order to get his share of pelts, particularly if he arrived late. As the *Rob Roy's* owners told Captain Daniel Cross in 1821: "After all you will find that the most industrious man will generally get the most furs. Some old N.W. Captains are too fond of lying in port 'to wait for better weather.' This does not answer & we doubt not you will never follow any bad examples."[13]

Some shipmasters preferred to cruise, others to sojourn. The latter strategy was better – at least while fur bearers were plentiful – because more skins were obtained. Few Indians were willing to chase a ship several miles offshore and then trade hurriedly, whereas a spring sojourner might meet at least 2,000 Nootkas in Nootka Sound in 1786 or 1792, 3,000–7,500 in five villages (including 2,500 at Chief Wickaninish's) in Clayoquot Sound in 1791, up to 2,000 Haidas at Kaigani Harbour in 1799, and as many as 2,000 Tlingits in Sitka Sound in 1805.[14] Moreover, trading "under sail" was more dangerous because of exposure to strong tides, high winds, and hidden rocks.[15] But not just any safe anchorage would suffice. As Captain Charles Bishop of the *Ruby* advised in 1795, "The Principal business is to look out for one [harbour] near the residence of the Chief as in that Situation you are shure of Procureing the Furs of the whole Tribe, and in this respect the Season must be consulted, for they shift their Habitations often."[16] As skins became scarcer, particularly at the most popular anchorages, sojourning perforce yielded to "trading from port to port" on the "cruising ground" of the coast.

Whether sojourning or cruising, smaller vessels were more manouverable than larger ones. Alexander Walker recommended good sailers of no less than 60 tons to prevent the wetting of skins and no more than 100 tons to navigate the coastal shallows and narrows and to minimize the number of hands.[17] Tacking along the windward coast also necessitated good sailers. In 1799 Captain Cleveland found that his thirty-eight-ton cutter *Caroline*, rigged fore and aft, was better suited to the narrow channels and tricky winds of the coast; he added, however, that at sea his ship was "very wet & uncomfortable, as well as unhandy."[18] But the coast was the most protracted and most important leg of the entire voyage, so small size prevailed. Sullivan Dorr asserted that coasters should be no more than 270 and no less than 200 tons; larger ships, he explained, were less adept at navigating the narrow, shallow, twisting channels of the coast, while smaller ships were more vulnerable to Indian attacks and stormy seas and carried insufficient cargo.[19] The small American vessels, not infrequently less than 100 tons, were also cheaper to build and to man – an important consideration for capital-short New England owners.[20] In addition, copper-bottomed coasters were best able to withstand worms and barnacles as well as groundings on the treacherous coast. "Vessels from 200 to 250 tons of light draft, are most adapted to the business, provided they sail well and are copper'd," said Dorr, adding that "many of our families Northwest Ships would have made their bottoms pay three or four fold if they had have been copper'd."[21] In 1828 Lieutenant Aemelius Simpson reconnoitered the coast trade for the HBC and reported that "a vessel of respectable force and sufficient capacity to carry a large outfit of goods, etc., with good sailing qualities is absolutely required for this business," tides being strong and anchorages few in the deep water of the northern coast.[22] He also stated that a steam vessel would be ideal, especially in view of the abundant wood fuel, and in 1836 the company's paddlewheeled steamer *Beaver* entered the coast trade (followed three years later by the RAC's steam-driven *Nikolay I*), but by then the maritime fur trade was virtually over. Occasionally smaller trading vessels were built on the coast itself as tenders; in 1792, for instance, three such craft were launched. In the early years of the coast trade, too, occasionally larger flagships were accompanied by smaller consorts for navigating shallower and narrower waters, such as the 171–ton *Prince of Wales* and its 50–ton smack *Princess Royal* in 1787–88. Finally, most ships carried boats – whale boats, jolly boats, longboats, bowers, pinnaces, kedges, yawls – for going ashore, probing unknown channels, and towing the mother ship.

Sighting an Indian village, shipmasters fired a cannon (or lit a bonfire ashore) to "alarm" the Natives and dropped anchor, sometimes also tying a hawser to a shoreline tree. The signal served as well to alert other vessels, as an officer of one ship noted: "It is a common signal on this Coast for any Vessel going into a harbour to fire a Gun and if there be a Vessel in the harbour to answer with another, then they may either come in or stay out just as they chuse."[23] Similarly, the log of the *Arab* noted on 18 June 1821 as it entered Kaigani Harbour: "Fir'd a Gun to aprise the Indians and any Ship that might ly in the Harbours of our approach."[24] The approach of the Natives presented a curious and fearsome spectacle to the Euroamericans. The carved and painted dugout canoes could be as long as the trading ships themselves and carry as many men, who were cloaked in furs, disfigured by scars, daubed with red ocher, coiffed in braids sprinkled with fish oil and eagle down, and adorned with nose and ear rings of shell and copper collars or bone necklaces. In the case of the northern Indians, the men were often tattooed and the women labreted (Fig. 5). "The [Haida] chiefs come off to the Ship with their heads powdered white as snow, with the down of sea fowls, & their faces painted with red, black & white colours, in various fancies," recorded the log of the *Atahualpa* in 1801.[25] The Natives greeted their visitors with an "agreeable" song, keeping time to a drum beat with their paddle strokes. When Captain Cook's two ships put in to Nootka Sound in 1778 they were met by thirty to forty canoes of Indians who "stood up in their Canoes, made many strange Motions, sometimes pointing to the shore & at other times speaking to us in a confused Manner very loud & shouting, & presently after they all sung in concert in a wild Manner, which some of our sailors compared to that of a Brother Tar on board who it seems in his time had cryed Potatoes about London" (although Cook's surgeon added that they sang "in concert in no disagreeable Stile").[26] As a sign of friendship they threw white feathers onto the sea, and as an even stronger sign a chief and a captain might eventually exchange surnames; a Nootka chief of Ahousat became Captain Hanna after the very first British Northwest Coastman, and Captain Bernard Magee of the *Globe* exchanged names with the Classet chief Utillah of Cape Flattery.[27] The canoes crowded around the ships, and trading was carried out over the side or on the deck; in the latter case only a few Natives, and often the chief alone, were allowed on board at one time for security reasons. The shipmasters were so keen to get skins that sometimes, like Captain Douglas of the *Iphigenia Nubiana* in 1788 on the northern coast, they traded sea-otter cloaks (cotsacks, also known as cutsarks or coatlusters) right off the backs of the Natives.[28]

The Indians were just as eager to trade as the Euroamericans. Apparently the Haida exceeded other northern Indians in "keenness in trade," perhaps because more of their furs were the more valuable sea otter and perhaps, too, because they had less opportunity for transmountain trade with interior Natives on the mainland. "They are fierce for trade," remarked an American missionary in 1829.[29] The southern Indians were likewise keenly commercial, Captain Vancouver observing that "their passion for traffick and exchange is irresistible."[30] One of the earliest shipmasters found in 1786 that Chief Maquinna's people had "more extensive acquaintance and experience in trade" and were "more avaricious" and "richer" than their neighbours.[31] Nootka possessiveness promoted trade. "Their jealousy of the rights of Property," noted the same shipmaster, "was excessive and extended to every object."[32] Captain Cook had been confounded by the same trait when his men tried unsuccessfully to cut grass, fell timber, or draw water in Nootka Sound free of charge; Captain King, who was ultimately to succeed Cook, declared that "no people had higher Ideas of exclusive property."[33] But they were still eager for *makook* – trade. As indicated earlier, salmon, the most esteemed food of the Nootkas, was one of the few things that they would normally refuse to barter, and very dearly when they relented.[34]

Often the chief handled all of the trade of his tribesmen, who might refuse to trade without him. For this reason the *Jefferson* obtained almost no skins in late spring of 1793 from Barkley Sound's Indians, who "frequently would tell us that [Chief] Wickenenish collected all there skins," and "no articles that we had would induce them to bring any skins for sail."[35] So out of economic as well as political necessity the chiefs had to be treated with respect and indulgence by shipmasters, being feted and allowed on deck and even in the cabin, where, as the *Atahualpa*'s log recorded, "They are not the most welcome visitors, as they eat & drink enormously, & Beg & steal all they can."[36] So much did Chief Concomly (Madsu) of the Chinooks expect and relish such treatment that he was styled King George by the fur traders.

In managing his people's trade a chief was disposing of communal resources, not only furs but also provisions, for which he was responsible. If he were bested in bartering, he lost not only wealth but prestige, too, and perhaps even rank and subjects as well. It was therefore important for him to strike a bargain. In this "harguing" (haggling) the tribeswomen had a decisive voice, particularly among the matrilineal northern Indians, with whom the Euroamericans had the most commercial intercourse. Many captains, such as Joseph Ingraham of the *Hope* in 1791, remarked what they considered to be the uxoriousness of the Haida men: "Here [Queen Charlotte Islands], in direct opposition to most other parts of the world, the women maintain a precedency to the men in every point insomuch as a man dares not trade without the concurrence of his wife. Nay, I have often been witness to men being abused by their wives for parting with skins before their approbation was obtained."[37] At Nootka Sound Alexander Walker found that at times it was "the Women, who managed the traffic, and who were more exorbitant in their demands than the Men."[38] And Lewis and Clark noted that the Chinooks, too, heeded their female compatriots: "Notwithstanding the Survile manner in which they treat their womin they pay much more respect to their judgement and opinion in maney respects than most indian nations; their womin are permited to Speak freely before them, and Sometimes appear to command with a tone of authority; they generally consult them in their traffic and act conformably to their opinions."[39] Upon enquiring why such "petticoat government" prevailed among the Haidas, Captain Sturgis was told by some men that the "women could talk with the white men *better* than they could, and were willing to talk *more*."[40] Certainly the women were adept traders. Captain Jacinto Caamaño found that Tlingit wives were better bargainers than their husbands, and Captain James Strange declared ruefully that whenever Nootka women were present during transactions he had to pay three times as much for skins.[41] Captain Sturgis recollected that one of the best-known female traders was "Mother" Connecor (so called because she regarded all whites as her children), who was the wife of a leading chief and, as a trafficker, "the keenest & shrewdest among the shrewd."[42]

Indian protocol required ceremonious introductions, gift exchanges, and price negotiations – as did the protocol of Euroamericans, too, at least for whomever they considered their equals. A skipper and a chief initiated trade by swapping presents; at Clayoquot Sound in the summer of 1788 Captain Meares was given forty sea-otter skins by Chief Wickaninish to start trade.[43] Such generosity had to be reciprocated fully, as Captain Ingraham learned from the Haidas: "Their presents are always [given] with an expectation of a return, and if this should not be of equal value, or what they esteem such, they would immediately demand their present again. I have often heard when a person gave anything away with an expectation of a return it was termed an Indian gift; this saying cannot be more completely verified than among these people."[44] Shipmasters soon discovered, too, that furs received in this way always cost more than those purchased in trade – perhaps because they were less likely to shortchange the Natives at the outset in order to stimulate traffic – so they tried to avoid gift exchanges, although they could not always be bypassed for fear of insulting the Indians and losing their business. While Captain Meares was at Nootka Sound in 1788 the Indians abruptly switched from trading to "making reciprocal presents," probably so as to get better value for their skin money.[45]

Before trading began it was likewise customary to fix a price for prime skins as a standard of value. This entailed "a great deal of haggling,"[46] and often only after several days of such "bantering" and window-shopping was a skipper able to "break trade," much to his and his crew's exasperation. (Incidentally, despite the emergence of the Chinook trading jargon, Sturgis, refering to the turn of the century, asserted that "all intercourse with the natives was carried on in their own language, which compelled us to acquire a competent knowledge of it for managing trade, but not sufficient for a critical examination."[47]) As the log of the *Vancouver* recorded in 1805, "It is a Custom amoung the Savages to trad Brisk after the Ship has Ben in harbor 2 or 3 Days."[48] In 1809 the *Hamilton* put in to Kaigani on Thursday, 8 November, and immediately had "a number of the Natives along Side but No trade" until Monday, the 13th.[49] At the beginning of August 1822 at Skidegate in the Queen Charlottes ("the pleasantest part of the Coast I have seen as yet & is not so high land as the other parts of the Coast") the *Rob Roy* encountered "a grate deal of talk and but little trade."[50] It was not uncommon for a week to pass before trading actually began. The Indians were, after all, skilful traders who viewed barter as more than simply a commercial transaction. To them it was also a political and social event that should not be hurried. Thus in March of 1801 the *Atahualpa* had "Natives under the stern of the ship from morning untill after dark in the evening, but they seem to prefer talking to trading"; four days earlier there had been "Natives on board as usual. They talk much & trade but little."[51] Captain Ingraham complained that the Indians were "tedious in [the] extreme about trading." "A man ought to be endowed with an uncommon share of patience to trade with any of these people," he opined, adding that "I let them take their own time, for to urge them on only enhanced the price of their skins."[52] That prospect was sufficient to make most shipmasters await the Indians' pleasure. Others would feign departure by preparing to weigh anchor in the hope of inducing the Indians to come to terms. "Got under Way & lay of[f] and on in order to make the natives trade," recorded the log of the *Hamilton* at Masset in May 1821.[53]

Auxiliary articles were added to the primary Euroamerican goods as small presents – *Saman Tauskins* to the Bay men of Fort Simpson – but were in fact part of the price of the goods. Since different individuals wanted different assortments, equivalents had to be established: an iron pot equalled an axe, a knife a file, a pocket mirror a pair of scissors. The Indians would try hard to obtain more than the equivalent. Captain Cook observed that the Nootkas were careful to regulate their trade with his two ships so as to ensure "that the price of their articles was always kept up while the Value of ours was lessening daily."[54] Captain Strange had a similar experience at Nootka Sound in 1786: "Altho' comparatively speaking the price [of skins] was moderate and even trifling, yet it was necessary to prevent a rise in the demand upon us, that we should maintain the importance and value of our own commodities. It required no small precaution and prudence to prevent the depreciation of our Currency. It was for the same reason necessary that we should not appear too easy and anxious to possess any of their articles."[55] As competition mounted, however, this sound advice was ignored and the value of Euroamerican trade goods fell accordingly as the price of Indian furs rose.

It was important that the attempts of the Natives to devalue Euroamerican goods be resisted, stressed Captain Sturgis, in order "to avoid trouble," that is, to avoid antagonizing those Natives who had already traded at the equivalent. He felt so strongly on this point that he once spent several hours in such a contest with a Haida woman over articles as trifling (to him) as a spool of thread and a sewing needle.[56] But this veteran Northwest Coastman was not alone in his concern for consistent terms of trade. Captain Bishop of the *Ruby* wrote: "I cannot help observing how Cautious a Trader should be how he begins trade on his Arrival ... for if he gives any thing Extraordinary at First, or if there is any thing new and uncommon in his Cargo, He must consider that the different Tribes communicate with each other, and he must Purchase every Skin at the Same Price and with the Same Articles, or meet with considerable delay and trouble noise etc."[57] Captain Bernard Magee of the *Jefferson* concurred: "Whin once an Etreordenary price is given for any articles – s. o. skins or Clamons in particular – it imedeatly takes light amongst them all – & accordingly the set value on the rest of thire trade – which is entirly owing to giveing more at one time then at an other."[58]

Similarly, Captain Ingraham warned that "anyone who trades on this coast may be sure if they adopt any particular custom they must afterwards adhere to it or give offense, which may often be a hindrance to trade."[59] The log of the brig *Lydia* recorded that on 1 February 1806 in the Queen Charlottes "the Natives came up to trade with the Skipper they told him they would trade with him if he would give them the same as he did at other places he told him he would not so they carried their skins away."[60] In the second week of June 1823 at Stikine the *Mentor* and *Owhyhee* found the Tlingits very reluctant to trade because they had heard that higher prices were being given to the south: "Both vessels have purchased at this place 80 Black skins after a great deal of trouble as they are more dificult to trade with than I have ever known them owing in a great measure to the high prices given to the south'd."[61] Again, in the spring of 1838 the HBC at Fort Simpson paid the Tlingits ten blankets but the Tsimshians only six for one sea-otter skin in order to match the Russian price at Sitka, although Chief Trader John Work was well aware that "having different prices for the different tribes trading here cause much trouble"; he added that "the Northern Indians [Tlingits] though told to do so will not keep what they get a secret but vaunt of it as soon as they go out and the others insist upon having as much." Consequently, the company had to raise the Tsimshians' price to seven to eight blankets per skin, otherwise they would sell their furs not to the Russians but to the Tlingits, who would then resell them to the Russians for ten blankets.[62] Predictably, when the company in 1840 took control from the Russians of St Dionysius Redoubt, which was replaced by Fort Stikine, and offered the standard (lower) price, the Tlingits were "very much dissatisfied" and "clamerous for the Ft. Simpson Tariff."[63] The Indians were equally insistent about the uniformity of their own prices. Thus in early April of 1799 the

Sitka and Hoodsnahoo Tlingits came to blows as a result of the latter trading skins to the *Caroline* for less than the former did.[64]

The Euroamerican traders were struck by the honesty of their Indian customers, at least initially (perhaps before they were corrupted by white malpractice).[65] To Captain King the Nootkas were "sharp & keen in their dealings, but open & honest in letting you examine their things."[66] Captain Vancouver's second lieutenant, Peter Puget, found that the southern Indians observed the "strictest honesty" in trade; the Nootkas, he added, "prefer the fair and Equittable mode of trading for whatever they want,"[67] although they were not above such tricks as blackening sea-otter pelts with charcoal – glossy black being the most desirable colour – or diluting animal oil with water.[68]

The Nor'westmen were more impressed with the Indians' commercial acumen. As traders the Natives proved not only as keen as the Euroamericans but also just as shrewd and just as sensitive to supply and demand, as well as equally vulnerable to fashion.[69] A picture of artless and gullible indigenes being duped by white carpetbaggers could scarcely be farther from the truth. And this fact was recognized early by the whites themselves. Captain Meares's "merchants proprietors" cautioned him in 1787: "Although you are abundantly provided with copper, iron, and other articles of trade, we must recommend to you the strictest oeconomy in the application of them; as it appears that the natives are such intelligent traders, that, should you be in the least degree lavish, or inattentive in forming bargains, they will so enhance the value of their furs, as not only to exhaust your present stock, but also to injure, if not ruin, any future adventure."[70] Apparently Meares did not sufficiently heed this sound advice, for he reported that "we found to our cost, that these people ... possessed all the cunning necessary to the gains of mercantile life," and at Clayoquot Sound "in all our commercial transactions with these people, we were, more or less, the dupes of their cunning: and with such peculiar artifice did they sometimes conduct themselves, that all the precaution we could employ, was not sufficient to prevent our being overreached by them."[71] A French visitor was struck by the fact that "the natives ... are not careless in business; they examine every thing with attention and intelligence, and never determine till after mature deliberation." "They do not conclude their bargains," he reiterated, "till after a long and minute examination of the commodities which are offered: the smallest defect escapes not the first glance of their eye, but makes them lessen the price of the article, or determines them to reject it entirely."[72] Sullivan Dorr advised his brother that "these cunning savages ... are great Merchant traders."[73] He warned that it was not possible, for example, to sell inferior muskets on the coast because "the Indians wont have other than good."[74]

Euroamerican traders were unanimous in their high opinion of the mercantile sharpness of the Tlingits, Haidas, Nootkas, and Chinooks – those with whom they had the most intercourse. An officer of the French merchant ship *La Solide* had this to say of the Tlingits of Sitka Sound in 1791: "They examined with the most scrupulous attention, turned about in every way, all that was presented to them, and they knew very well how to discover defects and point them out: on the other hand, they employed art and cunning in setting off their merchandise; and it may be said, that, in respect to interest and traffic, they have already made great strides in civilization, and that the modern Hebrews would, perhaps, have little to teach them." He added that "their obstinacy in not reducing their pretensions [demands], was such, that some of them were seen remaining constantly for two days together round the ship, with furs which they in the end carried on shore again, because their visitors refused to give the exorbitant price which they had not been ashamed to demand for them."[75] This view, with its ethnic prejudice, was reiterated by the American crew of the *Eliza*. They nicknamed one Sitka Tlingit broker "Hard and Sharp," "for no Jew in Christendom could be sharper than he was in buying and selling."[76] The 1837 post journal of Fort Simpson described the trading behaviour of some visiting Stikine Tlingits:

Mr. Kennedy [the post's Indian trader] busy all day trading with the Stikeen people and making very slow progress. They are very difficult to deal with, and hard to please in the quality of the goods. Our Duffle which is in great demand with them is done, they would take green blankets but the bars are not of a proper colour being of a different green instead of black as usual. The blue bar blankets are also objected to on account of the stripes being of a grayish instead of a dark blue, the Red bar blankets they will not have at all. The guns and in fact every other article they insist on having at a cheaper rate than we sell them.[77]

Captain Barkley's rating of the Tlingits was more succinct. "They are expert traders," he said flatly.[78] But no more so than the Haidas. According to Captain Ingraham, "The people of these [Queen Charlotte] isles in general possess a truly mercantile spirit"; they used "every effort and persuasion to obtain the best price" and would "not part with a single skin till they have exerted their utmost to obtain the best price for it."[79] The Scottish surgeon and botanist Dr John Scouler toured the coast in the middle 1820s and reported that "these

Islanders were the most acute & ingenious people we had seen on the coast."[80] In 1801 the *Atahualpa* found the Skidegate Haidas "very difficult to please" and "as sharp in their dealings as Boston market men." Also, "the natives have so much to say and require so great a price for their articles, that trade goes on but slowly."[81] Two decades later the *Rob Roy*'s logkeeper recorded that "these fellows are the hardest to deal with of any on the Coast."[82] In the middle 1820s the *Paragon* put in to Skidegate, "one of the best harbours on this Coast," and likewise reported that the local Natives were "the hardest to trade with on the Coast."[83] They were equally formidable to the HBC, as Lieutenant Simpson discovered in 1831:

The Indians [of Skidegate] collected about us in considerable numbers & offered a few Sea Otters & Beavers for sale but asked a very high price for them – One called Winqatis speaks a good deal of English & appears to have acquired a great deal of information about the value of goods – Speaks of dollars & invoices & precentages with as much freedom & apparent knowledge as a Merchant & will I have no doubt put the other Indians up to a good deal of nonsense which will render Trade with them very difficult & of little profit – My principal object in coming was to procure potatoes but on this too they put too high a value to procure them in any quantity.[84]

The Masset Haidas enjoyed a similar reputation. According to the log of the *Otter* in 1811, "These fellows thinks that they are the wisest people on this Coast, and they are just as much worse to deal with for they don't know what they would have, & it is impossible to please them."[85] In the middle 1830s the Kaigani Haidas were considered "the most difficult Indians on the coast to deal with,"[86] probably because they were in the best location for upping the bidding among competing Russian, American, and British traders. In 1837 the Russians promised to pay them as much as the British did, and the latter pledged to pay them a "little more" than the former.[87]

The Nootkas, too, "possessed all the cunning necessary to the gains of mercantile life" in the view of Captain Meares.[88] They likewise closely inspected Euroamerican wares, as Captain Strange ruefully discovered in 1786: "They would not part with any thing out of their hands, before they had received an equivalent; they never forgot to examine carefully our goods. Nor were they contented with their own opinion alone, but handing our goods to their friends, consulted with them respecting their quality, and what they should give in return." At the same time, the Nootkas extolled their own commodities: "The Natives remaining in their Canoes, exhibited their Goods also with all possible art; for they knew, as well as we did, how to put off their

Goods to the best advantage. If at any time Mr. Strange and they disagreed about the price, as frequently happened, they had recourse to a thousand little arts to make him give more. One would take up the Fur, and measuring it by extending his arms, would smooth it down with his hand, and expatiate on the fineness and colour of the Fur."[89] One of these "arts" was practised to good mercantile effect on some of Captain Vancouver's crewmen by a fourteen-year-old girl "at whose Shrine many were paying their addresses." She "contrived by an Excellent Management and distribution of her smiles to receive innumerable presents from her Admirers but without granting her favors to any one."[90] Captain Sturgis described another Nootkan artifice:

Some of the Chiefs, particularly those of Clayoquot near Nootka [Sound], were among the finest looking men I ever beheld. Tatoochzetticus and Tatoochakezetl, and others, were several inches over six feet in height, brawny, muscular, & remarkably broad across the chest. Either of them could extend his arms over seven feet, and much to our annoyance too, for cloth, with some other articles, was usually sold by the fathom, and it was often a matter of controversy who should be the measurer. In my own trade I was always disposed to take that office upon myself; the Indians often insisted upon having one with greater length of limb, and we were sometimes compelled to yield. When they got it into the hands of such as the two chiefs just named it was a sorry sight to see our Cloth disappearing at the rate of 7 or 8 feet to the fathom instead of some 5½ which we intended to give.[91]

The Chinooks, too, "were up to all the shifts of bargaining."[92] Lewis and Clark found that they were "close deelers, & Stickle for a verry little ... they are great higlers in trade and if they conceive you anxious to purchase will be a whole day bargaining."[93]

Owing to their skill as horse traders, the Indians often exacted higher prices for their furs than the Euroamericans had expected to pay. But other factors also inflated fur prices, including those listed by the *Atahualpa*'s supercargo on 27 May 1802: "the advanced season, the small quantity of peltry on board, being unacquainted with any other place where there was a probability of meeting with so large a lot, & the hazard of letting slip the opportunity of perchasing them, fearing some other vessel might come in & satisfy their demands."[94] But the principal determinant was Euroamerican competition. As Captain Cleveland learned by experience in 1799, "The Indians are sufficiently cunning to derive all possible advantage from competition, and will go from one vessel to another, and back again, with assertions of offers made to them, which have no foundation in truth, and showing themselves to be as well versed in the tricks of the trade as the greatest adepts."[95] The Natives were quick to take advantage of the presence of competitors to drive the best bargain. It was for precisely this reason that the HBC strove to eliminate American competition on the coast in the 1830s; it knew very well that "the Indians are too keen traders not to go to the best [highest bidder's] market."[96] One shipmaster commonly tailed another in the expectation that he could outcompete the other, just as in the continental fur trade rival companies often sited their posts near each other.[97] The Indians then went back and forth between the competing ships in order to raise the price of their skins. Indeed they were reluctant to open trade with a single vessel, preferring to wait until others arrived. When the *Atahualpa* reached Kaigani in 1802 it found that "the natives seem determined not to part with their skins until they are acquainted with ye. number of vessels on the coast this season."[98] As soon as the Indians heard of the arrival of other ships, their prices rose.[99] In early June 1799 three American skippers in Sitka Sound paid more than three times as much for skins as one of them had paid there in early April; indeed as a result of such inflation the Tlingits were "really confused, and so at a loss to know what to ask for, that they desisted from selling any more" in the expectation of even higher prices, and to avoid this "folly" the three captains agreed to halve their prices and share their returns equally.[100] At nearby Hoodsnahoo (or Khootznahoo, meaning "bear fort" in Tlingit) in the "straits" fur prices doubled between early April and late May of the same year.[101] Upon reaching the mouth of the Columbia in late 1805 Lewis and Clark found that Chinook prices were "emence," the Indians having been "spoiled" by competing fur-trading vessels. "Their prices are So high that it would take ten times as much to purchase their *roots* & *Dried fish* as we have in our possession," they lamented.[102]

More examples can be given. When the *Owhyhee* and *Convoy* entered the Columbia in the winter of 1828–29 "the English [Hudson's Bay Company] were getting six large Beavers for one Blanket and twenty for a musket, but [our] opposition has reduced it to ¼ of the former price."[103] At Kaigani in 1821 the *Arab* spent 7–10 July with another Boston ship, the *Mentor*, and had "a number of the Natives along side and on board but [they] would not Trade," anticipating a bidding war between the two vessels.[104] "Nothing please them better than to have two vessels thus opposing each other," observed Chief Trader Work.[105] In 1822 at the end of July at Sebastian the *Rob Roy* was outcompeted by the *Sultan*, which offered ten instead of eight yards of India cotton cloth for one skin, as well as presents of powder boxes which were twice as large as the *Rob Roy*'s (although three-and-one-half months earlier at Nass, in order to overcome very dull trade, eighteen yards of cloth had been given for a skin by the same *Rob Roy* – "the first Vessel that ever done it and commenced a brisk trade in furs").[106] (On 21 June at Sebastian the Indians had been "very saucy" and there had been "no trade as they want 7 fathom [14 yards] of cloth."[107]) To counter this tactic American shipowners assigned each of their vessels to a certain stretch of the coast and divided the take equally, at least until 1827, when presumably there were no longer enough sea otters to justify this practice.[108] But even when trading vessels were scattered the Indians "are soon acquainted with what vessels are at different parts ... and set a value on their furs accordingly."[109]

So effective was competition in raising prices that sometimes, as Captain Cleveland has already attested, the Indians would use the alleged arrival of other vessels as a trick to increase the value of their furs. The owners of the *Rob Roy* warned Captain Daniel Cross as follows: "You must remember that you are not always to believe all that is told you, but the best way is to let them [the Indians] think you believe them. The natives will often misrepresent things, particularly in relation to the prices which other vessels have given for furs, but when you fall in with our vessels you will know the real state of things."[110] At Fort Simpson the Tsimshians would "very often" falsely report that they had sighted an American ship "in hopes of receiving a better price for their Skins" from the HBC's post.[111] When two ships really did materialize in late August 1834, Chief Trader Peter Skene Ogden reported that "the Indians will not now trade as they expect better prices from the vessels," and in September, after the coasters had sailed, Ogden promptly reduced the price of marten pelts by one-half.[112] Again, on the evening of 9 February 1837 "2 canoes of Stikine Indians arrived [at Fort Simpson] with 70 or 80 Land Fur. they reported that they saw a Large Vessel standing in towards Tomgass, but am afraid this is a false report as they very often do so in hopes of receiving a better price for their Skins." "The Indians," added the post's journal, "will not part with the few Skins they have among them, in hopes of an opposition [American vessel] casting up."[113]

In order to get a higher price some chiefs "held back" their furs until the trading vessels were about to leave in September and were therefore anxious to dump their goods at lower prices and complete their furry cargoes[114] – an old Indian tactic, used, for example, at Kaigani in early March 1822, when the *Rob Roy* encountered "but Little Trade and not much prospect of doing much at this place as the Indians keep their furs for vessels going off the Coast at the close of the season."[115] As long as American competitors were present the HBC had to indulge the Natives and tolerate their cockiness and insolence. As Chief Trader Work stated in 1837, "These Stikeen men are daring scoundrels and require to be kept well down. But this plagued opposition [American and Russian competition] often deters us from being so severe as is necessary."[116]

The Indians, like the Euroamericans, also resorted to monopolization in order to prevent the price of their skins falling. Just as they refused to divulge the whereabouts of the inland Natives who supplied them with much of their peltry in order to safeguard their profitable intermediary role, so, too, did they control the traffic of a moored vessel, excluding other Indian sellers and not allowing them to participate directly until their own stock of skins had been exhausted, and even then only under certain restrictions.[117] While visiting the Nootkas, Captain Cook discovered that "they engrossed us intirely to themselves."[118] Whenever other Indians managed to break the monopoly, they charged less for their pelts.[119] When the *Prince of Wales* anchored in Nootka Sound in early July 1787 the "Natives flock'd about us in great numbers," wrote Captain Colnett, "making us entirely their guests, not suffering an Indian from any other part of the sound to trade with us, but thro' them."[120] Similarly, while spending the winter of 1786–87 in Prince William Sound, Captain Meares of the *Nootka* was "at first very much surprised" that the local Indians were well aware of the number of crewmen he had lost to scurvy and the location of their graves until he "soon after discovered that they obtained their intelligence from the constant watch they kept, to prevent any other bands of natives from coming to trade with us, without giving them a share of their profits, whatever they might be."[121] In response to shipmasters' inquiries, the Indian monopolists invariably characterized their suppliers as untrustworthy and ferocious. The Nootkas used the whites' abhorrence and dread of cannibalism to blacken the names of neighbouring tribes and thereby gain a competitive edge in trade.[122] Unfortunately, this ploy also reinforced the Euroamericans' perception of the Indians as savage brutes.

The higher Indian demand and the lower Euroamerican offer – the reverse from the Native point of view, of course – inevitably produced a compromise. In Sitka Sound in early 1799 the Tlingits offered one sea-otter skin for one musket but the *Eliza's* captain demanded from four to five skins; after three days of haggling the two sides settled on three skins.[123] Some skippers, like Captain Ingraham, feared that "should they [the Indians] raise their price from what they at present [1792] require, the trade will be no longer worthy of anyone's attention, for ruin must certainly follow."[124] But the Natives' response to supply and demand never reached that inelastic point. On the contrary, it was Euroamerican excess that glutted the market and dulled the trade. During the winter of 1788–89 at Nootka Sound, for instance, the market became so saturated with iron "toes" (spikes or chisels) that their value plummeted from three to ten for a skin.[125] The Indians, naturally, tried to keep fur prices as high as possible. In 1791 Captain James Colnett of the *Argonaut* observed that the Nootkas' skins were less dirty and more prime – and hence more valuable – than in 1789 because they were killing sea otters less promiscuously.[126] And it was not long before the Natives put price tags on other articles that were in demand by shipmasters. By 1829 Tongass was the only place on the northern coast where trading vessels could wood and water free of charge; elsewhere they had to pay in goods.[127]

The Euroamerican traders devised their own stratagems to counter the commercial wiles of the Indians. One such dodge was outright cheating in the form of diluted rum, defective muskets, weevily rice, and so on. Captain Eliah Grimes of the *Owhyhee* recommended to his owners that gunpowder be shipped to the coast in kegs, not barrels (4 kegs = 1 barrel), because in "emptying them into kegs [from barrels] we shall have to fill them all, whereas none of the [shipped] kegs are full by an inch or more and some two inches."[128] Doubtlessly, however, cheating afforded but short-term gains, since the Indians presumably detected such fraud before long and adjusted their prices and patronage accordingly. It certainly explains why they inspected Euroamerican trade goods so closely and shunned some shipmasters.

Ingratiation was a more effective artifice. Skippers tried to win the favour of fur-laden chiefs by giving them special presents, inviting them on board to dine and drink (often to the point of intoxication) in the ship's cabin, offering them passage to another village, teaching them the proper use of trade goods, and taking them to the outside world of Canton, Boston, or the Hawaiian Islands. On 26 May 1810 at Skidegate a Haida chief named Easter Kuner (or Easter Connor, whom the logkeeper of the *Rob Roy* in 1822 rated "the gratest begger I ever saw without exception," adding that "he is called the Largest Indian on the coast and is certainly the fatest I have seen"[129]) boarded the *Hamilton* with three of his slaves and spent the next several weeks sailing "from port to port" trying to sell his chattels.[130] Clucar, a Tlingit chief, voyaged to Canton and back and learned "tolerable English."[131] In 1810 he "gave Captain porter [of the *Hamilton*] his Sun for to go to boston" (although the boy subsequently changed his mind).[132] In 1794 the American crew of the *Thomas Jefferson* went so far as to plane, raise, and paint a mortuary pole and doctor a sick Indian at Cunneah's Harbour in the Queen Charlottes in the expectation of gaining favour.[133] Another device was prepayment for skins. In 1792 Captain John Kendrick paid Chief Wickaninish in advance for fifty to one hundred prospective skins in order to preclude their sale to rival shipmasters.[134] And in 1810 Captain Samuel Hill "engaged" the Tsimshian chief Quillaha to "save" skins for him.[135]

Less successful were attempts to establish permanent factories on the coast for year-round trading and to leave "resident agents" with the Natives to amass their furs. Several shipmasters were instructed to found permanent posts, for example, Portlock and Dixon in 1785–88 and Colnett in 1789–91. But they failed to do so – Meares's Fort Pitt (1787) and Gray's Fort Defiance or Washington (1789) at Nootka Sound notwithstanding – because of a shortage of personnel and matériel, a paucity of suitable sites with the requisite timber, water, farmland, and shelter (the Spanish missionaries at Nootka Sound reported that they were unable to form a mission because of insufficient arable land), and opposition from Indians and other Euroamericans alike (Sitka nearly failed for this reason). While agents were occasionally left behind during the summer or over the winter in order to "keep back" competition, they tired so quickly of the isolation and savagery that they left with the next ship; for example, John Mackay, surgeon's mate of the *Captain Cook*, was left at Nootka Sound in 1786 to recover his health and engross furs but was rescued by the *Imperial Eagle* in 1787 without having gained either.

Meanwhile, the tendency for competing vessels to bid fur prices up to "ruinous" levels continued. In 1799 a prime sea-otter skin cost four yards of blue broadcloth at the start and ten yards at the close of the season, and in 1801 it cost six yards at the beginning and twenty yards by the end of the season.[136] To defeat this "far fetched North West policy," as it was branded by Captain Sturgis,[137] shipmasters resorted to price-fixing. They had always helped each other in times of need – for example, in careening and graving their ships (hauling them on shore, cleaning them, and smearing them with pitch), forwarding mail, replenishing stores, exchanging information, borrowing craftsmen (armourers, carpenters, tailors), and even freighting furs, so cooperation was not new. On 1 September 1810 in Taddiskey (or Tattasco, or Taddy's Cove), or Meares Bay, or Haines Cove [Datzkoo Harbour on Dall Island in the Alexander Archipelago], the *Hamilton* bought seven casks of shrowton (oolachen oil) and some muskets from the *Enterprise*, paying in naval stores (pitch, tar, and turpentine); on the same day the *Hamilton* discharged one Euroamerican seaman, John Newton, who had been shipped at the

Hawaiian Islands, and two Hawaiian hands, who were to be returned to the islands on the *Enterprise* (which was about to leave for Canton via Honolulu), and engaged three Hawaiians from the same vessel.[138] And a couple of weeks later the *Derby* went on the rocks in Cocklane's (or Cockathane's) Harbour and the *Hamilton* went to her aid by unloading its own ballast and embarking the *Derby*'s cargo (30 casks of molasses, 16 casks of rice, and 5 bales of duffle) so as to lighten her and enable her to draw onshore for repairs to her bottom.[139] Another form of cooperation was more profitable – the freighting of cargo from the coast to the China market for a percentage of the sales. The *Alert*, plying the coast on 17 July 1817, "took in all to Gather [altogether] 10,017 sticks [short logs] of sandell wood from on Board the Ship Interprise [*Enterprise*] of New york"; on 2 August it was "Employed in taking furs on Board from the Ship Hamilton & Mentor on fraight for Canton"; and en route at Honolulu it loaded 2,029 logs of sandalwood from the *Bordeaux Packet* on 20 and 21 September, 700 logs from the *Cossack* on 25 September, and 2,109 logs from an unspecified ship on 4 October.[140] At the end of the 1824 season the *Rob Roy* hauled the *Volunteer*'s furs to Canton for 2 per cent of the sales.[141]

Collaboration readily followed such cooperation. Attempts to "regulate" trade – fix prices and share returns – began as early as 1799 but apparently did not become common until the 1810s with the depletion of sea otters. In June 1811 Captain Lemuel Porter of the *Hamilton* and Captain Andrew Blanchard of the *Katherine* "agread for to shear skins & take differant Routs, so Mr Gage & Mr Tilford exchanged burths" in order to keep a tally of each other's collection of skins.[142] At the beginning of the 1813 trading season Captain Suter of the *Atahualpa* "sent Mr. G Cooper on board [the *Packet*, Captain Bacon] to take an account of the skins, as we intend dividing what skins may be collected for the purpose of keeping the Price down as much as possible."[143] In the autumn of 1815 at Honolulu the masters of the *Hamilton* (William Martain) and the *Cossack* (John Brown) "agreed to Share Skins during the first winter [1815–16] – the Hamilton to take the Northward part of the Coast and the Cossack the South."[144] And on 10 April 1822 the *Rob Roy* "entered into an agreement with Capt Harris [of the *Lascar*] for a division of Skins to the first of September next," and on 18 April "engaged to divide Skins with Capt Martin [Martain of the *Hamilton*] until the middle of July"; at the end of June the *Frederick*, *Hamilton*, *Lascar*, *Owhyhee*, *Rob Roy*, and *Sultan* assembled at "Tumgass" (Tongass) to divide skins, share gunpowder, and smoke their holds, and on 13 July four of them left for different marts – the *Frederick* for Masset and North

Island, the *Owhyhee* for Kaigani and Pearl Harbour, and the *Rob Roy* and *Sultan* for Skidegate and Sebastian. On 8 May of the following year the logkeeper of the *Mentor*, originally of the *Rob Roy*, went on board the *Owhyhee* "to see fair play," that is, to oversee the division of skins and ensure fairness – a common practice.[145]

"Dividing skins" was rationalized by Bryant and Sturgis, perhaps the dominant firm in the coast trade in the 1810s, in their instructions to Captain George Clark of the *Borneo* in late 1817: "We suggest to you the propriety of making arrangements with [Captain James] Bennett [of the *Volunteer*] to divide skins, rather than enhance their value by attempting to outbid each other, which would be an unprofitable Contest, especially as the Owners of both vessels are partially the same."[146] The following summer they added: "Every one acquainted with the trade of the Coast must be aware how much easier it is to purchase Furs from the Natives when only a moderate price is given, than when it is enhanced by injudicious & unprofitable competition, and foolish attempts to 'outbid each other.'"[147] This injunction, the owners stressed again, applied especially to vessels "in the same interest [employ]."[148] Normally, colluding vessels plied different stretches of the coast, as Bryant and Sturgis also noted: "It will be for your interest to divide the Coast in such a manner as to have your vessels separate, & thus get a full share of all the Skins on every part of it, taking care not to fall in each others way oftener than is necessary to consult together."[149] The principal competitor of Bryant and Sturgis, Marshall and Wildes, likewise let their vessels operate "in division with" those of other owners. In 1822 they were informed by Captain Eliah Grimes of the *Owhyhee* as follows: "I have thought best for your interest to divide with the [five] vessels that remain on the Coast notwithstanding my cargo is better than the rest … in fact I could not have done otherwise without the Skins costing 20$ or more as the rest could give two fathoms [of cloth] and buy cheaper Skins than I can; even giving one more will always turn the scale with these people."[150] Grimes added that the five remaining captains, "for the interest of our owners," bought "the remains of Capt Martin's [William Martain's] cargo [from the *Hamilton*] as he was determined to give 9 & 10 fathoms for a skin with all the presents, in that case we should not have been able to have got a skin, we know for a fact that the natives have kept them back for that purpose."[151] Later the same year the Honolulu agent of Marshall and Wildes reported that "there are too many vessels on the coast to do much, they are all obliged to go in division."[152] And in the spring of 1835 even the American ships *Europa* and *Bolivar Liberator* and the British vessel *Lama* "acted in concert" in order to keep the price of beaver below three blankets for two pelts, dividing the returns equally.[153] A year later the American *La Grange*, Captain Snow, anchored at Fort Simpson, and the two sides "came to an understanding regarding the Tariff they [the Americans] made a kind of promise that they would not deviate from our [British] Tariff."[154] Actually, Captain Snow fixed a common price for skins with both the Russians at Sitka and the British at Fort Simpson.[155]

A variation of this tactic involved Sitka's Russians, who provided undepleted rookeries (some stretches of their colonial coastal waters) and expert hunters (Aleut or Kodiak kayakers), and Boston's Yankees, who furnished sound ships, with the two sides sharing the returns equally. Hence the following entry in the log of the *Otter* on 24 May 1810 in Sitka Sound:

At 5 P.M. we saw a number of Canoes [kayaks] (of a different construction from any that we have seen upon the Coast) hunting between us and the shore, and soon after discovered two Ships at anchor we immediately concluded that they were Russians from Coniac [Kodiak] who had brought these Asiatic Indians [Aleuts or Kodiaks] with their Canoes, or Bydarkies [bidarkas] ... we were soon visited by Capt. Winchip [Jonathan Winship] of the Ship Ocane [*O'Cain*] of Boston, he has sold his cargo to the Russian Governor [Alexander Baranov] at — and is now in company with the other Ship which belongs to the Russians, the Governor furnishes them with these Indians who are under pay from him and he gets one half the Skins that they kill & Capt. Winchip the other.[156]

By the middle 1810s this collaboration was ended by the over-hunting of the Russian-American Company's territorial waters and the improvement of its own shipping.

Collusion worked, however, only as long as the trade goods of the accomplices were more or less comparable in quality and variety. A trading vessel with superior goods had no need to share, being able to dominate the market on its own. In April 1799 the *Eliza*'s quantity and selection of goods were such that it could afford to offer the Hoodsnahoo Tlingits twice as much for skins as the *Caroline*.[157] Again, in April 1802 Captain William Cunningham of the *Globe* refused to divide skins with Captain Dixey Wildes of the *Atahualpa* because of the lower quality of the latter's clamons.[158] As Bryant and Sturgis told Captain Marcus Peirce of the *Griffon* in 1824: "In general it is desirable to avoid competition, but when you have a decided superiority in the quality, quantity and assortment of Cargo, advantage must be taken of it, for two or three dollars more or less in the price of prime Skins is of little consequence compared with the importance of making a large collection."[159]

Moreover, "par trade" (equal prices) did not always last because one confederate sometimes could not resist the temptation to exceed the fixed price and thereby reap a windfall of skins. In Sitka Sound on 3 June 1799 "the Captains of the three Vessels [*Caroline, Despatch, Hancock*] agreed not to give more Cloth than 2 fathoms for a Skin while altogether in this Port." This action was taken because the *Eliza* was offering three fathoms of cloth, so that, of course, "the Natives [were] not willing to sell them [skins] for two fathoms Cloth and a good Estuck [an assortment of household wares?]." But by 18 June the *Despatch*, despairing of getting any skins, had broken the accord by giving from three to four fathoms. A new round of competition ensued to the point that by 22 June "the Natives [were] not willing to sell them for 3 fathoms Cloth and an Iron Pot or 3 Great Coats and a Pot."[160] Additionally, a shipmaster might find that his partner did not exert himself as much as he himself did to get skins – hence a logkeeper's reference to "this cursed division."[161] In fact, American captains in particular were as liable to compete as to collude, as witnessed by the "general practice among traders on this coast ... always to mislead competitors as far as they can, even at the expense of truth."[162] The British tried to deceive the very first American coaster, the *Columbia Rediviva*, in 1788 in order to forestall American competition:

All the time these Gentlemen [Captain Douglas of the *Iphigenia Nubiana* and Captain Meares and Chief Mate Duffin of the *Felice Adventurer*] were onboard [the *Columbia Rediviva*] they fully employed themselves fabricating and rehursing vague and improvable tales relative to the coast of the vast danger attending its navigation of the Monsterous Savage disposition of its inhabitants adding it would be maddness in us so week as we were to stay a winter among them. Capt. Mears protested both vessells ever since they had been on the coast had not collected fifty skins; on our smileing (for we had been differently informed) he said it was a fact upon his sacred word and honour, so intent was this Gentleman in deceiving us that he hesatated not to forfit his word and Honour to what we were convinced was a notorious falsity. The fact was they wished to frighten us off the Coast that they alone might menopolise the trade but the debth of there design could be easily fathemed.[163]

There was also the danger that the Indians might retaliate by withholding their furs until the free market had been restored.

Another Euroamerican tactic was the finding of "new" Indians, that is, those who had had little or no contact with trading vessels, since "not having been visited by Ships often they are not so knowing and Clammorous and of Course the Skins purchased proportionally cheap."[164] In 1799 the *Caroline* and *Eliza* were able to collect more skins than other vessels on the coast (together they accounted for 5,000 of the 11,000 taken by seven ships that year)[165] partly because they arrived early and partly because they tapped Sitka Sound's Tlingits, who had heretofore been unexploited (the Russians were to appear later the same year and erect New Archangel). Again, the log of the *Lydia* recorded in early June 1806 that Captain Hill was "poaking about in every Hole & Corner where No other Ships goes" in an attempt to locate untapped Indians.[166] Inevitably, however, "new" Indians quickly became "old" Indians who possessed fewer skins and demanded higher prices. Nevertheless, it remained true that it was easier and cheaper for a shipmaster to trade with those Indians who had less rather than more contact with trading vessels. As Lieutenant Simpson recorded in his log in 1831, "I find generally that in the Ports most frequented by Vessels the prices are higher than the others and the Indians much more difficult to deal with & more presuming."[167]

A similar stratagem was the bypassing of Indian traders in order to deal directly – and more cheaply – with their suppliers. Many, if not most, of the skins that were traded by the Natives of the outer coast had not been bagged by them but gained from more distant inland tribesmen by barter or even plunder. That is what happened when, after exhausting his stock of furs, a chief would ask a shipmaster to wait a few days until he had procured more. Captain Portlock, one of the earliest British coasters, reported that "the Indians, on leaving the ship, gave us to understand that their neighbourhood was drained of furs, but that they would go to procure more in the adjacent country," and the first American venture discovered that "tribes who have intercourse with the European traiders extend there trafic to those more remote collecting skins for the next vessell that may come."[168] The Chinooks paddled up the Columbia in the autumn and obtained elk hides (clamons) for as little as one-twentieth of the value at which they traded them to coasters at the mouth of the river.[169] In addition, they traded Euroamerican goods for interior furs which they then sold to Nor'westmen at a profit of nearly 50 per cent;[170] one-eyed Chief Concomly's Chinooks sold skins to the Astorians in 1811 for double what they themselves had paid to Natives farther up or down the coast.[171] The Nootkas crossed Vancouver Island to get furs from the Kwakiutls "for a very trifling consideration in comparison to what they are afterwards sold to foreigners";[172] that is why the Kwakiutls of the village of Chief Cheslakees on the northeastern coast of the island "frequently explained" to Captain Vancouver's men in 1792 that their skins "would fetch more at Nootka [Sound] than we chose to offer."[173]

The first American coaster, Captain Gray, learned in 1791 that "there is a trade carried on between the [Haida] natives of the [Queen Charlotte] island[s] and main[land] no doubt the latter trade with more remote tribes."[174] In the fall, after salmon fishing, the Haidas canoed across Hecate Strait and bartered Euroamerican goods to mainland Indians at a profit of 200 to 300 per cent.[175] On 19 May 1794 at Cunneah's Harbour the Haidas told the *Jefferson* to wait ten days for the return of Chief Cunneah with skins from their "winter quarters" on the mainland. On 31 May "in the Evening arived Cawe [Cow] Cumeah Eldarze [or Altatsee] Skilkadee & other Cheeffs with a numerous fleet of Canoes from Tattasco on the main" with at least 800 skins (by then, unfortunately, the *Jefferson* had "little or nothing now left of our trading stock").[176] In 1799 Captain James Rowan of the *Eliza* discovered that not one-fiftieth of the skins that were available at Kaigani had actually been hunted by the local Haidas; they acquired the "mass" of them from an "eastern mine" for only half the price that they received from shipmasters. At first Chief Kow "inveighed" Captain Rowan not to go to this source, alleging that it offered only sickness, not peltry, but upon realizing that Rowan would not be dissuaded he begged him not to give his suppliers more than his own price of one fathom (two yards) of cloth per skin, which was half of what he got from American traders. Only a Captain Brown (apparently William Brown of the *Butterworth* in 1792) had been to this "mine" (Cocklane's Harbour), where he had obtained "a great many skins at half price."[177] The *Atahualpa* learned in the middle of March 1802 that the Haida chief Cocklane bought furs from another tribe nearby for two fathoms of cloth or one blanket per pelt and then sold them to American vessels for as much as five blankets each.[178] The *Atahualpa* waited two and one-half weeks at Cocklane's Harbour for Chief Cocklane to canoe to Nass on the mainland for more skins and return, trading vessels having yet to discover the availability of furs at the annual *sow-tow* (oolachen-oil) mart at the mouth of the Nass River.[179] Thus the logkeeper of the *Rob Roy* was wrong when he naively concluded in 1822 that the Cocklane Indians were "not so lazy as the Kigarnie [Kaigani]" Indians because, he supposed, they hunted for most of their skins.[180]

The Tsimshians told Lieutenant Simpson that they acquired land furs "from other Indians higher up the [Nass] River, who again say they procure them from others further in the interior, who they say have intercourse with Whites [HBC traders] who come to them upon Horses."[181] At Fort Simpson Chief Trader Work acknowledged that "most of the furs these [Tsimshian, Haida, and Tlingit] people get are obtained in trafic" with interior Indians.[182] (Interior furs could be distinguished from coastal furs by the method of curing, the former being stretched widthwise and the latter lengthwise.[183] Similarly, Tsimshian skins were "stretched in a different shape" from Haida skins.[184]) The Chilkat Tlingits traded muskets to interior Indians for fox and marten pelts and native copper.[185] The Stikine Tlingits spent the first half of summer – before salmon fishing – journeying inland to trade.[186] They made three or four trading expeditions annually to a "grand mart" 150 miles inland.[187] Lieutenant Simpson reported these expeditions in 1831: "The Stikeen Indians ascend [the Stikine River] by Canoes for six days when they arrive at a village the Indian name is Quinanai – they again go by land & Trade [ball and powder] with a Tribe named the Itaquanis who again Trade with the Indians of New Caledonia – from whom they procure their Furs."[188]

Increasingly trading vessels sailed farther up the labyrithine channels and inlets ("canals") in order to circumvent the Indian middlemen. As early as 1792 Captain Vancouver in Fitz Hugh Sound met the *Venus*, Captain Henry Shepherd, who, "having found the price of skins so exorbitant on the sea-coast, he had been induced to try this inland navigation, in the hope of procuring them at a less extravagant price."[189] Again, on 23 May 1806, the *Vancouver* "arrived at a Large Bay at the head of the tide in fresh Water Called By the Savages Stickeen farther in Land than ever aney Ship was before Except Vancouvers Discovery Ship"; consequently, in three days of trading, peltry, wildfowl, and herring were obtained "in grate plenty and Cheap."[190] Interception was in the interests of both the buyers and the sellers, of course, for the former expended less and the later received more for skins. Not all attempts were successful; witness the *Jenny*'s Captain Jonathan Bowers, who in 1800 after a bloody clash with Indians "up the sound" was forced "to go to the out ports, where he was under the necessity of giving treble price for skins."[191] Also, fortunately for the middlemen, not all of their sources of supply could be intercepted because some were accessible by canoe only.[192] The only coastal river which seagoing vessels could ascend was the Columbia (as far as Fort Vancouver), and even its entrance was obstructed by a notorious bar. The Indian middlemen tried to keep their sources a secret and to deceive the shipmasters by declaring that the waterways were impassable or the suppliers treacherous and murderous, while the captains tried to discover the location of the sources by plying the Indians with booze. In the summer of 1793, when off Caamano Point, Captain Vancouver told a Tlingit chief from Clarence Strait that he would first sail up Behm Canal; the Indian expressed not only disappointment but outright disapproval, too, saying that "we should neither meet with chiefs, skins, nor any thing worth our research; and that the people who resided in that quarter were great thieves, and very bad men"[193] – undoubtedly because they were the source of not a few of his furs, which, he feared, Vancouver would now get first, as well as pay too much for them.

Inevitably some suppliers were uncovered, either by accident or design, and their Native retailers were bypassed. The resultant frustration and resentment of the middlemen contributed to the deterioration of Indian-Euroamerican relations. After Vancouver Island's insularity was revealed by its namesake in 1792 Nootka-Kwakiutl trade was intercepted, and by the end of the decade trading vessels had more or less abandoned Nootka Sound, which itself had by then been hunted out anyway. Nootka anger, aggravated by periodic insults to Chief Maquinna, culminated in the capture of the *Boston* in 1803 and the killing of nearly all of its crew.[194] A visitor noted in 1825 that Nootka Sound was "completely neglected."[195] The Queen Charlotte Islands, the Washington Isles of the American traders, succeeded Vancouver Island as the locus of the coast trade, but already by 1799 they were yielding not half the skins that they formerly had, again because the coasters had intercepted the native trading expeditions, which brought most of the archipelago's supply from the mainland.[196] Then Sitka Sound became dominant until its fur supply was preempted by trading vessels sailing up Menzies Strait between Baranof (Sitka) and Chichagof Islands.[197] In the spring of 1799 the *Caroline* traded directly with the Stikine Tlingits, thereby avoiding the Hoodsnahoo Tlingit intermediaries; "some of them were so angry at our having been there [Stikine], that they would not sell us any Skins."[198] Eventually the only remaining untapped middlemen were the Indians of the mainland coast, and even some of their interior suppliers began to be intercepted by the HBC's Babine Lake and Conolly's (Bear) Lake posts in the 1820s. Similarly, Chief Concomly's Chinooks were bypassed by the middle 1810s. They had long kept their inland suppliers aloof by telling them that white shipmasters were evil men and would enslave them, but following contact with PFC and NWC traders in the ealy 1810s the suppliers canoed downriver every summer to the Columbia's mouth to truck directly with Euroamericans on ships or at Astoria (Fort George). By the 1830s only the interior suppliers of the Tlingits remained largely inaccessible to Euroamerican fur traders, maritime and continental alike.

The anger of the Indian middlemen was compounded in the 1830s, when the HBC succeeded in eliminating American competition and thereby reducing fur prices. Chief Trader Work reported from Fort McLoughlin in 1835 that "the disturbed state of the Indians and their discontent, arises from their being under the impression that our being established here is the cause of their not getting such high prices for their furs as formerly, in consequence of the Americans not visiting them so frequently, and also the loss of the Interior trade or a considerable part of it, as the Interior Indians dispose of their furs themselves at the fort, and they do not pass through the hands of the others as formerly."[199] At the same time, however, the company realized that "it might not be prudent all at once to reduce the price of furs too low as it might tend to discourage the Indians from exertion both in hunting and trafic for a time, and of course nurse [replenish] the furbearing animals but it might be nursing them for the first opponents to cast up."[200] By the end of the decade the latter worry, at least, vanished with the abandonment of the coast trade by American shipowners and the leasing of the mainland panhandle of Russian Alaska by the HBC.

7 Obstacles to Trade

The furs on the [Northwest] Coast this Year [1810] have been very scarce.

Captain John Ebbets to John Jacob Astor, 1810

The NW Coast has become very dangerous, without a large compliment [*sic*] of men and well armed.

Captain Eliah Grimes to Josiah Marshall, 1821

No nation, certainly, carries on so advantageous a trade with foreigners [as China], and yet there is no nation which imposes conditions so harsh, or multiplies vexations and every species of inconvenience with more audacity. There is not a cup of tea drank in Europe which has not been productive of humiliation to those who purchased it at Canton, and who have embarked and sailed over half the globe to bring this leaf to our markets.

Captain J.F.G. De La Pérouse, 1787

TO THE COAST

A trading voyage to the Northwest Coast from Boston, London, or even Okhotsk was seldom smooth sailing. The obstacles that faced the ship and its crew throughout the venture were more or less common to all long ocean voyages of the time, and included exasperating calms, fierce storms, unknown shallows, bloody mutinies, untrustworthy "savages," obstructive officials, disabling diseases, sudden accidents, boring routine – all of which could reduce crews, lengthen voyages, and lower profits. Of the twenty-five men who left Boston aboard the *Atahualpa* in 1800, two were transferred to another vessel, one left the ship at Maui, one fell overboard and drowned, one died of mussel poisoning on the coast, and one died at Canton of unknown causes.[1] Even seasickness was encountered, presumably mostly by novice seamen at the outset of a voyage. On the second day out of Boston in

April 1809 the *Otter's* carpenter recorded "6 or 7 Sea sick & S—g through there teeth."[2] Sailings were sometimes slowed by adverse elements. As the logkeeper of the *Hamilton* lamented on 5 August 1815 in the south Atlantic: "All of this day Calm Or the Next kin to it. Prospect of A damned Long passage."[3] In late 1826 it took the *Louisa* ninety-seven days to make Cape Horn from Boston (only 121½ miles per day), because of heavy weather, cross seas, head winds, and major leaks (necessitating up to 100 strokes of a hand pump per hour); it had to stop at Rio de Janeiro to plug a leak, and soaked trade blankets had to be dried. The ship took another seventy-one days to reach the Northwest Coast from the Horn, not arriving until 25 March 1827, a month after the beginning of the trading season.[4]

Violent storms were more recurrent and more dangerous than dead calms. One, probably a hurricane, struck the *Atahualpa* on 9 September 1800, six days out of Boston:

A most terrible storm rages with unabated fury, from the beginning to the end of this day, the amazing strength and violence of which, it is needless for me to attempt to describe. It is sufficient to observe, that every man on board of the ship (many of whom have spent the greatest part of their lives on the ocean) declare, that they never before experienced so severe and violent a gale of wind. Notwithstanding, the T[op] G[allant] Masts, yards, etc. etc. were got down on deck, the Lower yards lay several feet in the water for a considerable length of time.

It was almost resolved upon more than once to cut away the masts. The ax was kept ready for that purpose. Every moment threatened the destruction of our Ship, and a watery termination of our existence, & which must have been the inevitable consequence, of the least defect in the Hull of the vessel, her being so entirely new, gave room for apprehension. But happily my anxiety on that head was greatly relieved by being acquainted with the care and attention that was bestowed upon her, by *faithful* men.

Some water made its way into the Cabin, kept us constantly baleing out, soaked all the clothes in my Chest, wet and defaced a number of Books & did some other mischief. Three hogsheads [1 hogshead = 75⅔ gallons] of water on Deck were scuttled. Some live stock was lost. We came very near losing the Whale Boats, by the davys giving way. Indeed it seems a miracle that all the Boats, and every thing on Deck, was not washed away.[5]

During such storms hands could be washed off the decks or, more likely, blown from the masts. One particularly poignant case was recorded by the journal of the *Vancouver* on 13 August 1804: "Sea ran high at 6 o Cock AM the mait Sent 4 hands up to hand the main Sail and one John Nichols Sliped of the yard and overboard Every

Exertion Being [made] to Save [him] But in vain the poor Soul Swam after the Ship a Longe time but found that it was in vain took his hat from his head and twerled it over his head and then through it from him and gave up the ghost he was a native of Sweden City of Stockholm aged 29."[6] Another instance was recounted more matter-of-factly by the journal of the *Otter* on 15 July 1809: "About 10½ [10:30 P.M.] Tilly Hardy fell from the Main Top Sail Yard Over Board and was drowned, as the night was So dark and tempestous we could not lower the boat down, without endangering the lives of all that went in her, So with great reluctance we was oblidged to leave him to a watery grave."[7] At the beginning of April 1823, a week before returning to Boston, the *Hamilton* was struck twice by an Atlantic gale which left the ship in a "very shattered state" and caused "considerable" damage to its cargo.[8]

The worst storms on the "golden round," barring the ferocious typhoons of the China seas, were those of "dreaded" Cape Horn.[9] One voyager declared that "the dangers of C. Horn have been greatly exaggerated & we invariably find that the most experienced sailor talks le[a]st about them."[10] Yet most Nor'westmen, such as Captain Magee of the *Jefferson,* who experienced "these bausterous Seas for upwards of 30 days with containuely gails & Snow storms" in April 1792,[11] seem to have found that the cape's infamy was well deserved. The *Otter* in July 1809 in Drake Passage encountered "Cold Stormey weather and contrary winds which makes hard times for us in getting round this Cape Horn in these long dark and disagreeable nights of 17 hours in length."[12] Similarly, in early July 1821 Captain Grimes of the *Owhyhee* reported that "the weather off Cape Horn was very severe so much so I lost both boats, camboose house, spars, bulwarks, rose the starboard plankshire about ¾ of an inch, washed two men off deck, fortunately got on board again."[13] Usually, however, a trading vessel timed its departure from its home port so as to double the Horn in the southern hemisphere's summer, but even that season was far from placid. Rounding the Horn between 24 February and 14 March 1787, the *Prince of Wales* suffered "three heavy Gales & scarce a watch pass'd without rain, hail, or snow."[14] The experience of the *Vancouver* in December 1804 was not uncommon:

2 this 24 hours Wind sw Blew verry fresh handed all Sail Latter part Squalls of hail rain and Snow and Sever Could our Sails all frozen the riggin all ice and our Situation Deplorable By the vicsitudes of the weather

11 this 24 hours Wind nw Blew a gail Lay two under reefed foresail 16 hours Seas in mountains high and a Most terreable Sight to Behold as Ever i See

12 ... Several heavey Seas Brook on Board which wrecked the Ship verry much Some hail and Snow and verry Cold and Wet

20 ... Last Night I was taken Sick and fainted at the Wheel

23 ... Stood for the Sandwich Islands.[15]

In late 1805 the *Hazard* lost six men while rounding the Horn; four were washed overboard and two were frozen to death.[16] Likewise, in the mid-summer of 1811 the *Atahualpa* found "violent Winds & heavy Squalls & a heavy Sea Snow & Hail" off the Horn eighty-eight days out of Boston.[17] In the same waters during the mid-spring of 1821 the *Rob Roy* met "thick and heavy squalls of snow, hail, and rain" with, as usual, "a heavy swell from the Westward."[18] Here the veteran coaster *O'Cain* was swamped by heavy seas in late 1821 or early 1822 "and immediately went down & every soul on board of her."[19] The foul weather, incidentally, could extend some distance either side of the cape, as the HBC's ships *Vancouver* and *Cowlitz* experienced in 1841: "We have not yet reached the dreaded Horn, but have had regular Cape weather lately, constant squalls & Showers of sleet and snow, a rough sea & fickle winds."[20]

In doubling Cape Horn sailing ships were stymied not so much by the cold, ice, snow, hail, rain, currents, and waves as by the contrary winds. The *Otter*'s journal explained the problem: "We find as much difficulty in getting to the Northwd. & Westwd. on this [Pacific] Side the Cape, as we had in getting to the Southwd. & Westwd. on the other side, which threatens us with a very long passage and want of water."[21] The *Convoy* took from two to three weeks to round the Horn at the beginning of 1825, for instance.[22] The adverse winds necessitated long, hard hours for the men in the rigging to adjust the sails frequently. Thus the log of the *Atahualpa* noted on 2 January 1812: "4 hands on the sick list With Sore Hands."[23] The *Mentor*, after doubling the Horn on 7 November 1816, encountered nineteen consecutive days of strong winds and heavy seas between latitudes 55° and 60° s. that left several men with sore hands and three on the sick list.[24] And off Tierra del Fuego towards the end of 1826 Captain William Martain of the *Louisa* reported "all hands Well on bord but the tailor Exepting the General Complaint Among the whole Ships Company of sore hands ocasioned By the severity of the weather."[25] The *Louisa*'s logkeeper expressed relief at finally rounding the continent's southern tip on 22 January 1827, 106 days out: "This day Considered owerselves Clear of Cape horn thank God for his Kind Protection and Safe Keeping."[26]

Much more serious than sore hands was "the scurvy, that cruel scourge of maritime life."[27] Together with impressment and flogging (and perhaps buggery as well), scurvy was one of the chief banes of a sailor's existence. It was described by the *Amethyst*'s logkeeper, who had tended not a few scorbutic shipmates off the Spanish Main:

The common appearances of the Scurvey are large discolour'd Spots dispers'd on the whole body swell'd legs, putrid gums and above all, an extraordinary lasitude of the whole body especially after any exercise however inconsiderable and this lasitude, at last degenerates into a proness to swoon or faint on the least exertion of strength, or even the least motion. The disease also is attended with a strange dejection of the spirits, and with shiverings, tremblings, and a disposition to be seiz'd with the most dreadful terror's on the slightest accident, indeed it was most remarkable in all our experience of this malidy that whatever discourag'd the people or at any time damp'd their hopes, never failed to add new vigiour to the distemper, for it usually Kill'd those who were in the last Stages of it, and confin'd them in their bed's, who were before capable of some kind of duty.[28]

Captain Cook's voyages had demonstrated that the disease could be contained, but it nevertheless persisted, albeit less lethally. The British navy adopted citrus fruits as antiscorbutics in 1793, but their effectiveness depended upon the time of picking and the method of preparation; unripe fruit contains less vitamin c, which, moreover, is inactivated by pickling, salting, fermenting, heating, contact with metals like copper and iron, and prolonged exposure to air and sunlight. Ninety-nine days out of Boston and rounding Cape Horn in mid-September 1815, the *Hamilton* recorded "several of the People attacked with Symtoms of the Scurvy." "The Moast of the Crew i am Afraid is got An light tutch of the scurvey," added the ship's log.[29] The Honolulu commercial agent of Bryant and Sturgis reported at the beginning of 1827 that "the Brig Active, Capt Cotting, 145 days from Boston touch[ed] here in distress with six of his crew bad with the scurvy."[30] When the *Columbia Rediviva*, Captain Kendrick, reached the Northwest Coast in 1788 it had lost two men to scurvy "and most of the rest of the Crew were in an advanced state of that malignant Distemper."[31] When the same ship made the coast again in 1791 under Captain Gray on its second voyage, one-fifth of the crew was in the "last stage" of the disorder. Seven hands were "in a very advanced state of the scurvy; indeed, their is scarce a person on board the ship but what has felt, more or less, the banefull effects of this dreadfull distemper."[32] Scurvy forced Portlock's *King George* and Dixon's *Queen Charlotte* to divert to the Hawaiian Islands for curatives en route to the coast in 1786, and the remainder of their venture was dogged by the disease. When they reached the coast in the spring of 1787, they rescued the *Nootka*, Captain Meares, who had lost thirty-six of his fifty men to this "dreadful disorder" while wintering in Prince William Sound, and Portlock had to lend Meares two men to enable him to make the salubrious Hawaiian Islands.[33] The crews of the *Prince of Wales* and the *Princess Royal* were "extremely sick" with scurvy when they put in to Nootka Sound in early July 1787 eight and one-half months out of England; of the *Prince of Wales*'s crew of thirty-five, there were "only Eight including every Body able to stand the deck."[34] Voyages to the Northwest Coast from Asia were equally scorbutic. One-half of Captain Strange's men were incapacitated by scurvy by the time his two ships made Nootka Sound from Bombay in 1786,[35] and in late 1790–early 1791, en route from Canton to the coast, the *Gustavus* had as many as eight or nine of its thirty-one men sick of the disease at one time, and four died of it.[36]

Victims were usually soon restored by fresh air and fresh food, including such popular antiscorbutics as wild celery, wild parsley, wild leeks, and especially the decoction called spruce beer or tea – "tea boiled from the green *Spruce* boughs sweetned with Molasses."[37] Captain Portlock recalled that "to a puncheon [a cask of seventy-two imperial gallons] of [spruce] beer three gallons and a half of molasses were added; it was afterwards worked with prepared yeast."[38] John Nicol was signed on the *King George* by Portlock expressly for his utility as a brewer of spruce beer.[39] The effectiveness of this elixir depended upon the freshness of the green leaf buds and the duration of boiling. A much more bizarre remedy was vertical burial up to the hips for several hours! (John Boit, fifth mate on the *Columbia Rediviva*'s 1790–93 voyage, "found this method of great service."[40]) On 20 January 1799 the *Hancock* stopped at the Juan Fernández Islands and four scorbutic crewmen were interred in "good Soil" for a day.[41] The servants of the HBC dreaded the painful and disfiguring effects of scurvy, such as swollen and bruised arms and legs, bloody joints, bleeding gums, burst blood vessels, and lost teeth. They resorted to berries, which are rich in ascorbic acid, and potatoes, especially immature ("green"), fresh ("new"), and uncooked tubers. Aboard the *Hancock* in late 1798 "the Cap[t] by the help of eating Raw Potatoes Got Rid of every symton of the Scurvy."[42] Some measures were futile, such as that tried by the *Hamilton* in the summer of 1815 in the middle Atlantic: "All hands employed washing there Cloaths in fresh water & Cleaning of themselves in hope to keep off the scurvey."[43]

ON THE COAST

The Northwest Coast itself posed the most formidable obstacles – in both physical and cultural terms – to a successful trading voyage.

Physically "this labyrinth of waters," which Governor George Simpson of the HBC rated "the most extraordinary course of inland navigation in the world,"[44] presented a number of navigational hazards: persistent rain ("dirty weather"), high winds ("strong weather"), thick fogs (particularly around the Queen Charlottes), frequent overcast, strong currents and tides, and hidden rocks, all of which were very demanding of sailing ships and crews. (Simpson rated the command of the HBC shipping on the Northwest Coast the most dangerous post in the company's entire service.[45]) One of the first shipmasters on the coast found that his vessel's progress was "much retarded by contrary and variable Winds, and by a thick fog, which prevented us from seeing the Land, and from advancing with safety."[46] The variable winds were especially "baffling," as the *Atahualpa* found in 1802: "It is certainly not a little remarkable that an adverse wind constantly attends us which ever way we are bound!"[47] The brig *Otter* was equally stymied in 1810: "Standing off and on Queen Charlottes Islands and can get in no where, the wind so baffling that it head us off on all tacks ... The wind seems to baffle us upon all tacks for as soon as we get near a harbour it is sure to blow right out and prevent our getting in."[48] Even after managing to enter a harbour, a ship might find "no bottom." And leaving could be no easier than entering, as the *Otter* discovered on 24 June 1810 in trying to quit Clemencitty in Portland Inlet:

About 2 P.M. we got out of the harbour and endeavoured to get up to Nass but the wind being so light made very little progress, at 4 it fell calm and the flood tide swept us into a bay about 2 miles to the Eastd. of Clemencettee and with difficulty we kept off the rocks with the Boat [cutter] ahead towing but getting into shoal water, we let go the Anchor in 4 1/2 fathoms on the top of a reef to prevent our driving farther in, lowered down the jolly Boat and sent the second mate in her to look for a better place to Anchor in for the night & which he found about a Cable's length from us, we carried out the kedge warped up to it and let got [*sic*: go] the Anchor in 8 fathoms at high water, at Midnight being then about low water & the ebb tide having caused the Vessel to swing round she rubbed her Larboard side against a reef of rocks, we immediately carried the kedge out astern and haul'd her clear of it without sustaining any damage, At 8 A.M. weighed the kedge and carried it out ahead hove the Anchor up and warped up to the kedge intending to get under weigh from it but the wind coming right in with a very thick fog at the same time we let go the Anchor again to wait a more favourable opportunity for getting out, the Second Mate employed sounding through a passage between a number of small Islands & the shore, having found it clear returned on board, & at noon we began to get under weigh with a fine breeze from the Southd. & Westd.[49]

Such conditions necessitated not a little towing and sweeping to prevent a ship from drifting onto rocks and shoals (Fig. 6). In this respect the experience of the *Atahualpa* on 22 June 1812 was not unusual:

Cloudy Weather & passing showers, at 4 PM 1 canoe came along side with [*sic:* from] Keegarney which place they left 10 days since. they informed us that there had no ship been there except Capt Nye [of the *New Hazard*] at 6 we got under way with a breeze from the s.w. found it impossible to steer the ship without the Boat. sent her a head & got out the sweeps – Through the night baffling winds all round the Compass. all hands employd Towing to keep the ship off of the Rocks as it was impossible to get the ship into any Bay to get the anchor down. the Current runing in every direction & the ship would not mind her Helm Morning & Latter part the same Ship within one mile of the Harbour. the Current set us down again at Meridian [noon] the Boat ahead & the sweeps out pulling to try to get some place to anchor but all to no effect pt Highfield [Stikine] bg NE 4 Miles dist. saw none of the Natives.[50]

The next day began in a similar vein: "Gloomy weather & baffling airs, ship drifting down very fast. all much fatigued, being all night & nearly all day pulling at the sweeps & Boat. at 2 a heavy squall from the s enabled us to get off this place."[51] Year-round ventures compounded these hazards, for, as a Bay man declared, "a winter voyage on that rugged, stormy coast is both dangerous and unpleasant."[52]

The intricate network of narrow, winding channels in the "straits" was particularly demanding. The supercargo of the *Atahualpa* reported to its owner in 1801 that "the navigation here is more hazardous and the business worse than I expected, especially the inland navigation. Sunken rocks, strong tides, fogs, calms, no bottom for anchoring, and a large proportion of bad weather, are among the difficulties we are obliged to combat."[53] One of the *Otter*'s officers had a similar reaction in 1810: "This inland Navigation is rendered both difficult & dangerous on account of the frequent calms in the summer time & the strong and irregular tides at all times occasioned by the numberless Islands & sounds that lays about here in all directions."[54] In the same year the *Hamilton* struggled first up and then down the "straits," as attested by its log:

Monday 25 June 1810 This day Begins With light & variable Winds & Cloudy Weather all hands Employed towing & sweeping Ship up towards stickeen [Stikine] …

Thursday 28 June 1810 All of this day light & variable Winds with rain and showers 3 p^m got under Way from stickeen bound down the strates & all hands employed striving for to get the ship down But all in vain for there was No tide seting down & the winds draw principally up the strates.[55]

It was not until 8 July that the ship was finally able to leave the labyrinth after much beating to windward in the face of stiff gales. The *Atahaulpa* was confounded by the variable currents in 1812. Its logkeeper wrote: "I think it rather improper to get under way on a calm as the Current sets in so many different directions that it is almost impossable to keep the Ship off shore."[56] As well as relying on Captain Vancouver's charts and each other's logs, shipmasters turned to local experts. The favourite pilot of Captain Charles Derby of the *Caroline* in 1801 was a Haida or Tlingit named Scotsi.[57] The *Otter* employed a Stikine Tlingit as a pilot for a month at the beginning of 1810.[58] As late as 1825 trading vessels were still using Indians as pilots in the "straits."[59]

No less formidable was the bar at the mouth of the Columbia, where half a dozen ships were lost in the period of the maritime fur trade. Many others were delayed for days and even weeks by the breakers. The *Union* spent the last two weeks of July 1795 trying to enter the river but "the attempt was vain as the elements appear'd to have conspir'd against us," there being "an immense swell upon the bars."[60]

The elements were hard on vessels and their equipment. One hundred and ninety-seven days out of Boston Ebenezer Dorr of the *Hope* recorded in 1791 that "our Brig is now become very fowl with very long grass and bare whales [strakes] and the bottom to all appearance is covered with long barnacles."[61] The Northwest Coast was particularly demanding. Captain Grimes of the *Owhyhee* reported in 1822 that because of "so much wet weather" a ship's wood, canvas, and rope mildewed and rotted quickly.[62] And mooring in unsheltered waters with little or no bottom cost many cables and anchors. "I think a Vessel never ought to come on this Coast without five Cable[s] & Anchors at least," declared an officer of the *Tally Ho* in 1826.[63] These and the other difficulties of coastal navigation were summarized by Lieutenant Aemelius Simpson after he reconnoitered the coast trade for the HBC in 1828:

The spirit of opposition has made them [American shipmasters] undertake the Navigation of the Coast at all Seasons, which has led to the loss of a few Vessels, and placed them all frequently in dangerous situations. Experience has now made the Masters of these Vessels generally good Pilots for the Coast, and given them a knowledge of many good Ports which they can run for when caught in bad weather. This is however frequently attended with difficulty and danger from the Thick Foggy Weather that generally prevails, and great rapidity of the Tides. They therefore use great caution in sailing from Port to Port, waiting always for a favourable state of wind and weather, but it sometimes happens notwithstanding their caution, that they experience Gales before they have reached their Port, which places them in situations which oblige them to work off a Lee Shore; it is therefore necessary to have a good sailing Vessel and to be well formed in Sails and Stores as upon that depends their safety. They are frequently obliged to anchor in very exposed situations and foul bottom, which sunders the Chain Cable the only one that can serve in such a case, and the Anchors cannot be of too good a quality. Captain [Seth] Barker [of the *Volunteer*] informed me that he has lost six Anchors within a few seasons, and a consideration which always cuts upon the mind and works forcibly upon the apprehensions of a crew when placed in a difficult situation upon this Coast is that if so unfortunate as to suffer Ship Wreck they have little chance to escape from a cruel death by the hands of the savage Natives, or at least being reduced to the sad alternative of becoming their Slaves.[64]

The natural hazards of navigation were seldom compounded by defects in the trading vessels, since most of the ships were "tight" and "stiff." Only occasionally did faulty construction or long service make for a leaky or "crank" (unsteady) ship. Insufficient ballast (usually stones) could also make a vessel crank, and groundings and tempests could cause leaks that damaged cargo. Outbound to the coast in late 1824–early 1825 the *Convoy* was "very wet" because of a leak in the forecastle, with the "pumps much choked with coal."[65] The *Hancock* was "very Crank and likewise very leaky."[66] The entry for 16 June 1799 in its log reads: "A heavy sailing Ship, Uncommon bad Winds, no getting about the Coast with Dispatch, the Season advancing fast, makes our Prospects very unfavorable for a good Voyage but still have hopes."[67] But this was not the rule. Most ships were more like the brig *Owhyhee*, which was rated "the best vessel that was ever on the coast" by one of its owners.[68] And they were well served by the charts and journals of Captain Vancouver, who meticulously surveyed the coastal waters in the first half of the 1790s, as well as by their own experience.[69] Consequently, despite the appreciable navigational dangers, shipwrecks were rare (although groundings were not). The losses of the *Borneo* in 1819 and the *Convoy* in 1836 or 1837 with all hands and cargo were exceptional.[70]

The coastal elements had an adverse effect not only on ships but on their crews as well. The "dreary and inhospitable" tenor of "this

Wretched, Savage coast," "these Barberous coasts," the "wildest of the wild," depressed the spirits of some Nor'westmen.[71] "It is one vast wilderness and unbroken solitude," lamented one.[72] Another, Captain John Meares, wrote: "The American continent, in almost every part, presents nothing to the eye but immense ranges of mountains or impenetrable forests ... In some places the country appears to be level on the coast, but still the eye soon finds itself checked by steep hills and mountains, covered, as well as every part of the low-land, with thick woods down to the margin of the sea."[73] Nor'west Coast-men particularly decried the gloomy weather and the looming mountains. Most, like Joseph Ingraham, found that the "CLIMATE is exceedingly Temperate for the parrellel of Latt[d] ... [i]t is however very much subject to sudden changes & heavy Rains."[74] The *Rob Roy*, experienced "almost a continual gale of wind with rain & fog" from 3 July through 12 July 1822 at Tongass; and at the same harbour in the last two weeks of September and the first week of October the brig was beset by "heavy gales" and "torrents of rain."[75] The latter spell ended with a gale which the local Indians said "was as strong as they ever [k]new it":

During the night heavy Gales from the s.e. and morning commences with the Same. as we found She had drifted some at 8 Gale Freshens let go the best bower [anchor] and lowered Top Gallant Masts from 9 to 12 the Gale increased to a hurricane, the Brig still drifting with 3 anchors ahead sent down Fore & Main Yards. at 10 the vessel was very near the shore and must inevitably have gone on had not the Gale moderated in the afternoon more moderate but very heavy Squalls ends the same in the forenoon the wind blew in whirlwinds with heavy showers of rain & a pretty heavy swell the wind took the water up & blew it in sheets so that it resembled a snow storm & in the squalls the men in the tops could scarcely hold on.[76]

After the *Mentor*'s logkeeper transferred to the *Rob Roy* on 7 March 1823, he did not record a rainless day until 3 April.[77] Hence the reaction of an officer of the *Otter*, which – unfortunately in terms of both weather and trade – arrived on the coast in the autumn of 1809: "On this coast it is said to rain or snow three fourths of the Year and we have reason to believe it, for since we first made the land it has been snowing or raining seven eights of the time, we see the Sun perhaps once or twice a week and then not more than half an hour at a time."[78] Then one day "in the Morning the weather was Clear which opened to our view a range of high Mountains on each Side of us, there tops covered with Snow the Other parts with Spruce & Hemlock Trees down to the water's edge."[79] The towering mountains seemed more ominous in the less open "straits," where they were higher and barer:

we saw the land plainly made sail & stood on, the Straits growing narrower as we proceed to the Northd. & the immense height of the Mountains on each side Makes the distance from shore to shore look to be one half less than it really is, these Mountains assume a very different appearance from any that we have [seen] on any other part of the Coast, here they are destitute of trees except a few round the bottom, the middle parts are covered with a kind of turf, heath & a variety of bushes, their peaks are generally bare craggy rocks, very high & covered with snow, In the vallies, or rather gullies, are large beds of solid ice.[80]

Two days later the *Otter* "left Gillcat [Chilkat] astern of us I hope never to see it again."[81]

The spirits of the "Boston men" were lowered further by the extreme isolation and the monotonous routine, particularly if their ship remained on the coast over the winter, when there was less trade and worse weather. Occasional accidents and illnesses did not help. The log of the *Hamilton* records the following incident at Taddiskey on 18 January 1810: "william oating and addmiram [?] allen onshore cuting wood & the formers ax sliped & wounded the latter in the leg verry deep in to the bone."[82] Mr Allen survived this deep cut and returned to work a month later. Then on 2 November "addmiram allen assisting the Carpenters & the ax glanced and Wounded him bad in the ankle," and he did not return to duty until three weeks later.[83] Similarly, on 26 June 1817 John Groot of the *Alert* had his left leg broken by a falling tree while cutting wood ashore, and a week later his shipmate George Brown was seriously injured by a fall from a cask in the hold.[84]

The most prevalent diseases seem to have been venereal and respiratorial, the latter being promoted by the dankness of the coast. During the *Mentor*'s two trading seasons (1817–18) on the coast nearly every day one man, and sometimes two or three, was "in the sick list."[85] For most of the 1822 trading season from three to seven of the men of the *Owhyhee* were "most of the time sick" with violent colds, chest pains, or headaches, and Captain Grimes himself was "quite unwell and lame with rheumatism"; two hands died of tuberculosis.[86] The crew of the *Convoy* was decimated by disease in 1825. On 30 July Captain William McNeill reported "[Thomas] Low sick and off duty, who I fear has lost the sight of his eye entirely, having had the Venereal and Small Pox and I think it impossible to cure him."[87] By 2 September there were "five hands off duty and the Cook unwell, making our crew the weakest ever on the coast, having but Seven White Men in the Forecastle altogether and Four of them sick."[88] At New Archangel it took Russian newcomers two years to become "creolized," that is, acclimatized; meanwhile, they were "constantly" ailing.[89]

Mental disease was less common. During the winter of 1805–06 Captain Samuel Hill of the *Lydia* was not infrequently "sick and cross," with the result that there was less trading with the Indians and much discontent (to the point of mutiny) among the crew. He stopped the crew's allowance of grog and kept the best victuals for himself, his Hawaiian mistress, and his officers; he also sailed his ship carelessly and allowed too many Indians on board without enough supervision.[90] One of the officers complained that "when any person gets sick all the relief he can get is his allowance [rations] stopped," adding wryly that "Skipper Hill says it is impossible for a person to be sick in so healthy a climate but he has had his fill of it this last winter."[91] Evidently twice as much beef and pork were issued to the *Lydia's* eight officers as to the remaining sixteen hands.[92]

The latter, however, were better off than the crew of the *Hamilton* in 1821; at the end of May thirteen of them refused to work until they were given something besides salted halibut to eat.[93] Sometimes a vessel's provisions, especially salted meat, were spoiled by bacteria, vermin, or pests. Captain McNeill of the *Lama*, for instance, recorded on 31 May 1833: "P.M. sent the Powder on board the Dryad [a sister ship] & closed the Hatches for Smokeing having a great number of Mice on board destroying property of every kind."[94] Fresh foodstuffs – fish, deer, wildfowl – were available on the coast, but they were not always abundant. And mussels had to be used with care. In 1793 several of Captain Vancouver's crewmen were seized with mussel poisoning, and one died, and in 1799 from 115 to 135 of the RAC's essential Aleut sea-otter hunters succumbed to toxic mussels in Chatham Strait.[95]

A crewman's woes were occasionally worsened by a draconian captain, even though the latter had been admonished to be firm but fair. As Bryant and Sturgis told Captain James Harris of the *Lascar* in 1820: "Put the Crew on regular allowance and take care that they have full weight and measure. We earnestly desire you to treat them well – give them good language and good usage and they must be very bad if they make any difficulty. The success of the voyage depends very much on preserving peace & harmony on board & should you find any one particularly troublesome endeavor to get rid of him at the [Hawaiian] Islands and pay him off."[96] The same owners likewise warned Captain George Clark of the *Borneo* in 1817: "We would strongly impress on your mind, the necessity of regular discipline and perfect harmony, discord among officers has ruined many voyages, & it is to be particularly deprecated on such long ones as the present."[97] Bryant and Sturgis were insistent that "if you have any troublesome men or useless officers get rid of them soon as possible"[98] – meaning their discharge on the Hawaiian Islands, which very soon after Euroamerican contact became a dumping ground for malcontents and miscreants. Not a few crewmen were likewise discharged at Canton.

A shipmaster's ire could be aroused by illicit trading on the part of his men, who were expressly forbidden by their contracts to traffic on their own with the Indians. Both the sailors and the officers received wages, and the latter in addition shared in the proceeds of the voyage, their share varying with their rank. Because of their arrangement, it was in the officers' best interest to prevent private trading by the crewmen. On 4 June 1805 at Chuckenhoo (or Chucknahoo, the summer village of the Kasaan Tlingits) on Clarence Strait, Captain Porter of the *Atahualpa* discovered and confiscated 119 seaotter tails, 14 cub skins, and 2 prime skins which six hands had smuggled. The culprits "forfited their wages after three longe years hard Labour and Excessive fatigue."[99]

Most skippers seem not to have been overly heavy-handed. Perhaps the most notable exception was the *Lydia*'s Captain Samuel Hill (the father, incidentally, of the actor Yankee Hill). When a new first mate, Mr David Nye (who in 1810 was to become the unpopular master of the *New Hazard*), was obtained from the *Pearl* in the late winter of 1805–06, he was told by Captain Hill that "we was a damd Set of Rascals & he must treat us as such, he also told him he must knock us down with handsp[ike]s."[100] The same master was on the coast in 1810 in the *Otter*, and on 8 September he "flogged three men, the first for not rigging the royal yard right, the second for not sending the F.T.N. Std. sail tack down clear, the third because he told a kynackie [Hawaiian Islander] to strike 8 bells when it was but 7."[101] Captain James Bennett of the *Lydia* was denounced by one seaman, who wrote: "Pardon me if you think I go to[o] far with Capt Bennet, But I don't vary from the Truth – No man can form an Idea of his behavior. I make bold to say he is not capable of being Master of a vessel of any description – he treats all men with the greatest contempt particularly those in his powers."[102]

Shipboard discipline was strict, even harsh, particularly for such offences as falling asleep on the watch or getting drunk and cursing the captain.[103] The latter was usually prompted by the hard duty, as when the crew of the *Hamilton* spent Christmas Day of 1820 clearing the deck and sails of snow and fetching broomsticks ashore.[104] Even minor infractions were severely punished. On 22 September 1817 two crewmen of the *Mentor* "floged the cook From not cooking the Fish well," and on 21 May of the following year a crewman was tied to a starboard gun and given eighteen lashes "on the Bear Botem with a Cat and nin tails" by Captain Suter and then put in irons for flying into a rage and threatening another crewman.[105] Again, on 25 April 1820 Captain Dixey Wildes of the *Paragon*, homeward bound towards Boston, "gave the Cook one dozen lashes with a Cat for dirty Cooking."[106] Occasionally a skipper went too far, even by the standards of the time. In 1822 Bryant and Sturgis relieved Captain James Harris of the command of the *Lascar* for being "unnecessarily severe in the treatment of his officers & crew." Captain Harris had maltreated a cabin boy, and the owners advised the master not to return to Boston, where he would undoubtedly face a lawsuit, for during his absence from the city another skipper had been fined $4,000 in damages, plus court costs, for abusing a cabin boy.[107] A shipmaster's tyranny often resulted from his own drunkenness. The *Hope's* Captain Joseph Ingraham, for instance, was a "rum drinker" who was sufferable only "when he remains a sober man."[108]

In all fairness to the shipmasters, however, by the 1820s Nor'west crewmen were evidently less obedient and less competent than during the early years of the coast trade. Indeed it was for this reason that more and more Hawaiians were hired in lieu of Euroamericans. The Honolulu agent of Marshall and Wildes reported at the end of 1821 that "Capt Grimes [of the *Pedlar*] will be obliged to ship whoever he can get, good or bad and at high wages,"[109] and the following year Captain Brewster of the *Parthian* told the same owners that "every vessel has had more or less difficulty" hiring able seamen.[110] Also in 1822 Marshall and Wildes were informed by Captain Grimes (now of the *Owhyhee*) that his men were unruly and inept and that "in fact no vessel on the coast but what has had a great deal of trouble."[111] The logkeeper of the *Rob Roy*, which spent the winter of 1822–23 on the coast, blamed the "Corporeal Sistem Long nights & short days & rainy weather people tired & jealous of each other etc.," and he concluded that "in truth a vessell on this coast is a perfect hell to any person that is any ways peaceably inclined for the grumbling of crews (who ought to be shot) quarrels between the officers jealousy of others and an hundred other things make it worse than it really is."[112]

Whoever or whatever was to blame, the result was the same – occasional desertions and mutinies. Captain John Crocker managed the *Jenny* with such "club law" in 1802 that part of his crew deserted at Sitka, forcing him to leave the coast for the Hawaiian Islands for

replacements, and he got only 150 skins.[113] Of the fifty-four men who
served on the *Sultan* during its three-year voyage of 1821–24, one
left the ship at Sitka, one drowned at Tongass, and ten deserted
(seven at Honolulu and three at Acapulco).[114] Of the eighteen hands
of the *Convoy*, four jumped ship at Robinson Crusoe's Juan Fernández
Islands and two at Oahu en route to the coast in 1825.[115] Deserters,
however, risked slavery or death at the hands of the Natives, and they
could be replaced by Hawaiians. Perhaps for these reasons rebellious
hands seem to have preferred mutiny, although mutineers often eventually recanted and rejoined their ship, mutiny being a capital
offence. Captain Meares's 1788–89 voyage in the *Felice Adventurer* was
twice disrupted by mutiny in Nootka Sound, and on the second occasion eight ringleaders were put ashore; the mutineers were impatient
to "change the desart shore of Nootka, and the nauseating customs
of its inhabitants" for the delights of the Hawaiian Islands.[116] The
large (600-ton) French coaster *La Flavie*, flying the new tricolour flag
of the First Republic and seeking La Pérouse as well as furs (primarily
for liquor), was struck by mutinies at Petropavlovsk in 1792 and
Nootka Sound in 1793 which echoed the revolution, the mutineers
promising to submit their grievances to the new National Assembly
upon their return. At the beginning of May 1799 in Sitka Sound
thirteen crewmen of the *Hancock*, Captain Crocker, mutinied and left
the vessel; after a week in Tlingit territory six of them gratefully
returned, and the rest were eventually taken on by the American
cutters *Caroline* and *Dragon* and the Russian brig *Oryol*.[117] Also in
1799 the chief mate of the *Ulysses* led a "long and ruinous" revolt
against Captain Lamb until his vessel fell in with two other Boston
ships, whose skippers restored Lamb to command and confined the
mutineers.[118] The unstable Captain Hill nearly triggered a mutiny
aboard the *Lydia* in mid-December 1805 by discontinuing the rum
allowance.[119] In mid-October 1810 in Cocklane's Harbour there was
a mutiny aboard the same ship, now commanded by Captain Bennett, but it was suppressed with the help of the *Hamilton*, Captain
Porter.[120] Earlier that year several hands had rebelled on the *Guatimozin* but had returned to duty after a few days ashore.[121] Those
members of the *Mentor*'s crew who mutinied in November 1818 had
the good judgment to do so at Honolulu,[122] where both nature and
society were more hospitable than on the coast.

By the 1820s Nor'west crews had become even more unruly. Twice
within two days at the beginning of 1821 some hands on the *Hamilton*
refused to go "clambing" (clam gathering) on shore, and for three
days at the end of May thirteen crewmen refused to work until they

had something – such as rice – besides "Salt Halibot" to eat (they
were confined below deck until they relented from a want of fresh
air).[123] En route to the coast in 1822, Captain Samuel Chandler of
the *Pearl* "shot two men dead on board the Brig on the passage out
for mutiny and set some ashore at the Gallapagoss Islands."[124] In 1823
the *Mentor* was struck by mutiny again on March 11: "This day be it
remembered one of the crew of this ship took a loaded musket from
the arm chest forward with an intention to shoot the Captain [George
Newell] his name was Boston & in fact their was a mutiny on board
and in fact the whole of the sailors forward used very thortning
[obstructive] language language which would hang the whole of them
... Crawley struck the Capt once or twice & swore no man on board
should go in Irons also they swore revenge."[125] On 13 June in Clarence
Strait there was "a serious mutiny" aboard the *Owhyhee*, and two days
later one of the mutineers died "in consequence of the banging [beat-
ing] he received."[126] Captain Grimes reported to Marshall and Wildes
in mid-1822 that there were "no vessels on the coast but what has
had a great deal of trouble" with seamen who "resorted to pistols
knives axes & clubs."[127] Earlier that year at Whampoa several intoxicated *Arab* hands rebelled, complaining of mistreatment.[128] As late
as 1838 some crewmen of the HBC steamship *Beaver* refused duty to
protest serving under a foreign master, Captain William McNeill, an
American citizen.[129]

The Northwest Coast Indians, however, proved more intractable
than the crews of the trading vessels. Indeed the two most formidable
problems facing Nor'westmen arose on the coast itself, and they were
not unrelated: the rapid depletion of sea otters and the even more
rapid deterioration of Euroamerican-Indian relations. Initially the
Natives were curious, polite, and friendly – "a quiet inoffensive People
... naturally of a very peaceable disposition," according to Lieutenant
Puget.[130] The Euroamericans were as impressed with their honesty
and fairness in trade as they were with their skill in woodworking,
their devotion to their children, and the chastity of their wives and
daughters (they were just as unimpressed, incidentally, with the
stench of their houses, the picking and eating of one another's body
lice, and the disfigurement of labreted women, who earned the epi-
thet of "wooden lips" or "loblips" – whence Loblip [Milbanke] Sound).
From the beginning of contact, however, each side regarded the other
as socially, economically, spiritually, and artistically inferior. The
Euroamericans unquestionably felt racially superior, for the Natives
were after all not quite white in colour and certainly not Christian
in belief, and their inferiority was ostensibly confirmed by their lack

of farming and smelting, their inability to write, and their personal filthiness and shamelessness. Captain Cleveland referred to the northern Indians as "the most disgusting set of beings I ever saw."[131]

The attitude of common sailors was probably even less charitable, simply because their own ignorance begat prejudice. In the words of the logkeeper of the sealer *Amethyst*:

I have often heard the Character of Seamen very much extolled but experience teaches me the sad reverse. I am let [*sic*: led] to believe that this [*sic*: their] Humanity does not reach further than their Sunday. Viz Five leagues [15 miles] at Sea. and I think it may justly be accounted for in this way. They are the most ignorant Class of People in Existance and must remain so having no means for information. As soon as they are off the Ocean they are plung'd in intoxication, and vice in the most dirty places in City's and Towns and among their own Class of beings. It is absolutely impossible that Brutal Ignorance should be accepted for refined sentiments.[132]

At the Hawaiian Islands one of Captain Cook's officers, John Williamson, noted "yᵉ great wantonness of the inferior people on board a ship, & yᵉ idea they possess that it is no harm to kill an indian [Native]" (he said this by way of explaining why he had given strict orders to the men in his longboat not to fire on the Hawaiians without his express permission).[133] The Spanish naturalist José Moziño, who spent five months at Nootka Sound in 1792 (and who, like his countrymen, seems to have had a more enlightened view of the Indians, if only because they had much less commercial connection with them), wrote that "the sailors [of the fur trading vessels], either as a result of their almost brutal upbringing or because they envied the humane treatment the [Spanish] commandant [Bodega y Quadra] and other officers always gave the natives, insulted them at various times, crippled some and wounded others, and did not fail to kill several."[134] So whenever the Indians insisted upon being treated as equals, either in commercial or social situations, they were considered "saucy" or "daring and insolent" by their Euroamerican customers, who forgot that they had come to the Natives, not vice versa; conversely, those Indians who submitted were deemed "civil." Similarly, because they did not labour constantly and regularly, let alone hurriedly, the Indians were regarded as "indolent and lazy." Perceptions did vary, however. In 1792 the Salish chief Tetacu (or Tetacus, or Tetacui), "one of the most feared chiefs among those who live on these coasts [of the straits of Juan de Fuca and Georgia]," was given passage from Neah Bay to Esquimalt by the Spanish schooner *Mexicana*. This encounter led the Spaniards "to draw very different inferences about these Indians from what up to the present time voyagers have said about them. What they call ferocious treachery only seemed to us to be bold manliness." They added that Chief Tetacu enjoyed "the greatest respect and authority" by virtue of his "valour" and "talents."[135]

Prejudice rationalized abuse, which, moreover, was seemingly justified by the higher and higher prices demanded by the "savages" for their furs, as well as by their penchant for petty theft, their reliance on sneak attack, and their indulgence in slavery and, supposedly, cannibalism.[136] What one of Captain Cook's officers termed their "happy genius in the art of pilfering" seldom failed to gall and sometimes enrage shipmasters.[137] (Cook himself declared that the Nootkas were "as light fingered as any people we had before met with," and Captain King agreed that "we never met with more audacious theives," although he found them more persistent and cunning than adroit.[138]) The following comment by Captain John Green of the *Empress of China* on the thievishness of the crewmen of the French brig *La Jengat* at the Cape Verde Islands in 1786 would also have fit the coastal Indians: "These fellows are St. Peter's children – every finger a fish-hook, and their hand a grapnel."[139] Captain Meares marvelled at their prowess as petty thieves: "The natives [of Prince William Sound] ... never failed to exert their very extraordinary talents in the art of thievery. They would employ such a slight of hand in getting iron materials of any kind, as is hardly to be conceived. It has often been observed when the head of a nail either in the ship or boats stood a little without the wood, that they would apply their teeth in order to pull it out."[140] The larceny of the Indians also struck the very first American coasters, who found that the Chinooks "were a smart sett of active fellows but like all others without one exception on this Coast are addicted to thefts."[141] The *Rob Roy* was victimized by the Newhitty Indians in 1823: "They are the greatest thieves on the Coast yesterday they cut off & stole our Mizen Royal Sheets [sails] & clue line [a rope attached to the lower corner of a sail] on Larboard [port side] & cut away our main sheets clost up to the chocks & carried away the locks & thimble & our two gun aprons."[142] Captain Portlock, too, learned that the Natives "made no scruple of thieving." He added, however, that they stole "not only from strangers, but from one another," and he was certain that "with them thieving with dexterity is rather thought a grace than a disgrace; and the complete thief is a clever fellow, but the bungling pilferer is less admired."[143] Most commanders overlooked what Portlock regarded as "these trifling depredations,"[144] but some reacted violently.

From the standpoint of the Indians the trading vessels in their waters were drift liable to salvage, and they regarded the Euroamericans' cutting of wood and drawing of water on their shores as theft of their property, as well as trespass on their territory.[145] (Captain Cook was astonished by the possessiveness of the Nootkas: "I have no w[h]ere met with Indians who had such high notions of every thing the Country produced being their exclusive property as these."[146]) The result was much irritation, some tension, and occasional bloodshed. Witness an incident aboard the *Hamilton* on 12 July 1820 at Newhitty, Queen Charlotte Strait: "All Hands buizyly imployed tending trade & seting up fore Riging and giting reddy for sea one of the indins stole The carpenters rasp & was cot in the act in giting it From him made a bustle with the rest of the indins one pointed his musket at the carpenter and one or two others drew daggers Capt martain ordered the Guns cleared away which was in reddyness every man instantly Seized thear arms the indins was silanced without Any further difficulty."[147] A similarly volatile situation developed on board the *Rob Roy* on 10 April 1822 off Hoodsnahoo:

This day an unfortrunate affair happened on board our Brig it was this [Chief] Cowell was leaning over the side bargaining, for a hat with a fellow in a Canoe A 2nd Mate (Lampher) was standing by the side of him he (Lampher) observed to him he offered too much and Cowell said to him Chi ee a word which they use in a number of ways – contempt – not good etc when Lampher put his hand on him whether in anger or not I do not know – Cowell shoved him off Lampher got mad and pulled down his hair which was tied on top of his head and struck him, the pulling their hair is a thing they never will forgive and a disgrace which nothing but blood will wipe away Cowell was very mad and talked a grate deal about it ... he now tells him *frankly* he shall kill him the first opportunity. he is a great fighting character, and has killed a number for a less offence than this and will probably make true his words if he has a good opportunity, – a bad affair.[148]

Incidentally, the same officer, Mr Lampher, a month later was "put in irons for refusing to do duty before the mast and being saucy to the Captain," and he then "acknowledged he had done every thing he could to make difficulty between the Capt & crew," and at his own request he was transferred to the *Hamilton* on 16 May.[149] The *Rob Roy*'s logkeeper added that several years earlier at Nass the second mate and the boatswain of the *Hamilton* had been killed by the Tsimshians following a similar act of folly: "It was occasioned by the Clerks striking an Indian while trading with him."[150]

To common sailors in particular, with their plebeian prejudices and superstitions, the Indians – swarthy, tattooed, painted, greased, labreted, half naked, lousy, guttural, head-flattened – must have appeared savage and menacing.[151] Conversely, the fair Euroamericans with their outlandish attire, peculiar foods (especially salt) and beverages, gigantic boats, and noisy, smoky cannons and muskets must have seemed just as strange and fearsome. The American trader William Sturgis, who strongly empathized with the Indians, recollected a conversation with Chief Altatsee in this vein:

Their fancy for many articles could be traced to a desire to imitate their somewhat more polished [Euroamerican] visitors, and the absurdity, if any there was, lay in the manner in which they used them. When attacked upon this point they would dryly refer to some of our usages as equally absurd with their own. Talking one day upon such matters with Altadsee, a sarcastic old chief of the Hanslong tribe, I ridiculed the practice of covering their own & their childrens' garments with rows of brass & gilt button, & loading them with old keys to be kept bright at a great expence of labour. "Why," said he, "the white men wear buttons." "True," I replied, "but they are useful to us; the fashion to our garments requires buttons to secure them." "Ah," said he, "perhaps it is so; but I could never discover the usefulness of half a dozen buttons upon your coat tails; and, as for the waste of labour in scouring old keys, you are right; it is very foolish, and almost as ridiculous as the fashion, which I am told prevails in your country, of placing brass balls upon iron fences in front of your houses, to be polished every day & tarnished every night." "Truly," he added, "Eiyets Hardi & Hanslong Hardi cootnanong coonung." ("White people & Hanslong people are equally foolish.")

Sturgis added that "they have the good sense, Aye, and the good taste, too, to leave the female form in all its beautiful & graceful proportions, as it was fashioned by the great Creator, and neither destroy symmetry by artificial expansion, nor sacrifice health & endanger life by unnatural contraction."[152]

So it did not take much to create misunderstanding, suspicion, distrust, and enmity. The potential for conflict was mentioned by an American seaman during a visit to Nasparti Inlet in 1791: "On my landing, I gave positive orders to the boats crew, not to offer the least umbrage to the natives: and I verily believe they did not, though no doubt it is too often the case that sailors, when no officer is with them; from their ignorance of the language, either miscomprehend the natives, or the natives them; thus each deeming the other insulted, a quarrel ensues, and the officers who are on shore fall a sacrifice to it. as well in civilized, so in savage governments; from small causes, great evils spring."[153] Perhaps because the Euroamericans were "transient traders" they were wont to treat the Natives more callously and brutally than if, like the land fur traders, they had to live among them permanently; indeed probably most of the shipmasters and their hands did not make more than one visit to the coast. At any rate, owing to white mistreatment, the initial hospitality and friendliness of the Indians soon changed to antipathy and outright hostility. In addition, once the Euroamericans were no longer novel they were regarded as members of distant tribes and potential enemies, and as such they were fair game for theft or even murder.[154]

As the terms of trade changed dramatically on the coast in favour of the Indians because of intense competition (much more so than in the interior, where there was much less competition, and virtually none after 1821), Euroamerican ignorance, arrogance, and cupidity spawned a variety of abuses: the selling of defective goods, the seizure of skins, and the kidnapping of chiefs to force trade or to obtain ransom (in skins). Francois Péron, who was on the coast in 1796 as chief officer under Captain Ebenezer Dorr of the *Otter*, asserted that the acquisition of Indian furs by force or deceit and the excessive severity of Euroamerican punishment of Native misdemeanours or insults, real or imagined, were the causes of Indian hostility.[155] "They are a people more 'sinned against' than 'sinning'," declared William Sturgis, one of the most experienced and enlightened shipmasters.[156] The Natives, he said, were "victims of injustice, cruelty, and oppression, and of a policy that seems to recognize *power* as the sole standard of *right*." He explained white brutality:

Should I recount all the lawless & brutal acts of white men upon the Coast you would think that those who visited it had lost the usual attributes of humanity, and such indeed seemed to be the fact. The first expeditions were fitted out from different ports in India & China, and entrusted to such men as could be picked up ready to undertake a hazardous adventure. These were often men of desperate fortunes, lawless & reckless, who, on finding themselves beyond the pale of civilization and accountable to no one, pursued their object without scruple as to the means, and indulged every brutal propensity without the slightest restraint. They carried with them the general feeling in regard to Indians; considered them little better than brutes, and treated them accordingly. I do not exaggerate when I say that some among them would have shot an Indian for his garment of Sea Otter skins with as little compunction as he would have killed the animal from whom the skins were originally taken. The conduct of such men could not fail to provoke the vengeance of the natives, and give rise to the deadly feuds that followed. But even men of a different stamp – men whose general conduct elsewhere was irreproachable, and who would have shrunk with horror from shedding the blood of a white man, did not hesitate to take the life of an Indian for an offence which would scarce have called forth more than a rebuke had the offender been of their own colour.

Sturgis added that although "some who were engaged in this trade treated the Indians like human beings and kept up amicable intercourse with them," the general result was "the injustice, violence and bloodshed which has marked the progress of this intercourse from first to last."[157]

The Indians themselves were not innocents, as when they tried to sell water as oil to the *Hamilton* at Newhitty in 1820: "At 5 [p.m.] saw a number Of canoes coming acrost the [Queen Charlotte] sound up bord nets & begun trade In passing the kelp [containers of fish oil] in bord 1 bursted which happened to be Filled with water afterwards found a number in the same Manner stop trade ordered the indins un shore untill Morning."[158] The Nootkas had similarly tried to cheat Captain Cook's men by filling bladders of fish and train oil with water.[159] George Simpson was more condemnatory of Indian cheating. He wrote: "The natives ... still occasionally resort to fraud, practising every trick and devise to cheat their trader. One favourite artifice is to stretch the tails of land-otters unto those of sea-otters. Again, when a skin is rejected as being deficient in size, or defective in quality, it is immediately, according to circumstances, enlarged, or coloured, or pressed to order, and then is submitted, as a virgin article, to the buyer's criticism by a different customer. In short, these artists of the northwest could dye a horse with any jockey in the civilized world, or 'freshen up' a faded sole with the most ingenious and unscrupulous of fishermongers."[160] But the Natives were outdone by their visitors. Captain Vancouver deplored the cheating of the Indians by unscrupulous traders, and particularly the introduction of firearms. He found in 1793 that sometimes the Natives would "loudly complain" that "they had been illtreated in their traffic with white men," receiving faulty goods in exchange for their own of the "very best quality." Some muskets "burst into pieces on being fired," wounding or killing the holder, and "these defects have not arisen from ignorance or mismanagement on the part of the Indians, but from the baseness of the metal and imperfect workmanship of the firearms." Vancouver added:

Many of the traders from the civilized world have not only pursued a line of conduct, diametrically opposite to the true principles of justice in their commercial dealings, but have fomented discords, and stirred up contentions, between the different tribes, in order to increase the demand for these destructive engines. They have been likewise eager to instruct the natives in the use of European arms of all descriptions; and have shewn by their own example, that they consider gain as the only object of pursuit; and whether this be acquired by fair and honorable means, or otherwise, so long as the advantage is secured, the manner how it is obtained seems to have been, with too many of them, but a very secondary consideration.[161]

There is a touch of hypocrisy to Vancouver's complaint, however, for the *Rob Roy* was told in 1822 by the Haidas of Kaigani that they had paid the renowned navigator twenty skins for a musket which broke the first time it was fired.[162] They also said that the first trading vessel to come to Kaigani had been given ten prime skins for an iron pot which broke the first time it was put on a fire.[163]

Some shipmasters were not above such forms of deceit as short measure and adulteration (admixing, diluting). On 2 April 1806 at Taddiskey the local Haidas, who had been "tradeing briskly for Bread & Powder," became "verry angry" when they discovered that the *Lydia*'s Captain Hill was putting rope yarns in the bottoms of powder kegs, and the next day they refused to trade.[164] Two months later at Nass "the Natives tells him [Hill] He puts So mutch water in his Mols. [molasses] that they dont Like it they only ask him the same he gives at other places but he tells them No."[165] The unrepentant Hill was back on the coast in the *Otter* in 1810, and at the beginning of that year at Cumshewa's Harbour [Cumshewa Inlet] in the Queen Charlottes "the Indians came on board and began to barter their Skins for sundry Articles but as they pay more regard to quaintity than quality our molasses suits them best after it has had a large proportion of salt water put in it as we can then afford to give them two buckets full instead of one."[166]

Kidnapping and hijacking were two of the ruthless means to a furry end. Several times one hapless Haida chief, Altatsee, was enticed aboard ship, clapped in irons, and ransomed for skins.[167] Another Haida chief, Cow (or Keow), complained in 1799 and 1802 that in 1795 Captain William Wake of the *Prince William Henry* had imprisoned him and two other chiefs and ransomed each of them for 200 skins.[168] In June of the same year Captain John Boit of the *Union* seized a chief on the Queen Charlottes "for fear they [the Natives, who had "many skins ... but ... would not sell them"] wou'd not come of[f] again."[169] Sullivan Dorr rebuked Captains Crocker of the *Hancock* and Breck of the *Dispatch* for their unscrupulousness. "Crocker and Breck are such," he wrote, "that they should not have

charge of a Ship ... they ... had [been] taught ... to get skins by all
means, if not one way they must another, but skins they must have
by all means ... Crocker ... declared if he went on the coast and could
make a voyage by no other means he would by forceing them [the
Indians] to trade."[170] In 1802 at Masset on the Queen Charlottes
several Haida chiefs who were visiting the Philadelphia schooner
Hetty were abducted by Captain Jona Briggs and ransomed for 100
skins.[171] The captain was probably frustrated by the heavy competition that year, which saw eighteen vessels on the coast; indeed by May
he had obtained only 100 skins and at the end of the season he took
only 450 to Canton.[172] Captain Sturgis recalled that "Cunneaw, Cow
and Altatsee the principal chiefs on the Coast they [shipmasters] tre-
panned [lured] on board their ships, and, having seized and even
laid some of them in irons, forced them contrary to every principle
of honour or humanity to deliver up their Skins before they would
give them their liberty." He added that "this was the way some people,
not worthy of the name of Men (and who I thank Heaven cannot
call themselves Americans), took to make their fortunes."[173]

Notwithstanding Sturgis's comment, ruthlessness knew no national
distinctions. Captain Hill, an American, was perhaps the worst case.
In late May 1806 at Masset "at 2 PM Skipper Hill detained Six of the
Natives & told them they must Get him twenty Skins fifteen for a
man that fired upon us at Cassarn & five for what Some of the
Natives Stole themselves ... at 7 PM four Canoes came & fetched the
twenty Skins & gave them to Skipper Hill & he let the Six Prisoners
goe."[174] Captain Hill's misconduct during the next couple of days is
documented in the supercargo's log:

Sunday [May 25] Massett These 24 Hours Commences with heavy gales from
the Westward & pleasant Weather at 9 am Hove up & in Coming out the
Natives fired at us but did not reach us we in return gave them a broadside
into the Village in Standing over to the Southern Shore we got a ground &
laid there till flood tide ... we backed off & Came to ... & give them a couple
of big guns at 7 PM 1 Canoe Came alongside to trade he bought too tails
[worth] of Rum for brasskey [molasses] then he [Captain Hill] got his double
barrel Musket & his third officer with a blunderbuss on the Quarter [deck]
& told them to hand in their skins or he would fire into them they handed
up 5 Prime Skins 3 Cubbs & 9 tails he in return gave them 5 buckets of
Molasses & 1 musket presently after there Came another Canoe with four
Natives he got 6 Skins & 7 Tails & made them a present of two buckets of
molasses ... at 10 PM weighed main Sail & tacked out the Natives fired Smartly
at us but to no purpose ... Monday 26 ... at 6 PM Came to off Skidanis village
[Skedans] ... we had not been long at an anchor before the Natives Came

off to see us in a whale boat about a dozen of them the Cabin supper being
ready Skipper Hill invited too of them to Sup with him he then went down
he & his officers & the too Indians & Sent for three hands to come down
into the Cabin three Hands went & he told the too Indians they were Prisoners that they must fetch off the four guns that belonged to Capt Robertses
Schooner [the *Resolution*, 1793–94?] they had taken before & 100 Skins then
they may goe on shore again he Came on deck & told the other Natives they
must fetch the 4 big guns & 100 Skins for the too Indians he had in his
Cabin ... this is the Second Place he has Cut this caper ... Tuesday 27 Skin-
danis ... at 10 am Some of the Natives Came off one of them went down to
talk with there Countrymen & Said he would kill the first Ships Company
that he had a chance then Skipper Hill made him a prisoner for his Sauce
& he was to pay Some Skins for his Ransom ... Wednesday 28 Skidanis ... at
8 AM the Natives 6 of them ... Came off & fetched five Skins & gave them
to Skipper Hill they brought Some oil & Clemil [clemmels] instead of the
Skins but he would have nothing but the Skins themselves at 6 PM too of the
Natives Came off & fetched three more Skins & asked for their Comerades
but the Skipper Hill told them to make up the Hundred Skins the Natives
told him they had given him all the Skins they had got he has took three
Clemil in the lieu of three Skins they have offered him their whale boat &
told Him they Had nothing more to give him they Said they had been to
every Place Round to try to get the Skins he told them they ly he told them
He should get underway tomorrow if they dont fetch the Skins he should
carry them off & Sell them the Natives tell him they have dun the best they
can the Natives tell Him if He carries them away they will take the Hamilton
Capt Porter if they can Possibly at 7 PM three more of the Natives Came off
& fetched too more skins they took away too boxes of their Oil & the three
Clemil by the consent of the Skipper about 9 PM they Came & got the whale
boat they Said they was going to Sell her for Skins to the Cumshoewaws
[Cumshewa's] tribe ... Thursday 29 Skidanis ... Some of the Natives brought
off three Skins & Short time after they brought off one more Small Skin ...
the Skittegates People 6 of them Came along Side in a whale boat & fetched
5 More Skins & told the Skipper that was all they could get he told them
they Must fetch too Casks of Powder & five ... Muskets & Skins enough to
make up the Hundred ... he told them they must fetch Some Musquets &
powder & some more Skins they did fetch too Cegs of Powder one musket
& five more Prime skins he then gave them Six dutch brass Clamped muskets
& Let them goe the Natives offered the Skipper His Six muskets for one
Blanket a Little Molasses & a half a dozen biscuits but he would not when
he trades with the Natives for Skins he gives them too of these muskets for
one Skin he is acting verry unwisely in Staying Plundering the Coast he might
Have been off the Coast the first of april if he had been a mind to he had

22 Hundred Skins on board at the time but he seems as if he wants to loose the Brigg & all our Lives by his Carrying on ...[175]

By the beginning of summer, the supercargo added, "news of his Plunder is all over the Coast & the Natives is all up in arms about it expecting he is going to Serve them the same he has done more damage than any ship has this Some time the Natives was pretty Livid before he Cut Sutch Capers with them we Could goe on Shore amongst any of the Tribes to the Northward & not be afraid but Now it is dangerous to goe in to a harbour with the Vessel when she Lays within Musket Shot of them."[176] Such abuse bred distrust. On the day before Christmas 1805 on the northern coast some hands from the *Lydia* who were ashore cutting wood "let a tree foul on one of the Indens Conue and Stovs thas all to Peses at 6 PM the Indns fired to Muskets Bolls"; peace was not restored until the Bostonians agreed to pay the Natives for the canoe.[177]

These outrages were accompanied by what one first mate called "wanton cruelty,"[178] manifested in flogging, deadly warning volleys, and the indiscriminate punishment of an entire group for an individual's misdemeanour. Another officer similarly complained that "offenses of the Indians have been punished in a most bloody & unrelenting manner." "With respect to atrocity," he added, "they [American traders] can outdo the Indians in cruelty."[179] Two of the most egregious culprits were Captains Robert Gray and John Kendrick, who were probably the first Americans on the coast. In 1791 Kendrick not only introduced guns to the Haidas but killed up to fifty of them in a fight.[180] At the beginning of spring of the following year the one-eyed Gray burned the 200 houses of the Nootka village of Opitsat in Columbia's Cove (Clayoquot Sound) in retaliation for an abortive surprise attack on his ship. The settlement, according to one of Gray's officers, comprised at least 200 houses with much carved work "by no means *innelegant*"; "this fine Village," he added, "the Work of Ages, was in a short time totally destroy'd."[181] Two months later in Esperanza Inlet in the same sound Gray attacked another village, killing seven Indians and taking their sea otter skins "when the natives would not agree about the rate of exchange for furs with the Europeans, [and] these had used force to compel them." This outrage occurred because of the rapidly rising price of skins and the falling value of copper, both of which were the result of intensified competition. In these circumstances an uninformed shipmaster such as Gray "comes to trade, finds that the Indians have raised the price of the skins and that the rate they demand will result in great losses

... forgets the principles of justice, thinks that his operations cannot be checked, and makes use of force for his own advantage."[182] (At Nootka Sound in 1788 Maquinna had sold skins to Captain Meares at the rate of ten for one sheet of copper, but by 1792 the price had jumped to one skin for one sheet of fourteen pounds.[183]) Later yet in the same year in Gray's Harbour he massacred twenty whooping Chinooks who approached his ship in a war canoe. Later still Gray returned to Clayoquot Sound and killed or wounded more than twenty-five Nootkas as they neared his ship in a war canoe in the moonlight.[184] Then he sailed northwards and fought some Kwakiutls (Fig. 7). Meanwhile, on 13 June 1792 the *Butterworth*, Captain William Brown, had fired on Chief Wickaninish's people, killing several, including one of his brothers and two chiefs, for not receiving what Brown considered sufficient skins in return for his presents.[185] Little wonder that in the autumn Edward Bell, clerk of the *Chatham* of Vancouver's expedition, remarked that "few Ships have been on the Coast, that have not been attacked or attempted to be attacked, and in general many lives have been lost on both sides."[186] Perhaps the worst atrocities of the coast trade occurred in the early 1790s, and they may have been triggered by the American shipmasters' fear that the imminent settlement of the Nootka Sound controversy would exclude them, politically at least, from the fur traffic.[187]

Nevertheless, the carnage continued. In 1794 some of Wickaninish's men from the village of Seshart on Clayoquot Sound stole a canoe and thirty feet of cable from the *Jefferson*, so an armed party of fifteen crewmen went to the village and forced the Indians to return the canoe and part of the cable, whereupon the sailors fired on the Natives anyway (killing two or three and wounding two others), ransacked their village, razed some houses, and stove and stole a number of canoes.[188] In 1806 at Clayoquot Sound one of the *Vancouver*'s hands beat an Indian for nothing more than "asking a high Price for his oil."[189] And in early June 1821 at Skidegate as the result of a dispute over a trading debt – the local Haidas contending that they were owed twelve boxes of oil and Captain Martain of the *Hamilton* maintaining that he was owed four prime skins – the ship's pinnace with nine men was attacked by two canoes of Indians, and in the ensuing fracas two Natives were killed and three wounded and two Americans were wounded; not content with this outcome, the skippers of the *Hamilton* and *Lascar* fired cannon broadsides and musket volleys at the Haida village for an hour and again on departure.[190] Some skippers became so notorious for their dishonesty that it was not long before the Indians came to ask the identity of a ship's captain, and sometimes its flag ("King George Clue [ship] or Boston

Clue"?), before agreeing to trade.[191] Chiefs often refused to trade with shipmasters unless they exchanged hostages ("pledges") to guarantee mutual security, and Euroamerican castaways were invariably enslaved by the Indians rather than delivered to the next vessel. In the spring of 1810 the *Lydia* rescued at Classet, or Clahaset (Cape Flattery), thirteen Russians who had been shipwrecked and enslaved by Chief Wacash a year earlier.[192]

Not surprisingly, the Indians responded in kind to white violence,[193] "continually remembering their injuries, and never forgiving till they have obtained sufficient revenge," according to Captain Sturgis.[194] An anonymous compatriot agreed: "They never *forget* nor *forgive* offences," he asserted.[195] Their sense of revenge was not only strong but also "vicarious" in that it saw all whites as belonging to one tribe and therefore sharing in the guilt of any of its members. Thus, after being victimized by one vessel, they would seek revenge on the next, despite its "innocence." This "vicariousness" was the basis of the so-called "unprovoked" and "treacherous & unexpected" attacks of the Indians. The owners Bryant and Sturgis declared in 1815 that "we have little doubt that much of the Treachery of the Indians is but retributive Justice."[196] John Jewitt, the armourer who spent more than two years as a captive and slave of Chief Maquinna's Nootkas, was more emphatic:

For though they are a thievish race, yet I have no doubt that many of the melancholy disasters have principally arisen from the imprudent conduct of some of the captains and crews of the ships employed in this trade, in exasperating them by insulting, plundering, and killing them on slight grounds. This, as nothing is more sacred with a savage than the principle of revenge, and no people are so impatient under insult, induces them to wreak their vengeance upon the first vessel or boat's crew that offers, making the innocent too frequently suffer for the wrongs of the guilty, as few of them know to discriminate between persons of the same general appearance, more especially when speaking the same language. And to this cause do I believe, must principally be ascribed the sanguinary disposition with which these people are reproached, as Maquina repeatedly told me that it was not his wish to hurt a white man, and that he never should have done it, though ever so much in his power, had they not injured him. And were the commanders of our ships to treat the savages with rather more civility than they sometimes do, I am inclined to think they would find their account in it.[197]

Indian revenge began early in the trade. In 1789, in retaliation for stealing – mainly of drying linen – by some Haidas, Captain Kendrick seized two chiefs, tied them to his cannons, and threatened to blow them to pieces unless the stolen items were returned and, moreover, all of their furs were sold to him. The Indians complied, and two years later 100 to 200 of the same Indians attacked the same captain's ship at Coyah's Harbour on Houston Stewart Channel; the Natives suffered "a great slaughter" – about forty-five dead.[198] It is this incident which is commemorated in the so-called "Ballad of the Bold Northwestmen," issued as a broadside about 1795.[199] (Ironically and perhaps condignly, at the end of 1794 Kendrick was accidentally killed in Honolulu Harbour by a cannonball fired from the *Jackal*, which was saluting the *Lady Washington* at Kendrick's request with guns that had been mistakenly loaded with shot and whose own captain, William Brown, was killed by Hawaiians a month later.)

In the summer of 1793 in Behm Canal Captain Vancouver's boat party narrowly escaped destruction at the hands of a group of Tlingits bent on revenge for having been "ill-treated in their traffic with white men"; up to a dozen Indians were killed, and two of Vancouver's men seriously wounded, in the fray.[200] In the spring of 1801 some Haidas attacked the *Belle Savage* and killed five crewmen; that summer in retaliation the *Charlotte* kidnapped and executed five Haida chiefs, not all of whom had been implicated in the *Belle Savage* incident (in this instance the captain's thirst for revenge obviously exceeded his hunger for profit, for the chiefs could have been ransomed for prime skins); and in the autumn kinsmen of these innocent victims killed the captain of the *Globe*, Bernard Magee, and two of his crewmen near Skidegate.[201]

The seizure of the *Boston* in 1803 and the massacre of all but two of its crew (the prized armourer and carpenter) were "in fact the Bloody revenge of a long series of injuries" to Chief Maquinna, who in 1792 "complained greatly [to the Spaniards] of the conduct of the foreign vessels which traded on the coast, on account of certain wrongs which, he said, had been done to his people." In the very first year of trade, 1785, the very first trader, Captain Hanna of the *Sea Otter*, angry at the theft of a chisel, had inflicted "considerable slaughter" by firing on a canoe and killing from twenty to fifty Nootkas, who may have been trying to take advantage of the ship's small size (sixty tons) and small crew (thirty men). In 1785 or 1786 Maquinna had been invited aboard the same ship and given what the sailors said was a seat of honour, under which they had placed a charge of gunpowder, which was ignited, blowing the chief from his seat and leaving him with burns and scars which he showed to a Spanish officer in 1789. On another occasion an American or British skipper had ransacked Maquinna's house in his absence and taken forty skins; and a Spanish officer had executed three or four of his subchiefs.[202]

At Nass in 1810–11 the *Hamilton*, Captain Lemuel Porter, and the local Tsimshians conducted a two-year feud. It began on 15 July 1810: "A large number of the Natives suposed for to be about one hundred and upwards onbord & Alongside under pretence of trade for srowton [oolachen oil] but there intent was for to try to take the ship for they keep Coming up with thcre dagers sum of which was Drown out of the sheath & when wee found them with them & took them away sum Made resistance & then all in the Canoes took up there Musquets but when that they found that wee was redy with ower arms over the ships side at them they went off with out any damage."[203] On 21 May of the following year at Nass the third officer of the *Hamilton* and a Hawaiian hand were killed by musket fire when their party went ashore for water and was ambushed.[204] A week later the *Hamilton* returned to Nass in company with the *Katherine*; en route off Wales Point a "canoe Came alongside to sel Hollibote [halibut] with five Natives in her at Noon Made prisoners of 2 of them but Could not get the other 3 so killed them in the Canoe."[205] A month and a half earlier at Chilkat in Lynn Canal forty to fifty Tlingits, including thirteen chiefs, were killed in an attempt to wreak revenge on the *Otter*, whose second officer and boatswain were slain.[206] At the beginning of the 1822 trading season the *Rob Roy* was visited by Chief Shakes, "the greatest Chief of the N.W. Coast," according to the logkeeper, who added: "Shakes appears to be a pretty crafty fellow and it is said he intends taking the first vessel he possibly can to revenge the death of his wives father who was killed by Capt Hill of Brig Otter some time since [probably in 1810]."[207] In the same year the Nass Tsimshians were rated "the most powerfull tribe on the Coast and bad disposed" to Euroamerican traders; "they are grate hunters and sell a good many skins" (and one of their chiefs, Neacoot, was described as "a grate drunkard but the cleverist indian on the coast").[208] And so it went: Euroamerican affront begetting Indian revenge begetting Euroamerican retaliation begetting more Indian retribution. Native vengefulness was such that in 1840 the Chilkat Tlingits threatened the HBC's Fort Taku with retaliation for an altercation some twenty-five years earlier with Captain Hill in which from forty-five to one hundred Indians had been killed.[209]

No wonder that most shipmasters were cautious. Captain Sturgis recalled his safe way of trading:

Believing that the surest way to prevent an attack was to let the natives see me always prepared to repel one, I made a rule & adhered to it through all my voyages, that when many of them were along side, boarding nettings, some ten or twelve feet high should be kept hoisted – the arm chest, filled with loaded fire-arms, upon the forecastle – a barricado, a strong rail, across the deck near the foremast, upon which loaded swivels & blunderbusses were mounted & pointed to the quarter deck – All the officers and men, excepting two or three to assist me in trading, were stationed forward – Trade was carried on upon the quarter deck – A few Indians only were admitted on board at a time and they not permitted to go forward of the mainmast. By these precautions, and a conciliatory course towards the natives, I escaped collisions and preserved friendly relations with them throughout. But prudence & kindness did not, in all cases, ensure safety, for some discreet & estimable men fel victims to the too indiscriminate vengeance of the Indians.[210]

Occasionally the Indians even succeeded in capturing trading vessels and killing their crews. In 1801 in Fitz Hugh Sound 150 Haidas nearly seized the *Belle Savage*, killing three and wounding five crewmen.[211] In 1803 the Nootkas captured the *Boston* and killed twenty-five of its twenty-seven hands. American shipmasters told the Russians at Sitka that they had lost six ships to the Natives by 1805.[212] On 12 June of that year in Milbanke Sound the *Atahualpa* was attacked by 120 Tsimshians, who killed Captain Porter and nine of his men, including all of his officers, and wounded nine others; the ship and its cargo were saved, however.[213] Perhaps the bloodiest seizure occurred in 1811, when John Jacob Astor's 300–ton *Tonquin* was overrun at Clayoquot Sound; all 23 to 29 hands and up to 200 Nootkas perished.[214] (This attack may have been revenge for the abduction of up to twelve Nootkas by Captain George Ayres of the *Mercury* in 1810.) Ironically, "very often" the trading vessels were attacked with the very arms that they themselves had sold, and on the very day of the sale.[215]

Although a flotilla of fifty-foot war canoes bristling with two dozen armed and whooping Indians in warpaint must have been a daunting sight, most ships were well manned and well armed, and attacks were usually easily repulsed. Sometimes skippers were warned of planned attacks by the Natives themselves, usually chiefs, perhaps because they did not want to jeopardize their lucrative trading position. Chief Kow was regarded as "one of the Best Savages on this Coast" because he forewarned Captain Brown of the *Vancouver* in 1802 or 1803, Captain Ebbets of the *Alert* in 1803, and Captain Ebbets again of the *Pearl* in 1805 of planned attacks on their vessels by his own and other groups. For doing so in 1805 he had to take refuge aboard the *Pearl* to avoid being punished by his own people, "as they were Determined to Kill him for informing."[216] Chief Cunneah of the Haidas was another ally of the Bostonians; one of them described him in 1805 as "a verry old man upwards of one hundred yers old ... and the most humane Savage on this Coast and friendly."[217] Those few vessels that were overpowered were victims of surprise rather than frontal attacks – "they went on Voyages where they surpris'd the enemy in the Night [t]hey kill'd them as they caught them Sleeping," in the words of Joseph Ingraham.[218]

The principal danger was the large number of Indians so close to the ship during trading. There were 200 to 600 canoes trading alongside the *Gustavus* at Cloak Bay in late April 1791;[219] the *Hamilton* had 130 canoes alongside selling skins and oil at Nass on 28 May 1821 and about 2,000 canoes with "very troublesome" natives alongside at Newhitty on 10 July of the same year;[220] and on 22 May 1822 at Nass at least 500 canoes crowded around the *Rob Roy*.[221] Although outnumbered, the Euroamericans had larger vessels and heavier weapons. In the middle 1820s American coasters generally exceeded 200 tons, mounted several cannons and swivel guns, and carried a couple of dozen men with muskets, pistols, sabres, and daggers;[222] the *Alert* (1816–18), for example, carried thirty-five men and mounted ten guns.[223] Special precautions were taken: seldom putting into port singly, and otherwise standing offshore; not trading at night, and during the day allowing only a few canoes alongside at one time; permitting few or no Indians to come aboard; and insisting that the Natives be unarmed, with every crewman standing on guard and all cannons loaded with double grapeshot, a match burning at each of them. In 1801 the *Atahualpa* made the Indians "keep with their canoes, under our stern. The Cabin guns leveled directly at them."[224] Occasionally a ship, such as the *Otter* in 1809, took the extra precaution of "boarding the Tops over to prevent the Indians from seeing the men that are in them."[225] Boarding nets were much more common. By the 1820s the trade was more dangerous; consequently, as the Honolulu agent of Marshall and Wildes reported at the end of 1821, "all vessels on the coast now have got double crews."[226] The various defensive measures were described by Lieutenant Simpson in 1828:

The mode of defence adopted by the American vessels is more secure than one would at first suppose from seeing no shew of arms about the Decks, which is always looked upon by the Indians with an eye of suspicion, and displeasure; therefore to preserve their safety and not give offence to the Natives, their mode is certainly best calculated under these circumstances. In the first place they have Boarding Nettings with Crow foots and Tackles for hauling them out to each yard arm, and its after parts fixed to an outrigger lashed across the Stern, which gives them a sloping direction out from the vessel that renders it more difficult for the Indians to surmount. In the gangways they have ports fitted with hinges, which they can haul up and shut in at pleasure, and it is only thru this entry that the Indians have access, a hand being placed there to admit only those directed by the Captain, and when a sufficient number is on board the rest are excluded until some of those on board complete their Trade, when they return into their Canoes and make room for others to come on board; the Indians are all kept at aft the Main Mast, the after part of the vessel being kept clear of arms, and of every moveable article likely to be stolen (as an Indian cannot resist the temptation of stealing if a favourable opportunity offers); hands are placed on the gangways to prevent their passing firearms, and from the rail to the Fore Mast they have a Cross piece fitted into which they slip a few swivels which are pointed aft upon the Indians, and the Crew have arms in readiness in the event of a disturbance (an arm chest standing forward with arms and ammunition), tho no display is made of them, yet is understood by the Indians that such is the case, they therefore remain quietly aft and Trade their Furs; as a further precaution no Indians are allowed on board with arms, a search being made as they come on board to see that they have no Knives or other arms concealed under their blankets. The chiefs are allowed below to the Cabin to Trade, which is well arranged for the purpose as it is kept clear of every thing that could be removed by such visitors, there being no open apartments to which they have access and the principal Cabin has merely a Table and Chairs. A Trading room stands off the Cabin from which the Trader takes out the goods as he carrys on the Trade, and on the Furs being purchased they are put into the Trading room.[227]

Any hostilities usually ended in a stand-off, although the Indians suffered more casualties because of greater Euroamerican firepower. In a skirmish with the *Union* off Anthony Island in the Queen Charlottes in 1795 up to seventy Haidas, including Chief Coyah or Skoicheye, were killed; the shipmaster recorded that "I could have kill'd 100 more with grape shot but I let humanity prevail & ceas'd firing ... None of us was hurt ..."[228] The Natives could not, of course, overtake the ships at sea – unless they were becalmed or aground – and the whites dared not pursue the Natives on shore, where the thick woods and rugged mountains were ideally suited to the Indian strategy of stealth and ambush. "Stratagem and surprise form the offensive points of their military art," noted Captain Meares.[229] Some Indians could also retreat to the sanctuary of their formidable "touts" – wooden forts perched atop rocky promontories. They were described by an American seaman in 1791:

near to those head villages they have fortified towns or villages which they call "Touts" to which they retreat when invaded by a more powerfull enemy these are built on the most natural fortifications and much improved by art they endeavour to have only one means of access and this by a wooden pole with notches cut in it to admit the toe by which they ascend

when they are all up the pole is hauled after them they then with stones which these places are well supplied with annoy their enemy and are in general able to repel most any attack these places are also well supplied with provisions and water by which they can hold out a siege of several months if there enemy had the ability or skill to carry it on.[230]

One of Chief Shakes's "strongholds in War ... built on a Round Perpendicular Rock, with a Fighting stage, all round," was dubbed Fort Charles by Captain Bishop.[231] The Tlingit tout of Hakes off Hyuna's Harbour in Hoodsnahoo Sound comprised a stockade from 12 to 14 feet in height and 100 feet in circumference.[232] One Haida tout mounted eighteen cannons.[233]

Economic realities restricted the extent of white violence against the Natives. The Euroamericans realized that more bloodshed inevitably meant fewer Indians to hunt and trade. They also knew that excessive force might drive the Natives into the hands of rival Nor'westmen. Lieutenant Simpson felt that shipmasters were, if anything, too tolerant of the behaviour of their customers: "I do not consider these vessels very efficiently maned in the event of a rupture with the Indians, but as they generally sail two in Company the risk is less and the Indians are kept more in awe; when they apprehend danger they act with great caution, yet they behave with a degree of forbearance towards these Indians (as in certain situations they are necessarily very much in their power, particularly in small harbours) that has reduced the Whites very much in their estimation for bravery, and has made the life of a Trader upon this part of the Coast a most slavish one."[234] Yet as long as there was competition on the coast the Indians had to be indulged. As Chief Trader Work admitted ruefully in 1837, the "Stikeen men [Tlingits] are daring scoundrels and require to be kept well down. But this plagued opposition often deters us from being so severe as is necessary."[235]

Thus Euroamerican-Indian relations, initially cordial, soon became strained, with the mutual distaste periodically exploding in violence, mainly owing to prejudging, defrauding, and kidnapping on the part of white traders. Gun-running and rum-running aggravated the situation. Sullivan Dorr reported in 1801 that "small vessels ... are now obliged to keep together, the natives being so well armed that otherwise they would be inevitably shot off to a man at a single volley of Muskettry."[236] The *Juno's* Captain John D'Wolf, or "Nor'west John" (the uncle, incidentally, of *Moby Dick's* Herman Melville), declared in

1804 that the coast trade was a "dangerous business." He found that at Kaigani, one of the principal marts, "attacks were not rare when only one ship was in port."[237] The anxiety of crewmen was expressed by the journal of the *Vancouver* in 1805: "Lord What a figure Could be painted of our Doleful Situation on this Savage Coast where if By the hand of Providence we Should all Be inhumanely Butchered instantiously Good God Preserve us."[238] Captain Sturgis did not find the violence exceptional. By 1808 he had made four trips to the coast since 1799, and "these early visits," he recalled, "brought to my knowledge the injustice, violence, and bloodshed which have marked the progress of this intercourse from first to last."[239] Bryant and Sturgis cautioned Captain George Clark of the *Borneo* in 1817 to be very wary: "Your own experience will impress you with the necessity of constant vigilance and care to secure your vessel and crew from the treachery of the Natives, both on the coast and at the [Hawaiian] Islands."[240] The following year the same owners reminded Captain James Hale of the *Ann* of the "necessity of unremitted watchfulness and constant preparation when among the Natives."[241] By 1821, according to Captain Grimes, the coast had "become very dangerous, without a large compliment of men and well armed."[242] At the end of the summer of that year the *Pearl*, Captain John Meek, the *Arab*, Captain Thomas Meek, and the *Mentor*, Captain Lemuel Porter, arrived at Honolulu from the coast, where, a longtime Euroamerican resident of Oahu reported, "they have had much fighting with the Indians."[243] In 1825 the HBC's *William and Ann* was warned by the *Owhyhee*, Captain Kelly, of the danger: "He assured us that on every part of the coast the natives were hostile & would be ready to seize every opportunity of cutting of[f] those who went ashore & of surprising the vessel. The only exception to this hostile disposition was … Kagannie [where] the seamen went ashore without any precaution whatever, & the natives were allowed to visit the ship in as great numbers as they pleased."[244] The British company was apprised of the danger again in 1828 by Lieutenant Simpson:

Besides the peril of Ship Wreck I must also include the constant vigilance necessary to observe to prevent a vessels being cut off by the Natives who are ever upon the watch to avail themselves of any favourable opportunity to accomplish such an act, hardly a year passes that such an attempt is not made by the natives of some part of the Coast, indeed were it not for the constant jealousy existing among the several Tribes, which prevents their acting in concert, but on the contrary has the effect of defeating these hostile designs, it would not be possible to hold an intercourse with these people.

These circumstances makes it obvious how harasing and perilous an occupation the collecting of Furs upon this Coast is.[245]

By the late 1820s, according to Captain Auguste Duhaut-Cilly of the *Héros*, the Indians loathed the white traders, who, he wrote, "have sought by all manner of fraudulent schemes to deceive the natives, sometimes about matters of quantity, sometimes about the quality and character of the articles of exchange" and "have missed no opportunity in their practice of cheating and embittering the natives." He added that "the fatal word 'Revenge,' colourfully carved upon the prows of the Indian canoes, serves like the starry flag of the American Union to signal that the reign of trust and good will in this region has ended forever."[246] Little wonder that the Bay man John Work declared at the beginning of 1836 that the coastal Indians were "very numerous, treacherous, daring, savage, and ferocious in the extreme."[247]

The Tlingits became particularly hostile, perhaps partly because they were more numerous and better armed than other coastal Native groups and perhaps partly because they were in the best position to take advantage of Russian, American, and British competition for their furs. As early as 1792 Captain Charles Barkley of the *Halcyon* found the Tlingits of Sitka Sound to be "very daring" and "very difficult & tedious to deal with." They were "audacious in the highest degree," he added.[248] They struck Mrs Barkley, who was accompanying her husband, as "the most dangerous and mischevious set we had ever met."[249] In 1799 Captain Sturgis rated the Tlingits the most "deceiving, crafty and daring" Indians on the coast,[250] and they were deemed "exceedingly hostile & treacherous" by the Russians a quarter of a century later.[251] The Stikine Tlingits were especially formidable. They "are esteemed as the most numerous & warlike of any upon the coast," reported one of the *Atahualpa*'s officers in 1801.[252]

As Lieutenant Simpson noted, the Northwest Coast Indians fought amongst themselves as well as against Euroamericans, the internecine warfare usually resulting from attempts by one group to capture another's provisions or slaves (food producers).[253] And while they were fighting each other they were not hunting and trading, much to the chagrin of shipmasters. One of the bloodiest years seems to have been 1811. At Lahaina Roads on Maui Island in early 1812 Captain Suter of the *Atahualpa* "learnt very unpleasant news respecting the NW Coast, that the natives were at war with each other & that skins were remarkably dear & ships had been giving from Four to Five Fathoms [8–10 yards] of Duffil for a skin, & the natives had made many daring attempts to take several Ships & Capts Porter [*Hamilton*] Hill [*Otter*] & Bennet [*Lydia*] had fired upon them & each Vessel had lost 3 of their Men."[254] In June 1811 most of a party of Kaigani Haidas, including their well-known Chief Kow, were killed by Tsimshians at Nass while buying shrowton (oolachen oil).[255] Because of this strife Captain T. Brown, former master of the *Lydia*, was advised as follows: "Do not engage in the NW Business for times never was so Bad Before."[256] The same problem was encountered by the HBC after it established posts on the northern coast in the early 1830s. Chief Factor Peter Skene Ogden of Fort Simpson reported in the summer of 1835 that "we have not been able to procure any fresh salmon from the Indians this season owing to the quarrels among themselves."[257] In 1837 and 1838 the post's fur returns suffered from hostilities between Port Essington's Tsimshians and Masset's Haidas and between the Indians of Tongass and Port Stuart.[258] On 8 July 1838 the post journal of Fort Simpson recorded that "all their [Indians'] plagued quarrels" had diminished returns.[259]

Russia's 1821 decree prohibiting all foreign vessels from approaching within 100 miles of the Northwest Coast above 51° N. latitude was the cause of another disruption of the coast trade. Ships leaving Boston after 1 July 1822 were affected.[260] American shipowners were understandably upset, being "very unwilling to give up that trade knowing there may be money made with a suitable cargo,"[261] and they protested to Washington. "I hope our government will not suffer our valuable trade on the North West Coast to be taken from us by a nation who but a few years since were but a race of barbarians," wrote John Jones, the commercial agent of Marshall and Wildes (and later US consul) at Honolulu.[262] Jones believed that "Jack Debener's" [the Russians'] ban would double the selling price of sea-otter skins at Canton.[263] Bryant and Sturgis agreed: "We can hardly anticipate what will be the final result of these pretensions of the Russian Govt. but it will deter us from future adventures with present prospects. We think it may affect the value of Sea Otters in Canton, for it will be difficult to obtain them if this 'Ukase' [decree] is executed."[264] Yet the effect of the tsar's edict was minimal. In 1822 Bryant and Sturgis did "find it impossible to get insurance for a regular NW Voyage,"[265] and in the same year its *Pearl* was ordered off the coast by a Russian frigate; but subsequently the Russian government paid the owners some $15,000 in damages.[266] The dearth of Russian warships, the ingenuity of Boston shipowners, and the protests of the American government largely defeated the ban. As Bryant and Sturgis wrote to the *Rob Roy*'s Captain Daniel Cross in 1823:

The pretention of the Russian Government to all territories North of 51° is not sanctioned by our government yet it has alarmed People so much that few are disposed to adventure. We have *good reason to believe* that no attempt will be made by the Russians to execute their decree, unless it is in their own Ports & we advise you not to attempt to enter Norfolk [Sitka] Sound, nor any other Russian settlement, unless in case of extreme necessity. There would be little danger of a Russian Ship of War capturing you any where else, but 'tis best to avoid them when it can be done without injuring your voyage.[267]

If a Russian warship were to appear, coasters could take refuge inshore in constricted channels "where the Russians are unacquainted & cannot follow."[268] Captain Eliah Grimes of the *Owhyhee* had another strategy. It was "to make the natives acquainted with the proceedings of the Russians and get them to bring their skins to New Ettee [Newhitty] which is to the southward of their limits which may be easily done by giving them a trifle more as they are inveterate enemies of those people."[269] Because of Sitka's reliance upon American trading vessels for supplies, however, the Russians did not wholeheartedly enforce the decree. As one Hawaiian observer noted, "I do not believe they will proceed to this extremity [enforcement], since they must certainly have some unwillingness to raise the dander of brother Jonathan, who can do them much more harm than he can receive from them."[270] Soon Russia relented; as explained earlier, in 1824 and 1825 the tsar signed conventions with the United States and Great Britain, respectively, which retracted Russian America's southern boundary to 54° 40' N. latitude and readmitted foreign merchantmen to Russian America's coastal waters. Meanwhile, the Northwest Coast continued to see as many trading vessels during as before the ban (Table 1).

More problematical than the souring of Indian-Euroamerican relations was the wasting of sea otters, if only because the latter was one of the causes of the former. At first sea otters were plentiful, for they had not been over-hunted by the Indians. Lieutenant Puget was amazed by the "abundance" of otters on the coast in 1792–93.[271] (He logically surmised, incidentally, that if there really were a northwest passage between the coast and Hudson or Baffin Bays, then the creatures should also abound in the latter water bodies.) He saw an "Astonishing Quantity" along the northern coast in particular.[272] In the late 1780s a trading vessel could obtain up to 2,500 skins in one season with little difficulty. The Natives were literally stripped of furs, since, as Captain Dixon found, "the cloaths wore universally on the coast are made of skins sewed together in various forms."[273] Each of these robes or cloaks, termed "cotsacks" or "cutsarks" by the white traders, consisted of three to five sea-otter skins; they lent their name to Cloak Bay in the Queen Charlottes. And the Natives were eager to shed them. For Captain Dixon the Tlingits of Yakutat Bay "stripped themselves almost naked, to spin out their trade as far as possible."[274] No wonder that textiles, particularly blankets, became one of the most popular Euroamerican trade goods for the Indians.

The combination of abundance of sea otters and keenness for trade meant a high turnover. On the Queen Charlottes Captain Dixon procured 300 skins in half an hour in 1787, and in 1789 Captain Gray acquired 200 in a "very fue moments."[275] The number of trading vessels peaked initially at twenty-one in 1792 when, reported an American trader, "the northern coast is thronged with people well provided with cargoes."[276] "Active" traders realized profits of at least 30 per cent;[277] Captain Hanna, the very first trader, made up to 41 per cent on his 1785 venture in the *Sea Otter*.[277] These bumper years continued until the War of 1812, although the overdoing of the coast trade at the very beginning of the 1800s resulted in several "losing" voyages. The *Captain Cook* got 540 skins in one month of 1786, the *Hope* up to 1,800 in two months of 1791, the *Jenny* 2,000 in three months of 1794, and the *Eliza* 2,700 and the *Caroline* from 2,200 to 2,400 in three months of 1799.[279] More than once an outlay of $40,000 (vessel, outfit, crew) returned more than $150,000 for a profit of 275 per cent.[280]

As already noted, proceeds were large because there were three chances – not just one – to profit: the bartering of goods for furs on the coast, the selling of furs and buying of goods at Canton, and the disposing of Chinese goods in Boston. In 1819 a sea-otter skin cost three and one-half piaster's worth of cloth on the Northwest Coast and brought from forty to fifty piasters at Canton;[281] $881.75 worth of Californian skins belonging to Captain Grimes of the *Owhyhee* fetched just over $2,000 in goods at Canton in early 1822.[282] Apparently the Chinese goods brought double their Canton price in Boston in the middle 1790s, for Captain Boit of the *Union* stated that sea-otter skins were worth twice as much in the American as in the Chinese city.[283] The British ship *Jane*, 100 tons and 16 hands, expended £4,000 on outfit and crew and returned £20,000 on its 1794–96 voyage.[284] The American snow *Sea Otter* (1795–98) cost $3,658 to buy and $9,500 to outfit and man; it obtained 2,520 sea-otter skins and 2,755 tails, which were sold at Canton for $42,840 worth of teas, nankeens, silks, chinaware, and sugar.[285] Presumably the Chinese goods brought twice their Canton cost at Boston, where the shipowners paid $3,680.65 in duty, leaving a profit of some 400 per cent. In 1799 Captain Cleveland of the *Caroline* invested $9,000 in trade goods at Canton and procured 2,300 skins on the coast that fetched $55,100–$62,300 on the Chinese market;[286] and he would have made even more money, of course, if he had reinvested his proceeds in a cargo of China goods for the American market. The 1799–1801 expenses of the *Alert*, Captain William Bowles, totalled $34,689 and its earnings $84,282 for a net profit of $49,593 or nearly 150 per cent.[287] The 1801–02 voyage of the *Caroline*, Captains Derby and Sturgis, netted $73,034.[288] In 1805 Captain D'Wolf sold the 250-ton *Juno* and its cargo, valued together at $35,000 when it cleared Bristol, Rhode Island, in 1804, to the Russian-American Company at Sitka for $68,000 plus a 50–ton ship; the owners ultimately cleared $100,000 on the venture.[289] The two seasons (1805–06) on the coast of the *Vancouver* realized almost 5,000 skins – "a Noble Voyage" – which would have been worth $120,000 in Canton and fetched Chinese goods that would have brought $210,000 in Boston (an increase of 75 per cent on Canton) to defray the $30,000 cost of the cargo.[290] In 1806–10 the *Derby*, Captain Swift, incurred expenses of $100,790 ($56,653 for cargo, $20,026 for provisions, $15,000 for the ship, and $12,084 for wages and commissions) and realized revenues of $332,995 for a net profit of $232,205 or 230 per cent.[291] Perhaps the most lucrative voyage of all was that of the *Pearl*, Captain Suter, in 1808–09; its capital of $50,000 returned in two seasons 6,000 skins worth $284,000 gross.[292] And Suter was perhaps the most successful shipmaster. He captained the 1811–14 voyage of the *Atahualpa* and netted the owners nearly $120,000 on an investment of no more than $40,000.[293]

After the War of 1812 profit margins were undoubtedly smaller, given the depletion of sea otters, but a diligent skipper who made the coast early with an attractive assortment of trade goods could still do quite well. In 1827 the *Sultan* cleared some $35,000 for Bryant and Sturgis.[294] The most successful shipowners were W. H. Boardman, W. Boardman and P. Pope, E. Dorr and Sons, J. and T. Lamb, G. W. Lyman, T. Lyman, J. Marshall and D. Wildes, and J. and T. H. Perkins.[295]

The combination that generated a high turnover also led to over-hunting of the sea-otter resource and over-stocking of the Indian market. The extremely high value of sea-otter fur – more than three times as valuable as beaver fur at Canton at the beginning of 1811[296] – caused a fast rush and an early peak to the coast trade, as well as a quick slump in prices and a heavy toll of sea otters. The animal itself was particularly vulnerable. Its fertility is low – generally one offspring per dam per year, compared with litters of two to five or more for sables and beavers. As a Tlingit said to the Russians at Sitka, "cod lay eggs but otters are born in ones and twos, and because of this disparity alone they can be completely annihilated."[297] Perhaps because of this low rate of reproduction, the mother is exceptionally regardful of her young, so much so that she refuses to abandon her pup under any circumstances, with the fatal result in the era of the Northwest Coast fur trade that both were bagged; and since motherless pups cannot survive alone, they were caught, too. Also, because the dam's pelt is more valuable than her mate's, females bore the brunt of hunting. Furthermore, lacking the protective layer of body fat of other marine mammals, the creature retains a prime pelt all year as insulation against cool ocean waters, unlike the coat of land fur bearers; this fact invited year-round hunting and hastened depletion. The hunting proficiency of the RAC's Aleut and Kodiak kayakers accelerated the sea otter's demise, too. As early as 1802 the Tlingits of Frederick Sound in the central "straits" were complaining to shipmasters that they had few skins because Russian hunters had decimated the animal.[298] The overkill was forseen by the prescient Alexander Walker: "The indiscriminate ignorance and avidity of the Natives, will be continually exerted to supply the Traders, equally craving and rapacious. By this means the Numbers of the Animal will be reduced, and less valuable Skins brought into the Market."[299]

Already in 1810 Captain John Ebbets of the *Enterprise* informed the owner, John Jacob Astor, that "furs on the Coast this Year have been very scarce."[300] In 1812 Stephen Reynolds, an able seaman on the *New Hazard*, reported that skins were "remarkably scarce,"[301] and in the same year the adept Captain Suter made the following entry in the log of the *Atahualpa*: "Two or three canoes along side but nothing of any description for sale, this place [Milbanke Sound] appears to be the same as all others on the Coast with regard to Furs."[302] In 1821 Captain Brown wrote to Marshall and Wildes that "by the account from the NW Coast it is small doings there very few skins";[303] a year later Captain Grimes informed the same owners that "skins has become very scarce and dear."[304] The depopulation of sea otters continued apace. An American merchant in Honolulu, Stephen Reynolds, reported in 1827: "Skins Scarce on the coast. About 800 Sea Otters have been collected by the five vessels."[305] The next year saw no improvement; "Business very Dull there," he said.[306] Whereas Captain Bishop had found in 1795 that the waters around the Queen Charlottes "abound with Sea otters,"[307] Chief Trader Work noted in 1835 that "now scarcely any is to be found."[308] It is hardly surprising that, of the several phases or grades of *Enhydra lutris*, only that of the Northwest Coast, where competition was most intense, was hunted to extinction. (The sea otter has recently been reintroduced to the coast – Vancouver Island – from the Aleutian Islands.)

This carnage was reflected in the decline in the total number of skins taken by American vessels on the coast: from an unknown but probable peak in 1795 or 1796, when prices at Canton reached their lowest level, to 18,000 in 1800 and 15,000 in 1802 to annual averages of 14,837 in 1804–07 (17,445 in 1805), 9,592 in 1808–12, and 3,100 in 1813–14 to 4,300 in 1815, 3,650 in 1816, 4,177 in 1817, 4,500 to 4,800 in 1818, 3,000 to 3,500 in 1820 and 1821, 2,500 in 1822, 1,100 in 1826, 700 in 1827, and fewer than 500 in 1828.[309] Before 1801 the largest total collection in one season was 11,300 skins;[310] by the middle 1840s no more than 200 skins – of "very ordinary" quality, moreover – were taken annually by all trading vessels.[311] Collections by individual vessels likewise declined, although not without some variation, depending upon the shipmaster, the crew, the cargo, the itinerary, and the like. In 1791 the *Gustavus* procured 1,869 skins,[312] but in 1792 returns varied greatly from ship to ship, reflecting the first peak of competition, ranging from 1,700–1,800 for the *Columbia Rediviva* and her tender, the *Adventure*, and 1,100–1,200 for the *Margaret* to 700 for the *Jackal* and 450 for the *Hope*.[313] By 1794 collections had increased, with the *Jackal*, Captain William Brown, getting 4,000–5,000 and the *Jenny*, Captain John Adamson, more than 2,000.[314] In the two seasons of 1797–98 the *Hazard* obtained 3,600 skins, one of the largest collections so far.[315]

The overdoing of the coast trade at the turn of the century resulted in quite unequal collections. In 1799 the *Eliza* got 2,500–3,000 skins and the *Caroline* 2,396 but the *Ulysses* only 800 skins, the *Dispatch* 1,275, and the *Hancock* 1,785.[316] In 1800 the British vessels *Dove* and *Betsy* collected 2,200 and 1,800–2,000 skins respectively; the American ships *Alert*, *Jenny*, and *Alexander* acquired 2,690, 2,000, and 861 skins respectively.[317] In 1801 fifteen American vessels averaged 1,210 skins each, but their individual takes ranged from 150 to 2,800 with a mode of 700.[318] In two seasons from 1 March 1801 to 30 September 1802 the *Atahualpa* got 3,536 skins (including 2,297 prime pelts), 2,374 tails, 40 cotsacks, and 69 pieces, plus 129 beaver and land-otter pelts.[319] About 1,800 "black skins" were taken by the *Mary* in 1805; after "wintering over" in 1805–06 the *Atahualpa* obtained 6,000 skins and the *Caroline* 5,000.[320]

At the end of 1810 Captain Ebbets reported to his shipowner, John Jacob Astor, that "the furs on the Coast this Year have been very scarce."[321] In 1813 the *Atahualpa* under the proficient Captain Suter managed to get only 672 skins, but in 1817–18 the same skipper got 3,500 skins in two seasons with the *Mentor*.[322] In 1820 it was common, as the *Hamilton* discovered, to have "a grate number of indins Along side & onbord but no trade" or "a quantity of natives Along side & onbord but little trade" (partly because of Indian warfare).[323] The next year was no more productive, as evidenced by the log of the *Arab*: "A number of the Natives along side Trading … Bought a few Sea Otters and a number of Land Furs" (Tongass Harbour, 21 June); "we had some of the Natives along side but they were all very pore" (Cumshewa's Inlet, 2 July); "the Natives round us but pore as usal" (Tongass Harbour, 7 August).[324] The *Rob Roy* found 1822 no better: "No Skins to be had and no prospect of any bad bad business" (1 April); "this last cruse [one month long] has been bad enough we have not collected five skins & have had a devil of a banging [by stormy weather]" (18 September).[325] In the 1810s and 1820s a ship's collection seldom exceeded 1,000 and usually amounted to several hundred yearly. One thousand skins each were procured by the *Brutus* in 1818, the *Brutus* and *Volunteer* in 1819, and the *Rob Roy* in 1824 (a "good collection"), but in 1823 each of six American vessels collected only 350 skins.[326] (In 1816 Bryant and Sturgis told Captain Suter that 3,000 skins were needed to make a profitable voyage.[327]) At the same time the catch of fur seals was likewise declining – in Russian America from more than 62,000 skins in 1818 to fewer than 24,000 in 1828.[328]

All of these figures, however, should be treated with caution. Many are probably deflated, since a successful shipmaster would not want to encourage an inquisitive competitor by divulging his rich collection. As Clerk Edward Bell of Captain Vancouver's *Chatham* cautioned: "It was very difficult here to come at the truth of what numbers of skins ships collected; for the Masters of them and their mates & ships company, whether from a privilege they think they can claim by passing round Cape Horn, or from some unaccountable species of distrust or jealousy seldom agree in their accounts of their quantity on board, many of them, and often, varying hundreds of skins."[329] Another member of Vancouver's expedition, surgeon-botanist Archibald Menzies, concurred, reporting that the "general practice among traders on this coast … is always to mislead competitors as far as they can, even at the expense of truth."[330]

At the same time, naturally, that fewer skins were being taken on the coast, fewer were being shipped to Canton, where prices consequently began to rise. In 1800 some American shipmasters told Governor Alexander Baranov at Sitka that they had to get at least 1,500 skins in order to make a "saving" (profitable) voyage.[331] Apparently most did so until 1801; in 1799 six American vessels took 9,160–10,000 skins to Canton (an average of 1,527–1,833 each), in 1800

five took 9,800 (an average of 1,960 each), in 1801 eleven took
12,000–13,000 (an average of 1,091–1,182 each), and in 1802 fourteen took 14,000–14,600 (an average of 1,000–1,043 each).[332] Only
two of the one British and five American ships that took skins to
Canton in 1800 made a profit.[333] The three voyages of the *Atahualpa*
(1801–03), *Guatimozin* (1801–02), and *Vancouver* (1802–04), owned
by Theodore Lyman and associates, may have returned only 50 per
cent of the total cost (nearly $90,000) of their outfits.[334] Some
100,000 sea-otter skins were shipped from the coast to Canton from
1790 through 1799 (including 11,000 in 1799), 9,800 in 1800, 13,000
in 1801, 27,100 in 1802, and 129,655 from 1804 through 1818,[335]
making a total of 279,455 from 1790 through 1802 and from 1804
through 1818 or roughly 300,000 from 1790 through 1818 – virtually 10,000 annually for 30 years (plus those that the Russians sent
to Kyakhta). American shipments of sea-otter skins to Canton
dropped to 4,000 by 1820, and by 1831 to only 750 (and "principally
ordinary California" skins).[336]

One turning-point was the advent of stronger Russian competition
with the founding of Sitka in 1799 right on the northern coast, which
was by then becoming the focus of the trade. But a more compelling
constraint was the saturation of the Indian market by too many trading vessels and the resultant rising cost of furs – notwithstanding
Wike's assertion that it was not possible to saturate the Indian market.[337] (It was these rising prices that prompted some skippers to seize
skins outright.) As Captain Colnett's sailing orders of 1789 stated,
"the Number of Competitors that you will meet with on the Coast
will we fear somewhat diminish your collection of Furs as well as
enhance their price."[338] Already in 1787, only two years after the
British entered the coast trade, Captain Portlock found in Prince
William Sound that two of his countrymen, Captain Meares of the
Nootka and Captain Tipping of the *Sea Otter*, in the previous year
"had given such great prices in barter for skins, that the value of our
cargo was greatly reduced."[339] As a result, Portlock and Dixon got
only half of the number of skins that they had expected to get.[340] At
the end of the 1792 season, which saw the first peak in the number
of coasters, Captain Barkley encountered "such an extra-ordinary
competition," with "so many" vessels and prices "so high," that he
doubted that the trade was "worth following."[341] And in their eagerness for a quick and cheap killing some shipowners did not pay
enough attention to outfitting; the Spaniards told Captain Vancouver
in 1793 that the American coasters which had put in to Nootka
Sound that year were "in a most deplorable condition," lacking provisions, naval stores, and even trade goods.[342]

The second peak in 1801 saw even more reckless and ruinous competition, a veritable "Nor'west fever." "What a mania prevaild. among the American Merchants about 2 years since for North west voyages," exclaimed one participant in 1802.[343] Some owners, foreseeing an easy fortune, entered the trade "without either information or Capital";[344] Captain Jona Briggs of the schooner *Hetty* arrived on the coast in 1802 from Philadelphia expecting to obtain up to 3,000 skins, "notwithstanding he left home utterly ignorant of the coast & the manner in which the business is here conducted."[345] Some masters were too greedy and too foolish to respect the laws of supply and demand, so that whereas some prime skins were procured for articles that cost less than fifty cents in Boston, others were acquired for goods that cost nearly twice as much in Boston as the skins fetched in Canton.[346] In both cases the outcome was a "sinking," or "losing," voyage.

The uncompetitive quickly abandoned the business. Within two years of the second peak of 1801 the number of coasters had been halved (Table 1). The fewer owners as well as the fewer masters began to cooperate; the voyages of the *Hamilton* in 1809–12 and the *Lydia* in 1809–13 were sponsored by the same three separate firms of Theodore Lyman, J. and T. H. Perkins, and William Sturgis. As sea otters continued to dwindle, the weaker shipowners withdrew, leaving the overworked coast to fewer backers with more capital and more experience, so that by the 1820s only two or three firms were operating, their vessels acting in concert and staying year-round on the coast (one of them supplying goods and shipping skins, the others trading). Already by 1807 the firm of J. and T. H. Perkins, by their own admission, was dominant. In the summer of that year they informed Captain Benjamin Swift of the *Derby* that "we have at length got the NW Trade into our own hands ... & you will take advantage of this circumstance to raise the Price of the articles composing yr Cargo in barter for Skins ... acting in unison with [Captains] Suter [of the *Pearl*] and Whittemore [of the *Vancouver*]."[347] The owners were determined to exploit their position by raising not only the price of trade goods on the coast but also the value of sea-otter skins at Canton and of Chinese goods at Boston. In 1808 they advised their agency in Canton that "it is of the highest importance to endeavour to get the Price of Sea Otters up again & we have not any doubt, that with Your exertions & buying up small Parcells, you will succeed."[348] Later the same year they added that "if the [coast] Trade is open & many ships arrive in China, ship sparingly – If few arrive & you can get freight, ship largely."[349]

The fluctuating price of skins reflected the increasing number of trading vessels and the decreasing number of sea otters. At first the price of skins rose rapidly as the number of coasters accelerated to their first peak in 1792. Between 1787 and 1792 skins doubled in value on the western coast of Vancouver Island, the initial focus of traffic, thanks to "the avidity shewn by the rival adventures in this commerce, and the eagerness of an unrestrained throng of purchasers from different nations."[350] Captain Vancouver declared that such inflation "manifestly proved, that either a surplus quantity of European commodities had been since imported into this country, or more probably, that the avidity shewn by the rival adventurers in this commerce, and the eagerness of an unrestrained throng of purchasers from different nations, had brought European commodities into low estimation."[351] And evidently this doubling occurred within a single year – between 1791 and 1792.[352] At Nootka Sound in the autumn of 1792 the *Chatham*'s clerk, Edward Bell, found that a sheet of copper which had formerly fetched four skins now sometimes fetched only one, and that the first muskets to be traded had brought from six to seven skins but now only one to two.[353] Furthermore, the cost of skins doubled again between 1792 and 1795.[354] Little wonder that Captain Magee of the *Jefferson* complained in 1793 that skins were going "at a very extrevegent rate."[355] As early as 1796 shipmasters like John Boit were finding that a "voyage was not so lucrative as was contemplated at the commencement, owing to the rise [in cost] of skins on the coast & fall [in price] of the same at Canton."[356] It was for this reason that both voyages of the *Columbia Rediviva* were financial failures.[357]

In 1801, the year of the second peak in the number of coasters, Sullivan Dorr wrote to his father that "the trading ports all over the coast are furnished with an overstock of every species of trade, excepting eatables."[358] Consequently, skins were "excessively dear."[359] In the spring of that year, reported an officer of the *Atahualpa*, "the natives are astonished at the number of vessels that appear upon the coast," but not so much as to prevent them from asking "a very large price" for skins. "The Indians seem astonished at the number of ships they see, & they have sense enough to advantage by it, in demanding a large price for their furs." Competition was so keen that the high price – twenty yards of cloth instead of the usual four to eight – was paid; indeed by the end of May skins were "very scarce."[360] Sea-otter pelts continued to become fewer in number and higher in price. "Skins has become very scarce and dear," declared Captain Grimes of the *Owhyhee* in 1822,[361] and in 1827 Captain John Dominis of the same vessel voiced the same complaint to the owners: "The furs are very scarce every where, and particularly on this Coast. What we do get here is well paid for ..."[362] In two summers and one winter (1827–28) on the coast Captain William Martain, reputedly one of the ablest Nor'west skippers, was unable to procure more than 120 sea-otter and 800 beaver pelts, and the former cost eight times more than a decade earlier.[363] The only consolation for shipowners was the fact that, as sea-otter skins became less abundant on the coast, they became more valuable at Canton. As Bryant and Sturgis advised Captain James Hale of the *Ann* in 1818: "If your collection of Furs should not equal your expectation, do not be discouraged. If the whole quantity carried to Canton should be small the price there will doubtless be proportionably high. Only take care to get a full share of the whole collection and there is no doubt your voyage will prove a good one."[364]

As the cost of skins on the coast rose, the value of trade goods that were bartered for them fell, of course. Already in 1792 the Spanish at Nootka Sound asserted that the exchange value of copper had "declined through the competition of European vessels" – from half a large sheet for one skin in the spring of 1790 to one sheet in 1791 to two or three sheets in 1792.[365] (In 1791 British shipmasters traded sheets more than six feet long.[366]) Between the late 1780s and the early 1790s, that is, within four or five years, the worth of a sheet of copper fell from four skins to one and of a musket from six or seven skins to one or two.[367] Lieutenant Puget noted in 1793 that Nootka Sound skins, "though their Quality is inferior to many got on the Coast, are by far the Dearest," each costing fifteen shillings in goods.[368] Captain Cook's shipmates, by contrast, had bought skins there fifteen years earlier for only one shilling's worth of goods.[369] In 1799 at Sitka British traders complained that they could no longer compete with the Americans and would have to abandon the coast trade, because during the past decade the Yankees' presence had lowered the value of six yards of woollen cloth from six skins to one and of a musket from five skins to one.[370] On the northern coast a sea-otter skin's cost surged from two to four yards of blue broadcloth in 1799 to four to six yards in 1800, six to twenty yards in 1801, and fourteen to sixteen yards in 1802.[371] The peak year of 1801 was particularly volatile. Sullivan Dorr told his father that year that "you will be astonished at the extravagant prices given this season for skins, ten fathoms [twenty yards] of good blue cloth with a large present ... [or] two, three, nay four good musquetts with a large present."[372] On the Queen Charlottes a skin was worth one musket in 1801 but three muskets or five blankets in 1802.[373] On the northern coast a skin cost three blankets in 1800, four in 1812 (plus four bottles of molasses, two bottles of bread, one bottle of rice, an axe, "& other small presents"), five in 1823, seven (plus a present of rum, molasses, and rice) in 1835, and seven in 1839.[374] (According to another source, however, in 1823 as many as twenty blankets were paid for a skin.[375]) Renewed British competition drove the price as high as twelve blankets in 1833,[376] but thereafter the price fell somewhat as the "Boston opposition" waned.

Increasingly an assortment of goods was paid for a sea-otter skin. In 1822 Captain Grimes of the *Owhyhee* reported that the "standing price" of a skin on the northern coast was six yards of duffel, three blankets, two gallons of rice, and two gallons of molasses, plus small presents, or two muskets or two kegs of gunpowder with one to three gallons of rum.[377] Three years later the Haidas demanded and obtained seven blankets, one musket or one keg of gunpowder, and one axe from Captain William McNeill of the *Lama* for a skin.[378] Finally, Lieutenant Simpson found in 1828 that American shipmasters were paying the "extravagant rate" of ten $3\frac{1}{2}$-point blankets, two gallons of mixed rum, two gallons of molasses, and two gallons of rice or seven $3\frac{1}{2}$-point blankets and one gun for a sea-otter skin, and one $3\frac{1}{2}$-point blanket or six yards of cotton cloth or one gun for a beaver pelt; this price was more than double that of 1812.[379] Simpson's superior, his cousin Governor George Simpson of the HBC, was determined to lower this high "tariff" after eliminating American competition.

Skin prices not only rose steadily from year to year but also soared during a single season in response to competition. A sea-otter skin on the Queen Charlottes cost twice as much in iron collars at the close as at the start of the 1793 season.[380] In 1799 at Hoodsnahoo in the "straits" in late May the *Caroline* paid double what she had given there at the beginning of April, and in Sitka Sound in early June she paid treble what she had given there at the beginning of April (so the skippers of the *Caroline*, *Dispatch*, and *Hancock* agreed to fix a common price of 50 per cent less and to divide the returns equally).[381] In addition, of course, skin prices varied from place to place in the same season, again depending upon the extent of competition. In 1792 a skin cost ten iron chisels at Nootka Sound (the focus of competition), seven at Clayoquot Sound, five at Tatoosh Island, three at Zenith (on the Strait of Georgia?), and one in Queen Charlotte Sound.[382] And in 1796 the price of a skin was two yards of blue cloth on the southwestern coast of Vancouver Island opposite the Olympic Peninsula but six yards at busier Nootka Sound on the central-western coast of the island.[383]

The sea-otter traffic reached its "lowest ebb" at the close of the 1801 season, when the Indian market was glutted with textiles and muskets, because of the excessive prices given by as many as two dozen trading vessels. Now the Natives would accept only rice, molasses, and bread – "eatables" – and were even trading cloth and muskets back to the Euroamericans for biscuit.[384] Thereafter the inflation seems to have been arrested somewhat as more and more disillusioned owners abandoned the "savage"[385] coast for rosier prospects such as the Hawaiian sandalwood trade, the Californian hide-and-tallow trade, or Pacific sealing or whaling. Skin prices merely slowed their rise rather than fell, however, as the decreasing competition was offset by the diminishing peltry. In 1829 sea-otter skins were so uncommon and so valuable that one was worth ten beaver pelts, and a Haida in possession of a skin would dicker for at least two days and meanwhile demand special privileges, such as free access to the captain's cabin for eating, drinking, and lounging.[386] Lieutenant Simpson lamented in 1828 that "the spirit of opposition has tended very much too to spoil these Indians, the several Traders to ingratiate themselves with them, having granted indulgences and put up [with] such offences that has made the Natives take a very high footing with the Whites, and has lost for us the respect which we ought to command among Indians."[387] By then, although the coast trade was far from over owing to the taking of more and more land furs by trading vessels, the sea-otter trade was coming to a close. At the end of the 1827 season Marshall and Wildes were informed by their Honolulu agent that "the North West ships have done miserable enough the last year – not 150 Skins each, and what they have got cost on an avarage Thirty Dollars. That trade is finished for the present, no object for more than two vessels in one season."[388]

Given the hurdles and hazards of the coast trade, it is not surprising that Nor'westmen were glad when the hold had been filled with furs and they could leave the "savage" coast, especially with the attractions of the Hawaiian Islands ahead of them. One of the earliest traders, Captain James Colnett, wrote: "We sail'd in good health & if any of the Crews spirits had Flagg'd from the late Misfortunes a fair wind, leaving a Country half cover'd from the summit of its hills to the waters Edge with snow & no refreshments to be had, going to one supply'd with every refreshment a sailor wish'd but Grog revived them."[389] Captain Cleveland of the *Caroline* opined in 1799 that "the criminal who receives a pardon under the gallows, could hardly feel a greater degree of exultation" than a shipmaster leaving "this inhospitable coast."[390] An officer of the *Vancouver* was more specific: "8 [August, 1806] ... maid all haste that was possable to git out of Sight of this horrid Savage Land after 17 Months & 13 Days of rocks & Sholes & Daggers ice & Snow wit & Could & Nothing to Eate But Salt junk [hard salted beef] & Spruce tea."[391] The supercargo of the *Lydia* laconically expressed the common sentiment upon the ship's departure from the coast on 11 August 1806: "Thank god for getting Safe off the Coast."[392]

AT THE ISLANDS

Initially the Hawaiian Islands were a balmy, carnal larder for the coasters. It was not long, however, before the "isles of the blessed" had been blemished by the commercial, religious, and cultural pressures of Euroamerican traders, missionaries, castaways, and others. The risk of native attack actually lessened after the killing of Captain Cook, particularly once King Kamehameha I gained control of most of the archipelago. Nevertheless, in 1791 the coaster *Fair American* with 750 sea-otter skins was captured by Chief Kaiana, and five of the seven seamen, including Captain Simon Metcalf, were killed;[393] and as late as the end of 1794 the *Jackal*'s Captain William Brown and the *Prince Lee Boo*'s Captain Robert Gordon were killed and their ships captured by islanders (although both vessels were later recovered by surviving crewmen). As on the coast, these attacks were not unprovoked. In the early 1790s Captain Vancouver found that the Hawaiians were very displeased that "North-West American adventurers" had traded defective firearms and adulterated gunpowder for prime provisions; in the winter of 1792–93 the *Butterworth*, Captain William Brown, and the *Jackal*, Captain Alexander Stewart, sold some two dozen muskets to Kamehameha I which proved to be "such trash" and "so very bad that some of them burst on the first firing"[394] (significantly, both vessels were sister ships of the *Prince Lee Boo*, whose Captain Gordon was killed along with Captain Brown in 1794).

As the islanders became more "civilized" they, especially the chiefs, also became more self-indulgent and materialistic. By the late 1810s they had degenerated through overeating, overdrinking, and over-smoking – inflamed eyes and cankered skin were common – and the islands themselves had been scarred by the over-cutting of sandalwood trees. More important for the maritime fur traders was the sharp rise in the price of supplies as the number of producers decreased and the amount of Kamehameha I's exactions increased. As early as 1793 Captain Vancouver found that parts of Maui and Hawaii were "greatly impoverished and exhausted of supplies" and their lands "neglected" on account of the recruiting of soldiers by warring chiefs and the victualing of "half famished" trading vessels.[395]

In 1806 the supercargo of the *Lydia* complained that "we have traded very Little here at these Islands the King is got To nowing all his Cry is for [Spanish silver] dollars he asks Six dollars a piece for his hogs."[396] The *Behring* had a similar experience in 1814. "The Natives are unanimous in demanding dollars for almost every Article which they have for sale," stated its log, adding that "their demanding specie is not the greatest evil, the price has been enormously increased, Viz for a common sized Hog from four to six dollars & every thing else in proportion."[397] In 1818 Captain Hill of the *Packet* found that pigs and vegetables were "Scarce & Dear."[398] By 1825 the chiefs were demanding a "ridiculously high price" for provisions; hogs were now ten dollars each and vegetables "equally dear."[399] This was a far cry from 1791, when two iron spikes fetched a hog, or 1793, when Captain Vancouver's expedition bought up to ten hogs for one yard of red cloth.[400] What was even more frustrating for the Nor'westmen was the increasing inaccessibility – after the arrival of missionaries – of *wahines*. By 1826 female commoners were no longer readily available, thanks to the propagation of the virtues of chastity by the missionaries, who in 1825 had forbade native women from frequenting trading vessels.[401]

OFF CHINA

The voyage from the Hawaiian Islands across the western Pacific was uneventful. Approaching the Asian mainland, however, fur-trading vessels could encounter the "great winds" – typhoons – of the Philippine, East China, and South China Seas, especially between May and November, when most of these tropical cyclones swirled towards the coast out of mid-ocean. They could dismast, beach, or sink a ship. In October 1787 the *Nootka* was caught by a typhoon in the Typa and, having only one anchor left after a sojourn on the Northwest Coast, had to run ashore to escape destruction; in late September 1791 the *Gustavus* was nearly sunk by a typhoon in the East China Sea, three men being drowned and the cargo drenched; in October 1792 the *Lady Washington* was dismasted by a typhoon four days out of Macao en route to the Northwest Coast, one of its officers exclaiming that "the whole surface of the sea was cover'd with the Wrecks of Chinese *Boats*, and many of the poor fishermen was still hanging to peices of the Boats"; and sometime in 1800 the American schooner *Rover* was likely lost in a typhoon off China.[402] Another of these Pacific hurricanes struck Canton on 12 July 1801 and lasted seven hours; up to 10,000 lives were lost and 100 junks between Canton and Whampoa were wrecked.[403] Typhoons were particularly ferocious at the alteration of the northeast and southwest monsoons in April and October. But because most Northwest Coastmen made for Canton in the late autumn, and left for Boston in late winter, they usually avoided the typhoon hazard.

There was a greater threat from ladrones – daring and vicious Chinese and Malay coastal and riverine pirates/rebels in fast proas who exacted tribute from vessels and villages (*ladrones* translates as "robbers" in Portuguese).[404] As US Consul Edward Carrington reported to Secretary of State James Madison in 1807 from Canton, "The Coast of China and particularly the entrance to this Port, have for a long time been infested by China Ladrones or Pirates, in very alarming and considerable forces."[405] In the middle 1830s Canton's English-language yearbook reported that "from time immemorial, the southern Chinese coast has been infamous for the robberies on its waters," owing to the nature of the coast itself (numerous indentations, islands, and shoals, hidden harbours, and intricate passages), the extreme poverty and seafaring expertise of the lower classes, and the impotence of the imperial navy.[406] Seldom was the coast "free from foam," as the Chinese expressed it. The increasing severity of the problem at the end of the eighteenth century reflected growing social unrest in China,[407] with not a few of the malcontents turning to piracy.

The pirate threat peaked during the first decade of the nineteenth century, when they infested the shores of Kwantung Province, particularly the mouth of the Pearl River.[408] After 1801 the Ladrone (Wan-shan) Islands off the river's mouth became the headquarters of pirates who had left Annam after having failed to restore the Mongol Yuan dynasty there.[409] These corsairs actually besieged the Pearl River delta between 1804 and 1809.[410] "They plunder every thing in their power, as well on shore as at sea," wrote Captain Lisiansky, who added that "they will sometimes attack a vessel under the very batteries [of Macao]."[411] Lisiansky's commander, Captain Von Krusenstern, wrote: "These pirates have vessels of two hundred tons in their fleet, manned with one hundred and fifty or two hundred seamen, and mounting from ten to twenty guns; and the smallest of their boats carry thirty or forty men," so "In the road of Macao, and even in the Typa, vessels were not secure against their attacks; and the passage from Macao to Canton was particularly dangerous."[412] In the spring of 1804 the ladrones numbered 400 junks and 80,000 men, and they were strong enough to occupy the Typa anchorage for several weeks.[413] A year later there were 600–700 pirate vessels off the South China coast, and they even threatened the foreign factories at Canton.[414] A pirate confederacy flourished from 1805 to 1810; by

1809–10, when they virtually ruled the Southern Sea, there were 800 large and 1,000 small pirate sail on China's southern coast with 70,000 men.[415]

The large British Indiamen, high sided and well manned and armed, did not fear the ladrones,[416] but the smaller fur-trading vessels were more vulnerable. In the summer of 1809 pirates captured lighters between Canton and Whampoa and attacked the *Atahualpa* twice in the Pearl estuary; the first time Captain Sturgis outran some 200 pirate sail in Macao Roads and killed three pirates, and the second time the *Atahualpa* was in the company of four other American vessels.[417] The Manchu navy being weak, and the suppression of provincial rebellions taking priority, the pirates were not quelled until the spring of 1810, when, having split into two factions, they were curbed not by arms but by bribes.[418] Nevertheless, some pirates continued to plunder, ransom, and destroy, particularly near Hainan and Fukien. At the end of 1817 Bryant and Sturgis warned Captain Suter of the *Mentor* to beware of pirates: "When you arrive on the Coast of China be strictly on your guard against the Ladrones, who are prowling about in *small* Boats, and getting on board ship under pretense of furnishing Pilots, etc."[419]

Equally dangerous were British and French privateers, particularly in Sunda Strait separating Sumatra and Java.[420] More troublesome than dangerous were British warships whose commanders claimed the right of search for deserters at Canton, the Americans there being powerless to prevent such "violent outrages."[421] In 1805–07 ships of war of His Britannic Majesty detained and searched US ships at Whampoa and impressed British deserters, alias American sailors.[422] British naval supremacy became a menace during the War of 1812, when the fear of capture by the king's men of war kept many American merchantmen in their home ports. The captains of the coasters *Atahualpa*, *Lydia*, *Packet*, and *Pedler* were instructed by Bryant and Sturgis in early 1813 to "take down their Furs to Canton," proceeding "with all possible caution to avoid capture by the British."[423] They succeeded in doing so, but others were less fortunate. From 20 December 1812 to 23 November 1813 fourteen American merchantmen, including three from the Northwest Coast (the *Beaver*, *Katherine*, and *New Hazard*), were condemned (forfeited) at Canton.[424] Owing to the threat of capture, only two-thirds as many American vessels plied the coast trade in 1814 as in 1812 and 1813 and only one-half as many as in 1811 (Table 1). American turnover at Canton for the three seasons of 1812–13, 1813–14, and 1814–15 was but one-half that of 1811–12 and less than one-third that of 1809–10.[425] Added to the peril of ladrones, privateers, and warships were vigilant *guardas de costa* off New Spain. More than one clandestine Yankee coaster was impounded in Chile or California.

AT CANTON

The closer that the Northwest Coastmen got to Canton, the greater the obstacles that awaited them. The Pearl River itself offered no physical impediments; it had only a few mud shoals, which did little damage to grounded ships, and a very moderate current of up to four miles per hour.[426] But the pilots, who were taken aboard in Macao Roads, were not to be completely trusted, being "in general very ignorant of a ship, or the navigation from Macao to Canton,"[427] although they commonly charged $20 for their services. More damaging was the money – and the time – lost at Canton on sundry charges, bribes, and thefts. Admittedly, John Forbes, a Boston merchant with world-wide commercial interests, declared that "I never saw in this country [United States] such a high average of fair dealing as there [China]."[428] And John Cushing, the longtime American agent at Canton, recalled that "it was a place of business where he had had more facilities and less disputes than any other he was acquainted with." He added: "I can only say that the Americans never had much difficulty in business there; they have always gone on very regularly, and without any embarrassment [indebtedness], except on one or two occasions."[429] But these assertions were belied by the experiences of those American traders with less capital, particularly before 1800, whereupon the sea-otter trade began to come under the control of fewer merchants with more capital. As one of these smaller capitalists, Sullivan Dorr, remarked, "the Chineese are very vexatious" at "this de[te]stible place."[430] The Irishman Peter Dobell, who sojourned at Macao and Whampoa in 1798, 1803–10, and 1820, found that the mandarins were as corrupt as the commoners were frugal, industrious, sober, and congenial, and that their corruption resulted from their unchecked authority and niggardly remuneration. "No where under heaven," he wrote, "is the adage, 'every man has his price,' so well exemplified as in the Celestial Empire."[431]

Dishonesty and corruption were standard at Canton, on the part of both the lowest coolie and the highest mandarin. One observer advised the prospective trader "to deal with every man, comme s'il avait faire avec un Coquin," that is, as if he were dealing with a rogue. "You are entirely in their power & they will cheat you if they are inclined so to do," he added, so "be Vigilant, shew them by your Conduct that you are acquainted with the Trade & that you are a good judge of Goods."[432] The theft of inbound cargo from lighters between ship and factory was not uncommon.[433] First Mate John Boit, who accused the Cantonese "common folk" of poisoning the *Columbia Rediviva*'s pigs and scavenging chicken innards and rat carcasses from the river, asserted that "no Indians we had ever visited during the Voyage was more complete in the Art of theiving than the Chinese of the lower order on this River."[434] Probably they were driven by poverty and perhaps even by obliquity. Convicts were banished to Kwangtung Province in general and Hainan Island in particular, so the morality of the populace of Canton may have been lower than the Chinese average.[435]

More serious were the charges and extortions of officials. They were notoriously corrupt and greedy, and these traits led to the imposition of as many exactions as possible and to bribery and the evasion of regulations. At the turn of the century a French visitor decried "the indolence, the avidity, and the knavery of a Mandarin,"[436] and a Russian observer complained that "fraud and deceit are the prevailing practice here."[437] The Russian's commanding officer reported that the customs chief and hong merchant each extorted $5,000 from every fur-trading vessel.[438] The hongist was particularly grasping, arbitrary, and dilatory. He was described by Boit:

The Chinese *merchant* is very particular in his business, and very nice [exact] in his Calculations, and no part of his affairs appear to be unnotic'd by him. In making a bargain they are very *shrewd*, when closed they are *faithfull* as to quantity, but for quality you must be constantly on your guard or else 'tis certain the Goods will not turn out as expected, and the only satisfaction you will get from them Is that you ought to have looked sharper, and at the same [time] will try to Console you by this remark, that on another Voyage you will be better acquainted with the mode of doing business at Canton. Upon the whole, the Candour that is about the Chinese merchant makes some amends for the generall complaint against them, (that they *will* cheat you, if they can) therefore your business is to see (*that they shall not*).[439]

Sullivan Dorr concurred, and even more bluntly. "Chinamen lye from the Grand squeeze Gut of a Hoppo down to the lowest ... I know of no honest Chinamen," he declared, adding that "they [Chinese traders] are capable of such duplicity" and were "*arch rouges* [*sic*] *indeed*."[440] Dorr gave an example of the chicanery of the hongist Consequa in a letter to his father in 1799: "Consequai ... being a good adept at mixing teas ... it requires great circumspection in dealing with these fellows, and then you may be egregiously cheated, for over the packing place, some of them have trap doors through which they drop old good for nothing teas, in the dust of packing."[441] Two years later Dorr reported that green teas, particularly old ones, were sometimes dusted with Prussian blue or brown to enhance their colour, and that Bohea tea was "much adulterated" by the addition of inferior teas and apple, peach, and other leaves.[442] Other black teas, besides Bohea, were likewise subject to "the greatest deception" on the part of the Chinese, according to an American mechant, but he added that even in buying green teas it was advisable to "start" (open) several chests in each chop (1 chop = 120 chests) to check the uniformity of their contents, "as the common run of Hyson Chests will have good at Top, the middle indifferent, the bottom pure H[yson]. Skin [the chaff of Hyson – large, loose lumps or leaves]."[443] Another American merchant offered similar advice: "The Cooleys & Boatmen often play Tricks, & you should not be surprised if in a Cargo a Chest or two should prove pure Chaff. Young Hyson is now no more than some inferior Hyson broken or ground down."[444] Weighing, too, was subject to fraud. Dobell found that "as every thing, even to the smallest trifle, is sold in China by weight, and weighed by what is called a *tyching*, or steelyard, which is oftentimes false, the Chinese, who are exceedingly expert, will cheat strangers in spite of every precaution."[445] An American supercargo described some of the dishonest trading practices of Chinese vendors at Canton at the very end of the 1700s:

They have a great variety of fancy birds carried around for sale in their cages … but they are great cheats with them. While we were at Canton the mate of a vessel bought a cage-full of birds of various and beautiful plumage and was delighted to carry home such a beautiful variety of birds, when one evening a sudden shower came up and they were forgotten on deck, after which he found his birds all changed, the paint having washed off and not a handsome one among them. He opened his cage, let all his birds at liberty, d—d the Chinaman, and hove his cage overboard. A man should have his eye-teeth cut to come to Canton. The carpenter of our ship having paid eight dollars for a purchase, through the art of the Chinaman got into a dispute, when the carpenter demanded his money, and did not find out that, in lieu of his good, he had received counterfeit, until he had gone down on board of the ship when he found every dollar was a plated one. I made a contract for a hundred umbrellas and laying the sample one [a]side I gave a scratch with my nail on the handle as customary. The Chinaman brought it to our factory when I at once saw it was an inferior quality and without the scratch: that made me sure. I kicked the fellow down stairs for a villain. This is allowable here in such cases and the easiest way of getting satisfaction, but to do it is not exactly pleasing, for they are the most humble beings on earth, which rather gives it the appearance of a cowardly act, and one that I should not mention but to give you a little of the character of the people.[446]

Captain Dixon's appraisal of Canton's merchants was only slightly less negative. "A sharping, cheating disposition, *with some very few exceptions*, is generally prevalent amongst them," he wrote. Particularly the compradores were not to be trusted, he added, complaining that they "weigh every thing alive, and make use of every art to make their hogs, geese, ducks, etc. weigh heavy ... often cram them with stones, and give them salt and water to make them thirsty, and in short use every method in their power to defraud and over-reach their employers."[447] Another Occidental merchant agreed. "The Whampoa Compradores are great Cheats," he declared, "& all require a good Guarantee for their Conduct & particularly for the money you are obliged to advance as a gratuity for undertaking to furnish your Ship which is generally 200 Dollars for a Ship with Crew of 20 or 30 persons."[448] Such was the case because the authorities above the compradores extorted more than $500 from them for the privilege of supplying such a ship.[449] Consequently, provisions cost a merchantman double through a compradore;[450] in 1798–99 the officers of the *Neptune* figured that their compradore made a profit of 200–300 per cent, "that is, we suppose he buys for about one-quarter what he charges us."[451] In the middle 1790s the most trustworthy compradore, incidentally, was Attoy (or Atti) of Macao.[452]

Moreover, American traders lost money when hong merchants "very frequently" suffered "embarrassments" (bankruptcies) and were imprisoned or banished, since the Chinese authorities considered bankruptcy disgraceful and criminal.[453] The list of bankrupts included Howqua (Puiqua) in 1789, Eequa in 1790, Shy Kinqua in 1795, Munqua in 1797, Geowqua in 1798, Ponqua and Gnewqua in 1810, and Patqua (Exchin) in 1822; Munqua was so embarrassed that he killed himself, and Ponqua and Gnewqua were but two of five hongists who were bankrupted in the same year by over-extending credit to American traders.[454] Their financial difficulties arose from the periodic heavy exactions of rapacious officials; the high interest charges (up to 20 per cent per annum) of foreign lenders, liquid capital being scarce in China and the resultant high interest rates attracting foreign investors; the stiff competition from illicit traders, who evaded duties; and the general unprofitableness of their business.[455] Because they borrowed money at such high rates of interest, the hong merchants were anxious to invest all borrowed capital, leaving nothing for contingencies.[456] Their most profitable business was done with American traders, since they dealt mostly in specie ("plenty dollars") or furs ("soft gold"), not unsaleable cottons or woollens; that is why Howqua favoured American clients.[457] The hongists even had to buy both their appointments and retirements. Their position became so precarious and unenviable that usually only one-half to two-thirds of the hong openings were filled. In the 1820s there were only four hong merchants with whom it was considered safe to deal.[458] Thus there was a gradual concentration of Canton hongists, just as there was of Boston merchants in the coast trade.

The American "round eyes" themselves, at least some of them, were partly to blame for the plight of the hong merchants. Those ship-owners who were short of capital occasionally took loans or advances from the hongists and then defaulted. The US consul at Canton reported in 1795 that American traders had become notorious because some shipmasters were both fools and rogues; he cited Captain Ingraham's debt of $43,821 to Consequa as an example. He added: "It is absolutely necessary some steps should be taken to retrieve the character of the Americans here. Such villainies have been practised as have sickened the Chinese from having any dealings with them on that liberal scale they would otherwise adopt."[459] Again, in 1814 Ponseequa went so far as to petition President James Madison to help him recover debts that were owed to him by some American traders who had been given credit because "during recent years, the Americans had brought in fewer imports, so they could not pay their debts either in cash or in kind."[460] The "fewer imports" included, of course, fewer sea-otter skins.

Although the skins brought "very high prices" at Canton, particularly at first, they were eroded by various transaction costs, which were "very heavy."[461] "The Chinese always, as we say here, squeeze hard," reported an American supercargo, "that is, make you pay well" for anything.[462] Although all duties on imports and exports were paid by the Chinese merchants, their amount still formed part of the price of goods – as much as 50 per cent[463]. Charles Marjoribanks, a veteran servant of the EIC, testified that in the middle 1820s the Chinese import duty was 1⅓ taels, or 8 shillings, 9 pence, or $1.94 per hundred for sea-otter skins, and 6⅛ taels, or £2/–/10, or $8.89 per hundred for beaver pelts[464] (assuming 1 tael = 6 shillings, 6 pence and £1 = $4.44).[465] In 1822 the Perkins and Russell firm cited an import duty of 10 cents per fur and an export duty of four or five times this amount at Canton, plus "heavy transit Duties & Extortions" from Canton to the interior of China.[466]

High duties were compounded by high port charges, which had to be paid before a merchantman could open hatches. The measurement, or tonnage, fee was ten dollars per ton and totalled up to $3,000 for an American coaster.[467] A ship was measured by multiplying its length by its width and dividing the product by ten (depth was not considered).[468] (According to Parkinson, however, the Chinese multiplied the distance between the centre of the foremast and the centre of the mizzenmast by the ship's extreme width at the gangway, multiplied the result by the half-width, and then divided by ninety-four.[469]) The fee discriminated against the smaller (280–300 ton) American coasters because it was not pro-rated for vessels of less than 400 tons; however, when American ships in general became narrower and deeper, as well as longer, in the 1810s they probably paid less for their capacity than Indiamen. Also, the Hoppo appropriated a certain number of the best furs from a ship's cargo (or demanded a sum of money instead from the ship's security merchant).[470] In addition, the cumshaw ("golden sand"), or gratuity, for provisions had to be rendered, lighters and a warehouse had to be rented, and coolies, an interpreter, and a security merchant had to be paid as well as bribed with gifts. Cumshaw signified present, and it originated in the payment made by the earliest foreign vessels for the privilege of entering the port.[471] It amounted to 1,900–1,950 taels (more than £600 or $2,700) for all ships, regardless of size, so that the smaller American craft were more likely to try to avoid it by smuggling.[472] Port charges for an American vessel amounted to at least $4,500 in 1789–90, $5,000–$5,500 in 1801–02, and $7,000–8,000 in the 1820s.[473] In the winter of 1789–90 the *Columbia Rediviva*, Captain Gray, received $21,400 for 700 pelts and 300 pieces of fur but expended $10,158.50 for port, factory, and commission charges, leaving $11,241.50 for investment in a return cargo of China goods.[474] All in all, a trading vessel's expenses at Canton could equal up to one-half of the value of its cargo of furs.[475] In 1807 a ship of 300 tons with thirty men staying three months paid some $7,500, including $2,600 for cumshaw, $200 for a compradore, $40 for pilotage inwards and $56 for pilotage outwards, $216 for a linguist, and $500–1,000 for factory rental.[476] Around 1820 a large ship staying from two to three months paid $6,000–10,000.[477] These exhorbitant charges could have meant that traders profited not from the sale of skins at Canton but from the sale of Chinese goods from Canton in Europe and the United States were it not for the apparent evasion of some or all of the charges by the traders with the complicity of the Chinese; in 1798 the *Neptune* evaded the cumshaw by rendering "a couple bottles New England rum."[478] As one longtime New England China merchant recalled, because of the rampant corruption of officials, "in very few cases did the private trader at Canton pay the regular imperial charges."[479] Bribe-taking was simply commonplace. Moreover, from 1824 American ships could lawfully avoid all of the measurement and part of the cumshaw by bringing rice to Canton to help feed China's burgeoning population, so en route they often stopped in the Philippines for that commodity.[480] And from 1833, when a severe famine struck China, ships carrying rice only were exempted from all port charges.[481]

The heavy port charges were exacerbated by the long time it took – two or three months was not unusual – to complete a transaction at Canton. Although one shipmaster stated that trade was conducted with more dispatch than at any other port in the world,[482] most Nor'westmen found otherwise. The longer their business took, the costlier chandlering, warehousing, and interpreting became, of course. And overstayers had to pay demurrage. Traffic was further protracted by occasional short-term trade bans, usually imposed by the Chinese authorities after their countrymen had been killed in brawls with Euroamerican sailors, as in 1820 and 1822, or by the EIC in retaliation for the irresolution of longstanding grievances, as in 1814 and 1821. During the 1821–22 trading season "all business" was halted for two months over the accidental drowning of a Chinese woman and the summary strangulation of the responsible American sailor by the Chinese authorities.[483] Probably the most serious hiatus occurred in 1791, when on 13 March the Chinese imposed a ban on the importation of sea-otter skins, "as they were at war with Russia and they supposed by stopping the fur trade they would injure that nation," having "a mistaken idea that all fur ships were in some measure concerned with the Russians."[484] Eventually the Chinese realized their mistake, and besides, as Captain Marchand noted, "the taste of the Chinese for furs is so decided, so general," and they lifted the ban on 1 June 1792.[485] Because of the prohibition only half as many ships traded at Canton in 1791–92 as in 1790–91,[486] although some coasters resorted to smuggling. Unfortunately for the French, *La Solide*, Captain Marchand, arrived with its skins during the ban, as did some Spanish skins.

As a result of the prohibitions and exactions, smuggling was rampant.[487] The most popular anchorage for clandestine trade was Dirty Butter, or Lark's, Bay on an island just southwest of Macao. Here ships were able "to save the payment of duties on their cargoes, since the bay was out of the reach of Chinese authority at that time."[488] Smuggled skins brought twice as much there as licit skins did at Canton.[489] Dirty Butter Bay, however, as one American smuggler complained, was "if possible ... a more lonely Situation than upon the N.W. Coast."[490] More important, it was frequented by pirates and opium-runners. Thus the owners of the *Hope*, J. and T. H. Perkins, instructed the supercargo "on arrival in China best sell the furs down the River, to avoid charges", but added: "Never trust a Chinese with property out of sight, as they are free from the inducement to be honest with which they are bound at Canton. Your guns and boarding nettings should be ready night and day."[491] (The *Hope* spent three months at Lark's Bay in the winter of 1791–92 with five other coasters: the *Hancock, Fairy, Grace, Gustavus,* and *Washington*.[492])

Naturals disasters like typhoons, floods, and fires caused further delays. Fires were "very common" in Canton,[493] and they were especially frequent in the suburbs during the NE monsoon. The "great fire" of 1–2 November 1822 was the worst. It destroyed 67 or 68 of the 70 foreign residences, 8,000–12,000 Chinese buildings in the city's western suburb, including 7,000 outside shops, 30,000 chests of tea, and several thousand piculs of sandalwood; the loss of property totalled $12–15 million, including $1,500,000 worth belonging to the EIC.[494] The log of the American ship *Caledonia* contains a vivid description of this disaster:

On the first of November, after a long spell of dry weather & during the prevalence of a brisk North wind, at ten o'clock at night a fire broke out, in the western suburb of Canton about a mile north of the Factories. By midnight it had spread to an alarming extent & some anxiety for the safety of the factories began to be felt. At 1 AM an order for men & boats was despatched to the Ships at Whampoa. At 3 AM the fire was within half a mile of the Factories & their destruction seemed inevitable. Chop boats were procured by the Foreigners & many of them began to embark their property. By 5 AM the consternation became general & the arrival of assistance from the shipping importunely looked for. Owing to the tides being contrary both to & from Whampoa the officers & men from the ships did not begin to arrive until 7 o'clock. they were the means of saving much property as the fire had then reached the rear of the Factories which, except three, were in a few hours laid in ruins.

From the Factories the flames took a direction along the river side to the Westward for two miles extending ½ to ¾ of a mile back from the shore. Towards evening it ceased to spread but the fire was vivid all night & was not entirely extinguished for four or five days.

The Chinese authorities state the destruction of 10,500 houses, of which 3000 were shops & many were houses. Of about 70 Factories occupied by Foreigners three in the Greek hong are all that remain; they are occupied by B.C. Wilcocks Esq. American Consul, and Mr. Berry and Maignac British merchants.

The loss of property has been immense. The Eng. Company's loss is stated at half a million Sterling, chiefly in Cloths and Long ells. Manqua, Hong merchant, had a large amount in Company Teas ready for shipping which were all burnt. Nearly all the Crape dyers shops & several large Crape warehouses were destroyed. Upwards of 20,000 chests of Black & 10,000 chests of Green Teas were lost. Several Chinese mostly small footed females lost their lives. A seaman of the America of New York perished. Part of his body was found among the ruins.

A Police guard was encamped near the foot of Hog lane to keep the mob from plundering. The English also have a guard, drafted from the Crews of their ships which was more efficient.

The Specie from the Factories was sent to the ships at Whampoa.

Throughout this scene of destruction there was no attempt made by the Chinese to check the fire. Unless occupied in removing their goods they were looking on with a degree of apathy almost incredible. Certainly by pulling down a few houses in the first instance & attending to extinguish the sparks which were very thick the loss might have been confined to a few thousand dollars, instead of extending as it has to several lives, millions of property & the utter ruin of many industrious subjects.[495]

Delays at Canton were costly for merchantmen. According to Sullivan Dorr, the cost of delay to an American trader amounted to about $100 per day.[496] And the longer the delay, the greater the risk of the crewmen taking sick and the ship missing the monsoon. Canton's morbidity was evidenced by the number of crewmen "in the sick list," commonly from one to four daily. Captain Von Krusenstern declared that "in no parts of the world did the small pox commit such ravages as in China,"[497] and Canton was likely an epicentre of the disease, which was but one of several that struck seamen there. Smallpox was an annual epideme in Canton Province, and it was usually most virulent from February (when most coasters were still there) to June.[498] Smallpox vaccine was introduced to China in 1805 by Dr Pierson, second physician at the factory of the East India Company, and Dr Balmis, a Spanish physician from Manila, but it had to be reintroduced on at least two occasions thereafter.[499] "Bloody flux" (dysentery) was more common, usually resulting from the abrupt change from salted to fresh food upon docking. In the 1798–99 season, eight or nine crewmen of the sealer *Neptune* went "down with the flux" at Whampoa, and four of them died.[500]

More serious was the decline of fur prices at Canton (Table 9), for the "round eyes" were willing to suffer the frustrating regulations, exhorbitant exactions, and insulting indignities only so long as there were large profits to be made. But, as Captain Lisiansky noted, "such immense quantities are imported by American ships, that the market is often glutted with them."[501] As supply rose from the middle 1780s, demand and hence prices fell, reaching their lowest level in the early and middle 1790s, and falling almost as low again a dozen years later – in each case several years after peaks in the number of trading vessels on the coast. At the end of 1785 a single coaster brought 560 sea-otter skins to Canton, where they fetched $43 each; at the end of 1791 six vessels anchored at Whampoa with 11,000 skins, which brought only $25 apiece; and in 1805 six ships took up to 23,000 skins to Canton, where this glut further lowered the price to $18 per skin.[502] Between 1785 and 1792 the price of skins fell threefold at Canton (and rose fourfold on the Northwest Coast).[503] Conversely, however, with the depletion of sea otters on the coast supply decreased and demand and hence prices increased at Canton. As the Russians told Lieutenant Simpson at Sitka in 1827, "sea Otters were becoming scarce to the Northward, but ... they commanded ... a price high in proportion as the quantity decreased."[504] By 1845–46 the top price at Canton for a prime pelt ($150) even exceeded that ($120) which had astonished Captain King in 1779–80.[505] Prices had come full circle and more. Captain Von Krusenstern was largely correct when he predicted in 1810 that "it is probable that the price of a sea-otter skin will never be less than eighteen or twenty piasters," since "it finds as certain a market with the Chinese as cotton, tin, and opium."[506] The higher prices for the fewer skins allowed fur traders to stay in business, although as late as 1821–22 the Canton price of $40 was, for the *Rob Roy* at least, "good but more is necessary to make a voyage."[507]

As Table 9 indicates, the value of imports, including sea-otter skins, as well as the value of exports, fluctuated appreciably at Canton from year to year, season to season, month to month, and even week to week, depending largely upon the amount imported and the amount exported.[508] Skins marketed late in the season (say February and March) brought only one-third as much as those marketed in December and January, and even the latter fetched no more than $30 each in 1792–93 because already "there are a great many at market and many more expected."[509] Skins averaged $35 in 1815–16 (Table 9) but at the end of that season (by which time the market had been sated) the *Behring's* brought only $7.30.[510] Smuggled skins, which paid no duties, also brought more – $50–70 each in 1789–90[511] compared with a seasonal average price of $30 for lawful skins (Table 9). Quality was a factor, too, of course. For instance, Northwest Coast otter skins fetched more than those from California – $60–75 versus $45–55 in 1831–32.[512] Prices were also affected by the medium of exchange. Skins brought less if they were sold for money rather than goods – $25 in cash versus $27 in kind in the autumn of 1799 and $23 versus $26 at the end of the same year.[513] In paying for Chinese goods in money either the price was lower or the quality was higher by 10 to 20 per cent, "so that if you send a money Ship you may expect the best of goods at less prices than for skins," Sullivan Dorr reported.[514] He stressed that a "rich" ship, that is, one laden with silver dollars, would fare better at Canton than a vessel with a cargo of furs: "At all times you may expect inferior goods for Otter Seal or any other Skins and cargo, unless you accept the price at which they can be consolidated into money or receive goods in exchange at an extravagant price, so as to make the difference bear between the price of goods bartered with a Hong Merchant and the real cash price of teas, so that in barter one generally loses in quality what he gets in price in fact much more."[515] In selling for goods it was also possible to be cheated. "Paying in skins," Dorr warned, "you give 10 or 20 per Cent higher [for teas] and I really believe they calculate upon cheating in the quality of teas as much more, by which you can see that skins are not dollars."[516] He added: "Barter business in the Country [China] is attended with great uncertainty as it respects the quality of goods had in return, and I assure you that I can transact business with specie 10 to 20 per Cent better, and with certainty in point of the quality of the Merchandize received in return, for there is few or no Hong Merchants but that will avail himself of those little and mean advantages which being in his power gives him."[517]

Volume, however, remained the chief determinant of Canton's prices. The market there was periodically overdone by too many, or underdone by too few, imports. The 2,986 sea-otter and 34 fox skins brought to Canton by the *King George* and *Queen Charlotte* in January 1788 fetched $54,857, which was less than half the expected amount because the market was "quite glutted" (when the two ships arrived sea-otter skins were selling for $80–90 each but by the time the EIC's supercargoes sold them they brought only $20 apiece).[518] China's suspension of the Kyakhta trade, its source of Russian sea-otter skins, from 1788 until 1792 raised fur prices at Canton by 20 per cent, much to the delight and benefit of American and British Nor'westmen.[519] Before the ban was lifted on 1 June 1792, Captain Kendrick had to sell the *Lady Washington*'s 1,000 skins clandestinely in March of that year at Dirty Butter Bay for $21 each,[520] which was less than he had anticipated, the penalties for smuggling being "very severe."[521] The resumption of the Kyakhta trade led to a glutting of the Chinese market, the East India Company reporting that the trade in furs at Canton was "greatly overdone" in 1793–94.[522]

Prices were particularly depressed at the turn of the century, when Canton was flooded with furs, ginseng, specie, and other goods by Euroamerican traders eager to tap the vaunted Chinese market. In the autumn of 1799 the cost of nankeens increased by one-sixth and of Bohea tea by one-eighth within ten days in response to greater demand "since the arrival of so many ships."[523] Even more ships came in 1800 and prices continued to rise, although after 1 December advised Dorr, "if the contracts have not absorbed all the [available Chinese] goods, what remains can be obtain'd 20 to 33 Per Cent cheaper, because the Nankin and Pekin Merchants want to close Sales settle accounts and be off."[524] The supply of Chinese goods frequently varied, however, so prices "are very precarious continually fluctuating."[525] On the other hand, the value of Euroamerican goods decreased as more and more were brought by more and more ships. At the end of 1800 Dorr reported that "the [hong] Merchants say there never was known so great a redundance of every kind of article at this market."[526] By the fall of 1801 "such a redundancy [of goods] never was known," and in 1802 "this market is inundated with everything, so that no one article brings any proffit."[527] The situation became even worse during the following several years, Dorr explaining that the the Peace of Amiens of 1802 between England and France temporarily halted the European wars and "extended its effects to the remotest corners of the world commerce reverting to its old channel has already not only caused the markets of the Spanish American possessions to be glutted but all the East is inundated with European and American productions."[528] Canton was surfeited with furs in particular. Up to 10,000 sea-otter skins (9,160 American and 800 British) were brought in 1799–1800, 9,400 (6,450 American and 2,950 British) in 1800–01, 12,000 in 1801–02, and 14,600 in 1802–03.[529]

In the autumn of 1800 the fur market was so overdone that one hongist opined that "skins are bought now upon speculation."[530] By the end of October an influx of 200,000 fur-seal skins had reduced their price to 75 cents, which "will little more than pay port charges."[531] It was "a flemish [unprofitable] business," declared Dorr, adding that "the business is compleatly done over."[532] He estimated that Canton's "annual call" for fur-seal skins was 70,000 to 100,000, whereas at least 353,000 were brought in 1800–01, 569,000 in 1801–02, and 280,000 in 1802–03.[533] In August 1801 Canton was so sated with furs, especially fur-seal skins, that the Chinese would not accept them in exchange for silks or nankeens, which could be had for specie only.[534]

The torrent of sea-otter and fur-seal skins likewise lowered the value in China of furs imported from Europe. Already by 1786–87 furs from the Northwest Coast had "not a little reduced the price of furs brought here [Canton] from Europe."[535] Fur prices were sometimes further diminished by lessened demand in China, resulting, for example, from internal disturbances.

American traders were wont to drug not only the Northwest Coast Indian and Canton Chinese markets but their home market as well. As William Sturgis remarked to John Cushing, "the Yankees always over do the market wherever they go" in their eagerness to make money.[536] In 1806 and 1807 the American tea market was so overstocked that "at the prices now going in Boston the first cost of Teas (charges included) cannot be realized," so that "regular Traders can make nothing – They lose money."[537] The solution was to switch to other trade goods and to lend money in Canton at interest rates of up to 18 per cent per year until the tea glut was reduced. Again in 1818 silks (especially) and nankeens were more profitable than teas in the United States.[538] American trade with China was overdone yet again in 1825 and 1826, particularly in teas; consequently, in 1826 and 1827 the United States exported from one-quarter to one-third as much tea as it imported, mainly to Rotterdam, Hamburg, and Paris, and in the same two years, respectively, twice as much and five times as much tea was exported from the United States to Europe as from Canton to Europe.[539] Periodic financial panics in the United States, as in 1819, 1827, and 1837, also discouraged trade, since interest rates soared and made venture capital too costly.

The vicissitudes of the China trade were such that it gained the reputation of a very risky, if not unprofitable, business. As Sturgis told Cushing, "We have been so constantly in the habit, for many years past, of complaining how ruinous the China Trade is that it has become quite an old story."[540] This remark implies that the trade's problems were perhaps exaggerated and that astute investors, such as Sturgis and Cushing themselves, could prosecute it profitably. In doing so they avoided the problems by adjusting to them, and in the process the Northwest Coast trade – as dynamic as any other – changed constantly and appreciably.

8 Changes in Trade

The principal object of your cruize on the N.W. Coast is the
collection of Land Furs.
>
> Marshall and Wildes to Captain John Dominis
> of the *Owhyhee*, 1827

Like the price of skins, the coast trade was anything but static. From
its inception until its demise traffic changed constantly and rapidly,
especially during the period of greatest competition – from 1791
through 1802 – when over-pricing and over-hunting necessitated frequent adjustments. At first, following Captain King's advice, trading
vessels sailed in pairs to Nootka Sound, Cook Inlet, and Prince William Sound. These were the places where Cook had obtained furs
and which he had charted.[1] After 1788, however, British and American traders avoided "Cook's River [Inlet]" because by then the Russians "had got entire possession of the river," and within five years
they had "almost hunted out" the inlet.[2] Thereafter Nor'westmen concentrated on the coast between Cross and Puget Sounds, with occasional forays southwards to the Columbia River and northwards into
the "straits," where the Russians held sway *de jure* but not *de facto*.

During the early 1790s the foremost "mart for peltry" was Nootka,
or King George's, Sound, "an absolute collection of harbours and
coves, which are sheltered from the violence of all winds," in the words
of Captains Portlock and Meares.[3] Captain Clerke, Cook's second-in-
command, had noted approvingly that there "are a number of Coves
about the Sound, well enough calculated to render Vessels laying in
them perfectly free from danger, and where they may wood & water
with great facility."[4] Within the sound Friendly Cove was just that, at
least until the turn of the century, when Chief Maquinna's forbearance broke. American coasters, however, favoured the anchorage of
Mawinna, or Kendrick's Cove (now Marvinas Bay), on the western
side of the sound about five miles to the north; it was less affected
by winds and ocean swells, enjoyed better wind conditions for leaving,

and had a better bottom than Friendly Cove, although the latter had a better command of the sound.[5] There was plenty of timber and water as well as numerous Indian customers. Captain Clerke had praised the "vast abundance of excellent Timber" suitable for "Sticks" (masts and spars) – "as good as are to be procur'd in any part of the World."[6] Most important, the sound abounded in sea otters. "Great numbers were seen in different parts of the Sound," reported Captain Colnett in 1787.[7] The imperious Commandant Estéban Martínez, whose high-handed actions precipitated the Nootka Sound crisis in 1789, estimated that the British alone secured from 18,000 to 20,000 sea-otter skins in the sound in the last half of the 1780s.[8] It was visited by thirty ships in 1792, including twenty-one trading vessels; so much saluting with cannons resulted that Captain Vancouver's *Discovery* ran short of ammunition and had to get gunpowder from his Spanish opponents and British and American coasters![9] That year an American trader wrote: "Nootka sound being the head rendezvous for all Ships that trade on the Coast they make it a common practice to fall in with the Latitude of it, its being well Known for a good harbour and the Skins the best that is to be got on the Coast"; "they [the Nootkas] have the best Skins," he added, "cured the best and the plentifullest of any place on the Coast."[10] Such was the intensity of the first peak of competition, however, that by 1793 – only a year later – Nootka Sound had been hunted out, although Nor'westmen continued to frequent it because they could wood and water there without risk.[11] After 1803, when the Nootkas captured the *Boston*, few shipmasters resorted to the sound. It remained so neglected that a visitor found in 1825 that there was a "scarcity of European goods" among the Nootkas and even that "most of them were in a happy state of ignorance of rum & tobacco."[12]

The mouth of the Columbia remained a popular anchorage during the heyday of the coast trade, especially for wintering vessels like the *Ruby*, which in 1795–96 "passed thus much of the winter without feeling the Climate so cold as the *South* of England!"[13] As William Sturgis pointed out, it was visited "chiefly to obtain some articles, which are again sold to the Indians on the more northerly part of the Coast,"[14] principally elk hides but also salmon. (William Sturgis's kinsman, Josiah Sturgis, contended that the Columbia's salmon were deemed "the best in the world" and were caught "in great plenty"; they were so large that two of them were sufficient to feed for one day in 1818 the seventeen crewmen of the *Levant*, "and some of them perfect gormandizers."[15]) When Lewis and Clark reached the Columbia's mouth in late 1805, they were told by the Chinooks that a dozen trading vessels arrived twice a year (spring and autumn). One shipmaster, a Captain Davidson (probably the master of the American schooner *Rover*, which was lost on the China coast in 1801), hunted elk only and did not trade at all. Most did, however, and the Indians' favourite was a Captain Haley (perhaps a supercargo rather than a master) because he gave more presents than his rivals and thus dominated traffic. Lewis and Clark dubbed Baker's Bay Haley's Bay, which, they reported, was "spacious and commodious, and perfectly secure from all except the S. and S.E. winds," adding that "fresh water and wood are very convenient and excellent timber for refiting and reparing vessels."[16] The Chinooks, said Lewis and Clark, traded sea-otter skins, beaver pelts, fox skins, "tiger cat" [lynx] skins, elk hides, dried salmon, and shappelell for old muskets, gunpowder, ball and shot, copper and brass kettles, brass tea kettles and coffee pots, blankets, red and blue cloth, sheet copper and brass wire, knives, dentalia, buttons, and sailors' clothing; the Indians had also acquired the words "musquet," "powder," "shot," "knife," "file," "damned rascal," and "son of a bitch."[17] Fewer coasters visited the Columbia after the founding of Astoria (later Fort George) at the beginning of the 1810s.[18]

By the turn of the century the locus of the coast trade had shifted from the southern coast to the Queen Charlotte Islands and the Alexander Archipelago, whose Chatham Strait (between Admiralty Island on the east and Chichagof and Baranof Islands on the west) was described in 1794 by Joseph Whidbey, master of Captain Vancouver's *Discovery*, "as likely to be one of the most profitable places for procuring the skins of the sea otter, on the whole coast" because of the "immense number" of animals and the "abundance" of skins in the possession of the Indians.[19] Kaigani Harbour at the southern end of the archipelago quickly became the favourite American and British "rendezvous," which was defined by Captain D'Wolf as "a place of resort for traffic on the arrival of ships" with "many large villages in its vicinity."[20] Kaigani (the Spaniards' Nuestra Señora de los Dolores) was roomy, deep, and well sheltered from all except the S.E. and N.E. winds, with good facilities for wooding and watering.[21] In 1822 the logkeeper of the *Rob Roy* reported that the local Haidas "are considered to be the most friendly of any on the coast," although he added that "all of them are grate rascals and will steal any thing they can carry off convieniently."[22] Sitka, or Norfolk Sound, was also frequented, particularly in the 1790s; as early as 1792 Captain Barkley deemed it "the best place for Skins I ever was at."[23] Its "sea beavers" were already known to the Russians, who occupied it by the end of the decade, establishing their colonial headquarters there.

Thereupon the main venue of the coast shifted somewhat southwards. Lieutenant Simpson reported in 1828 that the part of the coast "most visited" by American trading vessels was that between Dixon Entrance and Queen Charlotte Sound. The chief rendezvous, he added, were still Kaigani (especially) and Tongass (on Annette Island at the entrance to Clarence Strait), where the only two tribes considered friendly to the Americans were found; occasionally vessels made a "Short Start" to other ports for furs.[24] As late as 1835 Kaigani was still the first port of call of American captains, whose "extravagant" prices, however, made the local Haidas the "most difficult Indians on the coast to deal with."[25] "Tumgass" (Tongass) was rated "one of the finest harbours in the world" by the logkeeper of the *Rob Roy* in 1822, with "excelent holding ground," although there were never more than three days without rain "or some kind of storm."[26] Also popular were Clemencitty (Tlehonsiti) on Tongass Island at the entrance to Portland Canal, and Newhitty (Nahwitti) on Cape Sutil at the western entrance to Goletas Channel. The latter was opened by Captain Asa Dodge of the *Alexander* in 1800, when he obtained 600 skins there at half the going price.[27] One American supercargo rated Newhitty "the prettiest & best harbour I have seen on the Coast."[28] All of these anchorages enjoyed the same basic requirements: several fathoms of water, "good bottom" (smooth and hard), wood for building and burning, fresh water, and, of course, Indian clients.

By the turn of the century, too, trading vessels were no longer sailing in tandem. At first they had sailed in company for safety and security against accidents, enemy ships, and hostile Natives – for example, the *Venus* (Captain Shepherd) with the *Halcyon* (Captain Barkley), and the *Three Brothers* (Lieutenant Alder) with the *Prince William Henry* (Captain Ewen) in 1792 – but this tactic soon changed because much time was lost by the two vessels "spoking their Noses into one anothers Buttocks," and many skins were missed because "one would [could] have been collecting the Skins to the Northward, while the other was doing the same to the Southward."[29] Later, too, there were fewer skins to share, and accumulated knowledge of the coast and the Indians made solo voyaging safer. Furthermore, no longer did vessels range up and down the coast in quest of golden fleece; greater competition induced them to remain longer in fewer places. Captain Ingraham learned the hard way that sojourning was better than cruising:

cruising ... I adopted on my first arrival on the coast, but I soon found it more to my advantage to remain awhile when in a good place. When cruising we went sometimes two or three days – nay once we were eight – without purchasing a skin; whereas while we were at anchor in Cummashawaa's [Cumshewa Inlet] not a day passed but we purchased more or less skins. We were situated between three tribes of the first consequence, and none of them would chase a ship four or five leagues off to trade away their skins in a hurry while they could come to us and trade at their leisure, which they are fond of, for many of them would wait alongside several hours – nay all day – to obtain their price. Besides this advantage a person is certainly in less danger at anchor in a good port than cruising among these isles where there are strong tides and sometimes heavy gales of wind.[30]

The *Hamilton's* two-year (1809–11) sojourn on the coast was typical. It confined its trade to fewer than a dozen harbours between Skidegate and Stikine, including especially Taddiskey, Nass, Kaigani, and Clemencitty, staying up to a week at a time.[31]

Keener competition also brought vessels closer to shore and prompted less trading over the side, with only chiefs on board, and more trading on the deck with more tribesmen as the shipmasters tried to ingratiate themselves. Eventually, however, as the Indians suffered more abuse and acquired more ordnance, trading "at arm's length" was restored.

At first, too, when pelts were plentiful, vessels were able to procure a full cargo of skins – up to 2,500 – in a single season (March through August) and proceed directly to Canton. As the number of competitors increased and the number of sea otters decreased, captains needed two seasons by the turn of the century to complete a cargo. By 1815 it took American coasters usually two and sometimes three years to get a full cargo for the China market.[32] The *Mentor* left Boston under Captain Suter in 1816 "provisioned and equip'd for a three years Voyage."[33] Masters of longer voyages, however, risked being undersold by captains of shorter ventures. A skipper who spent less time on the coast was able "to pay a more liberal price for Skins" ("and thus secure all the Skins that may be offer'd") because a shorter voyage was "a great saving in every point of view," for example, in insurance costs.[34]

Vessels took to wintering at the Sandwich Islands, only three weeks away from the coast, and, as the geography and ethnography of the coast became more familiar, on the coast itself. That meant finding a suitable winter anchorage, as the *Atahualpa* did at "Port George" just inside the entrance to "Canal de Principe" (Principe Channel) at the beginning of the winter of 1812–13: "Good bottom, an excellent place for getting wood & Water, & safe as to the Natives, it being very roomy & a good winter Harbour."[35] Actually, little fur trading was done during the winter months, the Indians having withdrawn to their winter quarters and temporarily abandoned trapping and trafficking. In the second and third weeks of December 1822, for instance, the *Rob Roy* collected only twenty-one black skins from the Natives.[36] Their Euroamerican customers simply bided their time, as recorded by the log of the *Griffon* on 30 November 1826: "Begins strong gales and s.e. weather, daylight moderate. Employed the boats to sweep for the lost anchor, and at 10 found it and took it on board to repair. Ends squally from s.w. and cloudy. As this day finishes the last of Nov. it is well to observe that the seamen have been employed sawing boards, cutting firewood, and other jobs as necessary, and the Mechanics at their respective jobs, during the working weather of this month."[37] The routine was boring and the weather depressing, but wintering vessels paid less ("winter prices") for any skins and gained a headstart in trade in spring. Lieutenant Simpson reported in 1828 that usually one or two American ships wintered on the coast. "It is competition that has driven them to the alternative of keeping the Coast during the Winter and returning to it so early in the Spring, as the business could otherwise be equally well accomplished by taking it at a more advanced period of the season," he wrote, adding that "their object is to get first to the Market."[38] The other American vessels wintered in Hawaii, leaving for the coast in late January or early February and arriving in late February or early March; they quit the coast for Hawaii in late September, since foul weather with strong southeastern gales began thereafter.[39] Firms with more than one ship in the trade commonly used one as a freighter and the others as year-round coasters. In 1826 Bryant and Sturgis sent the *Triton*, Captain Bryant, to the coast largely as a supply vessel, which enabled the *Volunteer* and *Griffon* to stay on the coast while it took their furs, plus Hawaiian sandalwood, to Canton after trading "in concert" with them for one season and visiting Sitka.[40]

Coastal wintering meant more exposure to the elements and the Natives and more dependence upon local foodstuffs. Deer, ducks, geese, clams, halibut, salmon, herring, berries, and birds' eggs were available, chiefly through the Indians, although the HBC's Fort Simpson found that "like all supplies from Indians it is precarious and cant be depended upon."[41] At Clayoquot Sound in September and October 1793 the *Jefferson*'s crew in September and October lived on "fresh grub" – fish, deer, and geese – as well as "salt provisions" [pork and beef] at the allowance of 1¾ pounds per man per day.[42] As the *Vancouver* discovered in 1805, the northern coast, particularly the Queen Charlottes, afforded venison, "which is hear in grate Plenty," "plenty of fine halubat and Salmon," "grate numbers" of wildfowl, and "grate quantiteys" of berries.[43] At Cocklane's Harbour in early March 1822 the *Rob Roy* had "a few Indians on board with Deer, Ducks, Geese & Swans for sale."[44] That summer at Skidegate the same vessel found "plenty" of "very nice" huckleberries, which enabled the logkeeper to have "some soft bread for supper for the first time on board the voyage."[45] Evidently there was no scarcity of deer, elk, and moose on the coast, and Dawson's caribou (now extinct) ranged the Queen Charlotte Islands. One seaman remarked that there was a "great plenty" of moose on "almost every part of the [northern] coast,"[46] while elk were more numerous to the south. The *Hamilton* in 1811 managed to buy sixty-six deer from the Haidas at Tucketsarn in eight days in the middle of winter[47] (the same ship in 1822 bought 159 sea fowl in one February day from the Tlingits at Stikine[48]). At the end of October 1836 at Fort Simpson the *La Grange* paid the Tongass Tlingits from three to four gallons of mixed rum, rice, or molasses for a prime deer.[49]

Forts McLoughlin, Simpson, Stikine, and Taku were "principally maintained" on "country provisions," primarily venison, fish, and potatoes.[50] The venison was bought "at so cheap a rate from the natives, that we absolutely make a profit on our consumption of provisions, the skin of the animals selling for much more than is paid for the whole carcase," according to Governor Simpson, who toured the posts in 1841.[51] Similarly, the Russians at Sitka depended upon the local Tlingits for venison, fish, and potatoes, buying as many as 1,118 deer in 1847, 138,096 pounds of halibut in 1851, and 1,060 barrels (at 4 rubles per 145–pound barrel) of potatoes in 1845![52] The venison came from Sitka blacktailed deer, which the Russians termed the *yaman* and the British the *chevreuil*. It was also a mainstay of Fort Taku, as Governor Simpson found in 1841: "The establishment was maintained chiefly on the flesh of the chevreuil, which is very fat, and has an excellent flavour. Some of these deer weigh as much as a hundred and fifty pounds each; and they are so numerous, that Taco has this year sent to market twelve hundred of their skins, being the handsome average of a deer a week for every inmate of the place. But extravagance in the eating of venison is here a very lucrative business, for the hide, after paying freight and charges, yields in London a profit on the prime cost of the whole animal.[53] Simpson added that the animal's flesh was "the finest meat I ever ate, with the single exception of moose."[54] It was eaten, too, at St Dionysius Redoubt, where the Russian commandant reportedly once traded 500 deer (presumably Sitka blacktails) from the Tlingits in fifteen days.[55]

Fish, however, were the staple, particularly "harcoo" (halibut) and "squagan," which one trader identified as a "bastard kind of salmon."[56] (In Haida "halibut" is *xakw* and "sockeye salmon" is *sgwáa-*

gaan.) "Harcoo and Squaggen is to Be got in Every Part of the Coast from the Savages for a Trifel," noted the journal of the *Vancouver* in 1806.[57] Some of the halibut bought by the *Vancouver* weighed 300–500 pounds each and some of the salmon 30–40 pounds each.[58] In early August at Cocklane's Harbour the same vessel purchased 4,000 squagan from the Tsimshians and salted them down.[59] In 1827 the *Griffon* bought squagon at Tongass for one leaf of tobacco each and salted them down in barrels.[60] So closely did Euroamerican traders associate sockeye salmon with the Nass River that they commonly referred to it as the Squagon River.

"Keeping" to the coast year-round allowed more opportunity for intracoastal trading by shipmasters. Some spent the winter at the mouth of the Columbia, where the weather was milder and calmer and where clamons were available. Other hunted sea otters on the coasts of New Albion and California, employing Tlingit and Haida marksmen. By the early 1820s it was deemed "much more profitable and much less risk" to ply the Northwest Coast from February until August and the Californian coast until December and then winter in Hawaii rather than stay the entire year on the coast.[61]

Eventually the duration of a Boston–Northwest Coast–Canton–Boston venture lengthened to as many as five years from two years or fewer initially. In turn, the longer trading period, combined with the deadlier hunting weapons, depleted the sea otters at an even faster rate. By the 1810s there were already so few otters left that American shipmasters were commonly "dividing the skins," that is, collaborating by trading on halves, with a crewman from each vessel aboard the other to monitor the increasingly valuable returns.[62] Vessels also cooperated in the procurement of supplies and the shipment of skins. At the end of the 1817 season the *Mentor* (Bryant and Sturgis) purchased 2,504 yards of blue duffle and one bale of blankets from the *Hamilton* (Lyman and associates) and *Alert* (Bryant and Sturgis) for 371 skins, shipped all of its furs to Canton on the *Alert*, and remained on the coast over the winter.[63] The "usual" charge, incidentally, for freighting furs from the coast to Canton was 2½ per cent of the sale in China, and from Hawaii to Canton 1¼ per cent of the same.[64] Similarly, in 1821 the *Hamilton* collaborated with the *Lascar*, *Mentor*, and *Pedler*: "Delivered Capt Meaks [Meeks of the *Pedler*] 48 prime sea oter skins to Capt porter [*Mentor*] 35 black cubs & 3 prime Received 19 prime tails from Capt Meaks ... received from Capt porter 2 pipes [eight 105-gallon barrels] of rice 2hhds [hogsheads, that is, four 105-gallon barrels] molasses & 1 bale & 3 peaces of blankets from Capt Meaks & 1 bale blankets from Capt harres

[Harris of the *Lascar*] ... Sent David Hartshorn onbord brig pedler to keep account of Furs Mr Spooner has returned onbord again [from inventorying skins on the *Pedlar*]."[65]

The growing Indian hostility triggered cooperation in defence, too. More and more vessels plied the coast "in company," just as they had in the early years of the trade. In the summer of 1821 the *Arab*, *Hamilton*, *Lascar*, *Mentor*, and *Pedler* traded together for mutual protection and probably for common pricing as well. In addition, the higher risks necessitated larger crews, and the same risks, added to the poorer prospects, made it more difficult for shipowners to sign up Euroamerican crewmen. American sailors also ran the risk of capture during hostilities like the War of 1812. As the US consul in Canton reported to Secretary of State James Munroe at the beginning of 1815, "I am sorry to say that in almost every instance the American Seamen prefer any other Service (except that of the Enemy [Great Britain]) to going on board of a Ship under the Flag of their own Nation."[66]

American shipowners were quick to realize that the Hawaiian Islands were a convenient and economical source of able seamen.[67] Nor'west Coastmen began taking on "Kanakas," or "canacers," as early as 1805, when the *Vancouver* shipped six islanders at Maui.[68] The Astorians of the doomed *Tonquin* hired twenty-four Hawaiians, a dozen for the ship and a dozen for Astoria.[69] (According to an Hawaiian source, in 1811 up to 100 Hawaiian men shipped to Astoria to work for the Pacific Fur Company.[70]) The *Hamilton* in the autumn of 1809 enlisted three islanders at Hawaii Island and in the autumn of 1815 engaged at Honolulu "six of the Natives to go in the ship to the N. W. Coast."[71] And in 1825 the *Convoy* got ten islanders at Oahu, while the *William and Ann* on its coastal excursion had thirteen Hawaiian hands, who probably formed at least half of the crew.[72] By 1827–28 it was standard practice for American coasters to complete their crews at the islands, and Kanakas generally formed up to one-half of all hands.[73] In 1827 up to 300 islanders worked on foreign ships.[74] The Hawaiians were used because they were skilled and cheap. A Russian naturalist observed in 1804 that they made "excellent sailors" and served on American trading vessels for $10–12 per month.[75] Another Russian observer remarked in 1818 that "the Sandwich Islanders like to work on European ships and the Americans, who always have several of them in their employ, praise them very highly as eager, obedient, reliable, and intelligent workers, and always loyal to their superiors." He added that so unquestioning was their loyalty that American skippers employed them partly in order to detect mutinous designs aboard ships bound for the coast.[76] The cheapness of "Stout Islanders" derived in part from their willingness to be paid in leftover goods not traded on the coast.[77] In September 1806 on Hawaii Island the *Lydia*'s Captain Hill "discharged one of the Natives that went on the Coast with us he gave him too Muskets 1 ax a Little Powder 1 Pair of Shoes & Stockings Some thread & Needles 3 Jack Knives & a Little Tobacco for 18 Months Services."[78] In 1821 Bryant and Sturgis instructed Captain Cross of the *Rob Roy*: "You will ship three or four islanders to make your whole number on board 21 or 22. Take care to get stout, healthy ones, & you will find them useful as the best men you have. Probably they may be got for about 8 or 9 dollars p month [about half an American crewman's wages] payable in such articles of trade as you may have when you come off the coast."[79]

Some shipmasters neglected or abused their Hawaiian hands, who, moreover, were not accustomed to the harsher elements of the coast. The journal of the brig *Otter* records the suffering of its "Kynackies" under the disreputable Captain Hill in 1810: "At 8 A.M.. this morning one of our Sandwich Islanders died he had the misfortune last winter [1809–10] to have his feet froze and lost four toes off one foot, as it had not got well he has never been able to walk about since, the others are now all lame with a swelling in their legs."[80] All but one of the "others" also had scurvy, and one of these on 11 November "took his departure for his long home."[81] Hawaiians worked at trading posts as well as on trading ships. In 1834 fourteen of Fort Simpson's fifty-nine men were islanders.[82] But Chief Factor McLoughlin, at least, believed that Hawaiians were not good hirelings, mainly because of their susceptibility to disease. He opined that "they are only fit to make up numbers on board of a Vessel or about an Establishment … they are very poor hands, on an average they are one tenth of their time off work from disease."[83] Presumably the same debilitation explains why the use of Asian hands in the early years of the coast trade did not last; twenty-nine of Captain Colnett's crew of sixty aboard the *Argonaut* at Nootka Sound in 1789 were Chinese (mostly craftsmen), and most of the crew of twenty-two of the *Venus* in the Straits of Juan de Fuca and Georgia in 1792 were Sulu Moros.[84]

As sea otters became scarcer, experienced and knowledgeable traders became more essential. Gone were the days at the turn of the century when maiden voyages to the coast were, as likely as not, also saving voyages. In late December of 1810 the veteran Captain Hill was able to get all of the skins at Lanacoon "as there is none of the other Vessels on the Coast knows where these Indians live in the winter."[85] In the late 1810s Bryant and Sturgis employed in their coast ventures Captain William Smith, who had "extensive knowledge of the Coast and long experience" on three of their vessels, the *Ann*, *Borneo*, and *Mentor*.[86] By the 1820s, with skins scarce and competition still keen, it was more important than ever that a coaster's trade goods be of the right variety and the best quality. Hence the following lament of the *Rob Roy's* logkeeper in 1822: "In the first place we had but one kind of Muskets on board the vessel (excepting Rifles) which in two weeks after our arrival were not worth a beaver skin each & not a half dozen of them was sold for the first two seasons [1822 and 1823] the locks of them were good for nothing."[87] When the HBC entered the coast trade at the end of the 1820s it soon bought not only a veteran American vessel, the *Lama*, but also a veteran American captain, William McNeill, both having made several trading voyages to the coast.

Successful shipmasters had to be especially sensitive to changing Native demands. Trade goods, particularly those demanded by the Indians but also those accepted by the Euroamericans, were among the first things to change – notwithstanding Wike's speculation that the Indians exhibited "exceptional uniformity of choice in European goods, within localities, over wide areas, and throughout time."[88] The Indians wanted goods for practical and especially aesthetic purposes. In dealing with the Nootkas in 1792 an American trader found that "they don't seem to covet usefull things but any thing that looks pleasing to the eye or what they call riches."[89] Generally the Indians preferred articles that could be readily counted and compared and were therefore suitable for potlatches, the gluttonous (and reciprocal) giveaways that proved the giver's wealth, power, rank, and prestige. Thus, portable, storeable, and uniform goods were desired.[90] But these goods varied in kind over time. In 1793 the *Jefferson* found that "the articles of thick Copper & Clemons was what they wanted in trade for their Skins ... and was what was in demand in all the places we visited in our way from Nootka sound [northwards]."[91] By the end of the century metals were no longer wanted. In 1799 the *Hancock* traded mostly cloth, clothing, and muskets for skins; in particular there was "a loud Cry for good Muskets."[92] When the *Atahualpa* left Boston for the coast in 1800 its cargo of trade goods consisted of the following: 5,796 yards of broadcloth, 181 greatcoats, 121 jackets, 124 pairs of trousers, 1,342 blankets, 1,980 yards of duck (a durable, closely woven, untwilled linen or cotton fabric used for sailors' trousers), 3,000 unknown units of gunpowder, 250 leather flasks, 150 cartouche boxes, 350 muskets, 20 pistols, 600 dozen buttons, 400 dozen knives, 100 dozen pairs of scissors, 301 iron pots, 240 frying pans, 623 gallons of molasses, 242 hats, 620 unknown units of iron, brass, copper wire, 480 axes and hatchets, 24 dozen hammers, 168 chisels, 47 saws, 480 files, 48 dozen spoons, 30 dozen combs, 771 looking glasses, 570 kettles and pans, 200 dozen cannisters, 49 dozen bottles, $362 worth of beads, 30 pounds of thread, and a few lesser items, all costing $20,905.[93] (Compare the list of trade goods "generally in demand" on the coast which was compiled about the same time by another trader.[94]) This variety is considerable, but textiles, arms and ammunition, utensils, and tools were clearly dominant.

At this time "eatables" – bread, molasses, rice – also became popular. In 1801 Sullivan Dorr reported that the most saleable goods were muskets, pistols, powder, ball, shot, lead, duffle, common cloth garments, bread, molasses, rice, whale oil, and clamons.[95] "Sugar, bread, Molasses and elements [sic: clements, i.e., clamons] are the best articles to buy skins with at present," he wrote, stressing that eatables led the list, a bucket of bread fetching one skin.[96] In the same year in a letter to his father Dorr reiterated the popularity of provisions and textiles: "The most valuable & saleable articles here [Northwest Coast] are *Molasses, Rice & Bread* & ... large thick *Duffil Blanketts* & broad blue & fancy coloured Duffil ... There have been great quantities of Molasses, Bred & Rice sold to the Natives this season & the former, in fact they become more & more improvident for their winter food then our Eatables command a charming barter. two Vessels have sold 15 hogsheads [thirty 105-gallon barrels] Molasses each this season & all more or less as the[y] could spare."[97] A year later Dorr again reported that "nothing answers so well as eatables."[98] When the *Vancouver* entered Clarence Strait in late July 1805 "grate numbers of Savages [Tlingits] Came of[f] and Began to trad verry brisk for Bread rice Blankets Molasse Powder Balls Shot and Cloth."[99] In 1806 William Sturgis, who knew the coast trade as well as any and better than most, suggested the following cargo to one of Sullivan Dorr's brothers for a coast venture:

There are a kind of Blankets imported to this country term'd Point Blankets – these are the best & most profitable Woolens which can be sent – the best sizes are 2½ & 3 points – in a common cargo 3,000 would not be too many – next to these are Blue Fearnoughts [stout woollen cloth used for outer garments] 6 or 7 gns. [?] wide, say 3,000 yds. – from 1 to 200 thick Blue Great Coats & large Pea Jackets, *lin'd throughout* – Fifty Hhds. [one hundred 105–gallon barrels] good molasses, which will bear reducing [diluting] – Thirty Tierces [thirty 42–gallon barrels] Rice & from 70 to 100 Hhds. [140 to 200 105–gallon barrels] Bread – Musketts need not be sent unless the best kind King's arms can be procur'd & then not more than 100 would sell – Powder in 25 lbs Kegs will ever be saleable – BB & mould Shott, say one Ton & Two of Bar lead – Brass Blunderbusses will sell well – Pistols do not answer

– 50 Barrells Beans might be sold advantageously & a few Bbls. common brown Sugar – Ermine Skins have been sold at an immense profit – how they will do in future is doubtful – I think however they might safely be sent – an assortment of Cutlery is always necessary, but not in great quantitys – 100 pss. [?] of Russia Sheetings [stout cloth of linen or cotton used for bed linen] will do well – 200 pss. of coarse Gurrahs [plain India muslins] will also be necessary – Common Blue Cloth with white list [edging] is not so saleable as formerly, a small quantity, however, might be sold – Trinkets of different kinds, such as Beads etc sometimes answer – but the taste of the natives in this respect is so fluctuating & capricious that certain provision cannot be made – Iron & brass wire – looking Glasses etc., are generally sent to make up a variety –

A Cargo exported in this way would suit that market at the present moment & most of the articles I have mention'd must ever be saleable so long as the trade is prosecuted.[100]

Sturgis's confident prediction was more or less correct. In 1822 the leading trade goods were blankets, duffle, red and especially blue cloth, gurrah, India chintz, muskets (particularly Speak rather than French or Kendrick muskets), fowling pieces, ball and shot, gunpowder, indigo dye, vermilion, pearl buttons without brass eyes, chisels, adzes, coloured rum, rice, and molasses.[101] Similarly, the *Active* and *Louisa* left Boston for the coast in 1827 with mostly molasses (7,350 gallons), rice (13,860 gallons), flour (43,260 gallons), tobacco (2,310 gallons), rum (6,510 gallons), gin (1,050 gallons), blankets (33 bales), axes (20 boxes), beads (2 casks and 6 boxes), textiles (duck, broadcloth, duffle, gurrah, calico, gingham), firearms (muskets, fowling pieces, pistols, rifles, blunderbusses), ammunition (bullets, shot, lead, powder), paints, iron and steel, and hollowware vessels (as opposed to flatware), all worth $7,000.[102] These two ships were on the coast in 1828, when Lieutenant Simpson reported that the "American adventurers" brought chiefly blankets, duffles, cottons, calicoes, "slops" or made clothing (frock coats, waistcoats, trousers, shirts, hats, shoes, handkerchiefs), arms, ammunition, rum, axes, knives, beads, bracelets, mirrors, buttons, fish hooks, vermilion, and tobacco.[103] Guns and rum, he said, were the articles "upon which the Indians place the greatest value."[104] Finally, in 1829 a shipmaster asserted that blankets, blue cloth, fearnought, muskets, powder, shot, and traps were the "leading articles."[105]

Thus, metals, the dominant trade goods of the early years of the coast traffic, were soon superseded by textiles and provisions, and the latter were eventually overshadowed by firearms and spirits, with textiles remaining important. And as competition increased, better grades of these trade goods were offered by shipmasters in order to outsell their rivals. The muskets that were sent on the *Mentor* in 1816 were "unequalled by any ever shipped from this Country," according to the owners, Bryant and Sturgis.[106] In 1822 Captain Grimes of the *Owhyhee* recommended to its owners, Marshall and Wildes, that if fowling pieces were to be sent they should be "the English cocking ps Iron mounted, coloured pegging blue – silver thumb ps and silver round the Hides that keep the barrel in the stock large bores size of a kings arm or larger [for hunting bigger game such as sea otters]."[107] By then French or Kendrick muskets would not sell very well but superior Speak muskets would.[108] Also, Grimes advised, any blankets should be woven with a double wale and have a nap on both sides.[109]

At first – in the last half of the 1780s – the Indians demanded principally iron, copper, and coloured glass beads, although beads, like all trinkets, were accepted mainly as introductory and conciliatory gifts. The use of beads as trade goods seems to have been limited to Cook Inlet and Prince William Sound, where they were popularized by the Russians and where five blue beads obtained one sea-otter pelt in 1786, although by then they had already been spread by intertribal traffic as far south as Nootka Sound.[110] The first Spanish visitors found iron and copper already present among the Haidas and Nootkas in 1774. They may have procured the iron through long-distance trade across Bering Strait from Russian posts in Siberia or across the cordillera from HBC posts in Rupert's Land or along the coast from Spanish missions in Mexico.[111] Some may even have drifted across the North Pacific from Japan in the flotsam of junks.[112] Some native copper was procured from the upper reaches of the White and Chitina Rivers. It was described by William Sturgis in 1799 on his first voyage to the coast on the *Eliza* and the *Ulysses*: "The copper that abounds of Chilcart [Chilkat] … they [the Indians] found in lumps in the fresh water rivers … Vessels that have been there have often seen the copper as it was found in its natural state, perfectly pure, and in lumps of ten, eleven and twelve pounds. They then laid it on a flat stone and pounded it into a sheet about two feet square in which form they sold it. The purchaser again sold it further South, and, increasing in its value as it went, it would sometimes get as far to the Southward as Nootkah."[113] Subsequently Sturgis found among the northern Indians chunks of such virgin copper weighing from fifty to sixty pounds.[114] These traditional sources of iron and copper could not satisfy Indian demand, however, so the Natives pressed the trading vessels; they especially wanted iron, probably because it was more suitable than copper for use in weapons and tools and because it was rarer than copper on the coast. "The article which the natives esteem most is iron," declared Captain Meares in 1786.[115] When Captain William Douglas of the *Iphigenia Nubiana* had exhausted his stock of iron bars and spikes in 1789, he resorted to cutting up his ship's hatch bars and chain plates in order to meet the unabated Indian rage for the metal (but when these proved too brittle to be worked, the Haida customers refused to accept any more).[116] Wrought was preferred to unwrought iron, since the non-metallurgical Indians tended to work it cold. Wrought iron cost the ship armourers time, labour, and sea coal but brought twice as many Haida pelts as unwrought metal.[117] Iron was fashioned into "collars" (necklets) and "toes" (chisels or spikes). Toes, or "John Porter's chisels" after the blacksmith who first made them aboard the *Captain Cook* in 1786, were five inches long and very broad towards one end. They acquired "great celebrity" among the Indians, who used them to chisel canoes, plane boards, and carve articles.[118] A sea-otter skin could be had for a single iron toe in 1789, but inflation was such that only two years later forty were demanded.[119] Iron was also used for fishhooks, arrowheads, and lancetips in place of stone, shell, and bone – among the northern Indians fifteen-foot lances or pikes were their most lethal weapons – as well as for blades for chisels, adzes, and knives, particularly sheath daggers (sharp foot-long dirks slung from the neck), but not for axes or hatchets.

Copper would "answer" almost as well as iron. The Nootkas' demand for copper, tin, pewter, and brass from Captain Cook's men was such that they called Nootka Sound "Cheepocs Sound" after the Nootkan word for "copper."[120] Copper in particular and iron were the "uniform and steady object" of the Nootkas in 1786, when a single one-quart copper kettle fetched five skins.[121] Upon reaching Nootka Sound in early July of 1787 Captain Colnett of the *Prince of Wales* (with the smack *Princess Royal*, Captain Duncan) found Captain Barkley of the *Imperial Eagle* already there; Colnett's "chief Barter" comprised only "little trinkets & Buttons," so that "for having no Copper which was the only exchange the Natives took for their Skins he [Barkley] engross'd the whole trade & ruined ours."[122] Captain Dixon found in 1787 that "copper is almost the only article in request" among the Nootkas;[123] again in 1788 "copper was all there [*sic*] cry," and still in 1792 "the rage was copper."[124] The Spaniards, whose main interest was exploration rather than commerce, traded primarily copper sheets (and Monterey shells) for otter skins. Their copper sheets measured twenty-six inches in length, twenty-two inches in width, and a *real* coin in thickness and apparently weighed fourteen pounds.[125] As in the case of other trade goods, copper's value could vary considerably from place to place and even from month to month in the same season. In 1793 a copper sheet weighing sixty pounds brought one skin at Clayoquot Sound in mid-June, six skins on the Queen Charlottes in mid-July, and two skins (or four clamons) at the Columbia's mouth in August.[126] Copper was used for bracelets, ear and hair ornaments, and robe bangles. And from sheet copper the Haidas in particular wrought the famous "coppers" or shields that loomed so large in the potlatches of the nineteenth century.[127] In the middle 1830s a Chilkat Tlingit copper shield measured two and one-half feet long and one foot wide "with figures of men and animals engraved upon it." Worth nine slaves, it was bequeathed from father to son as a precious heirloom.[128]

The white "iron men," as they were called by the Haidas, soon satisfied the Natives' demand for metal, which, after all, was fairly durable. Already by the summer of 1791 at Clayoquot Sound "iron they would scarcely take as a gift."[129] A year later Captain Vancouver found that iron had become a "mere drug" on his island.[130] In early 1793 iron collars were "much on the decrease in value"; in the middle of the year no furs and only halibut could be bought for toes on the Queen Charlottes, and at the mouth of the Columbia there was "no demand" at all for iron.[131] By 1795 among the Nootkas and Haidas "iron they wont take as presents & Copper is not much better."[132]

By then cotton cloth had become the "commanding inducement" on the coast. Before the end of the decade it was joined by ready-made clothing, especially greatcoats, blankets, and duffles, and both remained in demand until the end of the coast trade. Already in 1791 Captain Colnett discovered that "neither Man, women, nor Child, that could procure a Blanket but would buy one. And those that had old ones wish'd for new."[133] In 1826 Dixey Wildes assured his partner, Josiah Marshall, that "*blankets* are the staple article," while one of their shipmasters declared that blankets and duffles were "the most essential articles of trade."[134] At late as 1838 Russian America's Governor Ivan Kupreyanov reported from Sitka that "without them [blankets] trade with the Tlingits is not profitable."[135] The longstanding demand for textiles is explained by the fact that they were not particularly durable. Moreover, they were needed to replace the fur garments that the Indians traded right off their own backs; Captain Clerke had noted in 1778 that from sea-otter fur the Nootkas "formed a great, & by them the most esteem'd part of their dress."[136] Clothes were perhaps first traded in the spring of 1794 by the *Jefferson* on the Queen Charlotte Islands, where they "were bought up by the natives with the greatest avidity."[137] En route from Boston to the coast in 1794–95 the *Union*'s tailor was "steadily employ'd making coats for trade."[138] The greatcoats sold by the *Atahualpa* on the Queen

Charlottes in 1801 were "of very thick cloth, well lined, & bound with bright red cloth"; the thickest were "very much in demand."[139] Cheap, ready-made seamen's clothing was still in "great demand" on the northern coast in the late 1820s.[140] Many visitors were amused by the bizarre sight of Indians bedecked in Euroamerican garb. A Russian naturalist observed at Sitka Sound that "it is no uncommon thing here to see Indians dressed like Europeans," woollen frocks of red and blue being favoured.[141] Thick blankets and duffles were especially suited to the cool climate. Both, too, were used to make "button blankets," ceremonial robes designed by men and sewn by women, with pearl-shell buttons or sometimes appliquéd red flannel usually outlining a family crest; they displayed a family's or clan's origins and privileges.[142]

The value of textiles in skins varied, of course, from time to time and place to place but generally increased with the intensification of competition and the depletion of sea otters. In 1796 a skin cost two yards of blue cloth at Clayoquot Sound and six yards at Nootka Sound, which harboured more trading vessels.[143] In 1799 at Sitka Sound a skin fetched two yards of blue broadcloth at first, but by the end of the season this price was doubled by competition.[144] Three yards of cloth were paid for a skin in 1819 and four yards in 1822.[145] The usual price of a skin was twelve yards of cotton cloth by 1826, when the Tlingits were "holding back" their prime skins for fourteen yards, and for up to eighteen yards in 1827.[146] In the summer of 1812 on the Queen Charlottes the proficient Captain Suter paid four three-point blankets, plus four buckets of molasses and rice, two buckets of bread, an axe, and "other small presents," or ten yards of duffle, plus two buckets of molasses, two buckets of rice, and "other presents," for one sea-otter skin.[147] In 1822 a skin cost three blankets or six yards of duffle or two gallons of molasses or two gallons of rice or two muskets or one fowling piece or two kegs of gunpowder.[148] On the northern coast in 1834 the HBC paid from six to eight blankets for a prime skin, and in 1837 the usual price of a skin was eight (HBC) or ten (RAC) blankets plus presents (and one blanket plus presents for a beaver pelt).[149] Textile prices varied partly because some blankets were thinner and lighter than others (that is, they had fewer points) and duffles dyed logwood-blue would "lose their colour by water" whereas those dyed indigo blue would not.[150] As for clothing, in 1793 a skin brought a greatcoat or a waistcoat and a pair of trousers at Barkley Sound and a greatcoat or a jacket with trousers on the Queen Charlottes and at the Columbia.[151]

Firearms – "magic sticks" to the Kwakiutls – were introduced shortly after textiles. At first the Indians were frightened by these noisy, smoky weapons. Captain Dixon noted in 1787 that "the sight of a few muskets kept them in a kind of awe" and was sufficient to prevent an attack.[152] This fear was short-lived, however, for greedy shipmasters could not long resist the temptation to trade away their putative advantage. The villainous Captain Kendrick seems to have initiated this folly in 1788, when he furnished Chief Wickaninish with more than two hundred muskets, two barrels of gunpowder, and a "considerable" amount of shot and Chief Maquinna with ten muskets and one swivel gun; by the autumn of 1792 Wickaninish had 400 men armed with muskets and well stocked with ammunition, thanks largely to Kendrick.[153] The American trader Joseph Ingraham told the Spanish commandant at Nootka in 1789 that "Maquinna Calli-cum, Wakanannith [Wickaninish] and a few others are in possession of Fire arms suficient to keep them Superior to other savage tribes but not to Attack a Ship indeed none but chiefs have knoledge enough of them to defend themselves [t]hey are however eager to possess them and almost continually beging for powder [w]hen the [Lady] Washington [Kendrick's sister ship] sail'd from [F]riendly Cove the natives in Ugot [the local Nootka village] beg'd Cap. Gray not to Sell any other Tribe a Musquet or any fire arms whatever that put themselves on a footing for Defence against the Natives of this sound."[154] This plea fell on deaf ears, of course. The Nootkas' demand for ordnance was such that in 1790 at Clayoquot Sound Captain Colnett found that "few Bargains can be made without it," and he correctly predicted that "the only articles of trade that will answer on this part of the Coast in a season or two, are arms, ammunition, and Clothing."[155] Within two years the Nootkas were favouring mus-kets and ammunition over copper and clothing; an American trader reported that "they will not sell a single Skin but for Copper or Muskits or Powder and Shot."[156] By 1793, asserted Lieutenant Puget, "in the Place of Bows and Arrows they have substituted Musquets & it is rather rare to see the former in their possession."[157] He added that the chief suppliers of firearms were American traders, who had been seduced by Indian promises to traffic with them exclusively in return for an annual supply of muskets and ammunition.[158]

It was not long before intertribal trade had diffused guns up and down the coast. By 1792 the Coast Salishes were not yet armed with guns, perhaps because their Native neighbours were wont to wage war rather than trade with them, but the Kwakiutls of the Strait of Georgia had been "amply provided" with muskets by the Nootkas through trans-island trade.[159] Muskets were being sold to the Haidas as early as 1792;[160] by the end of that trading season the Tlingits had "plenty" of guns, and among them ammunition was "always the first demand."[161] (The *Halcyon*'s Captain Barkley reiterated that "powder and shot was always the first thing they [Sitkan Tlingits] wanted," but he noted, too, that they were "very proud of their spears, which are very formidable weapons ... and they are very expert in the use of them, and informed us they liked them better than muskets, because they were sure to hit with them, whereas the fire arms made a great noise but did not always do execution."[162]) A year later Captain Vancouver observed that "most" of the northern Indians were "well armed."[163] "Musquests Powder etc. was their first demand," recorded his second lieutenant, Peter Puget.[164] Puget stated that the Tlingits of Clarence Strait had obtained their firearms from Captain Magee of the *Margaret*; "it is principally from these Americans," he contended, "that the Indians are so well furnished with such excellent weapons, which I sincerely hope, if ever they are used in an hostile Manner, it may be against those people who supplied the Indians with them."[165] In the summer of 1795 Captain Bishop trafficked with some Indians in Portland Canal who "appeared to have seldom seen a Ship by their curiosity and surprize" but who "understood the use of Powder and Arms," which "formed the Principal medium of our Barter."[166]

By then the market was already glutted, Captain Magee having found the previous year that "muskets has got to be of little value on every part of the Coast – will command not more than one skin in any part of it," whereas two years earlier they had brought six skins from the Nootkas.[167] At the end of the decade, however, there was a resurgence in demand, perhaps because of a desire to obtain newer and better models. "Musketts is the cry on the coast," reported Sullivan Dorr in 1799, "they have a surcharge [surfeit] of cloth."[168] On the Queen Charlottes the *Hancock* found mostly "a loud Cry for good Muskets," so much so that one fetched from two to five skins from the Haidas.[169] This renewed demand was soon overmet, and by 1801 the going rate on the islands was back to one skin for one musket.[170] Agent Dorr reported from Canton that in general on the coast a musket brought four or five skins in 1800 but in 1801 one skin cost from two to three muskets and in 1802 from three to six.[171] Guns nevertheless remained a staple trade good, owing to their utility as a weapon and their symbolization of wealth. Every trading vessel carried an armourer to repair not only its own but also Indian firearms, as well as to forge made-to-measure articles like iron toes and collars. In the early 1820s American traders got one-third of their sea-otter skins for guns (and the rest for blankets and woollen cloth).[172] In 1822 a skin was worth two muskets or one fowling piece or two kegs of gunpowder.[173] The standard price in 1827 was two beaver pelts for one musket, and in 1831 one keg of gunpowder for one sea-otter skin.[174]

The gun trade soon backfired, since the muskets and pistols were used by the Indians mainly for warfare, not only among themselves but against whites as well; the Nootkas, at least, likewise preferred guns to bows and arrows for hunting land animals and shore birds.[175] "The shameful practice of putting Fire Arms and Ammunition into their Hands," stated Lieutenant Puget in 1793, "have made some of the Tribes so formidable, that several of the Traders who are weakly manned cannot enter their Harbours with Safety." Chief Wickaninish, he added, was "reported to have four Hundred Hand of Arms and Indians regularly trained to use them."[176] Guns proliferated to such an extent that in 1810 Captain Hill of the *Otter* was able to buy "two very fine Brass Swivels [small cannons mounted on swivels]" from a Nass Chief.[177]

The Natives mastered firearms quickly. Already by 1792, complained Captain Gray hypocritically, the Nootkas had become "expert marksmen and exeedingly troublesome."[178] The Spanish botanist José Moziño concurred, declaring that "they handle all the European arms of flints, sabers, and swords with special dexterity."[179] In the same year the Kwakiutls met Captain Vancouver "with Muskets which they could handle & use with much ease & great dexterity."[180] And the Indians were soon knowledgeable enough to accept only the best guns. In 1802 the "best of Kings arms [regular army muskets] or handsome fowling pieces [light rifles for shooting wildfowl]" were the only guns that the northern Indians would buy.[181] Three years later Captain D'Wolf observed that "from long intercourse with American traders, the natives had become extremely expert in the use of the muskets, in the choice of which they showed great judgment and sagacity, and invariably selected a king's arm in preference to the most finished fowling-piece."[182] "Both sexes [of Sitkan Tlingits]," he added, "are expert in the use of fire-arms, and are excellent judges of their quality."[183] Their Chief Kotlean, who was an "excellent" marksman, owned twenty of the "best" muskets and even some small cannons.[184] At this same time Lewis and Clark found that the Chinooks were "well armed with good Fusees [light muskets]."[185] (Lewis and Clark added, however, that most of the Chinook guns were old and inferior American and British muskets, and even their few good pieces were in bad condition because they did not take proper care of them [substituting gravel for shot, for example]; the bow and arrow was still their chief weapon.[186]) Another American visitor noted in 1818 that the Northwest Coast Indians were "with a musket, the best of marksmen."[187] And a decade later Lieutenant Simpson reported that the northern Indians had guns of "fine quality" as well as a "good supply" of ammunition.[188] Apparently the only restraint shown by shipmasters was their reluctance to trade blunderbusses, which fired several balls at one time (whereas muskets, with a smaller bore and a longer range, fired only one ball at a time).

Armed with plenty of superior guns – besides lances, bows and arrows, sabres, and daggers – and adept in their use, the Indians were a potent force. (Robin Fisher has questioned the assumption that the introduction of firearms had a devastating effect on the Northwest Coast Indians, arguing that guns were not necessarily superior to traditional Native weapons [given the nature of flintlock muskets and the character of Indian warfare] and that the Indians wanted to possess guns for economic rather than military purposes; Joan Townsend has posited a similar case for Russian America.[189]) Many skippers wanted to stop the arms trade but failed to do so for reasons cited by Chief Trader John Work in 1838 in a reply to a proposal from Chief Factor John McLoughlin at Fort Vancouver to ban the sale of ordnance at Fort McLoughlin and southward:

But doing so would be an act of inhumanity by leaving those Indians defenceless and unprepared to repel the frequent attacks of the natives from the northward, from whom, owing to the vicinity of the Russians, these articles cannot be withheld without very serious loss to the trade. Besides stopping the supply of ammunition would disable the Indians from hunting Sea Otter, Beaver, and land Otters which are chiefly killed by shooting them, and moreover the supply of deer for provisions at Fort McLoughlin would cease; and there can be no doubt a great deal of discontent would be created among the Indians.[190]

By way of compromise it was decided to lower the price of a beaver pelt from one gallon to one quart of gunpowder (and shot in proportion), so that "notwithstanding this advance in price [of ammunition] the Indians will still be able to procure the means of defence and to hunt, and not have enough to trade to the prejudice of our Establishments in the Interior [New Caledonia] and to the Southward."[191]

Alcohol and tobacco were nearly as pernicious as firearms. Both were introduced at the turn of the century. Before the arrival of Euroamerican traders the Haidas and perhaps the Tlingits cultivated a variety of chewing tobacco, and the Yuroks grew and smoked tobacco. The remaining Indian groups soon became addicted to this carcinogen. When Lewis and Clark sojourned among the Chinooks in the winter of 1805–06, for example, they found them "excessively fond" of pipe smoking. They both inhaled and swallowed the tobacco smoke, which rendered them inebriate and flatulent.[192] Intoxicants were unknown to the Northwest Coast Indians before white contact. They were soon introduced by shipmasters on the assumption that bibulous customers were more likely to trade, and to trade less punctiliously, than abstinent clients. The initial Native distaste for alcohol (and salt) was overcome by persistent offerings by explorers in a spirit of friendship and by traders bent on ingratiation and habituation. By the turn of the century it was used in large amounts as a trade good.[193] In 1799 the Haidas would accept "lambs" (rum) as a present, although they would not buy it.[194] Thereafter "Indian rum" – from one-quarter to one-half rum and the rest water – was commonly given to open trade. Lieutenant Simpson admitted in 1831 that "I cannot do business without it."[195] When the *Boston* cleared for the coast in 1802, its cargo included 1,260 gallons of rum (and 3,000 guns).[196] In one April week in 1833 at Active Cove in Milbanke Sound the *Lama* dispensed 410 gallons of "Indian grog" from one cask of pure rum while procuring 1,200 land furs.[197] Grog was so plentiful on the coast that in 1818 some crewmen of the *Mentor* were able to buy rum from the Indians themselves at Taddiskey on the Queen Charlottes.[198]

Alcoholism was inevitable. The supercargo of the *Atahualpa* noted at Kaigani in 1802 that "here, and at other places where trading vessels frequent, drunkeness is not uncommon."[199] Liquor also made the Indians more prone to quarreling and less prone to hunting. At Fort Simpson on 4 February 1835, the HBC "stopt the sale of Liquor as a punishment to the Chiefs who appear very much inclined to quarrel when intoxicated," and the rum trade was not resumed until a week later.[200] Again, at the end of May 1837 the post journal recorded: "Mr. Kennedy [the Indian trader] still kept busy trading with the Indians, the run on rum is immense the vagabonds are drinking awfully." A week later it added: "The Indians are so much occupied drinking that they dont take time to either hunt or fish. The quantity of liquor they are trading is immense they have consumed two puncheons [144 gallons] of rum within the last fortnight or three weeks."[201] Some of the liquor figured in potlatches, as the post journal noted at the end of May 1838: "Cacax and a party of his people arrived from Pearl Harbour early in the morning and traded 25 beaver and a few Martens principally for rum. The great feast and ball which they are going to give and which has been so long talked of is to take place shortly, the liquor traded today is intended for it. It is said it will be a grand concern of the kind. Cacax wishes to set himself up as a man of great consequence, to effect which giving these feasts is generally one of the means employed."[202] A Protestant missionary warned the northern Indians in 1829 of the evils of "demon rum" but admitted that "on board the ship of a north-west trader is a place very unsuitable to preach temperance to an Indian."[203] At that time rum and guns were held in the "greatest estimation" by the Natives and yielded shipmasters the "greatest profit."[204]

As a trade item grog enjoyed the additional advantage of cheapness. For this reason rum was particularly favoured by the Russians, who themselves had a well-deserved reputation for intemperance. During the first half of the 1830s, because of the high prices demanded by Tlingits in the "straits" as a result of American liberality, the RAC preferred to trade rum since it was sold at 180 per cent above cost; a large beaver pelt could be bought for one and one-half gallons of rum costing officially twenty but actually only seven silver rubles (less than five dollars).[205] At this time the rival HBC gave from one and one-half to two gallons of "Indian grog" (⅜ rum, ⅝ water) for a large beaver skin.[206] (At Fort Simpson in 1837 "Indian rum" likewise comprised three parts water and one part rum.[207]) And the Honourable Company, too, realized rum's value. Clerk Donald Manson, who was in charge of Fort McLoughlin, reported to Governor Simpson in 1834 that, because it was diluted, "rum is a very cheap article of Trade." He added that "the natives of Millbank Sound [Fort McLoughlin] are not yet so fond of liquor as their more northern neighbours, consequently the Returns of this Establishment will appear dearer than those to the northward."[208] Because they were traded mostly for dry goods, skins cost the HBC from four to five times more at Fort McLoughlin than at Fort Simpson, where they were bartered mostly for cheaper rum, rice, and molasses, "which are in great demand among those indians who have had more communication with the Americans."[209] Manson felt that "our opponents being always well stocked in it [liquor] when on the Coast, I cannot see wherefore we should not consider our Interest also by encouraging its sale." He was confident that then "the Natives here would soon become as fond of it as to the northward."[210] In 1842, after the Americans had withdrawn from the coast trade, the HBC and the RAC agreed to ban the trading of booze but within a few years this pact was broken and toping continued to wreak physical, social, and economic havoc.

Liquor was introduced about the same time as molasses, rice, bread, and "Indian sugar," which was half sugar and half bran – again note the possible pejorative connotation of the adjective "Indian" to mean "adulterated" or "bogus," as in "Indian giver" or even "Indian summer," the irony being, of course, that the deceit was practised by whites. (Molasses were diluted with an equal amount of salt water.[211]) These Euroamerican foodstuffs became popular as more and more trading vessels wintered on the coast and thus were able to cater to hungry Indians during the leaner winter months. (For example, the *Hamilton* was able to trade fish oil for skins in late winter.[212]) Initially the Nootkas, at least, detested salt and liquor but relished rice and biscuit.[213] As early as 1793 Captain Vancouver found that "bread and molasses were the greatest treat we could give" to the Tlingits of Clarence Strait; one of their chiefs, Onnnistoy, deemed this treat a "very acceptable" present.[214] The Haidas acquired a taste for molasses with rice in March 1799, when Captain James Rowan of the *Eliza* gave some to a number of hungry tribesmen who had been detained three days without food at Kaigani by a gale.[215] Before long they even preferred molasses to rum and would trade a prime sea-otter skin for four bottles of "brassis."[216] Demand was such that around 1800 one trading vessel made the coast with 601 gallons of molasses and six casks of rice (plus 534 gallons of rum).[217] In 1802 one of the owners of the *Alert*, J. Lamb, Sr, assured one of its officers, his son J. Lamb, Jr, that "you will have molasses & rice in plenty on the Coast to sweeten the tawny stomachs of those savages."[218] Molasses with rice or bread was the best seller on the coast that year, when it was reported that "musquets & cloth are mere drugs on the market" and "bread, rice & molasses are all the cry."[219] In 1801 ten gallons of either molasses or rice fetched a skin, and "more was wanted than the quantity on the coast ... $1000 in rice & molasses, was of more value & would bring a greater number of skins than $10,000 would bring in cloth etc."[220] A hogshead of bread brought two or three skins on the northern coast in 1801 and five skins in 1802.[221]

Concoctions of molasses with rice or bread remained in demand until the close of the coast trade simply because the Indians relished them, particularly in winter, when their own food sources were rather meagre. Molasses, honey, rice, and bread "they gorge unmercyfully," noted an 1805 visitor.[222] These foodstuffs even generated potlatches, as another visitor recorded in 1811: "Yesterday the Chief bought a pipe & a barrel of bread and 6 buckets of Molasses, it was all carried ashore [at Chuckenhoo] to his house in our [jolly] boat, and all the Indians that was here invited to a feast of bread & molasses."[223] In 1825 molasses with bread was still "of all things the most delicious to an Indian palate."[224] And in 1833 even among the Coast Salishes around Fort Nisqually "Rum, Bread & Molasses in their Eyes is a great desideratum."[225] Like rum and tobacco, molasses was eventually given as a present rather than traded for skins.[226]

Other Euroamerican wares like wire and paint were traded but never as heavily as guns and textiles. Trinkets – "trifles" or "gewgaws"

– probably had the longest life of all trade goods, although they were actually of "little value" and sometimes even despised.[227] According to Captain Sturgis, the favourite trinkets of the Indians in the early 1800s were haliotis ear pendants, arm and leg bracelets of iron or more commonly brass, wire, brass, and gilt finger rings, neck chains of iron wire ("jack chains," made from stout iron wire with links the size of those in the curb chain of a bridle, from which snaffle bridle bits, keys, and buttons were hung), metal buttons and brass thimbles (both of which were fastened to their robes), keys (which were suspended from their bodies and attached to their garments), black, white, and red pigments (especially red lead and Chinese vermilion), and haiqua nose pieces.[228] Most "small presents" were ornamental personal effects, such as beads, which were worn as necklaces, bracelets, and anklets. Russian blue beads seems to have been the most popular, spreading as far south as Nootka Sound.[229] In 1786 the Natives of Prince William Sound sold sea-otter skins to Captain Strange for five blue beads each.[230] But this transaction was exceptional. "Small" trade in beads, buttons, "China cash" (holed Chinese coins), spoons, nails, fishhooks, scissors, mirrors, combs, handkerchiefs, and the like served two functions: as gifts to broach trade and as barter for provisions. In 1787 such goods were accepted as ceremonial gifts only, but by 1791 such goods "were hardly accepted as a free gift, or by way of closing a bargain."[231] A year later Captain Vancouver's expedition found that the Indians would accept bagatelles as presents but not in exchange for anything.[232] In fact, such was normally not the case, because from the beginning they could be swapped for provisions (fish, venison, wildfowl, berries, wappatoos ["swamp potatoes"], greens) and water, and this barter increased as more and more vessels wintered on the coast and hence had to replenish their "sea stock." In the early 1790s one nail bought one "harcoo" (halibut) from the Haidas or two salmon from the Chinooks.[233] In addition, whale oil was obtained for ships' lamps. At Nootka Sound in 1778 Captain Clerke bought more than 100 gallons of whale oil "to burn in Lamps"; he also found that it was "indeed by no means ill-flavour'd or disgusting to the Palate."[234]

Besides bringing Euroamerican goods to the coast, the maritime fur traders also bought and sold local goods that had long supported intertribal trade: Monterey and dentalium shells, ermine skins, elk hides, oolachen oil, and slaves – anything that could be exchanged for furs. At Clayoquot Sound in 1790 the Nootkas paid one sea-otter skin for ten Monterey shells; on the northern coast in 1802 200 dentalium shells fetched one skin, and in 1835 the Bella Coolas gave a large beaver pelt for twelve feet of good or sixty feet of poor dentalia (in 1793 they had given Captain Vancouver's crew-men one sea-otter skin for four Monterey shells); four ermine skins, or "clicks," fetched a prime sea-otter skin from the Haidas in 1799; and an elk hide brought one skin and one marten cloak in 1793 from the Tsimshians and from one to three skins (depending upon the size of the hide) from the Haidas in 1794 and 1802.[235] Both Monterey and dentalium shells were coveted by the Indians up and down the coast and inland as well. At the mouth of the Columbia in the winter of 1805–06 Lewis and Clark found "common coarse blue and white beads" which were made from Monterey and den-talium shells, respectively, and which were worn by the Chinooks as bracelets, necklaces, anklets, earrings, and nose rings. The blue or "chief's beads" were the Chinooks' favourite commodity, but the white shells still remained a standard of value among them.[236] Gov-ernor Simpson noted that "these articles, thus practically corre-sponding with the cowries of the East Indies, are used as small change all along the coast and in many parts of the interior; and they are also applied to more fanciful purpose in the shape of necklaces, ornaments for the hair, and so forth, while occasionally a large haiquay may be seen balancing itself through the cartilage of a pretty girl's nose."[237] (Polished wooden nose pieces were jocosely called "spritsail yards" by sailors of the trading vessels.[238])

This shell money became a circulating medium from Unalaska to the Columbia, owing to the scarcity, computability (always forty to a string), durability, and portability of the shells, each from one to one and one-half inches long, white, hard, smooth, curved, and tapered.[239] While wintering in Clayoquot Sound in 1793–94 the *Thomas Jefferson*, Captain Josiah Roberts, bought 160 fathoms (960 feet) of haiqua at the rates of one short jacket for one fathom, one iron sword for one and one-half to two fathoms, and one musket for six fathoms. The ship's logkeeper, Bernard Magee, noted that haiqua were "in great demand on the south coast," where the Chinooks in the previous summer had offered a skin for a fathom-long string.[240] Similarly, in Columbia Cove the *Vancouver* in 1806 purchased "a g[r]ate Quantity of hyakwaw and Quiller [pearl shell] Which is verry Sailable among the Northern indians."[241] Haiqua were "very much enquired for" by the Indians around Kaigani in 1801.[242] Lewis and Clark found that the lower Columbia River Indians were "extrava-gantly fond" of dentalium "beeds." "They prefer beeds to any thing" and "for those beeds they will dispose of any article they possess," they noted.[243] The Sahaptin Indians of the Columbia-Snake conflu-ence pierced their noses and inserted an ornament of dentalium[244] and hence were dubbed the Nez Percés. Lewis and Clark noticed haiqua as far east as the Rockies.[245] The Aleuts, too, prized "sea teeth," or *tache*.[246] The Native demand for haiqua was such that American traders had some imitated in porcelain in England. They "were so well executed both as to form, size, and polish, that they had a perfectly natural appearance," but the Tlingits "detected the fraud, treated the pretended shells with the utmost contempt, and the speculation proved entirely abortive" (the same observer wrote that the Tlingits likewise "understand the qualities of a good gun so well, that it is impossible to impose a bad one upon them").[247] The popularity of haiqua persisted. In the spring of 1825 the *Convoy* bought 5,000 near Newhitty.[248] Three years later Lieutenant Simpson noted that the shells were regularly purchased from the Newhitty Indians and were a "good article of trade" with the northern Indians.[249] At Fort Nisqually the HBC acquired 170 fathoms of haiqua between 1 March 1834 and 20 January 1835.[250]

Ermine fur was prized by the Indians of the northern coast, principally as adornment in ceremonial dress. This esteem prompted the *Pearl*, Captain Ebbets, and the *Vancouver*, Captain Brown, to take ermine skins to the coast – coals to Newcastle – in 1805.[251]

Elk hides were more utilitarian and more common. The hides were bleached white in the sun and folded double or treble into a tough cape that covered a warrior from his neck to his heels, with an opening on the side for the fighting arm. Captain Bishop described them: "Leather War Dresses ... are made from the Hide of the Moose Deer [elk] which are very large and thick. This is dressed into a kind of White leather, and doubled, & is when Properly made up, a compleat defence against a Spear or an Arrow and Sufficient almost to resist a Pistol Ball."[252] Called "clemmels" by the Tlingits, "clemens" or "clamons" by the Haidas, "clemals" by the Chinooks, and "clammels" by the Euroamerican traders, they seem to have lent their name to Clemencitty, or Clement City (Tlekhonsiti Harbour on Tongass Island), one of the main rendezvous on the northern coast. Clammels were "much called for" on the northern coast in particular because of the frequent intertribal warfare of the Natives.[253] They came mostly from the lower Columbia, especially the Willamette Valley. Shipmasters soon realized their value. Captain Roberts of the *Thomas Jefferson* in the summer of 1793 "had good information of Clamons to be procured [at the Columbia] & has been purchased by several for 3 Chisils apeace & afterwards bartered for the sea otter skin for skin" – and this at a time when only halibut could be bought with chisels on the Queen Charlottes.[254] By the end of the year the *Jefferson* had obtained 124 clammels from the Nootkas and Chinooks "for the trade to the North – in the [following] spring – the natives there being so desireous of the Moose skins dressed – which they wear allwise going to war or any combatt – as it [is] a sufficient proofe against the force of an arrow."[255] The ship wintered in Clayoquot Sound, where it was found that a sea-otter skin could be had for one clammel or forty chisels.[256] Similarly, in late 1795 and early 1796 Captain Bishop of the *Ruby*, while wintering at the mouth of the Columbia, procured 200 clammels, which he expected to barter for 700 sea-otter skins.[257] And in a month at Newhitty at the end of the 1801 trading season the *Atahualpa* bought up to 100 clammels, most of them "of an inferior quality," however, to those of the Columbia.[258] (The Chilkat Tlingits made and traded a garment that was similar to a clammel. Called a *siskquo* or *chisquo*, it was fashioned from mountain sheep skins or moose hides, two or three of which were sewn together to form a loose cloak that was "greatly esteemed" by both Tlingits and Haidas for everyday rather than military use.[259])

The Columbia offered not only clammels but also oolachen, "very closely resembling the sardine in richness and delicacy."[260] "Eulachon" were praised by both Lewis and Clark: "They are so fat they require no additional sauce, and I think them superior to any fish I ever tasted, even more delicate and lussious than the white fish of the lakes which have heretofore formed my standart of excellence among the fishes."[261] The main source of "shrow" for shipmasters and northern Indians, however, was the early spring run in the Nass River (which the Indians called *Ewen Nass*, meaning either "great food depot" or "great satisfier of the belly" in Tlingit). The *Atahualpa* in 1802 was one of the first trading vessels to note at Cocklane's Harbour that "all the Tribes in this vicinity repair thither for the purpose of procuring large quantities of a small fish, not unlike herrings, which serves them for food during the summer." It was likewise noted that "an oil they call sow-tow is extracted from these small fish & is an article of trade much in demand among the neighbouring tribes.[262] (In Haida oolachen is *sáaw* and oolachen grease or oil is *satáw*.) Similarly, in early April 1810 the *Otter* found that the Tsimshians of "Nass Sound" (Observatory Inlet) "are all employed in catching Shrow for their Summers provision, the Shrow are small fish that goes up the Inlets in the Spring and which they catch with nets in great abundance, they are very fat and serve for the double purpose of eating, & making Oil."[263] Indeed they were so preoccupied with catching and trading oolachen to visiting Haidas, whose "vast number of Canoes" left Nass "loaded with dried Shrow packed in boxes," that they did little fur trading.[264] In the words of the ship's journal for 27 June: "The weather cloudy & showery, the Indians are coming & going between us & the shore all the time but they bring very few skins with them, they have been so busy about the Shrow-tow fishery these 6 weeks back that they could not spare time to go a hunting, the Shrowtow is a great source of riches to the Nass Indians as it supplys them plentifully for provisions during the summer and enough to sell to other Tribes that comes and buys the shrow of them, for cloth and other articles that they purchase from the ships for their otter Skins."[265] In the same year the *Hamilton* observed 300 canoes arriving at "Nass Roads" in one day in the middle of March and another 300 in one day at the beginning of April.[266] The crew had to be wary in the midst of so many Indians, as on 3 June when from 200 to 300 were alongside "trading with srow tow & they were sumthing insolant but we desided them with out any damage on oather side."[267] Again, on 15 July: "A large number of the Natives suposed for to bee about one hundred or upwards onbord & Along side under pretence of trade for srow tow but there intent was for to try to take the ship for they keep coming up with there dagers sum of which was Drawn out of the sheath & when wee found them with them & took them away sum Made resistance & then all in the Canoes took up there Musquets but when that they found that wee was redy with ower arms over the ships side at them they went off with out any damage."[268]

Shipmasters eventually emulated the Tsimshian chiefs of Nass, for oolachen was in demand "not only as a luxury for the great, but also as a necessary of life to all classes."[269] The *Hamilton* in 1821 bought 60 boxes of shrowtow, or shrowton, on 4 May and another 60 boxes on 6 May but it must have purchased much more both that year and the previous year because it transferred 1,290 "kelp" (a container for oil of unknown capacity, possibly a scabbard) of oil to the *Ann* and 1,266 to the *Volunteer* on 24 July 1820, 800 to the *Arab* and 1,000 to the *Pedler* on 4 August 1821, 600 to the *Mentor* and 3,300 to the *Lascar* on 20 August 1821, 1,648 to the *Sultan* on 24 September 1821, and 1,361 more to the same ship on 25 September.[270] The *Tally Ho* on 13 June 1826 bought sixty boxes of shrowton at Nass for trade at Skidegate and Lanacoon on the Queen Charlottes.[271] The oil was as saleable as the fish itself. John Work described oolachen oil as "a great article of commerce among the natives and constitutes a principal article of food and is considered a great delicacy."[272] His superior, Governor Simpson, sarcastically concurred:

This fish yields an extraordinary quantity of very fine oil, which, being highly prized by the natives, is a great article of trade with the Indians of the interior, and also of such parts of the coast as do not furnish the luxury in question. This oil is used as a sauce at all their meals – if snapping at any hour of the day or night can be called a meal – with fish, with seaweed, with berries, with roots, with venison, etc. Nor is it less available for the toilet than for culinary purposes. It is made to supply the want of soap and water, smearing the face or any other part of the body that is deemed worthy of ablution, which, when well scrubbed with a mop of sedge, looks as clean as possible. In addition to this essential business of purifying and polishing, the oil of the ullachan does duty as bear's grease for the hair; and some of the young damsels, when fresh from their unctuous labours, must be admitted to shine considerably in society.[273]

In the early 1840s the Tsimshians brought more than 30,000 gallons of oolachen oil to Fort Simpson annually.[274]

Slaves were another coastal trade good that Nor'westmen came to adopt, the slave trade having come into existence long before the advent of Euroamerican traders. One-third of the Indian population of the entire Northwest Coast comprised slaves, who were mostly born into their station.[275] They were the lowest rank of Native society and came the closest to forming a distinct caste. Slaves were mere chattels who could be sacrificed by their owners, particularly upon the death of the latter, or ransomed by their relatives. Upon the death of a notable or one of his/her relatives among the northern Indians, the slaves of that person were customarily killed.[276] Sometimes, too, a quarrel was settled by the killing of slaves belonging to the disputants, the intent being "to make up the matter by showing who was the richest and could best afford the loss."[277] The possession of slaves was prestigious in that it demonstrated the military success or the material wealth of their owners, since most slaves were war captives rather than debtors and since only the wealthy could afford to buy them. Slaves were economically desirable, too, for they were obliged to "labour severely" in menial and heavy tasks, food gathering in particular. Chief Factor James Douglas described their lot in 1840:

The wealth and consequence of all classes [of the northern Indians] from the stripling, to the highest chieftains, are measured by the number of such dependents, who tho' in many cases kept for the mere purpose of display, are also exceedingly useful as fishermen and hunters, while they constitute a body guard of generally faithful adherents, ready to protect their master or murder his enemies at the slightest intimation of his will without question or scruple. In fact Shakes the most influential Stekine Chief has no followers of his own tribe and merely a retinue of 24 slaves, who paddle his canoes, fish, hunt and perform for him every menial office, live under the same roof, and in short uphold his cause with their ever ready swords and spears. The ladies too, slovenly as they are in their general habits, cannot condescend to exercise their tender hands, at any kind of work, and must also have their train of attendants to relieve them of domestic drudgery, which in their opinion is degrading and would involve the loss of caste.[278]

George Simpson noted in 1824–25 that Chinook slaves were "made to Fish, hunt, draw Wood & Water in short all the drudgery falls on them ... indeed I conceive a Columbia Slave to be the most unfortunate Wretch in existence."[279] Most slaves were women or children, who were not expected to fight in wartime; besides, men were too ready to seek escape or revenge and thus were often executed. The likelihood of escape, ransom, or rescue was slim, since, as the *Atahualpa's* journal for 1802 stated, "the prisoners taken are sold to the most distant tribes they are acquainted with, then resold to others more distant, in order to prevent a possibility of their being rescued or ever returning."[280] Slaves were traded up and down the coast and across the mountains to the interior. Fort Simpson's post journal recorded that slaves were "the articles most in demand with the Inland Indians," and in particular were they "a great article of trafic in the interior of Stikeen where they [Stikine Tlingits] get the most of their furs."[281] Indeed the traffic in slaves was the cause of "a great deal of predatory warfare" among the northern Indians.[282] The chief victims, apart from the Californian Indians, seem to have been the Coast Salishes, who were periodically terrorized by flotillas of Kwakiutl, Haida, and even fellow Salish slavers; the Cowichan Salishes, for example, crossed Georgia Strait and ascended the Cowichan (Fraser) River every late summer to get salmon and slaves and returned to Vancouver Island in early fall. Whatever their origin, slaves were valuable pieces of property. In February 1811 a Haida chief sold a slave – "a fine boy about 10 years old" – at Lanacoon for fifteen clammels, four sea-otter skins, and two blankets.[283] George Simpson found in the middle 1820s that slaves "form the principal article of traffick on the whole of this Coast and constitute the greater part of their [Indians'] Riches."[284] Another Euroamerican visitor of the 1830s, John Dunn, who in the summer of 1834 was an assistant to Donald Manson, the clerk in charge of Fort McLoughlin,[285] wrote that the Bella Coolas "deal in slaves, purchased from the southern tribes – the original kidnappers – and then sell them, at a profit, to the northern tribes, who come down to purchase them. A full-grown, athletic slave, who is a good hunter, will fetch nine blankets, a gun, a quantity of powder and ball, a couple of dressed elk skins, tobacco, vermillion paint, a flat file, and other little articles."[286] To the Tlingits at this time a slave was worth two sea-otter or twenty-five beaver skins.[287] Wealthy Tlingits owned from thirty to forty slaves, who constituted up to one-third of the total Tlingit population in the early

1840s.[288] The Taku Tlingits prized slaves more than any other commodity, and some tribesmen owned as many as twenty, who were worth from eighteen to twenty beaver skins each. Most were war captives, and "many predatory excursions" were undertaken not to avenge wrongs but to acquire slaves.[289] The Nootkas, too, regarded slaves as their most valuable property; in 1803 Chief Maquinna owned up to fifty, and one was worth sixty feet of haiqua.[290]

By at least the turn of the century shipmasters were taking advantage of this additional medium of exchange for furs, buying slaves at the mouth of the Columbia and in the Strait of Juan de Fuca and selling them on the northern coast. Occasionally they even traded Hawaiian women as slaves. Captains were reluctant to admit to slaving, especially in writing; one exception was a testimonial of one of the officers of the *Lydia* in 1812: "We are continually engaged in the slave trade whenever we go to the South we bring a number and dispose of them to the highest Bidder."[291] Aemelius Simpson found in 1828 that American coasters trafficked in slaves, "purchasing them at a cheap rate from one tribe and disposing of them to others at a very high profit." He concluded sanctimoniously that "it is upon illicit and inhuman branches of Trade that the American adventurers make their greatest profits ... viz. Arms, Ammunition, Rum, and Slaves."[292] One slave fetched from one to two sea-otter skins from the Nootkas in 1791, three skins from the Haidas in 1799, three to eight skins from the Haidas in 1811, and ten beaver pelts or fifteen elk hides from the Tsimshians in 1835.[293]

Slaves were often used as concubines and prostitutes, whose charms served the same propitiatory purpose for the Indians as trinkets did for the Euroamericans. The earliest Nor'westmen invariably remarked the fidelity and modesty of the Native women. Lieutenant Puget asserted that they "hold Chastity as one of the Cardinal Virtues."[294] The deportment of Nootka women, who "have a great share of Modesty,"was "uniformly exemplary"; only female slaves were prostituted.[295] The uxorious Nootka men ostentatiously offered to barter their wives and daughters but did not complete the transaction, intending only to mock the Euroamericans who often tried to debauch the women with bribes but were nearly always spurned.[296] "Still they were not all *Dianas*," noted an American seaman in 1791, probably referring to slaves.[297] The very first white visitors to the sound, Captain Cook's crews, had a similar experience. One of the first officers wrote that "they [Nootka girls, presumably slaves] were offer'd by the Men for dalliance to our People, and by some accepted, though but by few; this connection was by no means general."[298] The *Discovery*'s surgeon, David Samwell, was more explicit:

tho' some of them [Nootka girls] had no bad faces yet as they were exceedingly dirty their Persons at first sight were not very inviting, however our young Gentlemen were not to be discouraged by such an obstacle as this which they found was to be removed with Soap & warm water, this they called the Ceremony of Purification and were themselves the Officiators at it, & it must be mentioned to their praise that they performed it with much piety & Devotion, taking as much pleasure in cleansing a naked young Woman from all Impurities in a Tub of Warm Water, as a young Confessor would to absolve a beutiful Virgin who was about to sacrifice that Name to himself.

Samwell added that the "price of the Prostitution ... was commonly a Pewter plate well scoured for one Night," so that the Nootka girls thus "found means at last to disburthen our young Gentry of their Kitchen furniture, many of us after leaving this Harbour not being able to muster a plate to eat our Salt beef from."[299]
    As Indian demands increased, slave girls and eventually perhaps wives and daughters, too, were readily prostituted. So it was not really necessary for Captain Hugh Moore of the *Phoenix* to bring a "Lady of pleasure," an "Indian wench" from Bengal, with him to the coast in 1794 or for Captain Hill of the *Lydia* to have an "Attoi [Kauai] Lady" on board in 1805–06 on the northern coast,[300] although seamen invariably preferred Polynesian to Northwest Coast Indian damsels (considering the former prettier and cleaner); in early 1793 Captain Vancouver returned to Niihau in the *Discovery* two teenaged girls who had been kidnapped a year earlier by the *Jenny*, Captain James Baker.[301] When the *Aranzazu* under Captain Jacinto Caamaño sojourned at Bucareli Bay in 1792 he found that "the natives [Tlingits] were greatly surprised at our abstaining from any commerce with their women, whom they brought with them, for that purpose, since they are accustomed to the English, and others, who trade in these parts, not only accepting, but also demanding, and choosing, them."[302] (He was surprised because the Spaniards tended to avoid sexual contact with the Indian females, or at least to have much less such contact with them than the Americans, British, and Russians did.) The Haidas also offered trading vessels a "lady for the night," usually from their slaves.[303] Captain Colnett reported in 1787 that "as to their Chastity it may be compared to those of the Sandwich & Friendly [Tonga] Isles, their favours purchas'd at a very easy rate, but this I do not think a common failing of theirs, when we first arrived among them Iron was very scarce, & they had no Skins to purchase it of us, they robb'd us of every hook & Thimble out of [the] rigging they could come at but still their wants were great, they soon found

that their Women was the next thing coveted to their Furs, and the Men & parents, whom they are under great subjection to readily barter'd them, we soon had many Ladies desirous of disposing of themselves & the numbers so increas'd that they had no purchaser."[304] An American sailor noted in 1791 that "the females was not very Chaste, but their lip pieces was enough to disgust any Civilized being, however some of the Crew was quite partial."[305] And in the same year another American seaman reported from the Queen Charlottes that his ship had "well Featread" Haida girls on board between the ages of ten and twenty, their "fathers" (owners) instructing them "how to be have while our men had to dow with them."[306] Three years later the *Thomas Jefferson* was similarly serviced at the Queen Charlottes: "The afternoon being very rainy the [Haida] Canoes left us Early leaving on board 8 or 9 of the fair – no fair priestesses of venus to assist & accommodate those whose inclinations now laid them to a discharge of those rites & obligations so peculiarly due to that divinity."[307] These "fair guests" spent two nights on the ship.[308] The *New Hazard* celebrated New Year's Eve 1811 in like fashion in Kaigani Strait, its logbook recording dryly: "Plenty girls on board. Pleasant night."[309] In the summer of 1822 Captain Cross of the *Rob Roy* kept a Kaigani girl on board.[310] Lieutenant Simpson reported in 1828 that the women of the Kaigani Haidas and Tongass Tlingits "freely grant favours, for which they are liberally rewarded generally" by American traders.[311] As more and more trading vessels wintered on the coast, the sexual demands of their crews mounted, resulting in more and more whoring. In 1817 a British trader found that Trinidad Bay on the shore of New Albion was the "only place on the coast where we could not induce the females to visit the ship."[312]

Chinook women seem to have been particularly licentious. John Boit, the young fifth mate of the *Columbia*, found in 1792 that "the women are very pretty. they ... wear a leaf Apron (perhaps 'twas a fig leaf). But some of our gentlemen, that examin'd them pretty close, and *near*, both *within* and *without* reported that it was not a leaf but a nice wove mat in resemblance!!"[313] Lewis and Clark likewise found that many of the Chinook women were attractive and wanton. They went so far as to assert that "those people appear to view sensuality as a necessary evill, and do not appear to abhore this as crime in the unmarried females."[314] They added that the men were even willing to prostitute their wives and daughters for a fishhook or a strand of beads.[315] George Simpson had a similar reaction in the middle 1820s, when he reported that unmarried Chinook women were allowed "to indulge the full scope of their inclinations," and chastity was regarded as a virtue by only "Ladies of the very first rank" who were intended by their parents to become the "country wives" of Euroamerican traders. Even married women, from the "Princess of Wales [Chief Factor Donald McKenzie's concubine] downwards," could be had for the right price. Simpson added that the Chinook women at Fort George "let out" their female slaves as prostitutes for the new recruits of the HBC.[316]

Such intercourse not only allayed the sexual appetites of Nor'westmen but occasionally saved their lives, too, as when one of the Chinook prostitutes aboard the *Lydia* forewarned the crew of a plan by her people to seize the ship[317] (apparently Captain Hill's reputation for unscrupulousness had preceded him all the way down the coast). Yet sexual contact also had tragic results. One was the Euroamerican perception of all Indian women as lascivious and promiscuous sex objects – part of what might be termed the unflattering "squaw" image. Another was the introduction and diffusion of what one logbook called the "ladies disorder" (venereal disease) and its attendant physical suffering and genetic damage (although an indigenous form of the "pox" may have been present prior to the coming of Euroamericans). The Nootkas had contracted syphilis by 1791. That year the *Columbia Rediviva* found that Chief Cassacan of Nittenat, or Nitinat, was "troubled with the venereal to a great degree," having caught it from a slave girl who had been infected by a shipmaster "sometime since" (the latter had paid several sheets of copper for the girl but upon his departure had sent her ashore).[318] The disease seems to have been especially prevalent among the Chinooks, perhaps because a permanent white settlement (Astoria, later Fort George) was established early among them. "Pocks & venereal is common amongst them," declared Lewis and Clark.[319] "Many" of their men caught "Louis Veneri" (*Lues venerea*: "syphilis" in Latin) from Chinook women.[320] In the middle 1820s George Simpson found that the Chinooks were "wonderfully healthy being rarely afflicted by any other than *Imported Diseases*"; nine out of ten Bay men at Fort George had been treated with mercury for syphilis.[321] (Hence the saying "One night with Venus and three years with Mercury.") By the early 1840s it was "very prevalent" among the northern Indians.[322]

Yet another legacy was the appearance of mixed-blood offspring in the mold of the Creoles of Russian America and the Métis of Canada. Lewis and Clark at Fort Clatsop in 1805–06 and Ross Cox at Astoria in 1811–12 encountered a *lusus naturae* ("freak of nature"), a fair-skinned, red-haired, freckle-faced crossbreed named Jack Ramsay whose father, a British sailor, had deserted and taken a Chinook wife, by whom he had several children before dying around 1792.[323] Jack Ramsays were not uncommon. After visiting Tlingit territory in 1827–28 Aemelius Simpson reported that "there is a half breed population growing up among them."[324] The "long Female intercourse" of the American traders, he added incidentally, gave them "much influence" over the Indians, forming "a sort of tie or connexion between the Shipping and these people, which accounts for their friendly disposition towards the Americans."[325] In the middle 1830s another Bay man found that "amongst these [northern] tribes are numbers of American half-breeds, both men and women: some of the latter as fair as English females: some with light hair, and some few with quite red hair."[326] At that time the Kaigani Haidas on North Island had as their chief a crossbreed named George Bennett – reputedly the son of Captain James Bennett of Boston, who was on the coast three times in the 1810s – and he spoke English "very well."[327]

This population of mixed bloods would have been more numerous and might have persisted had it not been for infanticide on the part of their mothers. In the 1810s at the mouth of the Columbia the Euroamerican fathers of mixed offspring insisted that their heads, contrary to Chinook custom, not be flattened; consequently, their mothers killed them rather than see them ranked as slaves, who were distinguished by unflattened heads.[328] At the end of the 1820s a missionary learned that among the northern Indians the babies sired by white traders of unmarried Native girls were often killed at birth.[329] He was told by the Haida chief Cow that "all the young women of the tribe visit ships for the purpose of gain by prostitution, and in most cases destroy their children, the fruit of this infamous intercourse."[330] The mixed-blood children of slave girls would, as slaves, have led rather risky lives anyway, and, as mixed bloods, they may well have been undervalued even more by Natives and whites alike (witness the negative connotation of the Euroamerican term "halfbreed").

Thus the kind and price of goods traded to the Indians varied from time to time and even from place to place. The change could be quite abrupt. One of the earliest maritime fur traders complained that "these Americans [Natives] showed great inconstancy in their desires after different commodities, an article of Trade being one Day in high estimation, and next Day totally despised."[331] This variability is what Captain Dixon had in mind when he lamented, "so uncertain is the fur trade on this inhospitable coast."[332] For the same reason Captain Meares was vexed in 1788: "The fickleness that they [Nootkas] at times discovered in their traffic, was occasionally very troublesome. At one time copper was their favourite object; at another, iron was the only commodity in estimation among them;

beads would also have their turn of preference."[333] Again, in 1791 the Nootkas demanded copper but the Haidas iron.[334] In the same year the Indians eagerly accepted iron collars fashioned by Captain Ingraham's armourer, giving three prime sea-otter skins for a collar, but a year later they scorned them, offering only one skin.[335] Also in 1792 a skin cost ten toes at Nootka Sound, seven at Clayoquot Sound, five on Tatoosh Island, and one at Queen Charlotte Sound.[336] A successful shipmaster had to be both perspicacious and lucky. At the turn of the century, when competition was at its height, the kind and price of trade goods fluctuated greatly.[337] In 1804 Captain Sturgis traded ermine skins (from Leipzig's fur mart) for sea-otter skins at the rate of five for one (or $1.50 for $50), but within two years a hundred ermine skins would not fetch one sea-otter skin.[338] Thereafter, however, reckless skippers were weeded out and the trade settled down into a less frenetic and more stable pattern dominated by guns, blankets, and cloth, plus rum, tobacco, and molasses with rice or bread. Nevertheless, as late as 1831 a shipowner was obliged to remind one of his shipmasters that "the getting together of a cargo adapted to the NW trade is an undertaking accompanied with no small labour & not a little vexation particularly if pressed for time."[339] At the same time, a shipmaster would sell almost anything to the Indians, provided they paid in furs; in 1822 at Stikine the *Rob Roy* traded its whaleboat to Chief Shakes for four prime skins.[340]

The sort of goods traded to the Euroamericans likewise changed over time. As competition increased, fewer superior and more inferior skins were taken. Profits were thereby lowered, for at Canton in 1789 a prime skin (large and dark) brought five times as much as an inferior one (smaller and lighter and perhaps dirty, lousy, and torn).[341] Also, as the population of sea otters dwindled, more land furs, mainly beaver pelts, were traded (as well as more fur-seal skins, which were worth only one-fiftieth as much as sea-otter skins at Canton in 1789).[342] As early as 1805 one trading vessel, the *Atahualpa*, left the coast for Canton carrying one-half as many beaver (3,000) as sea-otter (6,000) skins.[343] Bryant and Sturgis instructed Captain Clark of the *Borneo* as follows in 1817: "When on the coast turn your attention to any kind of furs which may offer all are worth collecting."[344] In fact, in a very strict sense the maritime fur trade was no longer maritime after about 1820 because it was no longer based primarily upon marine fur bearers, although ships were still used. The log entry of the *Arab* for 21 June 1821 at Tongass was common to all coasters: "Bought a few Sea Otters and a number of Land Furrs."[345] In 1822 American coasters collected 2,500 sea-otter skins but 3,000–4,000 land furs.[346] In 1823 the bulk of the annual shipment of coast furs by Marshall and Wildes from Honolulu to Canton was land furs: beaver, land otter, and marten.[347] When Captain John Dominis of the brig *Owhyhee* left Boston for the coast in 1827, he was instructed by the owners that "the principal object of your cruize on the n. w. Coast is the collection of Land Furs."[348] As the *Owhyhee* was clearing Boston, the *Louisa* was quitting the coast after spending eighteen months "in pursute of sea otter and land furs," in the words of its log.[349] The Honolulu commercial agent of Marshall and Wildes reported laconically and understatedly in 1828: "Land furs rather increasing."[350] That trading season Captain Cotting of the *Active* obtained only 102 sea-otter skins but 1,400 land furs.[351] The same season saw the best American coaster get only one-sixth as many sea-otter as beaver pelts.[352] By taking more land furs American ship-masters were, of course, diverting the returns of the inland (New Caledonia) posts of the HBC, and it was this encroachment upon the company's monopoly of the continental fur trade that brought the British back resolutely into the coast trade in the late 1820s.

The Russians, too, were forced to take more and more land furs, but their Alaskan hinterland was large enough that they did not have to encroach upon the adjoining sources of British furs in the upper Yukon River basin. In 1828 Governor Peter Chistyakov reported to the RAC's head office that the sea otter, which he called the main object of the company's business and its chief source of profit, had been "almost completely depleted" on the coast of the colony. Although this depletion had occurred some time ago, he said, it had not been felt because of the high prices for not only sea otter but other furs as well; now, however, it was noticeable because of lower prices for some furs, particularly foxes, so that it was necessary to get more beaver and land-otter skins on the mainland.[353]

The changing composition of collections (as well as other changes) was evidenced at Canton. Of the thirty-eight American ships that put in to Canton between 6 June 1816 and 26 February 1817 only four had plied the Northwest Coast and of these only two brought any sea-otter skins (3,781 altogether), while the four also brought 26,431 fur-seal, 1,564 beaver, and 1,250 land-otter skins.[354] By the early 1820s American vessels were taking 3,000–5,000 beaver pelts annually to Canton, whose yearly demand ranged from 12,000 to 15,000.[355] The problem with pelts other than those of the sea otter was their much lower value in China. In the autumn of 1800 at Canton sea-otter skins were worth $20 but land-otter skins $5–7, beaver skins $4–4.50, and fur-seal skins $0.75.[356] The reason for the differential, as the American trading house of Perkins and Russell explained, was the "little demand either for Land furrs or seal skins in the northern provinces."[357] The same firm reported at the beginning of 1820 from Canton that "land furrs are exceedingly dull & there appears to be no inclination whatever on the part of the furr dealers to purchase them at any price," adding that "we have no idea whatever of realizing more than three or three & a half dollars for the Beavers & about the same for the Land Otters."[358] Perkins and Russell, which had been marketing NWC beaver pelts at Canton, advised the Canadian concern that at these prices it would be to their advantage to sell their furs in the United States instead.[359] In 1821 marten skins were worth five times as much at Boston as at Canton.[360]

As sea otters diminished, the trading vessels bartered from the Indians, or procured by themselves, alternative coastal products: timber, provisions, concubines, and even curios. Wood was an obvious alternative, given the munificence of the temperate rain forest. An early visitor, Captain Meares, had noted that "the coast every where abounds with timber for ship-building, and which would form the finest masts and spars in the world." "Indeed," he added, "the woods of this part of America are capable of supplying, with these valuable materials, all the navies of Europe."[361] But the Hawaiian Islands, with their growing *haole* population, were the most convenient market. The *Hamilton* took planks and spars from the coast to Honolulu (for King Kamehameha I) as early as the fall of 1811.[362] By the 1820s the crews of coasters were regularly going ashore to cut "board logs." The *Convoy* arrived at Honolulu from the coast in the autumn of 1825 and discharged a deck load of spars, five raft loads of firewood, fifty-five cedar boards, and sixteen barrels of fish.[363] The HBC's Lieutenant Simpson found in 1828 that "a great part of the Crew" of American coasters "is occupied in cutting down and squaring Timber, the Logs are then brought on board and sawn into planks, with which and Spars they fill up their vessels for the Sandwich Islands, where it commands a very high price." (Similarly, a year later the missionary Jonathan Green noted that "more or less boards" were sawn on the coast for Hawaiian buyers.[364]) Simpson added that they also cured salmon on the coast for the islands, buying the fish from the Indians "for a mere trifle, principally leaf Tobacco in small quantities."[365] In the same year the Honolulu agent of Marshall and Wildes reported that spars, masts, firewood, and fish from the coast were being sold in Hawaii.[366] By 1830 American vessels were taking house frames, fish, and potatoes from the coast to Hawaii for sale.[367] (In early 1835 an American ship owned by William French, a foreign resident and merchant of Honolulu, even cut logs, planks, and masts at Sitka's sawmill and grossed up to 11,000 piasters, 20 per cent of which was paid to the Russian-American Company for the use of the wood and mill.[368]) Tongass Harbour on Revillagigedo Channel, then the most popular wintering place for American ships, was reputed in the middle 1830s "to be the best on this [northern] part of the coast whence to obtain spars, and other wood, for shipping."[369] The "other wood" included red-cedar shingles, some wintering American coasters getting "as many of them as possible" for the Hawaiian market.[369] (Shingles were also made at Fort Simpson, where, in the second week of July 1837 nine shingle makers made 13,134 shingles – an average of 2,189 per day for six days![371]) By then the HBC was also exporting "country produce," mostly timber and fish, to Honolulu from Forts Vancouver and Langley. The only drawback was noted by Bryant and Sturgis: "NW Coast vessels [upon leaving the coast] generally have a great deal ... of all such lumber & trash as is of no great value"[372] by comparison with sea-otter skins.

Whereas shipmasters simply helped themselves to the coastal rain forest, they had to buy salmon, venison, and potatoes from the Indians, who did most of the fishing, hunting, and gardening. The *Hamilton* bought 66 deer from the Kaigani Haidas during an eight-day period at the end of January 1811, and the same vessel bought 159 sea fowl from the Stikine Tlingits in one day in February 1822.[373] The *Owhyhee*, Captain Dominis, bought halibut, cod, herring, salmon, clams, venison, ducks, and geese from the Natives during the 1827 trading season.[374] Garden vegetables seem to have been introduced quite early at several places, although with little success. In June 1791 Captain Gray left potatoes and onions with the Indians of Clayoquot Sound and showed one of Chief Wickaninish's brothers the "method of cultivation"; the next day, however, they were uprooted by the Indians and brought to the ship for sale.[375] In the summer of 1795 Captain John Boit of the sloop *Union* observed at Friendly Cove in Nootka Sound "many potatoes, beans, cabbages—being the remains of the beautiful Spanish gardens."[376] Six years later the *Atahualpa* anchored in Friendly Cove and found the local Nootkas growing turnips and onions.[377] The ship's crew also discovered wild apple trees at Newhitty, and they had corn, beans, potatoes, celery, lettuce, and parsley planted there.[378] The next year the same vessel likewise found wild apple trees at the Tlingit village of Eelyecanoom in Clarence Strait.[379] The journal of the *Vancouver* noted in 1805: "There is to Be found in Several places on this Coast peas, beans, potatoes, Black Cherries, Small Sower Apples, Calavacses [pulses], and a grate numbers of Difft. Kinds fruets."[380]

Particularly the potato was favoured by the northern Indians, who lacked wappatoo and camas roots. The tuber was well suited to the light, sandy soils and the cool, moist summers of the coast and was consistent with Native root gathering. The Tlingits began to cultivate potatoes in the middle 1820s, apparently later than the Tsimshians or Haidas, for a Russian navigator reported from Sitka in 1827 that "the cultivation of potatoes and other vegetables, already widespread among tribes who live further south, is now beginning to become popular here."[381] By the early 1840s the Tlingits were selling potatoes – as well as halibut and venison from Sitka blacktailed deer – in large amounts to the Russians, and even taking jobs at the colonial capital.[382] The steamship *Nikolay I* bought up to 100 kegs of potatoes from the Tlingits of the "straits" in the autumn of 1841.[383] The Koloshes, as they were termed by the Russians, proposed the regular sale of potatoes to the tsar's men, who agreed.[384] By 1840 the RCA was outlaying $6,000 worth of goods yearly for "country Provisions" at Sitka.[385] The Tsimshians also adopted the potato, perhaps from the Tlingits, but it was the remarkable Haidas who seem to have adjusted the most successfully to the changing commercial conditions and to have embraced the potato most enthusiastically. As early as 1795 a shipmaster observed that they "have several Spotts of Land clear'd in which there appear'd to be something sow'd,"[386] although the "something" may have been tobacco rather than potatoes. In the middle 1820s Dr John Scouler, ship surgeon on the HBC's ill-fated *William and Ann* (lost at the mouth of the Columbia in 1829), noted that the cultivation of potatoes was "very general" among the Haidas.[387] He asserted that they were not taught potato growing by Euroamericans.[388] If that were indeed the case, presumably they adopted it from their Tlingit neighbours, who had in turn adopted it from the Russians. The Reverend Green, however, who in 1829 found potatoes of a "most excellent quality" on the Queen Charlottes, which he praised as the "garden of this [northern] part of the coast," declared that "some years since" a white trader had left some English potatoes on the islands and told the Haidas how to cultivate them. Thereafter, he added, trading vessels were able to buy "excellent" tubers at low prices.[389] Similarly, in the middle 1830s the Bay man John Dunn found that most Haidas had large potato gardens next to their dwellings. He asserted that "this vegetable was first given to them by an American captain; and is now grown in abundance."[390] About this time Chief Factor John McLoughlin of Fort Vancouver rated the Haidas the best potato growers on the coast.[391]

Regardless of whomever showed the Haidas how to grow potatoes, nobody had to tell them how to hawk them. By the middle 1820s they were selling them to Indians and Euroamericans alike. The *Rob Roy* bought "some new potatoes" at Cumshewa's Harbour on 22 July 1822 and some more at Skidegate on 11 and 12 September (six barrels) and 4 November.[392] Apparently the Haidas charged plenty, because the ship's logkeeper wrote: "'Whoever can make two ears of corn or two blades of grass grow upon a spot of ground where only one grew before deserves better of mankind and does more essential service to his country than the whole race of politicians put together.' This may be true Doct Franklin; but the man that gave the Cumshewar Indians potatoes to plant, all things considered did his country no essential service if he was an American."[393] Scouler asserted that "their staple article is the potato, which they sell in great quantities to the mainland tribes [Tsimshians]. In the autumn, there is quite a competition among the Haidahs who shall carry early potatotes to the mainland. Fleets of from forty to fifty canoes arrive early in September, and proceed to the different villages of the Chimmesyan nation, and the potato-fair seldom ends without more or less fighting."[394] The Haidas sometimes sold from 500 to 800 bushels of potatoes at the annual Nass fair.[395] In 1826 the *Griffon* bought "a few barrels" of Haida potatoes in late February, and at the end of August the *Tally Ho* purchased two hogsheads (four 26¼-gallon casks) at Skidegate.[396] Also at Skidegate a HBC trading vessel bought three puncheons (three 72–gallon barrels) of new potatoes in mid-August 1831.[397]

Throughout the 1830s the Haidas sold potatoes to American vessels and HBC posts, particularly Fort Simpson, which bought from 500 to 800 bushels yearly.[398] In the autumn of 1835 the post harvested 204 bushels of its own potatoes ("good & very large") and purchased 784 bushels from the Haidas and Tsimshians "at a very moderate price, 2 quarts mixed Rum [four parts water, one part rum] & 2 Hds [hands] Leaf Tobacco, or 8 Hds do do for [one keg of] 1½ Bush."[399] (The fort's autumn 1837 potato crop, fertilized with seaweed, amounted to 651 bushels, which would have been at least 50 bushels greater had it not been for thieving Indians and foraging crows.[400] The autumn 1837 potato crop at Fort McLoughlin was 800 bushels, which was "short of expectations."[401]) The extent of the dependence of Fort Simpson's twenty men upon Native provisions is illustrated by the post's purchases from the Haidas and Tsimshians in 1837 (when it produced 651 bushels of its own potatoes): 842 bushels of potatoes, 568 deer (venison was the fort's most common fresh food), 60 beaver, 621 pounds of meat (perhaps mountain sheep or goat), 178 geese, 90 ducks, 1 swan, 2,236 eggs, 1,113 halibut, 7,918 salmon, 58 cod, 240 flounder, 61 bushels of small fish (perhaps sardines), 36 crabs, 212½ pounds of grease, 24 gallons of cranberries, and 36 blueberry cakes.[402] (Similarly, in the two months from 20 October through 14 December 1834 Fort Simpson obtained from the

Indians 274 deer, 632 pounds of grease, 32 gallons of whale oil, 60 boxes of dried berries, 2 bushels of cranberries, 13 pieces of dried meat, 3 dried beaver [for meat], 18 geese, 14 ducks, 4 bushels of potatoes, and 1,016 dried salmon, so that it was not until the beginning of 1835 that the post had to resort to "salt provisions" [the first time since the departure of the *Dryad* on 23 October].[403] In June and July 1837 the post bought 2,236 eggs alone from the Indians.[404]) In September 1838 465 bushels of potatoes were purchased from the Haidas.[405] Fort Stikine, too, benefitted from Haida gardening. In one week of October 1840 the post bought 100 bushels of potatoes from the Kaigani Haidas.[406] The only shortcoming of Indian potatoes was the fact that they were sometimes harvested too early (in September) and consequently were not very large and did not keep well.[407]

When the Reverend Green visited the Haidas in 1829, he found them offering for sale not only potatoes but also "slate-stone" (argillite) pipes, "grass" (reed) hats, fish, fowl, eggs, and berries, besides furs.[408] Dr Scouler, who was on the coast in 1825 but obtained his information about the Haidas from a fellow physician, William Tolmie, in the middle 1830s, wrote that the Queen Charlotte Islanders carved "drinking-vessels, tobacco-pipes, etc., from a soft argillaceous stone, and these articles are remarkable for the symmetry of their form, and the exceedingly elaborate and intricate figures which are carved upon them."[409] Indeed, he added, "they fabricate most of the curiosities found on the coast."[410] They also made and exported canoes.[411] Scouler explained that the Haidas had been reduced to the commercial production of curios by the depletion of sea otters; formerly, when the animals had abounded, the Haidas had been "among the most wealthy on the coast."[412] Even the condescending George Simpson was impressed by Haida craftsmanship: "They are remarkably clever and ingenious. They carve steamers, animals, etc. very neatly in stone, wood, and ivory, imitating, in short, every thing that they see, either in reality or in drawings; and I saw, in particular, a head for a small vessel that they were building, so well executed, that I took it for the work of a white artificer. One man, known as the Arrowsmith [Aaron Arrowsmith, a leading British cartographer] of the north-east [*sic*: northwest] coast, had gone far beyond his compeers, having prepared very accurate charts of most parts of the adjacent shores."[413] The argillite carvings, soon to be sought by public museums and coveted by private collectors, may have begun to appear around 1820.[414] Until the middle 1860s mostly pipes were carved.[415] They were produced as trade goods to replace the fragile clay pipes that other Indians had obtained from Euroamerican traders and to replace the sea-otter skins that the same traders demanded. All Haida argillite came from a single quarry on Slate-chuck Mountain near Skidegate that was probably found and used by the Indians during the first or second decade of the 1800s. It is still the source of the fine argillite pieces that are carved and sold by Haida craftsmen today.[416]

The Northwest Coast trade was, of course, an offshoot of the China trade and as such was affected by changes in the latter, which was, if anything, transformed even more than the former during the first third of the nineteenth century. As on the Northwest Coast, so too on the South China Coast did new merchants and new commodities become dominant. Until the end of the eighteenth century the main feature – and basic problem – of trade between China and the West was its onesidedness. The Occident afforded a ready market for Chinese goods, but the self-sufficient (and ethnocentric) Chinese Empire had little demand for Western raw materials or manufactured goods, which were generally inferior to Chinese products anyway. The Chinese did accept specie (gold and silver in bullion and coin), mostly silver dollars minted in the Iberian Peninsula and New Spain. The result was a drain of precious metals to China; by the early 1790s the China trade was, according to a British Nor'west trade backer, "a drain to the Nation of upwards of a Million and a half of specie annually."[417] Towards the end of the century, however, the supply of European silver became uncertain and the demand for Chinese teas increased, so that raw cotton and opium from India, furs from the Northwest Coast, sandalwood from the South Sea Islands, and other articles began to replace specie. By 1804 Chinese demand for these substitutes was such that the flow of specie was reversing.[418]

Before long the traders likewise changed. The opening of the India trade to private merchants in 1813, and the coming of peace to Europe in 1815, brought many newcomers to Canton.[419] They imported more and more opium and fewer and fewer traditional items like "Straits produce" (pepper, tin), India cotton, furs, sandalwood, and "sing-songs" (small automata). This private "country trade" between India, the Eastern Archipelago, and China, along with the "privilege tonnage" (private personal trade) of the captains of the East Indiamen, increasingly infringed the John Company's monopoly on Britain's China trade. By the early 1830s more than one-half of British trade with China was in private hands.[420] Finally, in 1834 the EIC's monopoly was terminated. This measure did not, however, lead to the expected boom in trade, and so criticism was turned against the constraints of the Canton system. Meanwhile, China was being mishandled by a series of inept emperors following the abdication of the able Chien-lung in 1796. More important, the country was being bled by opium imports – economically and socially costly – and its attempt in 1836 to enforce the ban on this traffic sparked the Opium War. This conflict, which underlined the naval weakness of the Manchu "paper tiger," was ended in 1842 by the Treaty of Nanking, which opened four new ports to foreign traders, abolished the Cohong monopoly, and limited import duties.[421] The "foreign devils" had finally succeeded in bringing the haughty mandarins to their knees. And the Celestial Empire was now darkened by commercial exploitation and territorial encroachment on the part of the European powers, whose gains were formalized in a series of "unequal treaties." Chinese resentment was to simmer for more than half a century before flaring into the xenophobia of the Boxer Rebellion.

American as well as British trade with China changed fundamentally. Before the War of 1812 the United States' "East India trade" had been conditioned primarily by the protracted European wars, the Northwest Coast sea-otter trade, and the South Sea traffic. However, the Treaty of Ghent ended the Napoleonic Wars in 1815, whereupon the United States was no longer the world's neutral carrier. Sandalwood and *bêche de mer* remained more or less bouyant until the late 1820s, but the maritime fur trade ceased to be an influential factor after 1820, owing to the depletion of sea otters, stiffer Indian demands, and renewed British and Russian competition. Nevertheless, peace did stimulate American-Chinese commerce by ending the hostilities (and such irritants as search and seizure). Moreover, tea and silk prices had risen during the War of 1812, and peace released accumulated demand.[422] As Colonel Thomas H. Perkins informed his Canton agency in late 1815:

Three years of war, and twice that number of restrictions upon commerce, had made our people very rigidly economical; and they bought only what was necessary, not what was luxurious. In place of a silk gown or pelisse, they purchased cotton for the first, and dispensed with the last altogether. So with tea. Although they did not wholly forego it, they were careful in the use of it; and now, to make up for lost time, they feel as if they may indulge in the fashions of the city, and gratify their palates with the beverages of the East. This being the case it will take a long time to overstock the market ...[423]

Also, trade barriers had been lowered in Europe; the United States market was larger and richer than it had been in 1790; and – what was especially germane to the Northwest Coast trade – Americans now had more commercial capital and specie and therefore did not need furs as urgently as before as substitutes for gold and silver.[424]

American exports to China changed from specie (mostly milled dollars from Spanish America, Portugal, and Gibraltar) and furs (mostly fur-seal and sea-otter skins) to bills of exchange on England, Turkish opium (which was cheaper than Indian opium at Canton), cotton goods (from England and the United States), quicksilver, rice (from Batavia and Manila), Chilean copper, and English manufactures (mainly woollens).[425] After 1815 bills on London increasingly supplanted specie as first English and then American manufactures, plus opium, were traded. Eighty per cent less specie was exported to China by the United States in the 1830s than in the 1820s.[426] As the volume of furs (from the middle 1810s), silver (from the middle 1820s) and sandalwood and ginseng (from the late 1820s) fell, the volume of Turkish opium and American cotton goods (from the middle 1820s) rose. American cottons began to be exported to China in 1826, and they gradually displaced English cottons in American bottoms.[427] American success at marketing English manufactures at Canton raised outcries from merchants and demands for an end to the EIC's monopoly.[428] So successful were American exporters that the total value of the United States' exports to China increased rather than decreased during the first third of the 1800s, despite the decline in shipments of precious silver and valuable sea-otter skins. Trade from the Northwest Coast to China was "falling off" by 1830, when it was valued at some $500,000.[429] Only one American ship every two years was sailing from the coast to Canton.[430] American imports from China remained more or less the same and included teas (whose grade steadily improved), silks, nankeens (white, blue, and brown cotton fabrics), cassia (a substitute for cinnamon), and chinaware (often used as ballast). But imports of teas, nankeens, and chinaware plummeted as Americans turned to coffee, English and American cottons replaced nankeens, and European supplanted Chinese porcelain. Indeed the Americans came "to regard China as a limitless market in which to sell rather than as a limited market in which to buy."[431] The Middle Kingdom met its mounting trade deficit with specie. Although the export of gold and silver bullion from China was illegal, it could be smuggled out by the outside merchants.[432] Consequently, the country was much poorer in 1830 than in, say, 1810, so that its demand for foreign goods fell and the Chinese market became overstocked.[433] Little wonder that Western traders pushed opium and that the Chinese authorities banned it and finally blocked it, albeit in vain.

Fewer American ships made China from the Northwest Coast not only because fewer furs were available but also because fewer shipowners were involved. And, reflecting decreased competition and increased cooperation, they pooled their collections for delivery to Canton in order to cut costs. As was the case on the Northwest Coast at the very beginning of the century, so it was on the South China Coast after the War of 1812 – a period of intense speculation among American merchants hoping to get rich from the revival of the China trade. The result was the same: commercial failures. Too many inexperienced merchants entered the trade, the market became overstocked, and bankruptcies followed. These failures led in turn to the consolidation of the trade out of the hands of numerous small firms in most northeastern us ports and into those of a few large concerns in Boston, New York, and Philadelphia. By 1825 four American firms handled seven-eighths of their country's China traffic, and by 1829 one house, Thomas H. Perkins and Company of Boston, controlled one-half.[434]

At the same time – in fact, even earlier – supercargoes, who travelled with American ships and conducted their transactions at Canton, were gradually replaced by permanent commercial houses which either dealt on commission or represented directly a mercantile firm headquartered in the United States, for example, the branch established at Canton in 1803 by Perkins and Company in charge of John P. Cushing, then a youth of sixteen. By 1815 supercargoes had nearly disappeared.[435] Conversely, whereas there were "very few" American houses of business at Canton around 1810, there were a "great number" by 1826.[436]

Colonel Perkins's optimism of 1815 notwithstanding, the periodic and seemingly inevitable commercial crisis struck in 1826–27 as a result of the traffic being "overdone very much" that trading season.[437] Tea prices in New York fell by up to one-third in the last half of the 1820s, and American trade turnover with China declined by the same amount and did not recover until 1833.[438] Thomas H. Smith, one of New York's foremost tea merchants, went broke, owing three million dollars in duties alone.[439] Between 1827 and 1830 the number of American commercial agencies at Canton decreased by one-third.[440] By then both the old China trade and the old Northwest Coast trade were dying. The *coup de grâce* was to come a decade later with the depression of 1841–43, perhaps the century's worst. Before that final blow, however, a new Northwest Coast trade, exploiting new products and new markets, was built from the wreckage of the old.

9 The New Northwest Trade

You will of course turn your attention to the collection of any article which you think will afford a profitable result. Furs of every description as well as Sea Otter Skins are an object as they may all be advantageously disposed of in China. When leaving the Coast it would be well to take a large number of Spars between Decks which will find a good Market at Canton in fact no object is too large or too small to merit your attention on a Voyage like the present.

Bryant and Sturgis to Captain Suter of the *Mentor*,
6 August 1816

In response to a variety of pressures – mainly biological and commercial – the maritime fur trade of the Northwest Coast became less and less monolithic, so much so that after 1800 it was no longer solely a sea-otter traffic and no longer confined to the Northwest Coast; only the maritime (shipping) element remained constant. A Northwest voyage became a congeries of ventures throughout the Pacific (and the toponym "Northwest Coast" even came to refer to the entire western coast of North America), and the shipmaster was given considerable latitude by the owners so that he could adjust quickly to the increasing vicissitudes of commerce wrought by over-trading, revolutionary upheaval in Spanish America, domestic discord and external pressure in China, and intensifying imperial ambitions on the islands and shores of the Pacific.

Diversification was led by American traders, who wisely decided to spread their commercial risk, although at least one Bostonian, Captain Sturgis, initially believed that "a North West Voyage should never be blended with any other" because it was such a trying venture that it required a skipper's "undivided attention."[1] The dwindling of sea otters eventually made Sturgis change his mind, as attested by the above epigraph. Bryant and Sturgis were not alone, of course. About the same time J. and T. H. Perkins and Company instructed

Captain Hill of the *Ophelia* to procure a cargo of copper at Valparaíso or, failing that, whale teeth on the Galápagos or, failing that, sandalwood on the Hawaiian Islands (taking care to avoid the "spurious or bastard wood") or, failing that, fur-seal skins at Sitka or, failing that, coffee at Batavia (Jakarta).[2] A Nor'west venture had become, as one Boston shipowner expressed it, "a voyage of adventure," and "in fact no object is too large or too small to merit ... attention."[3]

By now (middle 1810s) American Nor'westmen were scouring the entire Pacific in search of trade goods: beetle nut from Java, sugar from Manila, sandalwood from Fiji, fur-seal skins from the Juan Fernández Islands, tortoise shell and whale teeth from the Galápagos, *bêche de mer* (trepang), bird nests, coral moss, mother-of-pearl, and anything else that would catch an eye and open a purse in Canton.[4] As a HBC servant recognized, "The Americans never calculate on making more than a part of their voyage on the coast."[5] The Galápagos giant tortoise was preferred by sailors because it was "by far the largest, best, and most numerous of any place."[6] It was easily caught and weighed up to 400 pounds, and its abundant meat, which could keep for a year without spoiling, was "of as sweet and pleasant a flavour as any."[7] *Bêche de mer*, a large sea cucumber, was found on shallow reefs in tropical seas; after boiling and drying, it was savoured in soups by Chinese customers. The *bêche de mer* traffic flourished in the 1820s and 1830s, largely in the hands of Salem shipmasters, who sold most of their catch at Manila.[8] (According to a Russian source, from 25 to 50 and sometimes up to 100 piculs of trepang per year were sold at Canton in the 1820s for 60 piasters per picul.[9]) But resources of *bêche de mer*, tortoise shell, pearl shell, bird nests, and such were limited. A year's (1821) collection of *bêche de mer* on Fanning Island, for example, amounted to only 2,667 pounds.[10] Nevertheless, scarce resources meant high prices. In the spring of the same year at Canton bird nests brought $1,400–3,400, tortoise shell $500, *bêche de mer* $30, and pearl shell $15 per picul (1 picul = 133⅓ pounds).[11] Even Chilean copper fetched three times its Valparaíso price at Canton in the late 1810s.[12]

It did not take long for the Northwest Coast trade to diversify, the Yankee shipowners and shipmasters being ever ready to try new opportunities. Perhaps the first sideline was sealing.[13] As early as the late 1780s American Nor'westmen began to take fur seals on the Falklands, South Georgia, Staten Land, Juan Fernández, Más Afuera, St Ambrose, St Felix, and other islands in the southwestern Atlantic and southeastern Pacific off the coast of South America. These islands were conveniently situated on their route to the Northwest Coast, and they provided fresh food, fresh water, and relaxation as well as fur seals. Besides, the principal rookeries of the northern fur seal, the Pribilof and Commander Islands in the Bering Sea, were securely in Russian hands. Sealing voyages were also undertaken as ends in themselves by a number of firms out of a variety of ports, including Boston. The seal skins were obtained by slaughter, not barter, the sealing grounds being largely unpopulated. In two summer months of 1792 the *Jefferson* killed and cured up to 13,000 fur seals on St Ambrose Island.[14] Sealing on Más Afuera (or Alejandro Selkirk in honour of Robinson Crusoe's prototype) has been better documented.[15] Between 1800 and 1804 from ten to twenty sealing ships visited the island annually.[16] In one year fourteen ships sealed there at the same time, and in 1802 there were 200 men sealing on the island.[17] The resultant toll was staggering. Between 1793 and 1807, 3,500,000 fur seals were killed.[18] In 1798 one shipmaster counted up to 700,000 animals on the island, and in a subsequent year up to 1,000,000 skins were taken.[19] A merchant asserted that by 1801 the "Seal [had been] most all Killed" on what was commonly known as Massafuero.[20] The fur seals were clubbed and skinned, and the skins were dried or salted and shipped to Canton (dried skins kept better in a ship and each brought 25–50¢ more than "pickled" skins at market[21]). Depending upon supply and quality, fur-seal skins fetched as much as $3–4 or as little as 35¢ but generally $1 each at Canton.[22] From 1815 through 1821 Canton imported some 60,000 fur-seal skins yearly at an average cost of $1.50 each.[23] Little wonder that the population of fur seals diminished at least as precipitously as that of sea otters, and probably more so, and the trade in their fur plummeted accordingly. Indeed by the time that sea otters had been depleted, fur seals had suffered the same fate, so sealing did little to offset the decline of the sea-otter trade.

More important in this regard was the sandalwood traffic.[24] The period from the early 1810s to the middle 1820s saw the booming of this business, just as it witnessed the waning of the sea-otter trade. Sandalwood is an aromatic wood from a small tree in the tropics and subtropics. It was, as a Russian shipmaster noted, "so much and so highly esteemed in China,"[25] mainly for incense sticks (in joss houses) and fine furniture. The principal sources in the Pacific were Fiji, the Marquesas, and the Hawaiian Islands. The trees had to be selected, felled, and prepared carefully in order to maximize sales, as Bryant and Sturgis warned Captain Clark in 1817: "When among this group [Marquesas], you will procure all the wood you can obtain giving a preference to that which is about 10 or 12 inches in circumference & 4 or 5 feet long. Particular attention is requisite, in selecting the Wood, as some Kinds are of but little value in Canton; if the *Sap* is not taken off before you purchase it, let it be done on board; as the Sap is of no value it would be useless to fill your Ship with it, to the exclusion of good wood. Only the *heart* is valuable."[26] Hawaiian sandalwood was sawn, not axed, to avoid chip wastage,[27] and because of its stronger fragrance freshly felled (light yellow) wood brought higher prices in China than wood which had been felled a year or two (dark yellow). Sandalwood was so heavy – a log measuring seven feet in length and five and one-quarter inches in thickness weighed a picul[28] – that ballast was unnecessary when it was shipped; the large logs could be stored in the lower hold and the small logs and furs above, making the vessel "stiff enough."[29] (An 1828 French visitor, however, reporting that the embarkation of sandalwood was a protracted and demanding process, noted that ballast was also loaded: "After supplying the ship with ballast by a sixth of its tonnage, loading is begun at the ship's two ends; pieces of wood all the same length are stowed in layers in the hold under the deck, and then other pieces that can be so accommodated are inserted into the stacks by hammering them in place strongly with a mallet."[30])

Sandalwood grew on all of the Hawaiian Islands but was most accessible on Kauai.[31] The best grew on Oahu, Maui, and Kauai, and the most on Hawaii but it was inferior.[32] The trade began in 1790, when Captain William Douglas of the schooner *Grace* left two men on Kauai to collect wood; he took more than thirty tons to Canton, but it did not sell well because of its inferior quality.[33] (Also in 1790 Captain John Kendrick of the *Lady Washington* left a crewman, T. Ridley, on Maui to procure sandalwood but the ship did not return for him and he left with Captain Ingraham of the *Hope* in the spring of 1791.[34]) Heretofore Canton had been supplied with superior sandalwood from Malabar and Timor, but as it became scarcer it was supplanted on the Chinese market by Hawaiian sandalwood, although the latter was much poorer and cheaper than that of Malabar or even Timor, and both Hawaiian and Marquesan wood fetched only one-third as much at Canton.[35] (Hawaii was known in China as *Tan Heung Shan*, "the fragrant mountains," because of its odourous sandalwood.) Moreover, the superior trees on the islands were being exploited in place of the inferior trees by the end of the 1790s.[36] Sandalwooding was very labourious. The heavy logs were sawn into pieces from one and one-half to eight feet long and from one to eighteen inches thick, and carried on the heads, shoulders, and backs of men, women, and children – sometimes in parties of up to 5,000 haulers – from the mountain forests in the interior as many as eighteen miles to the coastal depots, where the wood's aroma increased as it dried.[37] (The preference was for logs from ten to twelve inches round and from four to five feet long.³⁸) In 1823 a missionary counted 2,000–3,000 men carrying from one to six pieces of sandalwood each from the interior mountains of Hawaii Island to Kohala on the northern coast.³⁹ Sandalwooding continued throughout the year and occupied from one-quarter to one-third of the Native population in the late 1820s.⁴⁰ The wood was sold by weight.

All Hawaiian sandalwood belonged to the king, and Kamehemaha I, after uniting the islands under his central authority, used it as a source of Spanish silver dollars for increasing his wealth and modernizing his army and navy and thereby consolidating his control. By 1810 sandalwood was being "frequently purchased for the China market" together with pearls and mother-of-pearl,⁴¹ providing Nor'westmen with yet another profitable reason for stopping at the islands. On 4 August 1812 the king agreed to give Jonathan and Nathan Winship and William Davis, all veteran Northwest Coastmen, a ten-year monopoly on sandalwood (and cotton) exports from his realm in return for one-quarter of the proceeds, and later that year their three ships (the *Albatross*, *Isabella*, and *O'Cain*) left for Canton with wood and ten Hawaiian men each for unloading. On 18 September 1814, however, His Majesty broke the contract, one day after Davis's death, and open competition ensued.⁴² From 1816 through 1818 Kamehemeha bought six Euroamerican ships for sandalwood,⁴³ and in 1819 he made an unsuccessful attempt to circumvent American traders by shipping sandalwood directly to Canton (where the cargo was refused access and had to be sold at a loss at Macao). In the same year he was succeeded by his self-indulgent son Liholiho, Kamehameha II, who opened the sandalwood trade to his vassal chiefs. Together they overcut and oversold and sparked the boom years of the first half of the 1820s, when trees were felled indiscriminately in order to finance their extravagance. In 1820 the Bryant and Sturgis vessel *Cleopatra's Barge* was exchanged for sandalwood worth more than $60,000, or six times its original cost.⁴⁴ The commoner loggers were weakened by the hard labour, which, moreover, left them insufficient time to procure food.⁴⁵ The king himself made 30,000–40,000 piasters annually from sandalwood in the early 1820s.⁴⁶ Some chiefs were soon indebted by promissary notes; by the beginning of 1822 they owed 22,500–23,000 piculs ($225,000–230,000).⁴⁷ Their slowness in paying their sandalwood debts incurred us gunboat diplomacy. In 1826 the schooner *Dolphin* and the sloop of war *Peacock*, and in 1829 the sloop of war *Vincennes*, showed the flag at Honolulu in a partially successful attempt at intimidating the king and his chiefs into paying their American creditors. At the end of 1826 Kamehameha II, in order to liquidate his own debts, levied a special tax on every native islander, payable in sandalwood (½ picul per person) or cash ($4 per male and $1 per female).[48] The resultant spate of felling virtually eliminated the tree.

The American traders were just as greedy as the Hawaiian rulers. The financial panic of 1819 made it more difficult for Yankee merchants to obtain specie for the China trade and forced them to rely more on kind, especially fur and sandalwood (as well as opium), as a medium of exchange. And as sea otters and fur seals were depleted, sandalwood increasingly replaced their skins on the Canton market. In the late 1810s and early 1820s American traders bought Hawaiian sandalwood for $10 and sold it at Canton for $12–15 per picul; their profit margin, however, was actually larger because they paid for the wood in goods, which they quoted at "very high prices."[49] (Earlier, at the end of 1815, when demand was lower, the price was likewise lower – $8.50 per picul.[50] By 1826 American merchants who were trading between Honolulu and Canton were making an annual profit of 33⅓ per cent on their investment.[51]) The trade peaked in 1821, when 30,000 piculs of sandalwood – "twice as much as is annually consumed" at Canton – were shipped from Hawaii to China; in the 1821–22 trading season the price in China was $9 per picul, which was deemed "Good."[52] Thereafter Honolulu's shipments and Canton's prices fell as the source was overcut and the market was overdone: 15,000 piculs in 1822 at $10 per picul, 10,000 in 1823 at $8.50, and 7,000 in 1824 at $9.[53] The diminishing supply raised Canton's prices to $10–13 per picul in 1827, and this increase, plus the king's sandalwood tax, resulted in a shipment of 13,000 piculs that year.[54] Yet the resurgence was short-lived. By 1828, owing to the declining quality of Hawaiian sandalwood and a large importation of Indian sandalwood, the selling price at Canton had fallen to $7 per picul, which was $1 less than the buying price in Hawaii in goods in 1828 (and the same as the buying price in 1829).[55] (The cost of freighting sandalwood from Honolulu to Canton was $2 per picul in 1821 and $1.50 in 1822.[56]) At the beginning of 1829 the wood fetched only $4.75 per picul at Canton, and a merchant correctly forecast that this low price would "go yet lower," for a year later it reached $4.25.[57] In 1831 Boardman and Company warned one of its shipmasters: "Don't touch it on any account even if given you," and a year later the same firm told the same captain: "Sandal wood worth nothing in Canton."[58]

The Hawaiian Islands were quickly stripped of sandalwood, which, moreover, was "a plant of slow growth."[59] A French visitor noted in 1819 that sandalwood was "already becoming difficult to obtain" and the "forests are being destroyed."[60] The Honolulu agent of Marshall and Wildes reported in 1822 that "the wood on Atoi [Kauai] is almost exhausted."[61] At the beginning of 1823 he added: "Wood comes in slow indeed, in fact it has been almost all cut from this Island [Oahu] and what they get now is rather small & inferior."[62] For this reason only half as much sandalwood was exported from the islands in 1822 as in 1821.[63] Also, all of the Hawaiian sandalwood that reached the Canton market in the 1822–23 season was "poor" in quality, "being a large proportion of small wood & roots," thereby lowering its selling price to as little as $6 per picul from $10 the previous season.[64] The final blow was struck in 1827, when up to 30,000 piculs were cut.[65] John Jones, who doubled as the United States consular agent and the commercial agent of Marshall and Wildes in Honolulu, explained this momentary resurgence of logging: "The allowing the native Kanackers to receive a proportion of all the wood they may cut is a great inducement to exertion and brings a large quantity of wood into the market for sale, indeed this indulgence [by the king] has produced a complete change in the feelings and habits of this people, each one is anxious to get all the wood he can, and thinks of nothing but accumulating property."[66] Another commercial agent, James Hunnewell, reported to Bryant and Sturgis that "the past summer [of 1827] the mountains have been glean'd for Sandal Wood, which has brought a great quantity of poor wood to market ... after next summer I expect Sandal Wood will be very scarce at the islands."[67] Two years later Hunnewell wrote that "Sandal Wood is an article which has become so scarce here, that we get little other [than] Chips, the gleanings of the mountains, the refuse of better days."[68] Already by 1828, when only 5,000 piculs were cut, "it had to be fetched from the most inaccessible parts of the mountains" of the archipelago.[69] By 1830 sandalwood had been exhausted on both the Hawaiian and Fijian archipelagos, as it had been on the Marquesas by 1817.[70]

Just as the Canton market was flooded with sandalwood, so was the Hawaiian market swamped with goods in exchange for wood. American buyers and Hawaiian sellers wanted too much too soon; such concepts as "inflationary spiral" and "sustained yield" were unknown. An American shipmaster complained in 1821 that "Sandalwood fever" had reached such a pitch that "every one here is ready to cut his neighbors throat, truth never is spoken, treachery is the order of the day, I am disgusted with my fellow man."[71] His disgust was echoed by James Jones: "Every foreigner in this country is ready to cut his neighbours throat, truth is a stranger here, the Sandal wood fever will deprive some of their reason."[72] Too many goods chased too few trees, the king and his chiefs being as greedy for Euroamerican commodities as the American traders were for san-

dalwood. The local market quickly became overstocked with Euroamerican consumer goods, and Hawaiian indebtedness mounted. Jones
reported the situation to Marshall and Wildes in 1821: "The Sandwich Islands are not what they were two years ago they are glutted
with merchandize, and vessels more than they know what to do with
...; they are sick of trading, all their [king's and chiefs'] subjects are
complaining and endeavoring to influence them to purchase no
more."[73] By then the king and his chiefs owed American merchants
at least 18,000 piculs of sandalwood.[74] At the end of the same year
Jones advised that "Rum and Cloth are the only articles in demand
and even those articles pay only a moderate profit."[75] He added that
"the days for making a voyage to the S. Islands have past, the natives
are now too much enlightened, they know well the value of every
article, if they do not there are plenty of canting, hypocritical missionaries to inform them, even though unasked."[76] Two years later
Jones blamed the Congregational-Presbyterian missionaries even
more vitriolically for the depression of the local market:

Trade never will again flourish at these Islands until these emissaries from
the Andover [Theological Seminary in Massachusetts] mill are recalled, they
are continually telling the King & Chiefs that the white people traders are
cheating & imposing on them, consequently have depreciated the value of
most articles. I believe it is a fact generally acknowledged by all here, that
the natives are fifty percent worse in every vice since the missionaries began
their hypocritical labour here; these blood suckers of the community had
much better be in their native country gaining their living by the sweat of
their brow, than living like lords in this luxurious land, distracting the minds
of these children of Nature with the idea that they are to be eternally damned
unless they think and act as they do.[77]

Consequently, Jones added, the Hawaiians "do not purchase now as
formerly ... saying they have property and let their goods moulder
away, it is now only as they want to consume that they buy therefore
no large sales can be effected at one time."[78] Nevertheless, "every thing
new and elegant will sell and at a good profit," although "coarse
articles are of no use."[79] But the selling boom was over. As late as the
end of 1829 Hunnewell noted that "the Sandwich Island market is
overrun with goods (particularly cotton goods) and retail prices
fallen."[80] By then the sandalwood trade had more or less ended.
   American Northwest Coastmen pursued other sidelines closer to
the sea-otter grounds. Smuggling along the Pacific coast of the Spanish
Main – putting into port on the pretext of "under stress of weather"
– was a profitable supplement. This clandestine traffic was conducted

"with very little Risk and not much delay" and netted profits of up to 200 per cent.[81] It peaked in the 1810s, as the sea-otter traffic was waning, and faded in the early 1820s, as the viceroyalties of Spanish America – beginning with Chile in 1818, New Granada in 1819, and Peru and New Spain (México) in 1821 – became independent and opened their ports to lawful foreign trade. The American smugglers concentrated on Alta California. Its Franciscan missions produced surplus grain, beef, tallow, and hides but they (and the presidios) were woefully short of goods, being neglected by New Spain. In 1817 the Russian ship *Rurik* visited Alta California and found that "for six or seven years during the internal wars between Spain and its colonies it has languished forgotten, without any imports from Mexico," so that "a smuggling trade ... is all that provides this province with the most indispensable necessities."[82] In the middle of the first decade of the century American ships annually marketed $25,000 worth of goods and specie in Alta California.[83] In return the American traders took grain, beef, and sea-otter skins. The provisions were easily bartered for fur-seal skins to Sitka's Russians, who were perennially short of supplies. The sea-otter pelts helped to offset the diminishing collections on the Northwest Coast. From 1803 through 1813 the Americans even poached along the California coast on halves with the Russians, the latter providing Aleut and Kodiak hunters and kayaks and the former ships. The ten joint ventures yielded the tsar's men 13,266 skins or more and the Boston men at least as many.[84] In 1821 the RAC began to hunt on halves with the Mexican authorities but with little profit because by then few sea otters were left, and their fur was less valuable than that of the northern otter.[85] These southern sea-otter skins were lower in quality but "much cheaper" than northern skins.[86] They could be bought from the Spaniards for $2 each in 1793,[87] when they were worth $25 at Canton (see Table 9). Californian's coastal Indians were less dangerous and its rookeries less depleted than those of the Northwest Coast, and Spanish coastal defences were weak. As Captain John Ebbets reported to John Jacob Astor at the end of 1810, "The killing [of] Sea Otter in California is been attended with little danger and much profit."[88]

With the ending of smuggling (but not poaching) in 1821, American traders met Alta California's demand for manufactured goods in return for silver dollars, hides, and tallow. Changing demand and supply meant changing itineraries, as Captain Eliah Grimes of the *Owhyhee* informed Marshall and Wildes in 1822: from February through July on the Northwest Coast, from August through November on the California coast, and from December through January in the Hawaiian Islands.[89] The summer-autumn leg could be lucrative, as Marshall's Honolulu agent reported in 1827: "California & Mexico afforded good trade the last year. French [William French, a prominent Honolulu merchant] took in three months on that coast $40,000."[90] The American traders brought mostly clothing, hats, cottons, silks, lace, cutlery, spirits, and sugar, which were bartered for hides and tallow, chiefly from the missions, whose *peninsular* padres were anxious to make as much as possible as soon as possible before being expelled by the revolutionary republican government, to which they refused to swear an oath of allegiance. The Americans generally disposed of their cargoes at a profit of from 200 to 300 per cent, provided they evaded the duties (25 per cent on sales and a tonnage fee of $2.50 per ton), which "in the present unsettled state of the Country they succeed in doing to a great extent ... by distributing presents and bribes to the official Men" (the captain or supercargo simply paid for a false list of sales, but to be able to do so one had to know both the language and the officials).[91] The hide-and-tallow trade proved particularly profitable, attracting such fur-trading firms as Bryant and Sturgis and others. "I shall probably fit out a vessel for Hides on California," wrote William Boardman to one of his shipmasters. "Money has been made there & I think will continue to be if a vessel is well managed."[92] In the same year (1832) California hides fetched $11–13 apiece in the eastern United States.[93] Within several years, however, supply dwindled as the productive missions were secularized by the Mexican authorities and deserted by the Indian labourers, and in the early 1840s the Boston market was glutted.

That left American shipmasters with but one adjunct to the sea-otter trade, and it lasted until they forsook the Northwest Coast altogether in the early 1840s. Just as they supplied California's missions, so, too, did they supply the Russian settlements far to the north. The first to test this market, however, were the British at the very beginning of the coast trade, and they did so on the Siberian side of the Pacific. In the summer of 1786 the EIC's *Lark*, Captain William Peters, sold some goods at Petropavlovsk, Kamchatka's entrepôt, to Grigory Shelikhov, a prominent Russian fur trader in the Gulf of Alaska. Subsequently Shelikhov sold the goods at Bolsheretsk for a profit of 50 kopeks on the ruble, while the *Lark* was wrecked on the Commander Islands with the loss of all but two of the crew of seventy.[94] Six years later the *Halcyon*, Captain Charles Barkley, tried to sell some goods (ironware, rum, anchors, cables, cordage) at Petropavlovsk at one-third the cost of their local counterparts but in vain, the port's commandant pleading insufficient authority and its merchants insufficient capital and credit.[95] The RAC, however, had much more of both, and by the time (1799) it was chartered to monopolize the administration and exploitation of Alaska the coast trade had fallen securely into American hands. Sitka, moreover, was much more conveniently located for Yankee coasters than Petropavlovsk or even the missions and presidios of Alta California, being found right on the Northwest Coast (Fig. 8). Russian America was chronically short of manufactures and especially provisions because of the remoteness of the motherland and the forbidding environment of the colony itself.[96]

A visiting Russian naval officer admitted in 1805, a year after Sitka's refounding, that "the settlement ... will always be a place of resort for ships trading on the coast; as the Russian company are ready to purchase flour, brandy, woollen cloth, and every necessary, at a profit of at least fifty per cent to the trader."[97] The traders were quick to respond, eight American and British vessels calling at "Shitgar" to barter in the first two years of its existence (1799–1800).[98] Thereafter until 1841 American ships put into Sitka regularly, exchanging provisions, textiles, and spirits for fur-seal skins, timber, and fish.[99] As at Honolulu, the American mark-up on these goods at Sitka was very high. During a July call at Sitka in 1806 for repairs and trade the *Vancouver* sold some guns "at an Exorbant Price."[100] It was for this reason that the Boston firm of J. and T. H. Perkins believed in 1808 that "some good Business might be done" by supplying Sitka, particularly since one of their shipmasters, Captain Benjamin Swift, was on friendly terms with the Russian governor, Alexander Baranov.[101] Baranov's compliance was essential, and American skippers went to considerable lengths to secure it. As Captain Ebbets informed Astor, "It would appear the Bostonians think this part of the world opens a wide field for speculation, as they leave no means untried to gain the esteem of G. B. [Governor Baranov], which I assure you is no easy matter."[102] Ebbets had recently put in to Sitka in the *Enterprise* and traded $26,884 worth of goods – mostly sugar, molasses, rice, bread, flour, tobacco, rum, brandy, cloth, clothing, and naval stores (tar, pitch, turpentine) – for pelts, primarily fur-seal skins.[103] The American traders ingratiated themselves with Baranov (Washington Irving's "rough, rugged, hospitable, hard-drinking old Russian ... a boon companion of the old roystering school, with a strong cross of the bear"[104]) the same way that they curried the favour of the governor, commandantes, and padres of Alta California – with gifts alias bribes. At Sitka particularly liquor was welcomed by the bibulous Russians. In Ebbets's words: "Without any we should have been unwelcome visitors. It is the *idol* of the common people, as they all drink an astonishing quantity, G. B. himself not excepted, and I assure you it is no small tax on a person's health that does business with him. A cargo of rum would, I believe, *sell*."[105]

Russian America's demands were such that some American coasters were selling as much to the Russians as they were buying from the Indians. "Nearly half" of the cargo of the *Mentor* (1816–19), Captain Suter, was "expressly calculated for supplying the Russians"; indeed, "much" of the cargo intended for Sitka could not be sold elsewhere. And the owners urged Suter to make the Russian colonial capital "*early in April* [1817]," before the arrival of other American suppliers, since "*the first Sale will be the best.*"[106] Similarly, Captain William Hammatt of the *Herald* was authorized by the owners in 1828 to sell as much as two-thirds of his coast trade goods (and even his ship) to the Russians.[107] In fact, from the middle 1820s up to one-half of all American coasters were mainly wholesalers of goods to the Russians. Everything on a Boston ship was for sale, including the vessel itself. Ships were coveted by the Russians, whose oceanic experience was slight, and by the Hawaiians, whose hegemonic King Kamehameha I had long desired a navy. The RAC purchased eight American (and one British) trading vessels from 1805 through 1827, when both Russian and British naval officers noted that the best and the cheapest ships in the company's fleet were those that had been bought from Americans.[108] In addition, the company hired foreign, including American, shipbuilders, shipmasters, navigators, and supercargoes.

The Sitka trade was especially heavy before 1815, that is, before the Russians began to obtain wheat and beef from Alta California's bountiful missions and other supplies from the homeland via more frequent round-the-world voyages. Competition among American captains to supply Sitka was so keen that by 1811 Governor Baranov was able to buy provisions for one-half the price that he had paid in 1803.[109] And he was able to buy more than enough. When Lieutenant Vasily Golovnin reached Sitka in the sloop *Diana* in the summer of 1810 he found an "abundance" of provisions there, the result of the "commercial spirit and speculations of the Americans."[110] He wrote:

Going to America we were afraid that we would find the company's settlements in the most wretched situation because of a lack of food, and that would really have been the case if citizens of the American republic had not sent their own ships to conduct trade along these shores and brought so many fresh provisions, such as wheat flour, rusks, rice, salted beef and pork, etc., which they bartered to Mr. Baranov for furs to the great benefit of the company. We even found all of the storehouses at Sitka filled with the necessities of life; some of the American ships had called at the Sandwich Islands and had brought from there a large quantity of salt and the root called taro, which, when dried and pounded, is like flour and just as nutritious, and especially when it is mixed with real flour is the bread or biscuit baked from this mixture very tasty. Besides the three American ships [*Enterprise*, *Isabella*, and *Lydia*] that we found at Sitka, one of which left soon after our arrival, two more [*Mercury* and *O'Cain*], also loaded mostly with fresh provisions, came during our stay here. Thus, the rye flour which we brought from Kamchatka for the company and which under different circumstances would have saved the residents from fatal starvation, was now superfluous ...[111]

Owing largely to American supplies, Baranov was able to tell an American friend, Abraham Jones, in the fall of 1816 that "here ... in all places under my command ... we enjoy abundance in every thing."[112] Thereafter the Bostonians found the Sitka market a little duller, as the Russians began getting more provisions from the Spanish missions and even their own colony (Fort Ross and Port Rumyantsev [Bodega Bay] with a couple of farms) in Alta California. As one American skipper cautioned another at the beginning of 1816, "I sincerely hope, that you have not embark'd in any more shipments to Shitka; the company have taken *new grounds*. no more skins are to be sold to foreigners. California supplies them with provisions."[113] Nevertheless, Sitka's demand for manufactured goods remained as a source of considerable profit. As the Honolulu commercial agent John Jones told his principal, Josiah Marshall, in 1827, "Amongst the Russians something will be done every year, they are always in want of certain articles for which they will pay a good profit."[114] Thus when Tsar Nicholas I unilaterally issued the 1821 decree banning foreign vessels from the coast of Russian America north of 51°, the colonial authorities were forced to overlook the ban in order to get sufficient supplies, and the company's head office petitioned for an exemption. As noted earlier, the ban was lifted in 1824 and Russian America's southern limit was retracted to 54° 40'.

In fact, the RAC was ambivalent about the Boston trade because the American suppliers infringed the company's monopoly on the fur trade in colonial waters, even poaching in Sitka Sound itself under the very guns of the Russian fort, usually under the cover of darkness. In the last two weeks of April 1812 the *Atahualpa* collected 124 beaver, 68 sea-otter, and 40 land-otter skins within view of Sitka.[115] In doing so, moreover, the Americans traded firearms to the Tlingits and allegedly incited them against the Russians. Also, the company was forced to pay for the American supplies in furs, the very object of its business. But the Russians had no choice, having nothing else to offer. All they could do was pay in less prized fur-seal skins rather than in sea-otter pelts. From 1799 – when both the RAC and Sitka were founded – through 1814 the company traded up to half a million fur-seal skins to foreign, primarily American, skippers.[116] (From

1786, when the Pribilofs, or Fur Seal Islands, were discovered by their Russian namesake, through 1827 the Russians killed up to 3 million fur seals on the islands.[117]) In 1813 the J. and T. H. Perkins brig *Lydia* (renamed the *Ilmen*) with some cargo was bartered to the Russians for 46,000 fur-seal skins.[118] In the same year the *Atahualpa* bought 46,000 fur-seal skins at Sitka, Unalaska, and the Pribilofs.[119] From 1818 through 1830 Sitka's Russians traded 215,357 fur-seal and 2,900 beaver pelts, plus cash, to Yankee coasters for provisions, manufactures, and four ships.[120] The Americans preferred furs to bills in rubles on St Petersburg or in sterling on London, and they also preferred beaver and land-otter to fur-seal skins because the Canton market was glutted with the latter.[121] But they took the fur-seal skins anyway, paying 1 ruble, 75 kopecks for each of them in the late 1820s at Sitka and selling them for up to 11 rubles each at Canton.[122]

The volume of American-Russian trade at Sitka was such that by the 1820s Russian America was experiencing a shortage of fur seals, and from 1831 American captains were paid in letters of credit on St Petersburg rather than in skins. (The Americans preferred bills in sterling on London to bills in rubles on St Petersburg because the latter were valued at fifty cents to the ruble in Sitka but were worth little more than twenty cents in the imperial capital.[123]) By then Yankee ships were visiting Sitka "very rarely."[124] The end came in 1839, when the HBC agreed to supply the Russian colony in place of the Bostonians.

The Sitka trade was beneficial to both parties, of course. The colonial capital's 800 residents (1827), including 300 Russians,[125] obtained necessary supplies of good quality at relatively moderate prices. In the late 1820s American imports accounted for 90 per cent of the living expenses of Sitka's officials and consumed two-thirds of the salaries of its workers; all of their rice, fine flour, sugar, molasses, tea, rum, and tobacco were provided by American traders.[126] And these imports were a substantial source of profit to the RAC, whose mark-up on them ranged from 56 to 82 per cent in 1836.[127] In addition to profiting from their own prior mark-up, the American suppliers obtained a substitute medium – fur-seal skins – for sea-otter pelts in the Canton market. Furthermore, they surreptitiously acquired sea-otter skins from the Tlingits in the channels near the colonial capital and at night in Sitka Sound itself.[128] The shipmasters also procured fresh water and firewood at Sitka, repaired their ships, and rested their crews.[129]

After trading with the Russians, the American captains dumped their remaining goods on the coast to the Indians at what the HBC termed an "extravagant rate," and it was only this dumping that kept the Bostonians competitive in the face of mounting British and Russian pressure in the 1830s. As Chief Trader John Work noted in 1835:

This is the way with the Americans, when they come to a winding up they part with every thing they have, and often at such low prices, as they say to, "*get rid of it,*" that it is exceedingly difficult to deal with the Indians afterwards. Indeed all along the Americans sell a quantity of articles, which stand them in cheap at such a low price, that the natives obtain them in such abundance that they lay little or no value upon them, particularly liquor and ammunition, especially the latter which is so essential to them in their hunting and continual wars, that little or no profit can be made on them to cover the loss, or at least very slight profit on woolens and other expensive goods. Unpromising as these circumstances render our affairs, there is little likelihood of its being otherwise so long as our opponents get worth their whiles for coming on the coast to to [sic] wind up a voyage, which is all they calculate upon, as they chiefly reckon upon the profit of their sales at the [Hawaiian] Islands, Sitka, and California.[130]

The changing pattern of the Northwest trade is exemplified by the contrasting voyages of the American schooner *Jane* in 1792–94 and the American brig *Arab* in 1820–24. The *Jane*, Captain Elias Newbury, sailed from Boston at the end of 1792, traded for sea-otter skins on the coast in the summer of 1793, went directly to Canton to sell the skins and buy Chinese goods, and returned to New England in the summer of 1794 after an absence of one and one-half years.[131] The *Arab*, Captain Thomas Meek, cleared Boston in late 1820, traded on the coast in the summer of 1821 for sea-otter skins, spent the autumn at the Hawaiian Islands to purchase sandalwood, and sailed to Canton to disembark eight chop-boat loads of sea-otter skins and sandalwood and to embark sugar, rice, molasses, and flour. It returned to Hawaii at the beginning of the summer of 1822 to get salt, sailed to Sitka to trade salt, sugar, rice, and rum for fur-seal skins, beaver pelts, firewood, spars, and planks, and returned to "the islands" in the fall, swapping lumber (and repairs to one of the king's ships) for sandalwood over the winter. Afterwards, in the late spring of 1823, it left for Canton, where it unloaded seven chop-boat loads of sandalwood, and returned to Honolulu in the autumn to purchase more sandalwood over the winter of 1823–1824, but it was sold early in the new year to the RAC at Sitka for 11,000 fur seal skins and become the *Baikal*.[132] The later voyages obviously lasted longer, entailed considerable improvisation, and involved a greater variety of trade goods.

As recounted earlier, in 1828 Aemelius Simpson of the HBC reconnoitered the coast trade to gather commercial intelligence, the company being determined to enter the fray and oust the Americans. His report, based upon both inspection and interview, encapsulates the new Northwest trade. He learned that half a dozen American trading vessels annually departed Boston in November for the Hawaiian Islands, which they reached in March to take on provisions and hands. From there they made the Northwest Coast in April and, usually sailing "two in company," traded until September, offering mainly blankets, duffels, cottons, calicoes, firearms, ammunition, rum, axes, knives, buttons, fishhooks, vermilion, made clothing (frock coats, waistcoats, trousers, shirts, hats, handkerchiefs, shoes), and Indian slaves, plus beads, bracelets, and looking-glasses for land furs and sea-otter skins. Chiefly small articles were bartered for land furs and large articles such as blankets and duffels for sea-otter skins. The vessels usually "kept" the coast for two years. One or two of them remained on the coast in winter, when pelts were obtained more cheaply. They wintered at Kaigani and Tongass, the principal rendezvous; here were found the only Indians who were on friendly terms with the Boston men. Occasionally a "Short Start" was made to other "ports" for furs. As Simpson noted, "It is competition that has driven them to the alternative of keeping the Coast during the Winter and returning to it so early in the Spring, as the business could otherwise be equally well accomplished by taking it at a more advanced period of the season." "Their object," he added, "is to get first to the Market." The other ships wintered at the Hawaiian Islands, leaving the coast in late September before the onset of foul weather with strong southeasterly gales and returning in late February or early March for an early start. The islands and mainland between Dixon Entrance and Queen Charlotte Sound formed the stretch of the coast that was "most visited" by the American traders. Here they took not only sea and land furs. Spars and planks were cut by "a great part of the Crew," and salmon was bought from the Indians "for a mere trifle" (mainly for leaf tobacco) and cured. The timber commanded "a very high price" ($200 per ten-foot plank) at Honolulu, as did the cured salmon ($10 per barrel). The vessels "frequently" put in to Sitka to exchange goods for fur-seal skins. By the end of July, when the Indians began moving to their fishing grounds, the coast had been "nearly swept of Furs." In September of their third year the Nor'westmen finally left the coast for "Owhyhee" to refit, discharge and engage crewmen, and purchase provisions, as well as to transfer their skins to an agent, who then shipped them to another agent at Canton, who in turn waited until the China market

was bullish before selling them and buying local goods for the home
market. At the Hawaiian Islands the coasters also sold the rest of
their goods and bought sandalwood, and sometimes they then made
a run to California's ports to dispose of any remaining commodities
and take on refreshments. They generally returned home via Canton
with a cargo of China goods after an absence of four and one-half
years.[133]

When Yankee merchants finally abandoned the coast trade in
1841, they had already discarded their other ventures: sealing, sandalwooding, smuggling, hiding and tallowing, and supplying Sitka.
But these adjuncts had successfully sustained their China trade for
three decades after the peak of the sea-otter traffic. The average
annual turnover (presumably excluding illicit opium) of American-
Chinese trade rose from approximately $7,800,000 in 1805–09 to
$9,200,000 in the 1810s and $12,300,000 in the 1820s before falling
to $10,200,000 in the 1830s and $6,300,000 in 1840–44.[134] Turnover
was actually higher after than during the heyday of the sea-otter
traffic because of the diversification of the Northwest trade in particular and the China trade in general (and perhaps inflation); it did
not decrease until the depletion of sandalwood by the late 1820s, and
it did not plummet until American withdrawal from the maritime
fur trade and the disruption of the Chinese market in the early
1840s. Long before then, however, the sea-otter trade had left its
mark on the Northwest Coast and the Hawaiian Islands in particular
but also on New England and even, perhaps, South China.

10 The Impact of the Trade

Taking the Sea Otter ... now engages all their [Nootkas'] Attention, that they may have a good Collection of Furs to purchase European Commodities.

Lieutenant Peter Puget, 1793

The Manners & Customs of the [Hawaiian] Islands are every day coppying more & more after the Europeans; Civilization is advancing with rapid strides, and former habits are almost forgotten. No longer is seen the Bow or the Spear, no longer is heard the shrill sounding Shell or ear piercing War Whoop. The Savage seems to have changed his Skin – The Aethiopian to have washed out his spots.

US Consul John C. Jones, Jr to Secretary of State
John Adams, 1821

The trade to the North West Coast of America has been, and probably will long continue, a very *valuable* branch of commerce, both in a national view, and as regards the individuals concerned in it. The Cargoes carried out, are of small value, many of the articles which compose them are of the growth, of manufacture of this country [United States], and the vessels return home, via China, with very valuable Cargoes of Teas, Silks and other products of the Chinese Empire, for which we should be compelled to send our specie, were it not for this trade.

William Sturgis to Captain Charles Morris, 1816

The maritime fur trade involved – and therefore affected – four widely separated and very different regions and peoples: the Northwest Coast itself and its Indians, the Hawaiian Islands and their Polynesians, South China and its Cantonese, and New England and its Yankees (and, one might add, Russia and the Russians). It is easier to assess the sea-otter trade's impact on the coastal Indians and the

Hawaiian Islanders because they were more isolated and hence subject to fewer economic and cultural contacts with outsiders than the South Chinese or New Englanders. Whereas the trade was but one of many such factors influencing American, British, Chinese, or Russian society, it was one of only a few conditioning the Indians and Hawaiians. Economically, socially, and politically they were more exposed to Euroamerican pressures than the Chinese, although even the latter were to prove militarily vulnerable.

THE NORTHWEST COAST

For the Northwest Coast Indians the trade was neither just destructive ("looting") nor just constructive ("enriching") but both.[1] It was positive in that the new goods and the new ideas were adapted by the Indians to suit their own needs, and they stimulated the development of their culture – perhaps even to the point of a so-called "climax" sometime in the first third of the nineteenth century. Generally Euroamerican goods supplemented rather than supplanted Indian products, and served to further, not initiate, changes. Thus, trinkets did not replace dentalia as valuables or ornaments; blankets did not replace cedarbark or even fur robes; muskets and pistols did not replace lances, bows and arrows, and knives; sails and rudders did not replace paddles in canoes (if only because sails were used before the wind only); fishing line did not replace harpoons, nets, or weirs; farming did not replace fishing or hunting; bread, rice, and potatoes did not replace smoked salmon, dried herring roe, pounded hemlock cambium, venison, and berries (although potatoes did help to overcome the coast's paucity of starchy foods); broken English or even the Chinook jargon did not replace Native languages; metal tools did not replace stone or bone implements; and so on. Yet all of these innovations were accepted and put to good use. And customs that disgusted Euroamerican traders – "steetgar" (labret) wearing, head flattening, corpse carrying, lice picking, hair greasing, body tattooing, funeral sacrificing, head and scalp taking – were not discontinued, although they became somewhat less common. In other words, the maritime fur trade did not revolutionize coastal Indian society, unlike plains Indian society, which was fundamentally altered by the introduction of the horse and gun.[2] After all, the Northwest Coast Indians were decidedly mercantile and commercial before white contact, and the fur traders came to them, not vice versa, and the Indians readily accepted them on their own terms.[3]

If the coast trade did not bring revolution, it certainly brought material prosperity – more accurately, more material prosperity –

because it meant increased business and therefore greater Native wealth (conversely, of course, as the coast trade declined the Indians became poorer, John Work noting at Fort Simpson in 1838, that "owing to the scarcity of furs the Indians are becoming poorer every year."[4]) The Euroamerican technological innovations increased Indian output; the introduction of metal tools facilitated woodworking and stimulated monumental art (totem poles, mortuary poles, plank houses),[5] and the adoption of firearms may have enhanced hunting. More wealth meant more ceremonies, which required more artistic products like totems, masks, rattles, amulets, and robes, which were also in demand by whites as curios. So native art boomed.[6] The increased demand for furs meant more hunting with better (at least more powerful, if not more accurate) weapons, as Lieutenant Puget noted at Nootka Sound in 1793, with the local Indians shooting, clubbing, and at night netting sea otters.[7] More hunting meant less time for food procuring, and this in turn may have led to more trading in slaves. The inflated demand for furs certainly meant more trading for pelts between the coastal and the interior groups, especially as sea otters decreased, and this in turn resulted in more "coastalization" of the inland Indians. For example, the Sekanis began to discard their bilateral descent system in favour of exogamous matrilineal phratries accompanied by crests and potlaches; the Babine Lake Carriers adopted phratry and crest systems, as well as the potlach and the labret; and the Athapaskans around Atlin and Teslin Lakes were so acculturated that they became known as Inland Tlingits.[8] The increased trafficking may have promoted more alliances, too, such as that between the Nootkas and the Kwakiutls, as one group strove to benefit commercially from another.[9] It undoubtedly generated more potlatching, since the greater wealth made possible more frequent and more lavish giveaways. In 1803 Chief Maquinna dispensed 400 yards of cloth, 100 looking-glasses, 100 muskets, and 20 kegs of gunpowder at a single potlatch.[10]

At first the intensified potlatching strengthened the position of chiefs like Maquinna of Nootka Sound, Wickaninish of Clayoquot Sound, Tatoosh of the Makahs, Concomly (Madsaw) of the Chinooks, Kotlean of the Sitka Tlingits, Kow of the Kaigani Haidas, Cunneah (Coyac) of the Kuista Haidas, and Cumshewa of the Cumshewa Inlet Haidas. Because they controlled hunting and trading, they grew richer and stronger. In order to enhance their commercial position some chiefs, such as Stonecliff (Legaic) of the Tsimshians and one-eyed Concomly, allowed their daughters to become the consorts or wives of white fur traders. Eventually, however, chieftainship was debased by a proliferation of chiefs. Now wealth could be acquired not only by hereditary clan chiefs but also by skilful individual hunters. These *nouveau riche* but untitled individuals tried to gain social status by throwing house-building potlatches, which gave them the title of household head, while the threatened hereditary clan chiefs, in order to safeguard their rights and bolster their prestige, resorted to boasting of their noble ancestry, names, totems, and crests, which had to be validated by potlatches.[11] The higher death rate resulting from gunfire, disease, and alcoholism likewise meant that more positions of rank became available for attainment by competitive potlatching (rivalry potlatches).[12] Vying among chiefs grew accordingly. In 1829 the Reverend Green observed that, among the northern Indians, chiefs had much less authority than formerly because wealth from the fur trade had created more chiefs, each with – perforce – smaller jurisdictions and fewer followers.[13] "Every man has influence in proportion to his property," he wrote, and the parvenu Haidas bragged to him that "we are all chiefs."[14] Chief Trader Francis Heron noted the same phenomenon at Fort Nisqually on Puget Sound in 1833: "The few articles of clothing brought [by the HBC to Fort Nisqually] for them [the local Coast Salish chiefs] are not exposed to view at all, as every one now is a Chief & expects to be [treated] & rewarded like the best of his neighbors without [re]ference to the quantity of Beaver – Indeed there is few of them now that can lay claim to any marked distinction [of this] kind, so many of them being ambitious of bringing in skins themselves."[15] A Soviet ethnographer has gone so far as to contend that among the Tlingits the accumulation of wealth furthered social stratification (even creating a special class of traders) and stimulated the transition from clan to class society, from matrilineality to patrilineality, from matrilocality to patrilocality, from kinship to territorial ties, from single-clan to multi-clan communities, and from communal to private property.[16]

The sea-otter trade may also have changed the pattern of Indian settlement. James Haggarty and Richard Inglis have argued that archeological findings and ethnohistorical sources indicate that on the western coast of Vancouver Island before white contact the Nootkas lived in numerous, small, independent groups in permanent villages within spatially limited and socially constrained territories; after contact, they amalgamated into larger and fewer seasonal villages (inland in winter at sheltered sites, on the outer coast in spring and summer, and on the inner coast at fisheries in the autumn) in order to take full economic advantage of the seasonal presence of trading vessels. Also, the new trade disrupted the traditional food-procurement schedule of offshore fishing and sea-mammal hunting in spring and summer, so that the Indians turned to more trade with their neighbours (and with trading vessels) for food and to shifting to the inner coast in September for salmon fishing.[17] If such were indeed the case, did it likewise occur among other Indian groups on the coast, and did the later year-round sojourns of the trading vessels further alter the pattern of Indian settlement?

The maritime fur trade brought the Indians not only to the outer coast but beyond to the world at large. Just as the Nor'west trade revealed the basic geography of the coast to the Euroamerican public and publicized its other resources, particularly timber and fish (although few permanent Euroamerican settlements resulted simply because none was needed by most white traders in order to get sea-otter skins), so did it reveal the wider world to the Indians of what the American anthropologist Alfred Kroeber called the "aloof" Northwest Coast. They were, so to speak, "cosmopolitanized," being taken aboard the ships as pilots, interpreters, and passengers on the coast and as tourists to the Hawaiian Islands, Canton, and Boston. As early as 1792 Captain Caamaño was amazed at the degree to which the Haida chiefs of Parry Passage, including Cunneah and his son, had become accustomed to European conventions and inventions. "They wandered all over the ship [the *Aranzazu*]," he reported, "without showing wonder at anything, nor was there any object of which they did not appear to know the use, until 9 o'clock, when I had them to supper with me. They ate of all that was on the table, showing no sign of dislike of anything, or wishing first to taste it; and were more at home in the management of fork and spoon than any Spanish squireen [petty squire]. They drank wine and spirits at first sight; and, altogether, their behaviour seemed to point to a considerable intercourse with Europeans." Caamaño added that they bore "comparison with the character and qualities of a respectable inhabitant of 'Old Castile'."[18] By 1825 the worldly Haidas were contemptuously rejecting diluted rum and demanding wine from trading vessels.[19]

Unquestionably, the sea-otter trade also had a negative impact on the Northwest Coast Indians. Their health was impaired by alcohol and tobacco and their numbers were reduced by epidemics and firearms. It has been estimated that the Indian population of the Northwest Coast fell from about 188,000 in 1774 to about 38,000 in 1874, for an annual decrease of approximately 1.5 per cent[20] (although the population estimates are questionable). Already by 1792 the Nootkas were "excessively" fond of brandy, wine, and beer, coffee and tea, sweets, bread, and beans.[21] Such dietary deterioration (bread and beans notwithstanding) soon affected the entire coast. Grog promoted sexual promiscuity, which in turn spread venereal disease, which in its own turn caused sterility and death. It was undoubtedly introduced in 1778 at Nootka Sound by Captain Cook's men, who were sexually active wherever they sojourned, especially at Tahiti and Hawaii but also at Nootka and Unalaska (where they found that vd had already been introduced by the Russians). Cook's sailors, like most Euroamerican visitors, found the Nootkan women much less appealing (homelier and dirtier) than their Polynesian sisters, but "notwithstanding these circumstances, some few of our gentlemen got the better of their feelings, so far as to admit them to their bed, in which case the poor creatures always underwent the ceremony of the mop and pail."[22] By 1792, noted the Spaniards at Nootka Sound, "the natives are already beginning to experience the terrible ravages of syphilis."[23] In 1811 syphilis and consumption (tuberculosis) were the most common afflictions of the Chinooks.[24] Mortality was increased by firearms; by supplementing knives and clubs, guns with their greater firepower made Indian warfare deadlier. Mainly for these reasons the Indian population of Nootka Sound may have dropped from as many as 3,000–4,000 in 1788 to as few as 1,500 in 1804.[25]

The most virulent of the epidemic diseases was smallpox, which periodically struck parts of the coast. It may have arrived with the first Euroamericans, namely, the Russians, whose Kamchatka Peninsula was devastated by the disease in 1768–69. (Smallpox killed from one-half to three-quarters of the peninsula's inhabitants in 1768–69, and from one-half to two-thirds of the remainder died in 1800 of yellow fever, which was introduced by the Kamchatka Regiment, which existed from 1798 to 1812.[26]) On the Northwest Coast the likeliest source of infection was the Spanish crew of either the *Santiago* and *Sonora* in 1775 or the *Favorita* and *Princesa* in 1779 (the first expedition of 1774 did not sail north of Vancouver Island and made shipside contacts but no landfalls). Captain Portlock found in 1787 that no Tlingits below the age of ten or twelve were scarred by smallpox, and he concluded that therefore it had been brought by a Spanish expedition.[27] "It cannot be doubted," reported Captain Marchand in 1791, "that the smallpox has been introduced into the countries which border on Tchinkitanay Bay [Sitka Sound]; for several individuals of both sexes bear unequivocal marks of it; and they explained very clearly to Surgeon Roblet, who questioned them concerning the cause of these marks, that they proceeded from a disorder which made the face swell, and covered the body with virulent pustules that occasioned violent itchings: they even remarked that the French must be well acquainted with it, since some of them also bore the marks of it."[28] Chief Saiginakh of the Sitkan Tlingits told the Russians that smallpox had struck them around 1770, when he was a boy, and had spread from the Stikine River and ceased at Sitka, leaving no more than one or two members of each family alive. They believed that the disease had been brought by a raven as punishment for their interminable internecine wars.[29] Similarly, some Tlingit elders told Captain Lütke in 1827 that the "coast was ravaged by smallpox about 1770 which left only one or two in each family untouched."[30] And the *Columbia Rediviva* found in 1791 that the Nootkas of Nittenat bore the pocks of the disease, which, the Indians said, had been contracted from the Spanish.[31] It was probably also brought from Canton, long an epicentre of the disease, by trading vessels returning to the coast rather than home. Captain Amasa Delano found smallpox at Canton in 1790 and 1793.[32] At the end of 1795 four of the *Union's* crew caught the disease there.[33] In the winter of 1828–29 Captain Martain of the *Louisa* lost four crewmen to smallpox at Canton, and for four to five days he had only four hands who were well enough to work.[34] When the vessel left Canton on 5 March 1829 for Boston three men were "laid up with the small pox," and on 7, 14, and 15 March the crew was employed "cleaning and clensing the ship in order to clear the small pox out of her."[35]

If the source of the disease is uncertain, its effect is not. British and American navigators of the late 1780s and early 1790s found the "indelible marks" – pitting and blindness – of this "scourge of mankind" among all the coastal Natives.[36] "The small pox most [southern Indians] have had, and most terribly pitted they are; indeed, many have lost their Eyes," noted one of Captain Vancouver's officers in 1792.[37] The large number of "deserted villages" found by Vancouver's expedition on the shores of Puget Sound and Georgia Strait, particularly "New Georgia" (the eastern side of Puget Sound), may have resulted from an epidemic of this disease (or seasonal movement or slave raiding).[38] In the same year the Spaniards were likewise struck by the fact that "many" of the Salishes around Boundary Bay were blind in one eye.[39] In the early summer of 1795 Captain Bishop found that Chief Shakes of the Tlingits had been reduced to a "Piteous object" by smallpox; in the late summer the disease was "raging" among the Haidas, whose Chief Kow told Bishop at Kaigani that "a few years since" smallpox had killed two-thirds of the Haidas.[40] Forty years later the Haidas told the Reverend Green that smallpox had made "great ravages among them" and "almost desolated their country"; they called it "Tom Dyer" after the sailor who had allegedly infected them.[41] The Chinooks, too, were ravaged – in 1776 or 1778 and again in 1801 or 1802, according to Lewis and Clark.[42] Similarly, the Astorian Ross Cox reported from the lower Columbia in 1812 that "about thirty years before ... the small-pox had committed dreadful ravages among these Indians."[43] At the beginning of the second decade of the century the entire coast was struck by another epidemic, possibly of smallpox, as the journal of the *Otter* recorded on 25 January 1811: "They [Stikine Tlingits] have all been very sick here as well as at every other place on the Coast there has been a general sickness among the Indians since last fall and all the winter, which I suppose is one great reason of the Skins being so scarce this season."[44] The same journal had noted the previous spring that the Haida village of "Skydance" (Skedans) was "once the largest & most populous of any on the N.W. Coast but [is] now reduced to a few huts."[45]

The worst outbreak of smallpox occurred towards the end of the maritime fur trade in 1835 on the northern coast. It seems to have begun in November 1835 at Sitka, where oldsters, Creoles, and Tlingits proved especially vulnerable. Between November 1835 and the middle of May 1836 at Sitka more than 400 Tlingits, all adults (nearly half of the settlement's Tlingit population), but only 12 Aleuts and Creoles (of more than 100 stricken) and one Russian died ("In January and February," reported a Russian officer, "the poor devils [Tlingits] dropped like flies [*pukh*, literally "down"]"); the Tlingit toll was higher at Khutsnahoo and Keku. In 1835–36 altogether about one-quarter of the Sitkan and Stikine Tlingits perished, the disease being less prevalent in other Tlingit areas.[46] It spread rapidly southwards nevertheless. The Bay man John Work reported from Fort Simpson in early 1837 that "the smallpox broke out among them [Indians] away to the Northward somewhere last spring [1836] and reached this place in September and is advancing on to the Southwards." "Great numbers of the Indians here died of it," he added.[47] The post journal of Fort Simpson monitored the disease in 1836 and 1837. Captain Snow of the *La Grange* informed the fort on 24 May 1836 that "the smallpox was raging to the North [Sitka & Stikine] and carrying off great numbers of the Natives."[48] On 2 November the Skeena Tsimshians reported that "a great number of the Indians are dying of the Small Pox."[49] Within a week or two, however, the disease was "not so violent or fatal as at first."[50] By 8 December it had "considerably abated" and "few ... have lately died of it," and by 27 December it was "not very severe" and "none are dying of it."[51] In the spring of 1837 the epidemic resurged. On 29 April the Nass Tsimshians reported that "a considerable number of the Indians in their quarter are still dying of the smallpox." "They still bring awful accounts of the ravages the smallpox have committed among the natives there they state that in ten houses there is not a man left alive

only some women and children have escaped."[52] A similar pattern
had been noted at Fort Simpson the previous autumn: "There are
now [October 19] only 6 of the Indian men [at the post] free from
the disease. The women, children and slaves appear to escape, have
not seen a single case occur in either, some of the women have cotch
[caught] it but does not appear to be so violent on them as on the
men."[53] More men died because they had more contact with white
carriers; also, the women and children, being together, could care
for each other. For the same reasons, among the Tsimshians the families of chiefs were ravaged more than the families of commoners.[54]

The epidemic may or may not have been hemorrhagic smallpox,
the most virulent type, which is fatal within four or five days of the
first symptoms. In the autumn of 1836 Fort Simpson's post journal
recorded that the Indian "Shagoony or better known by the name of
Mr Jackson died today [October 13] of the Small Pox he first began
to complain on the 28th Sept."[55] On 1 December a local chief's wife
died after only four days of illness. "She had all the symptoms of the
small pox," wrote the journal keeper, "though none of the symptoms
had made its appearance. This is the first case that has come under
my notice where death occured so early as the fourth day." But, he
added, "she was old and besides an habitual drunkard."[56] Another
Indian at the fort was struck by smallpox on 14 December, eruptions
appeared on the 17th, and on the 20th he died.[57] The HBC undertook
some vaccination. On 9 November 1836 a local chief and two of his
family were "innoculated"; in fact, they were vaccinated twice but
without "the desired effect owing I suppose to the matter [vaccine]
being old."[58]

According to the Nass Tsimshians, the epidemic "extended as far
to the interior as they usually go to trade, how much farther they
cannot say."[59] It killed one-third of the Indians north of Fort
Simpson[60]; the Tlingit population dropped from 10,000 to 6,000.[61]
This demographic disaster broke the back of northern Indian resistance to Euroamerican encroachment, both territorial and cultural.
(It was exceeded by the 1848 measles epidemic, which, according to
John Work, was brought to the Oregon Country by American immi-
grants and killed "great numbers" of Indians; indeed "in every quarter it was more fatal than the smallpox in 1836."[62]) The smallpox
epidemic also lowered fur returns, there being fewer Natives to hunt
and trade. The HBC's *Beaver* "made a very poor trade" on a visit to
Nass in April 1837 because "the Nass people had little or nothing,"
the reason being that "the Smallpox has been very severe among
them and carried off great numbers."[63] The company's coastal fur
returns of 1837 exceeded those of 1836 "but not so much as might

have been expected [in view of less American competition] on account of the prevalence of the smallpox the greater part of the fall [1837] and winter [1837–38] last season."[64] Smallpox was to ravage the coast again in 1852–53 and 1862–63.

The coast trade also promoted slavery, increasing the number, distribution, and exploitation of slaves;[65] the increased slave raiding in turn helped to depopulate such peripheral areas as the lower Fraser Valley and the Puget Sound Lowland.[66] The trade depopulated coastal waters, too, so much so that by the middle of the nineteenth century the sea otter was virtually non-existent on the Northwest Coast proper and found only at its northern (Aleutian Islands) and southern (California) extremes. Fortunately for the animal, as it was facing extinction the Euroamerican fashion for fur declined and the Chinese market for sea-otter skins in particular was disrupted; otherwise it might have been annihilated. Only very recently has the sea otter been reintroduced to the Northwest Coast (Vancouver Island's western shore). The depletion of the sea otter in turn altered its ecosystem. The animal's diet comprises at least fifty items, including fish, crabs, mollusks (such as abalone), squid, octopus, starfish, and sea urchins (which are eaten by lobsters and wolf eels, too). It also eats kelp (as do abalone), kelp crabs, kelp bass, kelp snails, sea hares, sea slugs, and especially sea urchins, the most voracious kelp eaters of all. So the sea otter is a controller of sea urchins and hence of kelp, or seaweed. Kelp itself is a valuable fish nursery, affording food and shelter for a variety of creatures (and it is the world's chief source of algin). Thus, when the sea otter declined, so did kelp, which was additionally harmed later in the nineteenth century by warm, toxic effluent from growing coastal cities. Furthermore, as the sea otter declined, abalone increased, the late 1800s becoming the heyday of the abalone fishery (as well as the sardine fishery). Today commercial abalone fishermen see the return of the sea otter as the return of unwanted competition.

Finally, the maritime fur trade conditioned Euroamerican-Indian relations along antagonistic lines. According to the preconceptions of most white traders, the Natives were heathen savages, and their appearance and behaviour simply reinforced that prejudiced view. Not being up to white standards, the Indians were considered second-rate, even subhuman, and this attitude rationalized abuse and discrimination. That attitude has long – far too long – poisoned relations, perhaps even biasing white reactions to Indian land claims.

The negative side of the Northwest trade would undoubtedly have been darker if there had been more posts with more administrating, more missionizing, and more colonizing. Fortunately for coastal

Indian culture, the Euroamerican maritime fur traders were mostly seasonal visitors, not permanent residents, and their transience allowed that culture to flourish in the first third of the nineteenth century.

THE HAWAIIAN ISLANDS

The political, economic, and social effects of the coast trade were even more marked in the Hawaiian Islands, probably because the Hawaiians – or at least Kamehameha I – were more receptive than the Northwest Coast Indians to Euroamerican incursion, including settlement. Admittedly, fur-trading vessels were not the only carriers of new goods, skills, and values to the archipelago but, explorers such as Cook aside, they were the first to arrive in force, and they outnumbered other visitors until at least the late 1810s or even early 1820s. Their initial impact was political, for the very ambitious and very capable Kamehameha – at the time of Cook's visit a royal attendant on Hawaii Island – succeeded in using them to conquer and unite the islands into a single kingdom under his rule (Fig. 9). In return for provisions, consorts, salubrity, and sandalwood the Euroamericans offered advisers, ships, and guns, and they were instrumental in Kamehameha's imperialist drive.[67] In the spring of 1789 Captain William Douglas of the coaster *Iphigenia Nubiana* gave Kamehameha firearms and ammunition, including a swivel gun mounted on the platform of a double canoe.[68] By the early 1790s Hawaiian chiefs were exhibiting such a "great avidity for procuring these destructive engines" that they were very reluctant to trade provisions for anything else.[69] When Captain Vancouver returned to Hawaii Island in early 1793 he learned that Kamehameha had prohibited, under pain of death, the disposal of any island products to Euroamericans for anything other than arms and ammunition (although this prohibition was not always observed).[70] Vancouver remarked the "insatiable desire" of the king's subjects for muskets and pistols.[71] In October 1795 the king was able to assemble 1,500 war canoes and more than 10,000 warriors at Oahu with 5,000 prime muskets and "many" swivels and cannons.[72] A British observer of this force reported that "the greater part of the Natives understood the using of Firearms equal to any men he ever saw."[73] Kamehameha's decisive victory earlier that year at the battle of Nuuanu Pali was gained with the help of Euroamerican tactical and technological advice. At that time hogs from Hawaii Island could be purchased for guns and ammunition only.[74]

By 1804 Kamehameha had some 30 cannons and 1,000 muskets and a "considerable quantity" of powder and ball;[75] by 1818 his arsenal had grown to 100 cannons and 6,000–8,000 men armed with guns.[76] He also developed a navy, although estimates of its sized vary from fifteen to forty vessels of light tonnage.[77] (One witness noted, however, that the king's ships were intended primarily for trade, not war,[78] because by then he had largely completed his conquest of the islands.) It impressed a missionary in 1823:

The natives possess no inconsiderable share of maritime and commercial enterprise. The king [Kamehameha II] and chiefs own fifteen or sixteen vessels, several of which, like the Nio, are brigs of ninety or a hundred tons burden. The greater part of them, however, are schooners of a smaller size.

The larger ones on a long voyage are commanded by a foreigner; but among the islands, they are managed and navigated by the natives themselves. A native captain and supercargo is appointed to each; the former navigates the vessel, while the latter attends to cargo.

The natives in general make good sailors; and although their vessels have greatly multiplied within the last few years, they find constant employ for them, particularly the small craft, which are continually plying from one island to another, while their larger ones are either chartered to foreign merchants, or make distant voyages on their own account.[79]

Kamehameha I welcomed intelligent and industrious foreigners, whom he employed in various capacities. He refused, however, to admit those who could not obtain a recommendation from their captains, and he particularly disliked loafers and drunkards.[80] A visitor noted at the end of 1802 that "he has European and American artificers about him of almost every description," and his own subjects had made "great progress" in mechanics and navigation.[81] A Scottish sojourner, Alexander Campbell, who was hired by the king in 1809 as a sailmaker, wrote that his employer had "a considerable number [of Euroamericans] in his service, chiefly carpenters, joiners, masons, blacksmiths, and bricklayers."[82] The chiefs, he added, were "always anxious to have white people about them."[83] (Apparently not all Euroamericans approved of this technological transfer, some of them believing that "the natives should be taught nothing that would render them independent of strangers," otherwise "ships would have no encouragement to call at the islands."[84]) In 1816 all of Kamehameha I's ships were commanded by American and British skippers, and half of his sailors were foreigners.[85] Two years later the king had 150 *haoles* in his service, compared with a dozen at the time of Captain

Vancouver's visits (1791–94).[86] Particularly useful foreigners were given lands and tenants (to use, not own) and some even the rank of chief. His most trusted Euroamerican advisers were two Englishmen, Isaac Davis and John Young, recruited in 1790 from the Yankee fur-trading vessels *Fair American* and *Eleanora*, respectively. Both acquired the influence and rank of leading chiefs, and Young served as the king's governor of Hawaii initially and Oahu subsequently (he died peacefully in 1835; Davis was poisoned to death in 1810 by Hawaiian plotters after he had foiled their conspiracy).

Because of his own abilities (physical strength, mental acuity, personal ambition) and his exploitation of foreign managerial and technological expertise (use of firearms, deployment of soldiers, construction of fortifications, shipbuilding), Kamehameha was able in 1795 to unite three of the four island chiefdoms – Hawaii, Maui, and Oahu – under his central authority. Only a sudden storm in Kauai Channel in 1796 and an infectious "squatting disease," probably cholera, on Oahu in 1804 prevented him from invading the northwestern chiefdom of Kauai-Niihau, whose ruler, Kaumuali, would be persuaded in 1810 by two American Nor'westers, the Winship brothers, to pay homage to the king in return for their ten-year monopoly on the archipelago's export of sandalwood and cotton. Upon Kamehameha's death in 1819 a rival chief, Kekouakalani of Hawaii Island, proposed to usurp the crown and kill all *haoles* because they had been responsible for enabling the late king to defeat his opponents (Kamehameha, moreover, had not made his horde of Euroamerican goods available to his vassal chiefs for fear of strengthening them.)[87]

"His Black Majesty" acquired a stock of foreign goods by exploiting the Nor'westers' desire for trade as well as their fund of knowledge. A visitor remarked his commercial acumen at the end of 1802: "He is not only a great warrior and politician, but a very acute trader, and a match for any European in driving a bargain. He is well acquainted with the different weights and measures, and the value which all articles ought to bear in exchange with each other; and is ever ready to take the advantage of the necessities of those who apply to him or his people for supplies."[88] The king imposed royal monopolies on the two items that were most in demand by American traders: provisions and sandalwood, and he even had a monopoly on the pearl fishery of Oahu's Pearl River. Also, Kamehameha sent a ship under his own flag to Canton in 1817 with a cargo of sandalwood; the voyage was a financial failure, owing largely to high harborage, tonnage, and pilotage fees, which the king then introduced at Honolulu, the favourite resort of American trading vessels. In 1818–19 a merchantman paid sixty Spanish silver dollars for mooring in the outer harbour and eighty for mooring in the inner harbour, plus one dollar for a pilot.[89] Such measures made Kamehameha a rich man. In 1809 Campbell declared that "he has amassed a considerable treasure in dollars, and possesses a large stock of European articles of every description, particularly arms and ammunition."[90] A Russian commander estimated the king's wealth at 200,000 Spanish silver dollars in 1818.[91] (A year later another visitor reported 300,000 piasters in the king's treasury.[92]) Upon his death his storehouses at Kaiakeakua (Kailua) on Hawaii were full of sandalwood, copper, iron, fishing nets, navigation instruments, liquor, gunpowder, cloth, and "other precious merchandise."[93]

Thus maritime fur traders helped to unite the Hawaiian Islands into a single kingdom and to make Kamehameha I politically and economically powerful. The price that the king paid was the commercialization and even commodification of his realm. Prior to Euroamerican contact Hawaiian trade was negligible, being limited to some barter.[94] But from the middle 1780s fur-trading vessels (as well as ships on voyages of exploration and discovery, and numerous whalers from 1819) created a sizeable demand for provisions, wood, water, salt, rope, and eventually sandalwood. By the middle 1820s at least 100 foreign ships were visiting the islands annually.[95] Initially iron and cloth, then knives, axes, guns, and ammunition, and finally ships and luxuries were dealt to the king and his chiefs as they came to emulate, under Euroamerican encouragement, some foreign tastes.[96] The chief imports were guns, ammunition, cloth, carpenter's tools, hardware, and sea-lion teeth in 1809 and naval equipment, war matériel, cloth, liquor, and piasters in 1819.[97] Accordingly, iron, cloth, and ships began to replace or supplement stone utensils, *kapa* (mulberry bark) garments, and canoes.[98] At first trade was conducted by means of barter but as it increased sandalwood and piasters became the media of exchange. By the early 1820s silver dollars had replaced feathered branches as the coin of the realm.[99] Foreign trade became so profitable that warfare decreased for fear of disrupting it,[100] and the Hawaiian economy became so commercialized that towards the end of Kamehameha I's reign a fine could be substituted for the death penalty for an infraction of the *kapu* (taboo: a sacred interdiction). Trade monopolies enriched the king and his chiefs, but they demanded more and more of the time and labour of the commoners; it was they who had to grow and rear the provisions and fell and haul the sandalwood.

To accommodate the Euroamerican demand for provisions new kinds of plants (pumpkins, melons, oranges, tobacco, cotton) and new breeds of animals (cattle, horses, sheep, goats) were introduced; especially cattle, horses, and goats thrived, with "immense herds" of feral cattle roaming Hawaii in the middle 1820s.[101] Particularly beans, cabbages, cucumbers, onions, pumpkins, radishes, and squashes – not esteemed by the Hawaiians themselves – were grown for foreign ships.[102] The alimentary demands of fur traders, sandalwooders, and whalers also led to an expansion of cultivation.[103] The same demands likewise helped to make Oahu (meaning "the gathering place") the most important of the Hawaiian Islands because of its superior fertility as well as its better harbour (Honolulu).[104] It was commonly known as "the garden of the Sandwich Islands," and visitors rated it the most fruitful and the most beautiful of the "Bright Islands."[105] Honolulu (meaning "safe harbour") was the only deep-water port in the archipelago and the only one that was safe in all seasons.[106] The harbour had a "fine sandy bottom" and was protected by a coral reef, which was broken by an ample channel.[107] Nearby there was a salt lake from which "fine, clear, hard, crystallized salt" was extracted.[108] The port's sole drawback was the lack of fresh water within several miles.[109]

By 1804 Kamehameha I had moved his court from Hawaii, the most populous island, to Honolulu in order to be closer to foreign traders (although he returned to the "Big Island" in 1812). By at least the late 1810s, owing to its sheltered situation, productive hinterland, and royal patronage, Honolulu was the foremost Hawaiian port, and most trading vessels were dropping anchor in – as the *Hamilton*'s log put it – "the Inner harbour in Whyteete [Waikiki] Bay Island of Woahoo [Oahu]" in the lee of what was then called Diamond Hill. In 1822 "Honoruru" reportedly had a population of from 2,000 to 3,000 with a dozen small brigs and schooners bringing provisions and sandalwood to the port from throughout the islands for foreign ships.[110] In 1823 a missionary reported 6,000–7,000 residents, including from twelve to fourteen foreign merchants, mostly Americans, with seldom fewer than three or four and sometimes thirty or more foreign vessels lying at anchor.[111] By 1825 there were some 10,000 inhabitants, including more than 300 Americans.[112] A year later Captain Ferdinand Von Wrangell visited Honolulu aboard the *Krotky* and found about twenty-five merchantmen in the harbour (all but one of them American) and one American warship, the corvette *Peacock*, whose commander, Thomas Jones, told Von Wrangell that "the harbor of Honolulu had become so important to American trade that the Government of the United States considered it necessary to guarantee for their mercantile interests the right of access to these islands free from the interference of England."[113]

Despite the expansion of agriculture and the shift to fertile Oahu, it was not long before provisions became costly in response to increased demand from fur-trading vessels. As early as the turn of the century victuals were no longer cheap. In 1801 a shipmaster found that on Hawaii Island provisions were "very dear, owing to so many vessels stopping here"; indeed they were no cheaper than in the Americas.[114] The situation was not much better on Oahu. At the end of 1802 a visitor reported that "although the island of Whahoo is one of the most fruitful ... and ... the natives supplied us with an abundance of all necessary articles, yet the demands of the sellers were much higher than we had either reason to expect, or could indeed afford."[115] Here provisions were from three to six times as expensive as on Kauai Island.[116] In 1809 Campbell noted that provisions were "by no means cheap," a large hog costing $5 or two axes or one and one-half yards of blue cloth.[117] Nevertheless, American fur traders continued to buy the provisions, affording them by simply raising the value of their own trade goods. After all, the Hawaiians wanted Euroamerican articles as much as the Euroamericans wanted Hawaiian products. Thus in 1818 Captain Golovnin found that at Kealakekua Bay (the site of Captain Cook's death on Hawaii Island) provision "prices were so high that it did not pay to buy anything," but he added that victuals were only dear in cash, not in goods, which were traded for foodstuffs by American skippers after inflating their real value by as much as sixteenfold.[118]

Demand was increased even more with the arrival of whaling vessels in 1819 and missionaries in 1820. Moreover, Kamehameha II and his chiefs were much more self-indulgent and profligate than his father, and in order to pay their mounting debts they charged higher prices for provisions and sandalwood. The commercial agent of Marshall and Wildes reported in the summer of 1821 that "the King, Queens, and Chiefs are at Woahoo devouring all before them, provisions of every description are dearer here than perhaps any part of the world."[119] He wrote in the autumn that "provisions are much dearer here [Honolulu] than in Boston market; every pound of pork we have bought has cost 16 cts, potatoes $4 a barrel other things in proportion."[120] "Labour too is also high," he added, "we have to pay one dollar per day for Conacars [Kanakas]."[121] In the summer of 1822 the same agent reported that the arrival of numerous whalers had further inflated prices: "During the summer the harbour has been crowded with whale ships, not less than say sixty; this has consequently made provisions scarce and dear, hogs twelve dollars, nothing but money, potatoes $3 pr barrel, no tarrow to be had."[122] In the autumn he wrote that "provisions of every description continue high, and nothing but dollars will command hogs, goats etc ... living here is much more expensive than in Boston."[123] At the beginning of 1823 he was more specific: "Every thing about twice what they might be bought for at home."[124] According to a Russian source, around 1827 the king made from 20,000 to 25,000 piasters annually from the sale of provisions to visiting vessels (up to 200 per year, each of which bought from 100 to 300 piasters worth of provisions, half of which went to the king and half to the owners) and from the lease of islanders as sailors on foreign merchantmen (at 10 piasters each per month, part of which went to the king).[125]

By then the Hawaiian Islands were not only less economical but also less populous, for the maritime fur traders brought new diseases and vices as well as new crops and animals. Diseases such as syphilis and smallpox and vices such as boozing and smoking, along with Kamehameha's unification campaign and the heavy labour of sandalwooding, took a heavy toll of Hawaiians. A Russian observer of 1804 summarized the morbidity of the islanders: "They are subject to many diseases, especially smallpox and venereal disease. On the bodies of many of them are disgusting scabs, boils, wounds, tumors, and warts, and others suffer from an eye ailment."[126] In that very year the *okuu*, probably a cholera epidemic, swept Oahu and decimated the king's army of invasion; Kamehameha himself was afflicted but survived and two of his most loyal chiefs succumbed.[127] Again in 1825 an unknown "epidemic disease" struck the entire archipelago, resulting in a "great mortality."[128] It was reported to Marshall and Wildes by their Honolulu agent: "The situation of the Islands is extremely bad, there has and is still raging a mortal malady many of the chiefs are dead and they are falling off daily ... the common people are dying by dozens & we cannot buy a potatoe for the reason that none are well enough to dig them from the ground & bring them to the water side – all business all occupations, all labour, all amusements have ceased."[129] In 1824 Kamehameha II and his queen caught measles on an official visit to London and died. Skin disease – the "itch" – was commonly noted by visitors, but it was not an imported ailment. As a Russian naturalist noted in 1804, the Natives "were covered with bruises and sores, probably the effect ... of drinking kava [an intoxicating beverage made from the fermented roots and stems of the shrubby pepper of the same name]."[130] In 1819 a French visitor found that "many" islanders bore scars and sores and that tuberculosis was common; he thought that the body lesions and sore eyes may have been associated with syphilis.[131] And one of the earliest missionaries to the Hawaiians, the Reverend Charles Stewart, asserted that "the majority are, more or less, disfigured by eruptions and sores; and many are as unsightly as lepers."[132] On Maui, he added, scrofula, ophthalmia, and elephantiasis were "very common."[133]

Captain Cook on his first visit at the beginning of 1778 had issued a "severe Injunction" against sexual intercourse between his crewmen and the Native women; no women were to be admitted to the two ships, and none of the crewmen who had recently been cured of, or was undergoing treatment for, venereal disease was to be allowed ashore, since Cook was determined "to prevent our contaminating an innocent People with that greatest plague that ever the human Race was afflicted with" (surgeon Samwell saw no signs of venereal disease on the Hawaiians, and no crewmen contracted the malady from them).[134] Despite the commander's injunction, some of his men did make sexual contact with women ashore, and some women did manage to board the *Discovery* at least, and the "dreadful distemper" was introduced, "the great eagerness of the Women concurring with the Desires of the Men."[135] When the expedition returned to the islands in the autumn of the same year the disease was "pretty universal among them" and even "raging."[136]

The Hawaiians partook "immoderately" of their own liquor, made from ti root, sugar cane, and sweet potato.[137] As early as 1809 kava was being replaced by ti root liquor – "rum" – whose distillation had been introduced by an escaped British convict from New South Wales.[138] Captain Von Kotzebue found in 1816–17 that "these islanders are passionately fond of spiritous liquors; they empty a bottle of rum at one draught, with the greatest ease, and it is inconceivable how much of it they can drink."[139] By 1819 the consumption of kava had diminished greatly,[140] and by 1822 gin was favoured over kava.[141] In the latter year a visitor found that heavy drinking was widespread.[142] The missionaries seem to have been particularly sensitive to what they regarded as unchristian Hawaiian habits. The Reverend Stewart lamented that much liquor was distilled locally and much was imported; "drunkenness is one of the most common vices of the people," he declared.[143] And the Reverend William Ellis estimated that inebriety was ten times more prevalent in 1823 than before contact.[144]

By the early 1820s not only heavy drinking but also heavy smoking was common,[144] the Hawaiians being as fond of puffing (pipes and cigars) as they were of boozing.[146] One Euroamerican sojourner even asserted that pipe smoking was universal by 1815.[147] In 1816–17 Captain Von Kotzebue observed that "the custom of smoking has become so prevalent, that little children begin to smoke, before they walk, and the adults carry it to such excess, as to fall down senseless, and frequently die of the stupor," the tobacco being "extremely strong."[148]

Presumably heavy drinking and heavy smoking impaired the health of the Natives and increased their mortality. Perhaps infanticide did, too. The missionaries Ellis and Stewart contended that up to two-thirds of all Hawaiian infants, mostly females, were killed (by being strangled or, more usually, by being buried alive) in their first (especially) or second year because they were ill, deformed, distressed, demanding, or burdensome.[149] "Parents seldom rear more than two or three, and many spare only one," wrote Ellis, who added that infanticide was practised by all except the higher class of chiefs.[150] It is uncertain, however, whether the practice had by then become more common than it had been before contact. If it had, it may have been partly induced by the burden of sandalwooding, which took the commoners away from their homes for weeks at a time and caused a neglect of cultivation,[151] as did the insistence of the missionaries on regular attendance at school and church. (In 1817 Von Chamisso observed that "for the sake of this [sandalwood] trade the chiefs were burdening the people with feudal service that is detrimental to agriculture and industry."[152]) By 1828, declared a French observer, the "old agricultural life" of the Hawaiians had declined by one-third.[153] This neglect may in turn have diminished their diet to the point where they could support fewer children. Also, the sparer diet, plus the harmful effects of heavy drinking and heavy smoking on reproduction, may have resulted in more disabled candidates for infanticide.

It is certain that many Hawaiians died in warfare, at least until Euroamericans had been accepted and Kamehameha had consolidated his central control. The worst – and one of the few – cases of Euroamerican atrocity was the Olowalu massacre of 1 February 1790, when Captain Simon Metcalfe of the *Eleanora* killed from 100 to 300 and wounded a "great many" Native men, women, and children of Maui with a close-range broadside of balls and nails in retaliation for the theft of a longboat and the murder of a sailor (several weeks later Metcalfe's son Thomas, commander of another fur-trading vessel, the *Fair American*, and all but one of his crew were killed at Hawaii Island).[154] One of the *Eleanora*'s crewmen, incidentally, the English-born John Young, remained in the islands and became an influential and renowned adviser to Kamehameha I, dying in 1835 at the age of ninety-one; and a survivor of the *Fair American*, another Englishman, Isaac Davis, also served as a trusted advisor of the king until his death in 1810. Many more islanders were undoubtedly slain during Kamehameha I's long and bloody struggle to dominate the archipelago, especially since the vanquished often committed suicide and prisoners of war were customarily executed. Captain William Broughton reported that the 1795 conquest of Oahu "and subsequent calamities" (like starvation) cost the lives of 6,000 of the king's followers.[155] His wars of conquest may have reduced the Hawaiian population by as much as one-third by 1804.[156] The missionary Hiram Bingham estimated that some 18,000 Hawaiians died directly and indirectly as a result of Kamehameha's campaigns between 1780 and 1796.[157] As late as 1825 at least 2,000 Natives died during a rebellion on Kauai,[158] which had stubbornly resisted Kamehameha's hegemony.

For all of these reasons (and others, including famine resulting from drought and warfare[159]) the population of the Hawaiian Islands was "singularly reduced."[160] Precise figures are lacking, however; only very rough estimates were made by residents and visitors. Lieutenant James King, who visited the islands twice in 1778–79 with Captain Cook, put the population at some 400,000,[161] but in 1818 Captain Golovnin stated that according to longtime Euroamerican residents, King's guess should be halved to about 200,000.[162] In 1821–23 the American consul and a British missionary both recorded 150,000 Hawaiians (as did a British visitor in 1825 [130,000–150,000] and a French visitor in 1828).[163] And in 1842, at the end of the maritime fur trade, a visitor estimated that there were 100,000 islanders.[164] Therefore, the archipelago's population may have decreased by one-quarter between the late 1770s and the early 1820s and by one-third between the early 1820s and the early 1840s, meaning that the greatest demographic impact of Euroamerican contact was felt during the heydays of sandalwooding, whaling, and missionizing, not that of fur trading.[165] The decrease of one-half for the entire period is close to the estimate of Romanzo Adams, an early Scottish settler, a pilot at Honolulu from 1823, and "a Chief, and universally known and esteemed," who in 1842 told a passenger on a HBC ship that "since the white man came amongst them [Hawaiians] they have degenerated, decreased about 40 p cent, and learned most of the vices of the white man, but few of his virtues."[166]

There is some evidence that Hawaiians may have degenerated morally after contact with maritime fur traders, although early visitors tended to idealize the pre-contact islanders as "noble savages," and all non-Christians were morally suspect in the eyes of the pious and prudish missionaries. On his second visit to the islands in 1824–25 Captain Von Kotzebue noted that the Natives were more indolent and dissolute than during his first visit eight years earlier.[167] A "great part" of the taro fields around Honolulu had been abandoned; fraud and theft were now common, and gambling was very popular.[168] Farming decreased as sandalwooding increased, and the onetime farmers may well have resorted to crime as a means of sustenance. Also, if the commoners were more dissipated, they may have been simply following the example of the royal family and some chiefs as well as white riffraff. As Marshall and Wildes were informed by their Honolulu agent in 1821, "King Rheo Rheo [Liholiho, or Kamehameha II] is only a boy, pleased with a rattle tickled with a straw, rum is his god, scarce have I seen him sober, he is flying from one Island to another, devouring all before him."[169] It is well to remember, however, that even before contact Hawaiian monarchs and chiefs were fond of bouts of eating, drinking, and idling.

What did begin to change under Euroamerican influence were Hawaiian beliefs, customs, values, clothes, foods – in other words, Hawaiian culture. Society became less theocratic and less ritualistic and more materialistic. The dank highlands were stripped of sandalwood in defiance of the traditional ethic of *aloha aina*, the feeling of affection and respect for nature, and especially the reverence for *mana*, the vital and sacred essence shared by all living things. All taboos were abolished, at least officially, by Kamehameha II in 1819; temples were razed, idols were broken and burned (or hidden), and priests became dutiless. The practice of human sacrifice (upon the death of a chief, for instance) was abandoned. The arrival of fundamentalist missionaries in 1820 further diminished ceremonialism. By 1822 the hula was seldom celebrated.[170] Already by 1804 tattooing was "much out of vogue,"[171] probably out of deference to Euroamerican sensibilities. By 1823 feasts (featuring baked dog) were "much less frequent than formerly,"[172] perhaps because of heavy sales of provisions to foreign ships and the impoverishment of commoners. Euroamerican clothing was adopted. In 1816–17 Captain Von Kotzebue found that some item of *haole* attire was considered *de rigueur* for Hawaiian men of all stations.[173] He wrote: "The rage is so great here, that no person can rest without having some articles of European dress; some only walk in a shirt, some in trousers, and others strut about in a waistcoat. The Americans buy up all the clothes which have become out of fashion, and then sell them here to great advantage."[174] American traders did the very same thing on the Northwest Coast, of course. At the end of 1821 the American consul reported from Honolulu that the archipelago's chief imports were textiles, hardware, guns, gunpowder, liquor, rice, and molasses.[175] This list would have fit the coast as well. But the Hawaiian nobles were more determined than the coastal chiefs to be *au fait*. Marshall and Wildes were assured by their Honolulu agent at the beginning of 1823 that "any thing that is new could sell here."[176] That sort of attitude was bound to erode Native culture.

One reason why the Hawaiian Islands were more affected by the maritime fur trade than the Northwest Coast is the fact that the fur traders landed more frequently and more permanently on the islands (and after 1819–20 they were joined by whalers and missionaries, who did not frequent the coast until the 1840s). The balmy and fertile archipelago was simply more attractive. William Ellis described the allure:

The descriptions which Captain Cook's Voyages contained, of the almost primitive simplicity, natural vivacity, and fascinating manners, of a people, who had existed for ages, isolated, and unknown to the rest of the world, were so entirely new, and the accounts given of the mildness and salubrity of the climate, the spontaneous abundance of delicious fruits, and the varied and delightful appearance of the natural scenery in the Sandwich and the other islands of the Pacific, were so enchanting, that many individuals were led to imagine they were a sort of elysium, where the highly favoured inhabitants, free from the toil and care, the want and disappointment, which mar the happiness of civilized communities, dwelt in what they called a state of nature, and spent their lives in unrestrained gratification and enjoyment.[177]

The "isles of the blessed" proved particularly irresistible to visiting seamen, who, tired of the harsh discipline, scorbutic diet, monotony, celibacy, and mortal dangers of long ocean voyages, "like so well to revel in a superfluity of the productions of nature without much labour ... [so] that a ship scarcely ever touches here without leaving one or more of its sailors behind."[178] The desertion of Euroamerican seamen at the Pacific's subtropical islands was not uncommon, it "being the natural turn of a sailor not caring where he lives so [long] as he has an easy life and his passions gratefied," in the words of Bernard Magee of the *Jefferson* at the Marquesas.[179] On 8 March 1812 as the *Atahualpa* was preparing to leave Honolulu for the coast nine crewmen swam ashore, and the captain "went on shore and found them drinking Rum and I flogd and sent them on Board."[180] The next day two of the deserters attempted a mutiny, which was suppressed, whereupon two other hands deserted, only to be returned a day later by the islanders; the leader of the abortive mutiny was then released, and six Kanakas were enlisted.[181] On 12 November 1819 seven sailors deserted from the coaster *Mentor* at Honolulu.[182] In mid-1827 the American consul reported that Oahu alone harboured from fifty to one hundred "lawless seaman [*sic*] of every nation, deserters from different ships."[183] Five years earlier the same informant had counted "not less than one hundred deserters from different whale ships" on the island, plus seventeen "established grog shops kept by white people."[184] "Woahoo is becoming one of the vilest places on the globe," he added.[185] An American shipmaster concurred, saying that "the off scourings of the earth is here."[186] So did a French shipmaster. "With almost no exception," he declared, "foreigners settled in these islands represent the dregs of all nations, and they have brought with them vices of every stripe."[187] As early as 1794 Captain Vancouver had expressed alarm at the "banditti of renegadoes" in the archipelago, mostly British and mostly on Hawaii (eleven) and Kauai Islands; although generally unsavoury, they were valued by the Native chiefs for their knowledge of firearms.[188]

The deserters were augmented by derelicts – seamen who had been dismissed on the islands by their captains in favour of cheaper Hawaiian hands. This ruthlessness was reported by the American consul at the end of 1821: "A practice has for many years existed, with the Commanders of Ships touching at the Sandwich Islands, either for supplies or trade, to turn on shore all Seamen, against whom they could alledge any trivial misconduct, and employ in their lieu Natives of the Islands, by this means lessening their postage Bills ... American Vessels have also been sold to the Natives & their Crews discharged, without any means of support, thus left to the protection & mercy of the Rude Savage."[189] Neither deserter (especially) nor derelict set a shining example to the Hawaiians of the merits of Euroamerican culture, and they helped to sully both the image and the reality of the island kingdom. Not that other foreign residents were blameless. Dixey Wildes wrote to his business partner in 1825 from Honolulu that "most of the [commercial] agents at the Sandwich Islands divide the 24 hours into three parts, Drinking, Gambling and Sleeping."[190] And a year later Captain Von Wrangell found the native Hawaiians more honest than the foreign merchants.[191]

In 1798 there were twenty-three foreigners on the islands, including some who had been there since 1790 (such as Davis and Young).[192] At one point in 1809 Oahu alone contained nearly sixty whites, two-thirds of them British and one-third American;[193] in early 1811 there were eight or ten settlers and about thirty idlers and drunkards on the island.[194] In 1817–18 the archipelago contained from 150 to 200 Euroamericans.[195] And in 1823 a missionary enumerated 100–200 runaways and vagabonds, 15–20 settlers, 10–15 missionaries, and 4 business agents.[196] In addition, of course, there were hundreds of seasonal visitors from fur-trading, sandalwooding, and whaling vessels.

Hawaiian culture was influenced, too, by islanders who went abroad to experience other societies. *Kanakas* (literally, "men") accompanied shipmasters to the Northwest Coast, Canton, Boston, and London as adept and loyal sailors and curious tourists. Perhaps the first was Kaiana, an ambitious and restless chief of Kauai who was taken (as Tianna) to China by Captain Meares in the *Nootka* in late 1787 and was returned by Captain Douglas in the *Iphigenia Nubiana* by way of the Northwest Coast at the end of 1788, whereupon he became a close ally of Kamehameha in his campaign of conquest of the entire archipelago; Kaiana's "extraordinary size and majestic appearance" so impressed the Chinese that they named him the "Great Stranger."[197] Two Hawaiian men left the islands aboard the *Columbia Rediviva* in September 1789 for Canton and Boston, where they arrived in August 1790; one of them, Joseph Ingraham's Opye (Kalehua), a native of Kauai, returned home on the *Hope* in May 1791 after six weeks in Boston. *Wahines*, too, were shipped as concubines, servants, and even chattels, such as Wynee, who left on the *Imperial Eagle* in 1787 to serve as maid and companion to Captain Charles Barkley's wife (until she was abandoned in Canton). A visitor to the Hawaiian Islands at the end of 1802 noted that some islanders had earned enough from voyages to the Northwest Coast to "acquire sufficient property to make themselves easy and comfortable, as well as respectable among their countrymen."[198]

SOUTH CHINA

It is not really possible to assess the impact of the maritime fur trade on South China, partly because the Chinese sources are inaccessible and partly because the fur traffic was but one inseparable part of the Canton trade (and, moreover, comprised many fur-seal as well as sea-otter skins). Charles Marjoribanks, a veteran servant of the EIC, believed that the Canton trade as a whole was more important to China than the Chinese cared to admit. He estimated that the emperor may have personally gained up to $2 million (£630,000) annually from it,[199] and he added: "The Chinese government has invariably ... professed to hold it in contempt but I believe great advantages result to the country generally from the foreign trade, from the encouragement which it gives to native industry, from the numerous natives employed in different ways in the transactions of foreign commerce, and from the very flourishing state of the southern provinces of the empire, among which I include the Tea provinces, which owe their prosperous condition very materially to the foreign trade."[200] But this estimate was in all likelihood exaggerated. Another company employee, John Davis, opined that "the influence of foreign trade does not extend very far inland from Canton."[201] It was important only to the tea growers of Fukien, the silk producers of Nanking, and the craftsmen of Canton, in addition to their middlemen.[202] Even so, sea-otter skins formed but a small part of this trade. Overall, foreign trade did not loom large in the Chinese economy, owing to the country's high degree of self-sufficiency, which stemmed in turn from its diversified agriculture, small-scale urban manufacturing, and extensive internal commerce. The Manchus feared that an expansion of foreign trade would disturb "the internal equilibrium of a traditionalist order," in the words of one specialist[203] (although given China's chronic internal unrest, it is debatable whether there was much "order" or even "equilibrium"). In addition, of course, ethnocentric Chinese culture was not about to be affected by contact with a few maritime fur traders, especially when they were carefully kept at bay at Canton. It is perhaps well to remember, too, that the principal buyers of sea-otter skins were not the Chinese masses but the much less numerous well-to-do of North China. Nevertheless, China's growing trade imbalance – stemming from the loss of more and more specie to pay for more and more opium, which the British grew in India and the Americans bought in Turkey in order to pay for Chinese goods – resulted in the economic incorporation of the country into the capitalist world system after 1830, and the first attempt at its political incorporation after 1840. But sea-otter skins played a minor role in this process.

NEW ENGLAND

Unlike old China, the young United States actively pursued foreign trade. Nevertheless, the American China trade was but one branch of the "East India" (Asian) traffic out of Salem, Boston, Providence, New York, Philadelphia, and Baltimore to Calcutta, Madras, Mauritius, Sumatra, Batavia, Manila, and Canton – a traffic that carried to the east a wide array of goods, including furs, rum, ammunition, lumber, ice, salt, Spanish silver dollars, iron, tobacco, opium, wine, ginseng, and tar and that brought home muslins, silks, nankeens, spices, cassia, chinaware, teas, sugar, and drugs. Asian trade was more romantic and exotic than important, however, never exceeding 10 per cent of the republic's foreign commerce.[204] And just as not all American East India traders were China traders, not all American China traders carried furs (let alone only sea-otter skins) to Canton.

Nevertheless, the China trade as a whole helped to accumulate a large amount of capital in a short time for the industrial development of the United States.[205] The rise of American manufacturing was further stimulated by rapid population growth (the country's population doubled from nearly 4,000,000 in 1790 to about 8,000,000 in 1815, and it doubled again to some 16,000,000 by 1835), urbanization (the number of cities multiplied tenfold between 1790 and 1850), and technological advancement (particularly the advent of mass production techniques and the development of machine tools and precision instruments).[206] In the second quarter of the 1800s the dominant group of stockholders in the New England textile industry were merchants – undoubtedly some of them China and Northwest Coast traders – attracted by the expected high profits and supposed safety of textile investment and repelled by the post-Napoleonic depression in commerce.[207] Capital was shifted "from wharf to waterfall."

Nor'west voyages, which enjoyed more popularity and more prestige among New England seamen than any other, no doubt because they were more profitable for owners, masters, and crews, made the fortunes of many Boston families.[208] Two such beneficiaries were William Sturgis and Thomas Handasyd Perkins. Sturgis went to sea in 1798 at the age of sixteen for $7 per month. A year later during his first visit to the coast he became chief mate of the *Ulysses*. In 1801 at the age of nineteen he succeeded to the command of the *Caroline* on the coast. By 1810 he had made five voyages to China and had sufficient experience and capital to enter into a partnership with John Bryant; it lasted until Sturgis' death in 1863 at the age of eighty-one. Between 1810 and 1840 Bryant and Sturgis accounted for more than one-half of American trade with China and the eastern side of the Pacific. Sturgis himself treated the Northwest Coast Indians fairly and respectfully, becoming conversant in their languages; his popularity among the coastal chiefs was reportedly "unbound."[209] Thomas Perkins invested in his first Nor'west venture in 1790 (the losing voyage of the *Hope*). Two years later he formed a partnership with his brother James under the name of J. and T. H. Perkins; it lasted until 1822, when James died. The firm's main business was the Northwest Coast and China trade. In 1804 they established an agency at Canton, Perkins and Company, under J. P. Cushing, a youth of sixteen years. The agency lasted until 1827, when Cushing left China.[210] Upon his return to Boston in 1828 Cushing invested his earnings in government bonds, railroads, banks, insurance companies, manufacturing companies, transportation companies, and real estate.[211] Indeed, just as Philadelphia's China merchants seeded their profits in shipbuilding, banking, insurance companies, land, manufacturing, railroads, and philanthropy,[212] so, too, did Boston's. Sturgis himself declared in 1846 that the coast trade had "brought wealth to those engaged in it, and was probably as beneficial to the country as any commercial use of an equal amount of capital has ever been."[213] The multiplier effect on New England's economy must have been appreciable.

Certainly it helped to rejuvenate Boston, the home port of almost all American Northwest Coastmen. Before the launching of the coast trade the city was depressed, American shipping having lost its British and West Indian markets. A churchman wrote to a friend in 1780: "The town of Boston is really poor. If some brighter prospects do not open, it is my opinion that we cannot subsist. You are sensible how much depends upon our trade."[214] Four years later a London newspaper reported much the same condition:

Boston was once the most flourishing place in America, and employed near five hundred sail of shipping, besides coasting and fishing vessels, which were numerous to a degree. Besides the trade which subsisted within themselves, they were to America what Holland has been to Europe – the carriers for all the other colonies. At present their distillery is entirely at a stand; their peltry and fur trade, once so considerable, is entirely over; the fishery is exceedingly trifling; instead of the vast exports of hemp, flax, tar, pitch, turpentine, staves, lumber and provisions ... only ... train-oil.[215]

But a decade later Boston had been transformed into a busy port, as one Thomas Pemberton noted: "There are eighty wharves and quays, chiefly on the east side of the town. Of these the most distinguished is Boston pier, or the Long Wharf, which extends from the bottom of State street one thousand and seven hundred and forty-three feet into the harbor. Here the principal navigation of the town is carried on; vessels of all burdens load and unload; and the London ships generally discharge their cargoes. It is the general resort of all the inhabitants, and is more frequented, we think, than any other part of the town."[216] He added that "it is reckoned that not less than four hundred and fifty sail of ships, brigs, schooners, sloops, and small craft are now [November 1794] in this port."[217] On just one day in 1791 seventy ships sailed from Boston for various parts of the world.[218] Some of these vessels were bound for China via the Northwest Coast.

Although many of the China goods imported by Bostonian merchants, especially tea, were re-exported to Canada, England, and the continent, some were sold locally, becoming standard consumer items. "India goods" enlivened and enriched the diet, dress, and furniture of New Englanders. Tea became cheaply and widely available as a fragrant and stimulating beverage, as did cassia, pepper, and sugar candy. Yellow nankeens brightened jackets and trousers, and so did handkerchiefs and gingham dresses. Colourful and graceful porcelains (cups, plates, bowls, tureens, pitchers) supplemented and replaced leather, metal, glass, and delft tableware and spawned a passion for fine chinaware. And sea chests, camphorwood desks, and smaller articles (fans, snuff boxes, shaving cases) adorned Yankee homes. But the only items from the Northwest Cost were a few chests, masks, rattles, pipes, and robes on display in public museums or private homes.

By the early 1840s little Cantonese willowware and few silks, nankeens, and crapes were being unloaded at Boston's wharves, having been ousted by English and French porcelains and English and New England cottons as well as fickle fashion. Only teas and spices remained, and even tea was losing ground to coffee, just as Boston was yielding to New York with the digging of the Erie Canal. Sea-otter fur was no longer in supply, although it was still in demand in North China, which had been less disrupted by foreign incursion than the Cantonese South. But this residual market was supplied by Russian, not American, traders. Yankee shipowners had reinvested in whaling and the hide-and-tallow trade. The Boston men had withdrawn from the Northwest Coast, where they had had no need to establish settlements anyway, and partly for that very reason they failed to gain it by the terms of the boundary treaty of 1846. They did receive the southernmost portion below the mouth of the Fraser River, but largely for strategic reasons (Puget Sound's harbours), and in 1867 they acquired the northernmost portion, but by purchase and mainly for political reasons (enlarging American, and outflanking British, dominion in North America). The middle portion of the coast went to the King George men, who had driven American shipmasters from its trade. One of the latter, Captain William Smith, who had plied the Nor'west trade for "many years" (and who had been interviewed by Lieutenant Aemelius Simpson on behalf of the HBC in 1827), was found old and poor at Santa Barbara in September 1840 by Captain William Phelps of the *Alert*. Phelps wrote: "Mr. Sturgis one of my owners was many years in the NW & Canton trade, and was intimate with Capt. Smith and in kindness to the old gentleman, desires his Capts. if they fall in with him to give him a home on board their Ships while on the coast, consequently he is transferred from one to the other, having spent so much of his life at sea, he can only live on Ship board. Has a most sovereign contempt for the land, and every body that lives on it, and wishes to die on board ship and be buried in his hammock in blue water."[219]

The maritime fur trade that had occupied Captain Smith for so long was dying with him. But it had persisted for more than half a century. During that time it had enriched Boston shipowners and contributed to the formation of the capital that enabled New England to evolve from an agrarian to an industrial society. It had intensified the trading proclivities of the Northwest Coast Indians and stimulated their culture if not to a climax then at least to a crescendo. It had exploited and publicized the natural advantages of the Hawaiian Islands and exposed the Hawaiians to overwhelming foreign influences. It had supplemented the Occident's commercial pressure on China at Canton, pressure that was to shatter its isolation and eventually topple its ruling dynasty.

And all of this happened because of a passion for the gorgeous fur of the hapless sea otter.

Tables

TABLE 1
Trading and Hunting Vessels on the Northwest Coast, 1785–1841

Year	British	American	Russian	Other	Total
1785	*Sea Otter*				1
1786	*Captain Cook* *Experiment* *King George* *Nootka* *Queen Charlotte* *Sea Otter* (Hanna) *Sea Otter* (Tipping)				7
1787	*Imperial Eagle* *King George* *Nootka* *Prince of Wales* *Princess Royal* *Queen Charlotte*				6
1788	*Felice Adventurer* *Iphigenia Nubiana* *North West America* *Prince of Wales* *Princess Royal*	*Columbia Rediviva* [*Eleanora*]	*Tri Svyatitelya*		[8]
1789	*Argonaut* *Iphigenia Nubiana* *North West America* *Princess Royal*	*Columbia Rediviva* *Eleanora* *Fair American* *Lady Washington*			8
1790	*Argonaut* [*Gustavus III*]	*Eleanora* *Grace* [*Polly*]		*Princesa Real* (Sp.)	[6]
1791	*Argonaut* [*Felice Adventurer*] *Gustavus III* [*Venus*]	*Columbia Rediviva* *Eleanora* *Fairy* *Grace* *Hancock* *Hope* *Lady Washington*	*Mikhail*	*La Solide* (Fr.)	[13]
1792	*Butterworth* *Fenis and St. Joseph* *Gustavus III* *Halcyon* *Iphigenia Nubiana* *Jackal* *Jenny*	*Adventure* *Columbia Rediviva* *Grace* *Hancock* *Hope* *Margaret*		*Feliz Aventurero* (Port.) *Florinda* (Port.) *La Flavie* (Fr.)	21

TABLE 1 (continued)

Year	British	American	Russian	Other	Total
	Phoenix				
	Prince Lee Boo				
	Prince William Henry				
	Three Brothers				
	Venus				
1793	*Butterworth*	*Amelia*		*La Flavie* (Fr.)	13
	Iphigenia Nubiana	*Hancock*			
	Jackal	*Jane*			
	Prince Lee Boo	*Jefferson*			
	Prince William Henry	*Margaret*			
	Three Brothers	*Lady Washington*			
1794	*Arthur*	*Eleanora*			[12]
	Jackal	*Fairy*			
	Jenny	*Jefferson*			
	Phoenix	*Lady Washington*			
	Prince Lee Boo	[*Nancy*]			
	Prince William Henry	*Resolution*			
1795	[*Jane*]	*Despatch*	*Aleksandr*		[12]
	Phoenix	*Mercury*	*Delfin*		
	[*Prince William Henry*]	*Union*	*Feniks*		
	Ruby		*Olga*		
			Tri Svyatitelya		
1796	*Arthur*	*Lady Washington*	*Olga*		[10]
	[*Prince William Henry*]	*Otter*	*Oryol*		
	Ruby	*Sally*	*Tri Svyatitelya*		
		Sea Otter			
1797	*Dragon*	*Amelia*	*Oryol*		7
		Despatch			
		Hazard			
		India Packet			
		Sea Otter			
1798	[*Dove*]	*Alert*	*Oryol*		[8]
	Dragon	*Alexander*	*Yekaterina*		
		Hazard			
		Jenny			
1799	[*Butterworth*]	*Caroline*	*Olga*		[12]
	Cheerful	*Despatch*	*Oryol*		
	Dove	*Eliza*	*Yekaterina*		
		[*Gowland*]			

TABLE 1 (continued)

Year	British	American	Russian	Other	Total
		Hancock			
		Ulysses			
1800	[Betsy]	Alert	Olga		[14]
	[Dove]	Alexander	Yekaterina		
	Nautilus	[Beaver]			
		[Belle Savage]			
		Betsy			
		Charlotte			
		Hazard			
		Jenny			
		[Rover]			
1801	Cheerful	Alert	Yekaterina		[25]
	[Mary Ann]	Atahualpa			
	Unicorn	Belle Savage			
		Betsy			
		Carlisle			
		Caroline			
		Catherine			
		Charlotte			
		Despatch			
		Enterprise			
		Globe			
		Guatimozin			
		Hazard			
		Lavinia			
		Litteler			
		Lucy			
		Manchester			
		[Mary]			
		Polly			
		Three Sisters			
		unidentified ship			
		vessel			
1802	Cheerful	Alert	Yekaterina		[18]
	Unicorn	[Amethyst]			
		Atahualpa			
		[Belle Savage]			
		Caroline			
		Catherine			
		Globe			
		[Greenwood]			
		[Hazard]			
		Hetty			
		Jenny			

TABLE 1 (continued)

Year	British	American	Russian	Other	Total
		Juno			
		Manchester			
		Mary			
		Vancouver			
1803		*Alert*	*Olga*		12
		Alexander			
		Boston			
		Guatimozin			
		Hazard (Rowan)			
		Hazard (Swift)			
		Juno			
		Lelia Byrd			
		Mary			
		O'Cain			
		Vancouver			
1804		*Atahualpa*	*Aleksandr*		11
		Caroline	*Rostislav*		
		Guatimozin	*Yekaterina*		
		Hazard (Rowan)	*Yermak*		
		Hazard (Swift)			
		Lelia Byrd			
		O'Cain			
1805	*Myrtle*	*Atahualpa*	*Maria*		[13]
		Caroline	*Rostislav*		
		Juno	*Yekaterina*		
		[*Katherine*]	*Yermak*		
		Lydia			
		Mary			
		Pearl			
		Vancouver			
1806	*Myrtle*	*Eclipse*	*Aleksandr*		[15]
		[*Grampus*]	*Nikolay*		
		Hamilton			
		Hazard			
		Lydia			
		[*Mary*]			
		[*Maryland*]			
		Mercury			
		O'Cain			
		Peacock			
		Pearl			
		Vancouver			

TABLE 1 (continued)

Year	British	American	Russian	Other	Total
1807	*Myrtle*	[*Amethyst*] *Atahualpa* [*Augustus*] *Derby* *Eclipse* *Guatimozin* *Hamilton* *Hazard* *Mercury* *O'Cain* *Peacock*	*Kodiak* *Nikolay* *Sitka*		[15]
1808	[*Otter*]	[*Amethyst*] *Derby* *Guatimozin* *Mercury* *Pearl* [*Triumph*] *Vancouver*	*Chirikov* *Kodiak* *Nikolay*		[11]
1809	[*Otter*] (Jobelin)	[*Amethyst*] [*Augusta*] *Hamilton* *Lydia* *Mercury* *O'Cain* *Otter* (Hill) *Pearl* *Vancouver*	*Chirikov* *Kodiak* *Konstantin*		[13]
1810		*Albatross* *Derby* *Enterprise* *Hamilton* *Isabella* *Katherine* *Lydia* *Mercury* *O'Cain* *Otter*	*Chirikov* *Yunona* *Konstantin*		[13]
1811		*Albatross* *Amethyst* *Enterprise* *Hamilton* *Isabella* *Katherine*	*Chirikov* *Yunona*		15

TABLE 1 (continued)

Year	British	American	Russian	Other	Total
		Lydia			
		Mercury			
		New Hazard			
		O'Cain			
		Otter			
		Pedler			
		Tonquin			
1812		[*Albatross*]			[12]
		Amethyst			
		Atahualpa			
		Beaver			
		Charon			
		Isabella			
		Katherine			
		Lydia			
		Mercury			
		New Hazard			
		Packet			
		Pedler			
1813		*Albatross*			11
		Atahualpa			
		Brutus			
		Charon			
		Isabella			
		Lydia			
		Mercury			
		O'Cain			
		Packet			
		Pedler			
		Tamaahmaah			
1814	*Columbia*	[*Brutus*]	*Ilmen*		[8]
	Forester	*Packet*			
	Isaac Tod	*Pedler*			
		Tamaahmaah			
1815	*Columbia*	*Albatross*	*Ilmen*		[12]
	Forester	*Brutus*	*Konstantin*		
		[*Cordelia*]	*Otkrytie*		
		Isabella			
		Lydia			
		O'Cain			
		Pedler			

TABLE 1 (continued)

Year	British	American	Russian	Other	Total
1816	*Columbia* *Colonel Allan*	*[Abaellino]* *[Albatross]* *Atala* *Avon* *Cossack* *Enterprise* *Hamilton* *Panther* *Sultan*			[11]
1817	*Columbia*	*Alert* *Alexander* *Atala* *[Avon]* *Brutus* *Eagle* *Enterprise* *Hamilton* *Lydia* *Mentor* *[Panther]* *Sultan* *[Traveller]*		*Le Bordelais* (Fr.)	[15]
1818	*Columbia*	*[America]* *[Bengal]* *Brutus* *Eagle* *Enterprise* *Hamilton* *Levant* *Mentor* *Savage* *Volunteer*	*Finlandia* *Platov*	*Le Bordelais* (Fr.)	[14]
1819		*Ann* *Borneo* *Brutus* *Clarion* *Eagle* *[Ellen Maria]* *Nautilus* *[Slyph]* *Volunteer*	*Baranov* *Finlandia*		[11]

TABLE 1 (continued)

Year	British	American	Russian	Other	Total
1820		Ann Arab Clarion Hamilton Levant Mentor Pedler Thaddeus Volunteer	Baranov Fortuna		11
1821		Alexander Arab [Becket] Frederick Hamilton Lascar Mentor Pedler Sultan	Chirikov Fortuna		[11]
1822		Arab Frederick Hamilton Hoqua Lascar Owhyhee Parthian Pearl Pedler Rob Roy Sultan	Fortuna Rumyantsev		13
1823		Arab Becket Frederick Lascar Mentor Octavia Owhyhee Parthian Pearl Rob Roy Sultan Volunteer	Fortuna Rurik		14

TABLE 1 (continued)

Year	British	American	Russian	Other	Total
1824		[Ann]	Fortuna		[15]
		[Becket]	Golovnin		
		Convoy			
		Frederick			
		Herald			
		[Mentor]			
		Owhyhee			
		Rob Roy			
		Sultan			
		Tamaahmaah			
		Triton			
		Volunteer			
		Washington			
1825	William and Ann	Convoy	Baranov		13
		Griffon	Fortuna		
		Lapwing	Rurik		
		Owhyhee			
		Paragon			
		Parthian			
		Rob Roy			
		Tamaahmaah			
		Volunteer			
1826	Dryad	Chinchilla	Fortuna		[11]
		Convoy	Rurik		
		Griffon			
		Louisa			
		[Owhyhee]			
		Sultan			
		Tally Ho			
		Volunteer			
1827	Cadboro	Active	Fortuna		16
	William and Ann	Albatross	Rurik		
		Chinchilla			
		Convoy			
		Courier			
		Diana			
		Griffon			
		Louisa			
		Owhyhee			
		Tally Ho			
		Triton			
		Volunteer			

TABLE 1 (continued)

Year	British	American	Russian	Other	Total
1828	Cadboro	Active		Kamolilani (Haw.)	13
		Chinchilla		Tamaolani (Haw.)	
		Griffon			
		Louisa			
		Owhyhee			
		Paragon			
		Parthian			
		Sultan			
		Volunteer			
		Washington			
1829	Cadboro	Active			12
	Ganymede	Alabama			
	William and Ann	Convoy			
		Griffon			
		Herald			
		Louisa			
		Owhyhee			
		Plant			
		Volunteer			
1830	Cadboro	Active			12
	Dryad	Convoy			
	Eagle	Griffon			
	Isabella	Louisa			
	Vancouver	Owhyhee			
		Sultan			
		Volunteer			
1831	Cadboro	Active			12
	Dryad	Bolivar Liberator			
	Little	Crusader			
	Vancouver	Diana			
		Griffon			
		Lama			
		Louisa			
		Smyrna			
1832	Cadboro	Active	Polifem	Victoria (Haw.)	15
	Dryad	Bolivar Liberator			
	Eagle	Convoy			
	Lama	Crusader			
	Vancouver	Diana			
		Griffon			
		Hamilton			
		Smyrna			

TABLE 1 (continued)

Year	British	American	Russian	Other	Total
1833	Cadboro Dryad Ganymede Lama Vancouver	Convoy Diana	Chichagov		8
1834	Cadboro Dryad Eagle Lama Nereide Vancouver	Bolivar Liberator Diana Europa Joseph Peabody La Grange	Chichagov Chilkat		13
1835	Cadboro Dryad Ganymede Lama	Bolivar Liberator Diana Europa	Chichagov Chilkat		9
1836	Beaver Cadboro Columbia Dryad Ganymede Lama Nereide	Bolivar Liberator Convoy Diana Europa Joseph Peabody La Grange Loriot Rasselas	Chichagov Chilkat		17
1837	Beaver Cadboro Lama Nereide	Hamilton Jones Loriot	Aktsiya Chichagov		9
1838	Beaver Columbia Lama Nereide	Joseph Peabody Suffolk	Chichagov		7
1839	Beaver Nereide Vancouver	Clementine Joseph Peabody Le Lorio Thomas Perkins	Chichagov Nikolay I		9
1840	Beaver Cadboro Columbia Vancouver	Alciope Don Quixote Joseph Peabody Lausanne	Nikolay I		9

TABLE 1 (continued)

Year	*British*	*American*	*Russian*	*Other*	*Total*
1841	*Beaver* *Cadboro* *Columbia* *Lama*	*Morea*	*Nikolay I*		6

Sources: [Allen], "Log of the Ship *Hamilton*," passim; [Anderson], "Historical Notes," passim; Anonymous, "*Griffon* Brig. Shipping Journal," passim; Anonymous, "*Joseph Peabody*, Brig. Shipping Logbook," passim; Anonymous, "Journal kept on board the Ship Paragon," passim; Anonymous, "Journal of a voyage kept on board Brig Lama," passim; Anonymous, "Logbook of the Ship Pearl," passim; Anonymous, "Logbook of the Snow Polly," passim; Bancroft, *History of the Northwest Coast*, 340–2; "Boardman Letterbook," 2:passim; Corning, "Letters of Sullivan Dorr," passim; Gibson, "Russian America in 1833," 9–10, 12; idem, *Imperial Russia in Frontier America*, 169–71; [Hammatt], C.H. Hammatt Journal, Bryant & Sturgis Papers, passim; Haskins, "Journal of a Fur Trading Voyage," passim; HBCA, B.223/b/24, 36v., B.223/c/1, 113v., 115–16, 120, D.4/121, 27v.; Howay, *List of Trading Vessels*, passim; Hunnewell Papers, passim; Khlebnikov, *Baranov*, passim; [idem], *Colonial Russian America*, passim; idem, "Khronologicheskaya tablitsa Sitkhi," passim; McNeill, "Journal of a Voyage kept onboard Brig Lama," passim; idem, "Journal of a Voyage to the N.W. Coast of North America," passim; Marshall Manuscripts, 1–2: passim; [Martain], "Ship Hamilton Log Book," passim; [idem], "Ship Louisa Log Book," passim; [Mitchell], *Journals of William Fraser Tolmie*, passim; Perkins & Company and Russell & Company Papers, 19:passim; Reynolds, "Journal," 1–2:passim; Rich, *Letters of John McLoughlin 1825–1838*, passim; idem, *Letters of John McLoughlin 1839–1844*, passim; [Suter], "Log of John Suter," passim; Tikhmenev, *History of the Russian-American Company*, 2:passim; Records of the Russian-American Company, USNARS, roll 34:150v., 155v., roll 36:212, roll 37:190v.–91, roll 38:146, roll 39:130v., 252v., 253v., 254v., roll 40:299v.–300, roll 42:445, roll 44:156, roll 45:169; USNARS, Despatches from United States Consuls in Honolulu, 1820–1903, roll 1, vol. 1: passim; Walker, "Supercargo's log of the brig *Lydia*," passim; [Work], *Journal*, 30–32.

This table includes only those ships (but not their tenders) that actually traded or hunted on – rather than merely cleared for – the coast, as well as only those whose sole or main purpose was the procurement of furs; thus, numerous British, Russian, and Spanish naval and scientific vessels are excluded, even though they did obtain some furs (for example, Captain Vancouver's expedition bought 200–400 sea-otter skins at the Kwakiutl village of Chief Cheslakees at the mouth of the Nimpkish River on Vancouver Island in 1792, and 180 from the Bella Coola Indians at Restoration Cove on Burke Channel on the mainland in 1793 [Lamb, *Voyage of George Vancouver*, 2:627n., 3:943]). The Russian ships were chiefly hunting vessels prior to 1832; the other bottoms were trading vessels, except some American ships in the first and second decades of the 1800s that hunted with the Russians on halves and some other American ships in the 1820s and 1830s that were largely freighters of goods to Sitka. Bracketed vessels denote uncertain voyages and bracketed figures uncertain totals.

TABLE 2
Value of American Exports to the Northwest Coast, 1789–1817

Year	Dollar Value	Year	Dollar Value
1789–90	$ 10,362	1803–04	$ 196,059
1790–91	3,380	1804–05	302,859
1791–92	2,483	1805–06	257,799
1792–93	1,586	1806–07	103,710
1793–94	5,383	1807–08	274,705
1794–95	44,063	1808–09	182,356
1795–96	23,510	1809–10	145,918
1796–97	15,607	1810–11	115,473
1797–98	79,515	1811–12	30,448
1798–99	72,941	1812–13	24,567
1799–1800	746,153	1813–14	0
1800–01	343,388	1814–15	170,985
1801–02	0[?]	1815–16	240,962
1802–03	58,500	1816–17	1,110,839

Source: Great Britain, *Sessional Papers* 7:186.

TABLE 3
Value of American Fur Sales at Canton, 1820–41

Season	Dollar Value	Season	Dollar Value
1820–21	$142,399	1830–31	$ 42,396
1821–22	78,158	1831–32	129,570
1822–23	100,910	1832–33	109,695
1823–24	89,939	1833–34	8,383
1824–25	33,130	1834–35	49,964
1825–26	45,110	1835–36	34,888
1826–27	100,986	1836–37	561
1827–28	101,764	1837–38	37,864
1828–29	80,180	1838–39	16,794
1829–30	10,306	1839–40	0
		1840–41	2,368

Sources: Anonymous, "Fur Trade with Canton," 226; United States, *House Document No. 35*, 8.

TABLE 4
Hudson's Bay Company Ships in the Coast Trade, 1825–41

Vessel	Tonnage	Launching	Purchase	Fate
William and Ann	161	1818	1824	lost (1829)
Cadboro	71	1826	1826	sold (1846?)
Eagle	193	1824	1827	sold (1837)
Isabella	195	?	1829	lost (1830)
Dryad	204	1825	1829	sold (1836)
Ganymede	214	1827	1830	sold (1837?)
Lama	150	1826	1831	sold (1837)
Nereide	253	1821	1833	sold (1840)
Beaver	109	1835	1835	sold (1874)
Columbia	308	1835	1835	sold (1850?)
Vancouver	?	1838	1838	lost (1848)
Cowlitz	?	1840	1840	sold (1851)

Sources: "Marine," HBCA, A. 7/1; Rich, Letters of John McLoughlin 1825–1838, passim; idem, Letters of John McLoughlin 1839–1844, passim.

TABLE 5
American and British Returns of Sea and Land Furs from the Coast Trade, 1835–38

Year	Sea Furs		Land Furs	
	American	British	American	British
1835	89	254	4,850	12,051
1836	43	130	2,197	12,930
1837	0	108	0	13,907
1838	0	136	0	14,011

Source: Work to Douglas, 28 October 1838, HBCA, B.223/c/1.

TABLE 6
Number of Foreign Ships Trading at Canton, 1787–1833

Season	American	British Company	British Private	Others	Total
1787–88	5	29	24	12	70
1788–89	4	26	24	12	66
1789–90	15	21	37	7	80
1790–91	6	25	21	7	59
1791–92	3	11	12	8	35
1792–93	6	16	23	12	57
1793–94	6	18	22	5	51
1794–95	7	21	23	7	58
1795–96	10	16	17	4	47
1796–97	11	23	17	3	54
1797–98	11	18	22	6	57
1798–99	13	16	16	6	51
1799–1800	18	15	15	4	52
1800–01	23	19	21	7	70
1801–02	36	26	6	3	71
1802–03	32	19	19	12	82
1803–04	23	18	25	4	70
1804–05	34–36	21	18	4	77–79
1805–06	41–42	17	36	7	100–101
1806–07	37–38	19	60	2	118–119
1807–08	30–33	14	37	0	81–84
1808–09	8	15	39	0	62
1809–10	37	14	26	2	79
1810–11	15–16	15	19	0	49–50
1811–12	25–27	19	25	0	69–71
1812–13	8–17	23	13	0	44–53
1813–14	?	20	18	0	?
1814–15	13	22	23	0	58
1815–16	21–30	24	23	5	73–82
1816–17	17–38	28	39	3	87–108
1817–18	33–39	16	39	0	88–94
1818–19	44–47	16	35	0	95–98
1819–20	39–43	24	17	0	80–84

TABLE 6 (continued)

Season	American	British Company	Private	Others	Total
1820–21	25–26	23	27	0	75–76
1821–22	42–45	21	36	0	99–102
1822–23	31–40	19	21	0	71–80
1823–24	34–35	21	24	0	79–80
1824–25	37–43	21	30	0	88–94
1825–26	42	22	39	0	103
1826–27	19–26	34	51	8	112–119
1827–28	20–29	28	42	0	90–99
1828–29	31	20	53	13	117
1829–30	40	25	47	17	129
1830 31	25	22	50	12	109
1831–32	41	25	68	14	148
1832–33	62	23	67	21	173

Sources: Great Britain, Sessional Papers 5:20; Morse, Chronicles of the East India Company, 2:136, 152, 173, 180, 193, 205, 256, 266, 278, 294, 311, 322, 348, 358, 389, 401, 416; 3:2, 27, 55, 77, 101, 131, 158, 175, 190, 206, 228, 243–4, 308, 331, 347, 369; 4:4, 53, 71, 89, 103, 123, 145, 162, 185, 223, 253, 325, 343.

TABLE 7
Fur Imports by American Vessels at Canton, 1804–34 and 1836–37

Season	Beaver	Fox	Fur Seal	Land Otter	Sea Otter	Others[1]	Total
1804–05	8,756	0	183,000	0	11,003	67,000	269,759
1805–06	34,460	0	140,297	0	17,445	3,400	195,602
1806–07	23,368	0	261,000	0	14,251	0	298,619
1807–08	11,750	2,009	100,000	0	16,647	0	130,406
1808–09	5,170	0	34,000	3,400	7,944	0	50,514
1809–10	20,000	3,500	0	15,000	11,003	0	49,503
1810–11	14,200	4,500	45,000	15,000	9,200	5,525	93,425
1811–12	20,000	0	173,000	12,000	11,593	149,736	366,329
1812–13	2,320	0	109,000	2,000	8,222	1,200	122,742
1813–15	3,928	284	59,000	7,045	6,200	0	76,457
1815–16	168	12,533	109,000	14,364	4,300	0	140,365
1816–17	1,579	9,932	27,000	5,467	3,650	17,000	64,628
1817–18	15,607	350	47,290	9,400	4,177	7,968	84,792
1818–19	15,172	3,050	91,500	8,578	4,714	40,000	163,014
1819–20	16,837	16,821	24,726	12,197	2,488	3,630	76,699
1820–21	2,870	8,967	13,887	5,927	3,575	9,254	44,480
1821–22	17,778	17,884	111,924	9,716	3,507	16,427	177,236
1822–23	21,451	20,410	11,330	16,318	2,953	7,420	79,882
1823–24	4,388	17,986	12,094	10,873	3,547	108,846	157,734
1824–25	2,532	19,479	52,043	18,532	1,921	6,267	100,774
1825–26	4,886	10,188	32,521	14,833	2,250	930	65,608
1826–27	4,950	12,852	36,822	14,525	1,662	0	70,811
1827–28	5,143	16,763	39,546	18,938	1,082	0	81,472
1828–29	6,127	30,292	28,285	16,354	1,062	0	82,120
1829–30	0	19,683	11,902	12,884	700	0	45,169
1830–31	0	5,263	6,022	6,454	329	0	18,068
1831–32	1,828	9,367	71	11,722	1,591	0	42,647
1832–33	1,810	11,903	4	13,203	494	18,253	45,667
1833–34	229	?	0	4,663	?	?	10,210
1836–37	1,465	1,198	0	6,773	560	0	9,996

Sources: Anonymous, "English and American trade," 284; Anonymous, "Fur trade," 558; Gutzlaff, Sketch of Chinese History, 2:Table 4; Morse, Chronicles of the East India Company, 4:384.
1 Muskrat, nutria, rabbit, and sable.

T A B L E 8

Commodity Composition (by Value) of American Imports at Canton, 1817–34[1]

Season	Furs	Opium	Sandalwood	Silver	Others[2]
1817–18	4.3%	8.4%	2.9%	78.8%	5.6%
1818–19	4.5	5.5	1.6	74.7	13.7
1819–20	2.8	1.2	1.2	77.2	17.6
1820–21	3.3	0	1.3	63.7	31.7
1821–22	6.7	5.8	3.7	64.1	19.7
1822–23	3.8	0	1.7	75.5	19.0
1823–24	4.3	2.1	1.1	64.9	27.6
1824–25	3.0	3.2	0.7	72.8	20.3
1825–26	3.3	0	0.4	73.6	32.7
1826–27	6.7	0.8	2.2	47.9	42.4
1827–28	4.2	13.9	3.7	42.5	35.7
1828–29	8.0	24.9	3.8	21.7	42.3
1829–30	4.9	12.8	1.1	28.7	52.5
1830–31	2.6	26.4	1.3	6.0	63.7
1831–32	5.5	7.2	0.2	21.9	65.2
1832–33	3.7	6.4	0.8	19.0	70.1
1833–34	?	12.2	?	16.7	?

Sources: Morse, *Chronicles of the East India Company*, 3:328, 344, 365, 383; 4:20, 67, 84, 99, 118, 139, 158, 181, 195, 248, 271, 339, 369, 384; Pitkin, *Statistical View of the Commerce of the United States*, Table 19, 304.

1   Excluding bills on London.

2   Mostly metals and textiles.

TABLE 9
Prices in Spanish Dollars of Prime Sea-Otter Skins at Canton for Various Years from 1779 to 1832[1]

Season	Price[2]	Season	Price[2]
1779–80	$50–70	1810–11	$21.50
1785–86	37–43	1812–13	23
1786–87	40–90	1815–16	35
1787–88	37.50–50	1817–18	33–34.50
1788–89	70–91	1818–19	30
1789–90	30	1819–20	35–50
1790–91	15–25	1820–21	35–38
1791–92	20–30	1821–22	40
1792–93	25–30	1822–23	45–48
1794–95	15–20	1823–24	38–50
1795–96	9–17	1824–25	30
1796–97	12	1825–26	38.50–45
1799–1800	23–27	1826–27	41–45
1800–01	18–22	1827–28	64
1801–02	20–21	1828–29	53
1802–03	20	1829–30	64
1805–06	17–19	1830–31	68
1807–08	17	1831–32	60–75
1808–09	30		

Sources: Anonymous, "Journal of a Voyage Round the World on the Brig Rob Roy," 6 December 1822; Boardman to Barker, 1 August 1831, 1 May and 8 September 1832, Boardman Letterbook; Bryant and Sturgis to Clark, 31 August 1818, Bryant and Sturgis to Suter, 16 August 1820, Bryant and Sturgis and Boardman and Pope to Barker and Pierce, 29 October 1827, and C. H. Hammatt Journal, 42, Bryant and Sturgis Papers; Choris, *Voyage pittoresque,* "Port San-Francisco et ses habitants," 7; Cleveland, *Narrative,* 1:100; Corning, "Sullivan Dorr," 170; idem, "Letters of Sullivan Dorr," 183, 190, 197, 198, 231, 290, 353; Dixon, *Voyage Round the World,* 316–19; Fleurieu, *Voyage Round the World,* 2:71–2; Haskins, "Journal of a Fur Trading Voyage," 255; Holmes, *Captain Cook's Final Voyage,* 154; Howay, "Letters Relating to the Second Voyage of the Columbia," 149; idem, *Journal of Captain James Colnett,* 237; idem, *Voyages of the "Columbia",* 129, 470, 488, 490, 491; idem, *List of Trading Vessels,* 117, 135; Goddard to Colville Jutting and Co., 1 April 1823, HBCA, A. 7/1; Allen to Hunnewell, 18 March 1829, Hunnewell Papers; Jackman, *Journal of William Sturgis,* 113, 115, 117, 120; Kaplanoff, *Joseph Ingraham's Journal,* 182; Lamb, "Notes on Trade with the Northwest Coast," 25, 53; Leder, "American Trade to China," 216–17; Lisiansky, *Voyage Round the World,* 281; Macnair, "Log of the Caroline," 200; Pitman and French to Marshall, 25 April 1823, Jones to Marshall and Wildes, 21 February and 12 March 1824, Sturgis to Marshall, 28 May 1826, Wildes to Marshall, 21 February 1827, Jones to Marshall, 4 October 1830, Marshall Manuscripts; Morse, *Chronicles of the East India Company,* 2:358, 4:91; Perkins to Perkins, 23 January and 25 February 1820, Perkins and Company to J. and T.H. Perkins, 30 December 1820 and 28 February 1821, Perkins to Perkins, 14 January and 28 February 1821, Perkins Letterbooks; J. and T.H. Perkins to McGillevray, 16 August 1809, in J. and T.H. Perkins, Foreign letters; Pipes, "Later Affairs of Kendrick," 100; Porter, *John Jacob Astor,* 1:454; Reynolds, Journal, 1:263; Rich, *Part of Dispatch,* 135; Roe, *Journal and Letters,* 109, 175, 182–3; USNARS, "Despatches from United States Consuls in Canton, 1790–1906," roll 1: Kendrick to Barrell, 28 March 1792, Howell to Barrell *et al.,* 11 May 1795,

Satement of the American Trade with Canton Season of 1823–24; Walbran, "Cruise of the Imperial Eagle," 14; Walker, *Account of a Voyage*, 199, 274n.

1   This table excludes pieces and tails, which were much less valuable than whole skins; for example, in 1802–03 prime skins brought $20 and tails $2 (Haskins, "Journal of a Fur Trading Voyage," 255).

2   Of all of the furs imported by Canton, sea-otter skins were by far the most valuable. In 1801–02 sea otters were worth $22, beavers $6, and fur seals $.80 (Morse, *Chronicles of the East India Company*, 2:358); in 1810–11 sea otters fetched $21.50, beavers $6.50, and fur seals $2 (Porter, *John Jacob Astor*, 1:454); and in 1824–25 sea otters brought $30, beavers $4.76, and land otters $4.32 (Morse, *Chronicles of the East India Company*, 4:91). By 1831 the Canton market for beaver and fur-seal pelts was so depressed that the former sold for $4–4.50 in Canton but $8 in Boston and the latter were "worth more in the United States than any where else" (Boardman to Barker, 7 October 1831, Boardman Letterbook); consequently, Captain Seth Barker of the *Hamilton* was ordered by the owner, William Boardman, to "get all your Furrs home excepting the Sea otters as the difference betwen the Canton & U States prices, is, in itself a voyage" (ibid.).

Notes

ABBREVIATIONS

AVPR Arkhiv Vneshney politiki Rossii [Archive of the Foreign Policy
      of Russia] (Moscow, USSR)
BCPA British Columbia Provincial Archives (Victoria)
  d. *delo* [archival file]
  f. *fond* [archival collection]
GAPO Gosudarstvenny arkhiv Permskoy oblasti [State Archive of
      Perm Oblast] (Perm, USSR)
HBCA Hudson's Bay Company Archives (Winnipeg)
 ms. manuscript
  n. note
 n.p. no pagination; no publisher
USNARS United States National Archives and Records Service
      (Washington, DC)
  v. verso

PREFACE

1 See Lamb, "Bibliography," 27–51.
2 See Fisher, "Arms and Men," 3–18; idem, *Contact and Conflict*, Chapter
  1; idem, "Indian Control," 65–86.
3 Fisher, *Contact and Conflict*, xiv.
4 Gibson, "Maritime Trade," 375–90.

INTRODUCTION

1 See, for example, Scouler, "Observations on the Indigenous Tribes,"
  218.
2 See Drucker, *Indians of the Northwest Coast*; idem, *Cultures of the North
  Pacific Coast*; Gunther, *Indian Life on the Northwest Coast*; McFeat, *Indians of the North Pacific Coast*; Suttles, *Northwest Coast*.

3 Dunn, *History of the Oregon Territory*, 290–1; Howay, *Voyages of the "Columbia"*, 194; Jackman, *Journal of William Sturgis*, 44.

4 Thwaites, *Original Journals*, 3:119, 122–3, 128, 130, 146, 149–50, 165–70, 172, 206–9, 309–10. Also see ibid., 4:276–7.

5 Ibid., 4:78–9.

6 [Colnett], "Voyage to the N.W. Side of America," 123v.; Fleurieu, *Voyage Round the World*, 1:206; Jane, *Spanish Voyage*, 48; Lamb, *Voyage of George Vancouver*, 2:548, 565; Scouler, "John Scouler's Journal," 196, 201; Wagner, *Spanish Explorations*, 256. Also see Amoss, "Little More than Kind," 292–305; Gunther, *Indian Life on the Northwest Coast*, 76, 259–60.

7 See Gustafson, *Salish Weaving*.

8 See Turner and Taylor, "Review."

9 Dixon, *Voyage Round the World*, 175, Howay, *Voyages of the "Columbia"*, 206. By contrast, the Yuroks, as an American seaman noted in 1788, "smoak tobacco out of a small wooden tube about the size of [a] Childs wistle" (Howay, *Voyages of the "Columbia"*, 29–30).

10 Howay, *Voyages of the "Columbia"*, 29–30.

11 Lamb, *Voyage of George Vancouver*, 4:1,357.

12 Haskins, "Journal of a Fur Trading Voyage," 234, 250. Also see ibid., 68.

13 Furgerson, "Journal of a Voyage from Boston to the Northwest Coast," 4 November 1810. Also see ibid., 2 November.

14 Walker, *Account of a Voyage*, 43, 80.

15 See Gunther, *Ethnobotany of Western Washington*; Stewart, *Cedar: Tree of Life*; Turner, *Food Plants of British Columbia Indians*.

16 Meares, *Voyages Made in the Years 1788 and 1789*, lxxi.

17 [Scouler], "John Scouler's Journal," 176.

18 See Stewart, *Indian Fishing*. Also see idem, *Artifacts of the Northwest Coast Indians*.

19 Meares, *Voyages Made in the Years 1788 and 1789*, Appendix A.

20 Green, *Journal of a Tour*, 85–6.

21 Goddard to Colville Jutting and Company, 1 April 1823, HBCA, A.7/1; Williams, *London Correspondence Inward*, 65.

22 Howay, *Voyages of the "Columbia"*, 284.

23 Meares, *Voyages Made in the Years 1788 and 1789*, 241.

24 Thwaites, *Original Journals*, 3:238, 4:99, 101.

25 [Sturgis], "Northwest Fur Trade," 534.

26 Walker, *Account of a Voyage*, 127, 146.

27 Meares, *Voyages Made in the Years 1788 and 1789*, 242–3.

28 Ibid., 243.

29 Fyodorova, *Russkaya Amerika*, 89.

30 Ibid., 88n., 89.

31 [Roe], *Journal and Letters*, 128.

32 Meares, *Voyages Made in the Years 1788 and 1789*, 253, 258; Moziño, *Noticias de Nutka*, 14.

33 Meares, *Voyages Made in the Years 1788 and 1789*, 260–1.

34 Haskins, "Journal of a Fur Trading Voyage," 34.

35 Meany, *New Vancouver Journal*, 8.

36 [Puget], "Log of the Proceedings of His Majesty's Armed Tender Chatham," 52.

37 Suttles, "Variation in Habitat and Culture," 536.

38 Meares, *Voyages Made in the Years 1788 and 1789*, 120–1.

39 [Ingraham], "Ingraham to Martínez," 17.

40 Newcombe, *Menzies' Journal*, 80–1.

41 See, for example, Heizer, "Introduction of Monterey Shells," 399–402. Also see Samuel, *Chilkat Dancing Blanket*.

42 Ross, *Adventures of the First Settlers*, 95–6.

43 [Sturgis], "Ms. of 3 lectures," lecture 2, 7.

44 [Sturgis], "Northwest Fur Trade," 34.

45 Lamb, *Voyage of George Vancouver*, 2:572–3.

46 Thwaites, *Original Journals*, 6:115–17. On the Chinooks, see Ruby and Brown, *Chinook Indians*.

47 Howay, *Voyages of the "Columbia"*, 397.

48 Thwaites, *Original Journals*, 3:217.

49 Lamb, "Notes on Trade with the Northwest Coast," 41–3.

50 Thwaites, *Original Journals*, 4:288–9. Also see ibid., 297.

51 Ross, *Adventures of the First Settlers*, 118.

52 Thwaites, *Original Journals*, 3:185.

53 Ibid., 343–4.

54 Ibid., 338.

55 Ibid., 81–2.

56 See Howay, "Origin of the Chinook Jargon," 225–50.

57 On late prehistoric and early historic Indian forts, grease trails, and trade in the Skeena River basin, see MacDonald, *Kitwanga Fort National Historic Site*.

58 Karamanski, *Fur Trade and Exploration*, 269–72.

CHAPTER ONE

1 Lisiansky, *Voyage Round the World*, 285.

2 Makarova, *Russians on the Pacific*, 209–17.

3 Dixon, *Voyage Round the World*, 322.

4 Khlebnikov, *Baranov*, 12–14.

5 Ibid., 15.

6 Khlebnikov, "Khronologicheskaya tablitsa Sitkhi," 2.

7 Ibid.

8 Ibid., 13.

9 Khlebnikov, *Baranov*, 34.

10 Ibid., 3.

11 Anonymous, "Ship Hancock Log Book," 26 April–9 May, 19 June 1799.

12 Ibid., 5.

13 Portlock, *Voyage Round the World*, 105.

14 [Khlebnikov], "Okhota," 1-1v.

15 Lamb, *Voyage of George Vancouver*, 4:1,309.

16 Golovin, *Civil and Savage Encounters*, 138.

17 Litke, *Voyage Around the World*, 1:59.

18 Records of the Russian-American Company, USNARS, roll 36:172–3.

19 Ibid., roll 42:403v., 446.

20 Anonymous to Loch Bros., 1823, HBCA, A.7/1.

21 Sladkovskii, *History of Economic Relations*, 60, 60n.

22 Meares, *Voyages Made in the Years 1788 and 1789*, lxxxvi.

23 Fu, *Documentary Chronicle*, 1:366.

24 Lisiansky, *Voyage Round the World*, 242.

25 Von Langsdorff, *Voyages and Travels*, 2:130.

26 Lamb, *Voyage of George Vancouver*, 4:1,337n.

27 Von Langsdorff, *Voyages and Travels*, 2:85.

28 Ibid., 113.

29 Lazarev, *Zapiski o plavanii*, 283.

30 Fyodorova, *Russkaya Amerika*, 112.

31 Jackman, *Journal of William Sturgis*, 80; Scouler, "Observations on the Indigenous Tribes," 219.

32 For more details on Russian participation in the maritime fur trade vis-à-vis the United States and Great Britain, see Gibson, "Russian Fur Trade." On Russian-Native relations in Russian America, see idem, "European Dependence Upon American Natives."

33 Lamb, *Voyage of George Vancouver*, 4:1,405.

34 Shaler, "Journal of a Voyage," 161.

35 Newcombe, *Menzies' Journal*, 128.

36 On Spanish interest in, and activities on, the Northwest Coast, see Archer, "Transient Presence"; idem, "Spanish Exploration and Settlement"; Cook, *Flood Tide of Empire*. Also see Gormly, "Early Culture Contact."

37 Milet-Mureau, *Voyage Round the World*, 1:457.

38 Moziño, *Noticias de Nutka*, 95–7.

39 Ibid., 95.

40 See Ogden, *California Sea Otter Trade*; idem, "Californias in Spain's Pacific Otter Trade."

41 Cook, *Flood Tide of Empire*, 108; Milet-Mureau, *Voyage Round the World*, 1:458; Shaler, "Journal of a Voyage," 151.
42 Cook, *Flood Tide of Empire*, 107–11; Ogden, "Californias in Spain's Pacific Otter Trade," passim.
43 Howay, *Voyages of the "Columbia"*, 31; Kaplanoff, *Joseph Ingraham's Journal*, 178.
44 Thurman, *Naval Department of San Blas*, 324–5.
45 See Ogden, "Russian Sea-Otter and Seal Hunting."

CHAPTER TWO

1 See Gough, "James Cook."
2 Holmes, *Captain Cook's Final Voyage*, 72.
3 Beaglehole, *Journals of Captain James Cook*, vol. 3, pt. 1:371–2.
4 Cook [and King], *Voyage to the Pacific Ocean*, 3:437; Lloyd and Anderson, *Memoir of John Trevenen*, 21–2; Munford, *John Ledyard's Journal*, 70.
5 Cook [and King], *Voyage to the Pacific Ocean*, 3:440.
6 Irving, *Astoria*, 13.
7 Lamb, *Voyage of George Vancouver*, 1:273–4.
8 Dixon, *Voyage Round the World*, xx-xxi; Fleurieu, *Voyage Round the World*, 1:lxxx; Portlock, *Voyage Round the World*, 2.
9 Anonymous, "New Fur Trade"; Dixon, *Voyage Round the World*, 315–16; Walker, *Account of a Voyage*, 199.
10 Walker, *Account of a Voyage*, 203.
11 On Hanna's voyages and his backer, see Lamb and Bartoli, "James Hanna and John Henry Cox."
12 Dixon, *Voyage Round the World*, 236.
13 Portlock, *Voyage Round the World*, 294, 382.
14 Dixon, *Voyage Round the World*, 303, 321.
15 Meares, *Voyages Made in the Years 1788 and 1789*, lxviii.
16 On the failure of British coast ventures on the King model between the middle 1780s and the early 1790s, see Mackay, *In the wake of Cook*, Chapter 3, especially 73–7. Mackay's weakly documented remarks on the Russian trade should be used with caution, however.
17 Dixon, *Voyage Round the World*, xviii-xix.
18 Meares, *Voyages Made in the Years 1788 and 1789*, lxix, 112, 120–1.
19 De Roquefeuil, *Journal d'un voyage*, 2:76.
20 Portlock, *Voyage Round the World*, 4.
21 Howay, *Journal of Captain James Colnett*, Appendix I, 297–305, Appendix II, 306–7.
22 Portlock, *Voyage Round the World*, 382.

23 O'Neil, "Maritime Activities," 265.

24 At the same time, the captains, officers, and supercargoes of the EIC's ships conducted a private trade at Canton in both imports and exports, including fur imports. Beaver skins were introduced to Canton through this private trade in 1785, fox and land-otter skins in 1786, and fur-seal skins in 1792; altogether 27,628 skins were imported privately in 1788, 108,471 (including 51,440 beaver and 48,936 fox and only 3,126 sea-otter) in 1798 (the peak year), and 14,.668 in 1813 (Pritchard, "Private Trade Between England and China," 133). The sea-otter skins were likely derived from British coasters.

25 "Account of Beaver Skins Returns from the Trade of the NWCO ...," 1 September 1823, HBCA, A.7/1.

26 Great Britain, Sessional Papers 7:92–3, 134. The licence granted by the EIC to the NWC in 1813 for the Isaac Tod is printed in full in ibid., 94–100.

27 United States, Senate Documents, 1, 6–7.

28 Keith, "Fort George on the Columbia," 14, 21, 23, 26.

29 Perkins and Company to the HBC, 10 September 1822, Perkins and Company and Russell and Company Papers.

30 Perkins and Company to J. and T.H. Perkins, 25 February, 11 March 1820, Perkins and Company and Russell and Company Papers. Also see Perkins and Company to J. and T.H. Perkins, 28 February 1821, Perkins and Company and Russell and Company Papers.

31 Perkins and Company to the HBC, 10 September 1822, Perkins and Company and Russell and Company Papers.

32 Keith, "Fort George on the Columbia," 25, Table 5.

33 Anonymous to Loch Bros., 15 July 1823, HBCA, A.7/1. Also see Merk, Fur Trade and Empire, 207–8.

34 Morison, Maritime History of Massachusetts, 65.

35 Portlock, Voyage Round the World, 4.

36 For an account by the captain of one of the British vessels that was seized at Nootka Sound, see Howay, Journal of Captain James Colnett.

37 Wagner and Newcombe, "Journal of Jacinto Caamaño," 273.

38 Von Krusenstern, Voyage Round the World, 2:332–3.

39 Kaplanoff, Joseph Ingraham's Journal, 105–6, 117, 119, 120, 127–9, 143–4.

40 Magee, "Log of the Jefferson," passim, especially 2 April, 17–19, 22 June, 8–9 July, 2 August 1794; Roe, Journal and Letters, 82, 97. On Haida wooden carving, sculpting, and building, see MacDonald, Haida Monumental Art.

41 "Journal of the Hudson's Bay Company," 1 November 1836.

42 Anonymous, "Ship Hancock Log Book," 20 July, 18 August 1799.

43 Ibid., 27–28 April 1799.

44 Jackman, *Journal of William Sturgis*, 65; [Sturgis], "Northwest Fur Trade," 536.

45 [Sturgis], "Ms. of 3 lectures," lecture 2, 8–10.

46 [Martain], "Ship Hamilton Log Book," Joseph Ford [to T. Brown], 1812, enclosure at end of log.

47 Tikhmenev, *History of the Russian-American Company*, 2:112.

48 Von Kotzebue, *New Voyage Round the World*, 2:64.

49 Sturgis to Cushing, 23 March 1812, Bryant and Sturgis Papers.

50 Finlayson, "Trip Across to the Columbia 1831," HBCA, E.12/2.

51 Morison, *Maritime History of Massachusetts*, 76–7.

52 Lamb, "Notes on Trade with the Northwest Coast," n.p.

53 Bryant and Sturgis to Suter, 6 August 1816, Bryant and Sturgis Papers.

54 Bryant and Sturgis to Clark, 1 December 1817, Bryant and Sturgis Papers.

55 Bryant and Sturgis to Hale, 31 August 1818, Bryant and Sturgis Papers.

56 Bryant and Sturgis to Suter, 20 June, 12 October 1820, Bryant and Sturgis Papers; Morison, "Boston Traders on Hawaiian Islands," 180–1.

57 [Martain], "Ship Louisa Log Book," [125], enclosure d.

58 [Suter], "Log of the ship Atahualpa," [1].

59 A. Simpson to McLoughlin, 22 September 1828, HBCA, B.223/c/1.

60 Lamb, "Notes on Trade with the Northwest Coast," n.p., 23.

61 A. Simpson to McLoughlin, 22 September 1828, HBCA, B.223/c/1.

62 Anonymous, "Account Book Ship Sultan," passim.

63 Bryant and Sturgis to Suter, 6 August 1816, Bryant and Sturgis Papers.

64 Bryant and Sturgis to Harris, 17 July 1820, Bryant and Sturgis Papers.

65 Fyodorova, *Russkaya Amerika*, 138.

66 [Dorr], ["Logbook of the *Hope*"], 27 November 1791.

67 [Allen], "Log of the Ship *Hamilton*," 23 November 1820.

68 Corning, "Letters of Sullivan Dorr," 182, 201.

69 Von Krusenstern, *Voyage Round the World*, 2:332.

70 Von Kotzebue, *New Voyage Round the World*, 2:65.

71 Cleveland, *Narrative*, 2:49.

72 MacNair, "Log of the Caroline," 69n., 75–8.

73 Despatches from United States Consuls in Canton, 1790–1906, USNARS, roll 1, Kendrick to Barrell, 28 March 1792.

74 Finlayson, "Trip Across to the Columbia 1831," HBCA, E.12/2.

75 Bryant and Sturgis to Suter, 6 August 1816, Bryant and Sturgis Papers.

76 Bryant and Sturgis to Clark, 1 December 1817, Bryant and Sturgis to Hale, 31 August 1818, Bryant and Sturgis Papers.

77 Bryant and Sturgis to Harris, 17 July 1820, Bryant and Sturgis Papers.

78 Von Kotzebue, *New Voyage Round the World*, 2:64.

79 Hill, *Trade and Commerce of Boston*, 117–18.

CHAPTER THREE

1 Pigot [to Ebbets], 7 January 1816, Astor Papers; Krooss and Gilbert, *American Business History*, 80–1.

2 Fleurieu, *Voyage Round the World*, 1:xcvii–xcviii.

3 Dennett, *Americans in Eastern Asia*, 6.

4 [Bond], "Letters of Phineas Bond," 540.

5 Dennett, *Americans in Eastern Asia*, 8.

6 Krooss and Gilbert, *American Business History*, 79.

7 Fleurieu, *Voyage Round the World*, 1:xcviii.

8 Munford, *John Ledyard's Journal*, 70, 201; Sparks, *Memoirs*, 174–210.

9 Beals, *For Honor & Country*, 86–9.

10 See Howay, *Voyages of the "Columbia"*.

11 Anonymous, "Return of American Vessels"; Lamb, *Voyage of George Vancouver*, 3:844n.; Dorr, "Journal of a Voyage from Boston round the World," 17 September 1790.

12 Anonymous, "Ship Hancock Log Book," 24 August 1798.

13 Anonymous, "*Griffon*, Brig. Shipping Journal," 24 October 1824.

14 [Martain], "Ship Louisa Log Book," 7 October 1826.

15 Bryant and Sturgis to Harris, 17 July 1820, Bryant and Sturgis Papers.

16 Bryant and Sturgis to Cross, 14 August 1821, Bryant and Sturgis Papers.

17 Anonymous, "Ship Hancock Log Book," 1–2 August 1798; McNeill, "Journal of a Voyage to the N.W. Coast of North America," 25 October 1824; Magee, "Log of the Jefferson," June 1792; [Suter], "Log of John Suter," 18 August 1816.

18 Dorr, "Journal of a Voyage from Boston round the World," 3 November 1790.

19 Anonymous, "Journal of a voyage perform'd on the Ship Amethyst," 2.

20 Anonymous, "Journal kept on board the Ship Paragon," 15–16 February 1819.

21 [Allen], "Log of the Ship *Hamilton*," 21 June 1821.

22 Anonymous, "Journal of a Voyage Round the World on the Brig Rob Roy," 9 November 1821.

23 [Brown?], "Journal from New London Towards the Falkland Islands," 20 December 1799.

24 Anonymous, "Journal of a voyage perform'd on the Ship Amethyst," 2.

25 Anonymous, "Journal kept on board the Ship Paragon," 15 May 1819.

26 Anonymous, "Journal of a Voyage Round the World on the Brig Rob Roy," 6 May 1823.

27 D'Wolf, *Voyage to the North Pacific*, 17; Hunnewell to Bryant and Sturgis, 31 August 1829, Hunnewell Papers; Kaplanoff, *Joseph Ingraham's Journal*, 1; Roe, *Journal and Letters*, 70.

28 [Allen], "Log of the Ship *Hamilton*," passim.

29 Furgerson, "Journal of a Voyage from Boston to the Northwest Coast," 15–20 July 1810.

30 Magee, "Log of the Jefferson," 1 August, September–October 1793.

31 [Martain], "Ship Hamilton Log Book," 19–21, 23–25 November 1810.

32 McNeill, "Journal of a Voyage to the N.W. Coast of North America," 19 July 1825.

33 Walker, *Account of a Voyage*, 178.

34 Ibid., 115; Fleurieu, *Voyage Round the World*, 1:221.

35 [Strange], *Journal and Narrative*, 21.

36 Howay, *Voyages of the "Columbia,"* 356; Magee, "Log of the Jefferson," 24 February 1793, March 1794.

37 Khlebnikov, "Khronologicheskaya tablitsa Sitkhi," 5; Lisiansky, *Voyage Round the World*, 265–6.

38 Meares, *Voyages Made in the Years 1788 and 1789*, lxxiii, 191.

39 Korn, "Shadows of Destiny," 28.

40 Howay, *Voyages of the "Columbia"*, 418.

41 Fleurieu, *Voyage autour du monde*, 1:410. Also see Fleurieu, *Voyage Round the World*, 2:8.

42 Stewart, *Visit to the South Seas*, 2:214–15.

43 Dixon, *Voyage Round the World*, 83.

44 Cook [and King], *Voyage to the Pacific Ocean*, 2:193–4, 199.

45 Lamb, *Voyage of George Vancouver*, 3:855–6.

46 [Brown?], "Journal from New London Towards the Falkland Islands," 18 July 1801.

47 Shaler, "Journal of a Voyage," 166.

48 Anonymous, "Voyage of an expedition," 35.

49 Von Kotzebue, *Voyage of Discovery*, 1:90–1, 327, 352.

50 [Rickman], *Journal of Captain Cook's Last Voyage*, 223, 226.

51 Howay, "Captains Gray and Kendrick," 260; idem, *Voyages of the "Columbia"*, 129; Meares, *Voyages Made in the Years 1788 and 1789*, 276.

52 Magee, "Log of the Jefferson," 30 March 1793.

53 Anonymous, "Ship Hancock Log Book," 8–14, 16–18 October 1799; Clinton, "Journal," 24 February 1805.

54 Bartlett, "John Bartlett's journal," 44; Dorr, "Journal of a Voyage from Boston round the World," 23 May 1791.

55 Portlock, *Voyage Round the World*, 146.

56 [Colnett], "Voyage to the N.W. Side of America," 171, 176.

57 Dixon, *Voyage Round the World*, 265–6.

58 Golovnin, *Around the World on the "Kamchatka"*, 213, 215–17.

59 Anonymous, "Journal of a voyage perform'd on the Ship Amethyst," 41–2.

60 Beaglehole, *Journals of Captain James Cook*, vol. 3, pt. 2:1,322; Holmes, *Captain Cook's Final Voyage*, 64.

61 Lamb, *Voyage of George Vancouver*, 2:475n.

62 Ibid., 3:811111.

63 Clinton, "Journal," 23–24 February 1805.

64 Roe, *Journal and Letters*, 101.

65 [Rickman], *Journal of Captain Cook's Last Voyage*, 294.

66 L., *Voyage Round the World*, 118.

67 Grant, *Life and Adventures of John Nicol*, 96–7.

68 Howay, *Voyages of the "Columbia"*, 418.

69 Ross, *Adventures of the First Settlers*, 46.

70 Dorr, "Journal of a Voyage from Boston round the World," 17 April 1791.

71 Franchère, *Journal of a Voyage*, 66; Hayes, *Log of the Union*, 70.

72 Beaglehole, *Journals of Captain James Cook*, vol. 3, pt. 2:1,083–5.

73 Lamb, *Voyage of George Vancouver*, 2:462.

74 Ibid., 475n.

75 Anonymous, "Log-book of the Brig Lydia," 26 August 1805.

76 Anonymous, "Journal of a voyage perform'd on the Ship Amethyst," 42.

77 Choris, *Voyage pittoresque*, "Isles Sandwich," 5–6, 9.

78 Von Chamisso, *Voyage Around the World*, 119, 312.

79 Campbell, *Voyage Round the World*, 188, 202.

80 Bartlett, "John Bartlett's journal," 45–6.

81 Anonymous, "Voyage of an expedition," 32.

82 Walker, "Supercargo's log of the brig *Lydia*," 41.

83 Howay, *Voyage of the "New Hazard"*, 46.

84 See, for example, Cleveland, *Narrative*, 1:97.

85 Anonymous, "Log-book of the Brig Lydia," 128.

86 Pierrepont, "Notes on the Trade of China," 20.

87 Maury Abstract Logs 1796–1861, USNARS, roll 72, target 2, volume 272, "Ship *Caledonia*," 31 December 1823.

88 Howay, *Voyages of the "Columbia"*, 129.
89 Dennett, *Americans in Eastern Asia*, 45.
90 Hunter, *"Fan Kwae" at Canton*, 103.
91 Gibson, "Observations on the Trade with the Chinese," [5].
92 Ibid., 34–5.
93 Ibid., 53.
94 Dobell, *Travels in Kamtchatka and Siberia*, 2:185.
95 Williams, "Recollections of China," 3.
96 Cleveland, *Voyages and Commercial Enterprises*, 72.
97 Hunter, *"Fan Kwae" at Canton*, 60.
98 Cumming, *Wanderings in China*, 2:54.
99 Pitman and French to Marshall, 1 December 1822, 1 February 1823, Marshall Manuscripts.
100 Meares, *Voyages Made in the Years 1788 and 1789*, lxxxvi.
101 Ibid.; Perkins to Smith, 15 November 1823, Perkins and Company and Russell and Company Papers.
102 Great Britain, *Sessional Papers* 5:122.
103 Latourette, "History of Early Relations," 29.
104 Meares, *Voyages Made in the Years 1788 and 1789*, lxxxvii.
105 Anonymous, "Fur trade," 557.
106 Meares, *Voyages Made in the Years 1788 and 1789*, lxxxvi.
107 Goddard to Colville Jutting and Company, 1 April 1823, HBCA, A.7/1.
108 Anonymous, "Fur trade," 553.
109 Anonymous to Loch Bros., 15 July 1823, HBCA, A.7/1.
110 Meares, *Voyages Made in the Years 1788 and 1789*, lxxxvii.
111 Fleurieu, *Voyage Round the World*, 1:xcviii–xcix.
112 Lamb, "Notes on Trade with the Northwest Coast," n.p.
113 Anonymous, "Logbook of the Ship Pearl," 23–24, 27, 30 December 1806, 1, 3, 8 January 1807.
114 [Allen], "Log of the Ship *Hamilton*," 5–7, 9–12, 14 December 1822.
115 MacNair, "Log of the Caroline," 200.
116 Cleveland, *Narrative*, 1:100; Von Krusenstern, *Voyage Round the World*, 2:331–2.
117 Von Krusenstern, *Voyage Round the World*, 2:332.
118 Pierrepont, "Notes on the Trade of China," 37.
119 Ibid.
120 Barkley, "Journal of the *Halcyon*," n.p.
121 Parkinson, *Trade in the Eastern Seas*, 118–19.
122 Hill, *Trade and Commerce of Boston*, 113.
123 Latourette, "Voyages of American Ships to China," 255–61.
124 Morison, *Maritime History of Massachusetts*, 261.
125 Dana, *Two Years Before the Mast*, 2:347, 442–3.

126 Morison, *Maritime History of Massachusetts*, 77.
127 "Statement of the Ship Dispatch's Accounts," 30 August 1796, Ebenezer Dorr Papers.
128 Myers, *Life, Voyages and Travels*, 408.
129 Rives, "Vessels Trading on the Northwest Coast," 295.
130 L., "On the Trade of the United States," 363.
131 Great Britain, *Sessional Papers* 7:10.
132 Krooss and Gilbert, *American Business History*, 87.
133 Howay, "Early Days of the Maritime Fur-Trade," 42–3.
134 Dennett, *Americans in Eastern Asia*, 41.
135 L., "On the Trade of the United States," 362.
136 Dennett, *Americans in Eastern Asia*, 41.
137 Rives, "Vessels Trading on the Northwest Coast," 295.
138 Krooss and Gilbert, *American Business History*, 77, 89 5.
139 Corning, "Letters of Sullivan Dorr," 280.
140 Ibid., 262, 280.
141 Jackman, *Journal of William Sturgis*, 117.
142 Corning, "Letters of Sullivan Dorr," 333, 354, 357.
143 Sturgis to Bennett, 27 November 1811, Bryant and Sturgis Papers.
144 [Martain], "Ship Hamilton Log Book," Joseph Ford [to T. Brown], 1812, enclosure at end of log.
145 Bryant and Sturgis to Perkins and Company, 25 March 1812, W. Sturgis to J. Sturgis, 26 March 1812, Bryant and Sturgis Papers.
146 Bryant and Sturgis to J. Sturgis and Company, 28 April 1824, Bryant and Sturgis Papers.
147 Bennett, *Americans in Eastern Asia*, 41; Latourette, "History of Early Relations," 55.
148 Great Britain, *Sessional Papers* 5:141.
149 Grimes to Marshall and Wildes, 11 August 1822, Marshall Manuscripts.
150 Marshall and Wildes to Grimes, 25 October 1823, Marshall Manuscripts.
151 Bryant and Sturgis to Suter, 6 August 1816, Bryant and Sturgis Papers.
152 Grimes to Marshall and Wildes, 5 November 1824, Marshall Manuscripts.
153 Reynolds, "Journal," 2:82, 256.
154 Jones to Marshall, 30 October 1827, Marshall Manuscripts.
155 Ibid.
156 Korn, "Shadows of Destiny," 36.
157 Bryant, Sturgis, and Pope to Pierce, 31 July 1828, Bryant and Sturgis Papers; Hunnewell to Bryant and Sturgis, 15 December 1829, Hunnewell Papers.

158 Bryant and Sturgis to Bennett, 16 March 1824, Bryant and Sturgis Papers; Jones to Marshall, 30 October 1827, Marshall Manuscripts; Dominis to Marshall, 14 June 1829, Marshall Manuscripts.
159 Dominis to Marshall, 14 June 1829, Marshall Manuscripts.
160 Boardman to Barker, 22 May 1832, Boardman Letterbook.
161 Boardman to Barker, 7 June 1831, Boardman Letterbook; Krooss and Gilbert, *American Business History*, 84.
162 [Morrison], *Chinese Commercial Guide*, 124.
163 Howay, "Early Days of the Maritime Fur-Trade," 44.

CHAPTER FOUR

1 Anonymous to Loch Bros., 15 July 1823, HBCA, A.7/1.
2 Records of the Russian-American Company, USNARS, roll 31:76.
3 Gibson, *Farming the Frontier*, 201, Table 30; Rich, *Letters of John McLoughlin 1825–1838*, 337–8.
4 McLoughlin to the Governor and Council of the Northern Department, 17 August 1827, HBCA, D.4/121.
5 Thompson to Marshall, 26 March 1829, Marshall Manuscripts.
6 Anonymous, "Documents," 1907:258.
7 McLoughlin to Rowand, [20 March 1830], HBCA, D.4/123.
8 McLoughlin to Simpson, 20 March 1830, HBCA, D.4/123.
9 "*Cadboro* and *Dryad* logs, 1827 [*sic*]," 1–2 July 1831, HBCA, C.1/218.
10 Boardman to Barker, 7 June 1831, Boardman Letterbook.
11 Boardman to Barker, 7 October 1831, Boardman Letterbook.
12 Lewes to Simpson, 2 April 1822, HBCA, D.4/116. Western (Pacific Slope) beaver, incidentally, were inferior to those of Rupert's Land – at least at first – partly because they were less well cured and beaten. The best Columbia Department beaver pelts came from the Flathead Country.
13 Simpson to the Governor and Committee, 10 August 1824, HBCA, A.12/1.
14 Simpson to Ogden, 14 March 1825, HBCA, D.4/7.
15 Merk, *Fur Trade and Empire*, 71–2.
16 Simpson to McLoughlin, 10 July 1826, HBCA, D.4/6.
17 Merk, *Fur Trade and Empire*, 73.
18 Ibid., 78, 83.
19 McLoughlin to the Governor and Council of the Northern Department, 20 March 1826, HBCA, D.4/119.
20 Simpson to the Governor and Committee, 20 August 1826, HBCA, A.12/1. Also see Simpson to McLoughlin, 10 July 1826, HBCA, D.4/6.
21 Simpson to McLoughlin, 10 July 1826, HBCA, D.4/6.
22 A. Simpson to Secretary Smith, 18 December 1827, HBCA, D.4/121.
23 Ibid.

24 A. Simpson to McLoughlin, 22 September 1828, HBCA, B.223/c/1.

25 Ibid.

26 Ibid.

27 Ibid.

28 Dominis to Marshall, 4 March 1829, Marshall Manuscripts.

29 Simpson to the Governor and Committee, 10 August 1826, HBCA, A.12/1.

30 McLoughlin to the Governor and Council of the Northern Department, 8 August 1826, HBCA, D.4/120; Rich, *Letters of John McLoughlin 1825–1838*, lxxi–lxxii, 29n.

31 Simpson to the Governor and Committee, 20 August 1826, HBCA, A.12/1.

32 Rich, *Letters of John McLoughlin 1825–1838*, 53.

33 "*Cadboro* log, 1826–27," 30 June 1827, HBCA, C.1/218.

34 Rich, *Letters of John McLoughlin 1825–1838*, 53.

35 Work to E. Ermatinger, 2 January 1828, Work Correspondence.

36 Rich, *Letters of John McLoughlin 1825–1838*, lxxiv.

37 Simpson to the Governor and Committee, 10 August 1832, HBCA, D.4/99.

38 Ibid.

39 Rich, *Letters of John McLoughlin 1825–1838*, 117–20.

40 Ibid., cxv.

41 "*Cadboro* and *Dryad* logs, 1827 [*sic*]," 22 July 1831, HBCA, C.1/218.

42 Simpson to the Governor and Committee, 10 August 1832, HBCA, D.4/99.

43 Ibid.

44 McLoughlin to Simpson, 20 March 1843, HBCA, D.5/8.

45 Rich, *Letters of John McLoughlin 1825–1838*, lxxii.

46 Ibid., 16–17, 35–6, 46–9, 79, 121–2, 140–1, 155–6, 160n., 233, 346–7.

47 "*Vancouver* log, 1831–32," 2 September 1831, HBCA, C.1/1,062.

48 Simpson to the Governor and Committee, 10 August 1832, HBCA, D.4/99.

49 Ibid.

50 Anonymous, "Documents," 1908:167.

51 McLoughlin to Simpson, 18 March 1834, HBCA, D.4/126.

52 Work to E. Ermatinger, 10 February 1838, Work Correspondence.

53 Connolly to the gentlemen of the Athabaska District, 2 September 1830, HBCA, D.4/125.

54 Simpson to the Governor and Committee, 10 June 1835, HBCA, D.4/100.

55 Ibid.

56 McLoughlin to Simpson, 20 March 1830, HBCA, D.4/123.

57 Simpson to the Governor and Committee, 10 August 1832, HBCA, D.4/99.

58 McLoughlin to Simpson, 18 March 1834, HBCA, D.4/126.

59 Simpson to the Governor and Committee, 10 June 1835, HBCA, D.4/100.

60 Rich, *Letters of John McLoughlin 1825–1838*, 123, 133.

61 Ibid., 61–2.

62 [Sturgis], "Examination of the Russian Claims," 399–400.

63 McLoughlin to the Governor and Council of the Northern Department, 20 March 1826, HBCA, D.4/119; A. Simpson to McLoughlin, 22 September 1828, HBCA, B.223/c/1.

64 Simpson to the Governor and Committee, 10 August 1832, HBCA, D.4/99.

65 Work to E. Ermatinger, 1 January 1836, Work Correspondence.

66 A. Simpson to McLoughlin, 22 September 1828, B.223/c/1.

67 McMillan to McLoughlin, 14 September 1827, HBCA, D.4/121.

68 Rich, *Letters of John McLoughlin 1825–1838*, 88.

69 Ibid., 104.

70 Simpson to the Governor and Committee, 10 August 1832, HBCA, D.4/99.

71 Ibid.

72 Ibid.

73 Ibid.

74 Rich, *Letters of John McLoughlin 1825–1838*, 129–30.

75 A. Simpson to McLoughlin, 22 September 1828, HBCA, B.223/c/1.

76 Dunn, *History of the Oregon Territory*, 229.

77 Rich, *Letters of John McLoughlin 1825–1838*, 330.

78 [Work], *Journal*, 56.

79 Ibid., 68–9. Also see ibid., 70–1.

80 Simpson to the Governor and Committee, 10 August 1832, HBCA, D.4/99.

81 Ibid.

82 See Gibson, *Farming the Frontier*.

83 Simpson to the Governor and Committee, 20 August 1826, HBCA, A.12/1.

84 McLoughlin to Simpson, 16 March 1831, HBCA, D.4/125.

85 Simpson to the Governor and Committee, 21 July 1834, HBCA, D.4/100.

86 Ibid.

87 Simpson to the Governor and Committee, 10 June 1835, HBCA, D.4/100.

88 McLoughlin to Simpson, 3 March 1835, HBCA, D.4/127.

89 Boardman to Barker, 7 October 1831, Boardman Letterbook.

90 Duncan Finlayson, "Trip Across to the Columbia 1831," HBCA, E.12/2.

91 McLoughlin to Simpson, 20 March 1827, HBCA, D.4/120.

92 Anonymous, "*Joseph Peabody*, Brig. Shipping Logbook," 9 May–2 June 1836.

93 "Fort Simpson (Nass) – Post Journal 1834–1838," 17 October, 8, 15–16 November 1836, HBCA, B.201/a/3.

94 [Work], *Journal,* 42.

95 Ibid.

96 "Fort Simpson (Nass) – Post Journal 1838–1840," 2 May 1838, HBCA, B.201/a/4.

97 "Fort Simpson (Nass) – Post Journal 1834–1838," 19 April 1837, HBCA, B.201/a/3.

98 Simpson to the Governor and Committee, 10 August 1832, HBCA, D.4/99.

99 McLoughlin to Simpson, 18 March 1834, HBCA, D.4/126.

100 See Gibson, "Bostonians and Muscovites."

101 Manson to Finlayson, 4 November 1834, HBCA, D.4/127.

102 [Work], *Journal,* 77.

103 *Alaska Boundary Tribunal. Case of the United States,* appendix, 232.

104 "Fort Simpson (Nass) – Post Journal 1834–1838," 26 July 1834, HBCA, B.201/a/3.

105 Davidson, "Relations," 39.

106 Litke, *Voyage Around the World,* 1:59.

107 Fyodorova, *Russkaya Amerika,* 135, 137.

108 Litke, *Voyage Around the World,* 1:59.

109 Records of the Russian-American Company, USNARS, roll 8:327v.–28, 330.

110 "Fort Simpson (Nass) – Post Journal 1834–1838," 2 October 1837, HBCA, B.201/a/3.

111 Simpson to the Governor and Committee, 25 November 1841, HBCA, D.4/110.

112 Simpson to the Governor and Committee, 10 August 1832, HBCA, D.4/99.

113 Simpson to the Governor and Committee, 21 July 1834, HBCA, D.4/100.

114 Ibid.

115 Rich, *Letters of John McLoughlin 1825–1838,* 317–22.

116 Simpson to the Governor and Committee, 6 July 1836, HBCA, D.4/103.

117 Davidson, "Relations," 43; "Fort Simpson (Nass) – Post Journal 1838–1840," 7 August 1838, HBCA, B.201/a/4; Morton, *History of the Canadian West,* 706–07.

118 Douglas to Simpson, 5 March 1839, HBCA, D.4/106.

119 Simpson to the Governor and Committee, 8 July 1839, HBCA, D.4/106.

120 Douglas to Simpson, 5 March 1839, HBCA, D.4/106.

121 Simpson to the Governor and Committee, 8 July 1839, HBCA, D.4/106.

122 "Remarks on the existing Agreement between the Hudson Bay Company and Russian American Company under date 6th February 1835," 30 October 1844, HBCA, A.12/2; "Remarks on existing agreement between the Hudsons Bay Company and Russian American Company dated 6 February 1839," 30 October 1844, HBCA, D.4/66.

123 Anonymous, "Documents," 1907:265.

124 Bagley, "Journal of Occurrences," 193, 265, 273, 277.

125 "Fort Simpson (Nass) – Post Journal 1834–1838," 4 June 1837, HBCA, B.201/a/3.

126 "Stikine – Post Journal 1840–1842," 13 June 1840, HBCA, B.209/a/1.

127 Manson to Simpson, 14 September 1843, HBCA, D.5/8.

128 Work to Ross, 9 September 1841, Fort Simpson. Correspondence outward.

129 Simpson to the Governor and Committee, 8 July 1839, HBCA, D.4/106.

130 Rich, *Letters of John McLoughlin 1839–1844*, 24.

131 Anonymous, "Documents," 1907:43.

132 Anonymous, "Documents," 1908:167.

133 Simpson to the Governor and Committee, 21 July 1834, HBCA, D.4/100.

134 McLoughlin to Simpson, 18 March 1834, HBCA, D.4/126.

135 Simpson to the Governor and Committee, 21 July 1834, HBCA, D.4/101; Simpson to the Governor and Committee, 10 June 1835, HBCA, D.4/102.

136 Simpson to the Governor and Committee, 10 June 1835, HBCA, D.4/102.

137 McLoughlin to Simpson, 20 March 1843, HBCA, D.5/8.

138 Simpson to the Governor and Committee, 25 November 1841, HBCA, D.4/110.

139 See Gibson, *Farming the Frontier*, 201, Table 30.

140 Work to McLoughlin, 9 September 1841, Fort Simpson. Correspondence outward.

141 Work to E. Ermatinger, 6 February 1844, Work Correspondence.

142 Simpson to the Governor and Committee, 25 November 1841, HBCA, D.4/110.

143 Simpson to McLoughlin, 21 June 1843, HBCA, B.223/c/1.

144 Dodd to Simpson, February 1844, HBCA, D.5/10; McNeill to Simpson, 23 February 1845, HBCA, D.5/13.

145 Work to E. Ermatinger, 6 February 1844, Work Correspondence.

146 Boardman to Barker, 7 October 1831, 8 September 1832, Boardman Letterbook.

147 Hughes, *Letters and Recollections*, 1:90–1.

CHAPTER FIVE

1 Fairbank, *Cambridge History of China*, vol. 10, pt. 1:35, 108–9; Hou and Yu, *Modern Chinese Economic History*, 82.
2 Eckstein, *China's Economic Development*, 109.
3 Great Britain, *Sessional Papers* 5:108.
4 Hart, *"These from the Land of Sinim"*, 51, 61.
5 Ibid., 60.
6 Ibid.
7 Fairbank, *History of China*, vol. 10, pt. 1:33; Le Fevour, *Western Enterprise in Late Ch'ing China*, 1.
8 Eckstein, *China's Economic Development*, 131–2.
9 Great Britain, *Sessional Papers* 5:69.
10 Greenberg, *British Trade and the Opening of China*, 41–6.
11 Ibid., 51–3.
12 Gibson, "Observations on the Trade with the Chinese," [6].
13 Great Britain, *Sessional Papers* 5:15.
14 Hunter, *"Fan Kwae" at Canton*, 40, 60.
15 Morse, *Chronicles of the East India Company*, 2:197, 4:59.
16 Hunter, *"Fan Kwae" at Canton*, 48.
17 Greenberg, *British Trade and the Opening of China*, 59.
18 Great Britain, *Sessional Papers* 5:19, 6:374.
19 Hunter, *"Fan Kwae" at Canton*, 48; Morse, *Chronicles of the East India Company*, 4:59; idem, *Trade and Administration*, 281; Quincy, *Journals of Major Samuel Shaw*, 24.
20 Great Britain, *Sessional Papers* 5:456.
21 Ibid., 18, 25.
22 Morse, *Chronicles of the East India Company*, 3:39.
23 Pierrepont, "Notes on the China Trade," 24–5.
24 Greenberg, *British Trade and the Opening of China*, 51; Hunter, *"Fan Kwae" at Canton*, 36.
25 Pierrepont, "Notes on the China Trade," 26.
26 Great Britain, *Sessional Papers* 5:14, 44, 60, 62, 248 [244].
27 Fairbank, *History of China*, vol. 10, pt. 1:164–5; Greenberg, *British Trade and the Opening of China*, 52–3.
28 Fairbank, *History of China*, vol 10, pt. 1:165.
29 Milburn, *Oriental Commerce*, 454–5.
30 Greenberg, *British Trade and the Opening of China*, 53–4; Hunter, *"Fan Kwae" at Canton*, 35; Morse, *Chronicles of the East India Company*, 1:164.
31 Gibson, "Observations on the Trade with the Chinese," [6–7].
32 Fairbank, *History of China*, vol. 10, pt. 1:169; Greenberg, *British Trade and the Opening of China*, 54.
33 Corning, "Letters of Sullivan Dorr," 190.

34 Hunter, *"Fan Kwae" at Canton*, 106; Quincy, *Journals of Major Samuel Shaw*, 183, 199, 349–50.

35 Pierrepont, "Notes on the China Trade," 33–4.

36 Corning, "Letters of Sullivan Dorr," 220.

37 Leder, "American Trade to China," 216–17.

38 Greenberg, *British Trade and the Opening of China*, 55–7.

39 Morse, *International Relations*, 1:34.

40 Morse, *Chronicles of the East India Company*, 2:353, 3:197.

41 Great Britain, *Sessional Papers* 5:103.

42 Fairbank, *History of China*, vol. 10, pt. 1:163–4.

43 Parkinson, *Trade in the Eastern Seas*, 58.

44 Fairbank, *History of China*, vol. 10, pt. 1:163; Morse, *Chronicles of the East India Company*, 2:425.

45 Latourette, "History of Early Relations," 23–4.

46 Delano, *Narrative of Voyages and Travels*, 540.

47 See Fairbank, *History of China*, vol. 10, pt. 1, Chapters 2–3.

48 On the British EIC, see Cotton, *East Indiamen*; Morse, *Chronicles of the East India Company*, 5 vols.; Parkinson, "East India Trade"; idem, *Trade in the Eastern Seas*.

49 Parkinson, *Trade in the Eastern Seas*, 1–8.

50 Parkinson, "East India Trade," 145.

51 Parkinson, *Trade in the Eastern Seas*, 121.

52 Ibid., 69–77.

53 Ibid., 78–89.

54 Great Britain, *Sessional Papers* 6:353–5, 359, 360–1.

55 Greenberg, *British Trade and the Opening of China*, 2.

56 Great Britain, *Sessional Papers* 7:113.

57 Greenberg, *British Trade and the Opening of China*, 3.

58 Quincy, *Journals of Major Samuel Shaw*, 229, 251–2, 298, 350, 353.

59 Pierrepont, "Notes on the Trade of China," 3.

60 Parkinson, *Trade in the Eastern Seas*, 94–5.

61 L., "On the Trade of the United States," 359. The popularity of tea was noted much earlier by a British Northwest Coast trader in words so similar that they may have been plagiarized: "It has long ceased to be a luxury among the great; and is become a kind of necessary of life among the poor" (Meares, *Voyages Made in the Years 1788 and 1789*, lxxxi–lxxxii).

62 Parkinson, *Trade in the Eastern Seas*, 94.

63 Greenberg, *British Trade and the Opening of China*, 3.

64 Parkinson, *Trade in the Eastern Seas*, 94.

65 Great Britain, *Sessional Papers* 6:363; Hunter, *"Fan Kwae" at Canton*, 93.

66 Great Britain, *Sessional Papers* 5:22–3, 34.

67 Ibid., 23.

68 Ibid., 6:360.

69 Ibid., 352.

70 Ibid., 5:18, 23.

71 Ibid., 23, 41, 47, 52.

72 Pierrepont, "Notes on the Trade of China," 33.

73 Great Britain, *Sessional Papers*, 6:360.

74 Ibid., 5:117.

75 Ibid., 6:351; Parkinson, *Trade in the Eastern Seas*, 60–2.

76 Hunter, *"Fan Kwae" at Canton*, 97; Parkinson, *Trade in the Eastern Seas*, 92–3.

77 Parkinson, *Trade in the Eastern Seas*, 89, 94.

78 Great Britain, *Sessional Papers*, 5:23, 307, 6:360.

79 Hunter, *"Fan Kwae" at Canton*, 33.

80 Pierrepont, "Notes on the Trade of China," 49–50.

81 Ibid., 47–8.

82 Great Britain, *Sessional Papers* 6:362, 463.

83 Ibid., 5:53; Pierrepont, "Notes on the Trade of China," 36.

84 Great Britain, *Sessional Papers*, 6:360.

85 On the dynamic role of the "country traders" in the Canton trade, see Greenberg, *British Trade and the Opening of China*.

86 Great Britain, *Sessional Papers* 5:25, 40, 44.

87 Fairbank, *History of China*, vol. 10, pt. 1:170.

88 Great Gritain, *Sessional Papers* 6:414.

89 See Forbes, "European Wars and Boston Trade."

90 Quincy, *Journals of Major Samuel Shaw*, 133, 218, 232.

91 Jameson, "Letters of Phineas Bond," 535.

92 Leder, "American Trade to China," 216–17.

93 Anonymous, "Return of American Vessels."

94 Jameson, "Letters of Phineas Bond," 611. On the development of New England's maritime business, see Morison, *Maritime History of Massachusetts*.

95 Jameson, "Letters of Phineas Bond," 635.

96 Ibid., 540.

97 Krooss and Gilbert, *American Business History*, 82. On Philadelphia's China trade, see Lee, *Philadelphians and the China Trade*.

98 Great Britain, *Sessional Papers* 6:369–70.

99 Ibid., 5:121.

100 Hunter, *"Fan Kwae" at Canton*, 118–19; also see Great Britain, *Sessional Papers* 5:121.

101 Great Britain, *Sessional Papers* 5:121.

102 Ibid., 80.

103 Corning, "Letters of Sullivan Dorr," 355.

104 Great Britain, *Sessional Papers* 5:88.

105 Corning, "Letters of Sullivan Dorr," 241.
106 Ibid., 188, 240–1.
107 Ibid., 181–2, 258, 280.
108 Ibid., 241.
109 Great Britain, *Sessional Papers* 6:443–4.
110 Morison, "Boston Traders in Hawaiian Islands," 185.
111 French to Marshall, 30 June 1821, Marshall Manuscripts.
112 Great Britain, *Sessional Papers* 6:448.
113 Ibid., 392, 5:193.
114 Ibid., 247; Hunter, *"Fan Kwae" at Canton*, 118.
115 Dennett, *Americans in Eastern Asia*, 63.
116 Great Britain, *Sessional Papers* 6:447.
117 Ibid., 5:123–4.
118 Pierrepont, "Notes on the Trade of China," 50–1.
119 Corning, "Letters of Sullivan Dorr," 272, 274; Great Britain, *Sessional Papers*, 5:54, 93.
120 Corning, "Letters of Sullivan Dorr," 332.
121 Great Britain, *Sessional Papers* 6:456.
122 Ibid., 362.
123 Ibid., 5:118.
124 Ibid., 98–101.
125 Ibid., 97.
126 Ibid.
127 Ibid., 96–7.
128 Ibid., 6:363.
129 Ibid., 5:96.
130 Ibid., 111.
131 Ibid., 112, 117.
132 Ibid., 117.
133 Ibid., 127, 6:368.
134 Ibid., 5:127.
135 Ibid., 356, 6:380.
136 Ibid., 367, 5:231, 442; Hunter, *"Fan Kwae" at Canton*, 94–5; Parkinson, *Trade in the Eastern Seas*, 89.
137 Great Britain, *Sessional Papers* 5:91–2, 6:360.
138 Ibid., 6:368.
139 Ibid., 363, 378, 442, 5:460.
140 Ibid., 354, 6:442.
141 Ibid., 438, 440, 5:89.
142 Ibid., 6:368.
143 Sterns, "Foreign Trade of the United States," 470–1.
144 Great Britain, *Sessional Papers* 5:361.
145 Ibid., 362.

146 Ibid., 93.
147 Corning, "Letters of Sullivan Dorr," 220.
148 Dennett, *Americans in Eastern Asia*, 56–7.
149 Great Britain, *Sessional Papers* 5:359.
150 Latourette, "History of Early Relations," 78n.–79n.
151 Great Britain, *Sessional Papers* 6:439.
152 Ibid., 438, 440.
153 Ibid., 377, 440, 5:77.
154 Ibid., 20, 6:370, 380, 439.
155 Corning, "Letters of Sullivan Dorr," 319, 346.
156 Ibid., 319.
157 Ibid., 184.
158 Ibid., 183–4, 202, 219, 271, 274–5, 278, 287, 320.
159 Ibid., 278, 287.
160 Gutzlaff, *Sketch of Chinese History* 2:Table 4.
161 Corning, "Letters of Sullivan Dorr," 324; also see Great Britain, *Sessional Papers* 5:108.
162 Cole, *Industrial and Commercial Correspondence*, Thomas Randall to Alexander Hamilton, 14 August 1791.
163 Corning, "Letters of Sullivan Dorr," 324–5, 339, 346.
164 L., "Trade of the United States," 365–6.
165 See Evans, "Ginseng."
166 Hence Boston's China ships proceeded to Canton via Cape Horn and Philadelphia's and New York's via the Cape of Good Hope. Before the opening of the coast trade, American ships had gone via the Cape of Good Hope; for example, in 1789, which was only the second year of American participation in the coast business, up to fifteen United States vessels put in to Canton, and all but one of them had come via the Cape, not the Horn, and all of them planned to return by that route (Howay, *Voyages of the "Columbia"*, 128–30; Meares, *Voyages Made in the Years 1788 and 1789*, lxxxviii.)
167 Great Britain, *Sessional Papers* 6:366.
168 Ibid.; Anonymous, "Imports and Exports," 470.
169 Great Britain, *Sessional Papers* 7:408.
170 Fleurieu, *Voyage Round the World*, 1:cn.
171 Latourette states that furs never constituted more than 15 per cent of the value of American imports at Canton but he cites no evidence for this assertion (Latourette, "History of Early Relations," 29n.).
172 Despatches from United States Consuls in Canton, 1790–1906, USNARS, roll 1, Imports at Canton by American Vessels from Season of 1804–5 to Season of 1809–10.
173 Pierrepont, "Notes on the Trade of China," 1.

174 Corning, "Letters of Sullivan Dorr," 220. There was no import duty on specie (Quincy, *Journals of Major Samuel Shaw*, 174).

175 Corning, "Letters of Sullivan Dorr," 245. On the use of silver, particularly that from New Spain, in the Canton trade, see Cheong, "Trade and Finance in China."

176 See Boxer, "Manila Galleon"; Schurz, *Manila Galleon*.

177 Fu, *Documentary Chronicle*, 2:613.

178 Ibid., 603.

179 Leder, "American Trade to China," 216–17.

180 Pitkin, *Statistical View*, 303.

181 Dennett, *Americans in Eastern Asia*, 20.

182 Great Britain, *Sessional Papers* 7:409.

183 Quoted by Dennett, *Americans in Eastern Asia*, 20.

184 Corning, "Letters of Sullivan Dorr," 185, 202.

185 Ibid., 296, 298, 302.

186 On the opium trade in general, see Collis, *Foreign Mud*. On the American opium trade, see Downs, "American Merchants"; Stelle, "American Trade in Opium," 2 pts.

187 Morse, *Chronicles of the East India Company*, 1:215–16.

188 Hunter, *"Fan Fwae" at Canton*, 65.

189 Ibid., 55.

190 Fairbank, *History of China*, vol. 10, pt. 1:172.

191 Great Britain, *Sessional Papers* 5:65, 6:364.

192 Perkins to Paine, 17 April 1820, Perkins Letterbooks.

193 Great Britain, *Sessional Papers* 6:420.

194 Fairbank, *History of China*, vol. 10, pt. 1:172.

195 Great Britain, *Sessional Papers* 6:375.

196 Ibid., 5:403.

197 Ibid., 15, 46, 63–4.

198 Ibid., 65.

199 Ibid., 6:419–20.

200 Dennett, *Americans in Eastern Asia*, 55.

201 Great Britain, *Sessional Papers* 6:433.

202 Ibid.

203 Ibid., 434.

204 Dennett, *Americans in Eastern Asia*, 52–3.

205 Ibid., 52.

206 Great Britain, *Sessional Papers* 7:111–12.

207 Ibid., 137, 153, 179.

208 Ibid., 220, 231.

209 Ibid., 153.

210 Ibid., 126, 152, 5:73.

211 Ibid., 7:133, 152, 179.
212 Despatches from United States Consuls in Canton, 1790–1906, USNARS, roll 1, Shillaber to the President of the United States, 20 April 1834.
213 Ibid.
214 Trowbridge, "Diary of Mr. Ebenezer Townsend, Jr.," 87–8, 96.
215 Dennett, *Americans in Eastern Asia*, 56.
216 Ibid., 61.
217 Fu, *Documentary Chronicle*, 2:612, 621–2; Great Britain, *Sessional Papers* 5:28–9.
218 Great Britain, *Sessional Papers* 5:95, 121.
219 Ibid., 128.
220 Ibid., 108.
221 Corning, "Letters of Sullivan Dorr," 278, 281–2.
222 Great Britain, *Sessional Papers* 6:371.
223 Ibid., 489, 7:61.
224 Ibid., 6:489.
225 Ibid., 487–9, 7:62.
226 Ibid., 6:374, 393.
227 Hill, *Trade and Commerce of Boston*, 80.
228 Great Britain, *Sessional Papers* 5:224.
229 Ibid., 223.
230 Ibid., 120, 6:371, 374.
231 Ibid., 371, 377.
232 Ibid., 371–2, 386–7.
233 Ibid., 5:109.
234 Ibid., 119–20.
235 Ibid., 120.
236 Ibid., 6:377–8.
237 Ibid., 386.
238 Ibid., 378, 5:116.
239 Ibid., 7:138.
240 Ibid., 5:124.
241 Ibid., 110, 7:63.
242 Corning, "Letters of Sullivan Dorr," 221.
243 Great Britain, *Sessional Papers* 5:81, 119, 223–4.
244 Fyodorova, *Russkaya Amerika*, 138.
245 Great Britain, *Sessional Papers*, 5:38, 106, 7:21, 39, 63.
246 Fairbank, *History of China*, vol. 10, pt. 1:169.
247 Great Britain, *Sessional Papers* 5:122.
248 Ibid., 18.
249 Ibid., 6:286.

250 Ibid., 5:79.
251 Ibid., 6:374.

CHAPTER SIX

1 Wagner, *Spanish Explorations*, 159.
2 Ibid.; [Bishop], *Journal and Letters*, 72; Dunn, *History of the Oregon Territory*, 251.
3 Anonymous, "Journal of a Voyage Round the World on the Brig Rob Roy," 5, 9 March 1822.
4 Lazarev, *Plavanie vokrug sveta*, 161; [Puget], "Log of the Proceedings of His Majesty's Armed Tender Chatham," 51v.; Records of the Russian-American Company, USNARS, roll 33:137.
5 Walker, *Account of a Voyage*, 178.
6 A. Simpson to McLoughlin, 22 September 1828 HBCA, B.223/c/1.
7 Furgerson, "Journal of a Voyage from Boston to the Northwest Coast," 26, 30 October 1810.
8 Bryant and Sturgis to Suter, 6 August 1816, Bryant and Sturgis Papers.
9 Corning, "Letters of Sullivan Dorr," 262.
10 Bryant and Sturgis to Suter, 12 October 1820, Bryant and Sturgis Papers.
11 Jackman, *Journal of William Sturgis*, 31, 113.
12 Cleveland, "Northwest Expedition," 24, 38.
13 Bryant and Sturgis to Cross, 14 August 1821, Bryant and Sturgis Papers.
14 Howay, *Voyages of the "Columbia"*, 382; Jackman, *Journal of William Sturgis*, 99; Jane, *Spanish Voyage*, 115; Lisiansky, *Voyage Round the World*, 237; Wagner, *Spanish Explorations*, 145–6; Walker, *Account of a Voyage*, 122.
15 Kaplanoff, *Joseph Ingraham's Journal*, 146–7.
16 [Bishop], *Journal and Letters*, 72.
17 Walker, *Account of a Voyage*, 193.
18 MacNair, "Log of the Caroline," 190.
19 Corning, "Letters of Sullivan Dorr," 237.
20 Dennett, *Americans in Eastern Asia*, 12.
21 Corning, "Letters of Sullivan Dorr," 188, 321.
22 A. Simpson to McLoughlin, 22 September 1828, HBCA, B.223/c/1.
23 Furgerson, "Journal of a Voyage from Boston to the Northwest Coast," 6 September 1810.
24 [Smith], "Arab (brig) Logbook," 18 June 1821.
25 Haskins, "Journal of a Fur Trading Voyage," 36.

26 Beaglehole, *Journals of Captain James Cook*, vol. 3, pt. 2:1,008.

27 Ibid., 143; Magee, "Log of the Jefferson," January 1794. Also see Bartlett, "John Bartlett's journal," 12.

28 Meares, *Voyages Made in the Years 1788 and 1789*, 321–4, 328–9.

29 Green, *Journal of a Tour*, 86.

30 Lamb, *Voyage of George Vancouver*, 2:546.

31 Walker, *Account of a Voyage*, 42.

32 Ibid., 47. Also see Cook [and King], *Voyage to the Pacific Ocean*, 2:284–5.

33 Beaglehole, *Journals of Captain James Cook*, vol. 3, pt. 2:1,407; Cook [and King], *Voyage to the Pacific Ocean*, 2:283–4.

34 Walker, *Account of a Voyage*, 43, 80.

35 Magee, "Log of the Jefferson," 31 May 1793.

36 Haskins, "Journal of a Fur Trading Voyage," 42–3.

37 Kaplanoff, *Joseph Ingraham's Journal*, 132. Also see [Bishop], *Journal and Letters*, 63; Haskins, "Journal of a Fur Trading Voyage," 32, 61; Howay, *Voyages of the "Columbia"*, 208; Jackman, *Journal of William Sturgis*, 34; Lamb, *Voyage of George Vancouver*, 3:1,055.

38 Walker, *Account of a Voyage*, 47.

39 Thwaites, *Original Journals*, 3:330.

40 [Sturgis], "Northwest Fur Trade," 537.

41 [Strange], *Journal and Narrative*, 25; Wagner and Newcombe, "Journal of Jacinto Caamaño," 205.

42 [Sturgis], "Ms. of 3 lectures," lecture 2, 13.

43 Meares, *Voyages Made in the Years 1788 and 1789*, 202.

44 Kaplanoff, *Joseph Ingraham's Journal*, 130.

45 Meares, *Voyages Made in the Years 1788 and 1789*, 120.

46 [Sturgis], "Northwest Fur Trade," 537.

47 [Sturgis], "Ms. of 3 lectures," lecture 2, 16.

48 Clinton, "Journal," 22 October 1805.

49 [Martain], "Ship Hamilton Log Book," [110].

50 Anonymous, "Journal of a Voyage Round the World on the Brig Rob Roy," 20 July, 2 August 1822.

51 Haskins, "Journal of a Fur Trading Voyage," 32, 207.

52 Kaplanoff, *Joseph Ingraham's Journal*, 132, 136.

53 [Allen], "Log of the Ship *Hamilton*," 172.

54 Cook [and King], *Voyage to the Pacific Ocean*, 2:278.

55 Walker, *Account of a Voyage*, 43.

56 [Sturgis], "Northwest Fur Trade," 537.

57 [Roe], *Journal and Letters*, 65.

58 Magee, "Log of the Jefferson," March 1794.

59 Kaplanoff, *Joseph Ingraham's Journal*, 203.

60 Walker, "Supercargo's log of the brig *Lydia*," 15v.

61 Anonymous, "Journal of a Voyage Round the World on the Brig Rob Roy," 7–13 June 1823.

62 "Fort Simpson (Nass) – Post Journal 1838–1840," 4 May 1838, HBCA, B.201/a/4.

63 "Stikine – Post Journal 1840–1842," 21 June 1840, HBCA, B.209/a/1.

64 MacNair, "Log of the Caroline," 169–70.

65 See, for example, Howay, *Voyages of the "Columbia"*, 195, 208; Lamb, *Voyage of George Vancouver*, 2:492, 527, 606, 627, 3:931, 940, 1,035, 1,042, 1,055; Portlock, *Voyage Round the World*, 113, 118, 264; Walker, *Account of a Voyage*, 62–3.

66 Beaglehole, *Journals of Captain James Cook*, vol. 3, pt. 2:1,396.

67 [Puget], "Log of the Proceedings of His Majesty's Armed Tender Chatham," 39v.; [Puget], "Log of the Proceedings of His Majesty's Ship Discovery," 134v.

68 Cook [and King], *Voyage to the Pacific Ocean*, 2:279; Walker, *Account of a Voyage*, 62.

69 See Fisher, "Indian Control."

70 Meares, *Voyages Made in the Years 1788 and 1789*, Appendix I.

71 Ibid., 141–2, 148.

72 Fleurieu, *Voyage Round the World*, 1:241, 301.

73 S. Dorr to E. Dorr, 16 August 1801, Ebenezer Dorr Papers.

74 Corning, "Letters of Sullivan Dorr," 232.

75 Fleurieu, *Voyage Round the World*, 1:192, 195.

76 Jackman, *Journal of William Sturgis*, 77–8.

77 "Fort Simpson (Nass) – Post Journal 1834–1838," 12 June 1837, HBCA, B.201/a/3.

78 Barkley, "Journal of the *Halcyon*," 3 October 1792.

79 Kaplanoff, *Joseph Ingraham's Journal*, 128, 130.

80 [Scouler], "John Scouler's Journal," 180.

81 Haskins, "Journal of a Fur Trading Voyage," 28, 30.

82 Anonymous, "Journal of a Voyage Round the World on the Brig Rob Roy," 1–2 December 1822.

83 Anonymous, "Journal kept on board the Ship Paragon," [7–8].

84 "*Cadboro* and *Dryad* logs, 1827 [*sic*]," 12 August 1831, HBCA, C.1/218.

85 Furgerson, "Journal of a Voyage from Boston to the Northwest Coast," 13 February 1811.

86 [Work], *Journal*, 21–2.

87 "Fort Simpson (Nass) – Post Journal 1834–1838," 2 October 1837, HBCA, B.201/a/3.

88 Meares, *Voyages Made in the Years 1788 and 1789*, 142.

89 Walker, *Account of a Voyage*, 40, 58–9.

90 [Puget], "Log of the Proceedings of His Majesty's Armed Tender Chatham," 49.

91 [Sturgis], "Ms. of 3 lectures," lecture 2, 5.
92 Ross, *Adventures of the First Settlers*, 88.
93 Thwaites, *Original Journals*, 3:278, 311–12.
94 Haskins, "Journal of a Fur Trading Voyage," 238.
95 Cleveland, *Narrative*, 1:74–5.
96 A. Simpson to McLoughlin, 22 September 1828, HBCA, B.223/c/1.
97 See Freeman and Dungey, "Spatial duopoly."
98 Haskins, "Journal of a Fur Trading Voyage," 195.
99 MacNair, "Log of the Caroline," 171–2.
100 Ibid., 187; Cleveland, *Narrative*, 2:90. Also see Jackman, *Journal of William Sturgis*, 114.
101 MacNair, "Log of the Caroline," 184.
102 Thwaites, *Original Journals*, 3:240, 248, 251.
103 Thompson to Marshall, March 26, 1829, Marshall Manuscripts.
104 [Smith], "Arab (brig) Logbook," 9.
105 [Work], *Journal*, 36.
106 Anonymous, "Journal of a Voyage Round the World on the Brig Rob Roy," 18 April, 31 July 1822.
107 Ibid., 21 June 1822.
108 A. Simpson to Smith, 18 December 1827, A. Simpson to McLoughlin, 9 March 1828, HBCA, D.4/121.
109 Kaplanoff, *Joseph Ingraham's Journal*, 203.
110 Bryant and Sturgis to Cross, 14 August 1821, Bryant and Sturgis Papers.
111 "Fort Simpson (Nass) – Post Journal 1834–1838," 9 February 1837, HBCA, B.201/a/3.
112 Ibid., 25 August 1835; [Work], *Journal*, 74.
113 "Fort Simpson (Nass) – Post Journal 1834–1838," 5, 9 February 1837, HBCA, B.201/a/3.
114 A. Simpson to Smith, 18 December 1827, HBCA, D.4/121.
115 Anonymous, "Journal of a Voyage Round the World on the Brig Rob Roy," 5 March 1822.
116 "Fort Simpson (Nass) – Post Journal 1834–1838," 22 August 1837, HBCA, B.201/a/3.
117 Walker, *Account of a Voyage*, 110. Also see Cook [and King], *Voyage to the Pacific Ocean*, 2:278.
118 Beaglehole, *Journals of Captain James Cook*, vol. 3, pt. 1:302. Also see ibid., 299.
119 Walker, *Account of a Voyage*, 111.
120 [Colnett], "Voyage to the N. W. Side of America," 118.
121 Meares, *Voyages Made in the Years 1788 and 1789*, xix.
122 Inglis and Haggarty, "Cook to Jewitt," 211. Also see Archer, "Cannibalism in the Early History of the Northwest Coast"; Wike, "A Reevaluation of Northwest Coast Cannibalism."

123 Jackman, *Journal of William Sturgis*, 34–5.

124 Kaplanoff, *Joseph Ingraham's Journal*, 203.

125 Howay, *Voyages of the "Columbia"*, 55.

126 Howay, *Journal of Captain James Colnett*, 281.

127 Green, *Journal of a Tour*, 76–7.

128 Grimes to Marshall and Wildes, 8 July 1822, Marshall Manuscripts.

129 Anonymous, "Journal of a Voyage Round the World on the Brig Rob Roy," 14 July, 6 August 1822.

130 [Martain], "Ship Hamilton Log Book," 26 May, 1, 7–9, 17, 19 June 1810.

131 Furgerson, "Journal of a Voyage from Boston to the Northwest Coast," 28 February 1810.

132 [Martain], "Ship Hamilton Log Book," 5 March 1810.

133 Howay, "Yankee Trader on the Northwest Coast," 90.

134 Meany, *New Vancouver Journal*, 39.

135 Furgerson, "Journal of a Voyage from Boston to the Northwest Coast," 3 March, 17 May 1810.

136 Jackman, *Journal of William Sturgis*, 113, 116–17.

137 Ibid., 71.

138 [Martain], "Ship Hamilton Log Book," 1 September 1810.

139 Ibid., 16–18 September 1810.

140 Leonard, "Ship Alert Log Book," 17 July, 2 August, 20–21, 25 September, 4 October 1817.

141 Anonymous, "Journal of a Voyage Round the World on the Brig Rob Roy," 24 September–7 October 1824.

142 Ibid., [170].

143 [Suter], "Log of the Ship Atahualpa," 10 January 1813. Also see Anonymous, ["Logs of the Ships *Atahualpa*, *Behring*, and *Isabella*, and the Brig *Pedler*,"], 10 January 1813.

144 [Martain], "Ship Hamilton Log Book," [318].

145 Anonymous, "Journal of a Voyage Round the World on the Brig Rob Roy," 10, 18 April, 30 June, 2–13 July 1822, 8 May 1823.

146 Bryant and Sturgis to Clark, 1 December 1817, Bryant and Sturgis Papers.

147 Bryant and Sturgis to Hale, 31 August 1818, Bryant and Sturgis Papers.

148 Ibid.

149 Bryant and Sturgis to the commanding officer of the *Lascar* or *Becket*, 13 August 1820, Bryant and Sturgis Papers.

150 Grimes to Marshall and Wildes, 8 July 1822, Marshall Manuscripts.

151 Ibid.

152 Jones to Marshall and Wildes, 10 October 1822, Marshall Manuscripts.

153 [Mitchell], *Journals of William Fraser Tolmie*, 312.

154 "Fort Simpson (Nass) – Post Journal 1834–1838," 19 May 1836, HBCA, B.201/a/3.
155 "Journal of the Hudson's Bay Company at Fort Simpson 1834–7," 17 May 1836.
156 Furgerson, "Journal of a Voyage from Boston to the Northwest Coast," 24 May 1810.
157 MacNair, "Log of the Caroline," 172.
158 Haskins, "Journal of a Fur Trading Voyage," 216.
159 Bryant and Sturgis to Peirce, 22 October 1824, Bryant and Sturgis Papers.
160 Anonymous, "Ship Hancock Log Book," 17 May, 3–4, 18, 22 June 1799.
161 Anonymous, "Journal of a Voyage Round the World on the Brig Rob Roy," 1 January 1823.
162 Newcombe, Menzies' Journal, 17.
163 Howay, Voyages of the "Columbia", 49.
164 [Roe], Journal and Letters, 71–2.
165 Jackman, Journal of William Sturgis, 113.
166 Walker, "Supercargo's log of the brig Lydia," 29.
167 "Cadboro and Dryad logs, 1827 [sic]," 2 August 1831, HBCA, C.1/218.
168 Howay, Voyages of the "Columbia", 45; Portlock, Voyage Round the World, 114–15.
169 [Bishop], Journal and Letters, 118–19.
170 Corney, Early Voyages in the North Pacific, 154.
171 Ross, Adventures of the First Settlers, 77.
172 Howay, Voyages of the "Columbia", 265.
173 Lamb, Voyage of George Vancouver, 2:627.
174 Ibid., 214.
175 Jackman, Journal of William Sturgis, 44.
176 Magee, "Log of the Jefferson," 19, 31 May, 1 June 1794.
177 Jackman, Journal of William Sturgis, 66–8.
178 Haskins, "Journal of a Fur Trading Voyage," 194.
179 Ibid., 208–14.
180 Anonymous, "Journal of a Voyage Round the World on the Brig Rob Roy," 5 March 1822.
181 A. Simpson to McLoughlin, 22 September 1828, HBCA, B.223/c/1.
182 "Fort Simpson (Nass) – Post Journal 1838–1840," 9 April 1838, HBCA, B.201/a/4.
183 A. Simpson to McLoughlin, 22 September 1828, HBCA, B.223/c/1.
184 Haskins, "Journal of a Fur Trading Voyage," 76.
185 [Khlebnikov], Colonial Russian America, 29.
186 "Fort Simpson (Nass) – Post Journal 1834–1838," 15 June 1837, HBCA, B.201/a/3.

187 Simpson, *Narrative of a Journey*, 2:210.

188 "*Cadboro* and *Dryad* logs, 1827 [*sic*]," 1, 13 July 1831, HBCA, C.1/218.

189 Lamb, *Voyage of George Vancouver*, 2:652.

190 Clinton, "Journal," 25–27 May, 23 August 1806.

191 Corning, "Letters of Sullivan Dorr," 231.

192 Jackman, *Journal of William Sturgis*, 89.

193 Lamb, *Voyage of George Vancouver*, 3:1,032.

194 See the memoir of one of the two survivors, John Jewitt, *Journal Kept at Nootka Sound*.

195 [Scouler], "John Scouler's Journal," 195.

196 Jackman, *Journal of William Sturgis*, 88.

197 Ibid., 88–9.

198 MacNair, "Log of the Caroline," 180.

199 [Work], *Journal*, 77.

200 A. Simpson to McLoughlin, 22 September 1828, HBCA, B.223/C/1.

CHAPTER SEVEN

1 Haskins, "Journal of a Fur Trading Voyage," 4.

2 Furgerson, "Journal of a Voyage from Boston to the Northwest Coast," 2 April 1809.

3 [Martain], "Ship Hamilton Log Book," 5 August 1815.

4 [Martain], "Ship Louisa Log Book," 7 October 1826–13 January 1827, 25 March 1827.

5 Haskins, "Journal of a Fur Trading Voyage," 5–6.

6 Clinton, "Journal," 13 August 1804.

7 Furgerson, "Journal of a Voyage from Boston to the Northwest Coast," 15 July 1809.

8 [Allen], "Log of the Ship *Hamilton*," 2, 4 April 1823.

9 Haskins, "Journal of a Fur Trading Voyage," 23.

10 [Scouler], "John Scouler's Journal," 63.

11 Magee, "Log of the Jefferson," April 1792.

12 Furgerson, "Journal of a Voyage from Boston to the Northwest Coast," 5 July 1809.

13 Grimes to Marshall, 5 July 1821, Marshall Manuscripts.

14 [Colnett], "Voyage to the N. W. Side of America," 82v.

15 Clinton, "Journal," 2, 11, 12, 20, and 23 December 1804.

16 Ibid., 9 August 1805.

17 [Suter], "Log of the ship Atahualpa," 27 December 1811.

18 Anonymous, "Journal of a Voyage Round the World on the Brig Rob Roy," 4–5 November 1821.

19 Ibid., 6 December 1822.

20 Lowe, "Journal of a Voyage," 3 December 1841, HBCA, E.25/1.

21 Furgerson, "Journal of a Voyage from Boston to the Northwest Coast," 25 July 1809.

22 McNeill, "Journal of a Voyage to the N.W. Coast of North America," 2–23 January 1825.

23 [Suter], "Log of the ship Atahualpa," 2 January 1812.

24 [Suter], "Log of John Suter," 45–54.

25 [Martain], "Ship Louisa Log Book," [54].

26 Ibid., 22 January 1827.

27 Meares, *Voyages Made in the Years 1788 and 1789*, 3. For an authoritative historical treatment of scurvy, see Carpenter, *History of Scurvy*.

28 Anonymous, "Journal of a voyage perform'd on the Ship Amethyst," 27–8.

29 [Martain], "Ship Hamilton Log Book," [303].

30 Hunnewell to Bryant and Sturgis, 4 January 1827, Hunnewell Papers.

31 Howay, *Voyages of the "Columbia"*, 51. Also see ibid., 118, 124.

32 Ibid., 183, 369.

33 Meares, *Voyages Made in the Years 1788 and 1789*, iii, xxxiv, xxxvi, xxxix.

34 [Colnett], "Voyage to the N.W. Side of America," 116; Walbran, "Cruise of the Imperial Eagle," 6–7.

35 [Strange], *Journal and Narrative*, 16, 17.

36 Bartlett, "John Bartlett's journal," 7, 20, 31.

37 Howay, *Voyages of the "Columbia"*, 390.

38 Portlock, *Voyage Round the World*, 217.

39 Grant, *Life and Adventures of John Nicol*, 92.

40 Howay, *Voyages of the "Columbia"*, 369.

41 Anonymous, "Ship Hancock Log Book," 20, 21 January 1799.

42 Ibid., 9 December 1798.

43 [Martain], "Ship Hamilton Log Book," 17 July 1815.

44 Simpson, *Narrative of a Journey*, 1:240–1.

45 Williams, *Hudson's Bay Miscellany*, 199.

46 Walker, *Account of a Voyage*, 39.

47 Haskins, "Journal of a Fur Trading Voyage," 231.

48 Furgerson, "Journal of a Voyage from Boston to the Northwest Coast," 13 June, 14 November 1810.

49 Ibid., 24 June 1810.

50 [Suter], "Log of the ship Atahualpa," 22 June 1812.

51 Ibid., 23 June 1812.

52 Work to E. Ermatinger, 1 January 1836, Work Correspondence.

53 Haskins, "Journal of a Fur Trading Voyage," iii.

54 Furgerson, "Journal of a Voyage from Boston to the Northwest Coast," 5 August 1810.

55 [Martain], "Ship Hamilton Log Book," 25, 28 June, 8 July 1810.

56 Anonymous, ["Logs of the Ships *Atahaulpa*, *Behring*, and *Isabella* and the Brig *Pedler*,"], 18 May 1812.

57 Haskins, "Journal of a Fur Trading Voyage," 93.

58 Furgerson, "Journal of a Voyage from Boston to the Northwest Coast," 30 January, 2 February 1810.

59 Anonymous, "*Griffon*, Brig. Shipping Journal," 30 May, 26 June 1825.

60 Hayes, *Log of the Union*, 55.

61 Dorr, "Journal of a Voyage from Boston round the World," 2 April 1791.

62 Grimes to Marshall and Wildes, 11 August 1822, Marshall Manuscripts.

63 [Underwood], "Journal on board Brig Tally Ho," 31 May 1826.

64 A. Simpson to McLoughlin, 22 September 1828, HBCA, B.223/c/1.

65 McNeill, "Journal of a Voyage to the N.W. Coast of North America," 6, 8 November, 26 December 1824.

66 Anonymous, "Ship Hancock Log Book," 25 February 1800.

67 Ibid., 16 June 1799.

68 Wildes to Marshall, March 1826, Marshall Manuscripts.

69 See, for example, Bryant and Sturgis and Boardman and Pope to Barker and Pierce, 29 October 1827, Bryant and Sturgis Papers.

70 "Fort Simpson (Nass) – Post Journal 1838–1840," 23 April 1838, HBCA, B.201/a/4; Perkins and Company to J. and T.H. Perkins, 23 January 1820, Perkins and Company and Russell and Company Papers.

71 [Bishop], *Journal and Letters*, 69, 91; Dixon, *Voyage Round the World*, 246; Jackman, *Journal of William Sturgis*, 48.

72 [Holbrook], *Sketches*, 10.

73 Meares, *Voyages Made in the Years 1788 and 1789*, 233.

74 [Ingraham], Ingraham to Martínez, May 1789.

75 Anonymous, "Journal of a Voyage Round the World on the Brig Rob Roy," 3–12 July, 17 September–5 October 1822.

76 Ibid., 5–6 October 1822.

77 Ibid., 7 March, 3 April 1823.

78 Furgerson, "Journal of a Voyage from Boston to the Northwest Coast," 28 December 1809.

79 Ibid., 3 November 1809.

80 Ibid., 10 October 1810.

81 Ibid., 12 October 1810.

82 [Martain], "Ship Hamilton Log Book," [117].

83 Ibid., [148, 150].

84 Leonard, "Ship Alert Log Book," 26 June, 4 July 1817.

85 [Suter], "Log of John Suter," passim.

86 Grimes to Marshall and Wildes, 8 July 1822, Marshall Manuscripts.

87 McNeill, "Journal of a Voyage to the N.W. Coast of North America," 30 July 1825.

88 Ibid., 2 September 1825.

89 Rossiisko-Amerikanskaya Kompaniya, *Otchyot*, 1860, 73.

90 Walker, "Supercargo's log of the brig *Lydia*," passim.

91 Ibid., 24v.

92 Ibid.

93 [Allen], "Log of the Ship *Hamilton*," 174–6.

94 McNeill, "Journal of a Voyage kept onboard Brig Lama," 31 May 1833.

95 Gibson, *Imperial Russia in Frontier America*, 14; [Khlebnikov], *Colonial Russian America*, 145; Lamb, *Voyage of George Vancouver*, 3:946–7.

96 Bryant and Sturgis to Harris, 17 July 1820, Bryant and Sturgis Papers.

97 Bryant and Sturgis to Clark, 1 December 1817, Bryant and Sturgis Papers.

98 Bryant and Sturgis to Suter, 20 June 1820, Bryant and Sturgis Papers.

99 Clinton, "Journal," 4 June 1805.

100 Walker, "Supercargo's log of the brig *Lydia*,," 20v.

101 Furgerson, "Journal of a Voyage from Boston to the Northwest Coast," 8 September 1810.

102 [Martain], "Ship Hamilton Log Book," Joseph Ford [to T. Brown], 1812, enclosure at end of log.

103 See, for example, [Allen], "Log of the Ship *Hamilton*," 5, 26 June 1821.

104 Ibid., 25 December 1820.

105 [Suter], "Log of John Suter," 22 September 1817, 21 May 1818.

106 Anonymous, "Journal kept on board the Ship Paragon," 25 April 1820.

107 Bryant and Sturgis to Harris, June 1822, Bryant and Sturgis to Newell, June 1822, Bryant and Sturgis to Harris, 6 May 1823, Bryant and Sturgis Papers.

108 Dorr, "Journal of a Voyage from Boston round the World," 15 February, 20 May 1791.

109 Jones to Marshall and Wildes, 23 December 1821, Marshall Manuscripts.

110 Brewster to Marshall and Wildes, 4 October 1822, Marshall Manuscripts.

111 Morison, "Letters on the Northwest Fur Trade," 176.

112 Anonymous, "Journal of a Voyage Round the World on the Brig Rob Roy," 1–2 December 1822, 1 January 1823.

113 Corning, "Letters of Sullivan Dorr," 326–7; Haskins, "Journal of a Fur Trading Voyage," 248.

114 Anonymous, "Account Book Ship Sultan," passim.

115 McNeill, "Journal of a Voyage to the N.W. Coast of North America," 3 February 1825.

116 Meares, *Voyages Made in the Years 1788 and 1789*, 128, 187–91.

117 Anonymous, "Ship Hancock Log Book," 2 May 1799; MacNair, "Log of the Caroline," 186.

118 Cleveland, *Narrative*, 1:90; idem, "Northwest Expedition," 40; MacNair, "Log of the Caroline," 189.

119 Walker, "Supercargo's log of the brig *Lydia*," 6–8v.

120 [Martain], "Ship Hamilton Log Book," 14 October 1810.

121 Haskins, "Journal of a Fur Trading Voyage," 39.

122 [Suter], "Log of John Suter," 227–8.

123 [Allen], "Log of the Ship *Hamilton*," 6–8 January, 30 May–2 June 1821.

124 Anonymous, "Journal of a Voyage Round the World on the Brig Rob Roy," 6 December 1822.

125 Ibid., 11 March 1823.

126 Ibid., 14, 16 June 1823.

127 Grimes to Marshall and Wildes, 8 July 1822, Marshall Papers.

128 [Smith], "Arab (brig) Logbook," 10 March 1822.

129 "Fort Simpson (Nass), Miscellaneous Items, 1831–1841," HBCA, B.201/z/1.

130 [Puget], "Log of the Proceedings of His Majesty's Armed Tender Chatham," 39v.; idem, "Log of the Proceedings of His Majesty's Ship Discovery," 133v.

131 MacNair, "Log of the Caroline," 193n.

132 Anonymous, "Journal of a voyage perform'd on the Ship Amethyst," 2–3.

133 Beaglehole, *Journals of Captain James Cook*, vol. 3, pt. 2:1,348.

134 Moziño, *Noticias de Nutka*, 84.

135 Wagner, *Spanish Explorations*, 210, 242–3.

136 See Archer, "Cannibalism in the Early History of the Northwest Coast."

137 Beaglehole, *Journals of Captain James Cook*, vol. 3, pt. 2:1,350. Cf. ibid., 1,351.

138 Ibid., 1,396, 1,407, pt. 1:297.

139 Quincy, *Journals of Major Samuel Shaw*, 137.

140 Meares, *Voyages Made in the Years 1788 and 1789*, xiii. Also see Dixon, *Voyage Round the World*, 183–4, for the pilfering propensities of the Tlingits of Sitka Sound.

141 Howay, *Voyages of the "Columbia"*, 33.

142 Anonymous, "Journal of a Voyage Round the World on the Brig Rob Roy," 1–3 July 1823.

143 Portlock, *Voyage Round the World*, 114, 249.

144 Ibid., 114.

145 Inglis and Haggarty, "Cook to Jewitt," 212.

146 Beaglehole, *Journals of Captain James Cook*, vol. 3, pt. 1:306.

147 [Allen], "Log of the Ship *Hamilton*," 121.

148 Anonymous, "Journal of a Voyage Round the World on the Brig Rob Roy," 10 April 1822.

149 Ibid., 15–16 May 1822.

150 Ibid., 18 April 1822.

151 The Euroamericans were particularly repelled by the dirtiness of the Indians and their dwellings. Yet the post journal of Fort Simpson recorded on 6 May 1838: "Gave the men a severe reprimand for from laziness leaving their fish for to rot & stink about their houses and raising a stench enough to create a pest. They require as much looking after to make them keep themselves clean as a band of the filthiest Indians would do" ("Fort Simpson [Nass] – Post Journal 1838–1840," 6 May 1838, HBCA, B.201 /a/4).

152 [Sturgis], "Ms. of 3 lectures," lecture 2, 8–9, 14.

153 Howay, *Voyages of the "Columbia"*, 192.

154 Duff, *Indian History of British Columbia*, 1:56.

155 [Péron], *Memoires*, 2:24, 78.

156 [Sturgis], "Examination of the Russian Claims," 400.

157 [Sturgis], "Ms. of 3 lectures," lecture 1, 1–2, lecture 3, 39–40.

158 [Allen], "Log of the Ship *Hamilton*," 122; Beaglehole, *Journals of Captain James Cook*, vol. 3, pt. 1:302, pt. 2:1,103.

159 Ellis, *Authentic Narrative*, 1:203.

160 Simpson, *Narrative of a Journey*, 1:188–89.

161 Lamb, *Voyage of George Vancouver*, 3:1,016.

162 Anonymous, "Journal of a Voyage Round the World on the Brig Rob Roy," 5 March 1822.

163 Ibid.

164 Walker, "Supercargo's log of the brig *Lydia*," 21. Also see ibid., 33.

165 Ibid., 29v.

166 Furgerson, "Journal of a Voyage from Boston to the Northwest Coast," 2 January 1810.

167 Jackman, *Journal of William Sturgis*, 53.

168 Ibid., 62; Haskins, "Journal of a Fur Trading Voyage," 220.

169 Hayes, *Log of the Union*, 45.

170 Corning, "Letters of Sullivan Dorr," 211.

171 Cleveland, *Voyages and Commercial Enterprises*, 212; Haskins, "Journal of a Fur Trading Voyage," 250.

172 Corning, "Letters of Sullivan Dorr," 327, 450.

173 Jackman, *Journal of William Sturgis*, 53.

174 Walker, "Supercargo's log of the brig *Lydia*," 26v.

175 Ibid., 27–28v.
176 Ibid., 33–33v. For another flagrant example of Euroamerican revenge and treachery, see [Holbrook], *Sketches*, 10–12.
177 Anonymous, "Logbook of the Ship Pearl," 24 December 1805. Also see Walker, "Supercargo's log of the brig *Lydia*," 9v.
178 Howay, *Voyages of the "Columbia"*, 377.
179 [Scouler], "John Scouler's Journal," 192.
180 Howay, *Voyages of the "Columbia"*, 379.
181 Ibid., 390–1.
182 Jane, *Spanish Voyage*, 22–3; Wagner, *Spanish Explorations*, 229–30.
183 Jane, *Spanish Voyage*, 90.
184 Howay, *Voyages of the "Columbia"*, 395, 401.
185 Magee, "Log of the Jefferson," 13 June 1793.
186 Lamb, *Voyage of George Vancouver*, 2:612n.
187 Meany, *New Vancouver Journal*, 41.
188 Ibid., March, 5, 8 April 1794.
189 Clinton, "Journal," 8 April 1806.
190 [Allen], "Log of the Ship *Hamilton*," 177. Also see Anonymous, "Journal of a Voyage Round the World on the Brig Rob Roy," 3 August 1821.
191 Jackman, *Journal of William Sturgis*, 36.
192 Furgerson, "Journal of a Voyage from Boston to the Northwest Coast," 5 June 1810.
193 See Howay, "Indian Attacks upon Maritime Traders."
194 Jackman, *Journal of William Sturgis*, 47.
195 Green, *Journal of a Tour*, 30.
196 Hill, "Journal and Log of Two Voyages," 8.
197 [Jewitt], *Narrative*, 93–4.
198 Howay, *Voyages of the "Columbia"*, 200, 240–1, 298, 379; [Liscome?], "Extracts from the Log of the Ship Margaret," 13.
199 Howay, "Ballad of the Bold Northwestman"; idem, "Ballad of the Northwest Fur Trade."
200 Lamb, *Voyage of George Vancouver*, 3:1,016, 1,017n.
201 Haskins, "Journal of a Fur Trading Voyage," 191–3; Jackman, *Journal of William Sturgis*, 118–19.
202 Archer, "Transient Presence," 29, quoting Estéban José Martínez, "Diario," 125; Barreiro-Meiro, *Coleccion de diarios*, 125; Dixon, *Voyage Round the World*, xvii; Jane, *Spanish Voyage*, 17; [Jewitt], *Narrative*, 91–3; Meares, *Voyages Made in the Years 1788 and 1789*, li-lii; Walker, *Account of a Voyage*, 189.
203 [Martain], "Ship Hamilton Log Book," [137].
204 Ibid., [168].
205 Ibid., [169].

206 Ibid., [168]; Hill, "Autobiography," 17.
207 Anonymous, "Journal of a Voyage Round the World on the Brig Rob Roy," 13 March 1822, 20–21 April 1823.
208 Ibid., 5 March, 25–26 August 1822. Also see ibid., 24 September–7 October 1824.
209 Douglas, "Diary of a trip to the Northwest Coast," 5, 17 August 1840.
210 [Sturgis], "Ms. of 3 lectures," lecture 3, 40.
211 Haskins, "Journal of a Fur Trading Voyage," 37, 39–40.
212 Tikhmenev, *History of the Russian-American Company*, 2:157.
213 Anonymous, "Log-book of the Brig Lydia," 112–13; Clinton, "Journal," 12–13 June 1805; Lamb, "Notes on Trade with the Northwest Coast," 43.
214 Franchère, *Journal of a Voyage*, 126–7.
215 Choris, *Voyage pittoresque*, "Port San-Francisco et ses habitants," 9.
216 Clinton, "Journal," 6 August 1805.
217 Ibid., 5 May 1805.
218 [Ingraham], Ingraham to Martínez, May 1789.
219 Bartlett, "John Bartlett's journal," 18–19.
220 [Allen], "Log of the Ship *Hamilton*," 174, 184.
221 Anonymous, "Journal of a Voyage Round the World on the Brig Rob Roy," 22 May 1822.
222 Rich, *Part of Dispatch*, 79.
223 Leonard, "Ship Alert Log Book," 29 August 1818.
224 Haskins, "Journal of a Fur Trading Voyage," 21 March 1801.
225 Furgerson, "Journal of a Voyage from Boston to the Northwest Coast," 24 October 1809.
226 Jones to Marshall and Wildes, 23 December 1821, Marshall Manuscripts.
227 A. Simpson to McLoughlin, 22 September 1828, HBCA, B.223/c/1.
228 Hayes, *Log of the Union*, 49–50.
229 Meares, *Voyages Made in the Years 1788 and 1789*, 267.
230 Howay, *Voyages of the "Columbia"*, 234. Also see ibid., 98.
231 [Roe], *Journal and Letters*, 94.
232 MacNair, "Log of the Caroline," 185.
233 Tikhmenev, *History of the Russian-American Company*, 2:157.
234 A. Simpson to McLoughlin, 22 September 1828, HBCA, B.223/c/1.
235 "Fort Simpson (Nass) – Post Journal 1834–1838," 22 August 1837, HBCA, B.201/a/3.
236 Corning, "Letters of Sullivan Dorr," 301.
237 D'Wolf, *Voyage to the North Pacific*, 2, 19.
238 Clinton, "Journal," 10 October 1805.
239 Loring, "Memoir of the Hon. William Sturgis," 443.
240 Bryant and Sturgis to Clark, 1 December 1817, Bryant and Sturgis Papers.

241 Bryant and Sturgis to Hale, 31 August 1818, Bryant and Sturgis Papers.
242 Grimes to Marshall, 5 July 1821, Marshall Manuscripts.
243 Gast and Conrad, *Don Francisco de Paula Marin*, 255.
244 [Scouler], "John Scouler's Journal," 191–2.
245 A. Simpson to McLoughlin, 22 September 1828, HBCA, B.223/c/1.
246 Korn, "Shadows of Destiny," 36–7.
247 Work to E. Ermatinger, 1 January 1836, Work Correspondence.
248 Barkley, "Journal of the *Halcyon*," 4 September, 3 October 1792.
249 Barkley, "Reminiscences," n.p.
250 Jackman, *Journal of William Sturgis*, 80.
251 Rich, *Part of Dispatch*, 79.
252 Haskins, "Journal of a Fur Trading Voyage," 60.
253 See Ferguson, "Reexamination."
254 [Suter], "Log of the ship Atahualpa," 27 February 1812.
255 [Martain], "Ship Hamilton Log Book," [171].
256 Ibid., Joseph Ford [to T. Brown], 1812, enclosure at end of log.
257 "Fort Simpson (Nass) – Post Journal 1834–1838," 20 August 1835, HBCA, B.201/a/3.
258 "Fort Simpson (Nass) – Post Journal 1838–1840," 6 May 1838, HBCA, B.201/a/4.
259 Ibid., 8 July 1838.
260 Bryant and Sturgis to J. Sturgis and Company, 6 May 1822, Bryant and Sturgis Papers.
261 Grimes to Marshall and Wildes, 10 January 1823, Marshall Manuscripts.
262 Jones to Marshall and Wildes, 22 November 1822, Marshall Manuscripts.
263 Jones to Marshall and Wildes, 21 December 1822, Marshall Manuscripts.
264 Bryant and Sturgis to J. Sturgis and Company, 6 May 1822, Bryant and Sturgis Papers.
265 Bryant and Sturgis to J. Sturgis and Company, 1 June 1822, Bryant and Sturgis Papers.
266 C. H. Hammatt Journal, 1823–1825, n.p., Bryant and Sturgis Papers. Also see Gast and Conrad, *Don Francisco de Paula Marin*, 271; [Smith], "Arab (brig) Logbook," 23 November 1822.
267 Bryant and Sturgis to Cross and Bryant, 18 October 1823, Bryant and Sturgis Papers.
268 Bryant and Sturgis to Newell, 20 June 1822, Bryant and Sturgis Papers.
269 Grimes to Marshall and Wildes, 10 January 1823, Marshall Manuscripts.
270 C. H. Hammatt Journal, 1823–1825, 28, Bryant and Sturgis Papers.

271 [Puget], "Log of the Proceedings of His Majesty's Armed Tender Chatham," 66.

272 Ibid., 71v.

273 Dixon, *Voyage Round the World*, 189. Also see Meares, *Voyages Made in the Years 1788 and 1789*, 321–4, 328–9.

274 Dixon, *Voyage Round the World*, 169.

275 Ibid., 201; Howay, *Voyages of the "Columbia"*, 96.

276 Howay, *Voyages of the "Columbia"*, 342.

277 Moziño, *Noticias de Nutka*, 97.

278 Walker, *Account of a Voyage*, 199.

279 Ibid., 66; Cleveland, *Voyages and Commercial Enterprises*, 51; Kaplanoff, *Joseph Ingraham's Journal*, xvii, 146; Jackman, *Journal of William Sturgis*, 106–7; Lamb, *Voyage of George Vancouver*, 4:1,407.

280 [Sturgis], "Northwest Fur Trade," 537.

281 Kelly, *Hawai'i in 1819*, 88.

282 Pitman and French to Marshall, March 1822, Marshall Manuscripts.

283 Hayes, *Log of the Union*, 64.

284 Myers, *Life, Voyages and Travels*, 70.

285 Lamb, "Notes on Trade with the Northwest Coast," 25, 27.

286 Cleveland, *Voyages and Commercial Enterprises*, 72; Corning, "Letters of Sullivan Dorr," 181, 183; MacNair, "Log of the Caroline," 68, 200.

287 Lamb, "Notes on Trade with the Northwest Coast," n.p.

288 Ibid., 39.

289 D'Wolf, *Voyage to the North Pacific*, 2, 32, 146.

290 Clinton, "Journal," 8 September 1806.

291 Lamb, "Notes on Trade with the Northwest Coast," 49, n.p.

292 [Sturgis], "Northwest Fur Trade," 537.

293 Howay, *Atahualpa*, 17, 28.

294 Hammatt to Hunnewell, 24 September 1827, Hunnewell Papers.

295 [Sturgis], "Northwest Fur Trade," 537.

296 Porter, *John Jacob Astor*, 1:454.

297 Fyodorova, *Russkaya Amerika*, 89.

298 Haskins, "Journal of a Fur Trading Voyage," 225–6.

299 Walker, *Account of a Voyage*, 146.

300 Porter, *John Jacob Astor*, 1:449.

301 Howay, *Voyage of the "New Hazard"*, 14n.

302 [Suter], "Log of the ship Atahualpa," 9 August 1812.

303 Brown to Marshall and Wildes, 6 July 1821, Marshall Manuscripts.

304 Grimes to Marshall and Wildes, 8 July 1822, Marshall Manuscripts.

305 Reynolds, "Journal," 2:82.

306 Ibid., 256.

307 [Roe], *Journal and Letters*, 62.

308 [Work], *Journal*, 40.

309 De Roquefeuil, *Journal d'un voyage*, 2:307–8; Jones to Marshall, 1 November 1826, 1 November 1827, 30 October 1828, Marshall Manuscripts; Perkins to Perkins, 13 October, 29 November 1822, Perkins and Russell Papers; [Phelps], "Solid Men of Boston," 6; [Sturgis], "Northwest Fur Trade," 536.

310 Corning, "Letters of Sullivan Dorr," 262.

311 [Sturgis], "Northwest Fur Trade," 536.

312 Bartlett, "John Bartlett's Journal," 40.

313 Lamb, *Voyage of George Vancouver*, 2:682n.

314 Ibid., 4:1,407–8.

315 Lamb, "Notes on Trade with the Northwest Coast," 35, 39.

316 Corning, "Letters of Sullivan Dorr," 181–2, 185, 198, 200; MacNair, "Log of the Caroline," 200.

317 Corning, "Letters of Sullivan Dorr," 227, 231, 243, 249; Haskins, "Journal of a Fur Trading Voyage," 52.

318 Haskins, "Journal of a Fur Trading Voyage," 127.

319 Ibid., "Blotter," 49.

320 Clinton, "Journal," 25 April, 12 July, 27 September 1805.

321 Porter, *John Jacob Astor*, 1:449.

322 Golovnin, *Around the World on the "Kamchatka"*, 127; [Suter], "Log of the ship Atahualpa," passim.

323 [Allen], "Log of the Ship *Hamilton*," 112, 116.

324 [Smith], "Arab (brig) Logbook," 21 June, 2 July, 7 August 1821.

325 Anonymous, "Journal of a Voyage Round the World on the Brig Rob Roy," 1 April, 18 September 1822.

326 Bryant and Sturgis to Bennett, 16 March 1824, Bryant and Sturgis Papers; Golovnin, *Around the World on the "Kamchatka"*, 127; Wildes to Marshall, 5 November 1824, Marshall Manuscripts; Perkins to Perkins, 23 January 1820 and C. H. Hammatt Journal, 1823–1825, 43, Perkins and Russell Papers.

327 Bryant and Sturgis to Suter, 6 August 1816, Bryant and Sturgis Papers.

328 Records of the Russian-American Company, USNARS, roll 32:55–55v.

329 Meany, *New Vancouver Journal*, 31.

330 Newcombe, *Menzies' Journal*, 17.

331 Tikhmenev, *History of the Russian-American Company*, 2:114. Also see De Roquefeuil, *Journal d'un voyage*, 2:309.

332 Corning, "Letters of Sullivan Dorr," 181–2, 185, 193, 198, 200, 302, 357; Howay, *List of Trading Vessels*, 36–52; Jackman, *Journal of William Sturgis*, 113, 115, 117, 120.

333 Corning, "Letters of Sullivan Dorr," 259.

334 Haskins, "Journal of a Fur Trading Voyage," 219, 221.

335 De Roquefeuil, *Journal d'un voyage*, 2:307–8; Fyodorova, *Russkaya Amerika*, 44, 88; Jackman, *Journal of William Sturgis*, 113, 115, 117, 120.

336 Boardman to Barker, 1 May 1832, Boardman Letterbook; Perkins to Perkins, 14 January 1821, Perkins and Russell Papers.

337 Wike, "Effect of the Maritime Fur Trade," 90.

338 Howay, *Journal of Captain James Colnett*, 23.

339 Portlock, *Voyage Round the World*, 218.

340 Ibid., 220, 382.

341 Barkley, "Journal of the *Halcyon*," 11 November 1792.

342 Lamb, *Voyage of George Vancouver*, 3:1,073.

343 Haskins, "Journal of a Fur Trading Voyage," 221.

344 Jackman, *Journal of William Sturgis*, 116.

345 Haskins, "Journal of a Fur Trading Voyage," 221.

346 [Sturgis], "Northwest Fur Trade," 537.

347 Perkins to Swift, 22 July 1807, J. and T.H. Perkins, Foreign letters, 1807–1815.

348 Perkins to Perkins, 29 March 1808, J. and T.H. Perkins, Foreign letters, 1807–1815.

349 Perkins to Perkins, 7 December 1808, J. and T.H. Perkins, Foreign letters, 1807–1815.

350 Newcombe, *Menzies' Journal*, 88.

351 Lamb, *Voyage of George Vancouver*, 2:627.

352 Howay, "Letters Relating to the Second Voyage of the Columbia," 139; idem, *Voyages of the "Columbia"*, 473.

353 Lamb, *Voyage of George Vancouver*, 2:612n.

354 Hayes, *Log of the Union*, 45.

355 Magee, "Log of the Jefferson," passim.

356 Hayes, *Log of the Union*, 119.

357 Quincy, *Journals of Major Samuel Shaw*, 34.

358 S. Dorr to E. Dorr, 16 August 1801, Ebenezer Dorr Papers.

359 Corning, "Letters of Sullivan Dorr," 284.

360 Haskins, "Journal of a Fur Trading Voyage," 41, 72, 74.

361 Morison, "Letters on the Northwest Fur Trade," 174.

362 Dominis to Marshall, 14 June 1829, Marshall Manuscripts.

363 Duhaut-Cilly, *Voyage autour du monde*, 2:320.

364 Bryant and Sturgis to Hale, 31 August 1818, Bryant and Sturgis Papers.

365 Newcombe, *Menzies' Journal*, 88; Wagner, *Spanish Explorations*, 88, 153, 165, 182, 189–90, 230.

366 Wagner, *Spanish Explorations*, 153.

367 Meany, *New Vancouver Journal*, 40.

368 [Puget], "Log of the Proceedings of His Majesty's Armed Tender Chatham," 42v.

369 Lloyd and Anderson, *Memoir of James Trevenen*, 21–2.

370 Tikhmenev, *History of the Russian-American Company*, 2:112.

371 Cleveland, *Narrative*, 1:72, 90; Haskins, "Journal of a Fur Trading Voyage," 74; Jackman, *Journal of William Sturgis*, 68, 113–17, 121; MacNair, "Log of the Caroline," 175, 183.

372 S. Dorr to E. Dorr, 16 August 1801, Ebenezer Dorr Papers.

373 Haskins, "Journal of a Fur Trading Voyage," 103, 194.

374 Anonymous, ["Logs of the Ships *Athahualpa*, *Behring*, and *Isabella* and the Brig *Pedler*,"], 4 August 1812; Jackman, *Journal of William Sturgis*, 115; Records of the Russian-American Company, USNARS, roll 28:245, roll 42:446; [Work], *Journal*, 21, 23.

375 C.H. Hammatt Journal, 1823–1825, 20, Bryant and Sturgis Papers.

376 McNeill, "Journal of a Voyage kept onboard the Honourable Hudson's Bay Brig Lama," 27 February, 21 September 1833.

377 Morison, "Letters on the Northwest Fur Trade," 177.

378 McNeill, "Journal of a Voyage to the N.W. Coast of North America," 3 August 1825.

379 A. Simpson to McLoughlin, 22 September 1828, HBCA, B.223/c/1; Howay, *List of Trading Vessels*, 93.

380 Magee, "Log of the Jefferson," 26 July 1793.

381 MacNair, "Log of the Caroline," 184, 187.

382 Howay, *Voyages of the "Columbia"*, 486.

383 [Péron], *Mémoires*, 1:295, 2:2.

384 Jackman, *Journal of William Sturgis*, 120.

385 For example, see Hayes, *Log of the Union*, 66; [Liscome?], "Extracts from the log of the Ship Margaret," passim.

386 Green, *Journal of a Tour*, 85–6.

387 A. Simpson to McLoughlin, 22 September 1828, HBCA, B.223/c/1.

388 Jones to Marshall, 30 October 1827, Marshall Manuscripts.

389 [Colnett], "Voyage to the N.W. Side of America," 155.

390 MacNair, "Log of the Caroline," 193n.

391 Clinton, "Journal," 8 August 1806.

392 Walker, "Supercargo's log of the brig *Lydia*," 38v.

393 Dorr, "Journal of a Voyage from Boston round the World," 26 May 1791. Also see Kaplanoff, *Joseph Ingraham's Journal*, 79–80.

394 Lamb, *Voyage of George Vancouver*, 3:797n., 818n.

395 Ibid., 856.

396 Walker, "Supercargo's log of the brig *Lydia*," 40v.

397 Anonymous, ["Logs of the Ships *Athahualpa*, *Behring*, and *Isabella* and the Brig *Pedler*,"], 15 March 1814.

398 Hill, "Journal and Log," 242.

399 Dampier, *To the Sandwich Islands*, 38.

400 Lamb, *Voyage of George Vancouver*, 3:800n.

401 Gast and Conrad, *Don Francisco de Paula Marin*, 299–301, 303–4; Polansky, "Baron Vrangel' Visits the Sandwich Islands," 19.

402 Bartlett, "John Bartlett's Journal," 51–3; Howay, *Voyages of the "Columbia"*, 420–1; Jackman, *Journal of William Sturgis*, 116; Meares, *Voyages Made in the Years 1788 and 1789*, xl.

403 Corning, "Letters of Sullivan Dorr," 276–7.

404 On Chinese piracy, see Boxer, "Piracy in the South China Sea"; Turner, *Account of the Captivity*; Yung, *History of the Pirates*.

405 Despatches from United States Consuls in Canton, 1790–1906, USNARS, roll 1, Carrington to Madison, 1807.

406 Anonymous, "Chinese Pirates," 62–3.

407 Fairbank, *History of China*, vol. 10, pt. 1:165.

408 Latourette, "History of Early Relations," 48.

409 Fu, *Documentary Chronicle*, 2:597.

410 Fairbank, *History of China*, vol. 10, pt. 1:165.

411 Lisiansky, *Voyage Round the World*, 269.

412 Von Krusenstern, *Voyage Round the World*, 2:276–7.

413 Morse, *Chronicles of the East India Company*, 2:422. Captains Lisiansky and Von Krusenstern reported 200,000 ladrones with 4,000 vessels (Lisiansky, *Voyage Round the World*, 269; Von Krusenstern, *Voyage Round the World*, 2:309).

414 Morse, *Chronicles of the East India Company*, 3:7–8.

415 Anonymous, "Chinese Pirates," 72, 82.

416 Morse, *Chronicles of the East India Company*, 2:290.

417 Ibid., 3:116–17; Latourette, "History of Early Relations," 49; Loring, "Memoir of the Hon. William Sturgis," 432; [Sturgis], "Journal of W. Sturgis, 1799," T. W. Ward to W. Ward, 29 September 1809.

418 Morse, *Chronicles of the East India Company*, 3:123, 144.

419 Bryant and Sturgis to Suter, 2 December 1817, Bryant and Sturgis Papers.

420 Latourette, "History of Early Relations," 49.

421 Ibid., 49–51.

422 Despatches from United States Consuls in Canton, 1790–1906, USNARS, roll 1:passim.

423 Perkins to Bennett, 14 February 1813, Bryant and Sturgis Papers.

424 Despatches from United States Consuls in Canton, 1790–1906, USNARS, roll 1, "A Return of American Vessels ..."

425 Latourette, "History of Early Relations," 51–2.

426 Great Britain, *Sessional Papers* 5:326 [316].

427 Delano, *Narrative of Voyages and Travels*, 408.

428 Hughes, *Letters and Recollections*, 1:86.

429 Great Britain, *Sessional Papers* 5:377–8.

430 Corning, "Letters of Sullivan Dorr," 242, 272.

431 Dobell, *Travels in Kamtchatka and Siberia*, 2:180.

432 Gibson, "Observations on the Trade with the Chinese," [1].

433 Morse, *Chronicles of the East India Company*, 2:148.

434 Howay, *Voyages of the "Columbia"*, 422.

435 Fu, *Documentary Chronicle*, 2:602.

436 Fleurieu, *Voyage Round the World*, 2:99.

437 Lisiansky, *Voyage Round the World*, 282.

438 Von Krusenstern, *Voyage Round the World*, 2:339.

439 Howay, *Voyages of the "Columbia"*, 423.

440 Corning, "Letters of Sullivan Dorr," 186, 207, 212.

441 Ibid., 180–1.

442 Ibid., 161–2.

443 Pierrepont, "Notes on the Trade of China," 37, 43.

444 Gibson, "Observations on the Trade with the Chinese," [11].

445 Dobell, *Travels in Kamtchatka and Siberia*, 2:133.

446 Trowbridge, "Diary of Mr. Ebenezer Townsend, Jr.," 93–4.

447 Dixon, *Voyage Round the World*, 314.

448 Pierrepont, "Notes on the Trade of China," 22.

449 Ibid., 22–3.

450 Fleurieu, *Voyage Round the World*, 2:72–3.

451 Trowbridge, "Diary of Mr. Ebenezer Townsend, Jr.," 92.

452 Pierrepont, "Notes on the Trade of China," 23.

453 Greenberg, *British Trade and the Opening of China*, 61.

454 Morse, *Chronicles of the East India Company*, 2:153, 181, 190, 261–4, 273, 299, 3:110–11, 4:57; Great Britain, *Sessional Papers* 7:171.

455 Greenberg, *British Trade and the Opening of China*, 63–9.

456 Great Britain, *Sessional Papers* 7:174.

457 Greenberg, *British Trade and the Opening of China*, 68.

458 Ibid., 86.

459 Despatches of United States Consuls in Canton, 1790–1906, USNARS, roll 1, Howell to Barrell *et al.*, 11 May 1795.

460 Fu, *Documentary Chronicle*, 1:392.

461 Gibson, "Observations on the Trade with the Chinese," [12].

462 Trowbridge, "Diary of Mr. Ebenezer Townsend, Jr.," 88.

463 Meares, *Voyages Made in the Years 1788 and 1789*, lxxvii.

464 Great Britain, *Sessional Papers* 5:59.

465 Ibid., 21; Bryant and Sturgis to Suter, 6 August 1816, Bryant and Sturgis Papers.

466 Perkins to Smith, 10 September 1822, 15 November 1823, Perkins and Russell Papers.

467 Corning, "Letters of Sullivan Dorr," 199.

468 Morse, *Chronicles of the East India Company*, 1:267.

469 Parkinson, *Trade in the Eastern Seas*, 341–2.

470 Lisiansky, *Voyage Round the World*, 281.

471 Hunter, *"Fan Kwae" at Canton*, 99.

472 Great Britain, *Sessional Papers* 5:33, 6:400.

473 Corning, "Letters of Sullivan Dorr," 262, 348; Great Britain, *Sessional Papers* 5:90; Howay, "Barrell Letters," 264.

474 Howay, "Captains Gray and Kendrick," 260, 264.

475 Howay, *Voyages of the "Columbia"*, 141.

476 Gibson, "Observations on the Trade with the Chinese," [12–14].

477 Dobell, *Travels in Kamtchatka and Siberia*, 2:170.

478 Trowbridge, "Diary of Mr. Ebenezer Townsend, Jr.," 85.

479 Forbes, *Remarks on China*, 16.

480 Great Britain, *Sessional Papers* 5:122, 247–8.

481 Hunter, *"Fan Kwae" at Canton*, 100.

482 Fanning, *Voyages Round the World*, 263.

483 Anonymous, "Journal of a Voyage Round the World on the Brig Rob Roy," 6 December 1822.

484 Kaplanoff, *Joseph Ingraham's Journal*, 177.

485 Fleurieu, *Voyage Round the World*, 2:72.

486 Ibid., 71.

487 Dobell, *Travels in Kamtchatka and Siberia*, 2:146.

488 Delano, *Narrative of Voyages and Travels*, 43.

489 Howay, *Voyages of the "Columbia"*, 129, 134.

490 Howay, "Captains Gray and Kendrick," 268.

491 Kaplanoff, *Joseph Ingraham's Journal*, xiv.

492 [Dorr], ["Logbook of the *Hope*"], 1 December 1791–2 March, 1792.

493 Von Krusenstern, *Voyage Round the World*, 2:315.

494 Hunter, *"Fan Kwae" at Canton*, 21; French to Marshall, 9 November 1822, Marshall Manuscripts; Morse, *Chronicles of the East India Company*, 4:65; Perkins to Perkins, 7 November 1822, Perkins to Williams, 15 November 1822, Perkins and Russell Papers.

495 The Maury Abstract Logs 1796–1861, USNARS, roll 70, target 3, volume 235, "Ship *Caledonia*," [161–63].

496 Corning, "Letters of Sullivan Dorr," 270.

497 Von Krusenstern, *Voyage Round the World*, 2:316–17.

498 P[earson], "Vaccination," 37.

499 Ibid., 36; Von Krusenstern, *Voyage Round the World*, 2:316–19.

500 Trowbridge, "Diary of Mr. Ebenezer Townsend, Jr.," 87, 103.

501 Lisiansky, *Voyage Round the World*, 281.

502 Dixon, *Voyage Round the World*, 232, 316–19; Howay, *List of Trading Vessels*, 5; Kaplanoff, *Joseph Ingraham's Journal*, 178, 182; Khlebnikov, *Baranov*, 50; Lisiansky, *Voyage Round the World*, 281; Walker, *Account of a Voyage*, 199.

503 Meany, *New Vancouver Journal*, 40.

504 Rich, *Part of Dispatch*, 75.

505 Cook [and King], *Voyage to the Pacific Ocean*, 3:437; [Sturgis], "Northwest Fur Trade," 536.

506 Von Krusenstern, *Voyage Round the World*, 2:331.

507 Anonymous, "Journal of a Voyage Round the World on the Brig Rob Roy," 6 December 1822.

508 Corning, "Letters of Sullivan Dorr," passim, especially 239.

509 Howay, *Voyages of the "Columbia"*, 135, 488.

510 Anonymous, ["Logs of the Ships *Atahualpa*, *Behring*, and *Isabella* and the Brig *Pedler*,"], 7 March 1816.

511 Howay, *Voyages of the "Columbia"*, 134.

512 Boardman to Barker, 1 May, 8 September 1832, Boardman Letterbook.

513 Cleveland, *Narrative*, 2:100; Corning, "Letters of Sullivan Dorr," 185; MacNair, "Log of the Caroline," 200.

514 Corning, "Letters of Sullivan Dorr," 234.

515 Ibid., 266.

516 Ibid., 212.

517 Ibid., 332.

518 Dixon, *Voyage Round the World*, 303, 321, 382.

519 Tikhmenev, *History of the Russian-American Company*, 1:115.

520 Howay, *Voyages of the "Columbia"*, 470; Pipes, "Later Affairs of Kendrick," 96–7.

521 Howay, *Voyages of the "Columbia"*, 480.

522 Morse, *Chronicles of the East India Company*, 2:256.

523 Corning, "Letters of Sullivan Dorr," 184.

524 Ibid., 224.

525 Ibid., 239.

526 Ibid.

527 Ibid., 287, 324.

528 Ibid., 329.

529 Ibid., 170–1, 181–2, 185, 193, 198, 200, 302, 357.

530 Ibid., 231.

531 Ibid., 226, 230.

532 Ibid.

533 Ibid., 170–71, 228–30, 235, 242–4, 248, 302, 357.

534 Ibid., 281.

535 Quincy, *Journals of Major Samuel Shaw*, 231, 345.

536 Sturgis to Cushing, 23 March 1812, Bryant and Sturgis Papers.

537 Perkins to Perkins, 13 May 1807, J. and T.H. Perkins, Foreign letters.

538 Bryant and Sturgis to Washing, 25 February 1818, Bryant and Sturgis to Sturgis, 31 March 1818, Bryant and Sturgis Papers.

539 Great Britain, *Sessional Papers* 6:366, 368.

540 Sturgis to Cushing, 23 March 1812, Bryant and Sturgis Papers.

CHAPTER EIGHT

1 Dixon, *Voyage Round the World*, xvii.
2 Meares, *Voyages Made in the Years 1788 and 1789*, 312; Tikhmenev, *History of the Russian-American Company*, 2:32.
3 Meares, *Voyages Made in the Years 1788 and 1789*, 234; Portlock, *Voyage Round the World*, 3.
4 Beaglehole, *Journals of Captain James Cook*, vol. 3, pt. 2:1,330.
5 Lamb, *Voyage of George Vancouver*, 4:1,406–7.
6 Beaglehole, *Journals of Captain James Cook*, vol. 3, pt. 2:1,323.
7 [Colnett], "Voyage to the N. W. Side of America," 121v.
8 Ibid., Appendix, v.
9 Lamb, *Voyage of George Vancouver*, 1:98, 4:1,399, 1,411, 1,416, 1,550–1.
10 Howay, *Voyages of the "Columbia"*, 485–6.
11 Moziño, *Noticias de Nutka*, 48, 91.
12 [Scouler], "John Scouler's Journal," 193.
13 [Roe], *Journal and Letters*, 122.
14 Miscellaneous Letters of the Department of State, USNARS, roll 35, Sturgis to Morris, 22 August 1816.
15 Sturgis, "Extract from the Journal of Josiah Sturgis," 2.
16 Thwaites, *Original Journals*, 3:226, 306–7, 327, 340–1, 345.
17 Ibid., 327–8, 344–5.
18 Sturgis, "Extract from the Journal of Josiah Sturgis," 5.
19 Lamb, *Voyage of George Vancouver*, 4:1,390.
20 D'Wolf, *Voyage to the North Pacific*, 17.
21 Wagner and Newcombe, "Journal of Jacinto Caamaño," 266.
22 Anonymous, "Journal of a Voyage Round the World on the Brig Rob Roy," 5 March 1822.
23 Barkley, "Journal of the *Halcyon*," 3 October 1792.
24 A. Simpson to McLoughlin, 22 September 1828, HBCA, B.223/c/1.
25 [Work], *Journal*, 21–2.
26 Anonymous, "Journal of a Voyage Round the World on the Brig Rob Roy," 1 July 1822.
27 Jackman, *Journal of William Sturgis*, 115.
28 Haskins, "Journal of a Fur Trading Voyage," 116.
29 Walker, *Account of a Voyage*, 191.
30 Kaplanoff, *Joseph Ingraham's Journal*, 146–7.
31 [Martain], "Ship Hamilton Log Book," passim.
32 Commonwealth of Australia, *Historical Records*, series 1, vol. 8, Captain Tucker to Secretary Croker, 28 June 1815.

33 Bryant and Sturgis to Suter, 6 August 1816, Bryant and Sturgis Papers.

34 Ibid.

35 Anonymous, ["Logs of the Ships *Atahualpa*, *Behring*, and *Isabella* and the Brig *Pedler*,"], 12 November 1812.

36 Anonymous, "Journal of a Voyage Round the World on the Brig Rob Roy," 10–21 December 1822.

37 Anonymous, "*Griffon*, Brig. Shipping Journal," 30 November 1826.

38 A. Simpson to McLoughlin, 22 September 1828, HBCA, B.223/c/1.

39 Ibid.

40 Bryant and Sturgis to Bryant, August 1826, Bryant and Sturgis Papers.

41 "Fort Simpson (Nass) – Post Journal 1838–1840," 4 September 1838, HBCA, B.201/a/4.

42 Magee, "Log of the Jefferson," September, October, November 1793.

43 Clinton, "Journal," 26 March, 4 April, 3, 4, 12 May, 4, 6, 8 July, 5, 18 August 1805.

44 Anonymous, "Journal of a Voyage Round the World on the Brig Rob Roy," 5, 9 March 1822.

45 Ibid., 16, 18 July 1822.

46 Furgerson, "Journal of a Voyage from Boston to the Northwest Coast," 19 May 1810.

47 [Martain], "Ship Hamilton Log Book," [155–6].

48 [Allen], "Log of the Ship *Hamilton*," 218.

49 "Fort Simpson (Nass) – Post Journal 1834–1838," 31 October 1836, HBCA, B.201/a/3.

50 Williams, *London Correspondence*, 61–4.

51 Ibid., 64.

52 Gibson, "European Dependence Upon American Natives," Tables 2, 3, and 4.

53 Simpson, *Narrative of a Journey*, 1:214.

54 Ibid., 227.

55 Douglas to McLoughlin, 1 October 1840, HBCA, B.223/b/28.

56 Furgerson, "Journal of a Voyage from Boston to the Northwest Coast," 31 August 1810.

57 Clinton, "Journal," 1 March 1806.

58 Ibid., 1, 18 March 1806.

59 Ibid., 7 August 1806.

60 Anonymous, "*Griffon*, Brig. Shipping Journal," 20–21, 23–27 July 1827.

61 Morison, "Boston Traders in Hawaiian Islands," 194.

62 Howay, *List of Trading Vessels*, 135.

63 [Suter], "Log of John Suter," 127.

64 Bryant and Sturgis to Cross, 14 August 1821, Bryant and Sturgis to Peirce, 22 October 1824, Bryant and Sturgis to Allen, 27 October 1827, Bryant and Sturgis Papers.

65 [Allen], "Log of the Ship *Hamilton*," 178.

66 Despatches from United States Consuls in Canton, 1790–1906, USNARS, roll 1, Wilcocks to Munroe, January 10, 1815.

67 See Duncan, "Kanaka World Travelers and Fur Company Employees", and idem, *Minority without a Champion*, for an account of Hawaiians in the maritime and continental fur trades of the Pacific Slope of North America. Also see Kittelson, "Hawaiians and Fur Traders."

68 Clinton, "Journal," 24 February 1805.

69 Franchère, *Journal of a Voyage*, 70.

70 Ii, *Fragments of Hawaiian History*, 87.

71 [Martain], "Ship Hamilton Log Book," 3 October 1809, 29 November 1815.

72 McNeill, "Journal of a Voyage to the N.W. Coast of North America," [1]; [Scouler], "John Scouler's Journal," 177.

73 Howay, *List of Trading Vessels*, 134; Korn, "Shadows of Destiny," 29; Rich, *Part of Dispatch*, 79.

74 Fyodorova, *Russkaya Amerika*, 134.

75 Von Langsdorff, *Voyages and Travels*, 1:187.

76 Golovnin, *Around the World on the "Kamchatka"*, 200–1.

77 Bryant and Sturgis to Hale, 31 August 1818, Bryant and Sturgis Papers.

78 Walker, "Supercargo's log of the brig *Lydia*," 40.

79 Bryant and Sturgis to Cross, 14 August 1821, Bryant and Sturgis Papers.

80 Furgerson, "Journal of a Voyage from Boston to the Northwest Coast," 17, 23 June 1810.

81 Ibid., 23 June, 11 November 1810.

82 "Fort Simpson (Nass) – Post Journal 1834–1838," n.d., HBCA, D.201/a/3, [lv.].

83 McLoughlin to the Governor and Council of the Northern Department, 20 March 1826, HBCA, D.4/119.

84 Howay, *Journal of Captain James Colnett*, 15–16; Wagner, *Spanish Explorations*, 293.

85 Furgerson, "Journal of a Voyage from Boston to the Northwest Coast," 25 December 1810.

86 Bryant and Sturgis to Clark, 1 December 1817, Bryant and Sturgis to Hale, 31 August 1818, Bryant and Sturgis Papers.

87 Anonymous, "Journey of a Voyage Round the World on the Brig Rob Roy," 5–9 March 1822.

88 Wike, "Effect of the Maritime Fur Trade," 90.

89 Howay, *Voyages of the "Columbia"*, 485.
90 Ibid.
91 Magee, "Log of the Jefferson," 26 July 1793.
92 Anonymous, "Ship Hancock Log Book," 19 July 1799 and passim.
93 Haskins, "Journal of a Fur Trading Voyage," [258].
94 See Myers, *Life, Voyages and Travels*, 408.
95 Corning, "Letters of Sullivan Dorr," 301.
96 Ibid., 284, 301.
97 S. Dorr to E. Dorr, 16 August 1801, Ebenezer Dorr Papers.
98 Corning, "Letters of Sullivan Dorr," 333.
99 Clinton, "Journal," 27 July 1805.
100 Sturgis to J. Dorr, October 1806, Ebenezer Dorr Papers.
101 Grimes to Marshall and Wildes, 8 July, 11 August 1822, Marshall Manuscripts; Morison, "Letters on the Northwest Fur Trade," 175, 177.
102 "Bill of Lading of the Ship Active," n.p.; "Bill of Lading of the Ship Louisa," n.p.
103 A. Simpson to McLoughlin, 22 September 1828, HBCA, B.223/c/1.
104 Ibid.
105 Thompson to Marshall, 26 March 1829, Marshall Manuscripts.
106 Bryant and Sturgis to Suter, 6 August 1816, Bryant and Sturgis Papers.
107 Grimes to Marshall and Wildes, 11 August 1822, Marshall Manuscripts.
108 Grimes to Marshall and Wildes, 8 July, 11 August 1822, Marshall Manuscripts.
109 Grimes to Marshall and Wildes, 11 August 1822, Marshall Manuscripts.
110 Walker, *Account of a Voyage*, 42, 138.
111 George MacDonald has postulated a shift of Indian population northwards from the northern coast and southwards from the central coast in the early 1770s in a Native attempt to get closer to the Russian and Spanish sources of iron, respectively (MacDonald, "Epic of Nekt," 79–80).
112 See Rickard, "Use of Iron and Copper".
113 Jackman, *Journal of William Sturgis*, 79–80.
114 [Sturgis], "Northwest Fur Trade," 536.
115 Meares, *Voyages Made in the Years 1788 and 1789*, xxxiv.
116 Ibid., 368.
117 Kaplanoff, *Joseph Ingraham's Journal*, 138.
118 Walker, *Account of a Voyage*, 109.
119 Howay, "Yankee Trader on the Northwest Coast," 84, 88; Howay, *Voyages of the "Columbia"*, 486.

120 Beaglehole, *Journals of Captain James Cook*, vol. 3, pt. 2:1,104.
121 Walker, *Account of a Voyage*, 42, 51–2, 108.
122 [Colnett], "Voyage to the N.W. Side of America," 118v.–19.
123 Dixon, *Voyage Round the World*, 245.
124 Howay, *Voyages of the "Columbia"*, 44; Meany, *New Vancouver Journal*, 5.
125 Jane, *Spanish Voyage*, 83; Wagner, *Spanish Explorations*, 189.
126 Magee, "Log of the Jefferson," 15, 16 June, 13 July, 7 September 1793.
127 Gunther, *Indian Life on the Northwest Coast*, 131.
128 Dunn, *History of the Oregon Territory*, 288.
129 Howay, *Voyages of the "Columbia"*, 187.
130 Lamb, *Voyage of George Vancouver*, 2:627.
131 Magee, "Log of the Jefferson," February, July–August, 7 September 1793.
132 Hayes, *Log of the Union*, 43.
133 Howay, *Journal of Captain James Colnett*, 281.
134 McNeil[l] to Marshall, 10 January 1826, Wildes to Marshall, March 1826, Marshall Manuscripts.
135 Records of the Russian-American Company, USNARS, roll 41:6v.
136 Beaglehole, *Journals of Captain James Cook*, vol. 3, pt. 2:1,325.
137 Magee, "Log of the Jefferson," 1 June 1794.
138 Hayes, *Log of the Union*, 7.
139 Haskins, "Journal of a Fur Trading Voyage," 30, 33.
140 A. Simpson to McLoughlin, 22 September 1828, HBCA, B.223/c/1.
141 Von Langsdorff, *Voyages and Travels*, 2:112.
142 See Jansen and Sargent, *Robes of Power*.
143 [Péron], *Memoirs*, 1:295, 2:2.
144 Cleveland, *Narrative*, 1:72, 90; Cleveland, "Northwest Expedition," 26, 28.
145 Kelly, *Hawai'i in 1819*, 88; Grimes to Marshall and Wildes, 8 July 1822, Marshall Manuscripts.
146 Anonymous, "*Griffon*, Brig. Shipping Journal," 15 May, 13 June 1826, 7 June 1827.
147 [Suter], "Log of the Atahualpa," 1, 4 August 1812.
148 Grimes to Marshall and Wildes, 8 July, 11 August 1822, Marshall Manuscripts.
149 Anderson, "McLoughlin, Fort. Report on District. 1834," HBCA, B.120/e/1; "Fort Simpson (Nass) – Post Journal 1834–1838," 3–4 October 1837, HBCA, B.201/a/3.
150 Bryant and Sturgis to Suter, 12 October 1830, Bryant and Sturgis Papers. On the point blanket, see Hanson, "Point Blanket."
151 Howay, "Yankee Trader on the Northwest Coast," 86; Magee, "Log of the Jefferson," 13, 15 July, 7 September 1793.

152 Dixon, *Voyage Round the World*, 184.
153 Lamb, *Voyage of George Vancouver*, 2:612n.; Moziño, *Noticias de Nutka*, 70–1.
154 [Ingraham], Ingraham to Martínez, May 1789.
155 Howay, *Journal of Captain James Colnett*, 202.
156 Howay, *Voyages of the "Columbia"*, 258, 485.
157 [Puget], "Log of the Proceedings of His Majesty's Armed Tender Chatham," 49v.
158 Ibid., 43, 85.
159 Moziño, *Noticias de Nutka*, 80–1, 88; Lamb, *Voyage of George Vancouver*, 2:623.
160 [Liscome?], "Extracts from the log of the Ship Margaret," 15.
161 Barkley, "Reminiscences," n.p.
162 Walbran, "Cruise of the Imperial Eagle," 23, 26.
163 Lamb, *Voyage of George Vancouver*, 3:1,011.
164 [Puget], "Log of the Proceedings of His Majesty's Armed Tender Chatham," 56v.
165 Lamb, *Voyage of George Vancouver*, 3:1,040n.
166 [Roe], *Journal and Letters*, 77.
167 Howay, *Voyages of the "Columbia"*, 486; Magee, "Log of the Jefferson," February 1794; Meany, *New Vancouver Journal*, 40.
168 Corning, "Letters of Sullivan Dorr," 207.
169 Anonymous, "Ship Hancock Log Book," 18 April, 30 June, 19 July 1799.
170 Haskins, "Journal of a Fur Trading Voyage," 103.
171 Corning, "Letters of Sullivan Dorr," 231–2, 301, 333.
172 Records of the Russian-American Company, USNARS, roll 28:245.
173 Grimes to Marshall and Wildes, 11 August 1822, Marshall Manuscripts.
174 Anonymous, "Journal of a Voyage in the Brig Owhyhee," [2]; "*Cadboro* and *Dryad* logs, 1827 [*sic*]," 13 July 1831, HBCA, C.1/218.
175 Moziño, *Noticias de Nutka*, 48.
176 [Puget], "Log of the Proceedings of His Majesty's Armed Tender Chatham," 39. Also see Meany, *New Vancouver Journal*, 39–40.
177 Furgerson, "Journal of a Voyage from Boston to the Northwest Coast," 21 November 1810.
178 Howay, "Letters Relating to the Second Voyage of the Columbia," 139; Howay, *Voyages of the "Columbia"*, 474.
179 Moziño, *Noticias de Nutka*, 16.
180 Newcombe, *Menzies' Journal*, 80.
181 Jackman, *Journal of William Sturgis*, 121.
182 D'Wolf, *Voyage to the North Pacific*, 19.
183 Ibid., 48.

184 Lisiansky, *Voyage Round the World*, 231, 239.

185 Thwaites, *Original Journals*, 3:229. Also see ibid., 240.

186 Ibid., 346, 348.

187 [Holbrook], *Sketches*, 14.

188 A Simpson to McLoughlin, 22 September 1828, HBCA, B.223/c/1.

189 See Fisher, "Arms and Men"; Townsend, "Firearms against Native Arms."

190 Work to McLoughlin, 2 May 1838, HBCA, B.201/a/4.

191 Ibid.

192 Thwaites, *Original Journals*, 3:322, 336.

193 See Howay, "Introduction of Intoxicating Liquors."

194 Jackman, *Journal of William Sturgis*, 57.

195 "*Cadboro* and *Dryad* logs, 1827 [*sic*]," 17 July 1831, HBCA, C.1/218.

196 [Jewitt], *Narrative*, 14.

197 McNeill, "Journal of a Voyage kept on board the Honourable Hudson's Bay Brig Lama," 22 April 1833.

198 [Suter], "Log of John Suter," 176.

199 Haskins, "Journal of a Fur Trading Voyage," 171.

200 "Fort Simpson (Nass) – Post Journal 1834–1838," 5, 11 February 1835, HBCA, B.201/a/3.

201 Ibid., 31 May, 7 June 1837.

202 "Fort Simpson (Nass) – Post Journal 1838–1840," 31 May 1840, HBCA, B.201/a/4.

203 Green, *Journal of a Tour*, 85.

204 A. Simpson to McLoughlin, 22 September 1828, HBCA, B.223/c/1.

205 Records of the Russian-American Company, USNARS, roll 36:175v.–76.

206 Manson to Simpson, 4 November 1834, HBCA, D.4/127; "Fort Simpson (Nass) – Post Journal 1834–1838," 29 December 1834, HBCA, B.201/a/3.

207 "Fort Simpson (Nass) – Post Journal 1834–1838," 30 July 1837, HBCA, B.201/a/3.

208 Manson to Simpson, 4 November 1834, HBCA, D.4/127.

209 Anderson, "McLoughlin, Fort. Report on District. 1834," HBCA, B.120/e/1.

210 Manson to Simpson, 4 November 1834, HBCA, D.4/127.

211 Phelps, "Solid men of Boston," 77.

212 [Allen], "Log of the Ship *Hamilton*, 159.

213 Walker, *Account of a Voyage*, 80, 187.

214 Lamb, *Voyage of George Vancouver*, 3:1,034, 1,040.

215 Jackman, *Journal of William Sturgis*, 114.

216 Ibid., 57.

217 Ibid., 131.

218 J. Lamb, Sr. to J. Lamb, Jr., 6 July 1802, in Lamb, "Notes on Trade with the Northwest Coast."

219 Haskins, "Journal of a Fur Trading Voyage," 216; Jackman, *Journal of William Sturgis*, 120.

220 Jackman, *Journal of William Sturgis*, 117–18.

221 Haskins, "Journal of a Fur Trading Voyage," 120, 249–50.

222 Clinton, "Journal," 22 October 1805.

223 Furgerson, "Journal of a Voyage from Boston to the Northwest Coast," 17 January 1811.

224 [Scouler], "John Scouler's Journal," 184.

225 Bagley, "Journal of Occurrences," 187.

226 D'Wolf, *Voyage to the North Pacific*, 19–20.

227 Walker, *Account of a Voyage*, 42–3. Also see Beaglehole, *Journals of Captain James Cook*, vol. 3, pt. 1:297, 302, 314.

228 [Sturgis], "Ms. of 3 lectures," lecture 2, 7–10.

229 Walker, *Account of a Voyage*, 42.

230 Ibid., 138.

231 Fleurieu, *Voyage Round the World*, 1:191; Portlock, *Voyage Round the World*, 284.

232 [Puget], "Log of the Proceedings of His Majesty's Ship Discovery," 94; Lamb, *Voyage of George Vancouver*, 2:627.

233 Howay, *Voyages of the "Columbia"*, 373, 397.

234 Beaglehole, *Journals of Captain James Cook*, vol. 3, pt. 2:1,324.

235 Haskins, "Journal of a Fur Trading Voyage," 218, 246; Howay, "Yankee Trader on the Northwest Coast," 87, 89; Howay, *Journal of Captain James Colnett*, 202; Jackman, *Journal of William Sturgis*, 65; Lamb, *Voyage of George Vancouver*, 3:938n.; Magee, "Log of the Jefferson," 9 May 1794; [Mitchell], *Journals of William Fraser Tolmie*, 313–14; [Puget], "Log of the Proceedings of His Majesty's Armed Tender Chatham," 59.

236 Ross, *Adventures of the First Settlers*, 95–6; Thwaites, *Original Journals*, 3:328, 345, 352–4, 4:187, 191.

237 Simpson, *Narrative of a Journey*, 1:196.

238 [Sturgis], "Ms. of 3 lectures," lecture 2, 11.

239 Scouler, "On the Indian Tribes," 242–3; Thwaites, *Original Journals*, 4:187, 191.

240 Howay, "Yankee Trader on the Northwest Coast," 88; Magee, "Log of the Jefferson," January, February 1794.

241 Clinton, "Journal," 18 March 1806.

242 Haskins, "Journal of a Fur Trading Voyage," 118.

243 Thwaites, *Original Journals*, 3:185, 328, 345. Also see ibid., 182, 185–6.

244 Ibid., 144. Also see Parker, *Journal of an Exploring Tour*, 143.

245 Thwaites, *Original Journals*, 3:144.

246 Von Langsdorff, *Voyages and Travels*, 2:40, 132.

247 Ibid., 132–3.

248 McNeill, "Journal of a Voyage to the N.W. Coast of North America," 30 April 1825.

249 A. Simpson to McLoughlin, 22 September 1828, HBCA, B.223/c/1.

250 Bagley, "Journal of Occurrences," 156–7.

251 Lamb, "Notes on Trade with the Northwest Coast," 45.

252 [Roe], *Journal and Letters*, 128.

253 Haskins, "Journal of a Fur Trading Voyage," 41; [Sturgis], "Northwest Fur Trade," 34.

254 Magee, "Log of the Jefferson," July 1793.

255 Ibid., November 1793.

256 Ibid., January 1794.

257 [Roe], *Journal and Letters*, 128, 156.

258 Haskins, "Journal of a Fur Trading Voyage," 119–26.

259 Ibid., 85, 229.

260 Simpson, *Narrative of a Journey*, 1:193. On oolachen, see Macnair, "Descriptive Notes"; Swan, "Eulachon or Candle-Fish."

261 Thwaites, *Original Journals*, 4:103. Also see Merk, *Fur Trade and Empire*, 103.

262 Haskins, "Journal of a Fur Trading Voyage," 205–6.

263 Furgerson, "Journal of a Voyage from Boston to the Northwest Coast," 7 April 1810.

264 Ibid., 26 June 1810.

265 Ibid., 27 June 1810.

266 [Martain], "Ship Hamilton Log Book," 21 March, 3 April 1810.

267 Ibid., 3 June 1810.

268 Ibid., 15 July 1810.

269 Simpson, *Narrative of a Journey*, 1:206.

270 [Allen], "Log of the Ship *Hamilton*," 24 July 1820, 4, 6 May, 20 August, 24–25 September 1821.

271 [Underwood], "Journal on board Brig Tally Ho," 13 June 1826.

272 Work to McLoughlin, 4 July 1842, Fort Simpson. Correspondence outward, 1841–1844.

273 Simpson, *Narrative of a Journey*, 1:193–4.

274 Work to McLoughlin, 4 July 1842, Fort Simpson. Correspondence outward, 1841–1844.

275 Simpson, *Narrative of a Journey*, 1:211.

276 "Fort Simpson (Nass) – Post Journal 1838–1840," 21 June 1838, HBCA, B.201/a/4.

277 Ibid., 16 July 1838.
278 Douglas, "Diary of a trip to the Northwest Coast," 26 August 1840.
279 Merk, *Fur Trade and Empire*, 101.
280 Haskins, "Journal of a Fur Trading Voyage," 180.
281 "Fort Simpson (Nass) – Post Journal 1834–1838," 11 June 1837, HBCA, B.201/a/3; "Fort Simpson (Nass) – Post Journal 1838–1840," 23 June 1838, HBCA, B.201/a/4.
282 "Fort Simpson (Nass) – Post Journal 1838–1840," 21 June 1838, HBCA, B.201/a/4.
283 Furgerson, "Journal of a Voyage from Boston to the Northwest Coast," 19 February 1811.
284 Merk, *Fur Trade and Empire*, 101.
285 McLoughlin to Simpson, 13 March 1835, HBCA, D.4/127.
286 Dunn, *History of the Oregon Territory*, 273.
287 Wrangell, *Russian America*, 32.
288 Lutké, *Voyage autour du monde*, 1:194; Simpson, *Narrative of a Journey*, 2:211.
289 Douglas, "Diary of a trip to the Northwest Coast," 14 July 1840.
290 [Jewitt], *Narrative*, 63, 73.
291 [Martain], "Ship Hamilton Log Book," enclosure at end of log.
292 A. Simpson to McLoughlin, 22 September 1828, HBCA, B.223/c/1.
293 Howay, *Voyage of the "New Hazard"*, 28–9; Jackman, *Journal of William Sturgis*, 55; [Mitchell], *Journals of William Fraser Tolmie*, 313; Wagner, *Spanish Explorations*, 190.
294 [Puget], "Log of the Proceedings of His Majesty's Ship Discovery," 134v.
295 [Colnett], "Voyage to the N.W. Side of America," 122v.; Walker, *Account of a Voyage*, 86–7.
296 Ibid., 42, 86–7.
297 Howay, *Voyages of the "Columbia"*, 371.
298 Beaglehole, *Journals of Captain James Cook*, vol. 3, pt. 2:1,326.
299 Ibid., 1,095.
300 Magee, "Log of the Jefferson," 27, 29 July 1794; Walker, "Supercargo's log of the brig *Lydia*," 37v.
301 Lamb, *Voyage of George Vancouver*, 2:688–9, 3:892–6.
302 Wagner and Newcombe, "Journal of Jacinto Caamaño," 207.
303 Jackman, *Journal of William Sturgis*, 60.
304 [Colnett], "Voyage to the N.W. Side of America," 136v.-37.
305 Howay, *Voyages of the "Columbia"*, 373.
306 Bartlett, "John Bartlett's journal," 16.
307 Magee, "Log of the Jefferson," 19 May 1794.
308 Ibid., 20 May 1794.

309 Howay, *Voyage of the "New Hazard,"* 59.

310 Anonymous, "Journal of a Voyage Round the World on the Brig Rob Roy," 29 August 1822.

311 A. Simpson to McLoughlin, 22 September 1828, HBCA, B.223/c/1.

312 Corney, *Early Voyages in the North Pacific*, 165.

313 Howay, *Voyages of the "Columbia"*, 399.

314 Thwaites, *Original Journals*, 3:239.

315 Ibid., 315.

316 Merk, *Fur Trade and Empire*, 99, 101.

317 Walker, "Supercargo's log of the brig *Lydia*," 38.

318 Howay, *Voyages of the "Columbia"*, 196.

319 Thwaites, *Original Journals*, 3:240.

320 Ibid., 4:170.

321 Merk, *Fur Trade and Empire*, 99

322 Cox, *Columbia River*, 170–1; Thwaites, *Original Journals*, 3:301.

323 Simpson, *Narrative of a Journey*, 1:207.

324 Rich, *Part of Dispatch*, 79.

325 A. Simpson to McLoughlin, 22 September 1828, HBCA, B.223/c/1.

326 Dunn, *History of the Oregon Territory*, 283.

327 Ibid., 287.

328 Merk, *Fur Trade and Empire*, 101.

329 Green, *Journal of a Tour*, 45, 51.

330 Ibid., 68.

331 Walker, *Account of a Voyage*, 108.

332 Dixon, *Voyage Round the World*, 229.

333 Howay, *Voyages of the "Columbia"*, 370–2; Kaplanoff, *Joseph Ingraham's Journal*, 105–6.

334 Meares, *Voyages Made in the Years 1788 and 1789*, 121.

335 Kaplanoff, *Joseph Ingraham's Journal*, xvi, xix, 105, 143, 192.

336 Howay, *Voyages of the "Columbia"*, 486.

337 See Jackman, *Journal of William Sturgis*, 113–21.

338 [Sturgis], "Northwest Fur Trade," 536–7.

339 Boardman to Barker, 7 October 1831, Boardman Letterbook.

340 Anonymous, "Journal of a Voyage Round the World on the Brig Rob Roy," 13 June 1822.

341 Howay, *Journal of Captain James Colnett*, 22.

342 Ibid., 22n., 283n.

343 Clinton, "Journal," 12 July 1805.

344 Bryant and Sturgis to Clark, 1 December 1817, Bryant and Sturgis Papers.

345 [Smith], "Arab (brig) Logbook," 21 June 1821.

346 Perkins to Perkins, 29 November 1822, Perkins and Company and Russell and Company Papers.

347 Grimes to Marshall and Wildes, 10 January 1823, Marshall Manuscripts.

348 Anonymous, "Journal of a Voyage in the Brig Owhyhee," [2].

349 [Martain], "Ship Louisa Log Book," [84].

350 Jones to Marshall, 30 October 1828, Marshall Manuscripts.

351 Cotting to Hunnewell, 28 July 1828, Hunnewell Papers.

352 Records of the Russian-American Company, USNARS, roll 31:76.

353 Anonymous, "O razprostranenii promyshlennosti," 1-1v.

354 Anonymous, "Return of American Vessels," n.p.

355 Perkins to Smith, 10 September 1822, Perkins and Company to the HBC, 10 September 1822, Perkins and Company and Russell and Company Papers.

356 Corning, "Letters of Sullivan Dorr," 230–1.

357 Perkins to Perkins, 25 February 1820, Perkins and Company and Russell and Company Papers.

358 Perkins to Perkins, 23 January 1820, Perkins and Company and Russell and Company Papers.

359 Perkins to Perkins, 7 April 1821, Perkins and Company and Russell and Company Papers.

360 Bryant and Sturgis to J. Sturgis and Company, 14 September 1821, Bryant and Sturgis Papers.

361 Meares, *Voyages Made in the Years 1788 and 1789*, 180, 224.

362 [Martain], "Ship Hamilton Log Book," 5 October 1811.

363 McNeill, "Journal of a Voyage to the N.W. Coast of North America," 2–5 November 1825.

364 Green, *Journal of a Tour*, 76.

365 A. Simpson to McLoughlin, 22 September 1828, HBCA, B.223/c/1.

366 Jones to Marshall, November 1828, Marshall Manuscripts.

367 Lambert to Hunnewell, 11 September 1830, Hunnewell Papers.

368 [Etholen], Etolin to Khlebnikov, 1/13, May 1835.

369 Dunn, *History of the Oregon Territory*, 286.

370 Anderson, "McLoughlin, Fort. Report on District. 1834," HBCA, B.120/e/1.

371 "Fort Simpson (Nass) – Post Journal 1834–1838," 15 July 1837, HBCA, B.201/a/3.

372 Bryant and Sturgis to Harris, 30 May 1822, Bryant and Sturgis Papers.

373 [Allen], "Log of the Ship *Hamilton*," 21 February 1822; [Martain], "Ship Hamilton Log Book," 25 January, 1 February 1811.

374 Anonymous, "Journal of a Voyage in the Brig Owhyhee," passim.

375 Howay, *Voyages of the "Columbia"*, 184.

376 Hayes, *Log of the Union*, 61.

377 Haskins, "Journal of a Fur Trading Voyage," 136.

378 Ibid., 128, 153.
379 Ibid., 234.
380 Clinton, "Journal," 6 August 1805.
381 Litke, *Voyage Around the World*, 1:91.
382 Chernykh, "Izvestiya iz Novoarkhangelska," 93. Also see Gibson, "European Dependence Upon American Natives."
383 Chernykh, "Izvestiya iz Novoarkhangelska," 93.
384 Ibid., 93–4.
385 Douglas, "Diary of a trip to the Northwest Coast," 21 May 1840.
386 [Roe], *Journal and Letters*, 64.
387 [Scouler], "John Scouler's Journal," 191.
388 Scouler, "On the Indian Tribes," 246.
389 Green, *Journal of a Tour*, 38, 76.
390 Dunn, *History of the Oregon Territory*, 294
391 Gibson, *Farming the Frontier*, 184.
392 Anonymous, "Journal of a Voyage Round the World on the Brig Rob Roy," 22 July, 11, 12 September, 4 November 1822.
393 Ibid., 9–10 December 1822.
394 Scouler, "Observations on the Indigenous Tribes," 219.
395 Ibid., 246–7.
396 Anonymous, "*Griffon*, Brig. Shipping Journal," 25 February 1826; [Underwood], "Journal on board Brig Tally Ho," 28–29 August 1826.
397 "*Cadboro* and *Dryad* logs, 1827 [*sic*]," 13 August 1831, HBCA, C.1/218.
398 Dunn, *History of the Oregon Territory*, 294.
399 "Fort Simpson (Nass) – Post Journal 1834–1838," 3–8, 19–20 October 1835, HBCA, B.201/a/3; [Mitchell], *Journals of William Fraser Tolmie*, 316.
400 "Fort Simpson (Nass) – Post Journal 1834–1838," 12 October 1835, HBCA, B.201/a/3.
401 Ibid., 22 December 1835.
402 "Fort Simpson (Nass) – Post Journal 1834–1838," 31 January, 28 February, 24, 29–30 March, 30 April, 31 May, 30 June, 31 July, 31 August, 30 September, 31 October, 30 November, 31 December 1837, HBCA, B.201/a/3.
403 Ibid., 26 October, 2, 9, 16, 23, 30 November, 1–7, 14 December 1834, 6 January 1835.
404 Ibid., 30 June, 31 July 1837.
405 "Fort Simpson (Nass) – Post Journal 1838–1840," 22 September 1838, HBCA, B.201/a/4.
406 "Stikine – Post Journal 1840–1842," 9–10 October 1840, HBCA, B.209/a/1.
407 "Fort Simpson (Nass) – Post Journal 1834–1838," 6 September 1837, HBCA, B.201/a/3; "Fort Simpson (Nass) – Post Journal 1838–1840," 15 September 1838, HBCA, B.201/a/4.

408 Green, *Journal of a Tour*, 86.

409 Scouler, "Observations on the Indigenous Tribes," 218.

410 Ibid., 219.

411 Ibid.

412 Ibid.

413 Simpson, *Narrative of a Journey*, 1:207.

414 Kaufmann, "Changes in Haida Indian Argillite Carvings," 2, 40–1.

415 Wright, "Haida Argillite Pipes," 8.

416 On Haida argillite carving, see Drew and Wilson, *Argillite: Art of the Haida*; Macnair and Hoover, *Magic Leaves*; Sheehan, *Pipes That Won't Smoke; Coal That Won't Burn*.

417 Richard Etches to Joseph Banks, 19 May 1792 in Howay, "Four Letters," 139.

418 Allen and Donnithorne, *Western Enterprise in Far Eastern Economic Development*, 15; Greenberg, *British Trade and the Opening of China*, 8–10.

419 Greenberg, *British Trade and the Opening of China*, 85.

420 Allen and Donnithorne, *Western Enterprise in Far Eastern Economic Development*, 16.

421 Ibid., 16–17.

422 Latourette, "History of Early Relations," 53–4.

423 Hill, *Trade and Commerce of Boston*, 115.

424 Latourette, "History of Early Relations," 53–4.

425 Ibid., 71–4.

426 Dennett, *Americans in Eastern Asia*, 73.

427 Ibid., 73–4.

428 Latourette, "History of Early Relations," 73–6.

429 Great Britain, *Sessional Papers* 5:232.

430 Ibid., 6:358.

431 Dennett, *Americans in Eastern Asia*, 70.

432 Great Britain, *Sessional Papers* 6:393.

433 Ibid., 449–50.

434 Dennett, *Americans in Eastern Asia*, 18.

435 Ibid., 70–1.

436 Great Britain, *Sessional Papers* 5:218.

437 Ibid., 219.

438 Ibid., 86; Latourette, "History of Early Relations," 63.

439 Latourette, "History of Early Relations," 63, 69.

440 Great Britain, *Sessional Papers* 5:121, 6:448.

CHAPTER NINE

1 Jackman, *Journal of William Sturgis*, 116.

2 J. and T.H. Perkins *et al.* to Hill, 30 June 1815, Bryant and Sturgis Papers.

3 Howay, *List of Trading Vessels*, 105.

4 On the collection of bird nests, *bêche de mer*, coral moss, and mother-of-pearl, respectively, see Fanning, *Voyages Round the World*, 459–66.

5 [Work], *Journal*, 56.

6 Delano, *Narrative of Voyages and Travels*, 375–6.

7 Ibid., 378.

8 Latourette, "History of Early Relations," 58–9.

9 Fyodorova, *Russkaya Amerika*, 135.

10 Jones to Marshall and Wildes, 10 August 1822, Marshall Manuscripts.

11 Perkins to Edes, 5 May 1821, Perkins and Company and Russell and Company Papers.

12 Hill, "Journal and Log," 6.

13 On fur seals and fur sealing, see Fanning, *Voyages Round the World*, 354–9.

14 Magee, "Observations on the Islands," 259.

15 See, for example, Delano, *Narrative of Voyages and Travels*, 305–8.

16 Ibid., 305–6.

17 Ibid., 306; Moulton, *Concise Extract*, 98.

18 Morrell, *Narrative of Four Voyages*, 130.

19 Fanning, *Voyages Round the World*, 118.

20 Corning, "Letters of Sullivan Dorr," 276.

21 Ibid., 209; Perkins and Company to the HBC, 10 September 1822, Perkins and Russell Papers.

22 Delano, *Narrative of Voyages and Travels*, 307. Also see Corning, "Letters of Sullivan Dorr," 209, 271, 281, 302, 353.

23 Perkins and Company to the HBC, 10 September 1822, Perkins and Russell Papers.

24 On sandalwood and sandalwooding, see Fanning, *Voyages Round the World*, 455–9.

25 Von Krusenstern, *Voyage Round the World*, 2:333.

26 Bryant and Sturgis to Clark, 1 December 1817, Bryant and Sturgis Papers.

27 Anonymous, "Puteshestvie na shlyupe 'Blagonamerenny'," 224.

28 Ibid., 223–4.

29 Bryant and Sturgis to Harris, 25 June 1822, Bryant and Sturgis Papers.

30 Korn, "Shadows of Destiny," 25.

31 Anonymous, "Puteshestvie na shlyupe 'Blagonamerenny'," 223; Golovnin, *Around the World on the "Kamchatka"*, 217.

32 Fyodorova, *Russkaya Amerika*, 134.

33 Delano, *Narrative of Voyages and Travels*, 399; Kaplanoff, *Joseph Ingraham's Journal*, 78, 84.

34 Dorr, "Journal of a Voyage from Boston round the World," 26 May 1791.
35 Anonymous, "Imports and Exports of Canton," 469; Fyodorova, *Russkaya Amerika*, 134.
36 Delano, *Narrative of Voyages and Travels*, 399.
37 Ellis, *Journal of William Ellis*, 214–15, 286–7; Fyodorova, *Russkaya Amerika*, 134; Golovnin, *Around the World on the "Kamchatka"*, 203, 214; Mathison, *Narrative of a Visit*, 458.
38 Bryant and Sturgis to Clark, 1 December 1817, Bryant and Sturgis Papers.
39 Ellis, *Journal of William Ellis*, 286.
40 Korn, "Shadows of Destiny," 22.
41 Campbell, *Voyage Round the World*, 200.
42 Gast and Conrad, *Don Francisco de Paula Marin*, 207, 213; Ii, *Fragments of Hawaiian History*, 88; Phelps, "Solid men of Boston," n.p.
43 Kuykendall, *Hawaiian Kingdom 1778–1854*, 87.
44 Jarvis, "Sandwich or Hawaiian Islands," 114.
45 Kuykendall, *Hawaiian Kingdom 1778–1854*, 89–90.
46 Anonymous, "Puteshestvie na shlyupe 'Blagonamerenny'," 224.
47 Kuykendall, *Hawaiian Kingdom 1778–1854*, 91.
48 Gough, *To the Pacific and Arctic with Beechey*, 196; Porter, *John Jacob Astor*, 1:666–7.
49 Golovnin, *Around the World on the "Kamchatka"*, 203; Lazarev, *Zapiski o plavanii*, 258.
50 Anonymous, ["Logs of the Ships *Atahualpa*, *Behring*, and *Isabella* and the Brig *Pedler*,"], 30 December 1815.
51 Polansky, "Baron Vrangel' Visits the Sandwich Islands," 21.
52 Anonymous, "Journal of a Voyage Round the World on the Brig Rob Roy," 6 December 1822; Bradley, *American Frontier in Hawaii*, 64–5; Ellwell to Marshall, 10 October 1821, Jones to Marshall and Wildes, 10 November 1821, 22 January 1822, Marshall Manuscripts; Despatches from United States Consuls in Honolulu, 1820–1903, USNARS, roll 1, Jones to Adams, 31 December 1821.
53 Jones to Marshall and Wildes, January, 24 October 1823, Wildes to Marshall, 5 November 1824, Marshall Manuscripts.
54 Jones to Marshall and Wildes, 30 November 1827, Sturgis to Marshall and Wildes, 9 December 1828 [*sic*: 1827], 20 January 1828, Marshall Manuscripts.
55 [Boelen], *Merchant's Perspective*, 76; Hunnewell to Sturgis, 18 December 1829, Hunnewell Papers; Sturgis to Marshall and Wildes, 12 December 1828, Marshall Manuscripts.
56 Jones to Marshall and Wildes, 23 December 1821, August 10, 1822, Marshall Manuscripts.

57 Green to Hunnewell, 10 February 1830, Hunnewell Papers; Sturgis to Marshall and Wildes, 9 January 1829, Marshall Manuscripts.

58 Boardman to Barker, 7 June 1831, 1 May 1832, Boardman Letter-book.

59 Ellis, *Journal of William Ellis*, 215.

60 Kelly, *Hawai'i in 1819*, 88.

61 Jones to Marshall and Wildes, 10 October 1822, Marshall Manuscripts.

62 Jones to Marshall and Wildes, January 1823, Marshall Manuscripts.

63 Ibid.

64 Pitman and French to Marshall, 1 February 1823, Marshall Manuscripts.

65 Jones to Marshall, 20 July 1827, Marshall Manuscripts.

66 Jones to Marshall, 30 September 1827, Marshall Manuscripts.

67 Hunnewell to Bryant and Sturgis, 28 October 1827, Hunnewell Papers.

68 Hunnewell to Bryant and Sturgis, 31 August 1829, Hunnewell Papers.

69 [Boelen], *Merchant's Perspective*, 76; Fyodorova, *Russkaya Amerika*, 134.

70 Latourette, "History of Early Relations," 58.

71 Morison, "Boston Traders in Hawaiian Islands," 188, 191.

72 Jones to Marshall and Wildes, 5 October 1821, Marshall Manuscripts.

73 Jones to Marshall and Wildes, 6 July 1821, Marshall Manuscripts.

74 Ibid.

75 Morison, "Boston Traders in Hawaiian Islands," 192.

76 Ibid.

77 Jones to Marshall and Wildes, 9 March 1823, Marshall Manuscripts.

78 Jones to Marshall and Wildes, 31 May 1823, Marshall Manuscripts.

79 Ibid. Also see Jones to Marshall and Wildes, 16 June 1823, Marshall Manuscripts.

80 Hunnewell to Bryant and Sturgis, 15 December 1829, Hunnewell Papers.

81 Hill, "Journal and Log," 52.

82 Von Chamisso, *Voyage Around the World*, 243.

83 Shaler, "Journal of a Voyage," 153.

84 Fyodorova, *Russkaya Amerika*, 46–7; [Khlebnikov], *Colonial Russian America*, 6–7; Khlebnikov, "Okhota," 3v.

85 Khlebnikov, "Okhota," 3v.

86 Wagner, *Spanish Explorations*, 294.

87 Magee, "Log of the Jefferson," 26 July 1793.

88 Porter, *John Jacob Astor*, 1:452.

89 Grimes to Marshall and Wildes, n.d. [1822?], Marshall Manuscripts.

90 Jones to Marshall, 30 October 1827, Marshall Manuscripts.

91 A. Simpson to McLoughlin, 9 March 1828, HBCA, D.4/121.

92 Boardman to Barker, 22 May 1832, Boardman Letterbook.

93 Boardman to Barker, 2 September 1832, Boardman Letterbook.
94 Sauer, *Account of a Geographical and Astronomical Expedition*, 279–81; Shelikhov, *Voyage to America*, 50–51.
95 Sauer, *Account of a Geographical and Astronomical Expedition*, 278.
96 See Gibson, *Imperial Russia in Frontier America*.
97 Lisiansky, *Voyage Round the World*, 233.
98 Alaska History Research Project, *Documents Relative to the History of Alaska*, 3:203.
99 See Gibson, "Bostonians and Muscovites on the Northwest Coast."
100 Clinton, "Journal," 18 July 1806.
101 J. and T.H. Perkins to Perkins and Company, 29 March 1808, in J. and T.H. Perkins, Foreign letters.
102 Porter, *John Jacob Astor*, 1:450.
103 Ibid., 435, 437.
104 Irving, *Astoria*, 465.
105 Porter, *John Jacob Astor*, 1:450–1.
106 Bryant and Sturgis to Suter, 6 August 1816, Bryant and Sturgis Papers.
107 Bryant and Sturgis to Hammatt, 29 July 1828, Bryant and Sturgis Papers.
108 A. Simpson to McLoughlin, 9 March 1828, HBCA, D.4/121; Lutké, *Voyage autour du monde*, 1:107.
109 Wheeler, "Empires in Conflict and Cooperation," 427.
110 Golovnin, *Puteshestvie na shlyupe "Diana"*, 327.
111 Ibid., 326–7.
112 [Baranov], Baranov to Johns [Jones], 4/16 October 1816.
113 Pigot to [Ebbets], 7 January 1816, Astor Papers.
114 Jones to Marshall, 30 October 1827, Marshall Manuscripts.
115 [Suter], "Log of the ship Atahualpa," 28 April 1812.
116 AVPR, f. Rossiisko-Amerikanskaya Kompaniya, d. 183, 1–1v., d. 192, 1.
117 Khlebnikov, "Okhota," 5.
118 [Suter], "Log of the ship Atahualpa," 29 October 1813.
119 Anonymous, ["Logs of the Ships *Atahualpa*, *Behring*, and *Isabella* and the Brig *Pedler*,"], 29 October 1818.
120 Fyodorova, *Russkaya Amerika*, 118.
121 Bryant and Sturgis to Suter, 6 August 1816, Bryant and Sturgis Papers.
122 Fyodorova, *Russkaya Amerika*, 115–18.
123 Bryant and Sturgis to Suter, 6 August 1816, Bryant and Sturgis Papers.
124 Records of the Russian-American Company, USNARS, roll 32:255v.
125 Lutké, *Voyage autour du monde*, 1:109.

126 Records of the Russian-American Company, USNARS, roll 31:326v.–27.
127 Ibid., roll 39:361v.-62v.
128 Corney, *Early Voyages in the North Pacific*, 159, 162.
129 Records of the Russian-American Company, USNARS, roll 27:139v.
130 [Work], *Journal*, 68–9. Also see ibid., 56, 70–1.
131 Howay, *List of Trading Vessels*, 19.
132 Ibid., 144–6; [Smith], "Arab (brig) Logbook," passim.
133 A. Simpson to McLoughlin, 22 September 1828, HBCA, B.223/c/1. Also
    see A. Simpson to McLoughlin, 9 March 1828, HBCA, D.4/121.
134 Latourette, "Voyages of American Ships to China," 269–71.

CHAPTER TEN

  1 On the impact of the maritime fur trade on the Northwest Coast Indi-
    ans, including the "enrichment thesis," see Wike, "Problems in Fur
    Trade Analysis." The notion of enrichment to the point of a cultural
    climax is quite controversial; for example, exactly what constitutes
    such a climax, and if one really does occur, is it precipitated by endog-
    enous or exogenous stimuli?
  2 Duff, *Indian History of British Columbia*, 1:57.
  3 Wike, "Effect of the Maritime Fur Trade," 92–107.
  4 "Fort Simpson (Nass) – Post Journal 1838–1840," 21 June 1838, HBCA,
    B.201 /a/4.
  5 See MacDonald, *Haida Monumental Art*.
  6 Duff, *Indian History of British Columbia*, 1:57, 59.
  7 [Puget], "Log of the Proceedings of His Majesty's Armed Tender Chat-
    ham," 49v.
  8 Duff, *Indian History of British Columbia*, 1:58; Harris and Ingram,
    "New Caledonia and the Fur Trade," 184–5.
  9 Wike, "Effect of the Maritime Fur Trade," 99–100.
 10 [Jewitt], *Narrative*, 39–40.
 11 Averkieva, "Tlingit Indians," 334.
 12 Duff, *Indian History of British Columbia*, 1:57–9.
 13 Green, *Journal of a Tour*, 45.
 14 Ibid., 46.
 15 Bagley, "Journal of Occurrences," 185.
 16 Averkieva, "Tlingit Indians," 319–20, 325, 331.
 17 Inglis and Haggarty, "Cook to Jewitt."
 18 Wagner and Newcombe, "Journal of Jacinto Caamaño," 215, 218.
 19 [Scouler], "John Scouler's Journal," 193.
 20 Boyd, "Demographic History," 135, 147.
 21 Moziño, *Noticias de Nutka*, 21–2.
 22 Ellis, *Authentic Narrative*, 1:216.

23 Jane, *Spanish Voyage*, 115.
24 Ross, *Adventures of the First Settlers*, 98.
25 [Jewitt], *Narrative*, 115, 142; Meares, *Voyages Made in the Years 1788 and 1789*, 229; Walker, *Account of a Voyage*, 122.
26 Gibson, *Feeding the Russian Fur Trade*, 196; Khlebnikov, *Baranov*, 104.
27 Portlock, *Voyage Round the World*, 271, 276.
28 Fleurieu, *Voyage Round the World*, 1:221.
29 Fyodorova, *Russkaya Amerika*, 82–3.
30 Litke, *Voyage Around the World*, 1:95–6.
31 Howay, *Voyages of the "Columbia"*, 196, 371.
32 Delano, *Narrative of Voyages and Travels*, 393.
33 Hayes, *Log of the Union*, 88, 91.
34 Martain to Hunnewell, 1 March 1829, Hunnewell Papers.
35 [Martain], "Ship Louisa Log Book," 5, 7, 14–15 March 1829.
36 Howay, *Voyages of the "Columbia"*, 371; Lamb, *Voyage of George Vancouver*, 2:528.
37 [Puget], "Log of the Proceedings of His Majesty's Ship Discovery," 134. Also see Newcombe, *Menzies' Journal*, 29, 35; Lamb, *Voyage of George Vancouver*, 2:528, 540, 559.
38 See Lamb, *Voyage of George Vancouver*, 2:538. Also see [Puget], "Log of the Proceeedings of His Majesty's Armed Tender Chatham," 66.
39 Jane, *Spanish Voyage*, 48.
40 [Roe], *Journal and Letters*, 71, 83, 91–2.
41 Green, *Journal of a Tour*, 39.
42 Thwaites, *Original Journals*, 4:50–1, 241.
43 Cox, *Columbia River*, 169.
44 Furgerson, "Journal of a Voyage from Boston to the Northwest Coast of America," 25 January 1811.
45 Ibid., 16 June 1810.
46 [Etholen], Etolin to Khlebnikov, 4/16 May 1836; [Rosenberg], Rozenberg to Khlebnikov, 29 April/11 May 1836; Records of the Russian-American Company, USNARS, roll 38:103v., roll 39:235v.
47 Work to E. Ermatinger, 15 February 1837, Work Correspondence.
48 "Fort Simpson (Nass) – Post Journal 1834–1838," 24 May 1836, HBCA, B.201/a/3.
49 Ibid., 2 November 1836.
50 Ibid., 19 November 1836. Also see ibid., 6 November 1836.
51 Ibid., 8, 27 December 1836.
52 Ibid., 29–30 April 1837.
53 Ibid., 19 October 1836.
54 Dunn, *History of the Oregon Territory*, 284.
55 "Fort Simpson (Nass) – Post Journal 1834–1838," 13 October 1836, HBCA, B.201/a/3.

56 Ibid., 1 December 1836.
57 Ibid., 14, 17, 20 December 1836.
58 Ibid., 9, 18 November 1836.
59 Ibid., 15 May 1837.
60 Rich, *Letters of John McLoughlin 1825–1838*, 271; Simpson, *Narrative of a Journey*, 1:207.
61 Z[avoiko], *Vpechatleniya moryaka*, 2:90.
62 Work to E. Ermatinger, 9 November 1848, Work Correspondence.
63 "Fort Simpson (Nass) – Post Journal 1834–1838," 14 April 1837, HBCA, B.201/a/3.
64 Ibid., 9 April 1838.
65 Averkieva, "Tlingit Indians," 331.
66 Wike, "Effect of the Maritime Fur Trade," 99.
67 Kuykendall, *Hawaiian Kingdom 1778–1854*, 23–7.
68 Meares, *Voyages Made in the Years 1788 and 1789*, 354–55.
69 Lamb, *Voyage of George Vancouver*, 2:476.
70 Ibid., 3:797.
71 Ibid., 818.
72 Hayes, *Log of the Union*, 72.
73 Ibid., 73.
74 Ibid., 70, 76–7.
75 Shaler, "Journal of a Voyage," 164.
76 Golovnin, *Around the World on the "Kamchatka"*, 191–2, 200, 223n.
77 Campbell, *Voyage Round the World*, 155–6; Franchère, *Journal of a Voyage*, 64; Ross, *Adventures of the First Settlers*, 39; Shaler, "Journal of a Voyage," 164; Turnbull, *Voyage Round the World*, 224; Von Langsdorff, *Voyages and Travels*, 1:187.
78 Campbell, *Voyage Round the World*, 212.
79 Ellis, *Journal of William Ellis*, 298.
80 Franchère, *Journal of a Voyage*, 67; Von Langsdorff, *Voyages and Travels*, 1:187.
81 Turnbull, *Voyage Round the World*, 223, 235–6.
82 Campbell, *Voyage Round the World*, 166.
83 Ibid.
84 Ibid., 140.
85 Choris, *Voyage pittoresque*, "Isles Sandwich," 7.
86 Golovnin, *Around the World on the "Kamchatka"*, 191.
87 Kelly, *Hawai'i in 1819*, 20–1.
88 Turnbull, *Voyage Round the World*, 223–4.
89 Golovnin, *Around the World on the "Kamchatka"*, 195; Kelly, *Hawai'i in 1819*, 90.
90 Campbell, *Voyage Round the World*, 212.
91 Golovnin, *Around the World on the "Kamchatka"*, 196.

92 Kelly, *Hawai'i in 1819*, 90.

93 Ibid., 8.

94 Kuykendall, *Hawaiian Kingdom 1778–1854*, 83.

95 Stewart, *Journal of a Residence*, xiii.

96 Ibid., 29.

97 Campbell, *Voyage Round the World*, 199–200; Kelly, *Hawai'i in 1819*, 88.

98 Mathison, *Narrative of a Visit*, 467.

99 Ibid., 453, 467.

100 Ibid., 455, 466–7.

101 Ellis, *Journal of William Ellis*, 291.

102 Ibid., 17; Stewart, *Journal of a Residence*, 146.

103 Mathison, *Narrative of a Visit*, 459.

104 Campbell, *Voyage Round the World*, 152–3.

105 Delano, *Narrative of Voyages and Travels*, 396; Korn, "Shadows of Destiny," 28; Stewart, *Journal of a Residence*, 26; Von Kotzebue, *Voyage of Discovery*, 1:319, 2:193. Also see Von Kotzebue, *New Voyage Round the World*, 2:158.

106 Ellis, *Journal of William Ellis*, 11.

107 Campbell, *Voyage Round the World*, 157.

108 Ellis, *Journal of William Ellis*, 12.

109 Campbell, *Voyage Round the World*, 133, 158.

110 Mathison, *Narrative of a Visit*, 448, 458–9.

111 Ellis, *Journal of William Ellis*, 11.

112 [Bloxam], *Diary of Andrew Bloxam*, 29–30.

113 Polansky, "Baron Vrangel' Visits the Sandwich Islands," 17–19.

114 Delano, *Narrative of Voyages and Travels*, 388.

115 Turnbull, *Voyage Round the World*, 204.

116 Ibid., 222.

117 Campbell, *Voyage Round the World*, 201.

118 Golovnin, *Around the World on the "Kamchatka"*, 177, 204.

119 Jones to Marshall and Wildes, 6 July 1821, Marshall Manuscripts; Morison, "Boston Traders in Hawaiian Islands," 187.

120 Jones to Marshall and Wildes, 5 October 1821, Marshall Manuscripts; Morison, "Boston Traders in Hawaiian Islands," 191.

121 Morison, "Boston Traders in Hawaiian Islands," 191.

122 Ibid., 196; Jones to Marshall and Wildes, 10 August 1822, Marshall Manuscripts.

123 Jones to Marshall and Wildes, 10 October 1822, Marshall Manuscripts.

124 Jones to Marshall and Wildes, January 1823, Marshall Manuscripts.

125 Fyodorova, *Russkaya Amerika*, 133–4.

126 Anonymous, "Voyage of an expedition," 33–4.

127 Lisiansky, *Voyage Round the World*, 112–113, 133. See Schmitt, "*Okuu.*"

128 Von Kotzebue, *New Voyage Round the World*, 2:243.

129 Jones to Marshall, 5 May 1826, Marshall Manuscripts.

130 Von Langsdorff, *Voyages and Travels*, 1:183.

131 Kelly, *Hawai'i in 1819*, 8, 57–8.

132 Stewart, *Journal of a Residence*, 155.

133 Ibid., 202.

134 Beaglehole, *Journals of Captain James Cook*, vol. 3, pt. 2:1,083.

135 Ibid., 1,083–4, vol. 3, pt. 1:266n.

136 Ibid., vol. 3, pt. 2:1,151; Ellis, *Authentic Narrative*, 1:170.

137 Kelly, *Hawai'i in 1819*, 61.

138 Campbell, *Voyage Round the World*, 146, 184–5.

139 Von Kotzebue, *Voyage of Discovery*, 1:331.

140 Kelly, *Hawai'i in 1819*, 83.

141 Mathison, *Narrative of a Visit*, 469.

142 Ibid.

143 Stewart, *Journal of a Residence*, 315.

144 Ellis, *Journal of William Ellis*, 275.

145 Mathison, *Narrative of a Visit*, 460.

146 Kelly, *Hawai'i in 1819*, 64–5.

147 Holt, *Hawaiian Journal*, 20.

148 Von Kotzebue, *Voyage of Discovery*, 1:306, 306n.

149 Ellis, *Journal of William Ellis*, 231–3, 316; Stewart, *Journal of a Residence*, 251–2.

150 Ellis, *Journal of William Ellis*, 231–2.

151 [Macrae], *With Lord Byron at the Sandwich Islands*, 41–2.

152 Von Chamisso, *Voyage Round the World*, 183.

153 Korn, "Shadows of Destiny," 21–2.

154 Bartlett, "John Bartlett's journal," 4–45; Lamb, *Voyage of George Vancouver*, 3:820–1.

155 Broughton, *Voyage of Discovery*, 71.

156 Shaler, "Journal of a Voyage," 163.

157 Bingham, *Residence of Twenty-One Years*, 49.

158 [Macrae], *With Lord Byron at the Sandwich Islands*, 7.

159 See Schmitt, "Famine Mortality."

160 Kelly, *Hawai'i in 1819*, 65. Also see Ellis, *Journal of William Ellis*, 16.

161 Cook [and King], *Voyage to the Pacific Ocean*, 3:128–9.

162 Golovnin, *Around the World on the "Kamchatka"*, 215, 217–19.

163 [Bloxam], *Diary of Andrew Bloxam*, 30n.; Korn, "Shadows of Destiny," 28; Stewart, *Journal of a Residence*, 141; Despatches from United States Consuls in Honolulu, 1820–1903, USNARS, roll 1, Jones to Adams, 31 December 1821.

164 Jarvis, "Sandwich or Hawaiian Islands," 123.

165 Robert C. Schmitt, former Hawaii state statistician and an authority on the state's historical demography, has estimated that the population of the islands approximated 200,000–250,000 in 1778, 165,000–195,000 in 1800, 135,000–145,000 in 1823, and 129,000 in 1831–32, and that the decrease was mainly the result of low fertility, high infant and adult mortality, and emigration, not epidemics, wars, famines, and human sacrifice (Schmitt, "New Estimates," 240, 242; also see idem, "Catastrophic Mortality").

166 HBCA, E.25/1,Lowe, "Journal of a Voyage," 14 February 1842, HBCA, E.25/1.

167 Von Kotzebue, *New Voyage Round the World*, 2:219.

168 Ibid., 217–20.

169 Jones to Marshall and Wildes, 5 October 1821, Marshall Papers.

170 Mathison, *Narrative of a Visit*, 471.

171 Shaler, "Journal of a Voyage," 168.

172 Ellis, *Journal of William Ellis*, 249.

173 Von Kotzebue, *Voyage of Discovery*, 1:329–30.

174 Ibid., 330.

175 Despatches from United States Consuls in Honolulu, USNARS, roll 1, Jones to Adams, 31 December 1821.

176 Jones to Marshall and Wildes, January 1823, Marshall Manuscripts.

177 Ellis, *Journal of William Ellis*, 1–2.

178 Von Langsdorff, *Voyages and Travels*, 1:187.

179 Magee, "Log of the Jefferson," November 1792.

180 [Suter], "Log of the ship Atahualpa," November 1792.

181 Ibid., 9–11 March. Also see Anonymous, ["Logs of the Ships *Atahualpa*, *Behring*, and *Isabella* and the Brig *Pedler*,"], 8–11 March 1812.

182 Gast and Conrad, *Don Francisco de Paula Marin*, 226.

183 Despatches from United States Consuls in Honolulu, USNARS, roll 1, Jones to Clay, 1 July 1827.

184 Jones to Marshall and Wildes, 16 November 1822, Marshall Manuscripts; Morison, "Boston Traders in Hawaiian Islands," 198.

185 Morison, "Boston Traders in Hawaiian Islands," 198.

186 Ibid.

187 Korn, "Shadows of Destiny," 35–6.

188 Lamb, *Voyage of George Vancouver*, 3:1,191–3.

189 Despatches from United States Consuls in Honolulu, USNARS, roll 1, Jones to Adams, 31 December 1821.

190 Wildes to Marshall, 27 March 1825, Marshall Manuscripts.

191 Polansky, "Baron Vrangel' Visits the Sandwich Islands," 19.

192 Bradley, *American Frontier in Hawaii*, 34.

193 Campbell, *Voyage Round the World*, 167.

194 Franchère, *Journal of a Voyage*, 67; Ross, *Adventures of the First Settlers*, 46–7.
195 Choris, *Voyage pittoresque*, "Isles Sandwich," 20; Golovnin, *Around the World on the "Kamchatka"*, 191.
196 Stewart, *Journal of a Residence*, 158–60.
197 Mortimer, *Observations and Remarks*, 51.
198 Turnbull, *Voyage Round the World*, 231.
199 Great Britain, *Sessional Papers* 5:15, 70, 103.
200 Ibid., 15.
201 Ibid., 104.
202 Greenberg, *British Trade and the Opening of China*, 44.
203 Ibid.
204 Krooss and Gilbert, *American Business History*, 86.
205 Dennett, *Americans in Eastern Asia*, 18.
206 Krooss and Gilbert, *American Business History*, 77–9, 91.
207 Davis, "Stock Ownership," 206–9.
208 Morison, *Maritime History of Massachusetts*, 76–7.
209 See Loring, "Memoir of the Hon. William Sturgis."
210 See Hunt, *Lives of American Merchants*, vol. 1.
211 Krooss and Gilbert, *American Business History*, 84.
212 Goldstein, *Philadelphia and the China Trade*, 40–5.
213 [Sturgis], "Northwest Fur Trade," 533.
214 Hill, *Trade and Commerce of Boston*, 71.
215 Ibid., 74.
216 Ibid., 90.
217 Ibid.
218 Anonymous, *Old Shipping Days*, 3.
219 Busch, *Alta California 1840–1842*, 74–5.

Bibliography

BIBLIOGRAPHIES

Grumet, Robert Steven. *Native Americans of the Northwest Coast*: *A Critical Bibliography*. Bloomington and London: Indiana University Press 1979.

Howay, F.W. "The Early Literature of the Northwest Coast." *Transactions of the Royal Society of Canada* 18 (1924):1–31.

– *A List of Trading Vessels in the Maritime Fur Trade, 1785–1825*. Kingston, Ont.: Limestone Press 1973.

Judd, Bernice. *Voyages to Hawaii before 1860*. Enlarged and edited by Helen Yonge Lind. Honolulu: University Press of Hawaii for Hawaiian Mission Children's Society 1974.

Lamb, W. Kaye. "A Bibliography of the Printed Writings of Frederic William Howay." *British Columbia Historical Quarterly* 8 (1944):27–51.

Langdon, Robert, ed. *American Whalers and Traders in the Pacific: A Guide to Records on Microfilm*. Canberra: Pacific Manuscripts Bureau, Research School of Pacific Studies, Australian National University 1978.

– *Where the Whalers Went: An Index to the Pacific Ports and Islands Visited by American Whalers (and Some Other Ships) in the 19th Century*. Canberra: Pacific Manuscripts Bureau, Research School of Pacific Studies, Australian National University 1984.

Latourette, Kenneth Scott. "Voyages of American Ships to China, 1784–1844." *Transactions of the Connecticut Academy of Arts and Sciences* 28 (1927): 237–71.

Maury Abstract Logs 1796–1861. Roll 1: Index and Supplement. National Archives Microfilm Publication M1160. Washington, DC: US National Archives 1981.

The Northwest Coast: A Century of Personal Narratives of Discovery, Conquest & Exploration from Bering's Landfall to Wilkes' Surveys 1741–1841. New York: Edward Eberstadt & Sons, n.d.

Snyder, James Wilbert, Jr. "A Bibliography for the Early American China Trade, 1784–1815." *Americana Illustrated* 34 (1940):297–345.

Strathern, Gloria M., comp. *Navigations, Traffiques & Discoveries 1774–1848*. Victoria: University of Victoria 1970.

PRIMARY SOURCES: UNPUBLISHED

[Allen, Peter]. "Log of the Ship *Hamilton*, Captain William Mart[a]in, from Boston towards the Northwest Coast of America, 1819–1823." Peabody Museum Salem (MA).

[Anderson, Alexander Caulfield]. "Historical Notes on the Commerce of the Columbia River, 1824 to 1848." Yale University Library (New Haven, CT).

Anonymous. "Account Book Ship Sultan 1821–1824." Hamilton Library, University of Hawaii at Manoa (Honolulu).

– "Directions for entering the Principal Harbours on the North West Coast of America, by different Commanders." BCPA, Ms. AB20.5 C76.

– "*Griffon*, Brig. Shipping Journal. Oct. 1824–July 1827." Essex Institute (Salem, MA), Log 1824 G4.

– "*Joseph Peabody*, Brig. Shipping Logbook. Jan. 1836–May 1838." Essex Institute (Salem, MA), Log 1836 J.

– "Journal kept on board the Ship Paragon ..." BCPA.

– "Journal of a Voyage in the Brig Owhyhee from Oahu to & from the Northwest Coast." California Historical Society (San Francisco), Ms. 091 J8.

– "Journal of a voyage kept on board Brig Lama ..." BCPA.

– "Journal of a voyage perform'd on the Ship Amethyst. Seth Smith Camman Jr. From Boston to the Coast of California. &c." Peabody Museum (Salem, MA), Logbook 43.

– "Journal of a Voyage Round the World on the Brig Rob Roy in the years 1821, 1822, 1823, 1824 and 1825." Nantucket Historical Association (Nantucket, MA).

– "Log-book of the Brig Lydia on a Fur-trading Voyage from Boston to the Northwest Coast of America 1804–1805 With the Return Voyage by Way of the Sandwich Islands and Canton Aboard the Ships Atahualpa and Swift 1805–1807." Yale University Library, Western Americana Ms. S–213.

– "Logbook of the Ship Pearl 1804–1808." Massachusetts Historical Society (Boston, MA).

– "Logbook of the Snow Polly 1800–1802." Massachusetts Historical Society (Boston, MA).

– ["Logs of the Ships *Atahualpa*, *Behring*, and *Isabella* and the Brig *Pedler*, 1811–16"]. Bancroft Library (University of California, Berkeley), Ms. P–K 211.

– "O razprostranenii promyshlennosti" ["Concerning the Expansion of Hunting"]. GAPO, f. 445, op. 1, d. 84.

– "Return of American Vessels that have entered the Port of Canton in China from June 6, 1816–May 25, 1817 with an Abstract of their Cargoes." Essex Institute (Salem, MA), Frederick Townsend Ward China Collection, Ms. C380 R439.

– "Ship Hancock Log Book." Houghton Library (Harvard University, Cambridge, MA).

– "The voyage of an expedition with two sailing-ships from Cronstadt via South-America to Alaska in 1803–04" [in Russian]. Turku University Library (Turku, Finland).

Arkhiv Vneshney politiki Rossii [Archive of the Foreign Policy of Russia (Moscow)]. f. RAK, ds. 183, 192.

Astor papers. Baker Library (Harvard Business School, Boston, MA), Ms. 766.

[Baranov, Alexander]. "Baranov to Johns [Jones], October 4/16, 1816." Yale University Library (New Haven, CT), Western Americana Collection.

Barkley, Capt. C.W. "Journal of the *Halcyon*." BCPA, Ms. M237.

Barkley, Frances. "Reminiscences." BCPA.

Bartlett, John. "John Bartlett's journal to North West Coast and China, 1790, on ship *Massachusetts*." Peabody Museum (Salem, MA).

"Bill of Lading of the Ship Active, July 20, 1826." Essex Institute (Salem, MA).

"Bill of Lading of the Ship Louisa, Oct. 5, 1826." Essex Institute (Salem, MA).

Boardman Letterbook. Baker Library (Harvard Business School, Boston, MA), Ms. 766.

[Brown, Norman B.?] "A Journal from New London Towards the Falkland Islands etc. etc." Sag Harbor Whaling and Historical Museum (Sag Harbor, Long Island, NY).

Bryant and Sturgis Papers. Baker Library (Harvard Business School, Boston, MA), Ms. 766.

Cleveland, Captain Richard J. "Northwest Expedition: Narrative of the Fur Trading Voyage of the Brig Caroline from China to the Northwest Coast of America January 10–September 13 1799." Yale University Library (New Haven, CT), Western Americana Ms. 90.

Clinton, Ebenezer. "Journal." Yale University Library (New Haven, CT), Western Americana Ms. 92.

[Colnett, James]. "A Voyage to the N. W. Side of America by J. Colnett." Great Britain, Public Record Office, Adm. 55/146.

Despatches from United States Consuls in Canton, 1790–1906. USNARS. File Microcopies of Records in the National Archives: no. 101, roll 1.

Despatches from United States Consuls in Honolulu, 1820–1903. Vol. 1. USNARS. File Microcopies of Records in the National Archives: no. 144, roll 1.

Dorr, Ebenezer. "A Journal of a Voyage from Boston round the World ..." John Carter Brown Library (Providence, RI).

– ["Logbook of the *Hope*, Sept. 14, 1791–Mar. 2, 1792."] Detroit Library, Burton Historical Collection, Ebenezer Dorr Papers.

Douglas, James. "Diary of a trip to the Northwest Coast, April 22–October 2, 1840." BCPA, Ms. AB40 D75.2A.

Dryad (Brig) Log, 1831. HBCA, Ms. C.1/218.

Duncan Finlayson – Journals, 1831–38. HBCA, Ms. E.12/2.

Ebenezer Dorr Papers. BCPA, Ms. 828.

[Etholen, Adolph]. Etolin to Khlebnikov, 1/13 May 1835. GAPO, f. 445, op. 1, d. 388.

– Etolin to Khlebnikov, 4/16 May 1836. GAPO, f. 445, op. 1, d. 388.

Fort McLoughlin Post Journal, 1833. HBCA, Ms. B.120/e/1.

Fort Simpson. Correspondence outward, 1841–1844. BCPA, Ms. AB20 sil2.

Fort Simpson (Nass) – Miscellaneous Items, 1831–41. HBCA, Ms. B.201/z/1.

Fort Simpson (Nass) Post Journal, 1834–40. HBCA, Ms. B.201/a/3–4.

Fort Vancouver (Columbia) Post Journal, 1826–50. HBCA, Ms. B.223/c/1.

Fort Vancouver (Columbia) Post Journal, 1840–41. HBCA, Ms. B.223/b/28.

Furgerson, Samuel. "Journal of a Voyage from Boston to the Northwest Coast of America, in the Brig Otter Samuel Hill Commander." Yale University Library (New Haven, CT), Western Americana Ms. 207.

Gibson, John. "Observations on the Trade with the Chinese," 1807. Library Company of Philadelphia, Robert Waln Notebooks.

Governor George Simpson – Correspondence Book Inwards, 1821–22, 1824–31, 1833–35. HBCA, Ms. D.4/116, 119–21, 123, 125–7.

Governor George Simpson – Correspondence Inward, 1843–45. HBCA, Ms. D.5/8, 10, 13.

Governor George Simpson – Correspondence Book Outwards (General), 1824–26. HBCA, Ms. D.4/6–7.

Governor George Simpson – Correspondence Book Outwards (General), 1844–45. HBCA, Ms. D.4/66.

Governor George Simpson – Official Reports to the Governor & Committee in London, 1832, 1834–36, 1839, 1841–42. HBCA, Ms. D.4/99–103,106, 110.

Haskins, Ralph. "Journal of a Fur Trading Voyage from Boston to the Northwest Coast of America in the Ship Atahualpa 1800–03." Yale University Library (New Haven, CT), Western Americana Ms. s–126.

– "Blotter for Ship Atahualpa, August 31, 1801" and "Ledger." Yale University Library (New Haven, CT), Western Americana Ms. s–126.

Hill, S. "Autobiography ..." New York Public Library.

– "Journal and Log of Two Voyages." New York Public Library.

Hunnewell Papers. Baker Library (Harvard Business School, Boston, MA), Ms. 733.

[Ingraham, Joseph]. "Joseph Ingraham to José Estéban Martínez, May 1789, Nootka Sound." Oregon Historical Society (Portland, OR), copy of typescript.

"Journal of the Hudson's Bay Company at Fort Simpson 1834–7." Bancroft Library (University of California, Berkeley), Ms. P–C 23.

Khlebnikov, K.T. "Khronologicheskaya tablitsa Sitkhi ..." ['A Chronological Table of Sitka ...']. GAPO, f. 445, op. 1, d. 413.

– "Okhota. O zverinom promysle Rossiisko-Amerikanskoy Kompanii" ["Hunting. Concerning the Fur Trade of the Russian-American Company"]. GAPO, f. 445, op. 1, d. 49.

Lamb, Horatio Appleton. "Notes on Trade with the Northwest Coast, 1790–1810." Houghton Library (Harvard University, Cambridge, MA), Ms. AMW 65.

Leonard, Spencer. "Ship Alert Log Book of Boston Lemuel Porter Esq. Commander Bound from Boston for the N W Coast of America & Canton Manilla England & Holland & Back to Boston." Old Dartmouth Historical Society and Whaling Museum (New Bedford, MA), Ms. 477.

[Liscome, Otis?]. "Extracts from the log of the Ship Margaret." Essex Institute (Salem, MA).

London Inward Correspondence from Governors of H.B.C. Territories – Sir George Simpson, 1823–45. HBCA, Ms. A.12/1–2.

London Locked Private Letter Book, 1823–46. HBCA, Ms. A.7/1.

McNeill, William H. "Journal of a Voyage kept onboard the Honourable Hudson's Bay Brig Lama during the years 1832, 1833." BCPA, Ms. AB20.5 L16j.

– "Journal of a Voyage kept onboard Brig Lama ..." BCPA, Ms. AB20.5 C76.

– "Journal of a Voyage to the N.W. Coast of North America kept on Board Brig Convoy ..." BCPA, Ms. AB20.5 C76 2.

Magee, Bernard. "Log of the Jefferson." Massachusetts Historical Society (Boston, MA).

Marshall Manuscripts. Houghton Library (Harvard University, Cambridge, MA), Ms. AMW 63f.

[Martain, William]. "Ship Hamilton Log Book 1809–1815." Essex Institute (Salem, MA).

– "Ship Louisa Log Book 1826–1829." Essex Institute (Salem, MA).

Maury Abstract Logs 1796–1861. USNARS. Roll 70, target 3, vol. 235 ("Ship *Caledonia*"); Roll 71, target 4, vol. 251 ("Ship *Levant*"); Roll 72, target 1, vol. 271 ("Ship *America*"); Roll 72, target 2, vol. 272 ("Ship *Caledonia*"); Roll 86, target 2, vol. 522 ("Brig *Nile*").

Miscellaneous Letters of the Department of State. 1 August–31 December 1816. USNARS. File Microcopies of Records in the National Archives: no. 179, roll 35.

Perkins, James and Thomas H. Foreign letters, 3 April 1807–5 January 1815. Massachusetts Historical Society (Boston, MA).

Perkins Letterbooks. Baker Library (Harvard Business School, Boston, MA), Ms. 766.

Perkins and Company and Russell and Company Papers. Baker Library (Harvard Business School, Boston, MA), Ms. 766.

Phelps, William Dane. "Solid men of Boston in the Northwest." Bancroft Library (University of California, Berkeley), Ms. P–C 31.

Pierrepont, Hezekiah B. "Notes on the Trade of China, taken chiefly from Observations made at Canton in the Season of 1796 & corrected in London June 1798." New York Public Library, Constable-Pierrepont Papers, Box 43.

[Puget, Peter]. "A Log of the Proceedings of His Majesty's Armed Tender Chatham ..." University of British Columbia Library (Vancouver, BC), Special Collections Division.

– "A Log of the Proceedings of His Majesty's Ship Discovery ..." University of British Columbia Library (Vancouver, BC), Special Collections Division.

Records of the Russian-American Company 1802–1867: Correspondence of Governors General. USNARS. File Microcopies of Records in the National Archives: no. 11, rolls 8, 27–8, 31–3, 36, 38–9, 41–2.

Reynolds, Capt. Stephen. "Journal." Peabody Museum (Salem, MA).

Roblet, Claude. "Extrait du journal du voyage autour du monde du navire le Solide de Marseille Capt le Marchand." Archives Nationale (Paris), Marine 3JJ390, Carton 1113, no. 2, pièces 1–4.

[Rosenberg, Nicholas]. Rozenberg to Khlebnikov, 29 April/10 May 1836. GAPO, f. 445, op. 1, d. 318.

Russian American Company – Miscellaneous Papers, 1824–1903. HBCA, Ms. F.29/2.

[Smith, William]. "Arab (brig) Logbook, June 15, 1821–Jan. 5, 1825." Bancroft Library (University of California, Berkeley), Ms. C–E 54.

Stikine Post Journal, 1840–42. HBCA, Ms. B.209/a/1.

Sturgis, Josiah. "Extract from the Journal of Josiah Sturgis kept on board the Ship Levant on a Voyage from Boston to the North West Coast and China in the Year 1818." Oregon Historical Society (Portland, OR), Ms. 153.

[Sturgis, William]. "Journal of W. Sturgis, 1799." Massachusetts Historical Society (Boston, MA).

– "Ms. of 3 lectures by Wm. Sturgis dealing with his voyages." Massachusetts Historical Society (Boston, MA).

[Suter, John]. "Log of John Suter, Captain, on the Ship *Mentor* of Boston toward the Northwest Coast of America, 1816–1820." Peabody Museum (Salem, MA).

– "Log of the ship Atahualpa." Massachusetts Historical Society (Boston, MA).

Thomas Lowe – Journal, 1841–42. HBCA, Ms. E.25/1.

[Underwood, Ebenezer]. "Journal on board Brig Tally Ho." BCPA, Ms. AB20.5 C76 2.

Vancouver (Schooner) Log, 1831–32. HBCA, Ms. C.1/1,062.

Walbran, Captain J.T., ed. "The Cruise of the Imperial Eagle." BCPA, Ms. AA20.5 L92W.

Walker, William, Jr. "Supercargo's log of the brig *Lydia* ... July 10, 1805–Jan. 3, 1807 ..." Yale University Library (New Haven, CT), Western Americana Ms. S–214.

Work, John. Work Correspondence. BCPA, Ms. AB40 W89A.

PRIMARY SOURCES: PUBLISHED

Alaska Boundary Tribunal. Case of the United States. Washington, DC: Government Printing Office 1903.

Alaska History Research Project. *Documents Relative to the History of Alaska.* College, AK: University of Alaska 1936. Vol. 3.

Andreyev, A.I. *Russian Discoveries in the Pacific and in North America in the Eighteenth and Nineteenth Centuries.* Translated by Carl Ginsburg. Ann Arbor: J.W. Edwards 1952.

Anonymous. "Documents." *Washington Historical Quarterly* 1 (1907):256–66.

– "Documents." *Washington Historical Quarterly* 2 (1908):161–8, 254–64.

– "English and American trade ..." *Chinese Repository* 6 (1837–38):280–6.

– "The fur trade ..." *Chinese Repository* 3 (1834–35):548–59.

– "Fur Trade with Canton, in China." *Congressional Globe* 13 (1844):226.

– "Imports and Exports of Canton." *Chinese Repository* 2 (1833–34):447–72.

– "New Fur Trade." *World,* 6 October 1788.

– "Puteshestvie na shlyupe 'Blagonamerenny,' dlya izsledovaniya beregov Azii i Ameriki za Beringovym-Prolivom s 1819 po 1822 god" ["A Voyage on the Sloop *Blagonamerenny* to Explore the Coasts of Asia and America beyond Bering Strait from 1819 to 1822"]. Pt. 3. *Otechestvennie zapiski* 67 (1849):215–36.

Bagley, Clarence B., ed. "Journal of Occurrences at Nisqually House, 1833 [1833–35]." *Washington Historical Quarterly* 6 (1915):179–97, 264–77; 7 (1916):59–75, 144–67.

Barreiro-Meiro, Roberto, ed. *Coleccion de diarios y relaciones para la historia de los viajes y descubrimientos: VI – Estéban José Martínez (1742–1798)* [*Collection of Diairies and Accounts for the History of Voyages and Discoveries: VI – Estéban José Martínez (1742–1798)*]. Madrid: Instituto Historico de Marina 1964.

Bartlett, John. "A Narrative of Events ..." In *The Sea, the Ship and the Sailor.* Edited by Captain Elliot Snow. Salem, MA. Marine Research Society 1925, 287–337.

Beaglehole, J. C. ed. *The Journals of Captain James Cook on his Voyages of Discovery.* Cambridge, UK: Hakluyt Society 1955–74. 5 Vols. in 4.

Bingham, Hiram. *A Residence of Twenty-One Years in the Sandwich Islands ...* Tokyo: Charles E. Tuttle 1981.

[Bloxam, Andrew]. *Diary of Andrew Bloxam Naturalist of the "Blonde" On Her Trip From England to the Hawaiian Islands 1824–25.* Honolulu: Bernice P. Bishop Museum 1925.

[Boelen, Jacobus]. *A Merchant's Perspective: Captain Jacobus Boelen's Narrative of his Visit to Hawai'i in 1828.* Translated by Frank J.A. Broeze. Honolulu: Hawaiian Historical Society 1988.

Broughton, William Robert. *A Voyage of Discovery to the North Pacific Ocean.* London: T. Cadell and W. Davies 1804.

Busch, Briton Cooper, ed. *Alta California 1840–1842: The Journal and Observations of William Dane Phelps Master of the Ship "Alert."* Glendale, CA: Arthur H. Clark 1983.

Campbell, Archibald. *A Voyage Round the World from 1806 to 1812* ... Edinburgh: Archibald Constable *et al.* 1816.

Chernykh, Ye. "Izvestiya iz Novoarkhangelska" ["News from New Archangel"]. *Zhurnal selskavo khozyaistva i ovtsevodstva* 1 (1843):91–4.

Choris, M. Louis. *Voyage pittoresque autour du monde.* Paris: Firmin Didot 1822.

Cleveland, Richard J. *A Narrative of Voyages and Commercial Enterprises.* Cambridge, MA. John Owen 1842. 2 Vols.

Cleveland, Richard Jeffry. *Voyages and Commercial Enterprises, of the Sons of New England.* New York: Burt Franklin 1968.

Cole, Arthur Harrison, ed. *Industrial and Commercial Correspondence of Alexander Hamilton* ... Chicago: Business Historical Society 1928.

Commonwealth of Australia. *Historical Records of Australia.* Canberra: Library Committee of the Commonwealth Parliament 1916. Series 1, Vol. 8.

Cook, Captain James [and King, Captain James]. *A Voyage to the Pacific Ocean.* London: G. Nicol and T. Cadell 1784. 3 Vols.

Corney, Peter. *Early Voyages in the North Pacific 1813–1818.* Fairfield, WA: Ye Galleon Press 1965.

Corning, Howard, ed. "Letters of Sullivan Dorr." *Proceedings of the Massachusetts Historical Society* 67 (1945):178–364.

– "Sullivan Dorr, An Early China Merchant." *Essex Institute Historical Collections* 78 (1942):158–75.

Cox, Ross. *The Columbia River.* Edited by Edgar I. and Jane R. Stewart. Norman: University of Oklahoma Press 1957.

Cumming, C.F. Gordon. *Wanderings in China.* Edinburgh and London: William Blackwood and Sons 1886. 2 Vols.

Cutter, Donald C., ed. *The California Coast*: A Bilingual Edition of Documents from the Sutro Collection. Norman: University of Oklahoma Press 1969.

Dampier, Robert. *To the Sandwich Islands on H.M.S. "Blonde."* Edited by Pauline King Joerger. Honolulu: University Press of Hawaii 1971.

Dana, Richard Henry, Jr. *Two Years Before the Mast*: A Personal Narrative. Large-paper limited edition. Boston and New York: Houghton Mifflin 1911. 2 Vols.

Day, A. Grove, ed. *Letter and Memorandum from Capt. George Dixon to Sir Joseph Banks Regarding the Fur Trade on the Northwest Coast, A. D. 1789.* "The White Knight Chapbooks: Pacific Northwest Series," No. 3. San Francisco: White Knight Press 1941.

De Roquefeuil, Camille. *Journal d'un voyage autour du monde pendant les années 1816, 1817, 1818 et 1819.* Paris: Ponthieu, Lesage, et Gide fils 1823. 2 Vols.

Delano, Amasa. *A Narrative of Voyages and Travels* ... New York, Washington, and London: Praeger Publishers 1970.

Dixon, Captain George [William Beresford]. *A Voyage Round the World*. London: Geo. Goulding 1789.

Dobell, Peter. *Travels in Kamtchatka and Siberia; With a Narrative of a Residence in China*. London: Henry Colburn and Richard Bentlcy 1830. 2 Vols.

Duhaut-Cilly, A. *Voyage autour du monde* ... Paris: Arthus Bertrand 1834–35. 2 Vols.

D'Wolf, John. *A Voyage to the North Pacific*. Fairfield, WA: Ye Galleon Press 1968.

Ellis, W. *An Authentic Narrative of a Voyage Performed by Captain Cook and Captain Clerke* ... London: G. Robinson, J. Sewell, and J. Debrett. 2 Vols.

Ellis, William. *Journal of William Ellis*. Tokyo: Charles E. Tuttle 1979.

Fanning, Edmund. *Voyages Round the World* ... London: O. Rich 1834.

Fleurieu, C.P. Claret. *Voyage autour du monde* ... Paris: L'imprimerie de la République 1796. 4 Vols.

– *A Voyage Round the World ... by Étienne Marchand*. London: T. Longman *et al*. 1801. 2 Vols.

Forbes, R.B. *Remarks on China and the China Trade*. Boston: Samuel N. Dickison 1844.

Franchère, Gabriel. *Journal of a Voyage on the North West Coast of North America during the Years 1811, 1812, 1813 and 1814*. Translated by Wessie Tipping Lamb and edited by W. Kaye Lamb. Toronto: Champlain Society 1969.

Fu, Lo-shu, comp. *A Documentary Chronicle of Sino-Western Relations (1644–1820)*. Tuscon: University of Arizona Press 1966. 2 Vols.

Fyodorova, S.G., comp. *Russkaya Amerika v "Zapiskakh" Kirila Khlebnikova: Novo-Arkhangelsk* [*Russian America in the "Notes" of Kiril Khlebnikov: New Archangel*]. Moscow: "Nauka" 1985.

Galvin, John, ed. *A Journal of Explorations Northward along the Coast from Monterey in the Year 1775*. San Francisco: John Howell 1964.

Gast, Ross H. and Conrad, Agnes C. *Don Francisco de Paula Marin: A Biography; The Letters and Journal of Francisco de Paula Marin*. Honolulu: Hawaiian Historical Society 1973.

Golovin, Pavel N. *Civil and Savage Encounters: The Worldly Travel Letters of an Imperial Russian Navy Officer 1860–1861*. Translated by Basil Dmytryshyn and E.A.P. Crownhart-Vaughan. Portland: Western Imprints 1983.

Golovnin, V.M. *Around the World on the "Kamchatka," 1817–1819*. Translated and edited by Ella Lury Wiswell. Honolulu: Hawaiian Historical Society and University Press of Hawaii 1979.

– *Puteshestvie na shlyupe "Diana" iz Kronshtadta v Kamchatku, sovershennoye pod nachalstvom flota leitenanta Golovnina v 1807–1811 godakh* [*A Voyage on the Sloop "Diana" from Cronstad to Kamchatka under the Command of Fleet Lieu-*

tenant Golovnin in 1807–11]. Moscow: Gosudarstvennoye izdatelstvo geograficheskoy literatury 1961.

Gough, Barry M. *To the Pacific and Arctic with Beechey* ... Cambridge, UK: Hakluyt Society 1973.

Grant, Gordon. *The Life and Adventures of John Nicol Mariner*. London: Cassell 1937.

Great Britain, Parliament. *Sessional Papers* 5 (1830), 6 (1830), 7 (1821).

Green, Jonathan S. *Journal of a Tour on the North West Coast of America in the Year 1829*. New York: Chas. Fred. Heartman 1915.

Hayes, Edmund, ed. *Log of the Union: John Boit's Remarkable Voyage To the Northwest Coast and Around the World 1794–1796*. Portland: Oregon Historical Society 1981.

[Holbrook, Silas P.]. *Sketches, by a Traveller*. Boston: Carter and Hendee 1830.

Holmes, Christine, ed. *Captain Cook's Final Voyage: The Journal of Midshipman George Gilbert*. Honolulu: University Press of Hawaii 1982.

Holt, John Dominis, ed. *The Hawaiian Journal of John B. Whitman 1813–1815: An Account of the Sandwich Islands*. Honolulu: Topgallant Publishing 1979.

Howay, F.W., ed. "Captains Gray and Kendrick: The Barrell Letters." *Washington Historical Quarterly* 12 (1921):243–71.

– "Four Letters from Richard Cadman Etches to Sir Joseph Banks, 1788–92," *British Columbia Historical Quarterly* 3 (1942):125–39.

– *The Journal of Captain James Colnett Aboard the "Argonaut"* ... Toronto: Champlain Society 1940.

– "Letters Relating to the Second Voyage of the Columbia." *Oregon Historical Quarterly* 24 (1923):132–52.

– *The Voyage of the "New Hazard"* ... Fairfield, WA: Ye Galleon Press 1970.

– *Voyages of the "Columbia" to the Northwest Coast 1787–1790 and 1790–1793*. Boston: Massachusetts Historical Society 1941.

Hughes, Sarah Forbes, ed. *Letters and Recollections of John Murray Forbes*. Boston and New York: Houghton Mifflin 1899. Vol. 1.

Ii, John Papa. *Fragments of Hawaiian History*. Honolulu: Bishop Museum Press 1983.

Jackman, S.W., ed. *The Journal of William Sturgis*. Victoria: Sono Nis Press 1978.

Jameson, J. Franklin, ed. "Letters of Phineas Bond, British Consul at Philadelphia, to the Foreign Office of Great Britain, 1787, 1788, 1789." *Annual Report of the American Historical Association for the Year 1896*. Washington, DC: Government Printing Office 1897. 1:513–659.

Jane, Cecil, trans. *A Spanish Voyage to Vancouver [Island] and the North-West Coast of America* ... London: Argonaut Press 1930.

Jarvis, James Jackson. "The Sandwich or Hawaiian Islands." Pt. 2. *Merchants' Magazine* 9 (1843):111–36.

Jewitt, John R. *A Journal, kept at Nootka Sound*. Boston: The Author 1807.

[Jewitt, John R.]. *Narrative of the Adventures and Sufferings of John R. Jewitt.* Fairfield, WA: Ye Galleon Press 1967.

Kaplanoff, Mark D., ed. *Joseph Ingraham's Journal of the Brigantine "Hope"* ... Barre, MA: Imprint Society 1967.

Kelly, Marion, ed. *Hawai'i in 1819: A Narrative Account by Louis Claude de Saulses de Freycinet.* Translated by Ella L. Wiswell. Honolulu: Bernice Pauahi Bishop Museum 1979.

[Khlebnikov, K.T.]. *Colonial Russian America: Kyrill T. Khlebnikov's Reports, 1817–1832.* Translated by Basil Dmytryshyn and E.A.P. Crownhart-Vaughan. Portland: Oregon Historical Society 1976.

Korn, Alfons L., ed. and trans. "Shadows of Destiny: A French Navigator's View of the Hawaiian Kingdom and Its Government in 1828." *Hawaiian Journal of History* 17 (1983):1–39.

L., C. *A Voyage Round the World, in the Years 1785, 1786, 1787, and 1788.* London: R. Randal 1789.

Lamb, W. Kaye, ed. *The Voyage of George Vancouver 1791–1795.* London: Hakluyt Society 1984. 4 Vols.

Lazarev, A. P. *Zapiski o plavanii ... [Notes of a Voyage ...].* Moscow: Gosudarstvennoye izdatelstvo geograficheskoy literatury 1950.

Lazarev, Andrey. *Plavanie vokrug sveta na shlyupe Ladoge v 1822, 1823 i 1824 godakh [A Voyage Around the World on the Sloop Ladoga in 1822, 1823, and 1824].* St. Petersburg: Morskaya tipografiya 1832.

Lisiansky, Urey. *A Voyage Round the World in the Years 1803, 4, 5, & 6.* Translated by the author. London: John Booth, Longman, *et al.* 1814.

Litke, Frederic. *A Voyage Around the World 1826–1829.* Translated by Renée Marshall and Joan Moessner. Kingston, Ont.: Limestone Press 1987. Vol. 1.

Lloyd, Christopher and Anderson, R.C., eds. *A Memoir of James Travenen.* London: Navy Records Society 1959.

Loring, Charles G. "Memoir of the Hon. William Sturgis." *Proceedings of the Massachusetts Historical Society,* first series, 7 (1864):420–73.

Lutké, Frédéric. *Voyage autour du monde.* Translated by F. Boyé. Paris: Didot Frères 1835–36. 3 Vols. and Atlas.

MacNair, H.F., ed. "The Log of the Caroline (1799)." *Pacific Northwest Quarterly* 29 (1938):61–84, 167–200.

[Macrae, James]. *With Lord Byron at the Sandwich Islands in 1825: Being Extracts from the MS Diary of James Macrae, Scottish Botanist.* Hil, HI: Petroglyph Press 1972.

Magee, Bernard. "Observations on the Islands of Juan Fernandez, Massafuero, and St. Ambrose ..." *Collections of the Massachusetts Historical Society, for the Year M,DCC,XCV* 4 (1795):247–60.

Mathison, Gilbert Farquhar. *Narrative of a Visit to Brazil, Chile, Peru, and the Sandwich Islands During the Years 1821 and 1822.* London: Charles Knight 1825.

Meany, Edmond S., ed. *A New Vancouver Journal*. Seattle: n.p. 1915.

Meares, John. *Voyages Made in the Years 1788 and 1789, from China to the North West Coast of America*. London: Logographic Press 1790.

Merk, Frederick, ed. *Fur Trade and Empire: George Simpson's Journal ... 1824–25*. Revised edition. Cambridge, MA: Belknap Press 1968.

Milet-Mureau, L.A., ed. *A Voyage Round the World, Performed in the Years 1785, 1786, 1787, and 1788, By the Boussole and Astrolabe, Under the Command of J.F.G. De La Pérouse*. London: G.G. and J. Robinson 1799. 2 Vols.

[Mitchell, Howard T., ed.]. *The Journals of William Fraser Tolmie*. Vancouver: Mitchell Press 1963.

Morison, Samuel Eliot, ed. "Letters on the Northwest Fur Trade." *Washington Historical Quarterly* 11 (1920):174–7.

Morrell, Benjamin. *A Narrative of Four Voyages ...* New York: J. and J. Harper 1832.

Morris, Grace Parker, ed. "Some Letters from 1792–1800 on the China Trade." *Oregon Historical Quarterly* 42 (1941):48–87.

Morse, Hosea Ballou. *The Chronicles of the East India Company trading to China 1635–1834*. Cambridge, MA: Harvard University Press 1926–29. 5 Vols.

Mortimer, Lieut. George. *Observations and Remarks Made During a Voyage ...* London: The Author 1791.

Moulton, William. *A Concise Extract, from the Sea Journal of William Moulton ...* Utica, NY: The Author 1804.

Mourelle, Don Francisco Antonio. *Voyage of the Sonora in the Second Bucareli Expedition*. Translated by Daines Barrington. Millwood, NY: Krause Reprint 1975.

Moziño, José Mariana. *Noticias de Nutka: An Account of Nootka Sound in 1792*. Translated by Iris Higbie Wilson. Toronto: McClelland and Stewart 1970.

Munford, James Kenneth, ed. *John Ledyard's Journal of Captain Cook's Last Voyage*. Corvallis: Oregon State University Press 1963.

Myers, Capt. John. *The Life, Voyages and Travels of Capt. John Myers ...* London: Longman *et al.* 1817.

Newcombe, C.F., ed. *Menzies' Journal of Vancouver's Voyage*. Victoria: Archives of British Columbia 1923.

Parker, Samuel. *Journal of an Exploring Tour beyond the Rocky Mountains ...* Minneapolis: Ross and Haines 1967.

[Péron, François]. *Mémoires du Capitaine Péron ...* Paris: Brissot-Thivars 1924. 2 Vols.

Pipes, Nellie B., ed. "Later Affairs of Kendrick; Barrel Letters." *Oregon Historical Quarterly* 30 (1929):95–105.

Polansky, Patricia, ed. "Baron Vrangel' Visits the Sandwich Islands in 1826 on the *Krotkii*." Translated by Robert Stanton. *Hawaiian Journal of History* 20 (1986):13–26.

Portlock, Captain Nathaniel. *A Voyage Round the World; But More Particularly to the North-West Coast of America: Performed in 1785, 1786, 1787, and 1788* ... London: John Stockdale and George Goulding 1789.

Quincy, Josiah. *The Journals of Major Samuel Shaw, the First American Consul at Canton*. Boston: Wm. Crosby and H.P. Nichols 1847.

Rich, E.E., ed. *The Letters of John McLoughlin ... 1825–1838*. Toronto: Champlain Society 1941.

– *The Letters of John McLoughlin ... 1839–1844*. Toronto: Champlain Society 1943.

– *Part of Dispatch from George Simpson Esqr Governor of Ruperts Land to the Governor & Committee of the Hudson's Bay Company London*. Toronto: Champlain Society 1947.

[Rickman, John]. *Journal of Captain Cook's Last Voyage to the Pacific Ocean on Discovery* ... London: E. Newbery 1781.

Rives, J.B. "Vessels Trading on the Northwest Coast of America, 1804– 1814." *Washington Historical Quarterly* 19 (1928):294–5.

Roe, Michael, ed. *The Journal and Letters of Captain Charles Bishop* ... London: Hakluyt Society 1967.

Ross, Alexander. *Adventures of the First Settlers on the Oregon or Columbia River* ... London: Smith and Elder 1849.

– *The Fur Hunters of the Far West*. Edited by Kenneth A. Spaulding. Norman: University of Oklahoma Press 1956.

Rossiisko-Amerikanskaya Kompaniya. *Otchyot Rossiisko-Amerikanskoy Kompanii Glavnavo Pravleniya za odin god ...* [*Report of the Head Office of the Russian-American Company for One Year ...*] St Petersburg: divers 1843–65. 1860.

Sauer, Martin. *An Account of a Geographical and Astronomical Expedition to the Northern Parts of Russia* ... London: T. Cadell, Jr. and W. Davies 1802.

[Scouler, John]. "Dr. John Scouler's Journal of a Voyage to N.W. America." *Oregon Historical Quarterly* 6 (1905):54–75, 159–205, 276–87.

Scouler, John. "Observations on the Indigenous Tribes of the N.W. Coast of America." *Journal of the Royal Geographical Society of London* 11 (1841):215–51.

– "On the Indian Tribes Inhabiting the North-West Coast of America." *Journal of the Ethnological Society of London* 1 (1848): 228–52.

Shaler, William. "Journal of a Voyage between China and the North-western Coast of America, Made in 1804." *American Register* 3 (1808):137–75.

Shelikhov, Grigorii I. *A Voyage to America 1783–1786*. Translated by Marina Ramsay. Kingston, Ont.: Limestone Press 1981.

Simpson, Sir George. *Narrative of a Journey Round the World*. London: Henry Colburn 1847. 2 Vols.

Sparks, Jared. *Memoirs of the Life and Travels of John Ledyard, from his Journals and Correspondence*. London: Henry Colburn 1828.

Stewart, C.S. *Journal of a Residence in the Sandwich Islands During the Years 1823, 1824, and 1825* ... Honolulu: University of Hawaii Press 1970.

– *A Visit to the South Seas* ... New York: John P. Haven 1831. Vol. 2.

[Strange, James]. *James Strange's Journal and Narrative* ... Madras: Government Press 1928.

[Sturgis, William]. "Examination of the Russian Claims to the Northwest Coast of America." *North American Review 15* (1822):370–401.

– "The Northwest Fur Trade." Edited by Elliot C. Cowdin. *Hunt's Merchants' Magazine* 14 (1846):532–8.

Thwaites, Reuben Gold, ed. *Original Journals of the Lewis and Clark Expedition 1804–1806.* New York: Arno Press 1969. Vols. 3–4, 6.

Tikhmenev, P. *Supplement of Some Historical Documents to the Historical Review of the Formation of the Russian-American Company.* Translated by Dimitri Krenov. Seattle: Works Progress Administration 1938.

Tikhmenev, P.A. *A History of the Russian-American Company.* Translated by Dmitri Krenov. Kingston, Ont.: Limestone Press 1979. Vol. 2.

Trowbridge, Thomas R., ed. "The Diary of Mr. Ebenezer Townsend, Jr., the Supercargo of the Sealing Ship 'Neptune,' on her Voyage to the South Pacific and Canton." *Papers of the New Haven Colony Historical Society* 4 (1888):1–115.

Turnbull, John. *A Voyage Round the World* ... 2nd edition. London: A. Maxwell 1813.

Turner, J.L. *Account of the Captivity of Mr. J.L. Turner amongst the Ladrones, in the year 1807.* London: n.p. 1810.

United States, Congress, Senate. *Senate Documents.* 24th Congress, 2nd Session, Vol. 1, No. 54.

Von Chamisso, Adelbert. *A Voyage Around the World with the Romanzov Exploring Expedition in the Years 1815–1818 in the Brig Rurik, Captain Otto Von Kotzebue.* Translated and edited by Henry Kratz. Honolulu: University of Hawaii Press 1986.

Von Kotzebue, Otto. *A New Voyage Round the World* ... London: Henry Colburn and Richard Bentley 1830. 2 Vols.

– *A Voyage of Discovery* ... London: Longman *et al.* 1821. 3 Vols.

Von Krusenstern, Captain A.J. *Voyage Round the World, in the Years 1803, 1804, 1805, & 1806.* Translated by Richard Belgrave Hoppner. London: John Murray 1813. 2 Vols.

Von Langsdorff, G.H. *Voyages and Travels in Various Parts of the World, During the Years 1803, 1804, 1805, 1806, and 1807.* London: Henry Colburn 1813–14. 2 Vols.

Wagner, Henry R. *Spanish Explorations in the Strait of Juan de Fuca.* New York: AMS Press 1971.

– and Newcombe, W.A., eds. "The Journal of Jacinto Caamaño." Translated by Harold Grenfell. *British Columbia Historical Quarterly* 2 (1938):189–222, 265–301.

Walker, Alexander. *An Account of a Voyage to the North West Coast of America in 1785 & 1786.* Edited by Robin Fisher and J.M. Bumstead. Vancouver and Toronto: Douglas and McIntyre 1982.

Williams, Glyndwr, ed. *Hudson's Bay Miscellany 1670–1870.* Winnipeg: Hudson's Bay Record Society 1975.

– *London Correspondence Inward from Sir George Simpson 1841–42.* London: Hudson's Bay Record Society 1973.

Williams, S.W. "Recollections of China Prior to 1840." *Journal of the North-China Branch of the Royal Asiatic Society* 8 (1874):1–21.

[Work, John]. *The Journal of John Work January to October, 1835.* Edited by Henry Drummond Dee. Victoria: Charles F. Banfield 1945.

Wrangell, Rear Admiral Ferdinand Petrovich. *Russian America: Statistical and Ethnographic Information.* Translated by Mary Sadouski. Kingston, Ont.: Limestone Press 1980.

Z[avoiko], Lieutenant V. *Vpechatleniya moryaka vo vremya dvukh puteshestvii drugom sveta* [*A Sailor's Impressions during Two Voyages Around the World*]. St Petersburg: Tipografiya Vnutrennikh del 1840. 2 Vols.

SECONDARY SOURCES

Amoss, Pamela. "A Little More Than Kin, and Less Than Kind: The Ambiguous Northwest Coast Dog." In *The Tsimshian and Their Neighbors of the North Pacific Coast*, edited by Jay Miller and Carol M. Eastman. Seattle: University of Washington Press 1984, 292–309.

Anonymous. "Chinese Pirates." *Chinese Repository* 3 (1834–35): 62–83.

– *Old Shipping Days in Boston.* Boston: State Street Trust Company 1918.

Allen, G.C. and Donnithorne, Audrey G. *Western Enterprise in Far Eastern Economic Development: China and Japan.* London: George Allen and Unwin 1954.

Archer, Christon I. "Cannibalism in the Early History of the Northwest Coast: Enduring Myths and Neglected Realities." *Canadian Historical Review* 61 (1980):453–79.

– "Spanish Exploration and Settlement of the Northwest Coast in the 18th Century." *Sound Heritage* 7 (1978):32–53.

– "The Transient Presence: A Re-Appraisal of Spanish Attitudes toward the Northwest Coast in the Eighteenth Century." *BC Studies* (Summer 1973):11–19.

Averkieva, Julia. "The Tlingit Indians." In *North American Indians in Historical Perspective*, edited by Eleanor Burke Leacock and Nancy Oestreich Lurie. New York: Random House 1971, 317–42.

Bancroft, Hubert H. *History of the Northwest Coast.* San Francisco: A.L. Bancroft 1884.

Boxer, C.R. "The Manila Galleon, 1565–1815: The Lure of Silk and Silver." *History Today* 8 (1958):538–47.

– "Piracy in the South China Sea." *History Today* 30 (1980): 40–4.

Boyd, Robert T. "Demographic History 1774–1874." In *Northwest Coast*, edited by Wayne Suttles, *Handbook of North American Indians*, vol. 7. Washington, DC: Smithsonian Institution 1990, 135–48.

– "The Introduction of Infectious Diseases among the Indians of the Pacific Northwest, 1774–1874." PHD dissertation, University of Washington 1985.

Bradley, Harold Whitman. *The American Frontier in Hawaii: The Pioneers 1789–1843*. Palo Alto, CA: Stanford University Press 1942.

Buell, Robert Kingery and Skladel, Charlotte Northcote. *Sea Otters and the China Trade*. New York: David McKay 1968.

Carpenter, Kenneth J. *The History of Scurvy and Vitamin C*. Cambridge, UK: Cambridge University Press 1986.

Cheong, W.E. "Trade and Finance in China, 1784–1834: A Reappraisal." *Business History* 7 (1965):34–56.

Collis, Maurice. *Foreign Mud*. London: Faber and Faber 1946.

Cook, Warren L. *Flood Tide of Empire: Spain and the Pacific Northwest, 1543–1819*. New Haven and London: Yale University Press 1973.

Cotton, Sir Evan. *East Indiamen: The East India Company's Maritime Service*. Edited by Sir Charles Fawcett. London: Batchworth Press 1949.

Davidson, Donald D. "Relations of the Hudson's Bay Company with the Russian-American Company on the Northwest Coast, 1829–1867." *British Columbia Historical Quarterly* 5 (1941):33–51.

Davis, Lance Edwin. "Stock Ownership in the Early New England Textile Industry." *Business History Review* 32 (1958):204–22.

Dennett, Tyler. *Americans in Eastern Asia*. New York: Barnes and Noble 1963.

Downs, Jacques M. "American Merchants and the China Opium Trade, 1800–1840." *Business History Review* 42 (1968):418–42.

Drew, Leslie and Wilson, Douglas. *Argillite: Art of the Haida*. North Vancouver: Hancock House 1980.

Drucker, Philip. *Cultures of the North Pacific Coast*. Scranton, PA: Chandler Publishing 1965.

– *Indians of the Northwest Coast*. Garden City, NY: Natural History Press 1963.

Duff, Wilson. *The Indian History of British Columbia*. Victoria: Provincial Museum of British Columbia 1964. Vol. 1.

Dulles, Foster Rhea. *The Old China Trade*. New York: AMS Press 1970.

Duncan, Janice K. "Kanaka World Travelers and Fur Company Employees, 1785–1860." *Hawaiian Journal of History* 7 (1973):93–111.

– *Minority without a Champion: Kanakas on the Pacific Coast, 1788–1850*. Portland: Oregon Historical Society 1972.

Dunn, John. *History of the Oregon Territory … 2nd edition*. London: Edwards and Hughes 1846.

Eckstein, Alexander. *China's Economic Development: The Interplay of Scarcity and Ideology*. Ann Arbor: University of Michigan Press 1975.

Evans, Brian L. "Ginseng: Root of Chinese-Canadian Relations." *Canadian Historical Review* 66 (1985):1–26.

Fairbank, John K., ed. *The Cambridge History of China*. London, New York, and Melbourne: Cambridge University Press 1978. Vol. 10, Pt. 1.

Fairbank, John King. *Trade and Diplomacy on the China Coast: The Opening of the Treaty Ports 1842–1854*. Cambridge, MA: Harvard University Press 1953–56. 2 Vols.

– "Tributary Trade and China's Relations with the West." *Far Eastern Quarterly* 1 (1941–42):129–49.

Ferguson, R. Brian. "A Reexamination of the Causes of Northwest Coast Warfare." In *Warfare, Culture, and Environment*, edited by R. Brian Ferguson. Orlando, FL: Academic Press 1984, 267–328.

Fisher, Robin. "Arms and Men on the Northwest Coast, 1774–1825." *BC Studies* (Spring 1976):3–18.

– *Contact and Conflict: Indian-European Relations in British Columbia, 1774–1890*. Vancouver: University of British Columbia Press 1977.

– "Indian Control of the Maritime Fur Trade and the Northwest Coast." In *Approaches to Native History in Canada*, edited by D.A. Muise. Ottawa: National Museums of Canada 1977, 65–86.

Forbes, John D. "European Wars and Boston Trade, 1783–1815." *New England Quarterly* 11 (1938):709–30.

Forbes, W. Cameron. "Houqua: The Merchant Prince of China 1769–1843." *Bulletin of the American Asiatic Association* 6 (1940):9–18.

Freeman, Donald B. and Dungey, Frances L. "A spatial duopoly: competition in the western Canadian fur trade, 1770–1835." *Journal of Historical Geography* 7 (1981):252–70.

Gibson, James R. "Bostonians and Muscovites on the Northwest Coast, 1788–1841." In *The Western Shore: Oregon Country Eassays Honoring the American Revolution*, edited by Thomas Vaughan. Portland: Oregon Historical Society 1975, 81–119.

– "European Dependence upon American Natives: The Case of Russian America." *Ethnohistory* 25 (1978):359–85.

– *Farming the Frontier: The Agricultural Opening of the Oregon Country 1786–1846*. Vancouver: University of British Columbia Press 1985.

– *Feeding the Russian Fur Trade: Provisionment of the Okhotsk Seaboard and the Kamchatka Peninsula 1639–1856*. Madison: University of Wisconsin Press 1969.

– *Imperial Russia in Frontier America: The Changing Geography of Supply of Russian America, 1784–1867*. New York: Oxford University Press 1976.

– "The Maritime Trade of the North Pacific Coast." In *History of Indian-White Relations*, edited by Wilcomb E. Washburn. *Handbook of North American Indians*, vol. 4. Washington, DC: Smithsonian Institution 1988, 375–90.

– "Russian America in 1833: The Survey of Kirill Khlebnikov." *Pacific Northwest Quarterly* 63 (1972):1–13.
– "The Russian Fur Trade." In *Old Trails and New Directions: Papers of the Third North American Fur Trade Conference*, edited by Carol M. Judd and Arthur J. Ray. Toronto: University of Toronto Press 1980, 217–30.
– "Smallpox on the Northwest Coast, 1835–1838." *BC Studies* (Winter 1982–83):61–81.
Goldstein, Jonathan. *Philadelphia and the China Trade 1682–1846: Commercial, Cultural, and Attitudinal Effects*. University Park, PA, and London: Pennsylvania State University Press 1978.
Gormly, Mary. "Early Culture Contact on the Northwest Coast, 1774–1795." *Northwest Anthropological Research Notes* 11 (1977):1–80.
Gough, Barry M. "Canada's 'Adventure to China,' 1784–1821." *Canadian Geographical Journal* 93 (1976–77):28–37.
– "James Cook and the Origins of the Maritime Fur Trade." *American Neptune* 38 (1978):217–24.
Greenberg, Michael. *British Trade and the Opening of China 1800–42*. New York and London: Monthly Review Press 1979.
Gunther, Erna. *Ethnobotany of Western Washington: The Knowledge and Use of Indigenous Plants by Native Americans*. Revised edition. Seattle: University of Washington Press 1973.
– *Indian Life on the Northwest Coast of North America*. Chicago and London: University of Chicago Press 1972.
Gustafson, Paula. *Salish Weaving*. Vancouver: Douglas and McIntyre 1980.
Gutzlaff, Rev. Charles. *A Sketch of Chinese History ...* London: Smith and Elder 1834. Vol. 2.
Hanson, Charles, E. "The Point Blanket." *Museum of the Fur Trade Quarterly* 12 (1976):5–10.
Harris, Donald A. and Ingram, George C. "New Caledonia and the Fur Trade: A Status Report." *Western Canadian Journal of Anthropology* 3 (1972):179–95.
Hart, Sir Robert. *"These from the Land of Sinim": Essays on the Chinese Question*. London: Chapman and Hall 1901.
Heizer, Robert F. "The Introduction of Monterey Shells to the Indians of the Northwest Coast." *Pacific Northwest Quarterly* 31 (1940):399–402.
Hill, Hamilton Andrews. *The Trade and Commerce of Boston, 1630 to 1890*. Boston: Damrell and Upham 1895.
Hou, Chi-ming and Yu, Tzong-shian, eds. *Modern Chinese Economic History*. Taipei: Academia Sinica 1979.
Howay, Frederick [sic]. *The Atahualpa*. Fairfield, WA: Ye Galleon Press 1978.
Howay, F.W. "The Ballad of the Bold Northwestman: An Incident in the Life of Captain John Kendrick," *Washington Historical Quarterly* 20 (1929):114–23.

– "A Ballad of the Northwest Fur Trade," *New England Quarterly* 1 (1928):71–9.
– "The Dog's Hair Blankets of the Coast Salish." *Washington Historical Quarterly* 9 (1918):83–92.
– "Early Days of the Maritime Fur-Trade on the Northwest Coast." *Canadian Historical Review* 4 (1923):26–44.
– "Indian Attacks upon Maritime Traders of the North-West Coast, 1785–1805." *Canadian Historical Review* 6 (1925):287–309.
– "The Introduction of Intoxicating Liquors amongst the Indians of the Northwest Coast." *British Columbia Historical Quarterly* 6 (1942):157–69.
– "Letters Relating to the Second Voyage of the Columbia." *Oregon Historical Quarterly* 24 (1923):132–52.
– "The Origin of the Chinook Jargon." *British Columbia Historical Quarterly* 6 (1942):225–50.
– "Potatoes: Records of Some Early Transactions at Fort Simpson, B.C." *Beaver* (1929):155–6.
– "A Yankee Trader on the Northwest Coast, 1791–1795." *Washington Historical Quarterly* 21 (1930):83–94.
Hunt, Freeman. *Lives of American Merchants.* New York: Hunt's Merchants' Magazine 1856. Vol. 1.
Hunter, W.C. *The "Fan Kwae" at Canton Before Treaty Days 1825–1844.* Taipei: Ch'eng-wen Publishing 1965.
Inglis, Richard I. and Haggarty, James C. "Cook to Jewitt: Three Decades of Change in Nootka Sound." In *Le Castor Fait Tout: Slected Papers of the Fifth North American Fur Trade Conference, 1985,* edited by Bruce G. Trigger, Toby Morantz, and Louise Dechêne. Montréal: Lake St Louis Historical Society 1987, 193–222.
Irving, Washington. *Astoria or Anecdotes of an Enterprise Beyond the Rocky Mountains.* Edited by Edgeley W. Todd. Norman: University of Oklahoma Press 1964.
Jensen, Doreen and Sargent, Polly. *Robes of Power: Totem Poles on Cloth.* Vancouver: University of British Columbia Press 1986.
Jopling, Carol F. "The Coppers of the Northwest Coast Indians: Their Origin, Development, and Possible Antecedents." *Transactions of the American Philosophical Society* 79 (1989):1–164.
Karamanski, Theodore J. *Fur Trade and Exploration: Opening the Far Northwest 1821–1852.* Norman: University of Oklahoma Press 1983.
Kaufman, Carole Natalie. "Changes in Haida Indian Argillite Carvings, 1820 to 1910." PhD dissertation, University of California at Los Angeles 1969.
Keith, H. Lloyd. "Fort George on the Columbia: A Reassessment of Financial Failure." Paper presented to the annual meeting of the Western History Association, Tacoma, WA, 13 October 1989.
Khlebnikov, K.T. *Baranov: Chief Manager of the Russian Colonies in America.* Translated by Colin Bearne. Kingston, Ont.: Limestone Press 1973.

Kirker, James. *Adventures to China: Americans in the Southern Oceans 1792–1812*. New York: Oxford University Press 1970.

Kittleson, David. "Hawaiians and Fur Traders." *Hawaii Historical Review* 1 (1963):16–20.

Krooss, Herman E. and Gilbert, Charles. *American Business History*. Englewood Cliff, NJ: Prentice-Hall 1972.

Kuo, Ping Chia. "Canton and Salem: The Impact of Chinese Culture upon New England Life during the Post-Revolutionary Era." *New England Quarterly* 3 (1930):420–42.

Kuykendall, Ralph S. *The Hawaiian Kingdom 1778–1854: Foundation and Transformation*. Honolulu: University of Hawaii Press 1947.

L., H.E. "On the Trade of the United States of North America with China." *Analectic Magazine* 14 (1819):359–66.

Lamb, W. Kaye. "The Mystery of Mrs. Barkley's Diary." *British Columbia Historical Quarterly* 6 (1942):31–59.

Lamb, W. Kaye and Bartoli, Tomás. "James Hanna and John Henry Cox: The First Maritime Fur Trader and His Sponsor." *BC Studies* (Winter 1989–90):3–36.

Latourette, Kenneth Scott. "The History of Early Relations between The United States and China 1784–1844." *Transactions of the Connecticut Academy of Arts and Sciences* 22 (1917):1–209.

– "Voyages of American Ships to China, 1784–1844." *Transactions of the Connecticut Academy of Arts and Sciences* 28 (1927):237–71.

Le Fevour, Edward. *Western Enterprise in Late Ch'ing China: A Selective Survey of Jardine, Matheson and Company's Operations 1842–1895*. Cambridge, MA: Harvard University East Asian Research Center 1968.

Leder, Lawrence H. "American Trade to China, 1800–1802: Some Statistical Notes." *American Neptune* 23 (1963):212–18.

Lee, Jean Gordon. *Philadelphians and the China Trade 1784–1844*. Philadelphia: Philadelphia Museum of Art 1984.

MacDonald, George F. "The Epic of Nekt: The Archaeology of Metaphor." In *The Tsimshian: Images of the Past: Views for the Present*, edited by Margaret Seguin. Vancouver: University of British Columbia Press 1984, 65–81.

– *Haida Monumental Art: Villages of the Queen Charlotte Islands*. Vancouver: University of British Columbia Press 1983.

– *Kitwanga Fort National Historic Site, Skeena River, British Columbia: Historical Research and Analysis of Structural Remains*. Ottawa: Parks Canada 1980.

Mackay, David. *In the Wake of Cook: Exploration, Science & Empire, 1780–1801*. London: Croom Helm 1985.

Macnair, Peter L. "Descriptive Notes on the Kwakiutl Manufacture of Eulachon Oil." *Syesis* 4 (1971):169–77.

Macnair, Peter L. and Hoover, Alan L. *The Magic Leaves: A History of Haida Argillite Carving*. Victoria: Provincial Museum of British Columbia 1984.

Makarova, Raisa V. *Russians on the Pacific 1743–1799*. Translated by Richard A. Pierce and Alton S. Donnelly. Kingston, Ont.: Limestone Press 1975.

McFeat, Tom, ed. *Indians of the North Pacific Coast*. Toronto and Montréal: McClelland and Stewart 1966.

Milburn, William. *Oriental Commerce* ... London: Kingsbury, Parbury, and Allen 1825.

Morison, S.E. "Boston Traders in Hawaiian Islands, 1789–1823." *Washington Historical Quarterly* 12 (1921):166–201.

– *The Maritime History of Massachusetts 1783–1860*. Sentry edition. Cambridge, MA: Riverside Press 1961.

[Morrison, J.R.]. *A Chinese Commercial Guide* ... 2nd ed. Macao: S. Wells Williams 1884.

Morse, Hosea Ballou. *The International Relations of the Chinese Empire*. Shanghai: Kelly and Walsh 1910. Vol. 1.

– *The Trade and Administration of the Chinese Empire*. Taipei: Ch'eng-wen Publishing 1966.

Morton, Arthur S. *A History of the Canadian West to 1870–71*. Edited by Lewis G. Thomas. 2nd edition. Toronto: University of Toronto Press 1973.

Ogden, Adele. *The California Sea Otter Trade, 1784–1848*. Berkeley and Los Angeles: University of California Press 1941.

– "The Californias in Spain's Pacific Otter Trade, 1775–1795." *Pacific Historical Review* 1 (1932):444–69.

– "New England Traders in Spanish and Mexican California." In *Greater America: Essays in Honor of Herbert Eugene Bolton*, edited by Adele Ogden and Engel Sluiter. Berkeley and Los Angeles: University of California Press 1945, 395–413.

– "Russian Sea-Otter and Seal Hunting on the California Coast 1803–1841." *California Historical Quarterly* 12 (1933):217–39.

O'Neil, Marion. "The Maritime Activities of the North West Company, 1813 to 1821." *Washington Historical Quarterly* 21 (1930):243–67.

P[earson], A[lexander]. "Vaccination." *Chinese Repository* 2 (1833–34):35–41.

Parkinson, C. Northcote. "The East India Trade." In *The Trade Winds: A Study of British Overseas Trade during the French Wars 1793–1815*, edited by C. Northcote Parkinson. London: George Allen and Unwin 1948, 141–56.

– *Trade in the Eastern Seas 1793–1813*. Cambridge, UK: Cambridge University Press 1937.

Pethick, Derek. *First Approaches to the Northwest Coast*. Vancouver: J.J. Douglas 1976.

– *The Nootka Connection: Europe and the Northwest Coast 1790–1795*. Vancouver: Douglas and McIntyre 1980.

Pitkin, Timothy. *A Statistical View of the Commerce of the United States of America* ... New Haven: Durrie and Peck 1835.

Polich, John Leo. "John Kendrick and the Maritime Fur Trade of the Northwest Coast." MA thesis, University of Southern California 1964.

Porter, Kenneth Wiggins. *John Jacob Astor: Business Man.* Cambridge, MA: Harvard University Press 1931. 2 Vols.

— "John Jacob Astor and the Sandalwood Trade of the Hawaiian Islands, 1816–1828." *Journal of Economic and Business History* 2 (1930):495–519.

Pritchard, Earl H. *The Crucial Years of Early Anglo-Chinese Relations, 1775– 1800.* Research Studies of the State College of Washington, vol. 4, nos. 3–4. Pullman: State College of Washington 1936.

— "Private Trade between England and China in the Eighteenth Century (1680–1833)." *Journal of the Economic and Social History of the Orient* 1 (1958):108–37, 221–56.

Rickard, T.A. "The Use of Iron and Copper by the Indians of British Columbia." *British Columbia Historical Quarterly* 3 (1939):25–50

Ruby, Robert H. and Brown, John A. *The Chinook Indians: Traders of the Lower Columbia River.* Norman: University of Oklahoma Press 1976.

Samuel, Cheryl. *The Chilkat Dancing Blanket.* Seattle: Pacific Search Press 1982.

Schmitt, Robert C. "Catastrophic Mortality in Hawaii." *Hawaiian Journal of History* 3 (1969): 66–86.

— "Famine Mortality in Hawaii." *Journal of Pacific History* 5 (1970):109–15.

— "New Estimates of the Pre-censal Population of Hawaii." *Journal of the Polynesian Society* 80 (1971):237–43.

— "The *Okuu* – Hawaii's Greatest Epidemic." *Hawaii Medical Journal* 29 (1970):359–64.

Schurz, William Lytle. *The Manila Galleon.* New York: E.P. Dutton 1939.

Sheehan, Carol. *Pipes That Won't Smoke; Coal That Won't Burn: Haida Sculpture in Argillite.* Calgary: Glenbow Museum 1981.

Sladkovskii, M.I. *History of Economic Relations between Russia and China.* Translated by M. Roublev. Jerusalem: Israel Program for Scientific Translations 1966.

Snyder, James Wilbert, Jr. "Spices, Silks and Teas – Cargoes of the Old China Trade." *America Illustrated* 36 (1942):7–26.

Stelle, Charles C. "American Trade in Opium to China prior to 1820." *Pacific Historical Review* 9 (1940):425–44.

— "American Trade in Opium to China, 1821–39." *Pacific Historical Review* 10 (1941):57–74.

Sterns, Worthy Putnam. "The Foreign Trade of the United States from 1820 to 1840." *Journal of Political Economy* 8 (1899–1900):34–57, 452–92.

Stewart, Hilary. *Artifacts of the Northwest Coast Indians.* Revised edition. North Vancouver: Hancock House 1981.

— *Cedar: Tree of Life to the Northwest Coast Indians.* Vancouver and Toronto: Douglas and McIntyre 1984.

– *Indian Fishing*: *Early Methods on the Northwest Coast*. Seattle: University of Washington Press 1977.

Suttles, Wayne. "Coping with Abundance: Subsistence on the Northwest Coast." In *Man the Hunter*, edited by Richard B. Lee and Irven DeVore. Chicago: Aldine Publishing 1968, 56–68.

–. ed. *Northwest Coast*. *Handbook of North American Indians*, vol. 7. Washington, DC: Smithsonian Institution 1990.

– "Variation in Habitat and Culture on the Northwest Coast." in *Akten des 34 Internationalen Amerikanistenkongresses, Wien, 1960*. Vienna: International Congress of Americanists 1962, 522–37.

Swan, James. "The Eulachon or Candle-Fish of the Northwest Coast." *Proceedings of the United States National Museum* 8 (1880):257–64.

Thrum, Thos. G., comp. "The Sandalwood Trade of Early Hawaii." *Hawaiian Annual* (1905):43–74.

Thurman, Michael E. *The Naval Department of San Blas: New Spain's Bastion for Alta California and Nootka 1767 to 1798*. Glendale: Arthur H. Clark 1967.

Tikhmenev, P.A. *A History of the Russian-American Company*. Translated by Richard A. Pierce and Alton S. Donnelly. Seattle and London: University of Washington Press 1978. Vol. 1.

Townsend, Joan B. "Firearms against Native Arms: A Study in Comparative Efficiencies with an Alaskan Example." *Arctic Anthropology* 20 (1983): 1–33.

Turner, Nancy J. *Food Plants and British Columbia Indians*: *Part I — Coastal Peoples*. Victoria: British Columbia Provincial Museum 1975.

Turner, Nancy J. and Taylor, Roy L. "A Review of the Northwest Coast Tobacco Mystery." *Syesis* 5 (1972):249–57.

Vastokas, Joan M. "Architecture and Environment: The Importance of the Forest to the Northwest Coast Indian." *Forest History* 12 (October 1969):12–21.

Vaughan, Thomas and Holm, Bill. *Soft Gold: The Fur Trade and Cultural Exchange on the Northwest Coast of America*. 2nd ed., rev. Portland: Oregon Historical Society Press 1990.

Wheeler, Mary E. "Empires in Conflict and Cooperation." *Pacific Historical Review* (1971):419–41.

Wike, Joyce Annabel. "The Effect of the Maritime Fur Trade on Northwest Coast Indian Society." PhD dissertation, Columbia University 1951.

– "Problems in Fur Trade Analysis: The Northwest Coast." *American Anthropologist* 60 (1958):1,086–101.

– "A Reevaluation of Northwest Coast Cannibalism." In *The Tsimshian and Their Neighbors of the North Pacific Coast*, edited by Jay Miller and Carol M. Eastman. Seattle: University of Washington Press 1984, 239–54.

Wright, Robin Kathleen. "Haida Argillite Pipes." MA thesis, University of Washington 1977.

Yung, Lun-Yuen. *History of the Pirates Who Infested the China Sea, from 1807 to 1810.* Trans. by C.F. Neumann. London: Oriental Translation Society 1831.

Index

ticipation in, 38; American profitability on, 57–8, 176–7, 293–4; reasons for post-1810 decline of, 59–61, 82–3; persistence of, 59–61; reasons for British re-entry into, 62–5; problems of British re-entry into, 65–72; British advantages in, 73–82; Russian disadvantages in, 78; American abandonment of, 77–80, 82, 186; price-setting in, 116–17; gift giving in, 117; necessity of consistent pricing in, 117–19; factors affecting prices in, 122–36; Euroamerican pricing stratagems in, 126–36; Euroamerican price-fixing in, 127–31; circumvention of Indian middlemen in, 132–5; disruption by Indian warfare of, 173–4; disruption by decree of 1821 of, 174–5; second peak of, 182; concentration of American shipowners in, 182, 249–50; decreasing value of Euroamerican goods in, 184–5; changing locus of, 204–7; changing trade goods in, 214–47; most popular trade goods in, 214–17; prostitution in, 235–9; increasing role of land furs in, 240–1; diversification of American participation in, 251–67; impact on Northwest Coast Indians of, 269–78; impact on Hawaiian Islands of, 278–91; impact on South China of, 291–2;

impact on New England of, 292–6
coatlusters: See cotsacks
Cohong: function of, 86; debasement of, 88; monopoly of, 88, 248
"collars": definition of, 218
Columbia Department: identity of, 62
Columbia River: discovery of, 38; as a rendezvous, 205–6
Columbia's Cove: identity of, 163
Commutation Act of 1784: terms of, 92
comprador: See compradores
compradores: function of, 52; dishonesty of, 194
conchas: See Monterey shells
Consoo Fund: purpose of, 88
convention of 1824: terms of, 62, 77, 175
convention of 1825: terms of, 64, 77, 175
Cook, Captain James: significance of third voyage of, 22–3; purpose of third voyage of, 22
Cook Inlet: Russian acquisition of, 204
copper: as a trade good, 217–19
coppers: size of, 184, 218, 219
cotsacks: definition of, 114, 175–6
"country dealers": See tea merchants
"country trade": definition of, 94; volume of, 94
"country traders": advent of, 89; role of, 94, 247
crape: definition of, 55
"creolization": definition of, 149

cumshaw: definition of, 196
Cunneah, Chief: character of, 168–9
Cunneah's Harbour: identity of, 29
Cushing, John: career of, 57, 97, 293–4
cutsarks: See cotsacks

Dalles, The: commercial importance of, 10
Davis, Isaac: Hawaiian career of, 280, 286
decree of 1821: purpose of, 62, 77, 263; impact of, 174–5
demurrage: definition of, 108
dentalia shells: description of, 9; use of, 9; as a trade good, 228–30
Dentalium Indianorum: See dentalia shells
Dentalium pretiosum: See dentalia shells
Dirty Butter Bay: role of, 197
Dixon, Captain George: voyage of, 24
"Down-Easters": definition of, 33
drawbacks: definition of, 37, 100
Dryad affair: See Stikine affair
duck: definition of, 214

"ear shells": See Monterey shells
Easter Conner: See Easter Kuner
Easter Kuner: reputation of, 126
East India Company: monopoly of, 25–6, 28, 37, 91, 94, 108, 247; functions of, 91; activities of, 91–4; tea trade of, 93–4, 99

Newhitty: location of, 207; advantages of, 207

New Spain: identity of, 259

Nez Percés: etymology of, 10

Nootkas: possessiveness of, 114, 156; trading skill of, 121–2

Nootka Sound: advantages of, 204–5

Nootka Sound controversy: cause of, 22

Norfolk Sound: *See* Sitka Sound

"Northermen": definition of, 33

Northwest Coast: location of, xi, 251; physical nature of, 3, 5, 38–9; resources of, 5–6; reasons for Spanish voyages to, 18; as contrasted with Hawaiian Islands, 50; navigational hazards of, 143–6

Northwest Coast Indians: distinctive cultural traits of, 3–4; pre-contact population of, 4; dogs of, 4; resource base of, 5–6; 1834 population of, 7; sea-otter use of, 7–8; pre-contact trade of, 7–11; seasonal movements of, 42, 43, 110–11; trading propensities of, 114; chief's management of trade of, 114–15; influential female voice in trade of, 115–16; trading protocol of, 116–17; initial trading honesty of, 119; trading skill of, 119–22; pricing stratagems of, 122–6; trading discontent of, 135–6; Euroamerican prejudice against, 153–5, 157, 277; larceny of,

155–6; Euroamerican mistreatment of, 157–65; cheating by, 159; revenge of, 165–8; Euroamerican military superiority over, 168, 169, 170; impact of coast trade on, 269–78; decrease of, 272–7; *See also* Bella Coolas, Chinooks, Haidas, Nootkas, Salishes, Tlingits, and Yuroks

Northwest Coastmen: *See* coasters

North West Company: China trade of, 26–7; HBC's absorption of, 26, 27, 62, 73

Northwest trade: *See* coast trade

Nor'Westers: *See* North West Company

Nor'west trade: *See* coast trade

Novoarkhangelsk: *See* Sitka

Nuestra Señora de los Dolores: *See* Kaigani

nutria de mar: *See* sea otters

Nuu-chah-nulth: *See* Nootkas

Oahu: etymology of, 282; advantages of, 282

oakum: defintion of, 44

okuu: identity of, 284

"Old Heads": definition of, 102

Olowalu massacre: occurrence of, 286

"on respondentia": definition of, 105

oolachen: use of, 9; as a trade good, 231–3

oolachen oil: as a trade good, 231–3

opium: Canton's smuggling of, 103–4; varieties

of, 104; impact of trade in, 247–8

outer anchorages: advent of, 89; location of, 104; role of, 104

"outside men": *See* outside merchants

outside merchants: functions of, 88–9; American preference for, 89, 97–8; riskiness of, 89

"par trade": definition of, 131

Pearl River (China): navigability of, 191

Perkins, Thomas Handasyd: career of, 293

Perkins and Company: worth of, 57–8; liquidation of, 95; China-trade dominance of, 250

Petropavlovsk: function of, 260

piaster: definition of, 57

picul: definition of, 93, 252

Pidgin English: description of, 53

pipe: definition of, 211

poaching: as an alternative to the sea-otter trade, 259, 263, 264

Portlock, Captain Nathaniel: voyage of, 24

Port Rumyantsev: identity of, 263

potato: Indian adoption of, 243–4; as a trade good, 244–6

"primage": definition of, 31

"privilege": definition of, 31

provisions: as trade goods, 215–16, 227, 243–6

puncheon: definition of, 45, 142, 225, 245

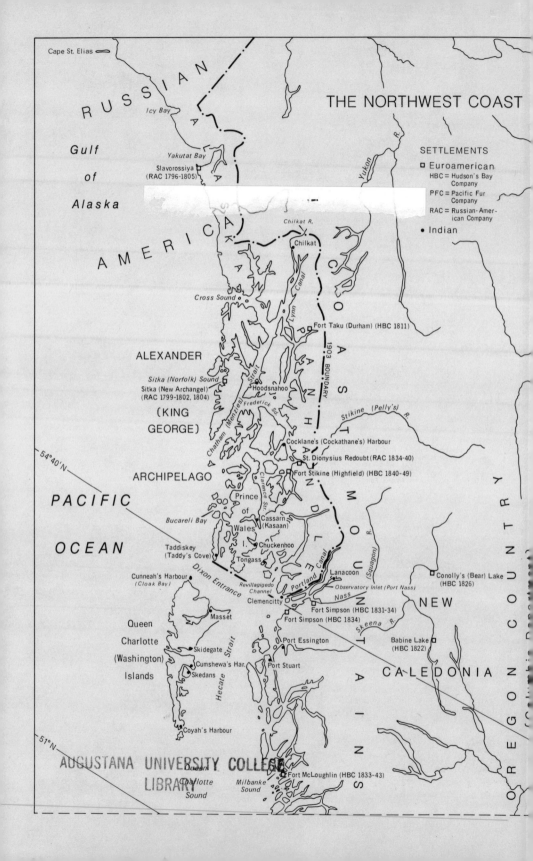

THE NORTHWEST COAST

Cape St. Elias

RUSSIAN

Icy Bay

Gulf

of

Alaska

Yakutat Bay
Slavorossiya
(RAC 1796-1805)

SETTLEMENTS

□ Euroamerican
HBC = Hudson's Bay
        Company
PFC = Pacific Fur
        Company
RAC = Russian-Amer-
        ican Company

● Indian

AMERICA

Chilkat R.

Chilkat

Cross Sound

Fort Taku (Durham) (HBC 1811)

ALEXANDER

Sitka (Norfolk) Sound
Sitka (New Archangel)
(RAC 1799-1802, 1804)

Hoodsnahoo

(KING

GEORGE)

Stikine (Pelly's) R.

Cocklane's (Cockathane's) Harbour
St. Dionysius Redoubt (RAC 1834-40)
Fort Stikine (Highfield) (HBC 1840-49)

54°40'N

ARCHIPELAGO

PACIFIC

Prince

of

Cassarn
(Kasaan)

Bucareli Bay

Wales

I. Chuckenhoo

Conolly's (Bear) Lake
(HBC 1826)

OCEAN

Taddiskey
(Taddy's Cove)

Tongass

Lanacoon

Cunneah's Harbour
(Cloak Bay)

Clemencitty

Observatory Inlet (Port Nass)

NEW

Masset

Nass

Fort Simpson (HBC 1831-34)
Fort Simpson (HBC 1834)

Skeena R.

Babine Lake
(HBC 1822)

Queen

Charlotte
(Washington)

Skidegate

Port Essington

Islands

Cumshewa's Har.
Skedans

Port Stuart

CALEDONIA

Coyah's Harbour

51°N

AUGUSTANA UNIVERSITY COLLEGE
LIBRARY

Queen
Charlotte
Sound

Milbanke
Sound

Fort McLoughlin (HBC 1833-43)

1903 BOUNDARY

Lynn Canal

Chatham (Menzies) Strait

Frederick Sd.

Clarence Strt.

Revillagigedo
Channel

Dixon Entrance

Portland Canal

(Squagoni) R.

Hecate Strait

OREGON COUNTRY
(Columbia Department)